THE SOLU SOLUTION

SURVEY OF ECON

Every 4LTR Press solution includes:

Visually Engaging Textbook

Online Study Tools

Tear-out Review Cards

Interactive eBook

Heading Numbers Connect Print & eBook

STUDENT RESOURCES:

- Interactive eBook
- Auto-Graded Quizzes
- Self-Assessments
- Flashcards
- Games: Crossword Puzzles & Beat the Clock
- Videos

- Exhibit Worksheets
- Graphing Workshops
- Answers to Self-Review
- Review Cards

Students sign in at **www.cengagebrain.com**

INSTRUCTOR RESOURCES:

- All Student Resources
- Engagement Tracker
- First Day of Class Instructions
- Instructor's Manual
- Test Bank
- PowerPoint® Slides
- Instructor Prep Cards

Instructors sign in at **www.cengage.com/login**

"I really like this book. It is so easy to read and understand. Plus, the format makes it easy to quickly find what I am looking for." — **Tina Iannone**, Student, *Tri County Technical College*

4LTR Press adds eBooks in response to a 10% uptick in digital learning preferences.

Engagement Tracker launches, giving faculty a window into student usage of digital tools.

1 out of every 3 (1,400) schools has adopted a 4LTR Press solution.

750,000 students are IN.

AUGUST 2010

NOVEMBER 2010

Third party research confirms that 4LTR Press digital solutions improve retention and outcomes.

CourseMate

Students access the 4LTR Press website at 4x's the industry average.

IN 2011

60 unique solutions across multiple course areas validates the 4LTR Press concept.

2,000

IN 2011

1 out of every 2 (2,000) schools has a 4LTR Press adoption.

APRIL 2011

Over 1 million students are IN.

AUGUST 2011

We're always evolving. Join the 4LTR Press In-Crowd on Facebook at www.facebook.com/4ltrpress

2012 AND BEYOND

SOUTH-WESTERN
CENGAGE Learning®

Survey of ECON, Second Edition
Robert L. Sexton

Senior Vice President, LRS/Acquisitions & Solutions Planning: Jack W. Calhoun

Editorial Director, Business & Economics: Erin Joyner

VP 4LTR & Learning Solutions Strategy, Institutional: Neil Marquardt

Sr. Acquisitions Editor: Steven Scoble

Product Development Manager, 4LTR Press: Steven Joos

Project Manager, 4LTR Press: Pierce Denny

Developmental Editor: Daniel Noguera

Editorial Assistant: Elizabeth Beiting-Lipps

Sr. Market Development Manager: John Carey

Marketing Coordinator: Ilyssa Harbatkin

Sr. Content Project Manager: Emily Nesheim, Holly Henjum

Managing Media Editor: Deepak Kumar

Media Editor: Sharon Morgan, Anita Verma

Manufacturing Planner: Kevin Kluck

Production Service: Integra

Sr. Art Director: Michelle Kunkler

Interior and Cover Design: Ramsdell Design

Cover Image: © Henrik Sorensen/ Getty Images, Inc.

Rights Acquisitions Specialist: Deanna Ettinger

For product information and technology assistance, contact us at
Cengage Learning Customer & Sales Support, 1-800-354-9706

For permission to use material from this text or product, submit all requests online at **www.cengage.com/permissions.**
Further permissions questions can be emailed to
permissionrequest@cengage.com.

Library of Congress Control Number: 2012945119

Student Edition ISBN-13: 978-1-285-08739-9
Student Edition ISBN-10: 1-285-08739-9

Student Edition package ISBN-13: 978-1-285-08730-6
Student Edition package ISBN-10: 1-285-08730-5

South-Western
5191 Natorp Boulevard
Mason, OH 45040
USA

Cengage Learning is a leading provider of customized learning solutions with office locations around the globe, including Singapore, the United Kingdom, Australia, Mexico, Brazil, and Japan. Locate your local office at: **www.cengage.com/global**

Cengage Learning products are represented in Canada by Nelson Education, Ltd.

For your course and learning solutions, **visit www.cengage.com.**

Purchase any of our products at your local college store or at our preferred online store **www.cengagebrain.com.**

Inside Front Cover and Page i Photography Credits:
Woman with magazine: © iStockphoto.com/sdominick; Stack of money: © iStockphoto.com/alexsl; College hangout: © iStockphoto.com/A-Digit; Laptop: © iStockphoto.com/CostinT; A+: © iStockphoto.com/photovideostock; Crowd: © iStockphoto.com/Leontura

Printed in the United States of America
1 2 3 4 5 6 7 16 15 14 13 12

BRIEF CONTENTS

CONTENTS

Money: © iStockphoto.com/Tomislav Forgo; Worker: © Exactostock / SuperStock;
Pills: © iStockphoto.com/Robert Chatterson; Rocket: © iStockphoto/setixela;
Arrows: © iStockphoto.com/Alex Slobodkin

© S_L/Shutterstock.com

4 Using Supply and Demand 68

© TONY RANZE/AFP/Getty Images

© Blue Jean Images/Alamy

5 Market Failure and Public Choice 100

People: © iStockphoto.com/Nicholas; Bagels: © iStockphoto.com/Peter Seager

8 Monopoly 160

9 Monopolistic Competition and Oligopoly 180

© J van der Wolf/Shutterstock.com

10 Labor Markets, Income Distribution, and Poverty 202

Angelina Jolie: © Helga Esteb/Shutterstock.com; Marilyn Monroe: © 20TH CENTURY FOX/THE KOBAL COLLECTION

© Zigy Kaluzny/Getty Images

16 The Federal Reserve and Monetary Policy 340

17 Issues in Macroeconomic Theory and Policy 362

© Emilia Szymanek/iStockphoto.com

18 International Economics 382

© Joerg Reimann/iStockphoto.com

© HUGH GENTRY/Reuters/Landov

Why do star football players have higher salaries than star surfers?

A good understanding of economics would allow you to answer such questions as: Why do 10 a.m. classes fill up more quickly than 8 a.m. classes during registration? Why is it so hard to find an apartment in cities such as San Francisco, Berkeley, and New York? Why is teenage unemployment higher than adult unemployment? Why is the price of your prescription drugs so high? Will higher taxes on cigarettes reduce the number of teenagers smoking? If so, by how much? Why do female models make more than male models? Do houses with views necessarily sell faster than houses without views? Why do people buy houses near noisy airports? Why do U.S. auto producers and sugar producers like tariffs (taxes) on imported goods? Is outsourcing jobs to India a good idea? Is globalization good for the economy? The study of economics improves your understanding of these and many other concerns.

Test your Economics *street-smart* **knowledge and see how you compare against other students! Scan here or visit CourseMate for Survey of ECON2.**

1

The Role and Method of Economics

As you begin your first course in economics, you may be asking yourself why you're here. What does economics have to do with your life?

Although we can list many good reasons to study economics, perhaps the best reason is that many issues in our lives are at least partly economic in character.

Economics is a unique way of analyzing many areas of human behavior. Indeed, the range of topics to which economic analysis can be applied is broad. Many researchers discover that the economic approach to human behavior sheds light on social problems that have been with us for a long time: discrimination, education, crime, divorce, political favoritism, and more. In fact, your daily newspaper is filled with economics. You can find economics on the domestic page, the international page, the business page, the sports page, the entertainment page, and even the weather page—economics is all around us.

However, before we delve into the details and models of economics, it is important that we present an overview of how economists approach problems—their methodology. How does an economist apply the logic of science to approach a problem? And what are the pitfalls that economists should avoid in economic thinking? We also discuss why economists disagree.

1-1 Economics: A Brief Introduction

SECTION CHECK 1

Keep the following questions in mind as you read through this section.

1. What is economics?

2. What is scarcity?

3. What are goods and services?

The study of economics is concerned with the choices we make when confronted with resource scarcity.

3

1-1a ECONOMICS—A WORD WITH MANY DIFFERENT MEANINGS

Some people think economics involves the study of the stock market and corporate finance, and it does—in part. Others think that economics is concerned with the wise use of money and other matters of personal finance, and it is—in part. Still others think that economics involves predicting what business conditions will be like in the future, and again, it does—in part. The word *economics* is, after all, derived from the Greek word *okionomia*, which referred to the management of household affairs.

Precisely defined, **economics** is the study of the choices we make among our many wants and desires given our limited resources. What are resources? **Resources** are inputs—land, human effort and skills, and machines and factories, for instance—used to produce goods and services. The problem is that our unlimited wants exceed our limited resources, a fact that we call **scarcity**. That is, scarcity exists because human wants for goods and services exceed the amount of goods and services that can be produced using all of our available resources. So scarcity forces us to decide how best to use our limited resources. This is **the economic problem**: Scarcity forces us to choose, and choices are costly because we must give up other opportunities that we value. Consumers must make choices on what to buy, how much to save, and how much to invest of their limited incomes. Workers must decide what types of jobs they want, when to enter the workforce, where they will work, and the number of hours they wish to work. Firms must decide what kinds of goods and services to produce, how much to produce, and how to produce those goods and services at the lowest cost.

economics the study of choices we make among our many wants and desires given our limited resources

resources inputs used to produce goods and services

scarcity exists when human wants (material and nonmaterial) exceed available resources

the economic problem scarcity forces us to choose, and choices are costly because we must give up other opportunities that we value

labor the physical and human effort used in the production of goods and services

land the natural resources used in the production of goods and services

capital the equipment and structures used to produce goods and services

human capital the productive knowledge and skill people receive from education, on-the-job training, health, and other factors that increase productivity

entrepreneurship the process of combining labor, land, and capital to produce goods and services

Local governments may have to decide between building a new park or a school. Consumers, workers, firms, and the government all face choices because of scarcity, which is why economics is sometimes called the study of choice.

1-1b SCARCITY AND UNLIMITED HUMAN WANTS

We may want or need "essential" items such as food, clothing, schooling, and health care. We may want many other items, such as vacations, cars, computers, and concert tickets. We may want more friendship, love, knowledge, and so on. We also may have many goals—perhaps an A in this class, a college education, and a great job. Unfortunately, people are not able to fulfill all their wants and desires, material and nonmaterial. As long as human wants exceed available resources, scarcity will exist.

1-1c SCARCITY AND LIMITED RESOURCES

The scarce resources used in the production of goods and services can be grouped into four categories: labor, land, capital, and entrepreneurship.

Labor is the total of both physical and mental effort expended by people in the production of goods and services. The services of a teacher, nurse, cosmetic surgeon, professional golfer, and electrician all fall under the general category of labor.

Land includes the "gifts of nature," or the natural resources, used in the production of goods and services. Economists consider land to include trees, animals, water, minerals, and so on, along with the physical space we normally think of as land.

Capital is the equipment and structures used to produce goods and services. Office buildings, tools, machines, and factories are all considered capital goods. When we invest in factories, machines, research and development, or education, we increase the potential to create more goods and services in the future. Capital also includes **human capital**—the productive knowledge and skill people receive from education and on-the-job training.

Entrepreneurship is the process of combining labor, land, and capital to produce goods and services. Entrepreneurs make the tough and risky decisions about what and how to produce goods and services. Entrepreneurs are always looking for new ways to improve production techniques or to create new products. They are lured by the chance of making a profit.

It is this opportunity to make a profit that leads entrepreneurs to take risks.

However, not every entrepreneur is a Bill Gates (Microsoft) or a Henry Ford (Ford Motor Company). In some sense, we are all entrepreneurs when we try new products or when we find better ways to manage our households or our study time. Rather than money, then, our profits might take the form of greater enjoyment, additional time for recreation, or better grades.

1-1d WHAT ARE GOODS AND SERVICES?

Goods are the items that we value or desire. Goods tend to be **tangible**—objects that can be seen, held, tasted, or smelled such as shirts, pizzas, or perfume. However, other goods that we cannot reach out and touch are called **intangible goods**. Intangible goods include equality, friendship, leisure, knowledge, security, prestige, respect, and health.

Services are intangible acts for which people are willing to pay, such as haircuts, dental cleanings, legal counsel, medical care, and education. Services are intangible because they are less overtly visible, but they are certainly no less valuable than goods.

All goods and services, whether tangible or intangible, are produced from scarce resources and can be subjected to economic analysis. Scarce goods created from scarce resources are called **economic goods**. These goods are *desirable but limited* in supply. Without enough economic goods for all of us, we are forced to compete. Scarcity ultimately leads to competition for the available goods and services, a subject we will return to often in this text.

What Are Bads?

In contrast to goods, **bads** are those items that we do not desire or want. For most people, garbage, pollution, weeds, and crime are bads. People tend to eliminate or minimize bads, so they will often pay to have

goods items we value or desire

tangible goods items we value or desire that we can reach out and touch

intangible goods goods that we cannot reach out and touch, such as friendship and knowledge

services intangible items of value provided to consumers, such as education

economic goods scarce goods created from scarce resources—goods that are desirable but limited in supply

bads items that we do not desire or want, where less is preferred to more, such as terrorism, smog, or poison oak

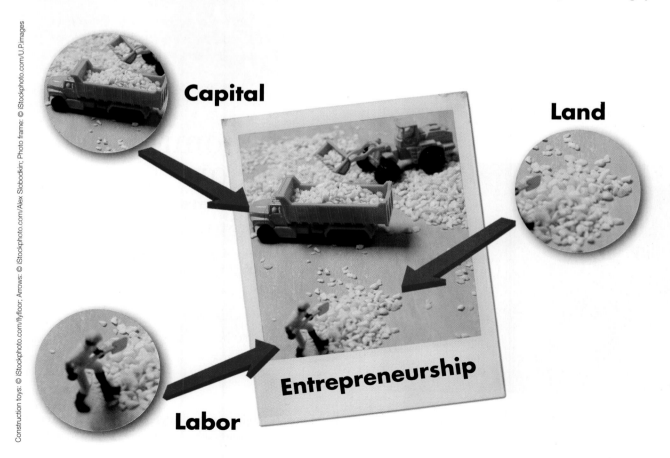

Capital

Land

Labor

Entrepreneurship

bads, such as garbage, removed. The elimination of the bad—garbage removal, for example—is a good.

1-1e DOES EVERYONE FACE SCARCITY?

We all face scarcity because we cannot have all the goods and services we desire. However, because we all have different wants and desires, scarcity affects everyone differently. For example, a child in a developing country may face a scarcity of food and clean drinking water, while a rich man in Beverly Hills may face a scarcity of garage space for his growing antique car collection. Likewise, a harried middle-class working mother may find time for exercise particularly scarce, while a pharmaceutical company may be concerned with the scarcity of the natural resources it uses in its production process. Its effects may vary, but no one can escape scarcity.

We often hear it said of rich people that "he has everything" or "she can buy anything she wants." Actually, even the richest person must live with scarcity and must, at some point, choose one want or desire over another. And of course, we all have only 24 hours in a day! The problem is that as we become more affluent, we learn of new luxuries to provide us with satisfaction. Wealth, then, creates a new set of wants to be satisfied. No evidence indicates that people would not find a valuable use for additional income, no matter how rich they became. Even the wealthy individual who decides to donate all her money to charity faces the constraints of scarcity. If she had greater resources, she could do still more for others.

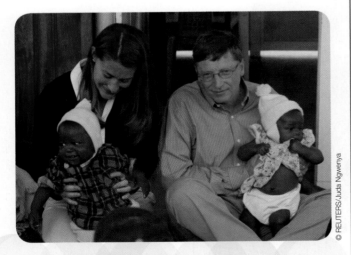

© REUTERS/Juda Ngwenya

Scarcity even exists for billionaires Bill and Melinda Gates.

1-1f WILL SCARCITY EVER BE ERADICATED?

It is probably clear by now that scarcity never has and never will be eradicated. The same creativity that develops new methods to produce goods and services in greater quantities also reveals new wants. Fashions are always changing. Clothes and shoes that are "in" one year will likely be "out" the next. New wants quickly replace old ones. It is also quite possible that over a period of time, a rising quantity of goods and services will not increase human happiness. Why? Because our wants may grow as fast as—if not faster than—our ability to meet those wants.

SECTION CHECK 1 ANSWERS

1. Economics is the study of the choices we make among our many wants and desires, given our limited resources. It is a problem-solving science that concerns itself with the choices we make in the face of scarcity.

2. Scarcity is the fact that our unlimited wants exceed our limited resources, so we must make choices.

3. Goods and services are things we value. They can be tangible (e.g., food, shelter) or intangible (e.g., love, compassion, intelligence).

1-2 Economic Behavior

SECTION CHECK 2

Keep the following questions in mind as you read through this section.

1. How is self-interest relevant to economics?

2. What is rational behavior?

3. Can we predict how people will respond to changes in incentives?

Economic behavior is usually determined by self-interest and rational behavior, which can help in predicting how people will react to changes in incentives.

1-2a SELF-INTEREST

Economists assume that individuals act *as if* they are motivated by self-interest and respond in predictable ways to changing circumstances. In other words, self-interest is a good predictor of human behavior in most situations. For example, to a worker, self-interest means pursuing a higher-paying job and/or better working conditions. To a consumer, it means gaining a higher level of satisfaction from limited income and time.

We seldom observe employees asking employers to cut their wages and increase their workload to increase a company's profits. Or how often do you think customers walk into a supermarket demanding to pay more for their groceries? In short, a great deal of human behavior can be explained and predicted by assuming people act as if they are motivated by their own self-interest.

There is no question that self-interest is a powerful force that motivates people to produce goods and services. But self-interest can include benevolence. Think of the late Mother Teresa, who spent her life caring for others. One could say that her work was in her self-interest, but who would consider her actions selfish? Similarly, workers may be acting in self-interest when they choose to work harder and longer to increase their charitable giving or saving for their children's education. That is, self-interest to an economist is not a narrow monetary self-interest. The enormous amount of money and time donated to victims of Hurricane Katrina is an example of self-interest too—the self-interest was to help others in need. However, our charitable actions for others are influenced by cost. We would predict that most people would be more charitable when the tax deductions are greater or that you may be more likely to offer a friend a ride to the airport when the freeway was less congested. In short, the lower the cost of helping others, the more help we would expect to be offered.

In the United States, individuals typically give more than $210 billion annually to charities. They also pay more money for environmentally friendly goods. Consumers can derive utility or satisfaction from these choices.

It is clearly not selfish—it is in their best interest to care about the environment and those who are less fortunate than themselves.

rational behavior people do the best they can, based on their values and information, under current and anticipated future circumstances

1-2b DO PEOPLE ACTUALLY ENGAGE IN RATIONAL BEHAVIOR?

Economists assume that people, for the most part, engage in rational behavior. Now, you might think that could not possibly apply to your brother, sister, or roommates. But the key is in the definition. To an economist, **rational behavior** merely means that people do the best they can, based on their values and information, under current and anticipated future circumstances. Economists assume that while people may not know with complete certainty which decisions will yield the most satisfaction they will select the one that they *expect* to give them the best results among the alternatives. Most people act purposefully. They make decisions with some *expected* outcome in mind. Their actions are rational and purposeful, not random and chaotic.

Consumers and producers all take purposeful actions when they decide what to buy or produce. They make mistakes and are impacted by emotion, but the point is that they make their decisions with

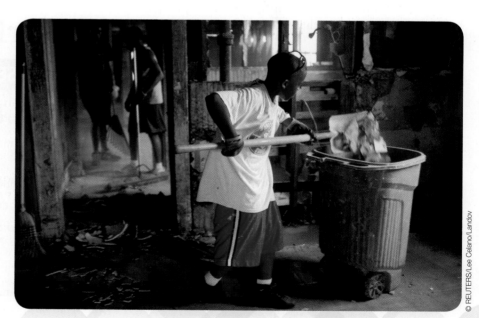

Enormous amounts of resources (time and money) were donated to the Hurricane Katrina victims. If individuals are acting to promote the things that interest them, are these self-interested acts necessarily selfish? Acting in one's own self-interest is only selfish if one's interests are selfish.

© REUTERS/Lee Celano/Landov

some expected results in mind. In short, rational self-interest means that individuals try to weigh the expected benefits and costs of their decisions, a topic we will return to in Chapter 2.

1-2c PEOPLE RESPOND TO CHANGES IN INCENTIVES

Because most people are seeking opportunities to make themselves better off, they respond to changes in incentives. That is, they are reacting to changes in benefits and costs. In fact, much of human behavior can be explained and predicted as a response to incentives. In the words of Levitt and Dubner, the authors of *SuperFreakonomics*, "People are people and they respond to incentives. They can nearly always be manipulated for good or ill, if only you find the right levers."

For example, a tax on cars that emit lots of pollution (an increase in costs) would be a negative incentive that would lead to a reduction in emitted pollution. On the other hand, a subsidy (the opposite of a tax) on hybrid cars—part electric, part internal combustion—would be a positive incentive that would encourage greater production and consumption of hybrid cars. Human behavior is influenced in predictable ways by such changes in economic incentives, and economists use this information to predict what will happen when the benefits and costs of any choice are changed.

In August of 2008, hip-hop mogul Sean "Diddy" Combs decided he will fly on commercial airlines instead of private jets because of soaring fuel prices. Incentives matter.

Because most people seek opportunities that make them better off, we can predict what will happen when incentives are changed. If salaries increase for engineers and decrease for MBAs, we would predict fewer people would go to graduate school in business and more would go into engineering. A permanent change to a much higher price of gasoline would lead us to expect fewer gas-guzzling SUVs on the highway. People who work on commission tend to work harder. If the price of downtown parking increased, we would predict that commuters would look for alternative methods to get to work that would save money. If households were taxed for water consumption in an attempt to conserve water, economists would expect people to use less water, and to use substantially less water than if they were simply asked to conserve water. Incentives matter.

SECTION CHECK 2 ANSWERS

1. Economists assume that people act as if they are motivated by self-interest and respond predictably to changing circumstances.

2. Rational behavior means that people do the best they can based on their values and information, under current and future anticipated consequences.

3. People respond to incentives in predictable ways.

1-3 Markets

SECTION CHECK 3

Keep the following questions in mind as you read through this section.

1. How does a market economy allocate scarce resources?

2. What is a market failure?

3. What are product and factor markets?

4. What is the circular flow model?

Let us look at markets, how they allocate resources, and what happens when they fail. We will then examine a model that illustrates market activities.

Although we usually think of a market as a place where some sort of exchange occurs, a market is not really a place at all. A **market** is the process of buyers and sellers exchanging goods and services. Supermarkets, the New York Stock Exchange, drug stores, roadside stands, garage sales, Internet stores, and restaurants are all markets.

Every market is different. That is, the conditions under which the exchange between buyers and sellers takes place can vary. These differences make it difficult to precisely define a market.

1-3a HOW DOES THE MARKET WORK TO ALLOCATE SCARCE RESOURCES?

Collectively, our wants far exceed what can be produced from nature's scarce resources. So how should we allocate those scarce resources? Some methods of resource allocation might seem bad and counterproductive—for example, the "survival of the fittest" competition that takes place on the floor of the jungle. Physical violence has been used since the beginning of time, as people, regions, and countries attacked one another to gain control over resources. We could argue that

Competitive markets are powerful, helping to make existing products better, improve production processes, and even create new products.

governments should allocate scarce resources on the basis of equal shares or according to need. However, this approach poses problems because of diverse individual preferences, the difficulty of ascertaining needs, and the negative work and investment incentives involved. In reality, society is made up of many approaches to resource allocation. For now, we will focus on one form of allocating goods and services found in most countries—the market economy.

efficiency when an economy gets the most out of its scarce resources

The market economy provides a way for millions of producers and consumers to allocate scarce resources. For the most part, markets are efficient. To an economist, **efficiency** is achieved when the economy gets the most out of its scarce resources. In short, efficiency makes the economic pie as large as possible.

Competitive markets are powerful—they can make existing products better and/or less expensive, they can improve production processes, and they can create new products, from video games to life-saving drugs. Buyers and sellers indicate their wants through their action and inaction in the marketplace, and it is this collective "voice" that determines how resources are allocated. But how is this information communicated? Market prices serve as the language of the market system. By understanding what these market prices mean, you can get a better understanding of the vital function that the market economy performs.

Markets may not always lead to your desired tastes and preferences. You may think that markets produce too many pet rocks, chia pets, breast enhancements, and face lifts. Some markets are illegal, such as the market for cocaine, the market for stolen body parts, the market for child pornography, and the market for pirated music. Markets do not come with a moral compass; they simply provide what buyers are willing and able to pay for and what sellers are willing and able to produce.

1-3b MARKET PRICES PROVIDE IMPORTANT INFORMATION

Market prices communicate important information to both buyers and sellers. These prices communicate information about the relative availability of products to buyers, and they provide sellers with critical information about the relative value that consumers place on those products. In short, buyers look at the price and decide how much they are willing and able to demand and sellers look at the price and decide how much they are able and willing to supply. The market price reflects the value a buyer places on a good and the cost to society of producing that good. Thus, market prices provide a way for both buyers and sellers to communicate about the relative value of resources. To paraphrase Adam Smith, prices adjust like an "invisible hand" to direct buyers and sellers to an outcome that is socially desirable. We will see how this works beginning in Chapter 3.

The basis of a market economy is voluntary exchange and the price system that guides people's choices and produces solutions to the questions of what goods to produce and how to produce and distribute them.

Wood—Georgia

Take something as simple as the production of a pencil. Where did the wood come from? Perhaps the Northwest or Georgia. The graphite may have come from the mines in Michigan and the rubber may be from Malaysia. The paint, the glue, the metal piece that holds the eraser—who knows? The point is that market forces coordinated this production activity among literally thousands of people, some of whom live in different countries and speak different languages. The market brought these people together to make a pencil that sells for 25 cents at your bookstore. It all happened because the market economy provided the incentive for people to pursue activities that benefit others. This same process produces millions of goods and services around the world, from automobiles and computers to pencils and paper clips.

The same is true of the iPod and iPhone. The entrepreneurs of Apple have learned how to combine almost 500 generic parts to make something of much greater value. The whole is greater than the sum of the parts.

1-3c COUNTRIES THAT DO NOT RELY ON A MARKET SYSTEM

Countries that do not rely on the market system have no clear communication between buyers and sellers. The

Graphite—Michigan

former Soviet Union, where quality was virtually nonexistent, experienced many shortages of quality goods and surpluses of low-quality goods. For example, thousands of tractors had no spare parts and millions of pairs of shoes were left on shelves because the sizes did not match those of the population.

1-3d MARKET FAILURE

The market mechanism is a simple but effective and efficient general means of allocating resources among alternative uses. However, when the economy fails to allocate resources efficiently on its own, it is known as **market failure**. For example, a steel mill might put soot and other forms of "crud" into the air as a by-product of making steel. When it does, it imposes costs on others not connected with using or producing steel from the steel mill. The soot may require homeowners to paint their homes more often, entailing a cost. And studies show that respiratory diseases are greater in areas with more severe air pollution, imposing costs that may even include life itself. In addition, the steel mill might discharge chemicals into a stream, thus killing wildlife and spoiling recreational activities for the local population. In this

Rubber—Malaysia

case, the steel factory does not bear the costs of its polluting actions, and it continues to emit too much pollution. In other words, by transferring the pollution costs onto society, the firm lowers its costs of production and so produces more than the ideal output—which is inefficient because it is an overallocation of resources.

Markets sometimes produce too little of a good—research, for example. Therefore, the government might decide to subsidize promising scientific research that could benefit many people—such as cancer research. When one party prevents other parties from participating in mutually beneficial exchange, it also causes a market failure. This situation occurs in a monopoly, with its single seller of goods. Because the monopolist can raise its end price above the competitive price, some potential consumers are kept from buying the goods they would have bought at the lower price, and inefficiency occurs. Whether the market economy has produced too little (underallocation) or too much (overallocation), the government can improve society's well-being by intervening. The case of market failure will be taken up in more detail in Chapter 5.

We cannot depend on the market economy to always communicate accurately. Some firms may have market power to distort prices in their favor. For example, the only regional cement company in the area has the ability to charge a higher price and provide lower-quality services than if the company were in a highly competitive market. In this case, the lack of competition can lead to higher prices and reduced product quality. And without adequate information, unscrupulous producers may be able to misrepresent their products to the disadvantage of unwary consumers.

In sum, government can help promote efficiency when there is a market failure—making the economic pie larger.

Does the Market Distribute Income Fairly?

Sometimes a painful trade-off exists between how much an economy can produce efficiently and how that output is distributed—the degree of equality. An efficient market rewards those that produce goods and services that others are willing and able to buy. But this does not guarantee a "fair" or equal distribution of income. That is, how the economic pie is divided up. A market economy cannot guarantee everyone adequate amounts of food, shelter, and health care. In other words, not only does the market determine what goods are going to be produced and in what quantities, but it also determines the distribution of output among members of society.

As with other aspects of government intervention, the degree-of-equity argument can generate some sharp disagreements. What is "fair" for one person may seem highly "unfair" to someone else. One person may find it terribly unfair for some individuals to earn many times the amount earned by other individuals who work equally hard, and another person may find it highly unfair to ask one group, the relatively rich, to pay a much higher proportion of their income in taxes than another group pays.

Government Is Not Always the Solution

However, just because the government could improve the situation does not mean it will. After all, the political process has its own set of problems, such as special interests, short-sightedness, and imperfect information. For example, government may reduce competition through tariffs and quotas, or it may impose inefficient regulations that restrict entry. That is, there is government failure as well as market failure.

> **product markets** markets in which households are buyers and firms are sellers of goods and services
>
> **factor (or input) markets** markets in which households sell the use of their inputs (capital, land, labor, and entrepreneurship) to firms

1-3e THE CIRCULAR FLOW MODEL

How do we explain how the millions of people in an economy interact when it comes to buying, selling, producing, working, hiring, and so on? A continuous flow of goods and services is bought and sold between the producers of goods and services (which we call firms) and the buyers of goods and services (which we call households). A continuous flow of income also moves from firms to households as firms buy inputs to produce the goods and services they sell. In our simple economy, these exchanges take place in product markets and factor markets.

1-3f PRODUCT MARKETS

Product markets are the markets for consumer goods and services. In the product market, households are buyers and firms are sellers. Households buy the goods and services that firms produce and sell. The payments from the households to the firms for the purchases of goods and services flow to the firms at the same time as goods and services flow to the households.

1-3g FACTOR MARKETS

Factor or **input markets** are markets in which households sell the use of their inputs (capital, land, labor, and entrepreneurship) to firms. In the factor market, households are the sellers and firms are the buyers. Households receive money payments from firms as compensation for the labor, land, capital, and entrepreneurship needed to produce goods and services. These payments take the form of wages (salaries), rent, interest payments, and profit.

EXHIBIT 1.1 The Circular Flow Diagram

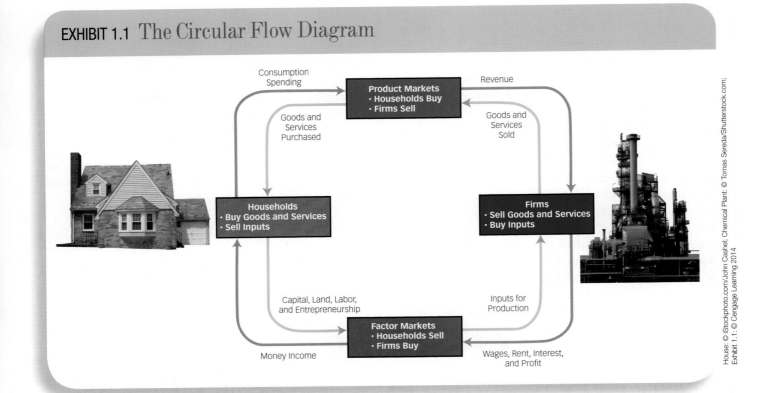

House: © iStockphoto.com/John Cashel; Chemical Plant: © Tomas Sereda/Shutterstock.com; Exhibit 1.1: © Cengage Learning 2014

1-3h THE SIMPLE CIRCULAR FLOW MODEL

The **simple circular flow model** is illustrated in Exhibit 1.1. In the top half of the exhibit, the product markets, households purchase goods and services that firms have produced. In the lower half of the exhibit, the factor (or input) markets, households sell the inputs that firms use to produce goods and services. Households receive income (wages, rent, interest, and profit) from firms for the inputs used in production (capital, land, labor, and entrepreneurship).

Look at a simple example to see how the circular flow model works. Suppose a teacher's supply of labor generates personal income in the form of wages (the factor market), which she can use to buy automobiles, vacations, food, and other goods (the product market). Suppose she buys an automobile (product market); the automobile dealer now has revenue to pay for his inputs (factor market)—wages to workers, purchase of new cars to replenish his inventory,

simple circular flow model an illustration of the continuous flow of goods, services, inputs, and payments between firms and households

rent for his building, and so on. So we see that in the simple circular flow model, income flows from firms to households (factor markets), and spending flows from households to firms (product markets). The simple circular flow model shows how households and firms interact in product markets and factor markets and how the two markets are interrelated.

SECTION CHECK 3 ANSWERS

1. Markets provide what buyers are willing and able to pay for and what sellers are willing and able to produce.

2. A market failure is said to occur when the economy is unable to allocate resources efficiently on its own.

3. In the product market, households are buyers and firms are sellers. In the factor market, households are sellers and firms are buyers.

4. The circular flow model illustrates the flow of goods, services, and payments among firms and households.

1-4 Economic Theory

SECTION CHECK 4

Keep the following questions in mind as you read through this section.

1. What are economic theories?
2. Why do we need to abstract?
3. What is a hypothesis?
4. What are microeconomics and macroeconomics?

Here we will examine economic theories, what they are, how they're developed, and how they're used.

1-4a ECONOMIC THEORIES

A **theory** is an established explanation that accounts for known facts or phenomena. Specifically, economic theories are statements or propositions about patterns of human behavior that occur expectedly under certain circumstances. These theories help us sort out and understand the complexities of economic behavior and guide our analysis. We expect a good theory to explain and predict well. A good economic theory, then, should help us better understand and, ideally, predict human economic behavior.

1-4b ABSTRACTION IS IMPORTANT

Economic theories cannot realistically include every event that has ever occurred. A theory weeds out the irrelevant facts from the relevant ones. We must abstract. A road map of the United States may not include every creek, ridge, and gully between Los Angeles and Chicago; indeed, such an all-inclusive map would be too large and too detailed to be of value. A road map designating major interstate highways will provide enough information to travel by car from Los Angeles

to Chicago. Likewise, an economic theory is more useful when it ignores the details that are not relevant to the questions that are being investigated.

Without abstraction or simplification, the world is too complex to analyze. For the same reason, economists make a number of simplifying assumptions in their models. Sometimes economists make very strong assumptions, such as that all people seek self-betterment or all firms attempt to maximize profits. Of course, this may not hold for every single person or firm. Only when we test our models using these assumptions do we find out if they were too simplified or too limiting.

theory a statement or proposition used to explain and predict behavior in the real world

hypothesis a testable proposition

1-4c DEVELOPING A TESTABLE PROPOSITION

The beginning of any theory is a **hypothesis**, a testable proposition that makes some type of prediction about behavior in response to certain changes in conditions based on our assumptions. In economic theory, a hypothesis is a testable prediction about how people will behave or react to a change in economic circumstances. For example, if we notice an increase in the price of oranges (per pound), we might hypothesize that sales of oranges will drop, or if the price of oranges (per pound) decreases, our hypothesis

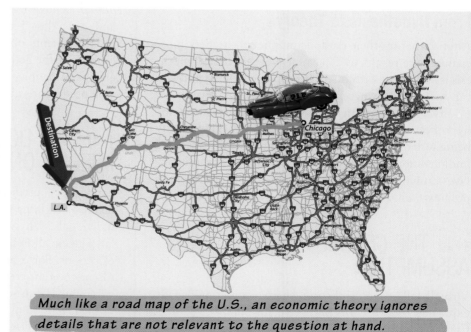

Much like a road map of the U.S., an economic theory ignores details that are not relevant to the question at hand.

might be that orange sales will rise. Once we state our hypothesis, we test it by comparing what it predicts will happen to what actually happens.

Using Empirical Analysis

To determine whether our hypothesis is valid, we must engage in **empirical analysis**. That is, we must examine the data to see whether our hypothesis fits well with the facts. If the hypothesis is consistent with real-world observations, we can accept it; if it does not fit well with the facts, we must "go back to the drawing board."

Determining whether a hypothesis is acceptable is more difficult in economics than it is in the natural or physical sciences. Chemists, for example, can observe chemical reactions under laboratory conditions. They can alter the environment to meet the assumptions of the hypothesis and can readily manipulate the variables (chemicals, temperatures, and so on) crucial to the proposed relationship. Such controlled experimentation is seldom possible in economics. The laboratory of economists is usually the real world. Unlike chemists in their labs, economists cannot easily control all the variables that might influence human behavior.

Economists are reluctant to use survey data because of the huge variance between how people say they behave and how they actually behave. Economists prefer to measure actual behavior, or revealed preference, not declared preference.

From Hypothesis to Theory

After gathering their data, economic researchers must evaluate the results to determine whether their hypothesis is supported or refuted. If supported, the hypothesis can be tentatively accepted as an economic theory.

Every economic theory is on life-long probation; the hypothesis underlying an economic theory is constantly being tested against empirical findings. Do the observed findings support the prediction? When a hypothesis survives a number of tests, it is accepted until it no longer predicts well.

1-4d THE *CETERIS PARIBUS* ASSUMPTION

Virtually all economic theories share a condition usually expressed by the Latin phrase **ceteris paribus**. A rough translation of the phrase is "letting everything else be equal" or "holding everything else constant." When economists try to assess the effect of one variable on another, they must keep the relationship between the two variables isolated from other events that might also influence the situation that the theory tries to explain or predict. The following example should make this concept clearer.

Suppose you develop your own theory describing the relationship between studying and exam performance: If I study harder, I will perform better on the test. That sounds logical, right? Holding other things constant (*ceteris paribus*), your theory is likely to be true. However, what if you studied harder but inadvertently overslept the day of the exam? What if you were so sleepy during the test that you could not think clearly? Or what if you studied the wrong material? Although it might look like additional studying did not improve your performance, the real problem could lie in the impact of other variables, such as sleep deficiency or how you studied.

1-4e WHY ARE OBSERVATION AND PREDICTION HARDER IN THE SOCIAL SCIENCES?

Working from observations, scientists try to make generalizations that will enable them to predict certain events. However, observation and prediction are more difficult in the social sciences than in physical sciences such as physics, chemistry, and astronomy. Why? The major reason for the difference is that the social scientists, including economists, are concerned with *human* behavior. And human behavior is more variable and often less readily predictable than the behavior of experiments observed in a laboratory. However, by looking at the actions and the incentives faced by large groups of people, economists can still make many reliable predictions about human behavior.

1-4f WHY DO ECONOMISTS PREDICT ON A GROUP LEVEL?

Economists' predictions usually refer to the collective behavior of large groups rather than to that of specific individuals. Why is this? Looking at the behaviors of a large group allows economists to discern general patterns of actions. For example, consider what would happen if the price of air travel from the United States to Europe was reduced drastically, say from $1,000 to $400, because of the invention of a more fuel-efficient jet. What type of predictions could we make about the effect of this price reduction on the buying habits of typical consumers?

What Does Individual Behavior Tell Us?

Let us look first at the responses of individuals. As a result of the price drop, some people will greatly increase their intercontinental travel, taking theater weekends in London or week-long trips to France to indulge in French food. Some people, however, are terribly afraid to fly, and the price reduction will not influence their behavior in the slightest. Others might detest Europe and, despite the lowered airfares, prefer to spend a few days in Aspen, Colorado, instead. A few people might respond to the airfare reduction in precisely the opposite way from ours: At the lower fare, they might make fewer trips to Europe, because they might believe (rightly or wrongly) that the price drop would be accompanied by a reduction in the quality of service, greater crowding, or reduced safety. In short, we cannot predict with any level of certainty how a given individual will respond to this airfare reduction.

What Does Group Behavior Tell Us?

Group behavior is often more predictable than individual behavior. When the weather gets colder, more firewood will be sold. Some individuals may not buy firewood, but we can predict with great accuracy that a group of individuals will establish a pattern of buying more firewood. Similarly, while we cannot say what each individual will do, within a group of persons, we can predict with great accuracy that more flights to Europe from Los Angeles will be sold at lower prices than at higher prices, holding other things such as income and preferences constant. We cannot predict exactly how many more airline tickets will be sold at $400 than at $1,000, but we can predict the direction of the impact and approximate the extent of the impact. By observing the relationship between the price of goods and services and the quantities people purchase in different places and during different time periods, it is possible to make some reliable generalizations about how much people will react to changes in the prices of goods and services. Economists use this larger picture of the group for most of their theoretical analysis.

Economists and Survey Data

Economists do not typically use survey data. Economists prefer to look at revealed preferences (how people actually behave) rather than declared preferences (how they say they behave).

Participants in surveys may consciously or subconsciously fib, especially when it costs almost nothing to fib. Measuring revealed preferences will generally give us more accurate results. For example, Professors Oster and Jensen, by measuring revealed preferences, found that rural Indian families who had cable TV had lower birth rates than those with no television.

microeconomics the study of household and firm behavior and how they interact in the marketplace

macroeconomics the study of the whole economy, including the topics of inflation, unemployment, and economic growth

1-4g THE TWO BRANCHES OF ECONOMICS: MICROECONOMICS AND MACROECONOMICS

Conventionally, we distinguish two main branches of economics: microeconomics and macroeconomics. **Microeconomics** deals with the smaller units within the economy, attempting to understand the decision-making behavior of firms and households and their interaction in markets for particular goods or services. Microeconomic topics include discussions of health care, agricultural subsidies, the price of everyday items such as running shoes, the distribution of income, and the impact of labor unions on wages. **Macroeconomics**, in contrast, deals

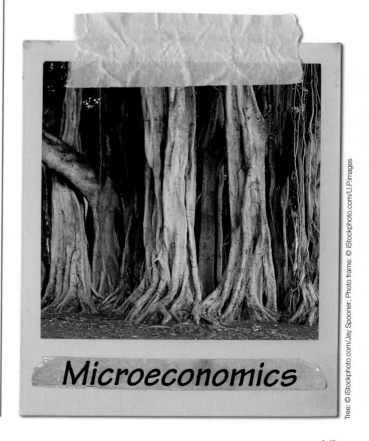

Microeconomics

aggregate the total amount—such as the aggregate level of output

correlation when two events occur together

causation when one event brings about another event

with the **aggregate**, or total economy; it looks at economic problems as they influence the whole of society. Topics covered in macroeconomics include inflation, unemployment, business cycles, and economic growth. To put it simply, microeconomics looks at the trees while macroeconomics looks at the forest.

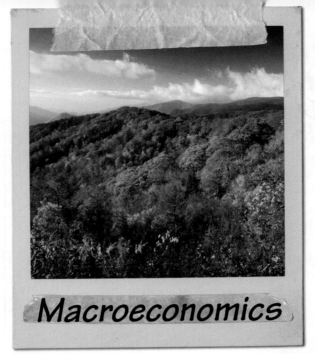

Macroeconomics

In our discussion of economic theory we have not yet mentioned that there are certain pitfalls to avoid that may hinder scientific and logical thinking: confusing correlation and causation, and the fallacy of composition.

1-5a CONFUSING CORRELATION AND CAUSATION

Without a theory of causation, no scientist could sort out and understand the enormous complexity of the real world. But one must always be careful not to confuse correlation with causation. In other words, the fact that two events usually occur together (**correlation**) does not necessarily mean that one caused the other to occur (**causation**). For example, say a groundhog awakes after a long winter of hibernation, climbs out of his hole, and sees his shadow—then six weeks of bad weather ensue. Did the groundhog cause the bad weather? In Europe, the stork population has fallen and so have birth rates. Does this mean that the one event caused the other to occur? It is highly unlikely.

It is also important to consider in which direction causality runs. A rooster may always crow before the sun rises, but it does not cause the sunrise; rather, the early light from the sunrise causes the rooster to crow.

SECTION CHECK 4 ANSWERS

1. Economic theories are statements used to explain and predict patterns of human behavior.

2. The world is too complex to analyze, so we must abstract to focus on the most important components of a particular problem.

3. A hypothesis makes a prediction about human behavior and is then tested.

4. Microeconomics focuses on smaller units within the economy—firms and households—and how they interact in the marketplace. Macroeconomics deals with the aggregate, or total, economy.

1-5 Pitfalls to Avoid in Scientific Thinking

SECTION CHECK 5

Think about the following questions as you read through this section.

1. If two events usually occur together, does it mean one event caused the other to happen?

2. What is the fallacy of composition?

Why Is the Correlation between Ice Cream Sales and Property Crime Positive?

Did you know that when ice cream sales rise, so do property crime rates? What do you think causes the two events to occur together? The explanation is that property crime peaks in the summer because of warmer weather, more people on vacations (leaving their homes vacant), teenagers out of school, and so on. It just happens that ice cream sales also peak in those months because of the weather. It is the case of a third variable causing both to occur. Or what if there were a positive correlation between sales of cigarette lighters and the incidence of cancer? The suspect might well turn out to be the omitted variable (the so-called "smoking gun"): the cigarette.

1-5b THE FALLACY OF COMPOSITION

Economic thinking requires us to be aware of the problems associated with aggregation (adding up all the parts). One of the biggest problems is the **fallacy of composition**. This fallacy states that even if something is true for an individual, it is not necessarily true for many individuals as a group. For example, say you are at a football game and you decide to stand up to get a better view of the playing field. This works as long as the people seated around you don't stand up. But what happens if everyone stands up at the same time? Then your standing up does nothing to improve your view. Thus, what is true for an individual does not always hold true in the aggregate. The same can be said of getting to school early to get a better parking place—what if everyone arrived early? Or studying harder to get a better grade in a class that is graded on a curve—what if everyone studied harder? These are all examples of the fallacy of composition.

SECTION CHECK 5 ANSWERS

1. The fact that two events are related does not mean that one caused the other to occur.

2. What is true for the individual is not necessarily true for the group.

1-6 Positive and Normative Economics

SECTION CHECK 6

Keep the following questions in mind as you read through this section.

1. What is a positive statement?

2. What is a normative statement?

3. Why do economists disagree?

Economists are asked to explain the world as scientists and improve the world as policy advisers. Positive analysis deals with factual statements trying to explain the world. Normative analysis deals with value judgments trying to improve the world.

1-6a POSITIVE STATEMENT

Most economists view themselves as scientists seeking the truth about the way people behave. They make speculations about economic behavior, and then, ideally, they assess the validity of those predictions based on human experience. Their work emphasizes how people do behave, rather than how people should behave. In the role of scientist, an economist tries to observe patterns of behavior objectively, without reference to the appropriateness or inappropriateness of that behavior. This objective, value-free approach, based on the scientific method, is called positive analysis. In positive analysis, we want to know the impact of variable A on variable B. We want to be able to test a hypothesis. For example, the following is a **positive statement**: If rent controls are imposed, vacancy rates will fall. This statement is testable. A positive statement does not have to be a true statement, but it does have to be a testable statement.

Keep in mind, however, that it is doubtful that even the most objective scientist can be totally value free in his or her analysis. An economist may well emphasize data or evidence that supports a hypothesis, putting less weight on other evidence that might be contradictory. This tendency, alas, is human nature. But a good economist/scientist strives to be as fair and objective as possible in evaluating evidence and in stating conclusions based on the evidence. In some sense, economists are like engineers; they try to figure out how things work and then describe what would happen if you changed something.

1-6b NORMATIVE STATEMENT

Economists, like anyone else, have opinions and make value judgments. When economists, or anyone else for that matter, express opinions about an economic policy or statement, they are indicating in part how they believe things should be, not stating facts about the way things are. In other words, they are performing normative analysis. **Normative statements** involve judgments about what should be or what ought to happen. For example, normative questions might include: Should the government raise the minimum wage? Should the government increase spending in the space program?

fallacy of composition the incorrect view that what is true for the individual is always true for the group

positive statement an objective, testable statement that describes what happens and why it happens

normative statement a subjective, contestable statement that attempts to describe what should be done

Should the government give "free" prescription drugs to senior citizens?

Positive versus Normative Analysis

The distinction between positive and normative analysis is important. While positive and normative analysis are different, policy prescriptions often incorporate both elements. Suppose researchers conclude, through positive analysis, that a higher minimum wage will lead to greater unemployment. That does not prove that a higher minimum wage is a bad idea. Proponents of the higher minimum wage may argue that the gains to the workers who get a higher wage offset the losses to employers and the unemployed workers. Opponents may argue the losses are greater than the gains. Ultimately, the decision will weigh heavily on normative analysis (political views and personal values). In short, positive statements are attempts to *describe* what happens and why it happens, while normative statements are attempts to *prescribe* what should be done.

1-6c DISAGREEMENT IS COMMON IN MOST DISCIPLINES

Although economists do frequently have opposing views on economic policy questions, they probably disagree less than the media would have you believe. Disagreement is common in most disciplines: Seismologists differ over predictions of earthquakes or volcanic eruption; historians can be at odds over the interpretation of historical events; psychologists disagree on proper ways to raise children; and nutritionists debate the merits of large doses of vitamin C.

The majority of disagreements in economics stem from normative issues; differences in values or policy beliefs result in conflict. For example, a policy might increase efficiency at the expense of a sense of fairness or equity, or it might help a current generation at the expense of a future generation. Because policy decisions involve trade-offs, they will always involve the potential for conflict.

How should the government distribute its funds? The space program? Higher minimum wage? Prescription drugs? This kind of decision requires normative analysis.

Often Economists Do Agree

According to a survey among members of the American Economic Association, most economists agree on a wide range of issues, including rent control, import tariffs, export restrictions, the use of wage and price controls to curb inflation, and the minimum wage. In fact, most economists would agree that the following statements are correct:

ECONOMISTS DO AGREE

1. A ceiling on rents (rent control) reduces the quantity and quality of rental housing available (93 percent agree).

2. Tariffs and import quotas usually reduce general economic welfare (93 percent agree).

3. The United States should not restrict employers from outsourcing work to foreign countries (90.1 percent agree).

4. Fiscal policy (e.g., tax cuts and/or increases in government expenditure) has a significant stimulative impact on an economy that is less than fully employed (90 percent agree).

5. Flexible and floating exchange rates offer an effective international monetary arrangement (90 percent).

6. The gap between Social Security funds and expenditures will become unsustainably large within the next 50 years if the current policies remain unchanged (85 percent agree).

7. The United States should eliminate agricultural subsidies (85 percent agree).

8. Local and state governments in the United States should eliminate subsidies to professional sport franchises (85 percent agree).

9. A large budget deficit has an adverse effect on the economy (83 percent agree).

10. A minimum wage increases unemployment among young and unskilled workers (79 percent agree).

11. Effluent taxes and marketable pollution permits represent a better approach to pollution control than imposition of pollution ceilings (78 percent agree).

12. Economists favor expanding competition and market forces in education (67.1 percent agree).

SOURCE: Richard M. Alston, J.R. Kearl and Michael B. Vaughn, "Is there Consensus among Economists in the 1990s?" *American Economic Review* (May 1992): 203-09; Robert Whaples, "Do Economists Agree on Anything? Yes!" *Economists' Voice* (November 2006):1-6.

SECTION CHECK 6 ANSWERS

1. Positive analysis is objective and free. They are testable statements. It describes what happens and why it happens.

2. Normative analysis involves value judgments and opinions about the desirability of various actions. It is not testable. These statements prescribe what should be done.

3. Disagreement is common in most disciplines. Most disagreement among economists stems from normative issues.

1-7 Why Study Economics?

Among the many good reasons to study economics, perhaps the best reason is that so many of the things of concern in the world around us are at least partly economic in character. A quick look at newspaper headlines reveals the vast range of problems that are related to economics—global warming, health care, education, and Social Security. The study of economics improves your understanding of these concerns. A student of economics becomes aware that, at a basic level, much of economic life involves choosing among alternative possible courses of action—making choices between our conflicting wants and desires in a world of scarcity. Economics provides some clues as to how to intelligently evaluate these options and determine the most appropriate choices in given situations.

The problem-solving tools you will develop by studying economics will prove valuable to you both in your personal and professional life, regardless of your career choice. In short, the study of economics provides a systematic, disciplined way of thinking.

1-7a ECONOMICS IS ALL AROUND US

The tools of economics are far reaching. In fact, other social scientists have accused economists of being imperialistic because their tools have been used in so many fields outside the formal area of economics, such as crime, education, marriage, divorce, addiction, finance, health, law, politics, and religion.

So while you might think that much of what you desire in life is "non-economic," economics concerns everything an individual might consider worthwhile, including things that you might consider "priceless." For instance, although we may long for love, sexual fulfillment, or spiritual enlightenment, few of us would be able to set a price for them. But even these matters have an economic dimension. Consider spirituality, for example. Concern for spiritual matters has led to the development of institutions such as churches, synagogues, and temples that conduct religious and spiritual services. In economic terms, these services are goods that many people desire.

Even time has an economic dimension. In fact, in modern culture, time has become perhaps the single most precious resource we have. Everyone has the same limited amount of time per day, and how we divide our time between work and leisure (including study, sleep, exercise, and so on) is a distinctly economic matter. If we choose more work, we must sacrifice leisure. If we choose to study, we must sacrifice time with friends or time spent sleeping or watching TV. Virtually everything we decide to do, then, has an economic dimension.

Living in a world of scarcity involves trade-offs. As you are reading this text, you are giving up other things you value, such as shopping, spending time on Facebook or texting your friends, going to the movies, sleeping, or working out. When we know what the trade-offs are, we can make better choices from the options all around us, every day. As George Bernard Shaw once said, "Economy is the art of making the most of life."

Who Studies Economics?

The study of economics is useful in many career paths. Here is a short list of some relatively well-known people who studied economics in college.

POLITICIANS, POLICY MAKERS, AND SUPREME COURT JUSTICES:

- George H. W. Bush, former U.S. President (Yale)
- Ronald Reagan, former U.S. President (Eureka College)
- Gerald Ford, former U.S. President (University of Michigan)
- Arnold Schwarzenegger, Body Builder/Actor/Governor (University of Wisconsin)
- Sandra Day-O'Connor, retired U.S. Supreme Court Justice (Stanford)
- Stephen Breyer, U.S. Supreme Court Justice (Stanford)
- Anthony Kennedy, U.S. Supreme Court Justice (Stanford and London School of Economics)
- Kofi Annan, former Secretary General of the United Nations (Macalester College)

BILLIONAIRES:

- Sam Walton, founder of Wal-Mart (University of Missouri)
- Warren Buffett, financier (Columbia School of Business, Masters in Economics)
- Meg Whitman, former President and CEO of eBay, Inc. (Princeton)
- Ted Turner, media tycoon (Brown)
- Steve Ballmer, CEO of Microsoft (Harvard)
- Donald Trump, real-estate/television mogul (University of Pennsylvania—Wharton)
- Paul Otellini, President and CEO of Intel (University of San Francisco)

CELEBRITIES:

- John Elway, former NFL quarterback (Stanford University)
- Mick Jagger, lead singer of The Rolling Stones (London School of Economics)
- Cate Blanchett, actress (Melbourne University)
- Scott Adams, cartoonist, creator of *Dilbert* (Hartwick College)
- Tiger Woods, golfer (Stanford)
- Bill Belichick, NFL head coach, New England Patriots (Wesleyan University)

According to Bob McTeer, former president and CEO of the Federal Reserve Bank of Dallas, "My take on training in economics is that it becomes increasingly valuable as you move up the career ladder. I can't think of a better major for corporate CEOs, congressmen (and women), or presidents of the United States. You've learned a systematic, disciplined way of thinking that will serve you well.

Chapter 1: Self-Review

Now that you're finished reading the chapter, review the questions below. You can write your answers in the space provided, then go online to see the answers at www.cengagebrain.com.

1-1 ECONOMICS: A BRIEF INTRODUCTION

1. What is the definition of economics?

2. Which of the following goods are scarce?
   a. garbage
   b. salt water in the ocean
   c. clothes
   d. clean air in a big city
   e. dirty air in a big city
   f. a public library

1-2 ECONOMIC BEHAVIOR

3. What does rational self-interest involve?

4. What is rational behavior?

1-3 MARKETS

5. What do market prices communicate to others in society?

6. Why does the circular flow of money move in the opposite direction from the flow of goods and services?

1-4 ECONOMIC THEORY

7. Why do economic predictions refer to the behavior of groups of people rather than individuals?

8. Are the following topics ones that would be covered in microeconomics or macroeconomics?
   a. the effects of an increase in the supply of lumber on the home-building industry
   b. changes in the national unemployment rate
   c. changes in the inflation rate
   d. changes in the country's economic growth rate
   e. the price of concert tickets

1-5 PITFALLS TO AVOID IN SCIENTIFIC THINKING

9. What types of misinterpretation result from confusing correlation and causation?

10. Do any of the following statements involve fallacies? If so, which ones?
    a. Because sitting in the back of the classroom is correlated with getting lower grades in the class, students should always sit closer to the front of the classroom.
    b. Historically, the stock market rises in years the NFC team wins the Super Bowl and falls when the AFC wins the Super Bowl; I am rooting for the NFC team to win for the sake of my investment portfolio.
    c. Gasoline prices were higher last year than in 1970, yet people purchased more gas, which contradicts the law of demand.

1-6 POSITIVE AND NORMATIVE ECONOMICS

11. Why is the positive/normative distinction important?

1-7 WHY STUDY ECONOMICS?

12. Why is economics worth studying?

A1-1 Appendix— Working with Graphs

Sometimes the use of visual aids, such as graphs, greatly enhances our understanding of a theory. It is much the same as finding your way to a friend's house with the aid of a map rather than with detailed verbal or written instructions. In this section we'll go over the basics of creating graphs and how graphs are used in economics.

A1-1a GRAPHS ARE AN IMPORTANT ECONOMIC TOOL

Graphs are important tools for economists. They allow us to understand better the workings of the economy. To economists, a graph can be worth a thousand words. This textbook will use graphs throughout to enhance the understanding of important economic relationships. This appendix provides a guide on how to read and create your own graphs.

The most useful graph for our purposes is one that merely connects a vertical line (the **Y-axis**) with a horizontal line (the **X-axis**), as seen in Exhibit 1.2. The intersection of the two lines occurs at the *origin*, which is where the value of both variables is equal to zero. In Exhibit 1.2, the graph has four quadrants, or boxes. In this textbook, we will be primarily concerned with the shaded box in the upper-right corner. This portion of the graph deals exclusively with positive numbers. Always keep in mind that moving to the right on the horizontal axis and moving up along the vertical axis both lead to higher values.

Y-axis the vertical axis on a graph

X-axis the horizontal axis on a graph

pie chart visual display showing the relative size of various quantities that add up to 100 percent

bar graph visual display showing the comparison of quantities

time-series graph visual tool to show changes in a variable's value over time

variable something that is measured by a number, such as your height

Using Graphs and Charts

Exhibit 1.3 presents four common types of graphs. The **pie chart** in Exhibit 1.3(a) shows the revenues received from various taxes levied on households and corporations. Each slice in the pie chart represents the percentage of finances that are derived from different sources—for example, personal income taxes account for 43 percent of the federal government's tax revenues. Therefore, pie charts are used to show the relative size of various quantities that add up to 100 percent.

Exhibit 1.3(b) is a **bar graph** that shows the unemployment rate by age and sex in the United States. The height of the line represents the unemployment rate. Bar graphs are used to show a comparison of quantities.

Exhibit 1.3(c) is a **time-series graph**. This type of graph shows changes in the value of a variable over time. This visual tool allows us to observe important trends over a certain time period. In Exhibit 1.3(c), we see a graph that shows trends in the inflation rate over time. The horizontal axis shows us the passage of time, and the vertical axis shows us the inflation rate (annual percent change). From the graph, we can see the trends in the inflation rate from 1913–2011.

A1-1b USING GRAPHS TO SHOW THE RELATIONSHIP BETWEEN TWO VARIABLES

Even though the graphs and chart in Exhibit 1.3 are important, they do not allow us to show the relationship between two variables (a **variable** is something that is measured by a number, such as your height). To more closely examine the structures and functions of graphs, let's consider the story of Josh, an avid skateboarder who has aspirations of winning the Z Games next year. He knows that to get there, he'll need to put

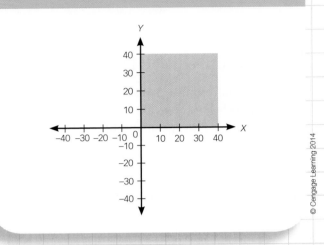

EXHIBIT 1.2 Plotting a Graph

© Cengage Learning 2014

EXHIBIT 1.3 Pie Chart, Bar Graph, and Time-Series Graph

a. Pie Chart—Tax Revenues—Federal Government, 2011

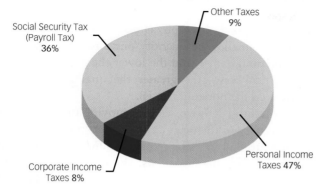

Other Taxes 9%

Social Security Tax (Payroll Tax) 36%

Personal Income Taxes 47%

Corporate Income Taxes 8%

SOURCE: *Economic Report of the President*, 2012.

b. Bar Graph—U.S. Unemployment, by Sex and Age, 2011

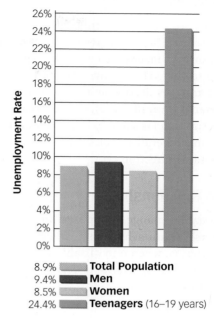

8.9% ▨ **Total Population**
9.4% ▨ **Men**
8.5% ▨ **Women**
24.4% ▨ **Teenagers** (16–19 years)

SOURCE: Bureau of Labor Statistics.

c. Time-Series Graph—Inflation in the United States, 1913–2011

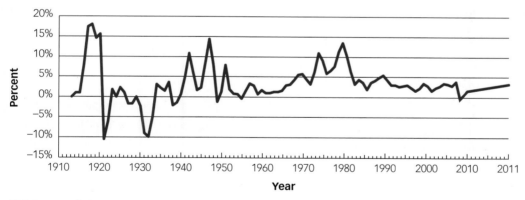

SOURCE: Bureau of Labor Statistics, Consumer Price Index.

© Cengage Learning 2014

in many hours of practice. But how many hours? In search of information about the practice habits of other skateboarders, he logs onto the Internet, where he pulls up the results of a study that looked at the score of each Z Games competitor in relation to the amount of practice time per week spent by each skateboarder. As Exhibit 1.4 shows, the results of the study indicate that skateboarders had to practice 10 hours per week to receive a score of 4, 20 hours per week to receive a score of 6, 30 hours per week to get a score of 8, and 40 hours per week to get a perfect score of 10. How does this information help Josh? By using a graph, he can more clearly understand the relationship between practice time and overall score.

A Positive Relationship

The study on scores and practice times reveals what is called a direct relationship, also called a **positive relationship**. A positive relationship means that the variables change in the same direction. That is, an increase in one variable (practice time) is accompanied by an increase in the other variable (overall score), or a decrease in one variable (practice time) is accompanied by a decrease in the other variable (overall score). In short, the variables change in the same direction.

A Negative Relationship

When two variables change in opposite directions, they have an inverse relationship, also called a **negative relationship**. That is, when one variable rises, the other variable falls, or when one variable decreases, the other variable increases.

A1-1c THE GRAPH OF A DEMAND CURVE

Let's now examine one of the most important graphs in economics—the demand curve. In Exhibit 1.5, we see Emily's individual demand curve for pizzas per month.

It shows the price of pizzas on the vertical axis and the quantity of pizzas purchased per month on the horizontal axis. Every point in the space shown represents a price and quantity combination. The downward-sloping line, labeled "Demand curve," shows the different combinations of price and quantity purchased. Note that the higher the price of the pizzas (as shown on the vertical axis), the smaller the quantity purchased (as shown on the horizontal axis), and the lower the price (shown on the vertical axis), the greater the quantity purchased (shown on the horizontal axis).

In Exhibit 1.5, we see that moving up the vertical price axis from the origin, the price of pizzas increases from $5 to $25 in increments of $5. Moving out along the horizontal quantity axis, the quantity purchased increases from zero to five pizzas per month. Point A represents a price of $25 and a quantity of one pizza, point B represents a price of $20 and a quantity of two pizzas, point C a price of $15 and a quantity of three pizzas, and so on. When we connect all the points, we have what economists call a curve. As you can see, curves are sometimes drawn as straight lines for ease of illustration. Moving down along the curve, we see that as the price falls, a greater quantity is demanded; moving up the curve to higher prices, a smaller quantity is demanded. That is, when pizzas become less expensive, Emily buys more pizzas. When pizzas become more expensive, Emily buys fewer pizzas, perhaps choosing to go to the movies or buy downloadable music instead.

EXHIBIT 1.4 A Positive Relationship

© Cengage Learning 2014

EXHIBIT 1.5 A Negative Relationship

© Cengage Learning 2014

A1-1d USING GRAPHS TO SHOW THE RELATIONSHIP AMONG THREE VARIABLES

Although only two variables are shown on the axes, graphs can be used to show the relationship among three variables. For example, say we add a third variable—income—to our earlier example. Our three variables are now income, price, and quantity purchased. If Emily's income rises—say she gets a raise at work—she is now able and willing to buy more pizzas than before at each possible price. As a result, the whole demand curve shifts outward (to the right) compared with the old curve. That is, the new income gives her more money to buy more pizzas. This shift is seen in the graph in Exhibit 1.6(a). On the other hand, if her income falls— say she quits her job to go back to school—she would have less income to buy pizzas. A decrease in this variable causes the whole demand curve to shift inward (to

the left) compared with the old curve. This shift is seen in the graph in Exhibit 1.6(b).

slope the ratio of rise (change in the Y variable) over run (change in the X variable)

The Difference between a Movement Along and a Shift in the Curve

It is important to remember the difference between a movement between one point and another along a curve and a shift in the whole curve. A change in one of the variables on the graph, such as price or quantity purchased, will cause a movement along the curve, say from point A to point B, as shown in Exhibit 1.7. A change in one of the variables not shown (held constant in order to show only the relationship between price and quantity), such as income in our example, will cause the whole curve to shift. The change from D_1 to D_2 in Exhibit 1.7 shows such a shift.

A1-1e SLOPE

In economics, we sometimes refer to the steepness of a line or curve on a graph as the **slope**. A slope can be either positive (upward-sloping) or negative (downward-sloping). A curve that is downward-sloping represents an inverse, or negative, relationship between the two variables and slants downward from left to right, as seen in Exhibit 1.8(a). A curve that is upward-sloping represents a direct, or positive, relationship between the two variables and slants upward from left to right, as seen in Exhibit 1.8(b). The numeric value of the slope shows the number of units of change of the Y-axis variable for each unit of change in the X-axis variable. Slope provides the direction (positive or negative) as well as the magnitude of the relationship between the two variables.

EXHIBIT 1.6 Shifting a Curve

a. Demand Curve with Higher Income

b. Demand Curve with Lower Income

© Cengage Learning 2014

EXHIBIT 1.7 Shifts versus Movements

© Cengage Learning 2014

EXHIBIT 1.8 Downward- and Upward-Sloping Linear Curves

a. Downward-Sloping Linear Curve

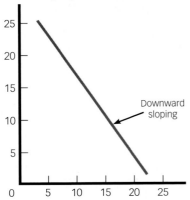

Downward sloping

b. Upward-Sloping Linear Curve

Upward sloping

© Cengage Learning 2014

Measuring the Slope of a Linear Curve

A straight-line curve is called a linear curve. The slope of a linear curve between two points measures the relative rates of change of two variables. Specifically, the slope of a linear curve can be defined as the ratio of the change in the Y value to the change in the X value. The slope can also be expressed as the ratio of the rise over the run, where the rise is the vertical change and the run is the horizontal change.

Exhibit 1.9 shows two linear curves, one with a positive slope and one with a negative slope. In Exhibit 1.9(a), the slope of the positively sloped linear curve from point A to B is 1/2, because the rise is 1 (from 2 to 3) and the run is 2 (from 1 to 3). In Exhibit 1.9(b), the negatively sloped linear curve has a slope of –4: A rise of –8 (a fall of 8, from 10 to 2) and a run of 2 (from 2 to 4) gives us a slope of –8/2, or –4. Notice the appropriate signs on the slopes: The negatively sloped line carries a minus sign and the positively sloped line, a plus sign.

EXHIBIT 1.9 Slopes of Positive and Negative Curves

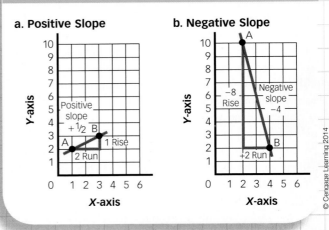

a. Positive Slope   b. Negative Slope

© Cengage Learning 2014

Finding the Slope of a Nonlinear Curve

In Exhibit 1.10, we show the slope of a nonlinear curve. A nonlinear curve is a line that actually curves. Here the slope varies from point to point along the curve. However, we can find the slope of this curve at any given point by drawing a straight line tangent to that point on the curve. A tangency is when a straight line just touches the curve without actually crossing it. At point A, we see that the positively sloped line that is tangent to the curve has a slope of 1: the line rises 1 and runs 1. At point B, the line is horizontal, so it has zero slope. At point C, we see a slope of –2, because the negatively sloped line has a rise of –2 (a fall of 2) for every run of 1.

Remember, many students have problems with economics simply because they fail to understand graphs, so make sure that you understand this material before going on to Chapter 2.

EXHIBIT 1.10 Slopes of a Nonlinear Curve

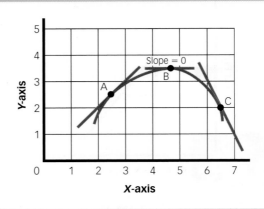

© Cengage Learning 2014

USE THE TOOLS.

- Rip out the Review Cards in the back of your book to study.

Or Visit CourseMate for:

- Full, interactive eBook (search, highlight, take notes)
- Review Flashcards (Print or Online) to master key terms
- Test yourself with Auto-Graded Quizzes
- Bring concepts to life with Games, Videos, and Animations!

Go to CourseMate for Survey of ECON to begin using these tools. Access at **www.cengagebrain.com**.

Complete the Speak Up survey in CourseMate at **www.cengagebrain.com**

 Follow us at **www.facebook.com/4ltrpress**

PART **1**

Economic questions

are all around you. Take for instance the people who lined up to buy opening day baseball tickets. Not only did it cost them money to purchase the tickets, but it also cost them time waiting in line—time that they might have spent doing other things. Choices like this one are all around us, and by studying economics we can better understand these choices and hopefully make better ones in the future.

Test your Economics *street-smart* knowledge and see how you compare against other students! Scan here or visit CourseMate for Survey of ECON2.

2
The Economic Way of Thinking

Studying economics may teach you how to "think better," because economics helps develop a disciplined method of thinking about problems.

A student of economics becomes aware, at a basic level, that much of economic life involves choosing one course of action rather than another—making choices among our conflicting wants and desires in a world of scarcity. Economics provides insights about how to intelligently evaluate these options and determine the most appropriate choices in given situations. *Most of economics really involves knowing certain principles well and knowing when and how to apply them.*

This chapter presents some important tools that will help you understand the economic way of thinking. The economic way of thinking provides a logical framework for organizing and analyzing your understanding of a broad set of issues, many of which do not even seem directly related to economics as you now know it.

The basic ideas that you learn in this chapter will occur repeatedly throughout the text. If you develop a good understanding of these principles and master the problem-solving skills inherent in them, they will serve you well for the rest of your life. Learning to think like an economist takes time. Like most disciplines, economics has its own specialized vocabulary, including such terms as *elasticity, comparative advantage, supply and demand, externalities, efficiency,* and *deadweight loss.* Learning economics requires more than picking up this new terminology; it also involves using its powerful tools to improve your understanding of a whole host of issues in the world around you.

2-1 Choices, Costs, and Trade-Offs

SECTION CHECK 1

Consider the following questions as you read through this section.

1. Why do we have to make choices?

2. What do we give up when we have to choose?

3. Why are "free" lunches not free?

In this section, we will discuss the costs, both monetary and nonmonetary, and the trade-offs that we must make when presented with choices.

2-1a SCARCITY FORCES US TO CHOOSE

Each of us may want a nice home, two luxury cars, wholesome and good-tasting food, a personal trainer, a therapist, and to enjoy it all in a pristine environment with zero pollution. If we had unlimited resources, and an ability to produce all the goods and services everyone wants, we would not have to choose among those desires. However, we all face scarcity, and as a consequence, we must make choices. If we did not have to make meaningful economic choices, the study of economics would not be necessary. The essence of economics is to understand fully the implications that scarcity has for wise decision making.

2-1b TRADE-OFF

In a world of scarcity, we all face trade-offs. In a world of scarcity, when we make a choice we choose from alternatives. This usually requires that we choose one thing that we value over another thing that we also value. In other words, we face a trade-off—or an exchange of giving up one thing to get something else. If you spend more time at work, you might give up an opportunity to go shopping at the mall or watch your favorite television show. Time spent exercising means giving up something else that is valuable—perhaps relaxing with friends or studying for an exam. Or when you decide how to spend your income, buying a new car may mean you have to forgo a summer vacation. Businesses have trade-offs, too. If a farmer chooses to plant cotton on his land this year, he gives up the opportunity to plant wheat. If a firm decides to produce only cars, it gives up the opportunity to use those resources to produce refrigerators or something else that people value. Society, too, must make trade-offs. For example, the federal government faces trade-offs when it comes to spending tax revenues; additional resources used to enhance the environment may come at the expense of additional resources to provide health care, education, or national defense.

2-1c TO CHOOSE IS TO LOSE

Every choice involves a cost. Anytime you are doing something, you could be doing something else. The next highest or best foregone opportunity resulting from a decision is called the **opportunity cost**. Another way to put it is that "to choose is to lose" or "an opportunity cost is the highest-valued opportunity lost." It is important to remember that the opportunity cost involves the next highest-valued alternative, not all alternatives not chosen. For example, what would you have been doing with your time if you were not reading this book? The next best alternative is what you give up, not all the things you could have been doing. To get more of anything that is desirable, you must accept less of something else that you also value.

Every choice you make has a cost, an opportunity cost. All productive resources have alternative uses regardless of who owns them—individuals, firms, or governments. For example, if a city uses land for a new school, the cost is the next-best alternative use of that land—perhaps a park. To have a meaningful understanding of cost, you must be able to compare the alternative opportunities that are sacrificed in that choice.

For example, time spent exercising costs time that could be spent doing something else that is valuable— perhaps relaxing with friends or studying for an upcoming exam. Trade-offs are everywhere. The famous poet Robert Frost understood that to live is to choose. In his poem, "The Road Not Taken," he writes, "two roads diverged in a yellow wood, and sorry I could not travel both."

Money Costs and Non-Money Costs

If you go to the store to buy groceries, you have to pay for the items you bought. This amount is called the *money cost*. This money cost is an opportunity cost because you could have used that money to purchase other goods or services. However, additional opportunity costs include the non-money costs incurred to acquire the groceries—time spent getting to the grocery store, finding a parking place, shopping for groceries, and waiting in the checkout line. The non-money costs are measured by assessing the sacrifice involved—the value you place on what you would have done with that time if you had not gone shopping. So the cost of grocery shopping is the price paid for the goods, plus the non-money costs incurred. Consider another example: Your concert ticket may have only been $50, but what if you had to wait in line for six hours in the freezing cold? Waiting and enduring the cold are costs, too. Seldom are costs just dollars and cents. Shopping at a large discount store may save you money on the price but cost you time waiting in long checkout lines. Also, buying food in bulk quantities may be less expensive per ounce but cost inventory space in your pantry, or the food may spoil before it is eaten.

opportunity cost the value of the best forgone alternative that was not chosen

Remember that many costs do not involve money but are still costs. Do I major in economics or engineering? Do I go to Billy Madison University or Tech State University? Should I get an MBA now or work and wait a few years to go back to school? Choices have present and future consequences. What if I decide *not* to study for my final exams? What future consequences will I bear? Flunk out of school? Not get into graduate school?

Policy makers, too, are unavoidably faced with opportunity costs. Consider airline safety. Both money costs and time costs affect airline safety. New airline safety devices cost money (for luggage inspection devices, smoke detectors, fuel tank safeguards, new radar equipment, and so on), and time costs are quite evident with the new security checks. Waiting in line costs time that could be used to do something else that is valuable. New airline safety requirements could also actually cost lives. If the new safety equipment costs are passed on in the form of higher airline ticket prices, people may choose to travel by car, which is far more dangerous per mile traveled than by air. Opportunity costs are everywhere! And the real cost of anything is what you have to give up to get it.

The Opportunity Cost of Going to College

The average person often does not correctly calculate opportunity costs. For example, the opportunity cost of going to college includes not just the direct expenses of tuition and books. Of course, those expenses do involve an opportunity cost because the money used for books and tuition could be used to buy other things that you value. But what about the non-money costs? That is, going to college also includes the opportunity cost of your time. Specifically, the time spent going to school is time that could have been spent on a job earning, say, $30,000 over the course of an academic year. Bill Gates, Tiger Woods, and Oprah Winfrey all quit college to pursue their dreams. Tiger Woods dropped out of Stanford (where he was pursuing an economics major) to join the PGA golf tour. Bill Gates dropped out of Harvard to start a software company. Oprah Winfrey dropped out of Tennessee State to pursue a career in broadcasting. At the early age of 19, she became the co-anchor of the evening news. LeBron James (Miami Heat), Kobe Bryant (LA Lakers), and Alex Rodriguez

(New York Yankees) understood opportunity cost; they didn't even start college, and it worked out well for them. Staying in or starting college would have cost each of them millions of dollars. We cannot say it would have been the wrong decision to stay in school, or never start college, but it would have been costly. Their opportunity cost of staying in or starting college was high.

Consider some other costs. What about room and board? That aspect is a little tricky because you would presumably have to pay room and board whether you went to college or not. The relevant question may be how much more it costs you to live at school rather than at home (and living at home may have substantial nonmoney costs). Even if you stayed at home, your parents would sacrifice something; they could rent your room out or use the room for some other purpose such as storage, a guest room, a home office, a sibling's room, and so on.

2-1d IS THAT REALLY A FREE LUNCH, A FREEWAY, OR A FREE BEACH?

The expression "there's no such thing as a free lunch" clarifies the relationship between scarcity and opportunity cost. Suppose the school cafeteria is offering "free" lunches today. Although the lunch is free to you, is it really free from society's perspective? The answer is no, because some of society's scarce resources will have been used in the preparation of the lunch. The issue is whether the resources that went into creating that lunch could have been used to produce something else of value. Clearly, the scarce resources that went into the production of the lunch—the labor and materials (foodservice workers, lettuce, meat, plows,

tractors, fertilizer, and so forth)—could have been used in other ways. They had an opportunity cost and thus were not free.

Do not confuse free with a zero money price. A number of goods—freeways, free beaches, and free libraries, for instance—do not cost consumers money, but they are still scarce. Few things are free in the sense that they use none of society's scarce resources. So what does a free lunch really mean? It is, technically speaking, a "subsidized" lunch—a lunch using society's scarce resources, but one that the person receiving does not have to pay for personally.

SECTION CHECK 1 ANSWERS

1. Scarcity means we all have to make choices.

2. When we are forced to choose, we give up the next highest-valued alternative.

3. Few things are free in the sense that they do not use any of society's scarce resources. A thing may still be scarce even though it costs consumers no money.

2-2 Marginal Thinking

SECTION CHECK 2

Keep the following questions in mind as you read through this section.

1. What do we mean by marginal thinking?

2. What is the rule of rational choice?

3. Why do we use the word "expected" with marginal benefits and costs?

2-2a MANY CHOICES WE FACE INVOLVE MARGINAL THINKING

Some decisions are "all or nothing," like whether to start a new business or go to work for someone else, or whether to attend graduate school or take a job. But rational people know that many decisions are not black and white. Many choices we face involve *how much* of something to do rather than *whether* to do

© Terrance Emerson/Shutterstock

something. It is not *whether* you eat but *how much* you eat. Or, how many caffe lattes will I buy this week? Or, how often do I change the oil in my car? Or how much of my paycheck do I spend, and how much do I save? Your instructors hope that the question is not *whether* you study this semester but *how much* you study. You might think to yourself, "If I studied a little more, I might be able to improve my grade," or "If I had a little better concentration when I was studying, I could improve my grade." That is, spending more time has an additional expected benefit (a higher grade) and an additional expected cost (giving up time to do something else that is valuable, such as watching TV or sleeping). These examples reflect what economists call **marginal thinking** because the focus is on the additional, or marginal, choices available to you. Or think of marginal as the edge—marginal decisions are made around the edge of what you are currently doing. Marginal choices involve the effects of adding or subtracting from the current situation. In short, they are the small (or large) incremental changes to a plan of action.

Businesses are constantly engaged in marginal thinking. For example, firms have to decide whether the additional marginal revenue received from increasing production is greater than the marginal cost of that production.

© @erics/Shutterstock.com

The question may not be whether you have coffee today, but rather how much coffee you will have.

marginal thinking
focusing on the additional, or marginal, choices; marginal choices involve the effects of adding or subtracting, from the current situation, the small (or large) incremental changes to a plan of action

rule of rational choice
individuals will pursue an activity if the expected marginal benefits are greater than the expected marginal costs

Always watch out for the difference between average and marginal costs. Suppose an airline had 10 unoccupied seats on a flight from Los Angeles to New York, and the average cost was $400 per seat (the total cost divided by the number of seats— $100,000/250). If 10 people are waiting on standby, each willing to pay $300, should the airline sell them the tickets? Yes! The unoccupied seats earn nothing for the airline. What are the additional marginal costs of a few more passengers? The marginal costs are minimal—slight wear and tear on the airplane, handling some extra baggage, and 10 extra in-flight meals. In this case, thinking at the margin can increase total profits, even if it means selling at less than the average cost of production.

Another good example of marginal thinking is an auction. Prices are bid up marginally as the auctioneer calls out one price after another. When bidders view the new price, the marginal cost, to be greater than the value they place on the good, the marginal benefit, they withdraw from further bidding.

In trying to make themselves better off, people alter their behavior if the expected marginal benefits from doing so outweigh the expected marginal costs, which is the **rule of rational choice**. Economic theory is often called marginal analysis because it assumes that people are always weighing the expected marginal benefits against the expected marginal costs. The term *expected* is used with *marginal benefits* and *marginal costs* because the world is uncertain in many important respects, so the actual result of changing behavior may not always make people better off—but on average it will. However, as a matter of rationality, people are assumed to engage only in behavior that they think will make them better off. That is, individuals will only pursue an activity if their expected marginal benefits are greater than their expected marginal costs of pursuing that activity one step further, $E(MB) > E(MC)$.

This fairly unrestrictive and realistic view of individuals seeking self-betterment can be used to analyze a variety of social phenomena.

Suppose that you have to get up for an 8 A.M. class but have been up very late. When the alarm goes off at 7 A.M., you weigh the marginal benefits and marginal costs of an extra 15 minutes of sleep. If you perceive

net benefit the difference between the expected marginal benefits and the expected marginal costs

the marginal benefits of 15 additional minutes of sleep to be greater than the marginal costs of those extra minutes, you may choose to hit the snooze button. Or perhaps you may decide to blow off class completely. But it's unlikely that you will choose that action if it's the day of the final exam—because it is now likely that the **net benefits** (the difference between the expected marginal benefits and the expected marginal costs) of skipping class have changed. When people have opportunities to make themselves better off, they usually take them. And they will continue to seek those opportunities as long as they expect a net benefit from doing so.

The rule of rational choice is simply the rule of being sensible, and most economists believe that individuals act *as if* they are sensible and apply the rule of rational choice to their daily lives. It is a rule that can help us understand our decisions to study, walk, shop, exercise, clean house, cook, and perform just about every other action.

It is also a rule that we will continue to use throughout the text. Because whether it is consumers, producers, or policy makers making decisions, they all must compare the expected marginal benefits and the expected marginal cost to determine the best level to consume, produce, or provide public programs.

Zero Pollution Would Be Too Costly

Let's use the concept of marginal thinking to evaluate pollution levels. We all know the benefits of a cleaner environment, but what would we have to give up—that

© Sergii Korolko/Shutterstock.com

How might the net benefits of waking up on time change between a normal day of class and the day of your semester exam?

is, what marginal costs would we have to incur—to achieve zero pollution? A lot! You could not drive a car, fly in a plane, or even ride a bicycle, especially if everybody else were riding bikes, too (because traffic congestion is a form of pollution). How would you get to school or work, or go to the movies or the grocery store? Everyone would have to grow their own food because transporting, storing, and producing food uses machinery and equipment that pollute. And even growing your own food would be a problem because many plants emit natural pollutants. We could go on and on. The point is not that we shouldn't be concerned about the environment, but rather that we have to weigh the expected marginal benefits of a cleaner environment against the expected marginal costs of a cleaner environment. This discussion is not meant to say the environment should not be cleaner, only that zero pollution levels would be far too costly in terms of what we would have to give up.

Optimal (Best) Levels of Safety

Like pollution, crime and safety can have optimal (or best) levels that are greater than zero. Take crime. What would it cost society to have zero crime? It would be prohibitively costly to divert a tremendous amount of our valuable resources toward the complete elimination of crime. In fact, it would be impossible to eliminate crime totally. Even reducing crime significantly would be costly. Because lower crime rates are costly, society must decide how much it is willing to give up. The additional resources for crime prevention can only come from limited supplies, which could be used to produce something else that people may value even more.

The same is true for safer products. Nobody wants defective tires on their car or cars that are unsafe and roll over at low speeds. However, optimal amounts of safety that are greater than zero are available. The issue is not safe versus unsafe products but rather *how much* safety we want. It is not risk versus no risk but rather *how much* risk we are willing to take. Additional safety can only come at higher costs. To make all products perfectly safe would be impossible, so we must weigh the benefits and costs of safer products. In fact, according to one study by Sam Peltzman, a University of Chicago economist, additional safety regulations in cars (mandatory safety belts and padded dashboards) in the late 1960s may have had little impact on highway fatalities. Peltzman found that making cars safer led to more reckless driving and more accidents. The safety regulations did result in fewer deaths per automobile accident, but the total number of deaths remained unchanged because more accidents occurred.

Speeding and reckless driving has a benefit in the form of getting somewhere more quickly, but it can also have a cost—an accident or even a fatality. Most people will compare the marginal benefits and marginal costs of safer driving and make the choices that they believe will get them to their destination safely.

2-3 Specialization and Trade

SECTION CHECK 3

Consider the following questions as you read through this section.

1. What is the relationship between opportunity cost and specialization?

2. What are the advantages of specialization in production?

As we go through this section, we will discuss specialization, the comparative advantage gained through specialization, and how trade allows us to take advantage of specialization.

2-3a WHY DO PEOPLE SPECIALIZE?

As you look around, you can see that people specialize in what they produce. They tend to dedicate their resources to one primary activity, whether it be child rearing, driving a cab, or making bagels. Why? The answer, short and simple, is opportunity costs. By concentrating their energies on only one, or a few, activities, individuals are **specializing**. This focus allows them to make the best use of (and thus gain the most benefit from) their limited resources. A person, a region, or a country can gain by specializing in the production of the good in which they have a comparative advantage. That is, if they can produce a good or service at a lower opportunity cost than others, we say that they have a **comparative advantage** in the production of that good or service.

specializing concentrating on the production of one or a few goods

comparative advantage occurs when a person or country can produce a good or service at a lower opportunity cost than others

2-3b WE ALL SPECIALIZE

We all specialize to some extent and rely on others to produce most of the goods and services we want. The work that we choose to do reflects our specialization. For example, we may specialize in selling or fixing automobiles. The wages from that work can then be used to buy goods from a farmer who has chosen to specialize in the production of food. Likewise, the farmer can use the money earned from selling his produce to get his tractor fixed by someone who specializes in that activity.

Specialization is evident not only among individuals but among regions and countries as well. In fact, the story of the economic development of the United States and the rest of the world involves specialization.

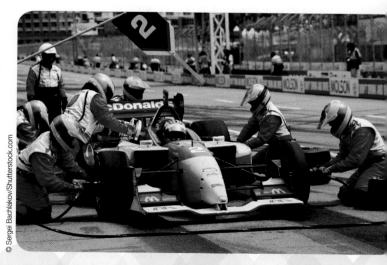

Without specialization and division of labor, this car and crew would not be as competitive. Imagine how much time would be lost if one person were changing four tires.

© Sergei Bachlakov/Shutterstock.com

Within the United States, the Midwest with its wheat, the coastal waters of the Northeast with its fishing fleets, and the Northwest with its timber are each examples of regional specialization.

2-3c THE ADVANTAGES OF SPECIALIZATION

In a small business, every employee usually performs a wide variety of tasks—from hiring to word processing to marketing. As the size of the company increases, each employee can perform a more specialized job, with a consequent increase in output per worker. The primary advantages of specialization are that employees acquire greater skill from repetition, they avoid wasted time in shifting from one task to another, and they do the types of work for which they are best suited. Furthermore, specialization promotes the use of specialized equipment for specialized tasks.

The advantages of specialization are seen throughout the workplace. For example, in larger firms, specialists conduct personnel relations, and accounting is in the hands of full-time accountants instead of someone with half a dozen other tasks. Owners of small retail stores select the locations for their stores primarily through guesswork, placing them where they believe sales will be high or where low-rent buildings are available. In contrast, larger chains have store sites selected by experts who have experience in analyzing the factors that make different locations relatively more desirable, such as traffic patterns, income levels, demographics, and so on.

2-3d SPECIALIZATION AND TRADE LEAD TO GREATER WEALTH AND PROSPERITY

Trade, or voluntary exchange, directly increases wealth by making both parties better off, otherwise they wouldn't trade. It is the prospect of wealth-increasing exchange that leads to productive specialization. That is, trade increases wealth by allowing a person, a region, or a nation to specialize in those products that it produces at a lower opportunity cost and to trade them for products that others produce at a lower opportunity cost. That is, we trade with others because it frees up time and resources to do other things that we do better.

In short, if we divide tasks and produce what we do *relatively* best and trade for the rest, we will be better off than if we were self-sufficient—that is, without trade. Imagine life without trade, where you were completely self-sufficient—growing your own food, making your

own clothes, working on your own car, building your own house—do you think you would be better off?

Suppose the United States is better at producing wheat than is Brazil, and Brazil is better at producing coffee than is the United States. The United States and Brazil would each benefit if the United States produces wheat and trades some of it to Brazil for coffee. Coffee growers in the United States could grow coffee in expensive greenhouses, but it would result in higher coffee costs and prices, while leaving fewer resources available for employment in more beneficial jobs, such as wheat production.

In the words of growth theorist Paul Romer, "There are huge potential gains from trade. Poor countries can supply their natural and human resources. Rich countries can supply their know-how. When these are combined, everyone can be better off. The challenge is for a country to arrange its laws and institutions so that both sides can profitably engage in trade." Standards of living can be increased through trade. In fact, the economy as a whole can create more wealth when each person specializes in a task that he or she does best. And through specialization and trade, a country can gain a greater variety of goods and services at a lower cost. So while countries may be competitors in the global market, they are also partners.

© KHAN PALASH/SIPA/Newscom

Bangladesh exports low-cost garments to mass-market retailers like Walmart. U.S. workers are a lot more productive in building airplanes and a little more productive in producing clothes than Bangladeshi workers. If the two countries divide the work according to comparative advantage, then the U.S. workers would specialize in the tasks at which they are most productive, airplanes. And the Bangladeshi workers would concentrate on the tasks where their productivity is only slightly less, clothing.

2-4 The Production Possibilities of an Economy

SECTION CHECK 4

Keep the following questions in mind as you read through this section.

1. What is a production possibilities curve?
2. What is efficiency?
3. What is the law of increasing opportunity costs?
4. How do we show economic growth on the production possibilities curve?

In this section, we will examine the production possibilities curve, the law of increasing opportunity cost, and how economic growth is generated.

2-4a THE PRODUCTION POSSIBILITIES CURVE

The economic concepts of scarcity, choice, and trade-offs can be illustrated visually by means of a simple graph called a production possibilities curve. The **production possibilities curve** represents the potential total output combinations of any two goods for an economy, given the inputs and technology available to the economy. That is, it illustrates an economy's potential for allocating its limited resources in producing various combinations of goods in a given time period.

The Production Possibilities Curve for Food and Shelter

production possibilities curve the potential total output combinations of any two goods for an economy

To illustrate the production possibilities curve, imagine living in an economy that produces just two goods, food and shelter. The fact that we have many goods in the real world makes actual decision making more complicated, but it does not alter the basic principles being illustrated. Each point on the production possibilities curve shown in Exhibit 2.1 represents the potential amounts of food and shelter that we can produce in a given period with a given quantity and quality of resources in the economy available for production.

Notice in Exhibit 2.1 that if we devote all our resources to making shelters, we can produce 10 units of shelter but no food (point A). If, on the other hand, we choose to devote all our resources to producing food, we end up with 80 units of food but no shelters (point E).

In reality, nations rarely opt for production possibility A or E, preferring instead to produce a mixture

EXHIBIT 2.1 Production Possibilities Curve: The Trade-Off between Food and Shelter

Combinations	Shelter (units)	Food (units)
A	10	0
B	9	20
C	7	40
D	4	60
E	0	80

© Cengage Learning 2014

increasing opportunity cost the opportunity cost of producing additional units of a good rises as society produces more of that good

of goods. For example, our fictional economy might produce 9 units of shelter and 20 units of food (point B) or perhaps 7 units of shelter and 40 units of food (point C). Still other combinations along the curve, such as point D, are possible.

Off the Production Possibilities Curve

The economy cannot operate at point N (not attainable) during the given period because not enough resources are currently available to produce that level of output. However, it is possible the economy can operate inside the production possibilities curve, at point I (inefficient). If the economy is operating at point I, or any other point inside the production possibilities curve, it is not at full capacity and is operating inefficiently. In short, the economy is not using all its scarce resources efficiently; as a result, actual output is less than potential output.

2-4b INEFFICIENCY AND EFFICIENCY

Suppose for some reason employment is widespread or resources are not being put to their best uses. The economy would then be operating at a point inside the production possibilities curve, such as I in Exhibit 2.1, where the economy is operating inefficiently. At point I, 4 units of shelter and 40 units of food are being produced. By putting unemployed resources to work or by putting already employed resources to better uses, we could expand the output of shelter by 3 units (moving to point C)

without giving up any units of food. Alternatively, we could boost food output by 20 units (moving to point D) without reducing shelter output. We could even get more of both food and shelter by moving to a point on the curve between C and D. Increasing or improving the utilization of resources, then, can lead to greater output of all goods. As you may recall from Chapter 1, an efficient use of our resources means that more of everything we want can be available for our use. Thus, *efficiency* requires society to use its resources to the fullest extent—getting the most from our scarce resources and wasting none. If resources are being used efficiently—that is, at some point along a production possibilities curve—then more of one good or service requires the sacrifice of another good or service. Efficiency does not tell us which point along the production possibilities curve is *best*, but it does tell us that points inside the curve cannot be best, because some resources are wasted.

2-4c THE LAW OF INCREASING OPPORTUNITY COST

As in Exhibit 2.1, the production possibilities curve in Exhibit 2.2 is not a straight line. It is concave from below (that is, bowed outward from the origin). Looking at Exhibit 2.2, you can see that at low food output, an increase in the amount of food produced will lead to only a small reduction in the number of units of shelter produced. For example, increasing food output from 0 to 20 (moving from point A to point B on the curve) requires the use of resources capable of producing 1 unit of shelter. In other words, for the first 20 units of food, 1 unit of shelter must be given up. When food output is higher, however, more units of shelter must be given up when switching additional resources from the production of shelter to food. Moving from point D to point E, for example, an increase in food output of 20 (from 60 to 80) reduces the production of shelters from 4 to 0. At this point, then, the cost of those 20 additional units of food is 4 units of shelter, considerably more than the 1 unit of shelter required in the earlier scenario. This difference shows us that opportunity costs do not remain constant but rise because more units of food and fewer units of shelter are produced. It is this **increasing opportunity cost**, then, that is represented by the bowed production possibilities curve.

> A skilled carpenter may be an expert at making shelters but a very bad farmer because he lacks the training and skills necessary for that occupation.

EXHIBIT 2.2 Increasing Opportunity Cost and the Production Possibilities Curve

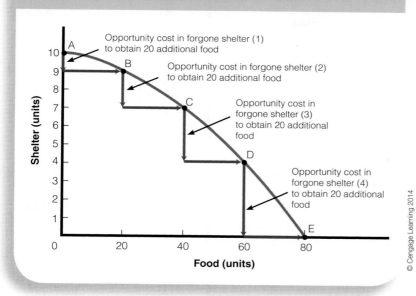

Opportunity cost in forgone shelter (1) to obtain 20 additional food

Opportunity cost in forgone shelter (2) to obtain 20 additional food

Opportunity cost in forgone shelter (3) to obtain 20 additional food

Opportunity cost in forgone shelter (4) to obtain 20 additional food

© Cengage Learning 2014

What Is the Reason for the Law of Increasing Opportunity Cost?

The basic reason for the increasing opportunity cost is that some resources and skills cannot be easily adapted from their current uses to alternative uses. And the more you produce of one good, the more you are forced to employ inputs that are relatively more suitable for producing other goods. For example, at low levels of food output, additional increases in food output can be obtained easily by switching relatively low-skilled carpenters from making shelters to producing food. However, to get even more food output, workers who are less well suited or appropriate for producing food (i.e., they are better adapted to making shelters) must be released from shelter making to increase food output. For example, a skilled carpenter may be an expert at making shelters but a very bad farmer because he lacks the training and skills necessary in that occupation. So using the skilled carpenter to farm results in a relatively greater opportunity cost than using the unskilled carpenter to farm. The production of additional units of food becomes increasingly costly as progressively lower-skilled farmers (but good carpenters) convert to farming.

In short, resources tend to be specialized. As a result, we lose some of their productivity when we transfer those resources from producing what they are relatively good at to producing something they are relatively bad at.

2-4d GENERATING ECONOMIC GROWTH

How have some nations been able to rapidly expand their outputs of goods and services over time, while others have been unable to increase their standards of living at all?

The economy can only grow with qualitative or quantitative changes in the factors of production—land, labor, capital, and entrepreneurship. Advancement in technology, improvements in labor productivity, or new sources of natural resources (such as previously undiscovered oil) could lead to outward shifts of the production possibilities curve.

In terms of the production possibilities curve, an outward shift in the possible combinations of goods and services produced indicates economic growth, as seen in Exhibit 2.3. With growth comes the possibility of having more of both goods than was previously available. Suppose we were producing at point C (7 units of shelter, 40 units of food) on our original production possibilities curve. Additional resources and/or new methods of using them, such as technological progress, can lead to new production possibilities, creating the potential for more of all goods or more of some with no less of others. These increases will push the production possibilities curve outward. For example, if we invest in human capital by training the workers

EXHIBIT 2.3 Economic Growth and Production Possibilities

making the shelters, it will increase the productivity of those workers. As a result, they will produce more units of shelter. Ultimately, then, we will use fewer resources to make shelters, freeing the resources to be used for farming, which will result in more units of food. Notice that at point F (future) on the new curve, we can produce 9 units of shelter and 70 units of food, more of both goods than we previously could produce, at point C.

2-4e GROWTH DOES NOT ELIMINATE SCARCITY

With all of this discussion of growth, it is important to remember that growth, or increases in a society's output, does not make scarcity disappear. When output grows more rapidly than population, people are better off. But they still face trade-offs; at any point along the production possibilities curve, to get more of one thing, you must give up something else. There are no free lunches on the production possibilities curve.

Capital Goods versus Consumer Goods

Economies that choose to invest more of their resources for the future will grow faster than those that do not. To generate economic growth, a society must produce fewer consumer goods (video games, DVD players, cell phones, cars, vacations, and so on) in the present and produce more capital goods (machines, factories, tools, education, and the like). The society that devotes a larger share of its productive capacity to capital goods than to consumer goods will experience greater economic growth. It must sacrifice some present consumption of consumer goods and services to experience growth in the future. Why? Investing in capital goods, such as computers and other new technological equipment, as well as upgrading skills and knowledge, expands the ability to produce in the future. It shifts the economy's production possibilities curve outward, increasing the future production capacity of the economy. That is, the economy that invests more and consumes less now will be able to produce and consume more in the future. In Exhibit 2.4, we see that Economy A invests more in capital goods than does Economy B. Consequently, Economy A's production possibilities curve shifts outward further than does Economy B's over time.

In Exhibit 2.4, we see that in 1970, Country B devoted 33 percent of its resources to capital accumulation while Country A devoted 20 percent of its resources. Both countries experienced economic growth from 1970–2012, but Country B grew more rapidly because it devoted a larger fraction of its resources to capital accumulation. Note that government-funded capital can also provide infrastructure (roads, schools, bridges, ports, dams, and so on), which makes private capital more efficient and helps the economy grow. The moral of the story is that developing countries can catch up to developed countries by using more of their resources to accumulate capital.

2-4f THE EFFECTS OF A TECHNOLOGICAL CHANGE ON THE PRODUCTION POSSIBILITIES CURVE

In Exhibit 2.5 on the next page, we see that a technological advance does not have to impact all sectors of the economy equally. There is a technological advance in food production but not in housing production. The technological advance in agriculture causes the production possibilities curve to extend out further on the horizontal axis, which measures food production. We can move to any point on the new production possibilities curve. For example, we could move from point A on the original production possibilities curve to point B on the new production possibilities curve. This would lead to 150 more units of food and the same amount of housing—200 units. Or we could move from point A to

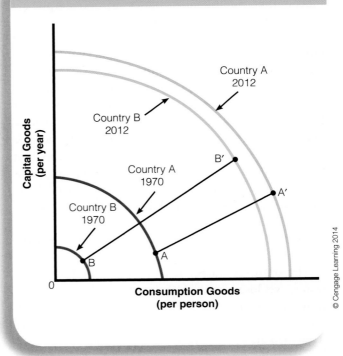

EXHIBIT 2.4 Economic Growth and Catching Up

© Cengage Learning 2014

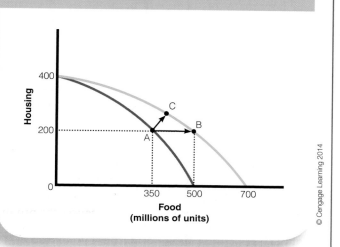

EXHIBIT 2.5 The Effects of a Technological Change on the Production Possibilities Curve

© Cengage Learning 2014

point C, which would allow us to produce more units of both food and housing. How do we produce more housing if the technological advance occurred in agriculture? The answer is that the technological advance in agriculture allows us to produce more from a given quantity of resources. That is, it allows us to shift some of our resources out of agriculture into housing. This is actually an ongoing story in U.S. economic history. In colonial days, about 90 percent of the population made a living in agriculture. Today it is less than 3 percent.

SECTION CHECK 4 ANSWERS

1. The production possibilities curve represents the potential total output combinations of two goods available to a society given its resources and existing technology.

2. Efficiency means that society uses its resources to the fullest extent—no wasted resources.

3. The law of increasing opportunity costs says that the opportunity costs of producing additional units of a good rise as society produces more of that good. This is indicated by a bowed production possibilities curve.

4. Economic growth is represented by an outward shift of the production possibilities curve.

2-5 Economic Systems

SECTION CHECK 5

Think about the following questions as you read through this section.

1. What goods and services will be produced?

2. How will the goods and services be produced?

3. Who will get the goods and services?

In this section, we will address the three economic questions every society must answer.

2-5a SCARCITY AND THE ALLOCATION OF RESOURCES

In the last section, we noted that each point on the production possibilities curve is efficient. But each economic system might answer certain economic questions regardless of the level of affluence of the society or its political structure. We will consider three fundamental questions that every society inevitably faces: (1) What goods and services will be produced? (2) How will the goods and services be produced? (3) Who will get the goods and services produced? These questions are unavoidable in a world of scarcity.

2-5b WHAT GOODS AND SERVICES WILL BE PRODUCED?

How do individuals control production decisions in market-oriented economies? Questions arise such as should society produce more baseball stadiums or more schools? Should Apple produce more iPhones or laptops? The government has a limited budget, too, and must make choices on how much to spend on defense, health care, highways, and education. In short, consumers, firms, and governments must all make choices about what goods and services will be produced and each one of those decisions has an opportunity cost—the highest-valued alternative forgone. In the marketplace, the answer to these and other similar questions is that people "vote" in economic affairs with their dollars (or pounds or yen). This concept is called

consumer sovereignty. Consumer sovereignty explains how individual consumers in market economies determine what is to be produced.

Televisions, DVD players, cell phones, iPods, camcorders, and laptops, for example, became part of our lives because consumers "voted" hundreds of dollars apiece on these goods. As TVs became more advanced, consumers "voted" fewer dollars on regular color TVs and more on high-definition TVs. Similarly, vinyl record albums gave way to tapes, and CDs to downloadable music as consumers voted for these items with their dollars. If consumers vote for more fuel-efficient cars and healthier foods, then firms that wish to remain profitable must listen and respond.

How Different Types of Economic Systems Answer the Question "What Goods and Services Will Be Produced?"

Economies are organized in different ways to answer the question of what is to be produced. The dispute over the best way to answer this question has inflamed passions for centuries. Should a central planning board make the decisions, as in North Korea and Cuba? Sometimes this highly centralized economic system is referred to as a **command economy.** Under this type of regime, decisions about how many tractors or automobiles to produce are largely determined by a government official or committee associated with the central planning organization. That same group decides on the number and size of school buildings, refrigerators, shoes, and so on.

What are you "voting" for with your dollars?

Other countries, including the United States, much of Europe, and, increasingly, Asia and elsewhere, have largely adopted a decentralized decision-making process where literally millions of individual producers and consumers of goods and services determine what goods, and how many of them, will be produced. A country that uses such a decentralized decision-making process is often said to have a **market economy.** Actually, no nation has a pure market economy. The United States, along with most countries, is said to have a **mixed economy.** In such an economy, the government and the private sector together determine the allocation of resources.

2-5c HOW WILL THE GOODS AND SERVICES BE PRODUCED?

Because of scarcity all economies regardless of their political structure, must decide how to produce the goods and services that they want. Goods and services can generally be produced in several ways. Firms may face a trade-off between using more machines or more workers. For example, a company might decide to move its production to a plant in another country that uses more workers and fewer machines.

A ditch can be dug by many workers using their hands, by a few workers with shovels, or by one person with a backhoe. Someone must decide which method is most appropriate. From this example, you might be tempted to conclude that it is desirable to use the biggest, most elaborate form of capital. But would you really want to plant your spring flowers with huge earthmoving machinery? That is, the most capital-intensive method of production may not always be the best. The best method is the least-cost method.

What Is the Best Form of Production?

The best or "optimal" form of production will usually vary from one economy to the next. For example, earthmoving machinery is used in digging large ditches in the United States and Europe, while in developing countries, shovels are often used. Why do these optimal forms of production vary? Compared with capital, labor is relatively cheap and plentiful in developing countries but relatively scarce and expensive in the United States. In contrast, capital (machines and tools, mainly) is comparatively plentiful and cheap in the United States but scarcer and more costly in developing countries. That is, in developing countries, production tends to be more **labor intensive**, or labor driven. In the United States, production tends to be more **capital intensive**, or capital driven. Each nation tends to use the production processes that conserve its relatively scarce (and thus relatively more expensive) resources and use more of its relatively abundant resources.

2-5d WHO WILL GET THE GOODS AND SERVICES PRODUCED?

In every society, some mechanism must exist to determine how goods and services are to be distributed among the population. Who gets what? Why do some people get to consume or use far more goods and services than others? This question of distribution is so important that wars and revolutions have been fought over it. Both the French and Russian revolutions were concerned fundamentally with the distribution of goods and services. Even in societies where political questions are usually settled peacefully, the question of the distribution of income is an issue that always arouses strong emotional responses. As we will see, in a market economy with private ownership and control of the means of production, the amounts of goods and services an individual can obtain depend on her or his income. Income, in turn, will depend on the quantity and quality of the scarce resources the individual controls. Income is also determined by the price others are willing and able to pay for what you have to sell. If you are a medical doctor and make $300,000 a year, that is income you will have available to buy goods and services. If you also own a condominium you rent out in Aspen, Colorado, you will have an even greater amount of income to spend on goods and services. For instance, markets reward education, hard work, and training. Education (years of schooling) and earnings are highly (positively) correlated. Also, people with unique and marketable skills, like media mogul Oprah Winfrey, can make lots of money. This basis for distribution may or may not be viewed as "fair," an issue we will look at in detail later in this book.

labor intensive
production that uses a large amount of labor

capital intensive
production that uses a large amount of capital

MARKET SIGNALS

Q&A

Q: Adam was a college graduate with a major in art. A few years ago, Adam decided that he wanted to pursue a vocation that utilized his talent. In response, he shut himself up in his studio and created a watercolor collection. With high hopes, Adam put his collection on display for buyers. After several years of displaying his art, however, the only one interested in the collection was his 18-year-old sister, who wanted the picture frames for her room. Recognizing that Adam was having trouble pursuing his chosen occupation, Adam's friend Karl told him that the market had failed. In the meantime, Adam turned to house painting (interior and exterior) and business was booming. Adam hired five workers and would often be painting all day and into the evenings and weekends. Do you think the market has failed?

You can find the answer on the next page.

MARKET SIGNALS

Q&A

A: No. Markets provide important signals, and the signal being sent in this situation is that Adam should look for some other means of support—something that society values. Remember the function of consumer sovereignty in the marketplace. Clearly, consumers were not voting for Adam's art. The market seems to be telling Adam, "less painting on canvas and more painting on walls, doors, and trim."

Castaway and Resource Allocation

In the movie *Castaway*, Chuck Noland's (played by Tom Hanks) plane crashes, leaving him stranded on a deserted island, and he has to find a way to survive. On the island, he must find answers to the *what*, *how*, and *for whom* questions. The *for whom* question is pretty easy: He is the only one on the island—he gets what is produced. The *what* question is pretty easy, too: He is trying to survive, so he is looking to produce food, shelter, and clothing. The *how* question is where this scene becomes interesting. Noland salvages several boxes from the plane crash. After a failed attempt to leave the island, he decides to open the boxes to see whether they contain anything useful. He first finds a pair of ice skates. He uses the blades of the ice skates as a knife to open coconuts, to cut a dress to convert into a fishing net, and to sharpen a stick to use as a spear for catching fish. He uses the laces from the skate

and the bubble wrap in the package to dress an injury. He uses the raft as a lean-to for his shelter. He builds a fire and even "makes" a friend out of a volleyball. In short, Noland must use his entrepreneurial talents to make the best use of the scarce resources to survive on the island.

Chuck Noland (Tom Hanks) had to make the best use of his scarce resources to survive on the island.

SECTION CHECK 5 ANSWERS

1. In a decentralized market economy, independent buyers and sellers decide what goods and services will be produced. In a mixed economy, government and the private sector make these decisions.

2. The best form of production is the one that conserves the relatively scarce (more costly) resources and uses more of the abundant (less costly) resources. When capital is relatively scarce and labor plentiful, production tends to be labor intensive. When capital is abundant and labor scarce, production tends to be capital intensive.

3. In a market economy, the amount of goods and services one is able to obtain depends on one's income. The amount of an individual's income depends on the quantity and quality of the scarce resources that he or she controls.

Chapter 2: Self-Review

Now that you are finished reading the chapter, review the questions below. You can write your answers in the space provided, then go online to see the answers at www.cengagebrain.com.

2-1 CHOICES, COSTS, AND TRADE-OFFS

1. Why does scarcity force us to make choices?

2. The price of a one-way bus trip from Los Angeles to New York City is $150.00. Sarah, a school teacher, pays the same price in February (during the school year) as in July (during her vacation), so the cost is the same in February as in July. Do you agree?

3. McDonald's once ran a promotion that whenever St. Louis Cardinals slugger Mark McGwire hit a home run into the upper deck at Busch Stadium, McDonald's gave anyone with a ticket to that day's game a free Big Mac. If holders of ticket stubs have to stand in line for 10 minutes, is the Big Mac really "free"?

2-2 MARGINAL THINKING

4. Which of the following activities require marginal thinking? Why?
   a. studying
   b. eating
   c. driving
   d. shopping
   e. getting ready for a night out

5. How could the rule of rational choice be expressed in terms of net benefits?

2-3 SPECIALIZATION AND TRADE

6. Farmer Fran can grow soybeans and corn. She can grow 50 bushels of soybeans or 100 bushels of corn on an acre of her land for the same cost. The price of soybeans is $1.50 per bushel and the price of corn is $0.60 per bushel. Show the benefits to Fran of specialization. What should she specialize in?

7. True or False: Autarky, a government policy under which countries choose not to trade with other countries, is the best way for an emerging nation to grow.

2-4 THE PRODUCTION POSSIBILITIES OF AN ECONOMY

8. True or False: Economy A produces more capital goods and fewer consumer goods than Economy B; therefore, Economy A will grow more rapidly than Economy B.

9. How does the production possibilities curve illustrate increasing opportunity costs?

10. If people reduced their savings (thus reducing the funds available for investment), what would that change do to the society's production possibilities curve over time?

2-5 ECONOMIC SYSTEMS

11. What are the three basic economic questions?

12. Why do consumers have to "vote" for a product with their dollars for it to be a success?

According to Thomas Carlyle,

a nineteenth-century philosopher, "Teach a parrot the term 'supply and demand' and you've got an economist." Unfortunately, economics is more complicated than that.

Test your Economics *street-smart* knowledge and see how you compare against other students! Scan here or visit CourseMate for Survey of ECON2.

3

Supply and Demand

I f Carlyle was hinting at the importance of supply and demand, he was right on target. Supply and demand is without a doubt the most powerful tool in the economist's toolbox. It can help explain much of what goes on in the world and help predict what will happen tomorrow. In this chapter, we begin with an introduction to markets. Every market has a demand side and a supply side. Buyers represent the demand side of the market and sellers represent the supply side. In this chapter, we will learn about the law of demand and the law of supply and the factors that can change supply and demand. We will also learn how markets with many buyers and sellers adjust to temporary shortages and surpluses, as prices move back to equilibrium. In addition, we will study the impact of a change in one or more of the determinants of supply and demand and see how it impacts the market price and quantity exchanged.

3-1 Competitive Markets

SECTION CHECK 1

Consider the question below as you read this section.

1. Who determines the demand and supply sides of the market?

The roles of buyers and sellers in markets are important. Buyers, as a group, determine the demand side of the market. Buyers include the consumers who purchase the goods and services and the firms that buy inputs—labor, capital, and raw materials. Sellers, as a group, determine the supply side of the market. Sellers include the firms that produce and sell goods and services and the resource owners who sell their inputs to firms—workers who "sell" their labor and resource owners who sell raw materials and capital. Through the forces of supply and demand, the interaction of buyers and sellers determines market prices and output.

In the next few sections, we will focus on how supply and demand work in a **competitive market**. A competitive market is one in which a large number of buyers and sellers are offering similar products, and no single buyer or seller can influence the market price. For example, in the market for wheat there are thousands of farmers who sell wheat and there are millions of consumers who use wheat. Because each buyer and seller must accept the price determined by the market, they are said to be *price takers*.

The supply and demand model is particularly useful in markets such as agriculture, finance, labor, construction, services, wholesale, and retail. In short, a model is only as good as its ability to provide accurate explanations and predictions. The model of supply and demand is very good at predicting changes in prices and quantities in many markets large and small.

SECTION CHECK 1 ANSWERS

1. Buyers determine the demand side of the market and sellers determine the supply side of the market.

3-2 Demand

SECTION CHECK 2

Keep the following questions in mind as you read through this section.

1. What is the law of demand?
2. What is an individual demand curve?
3. What is a market demand curve?
4. What is the difference between a change in demand and a change in quantity demanded?
5. What are the determinants of demand?

In the last couple of chapters we have discussed scarcity and trade-offs. Recall that most goods are scarce, so to acquire more of one requires giving up something else you value. That is, we weigh the expected marginal benefits against the expected marginal costs when we make choices involving scarce goods. Another implication of scarcity is that there are substitutes for most things. Once we recognize that people face trade-offs for goods and services that are scarce, it also changes our perception of the word "need." While economists do believe that people have genuine needs, we recognize that the concept of need can be very misleading in analyzing people's behavior.

3-2a WANTS VERSUS NEEDS

To an economist, the terms "wants" and "needs" are very different. In fact, it is difficult to objectively define a need. To most, a need is something you must have and don't currently possess. But it can be used to describe a trivial wish, a more serious want, or something that is essential for survival. A "need" can be more or less urgent, depending on the circumstances. Whenever you hear somebody say, "I need a new car," "I need a vacation," or "I need new clothes," always be sure to ask what the person really means.

During rush hour, there are often very congested freeways. Perhaps we should have an express lane for people who have urgent needs. What do you think of this idea? Imagine the number of people who would decide they faced urgent needs if the "urgent need" lane was much shorter than the other lanes. It would be fun to guess what might be defined as an urgent need when you are stopped by the urgent need police. It might include: "I am really in a hurry because I have to get home to clean up my apartment," or "I need to get back to the dorm to type my overdue term paper," or "I left the dog in the house." Many people would perceive their needs as more urgent than other people's urgent needs. This is a reason the concept of needs falls apart as a means of explaining behavior. It is impossible to make the concept of need useful when there is no clear way to define it and it cannot be compared among people.

Need as a concept ignores scarcity and the fact that choices may change with circumstances and trade-offs. In a world of scarcity, we have unlimited wants in the face of limited resources. That is, we all must make choices because we have competing wants and limited resources. Whenever we choose, we can satisfy one want only by leaving other wants unsatisfied. We might satisfy our want for a new car but it may leave other wants, like a trip to Hawaii or paying for tuition or rent, unfilled. That is, every want that is satisfied leaves other wants unsatisfied.

The concept of need implies thinking in all-or-nothing terms. That is misleading when people are confronted with trade-offs—less of one good for more of another. These trade-offs provide the foundation for the concept of demand. That is, the law of demand states that there is a negative relationship between the amount buyers will want to purchase and the price (sacrifice) they must make to obtain it. The concept of demand relates the amount people want to how much they must sacrifice to get it.

Sometimes observed behavior is so pervasive it is called a law; the law of demand is an example. According to the **law of demand**, the quantity of a good or service demanded varies inversely with its price, *ceteris paribus*. More directly, the law of demand says that, other things being equal, when the price (P) of a good or service falls, the quantity demanded (Q_D) increases. Conversely, if the price of a good or service rises, the quantity demanded decreases.

For example, a lower price may encourage consumers who were already buying the good to buy a larger quantity. Or the lower price may encourage people who could not afford to buy the product at the higher price to buy it now.

3-2b INDIVIDUAL DEMAND: AN INDIVIDUAL DEMAND SCHEDULE

The **individual demand schedule** shows the relationship between the price of the good and the quantity demanded. For example, suppose Elizabeth enjoys drinking coffee. How many pounds of coffee would Elizabeth be willing and able to buy at various prices during the year? At a price of $3 per pound, Elizabeth buys 15 pounds of coffee over the course of a year. If the price is higher, at $4 per pound, she might buy only 10 pounds; if it is lower, say $1 per pound, she might buy 25 pounds of coffee during the year. Elizabeth's demand for coffee for the year is summarized in the demand schedule in Exhibit 3.1. Elizabeth might not

EXHIBIT 3.2 Elizabeth's Demand Curve for Coffee

© Cengage Learning 2014

be consciously aware of the amounts that she would purchase at prices other than the prevailing one, but that does not alter the fact that she has a schedule in the sense that she would have bought various other amounts had other prices prevailed. It must be emphasized that the schedule is a list of alternative possibilities. At any one time, only one of the prices will prevail, and thus a certain quantity will be purchased.

An Individual Demand Curve

By plotting the different prices and corresponding quantities demanded in Elizabeth's demand schedule in Exhibit 3.1 and then connecting them, we can create the **individual demand curve** for Elizabeth, as shown in Exhibit 3.2. From the curve, we can see that when the price is higher, the quantity demanded is lower, and when the price is lower, the quantity demanded is higher. The demand curve shows how the quantity demanded of the good changes as its price varies.

3-2c WHAT IS A MARKET DEMAND CURVE?

Economists usually speak of the demand curve in terms of large groups of people—a whole nation,

law of demand the quantity of a good or service demanded varies inversely with its price, *ceteris paribus*

individual demand schedule a schedule that shows the relationship between price and quantity demanded

individual demand curve a graphical representation that shows the inverse relationship between price and quantity demanded

EXHIBIT 3.1 Elizabeth's Demand Schedule for Coffee

Price of Coffee (per pound)	Quantity of Coffee Demanded (pounds per year)
$5	5
4	10
3	15
2	20
1	25

© Cengage Learning 2014

market demand curve
the horizontal summation of individual demand curves

a community, or a trading area. That is, to analyze how the market works, we will need to use market demand. As you know, every individual has his or her demand curve for every product. The horizontal summing of the demand curves of many individuals is called the **market demand curve**.

Suppose the consumer group is composed of Peter, Lois, and the rest of their small community of Quahog, and that the product is still coffee. The effect of price on the quantity of coffee demanded by Peter, Lois, and the rest of Quahog is given in the demand schedule and demand curves shown in Exhibit 3.3. At $4 per pound, Peter would be willing and able to buy 20 pounds of coffee per year, Lois would be willing and able to buy 10 pounds, and the rest of Quahog would be willing and able to buy 2,970 pounds. At $3 per pound, Peter would be willing and able to buy 25 pounds of coffee per year, Lois would be willing and able to buy 15 pounds, and the rest of Quahog would be willing and able to buy 4,960 pounds. The market demand curve is simply the (horizontal) sum of the quantities Peter, Lois, and the rest of Quahog demand at each price. That is, at $4, the quantity demanded in the market would be 3,000 pounds of coffee (20 + 10 + 2,970 = 3,000), and at $3, the quantity demanded in the market would be 5,000 pounds of coffee (25 + 15 + 4,960 = 5,000).

In Exhibit 3.4, we offer a more complete set of prices and quantities from the market demand for coffee during the year. The market demand curve shows the amounts that all the buyers in the market would be willing and able to buy at various prices. For example, when the price of coffee is $2 per pound, consumers in the market collectively would be willing and able to buy 8,000 pounds per year. At $1 per pound, the amount collectively demanded would be 12,000 pounds per year. The market demand curve is the negative (inverse) relationship between price and the quantity demanded, while holding constant all other factors that affect how much consumers are able and willing to buy, *ceteris paribus*.

3-2d A CHANGE IN DEMAND VERSUS A CHANGE IN QUANTITY DEMANDED

Consumers are influenced by the prices of goods when they make their purchasing decisions. People prefer to buy more of a good at lower prices than they do at higher prices, holding other factors constant. Why? Primarily, it is because many goods are substitutes for one another. For example, an increase in the price of coffee might tempt some buyers to switch from buying coffee to buying tea or soft drinks.

Understanding this relationship between price and quantity demanded is so important that economists make a clear distinction between it and the various other

EXHIBIT 3.3 Creating a Market Demand Curve

a. Creating a Market Demand Schedule for Coffee

Price (per pound)	Peter	+	Lois	+	Rest of Quahog	=	Market Demand
					Quantity of Coffee Demanded (pounds per year)		
$4	20	+	10	+	2,970	=	3,000
$3	25	+	15	+	4,960	=	5,000

b. Creating a Market Demand Curve for Coffee

EXHIBIT 3.4 A Market Demand Curve

a. Market Demand Schedule for Coffee

Price (per pound)	Quantity Demanded (pounds per year)
$5	1,000
4	3,000
3	5,000
2	8,000
1	12,000

b. Market Demand Curve for Coffee

Market Demand Curve

Quantity (thousands of pounds per year)

© Cengage Learning 2014

change in quantity demanded a change in a good's own price leads to a change in quantity demanded, a move along a given demand curve

change in demand the prices of related goods, income, number of buyers, tastes, and expectations can change the demand for a good; that is, a change in one of these factors shifts the entire demand curve

factors that can influence consumer behavior. A change in a good's own price is said to lead to a **change in quantity demanded**. That is, it "moves you along" a given demand curve. The demand curve is drawn under the assumption that all things except the price of the good are held constant. However, economists know that price is not the only thing that affects the quantity of a good that people buy. The other factors that influence the demand curve are called *determinants of demand*, and a change in these other factors *shifts the entire demand curve*. These determinants of demand are called demand shifters, and they lead to **changes in demand**.

3-2e SHIFTS IN DEMAND

An increase in demand shifts the demand curve to the right; a decrease in demand shifts the demand curve to the left, as shown in Exhibit 3.5. Some possible demand shifters are the prices of related goods, income, number of buyers, tastes, and expectations. We will now look more closely at each of these variables.

3-2f THE PRICES OF RELATED GOODS

In deciding how much of a good or service to buy, consumers are influenced by the price of that good or service, a relationship summarized by the law of demand. However, sometimes consumers are also influenced by the prices of *related* goods and services—substitutes and complements.

Substitutes

Substitutes are generally goods for which one could be used in place of the other. To many, substitutes would include butter and margarine, domestic and foreign cars, movie tickets and video rentals, jackets and sweaters, Exxon and Shell gasoline, and Nike and Reebok shoes.

Suppose you go into a store to buy a couple of six-packs of Coca-Cola and you see that Pepsi is on sale for half its usual price. Is it possible that you might decide to buy Pepsi instead of Coca-Cola? Economists argue that many people would. Empirical tests have confirmed that consumers are responsive to both the price of the good in question and the prices of related goods. When two goods are substitutes, an increase in the price of one of the goods leads to an increase in the demand for the other good; and a decrease in the price of one of the goods leads to a decrease in the demand for the other good.

EXHIBIT 3.5 Demand Shifts

Decrease in Demand

Increase in Demand

Price

Quantity

D_3 D_1 D_2

0

© Cengage Learning 2014

Two goods are **substitutes** if an increase (a decrease) in the price of one good leads to an increase (decrease) in the demand for the other good.

Complements

Complements are goods that "go together," or are often consumed and used simultaneously, such as skis and bindings, peanut butter and jelly, hot dogs and buns, digital music players and downloadable music, and printers and ink cartridges. For example, if the price of motorcycles falls, the quantity of motorcycles demanded will rise—a movement down along the demand curve for motorcycles. As more people buy motorcycles, they will demand more motorcycle helmets—the demand curve for motorcycle helmets shifts to the right. In short, when two goods are **complements**, an increase (decrease) in the price of one good leads to a decrease (increase) in the demand for the other good.

3-2g INCOME

Economists have observed that generally the consumption of goods and services is positively related to the income available to consumers. Empirical studies support the notion that as individuals receive more income, they tend to increase their purchases of most goods and services. Other things held equal, rising income usually leads to an increase in the demand for goods, a rightward shift of the demand curve, and decreasing income usually leads to a decrease in the demand for goods, a leftward shift of the demand curve.

Normal and Inferior Goods

If demand for a good increases when incomes rise and decreases when incomes fall, the good is called a **normal good**. Most goods are normal goods. Consumers will typically buy more clothes, pizzas, and trips to the movies as their incomes rise. However, if demand for a good decreases when incomes rise or if demand increases when incomes fall, the good is called an **inferior good**. These goods include inexpensive cuts of meat, second-hand clothing, and retread tires, which customers generally buy only because they cannot afford more expensive substitutes. As incomes rise, buyers shift to preferred substitutes and decrease their demand for the inferior goods. Suppose most individuals prefer hamburger to beans, but low-income families buy beans because they are less expensive. As incomes rise, many consumers may switch from buying beans to buying hamburgers. Hamburgers may be inferior, too; as incomes rise still further, consumers may substitute steak or chicken for hamburger. The term *inferior* in this

Substitutes

Suppose there is a fall in the price of Pepsi; this would cause an increase in the quantity demanded for Pepsi, which is a movement down along the demand curve. Many Coke drinkers may switch to the relatively lower-priced Pepsi, causing a reduction in demand for Coca-Cola, which will shift the demand curve for Coca-Cola to the left. Alternatively, if there is an increase in the price of Pepsi, this causes a decrease in the quantity demanded of Pepsi, which is a movement up along the demand curve. At the new higher price for Pepsi, many Pepsi drinkers will switch to the relatively lower-priced Coca-Cola, shifting the demand curve for Coca-Cola to the right. In this example, Pepsi and Coca-Cola are said to be substitutes.

substitutes two goods are substitutes if an increase (decrease) in the price of one good causes the demand curve for another good to shift to the right (left)

complements two goods are complements if an increase (decrease) in the price of one good shifts the demand curve for another good to the left (right)

normal good a good for which demand increases if income increases and demand decreases if income decreases

inferior good a good for which demand decreases if income decreases and demand increases if income decreases sense does not refer to the quality of the good in question but shows that demand decreases when income increases and demand increases when income decreases. So beans are inferior not because they are low quality but because you buy less of them as your income increases.

3-2h NUMBER OF BUYERS

The demand for a good or service will vary with the size of the potential consumer population. The demand for wheat, for example, rises as population increases because the added population wants to consume wheat products, such as bread or cereal. Marketing experts, who closely follow the patterns of consumer behavior regarding a particular good or service, are usually very concerned with the *demographics* of the product—the vital statistics of the potential consumer population, including size, race, income, and age. For example, market researchers for baby food companies keep a close watch on the birth rate.

Complements

3-2i CONSUMERS' PREFERENCES AND INFORMATION

The demand for a good or service may increase or decrease suddenly with changes in people's tastes or preferences. Changes in taste may be triggered by advertising or promotion, a news story, the behavior of some popular public figure, and so on. Changes in taste are particularly noticeable in apparel. Skirt lengths, coat lapels, shoe styles, and tie sizes change frequently.

Changes in preferences naturally lead to changes in demand. A person may grow tired of one type of

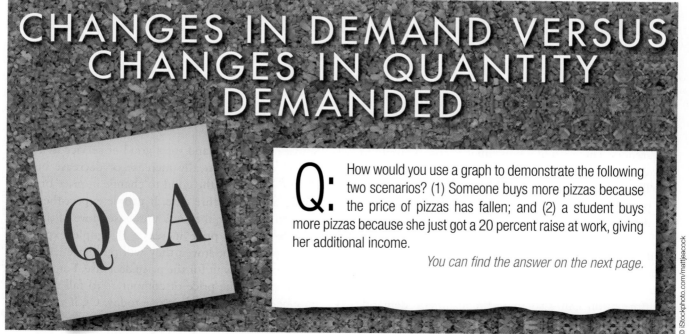

CHANGES IN DEMAND VERSUS CHANGES IN QUANTITY DEMANDED

Q&A

Q: How would you use a graph to demonstrate the following two scenarios? (1) Someone buys more pizzas because the price of pizzas has fallen; and (2) a student buys more pizzas because she just got a 20 percent raise at work, giving her additional income.

You can find the answer on the next page.

CHANGES IN DEMAND VERSUS CHANGES IN QUANTITY DEMANDED

Q&A

A: In the accompanying exhibit, the movement from A to B is called an increase in quantity demanded, and the movement from B to A is called a decrease in quantity demanded. Economists use the phrase "increase or decrease in quantity demanded" to describe movements along a given demand curve. However, the change from A to C is called an increase in demand, and the change from C to A is called a decrease in demand. The phrase "increase or decrease in demand" is reserved for a shift in the whole curve. So if an individual buys more pizzas because the price fell, we call it an increase in quantity demanded. However, if she buys more pizzas even at the current price, say $15, we say it is an increase in demand. In this case, an increase in income was responsible for the increase in demand, because she chose to spend some of her new income on pizzas.

Change in Demand versus Change in Quantity Demanded

recreation or food and try another type. People may decide they want more organic food; consequently, we will see more stores and restaurants catering to this change in taste. Changes in occupation, number of dependents, state of health, and age also tend to alter preferences. The birth of a baby might cause a family to spend less on recreation and more on food and clothing. Illness increases the demand for medicine and lessens purchases of other goods. A cold winter increases the demand for heating oil. Changes in customs and traditions also affect preferences, and the development of new products draws consumer preferences away from other goods. Compact discs replaced record albums, just as DVD players replaced VCRs. A change in information can also impact consumers' demand. For example, a breakout of *E. coli* or new information about a defective and/or dangerous product, such as a baby's crib, can reduce demand.

3-2j EXPECTATIONS

Sometimes the demand for a good or service in a given period will dramatically increase or decrease because consumers expect the good to change in price or availability at some future date. If people expect the future price to be higher, they will purchase more of the good now before the price increase. If people expect the future price to be lower, they will purchase less of the good now and wait for the price decrease. For example, if you expect the price of computers to fall soon, you may be less willing to buy one today. Or, if you expect to earn additional income next month, you may be more willing to dip into your current savings to buy something this month.

3-2k CHANGES IN DEMAND VERSUS CHANGES IN QUANTITY DEMANDED—REVISITED

Economists put particular emphasis on the impact on consumer behavior of a change in the price of a good. We are interested in distinguishing between consumer behavior related to the price of a good itself, which is the movement *along* a demand curve, and behavior related to changes in other factors, which is the shift of the demand curve.

As indicated earlier, if the price of a good changes, it causes a *change in quantity demanded*. If one of the other factors (determinants) influencing consumer behavior changes, it results in a *change in demand*. For example, there are two different ways to curb teenage smoking: raise the price of cigarettes, resulting in a reduction in the quantity of cigarettes demanded, or decrease the demand for cigarettes, resulting in a leftward shift in the demand curve for cigarettes. Both would reduce the amount of smoking. Specifically, to increase the price of cigarettes, the government could impose a higher tax on manufacturers. Most of this would be passed on to consumers in the form of higher prices (more on this in Chapter 4). Or to shift the demand curve leftward, the government could adopt policies to discourage smoking, such as advertising bans and increasing consumer awareness of the harmful side effects of smoking—disease and death.

SECTION CHECK 2 ANSWERS

1. The law of demand states that when the price of a good falls (rises), the quantity demanded rises (falls), *ceteris paribus*.

2. An individual demand curve is a graphical representation of the relationship between the price and the quantity demanded.

3. The market demand curve is the amount of a good that all buyers in the market would be willing and able to buy at various prices.

4. A change in demand shifts the entire demand curve. An increase in demand shifts the demand curve to the right; a decrease shifts it to the left.

5. The determinants of demand are the prices of related goods, income, number of buyers, tastes, and expectations. These factors can create a change in demand for a good—that is, a change in one of these factors shifts the entire demand curve.

3-3 Supply

SECTION CHECK 3

Keep the following questions in mind as you read through this section.

1. What is the law of supply?

2. What is an individual supply curve?

3. What is a market supply curve?

4. What is the difference between a change in supply and a change in quantity supplied?

5. What are the determinants of supply?

In a market, the answer to the fundamental question, "What do we produce, and in what quantities?" depends on the interaction of both buyers and sellers. Demand is only half the story. The willingness and ability of suppliers to provide goods are equally important factors that must be weighed by decision makers in all societies. As with demand, the price of the good is an important factor. Factors other than the price of the good are also important to suppliers, such as the cost of inputs or advances in technology. While behavior will vary among individual suppliers, economists expect that, *ceteris paribus,* the quantity supplied will vary directly with the price of the good, a relationship called the **law of supply**. According to the law of supply, the higher the price of the good (P), the greater the quantity supplied (Q_S), and the lower the price of the good, the smaller the quantity supplied.

The relationship described by the law of supply is a direct, or positive, relationship, because the variables move in the same direction.

3-3a A POSITIVE RELATIONSHIP BETWEEN PRICE AND QUANTITY SUPPLIED

Firms supplying goods and services want to increase their profits, and the higher the price per unit, the greater the profitability generated by supplying more of that good. For example, if you were a coffee grower, you would much rather be paid $5 a pound than $1 a pound, *ceteris paribus*. When the price of coffee is low, the coffee business is less profitable and less of the good will be produced. Some

law of supply the quantity of a good or service supplied varies directly (positively) with its price, *ceteris paribus*

© iStockphoto.com/mümin inan

produce more at higher prices than at lower prices.

3-3c THE MARKET SUPPLY CURVE

The **market supply curve** may be thought of as the horizontal summation of the supply curves for individual firms. The market supply curve shows how the total quantity supplied varies positively with the price of a good, while holding constant all other factors that affect how much producers are able and willing to supply. The market supply schedule, which reflects the total quantity supplied at each price by all of the coffee producers, is shown in Exhibit 3.7(a) on the next page. Exhibit 3.7(b) illustrates the resulting market supply curve for this group of coffee producers.

suppliers may even shut down, reducing their quantity supplied to zero.

3-3b AN INDIVIDUAL SUPPLY CURVE

To illustrate the concept of an **individual supply curve**, consider the amount of coffee that an individual supplier, Juan Valdes, is willing and able to supply in one year. The law of supply can be illustrated, like the law of demand, by a table or graph. Juan's **individual supply schedule** for coffee is shown in Exhibit 3.6(a). The combinations of price and quantity supplied were then plotted and joined to create the individual supply curve shown in Exhibit 3.6(b). Note that the individual supply curve slopes upward as you move from left to right. At higher prices, it will be more attractive to increase production. Existing firms or growers will

3-3d A CHANGE IN QUANTITY SUPPLIED VERSUS A CHANGE IN SUPPLY

Changes in the price of a good lead to changes in the quantity supplied by suppliers, just as changes in the price of a good lead to changes in the quantity demanded by buyers. Similarly, a change in supply, whether an increase or a decrease, can occur for reasons other than changes in the price of the product

---

individual supply curve
a graphical representation that shows the positive relationship between the price and quantity supplied

individual supply schedule a schedule that shows the relationship between price and quantity supplied

market supply curve a graphical representation of the amount of goods and services that suppliers are willing and able to supply at various prices

EXHIBIT 3.6 An Individual Supply Curve

a. Juan's Supply Schedule for Coffee

Price (per pound)	Quantity Supplied (pounds per year)
$5	80
4	70
3	50
2	30
1	10

b. Juan's Supply Curve for Coffee

Juan's Supply Curve

© Cengage Learning 2014

EXHIBIT 3.7 A Market Supply Curve

a. Market Supply Schedule for Coffee

Price (per pound)	Quantity Supplied (pounds per year)				
	Juan	+	Other Producers	=	Market Supply
$5	80	+	7,920	=	8,000
4	70	+	6,930	=	7,000
3	50	+	4,950	=	5,000
2	30	+	2,970	=	3,000
1	10	+	990	=	1,000

b. Market Supply Curve for Coffee

© Cengage Learning 2014

itself, just as changes in demand may be due to factors (determinants) other than the price of the good. In other words, a change in the price of the good in question is shown as a movement along a given supply curve, leading to a **change in quantity supplied**. A change in any other factor that can affect supplier behavior (input prices, prices of related products, expectations, number of suppliers, technology, regulation, taxes and subsidies, and weather) results in *a shift in the entire supply curve*, leading to a **change in supply**.

3-3e SHIFTS IN SUPPLY

An increase in supply shifts the supply curve to the right; a decrease in supply shifts the supply curve to the left, as shown in Exhibit 3.8. Anything that affects the costs of production will influence supply and the position of the supply curve. We will now look at some of the possible determinants of supply—factors that determine the position of the supply curve—in greater depth.

Input Prices

Suppliers are strongly influenced by the costs of inputs used in the production process, such as steel used for automobiles or microchips used in computers. For example, higher labor, materials, energy, or other input costs increase the costs of production, causing the supply curve to shift to the left at each and every price. If input prices fall, the costs of production decrease, causing the supply curve to shift to the right—more will be supplied at each and every price.

Prices of Related Goods

The supply of a good increases if the price of one of its substitutes in production falls, and the supply of a good decreases if the price of one of its substitutes in production rises. Suppose you own your own farm on which you plant cotton and wheat. One year, the price of wheat falls, and farmers reduce the quantity of wheat supplied, as shown in Exhibit 3.9(a) on the next page. What effect does the lower price of wheat have on your cotton production? It increases the supply of cotton. You want to produce relatively less of the crop that has fallen in price (wheat) and relatively more of the now more attractive other crop (cotton). Cotton and wheat are *substitutes in production* because both goods can be

> **change in quantity supplied** a change in a good's own price leads to a change in quantity supplied, a move along a given supply curve
>
> **change in supply** input prices, prices of related products, expectations, number of suppliers, technology, regulation, taxes and subsidies, and weather can change the supply for a good; that is, a change in one of these factors shifts the entire supply curve

EXHIBIT 3.8 Supply Shifts

© Cengage Learning 2014

produced using the same resources. Producers tend to substitute the production of more profitable products for that of less profitable products. So the decrease in the price in the wheat market has caused an increase in supply (a rightward shift) in the cotton market, as seen in Exhibit 3.9(b).

If the price of wheat—a substitute in production—increases, then that crop becomes more profitable. This leads to an increase in the quantity supplied of wheat. Consequently, farmers will shift their resources out of the relatively lower-priced crop (cotton); the result is a decrease in supply of cotton.

Other examples of substitutes in production include automobile producers that have to decide between producing sedans and pick-ups or construction companies that have to choose between building single residential houses or commercial buildings.

Some goods are *complements in production*. This means that producing one good does not prevent the production of the other, but actually enables production of the other. For example, leather and beef are complements in production. Suppose the price of beef rises and as a result cattle ranchers increase the quantity supplied of beef, moving up the supply curve for beef,

as seen in Exhibit 3.9(c). When cattle ranchers produce more beef, they automatically produce more leather. Thus, when the price of beef increases, the supply of the related good (leather) shifts to the right, as seen in Exhibit 3.9(d). Suppose the price of beef falls, and as a result, the quantity supplied of beef falls; this leads to a decrease, a leftward shift, in the supply of leather.

Expectations

Another factor that shifts supply is suppliers' expectations. If producers expect a higher price in the future, they will supply less now than they otherwise would have, preferring to wait to sell when their goods will be more valuable. For example, if a cotton producer expected the price of cotton to be higher next year, he might decide to store some of his current production of cotton and sell it next year when the price will be higher. Similarly, if producers expect now that the price will be lower later, they will supply more now. Oil refiners will often store some of their spring supply of gasoline for summer because gasoline prices typically peak in summer. In addition, some of the heating oil for the fall is stored to supply it in the winter when heating oil prices peak.

Number of Suppliers

We are normally interested in market demand and supply (because together they determine prices and quantities) rather than in the behavior of individual consumers and firms. As we discussed earlier in the chapter, the supply curves of individual suppliers can be summed horizontally to create a market supply curve. An increase in the number of suppliers leads to an increase in supply, denoted by a rightward shift in the supply curve. For example, think of the number of gourmet coffee shops that have sprung up over the last 15 to 20 years, shifting the supply curve of gourmet coffee to the right. An exodus of suppliers has the opposite impact, a decrease in supply, which is indicated by a leftward shift in the supply curve.

Technology

Technological change can lower the firm's costs of production through productivity advances. Human creativity works to find new ways to produce goods and services using fewer or less costly inputs of labor, natural resources, or capital. In recent years, despite generally rising prices, the prices of electronic equipment such as computers, cellular telephones, and high-definition (HD) televisions have fallen

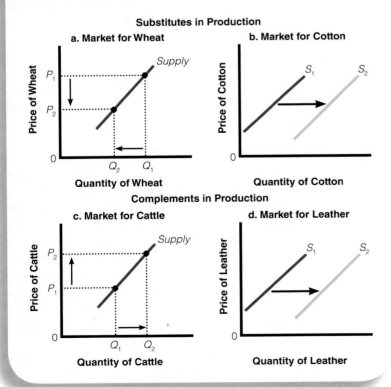

EXHIBIT 3.9 Substitutes and Complements in Production

Substitutes in Production

a. Market for Wheat

b. Market for Cotton

Complements in Production

c. Market for Cattle

d. Market for Leather

dramatically. These technological changes allow the firm to spend less on inputs and produce the same level of output. Human creativity works to find new ways to produce goods and services using fewer or less costly inputs of labor, natural resources, or capital. Because the firm can now produce the good at a lower cost, it will supply more of the good at each and every price, and the supply curve shifts to the right.

During the global recession of 2007–2009, oil demand dropped substantially. Early in 2009, as oil prices bottomed out, a situation known as contango developed, in which a large gap developed between oil prices trading on the daily spot market and future dated oil contracts. Traders bought oil on the spot market and parked it in tankers until the prices went back up. Floating storage worldwide peaked in April with nearly 90 million barrels sitting in oil tankers waiting to be sold.

Government (Regulation, Taxes, and Subsidies)

Supply may also change because of changes in the legal and regulatory environment in which firms operate. Government regulations can influence the costs of production to a firm, leading to cost-induced supply changes similar to those just discussed. For example, if new safety or clean air requirements increase labor and capital costs, the increased cost will result, *ceteris paribus,* in a decrease in supply, shifting the supply curve to the left, or up. However, deregulation can shift the supply curve to the right.

Certain types of taxes can also alter the costs of production borne by the supplier, causing the supply curve to shift to the left at each price. A subsidy, the opposite of a tax, can lower a firm's costs and shift the supply curve to the right. For example, the government sometimes provides farmers with subsidies to encourage the production of certain agricultural products.

Weather

In addition, weather can sometimes dramatically affect the supply of certain commodities, particularly agricultural products and transportation services. A drought or freezing temperatures will almost certainly cause the supply curves for many crops to shift to the left, while exceptionally good weather can shift a supply curve to the right. For example, unusually cold weather in California during the winter of 2006 destroyed billions of dollars worth of citrus fruit. Hurricane Rita disrupted oil and refining processes. Both events shifted the supply curve for those products to the left.

3-3f CHANGE IN SUPPLY VERSUS CHANGE IN QUANTITY SUPPLIED—REVISITED

If the price of a good changes, it leads to a change in the quantity supplied. If one of the other factors influences sellers' behavior, we say it results in a change in supply. For example, if production costs rise because of a wage increase or higher fuel costs, *ceteris paribus,* we would expect a decrease in supply—that is, a leftward shift in the supply curve. Alternatively, if some variable, such as lower input prices, causes the costs of production to fall, the supply curve will shift to the right.

CHANGE IN SUPPLY VERSUS CHANGE IN QUANTITY SUPPLIED

Q: How would you graph the following two scenarios? (1) The price of cotton rises; and (2) good weather causes an unusually abundant cotton harvest.

A: In the first scenario, the price of cotton increases, so the quantity supplied changes (i.e., a movement along the supply curve). In the second scenario, the good weather causes the supply curve for cotton to shift to the right, which is called a change in supply (not quantity supplied). A shift in the whole supply curve is caused by one of the other variables, not by a change in the price of the good in question.

As shown in the accompanying exhibit, the movement from A to B is called an increase in quantity supplied, and the movement from B to A is called a decrease in quantity supplied. However, the change from B to C is called an increase in supply, and the movement from C to B is called a decrease in supply.

Change in Supply versus Change in Quantity Supplied

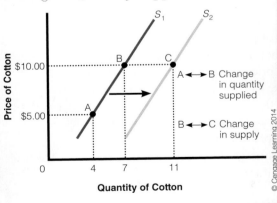

© Cengage Learning 2014

© iStockphoto.com/mattjeacock

3-4 Market Equilibrium Price and Quantity

SECTION CHECK 4

Keep the following questions in mind as you read through this section.

1. What is market equilibrium?

2. What are surpluses and shortages?

3. What happens to equilibrium price and quantity when the demand curve shifts? What happens when the supply curve shifts?

4. What happens when both supply and demand shift in the same time period?

5. What is an indeterminate solution?

Enough has been said for now about supply and demand separately. We now bring the market supply and demand together.

3-4a EQUILIBRIUM PRICE AND QUANTITY

The **market equilibrium** is found at the point at which the market supply and market demand curves intersect. The price at the intersection of the market supply curve and the market demand curve is called the **equilibrium price**, and the quantity is called the **equilibrium quantity**. *At the equilibrium price, the amount that buyers are willing and able to buy is exactly equal to the amount that sellers are willing and able to produce.* The equilibrium market solution is best understood with the help of a simple graph. Let's return to the coffee example we used in our earlier discussions of supply and demand. Exhibit 3.10 combines the market demand curve for coffee with the market supply curve. At $3 per pound, buyers are willing to buy 5,000 pounds of coffee and sellers are willing to supply 5,000 pounds of coffee. Neither may be "happy" about the price; the buyers would probably like a lower price and the sellers would probably like a higher price. But both buyers and sellers are able to carry out their purchase and sales plans at the $3 price. At any other price, either suppliers or demanders would be unable to trade as much as they would like.

Equilibrium is not some mythical notion. It is very real. Every morning fishermen bring in their fresh catch. Along the pier, they negotiate with

market equilibrium the point at which the market supply and market demand curves intersect

equilibrium price the price at the intersection of the market supply and demand curves; at this price, the quantity demanded equals the quantity supplied

equilibrium quantity the quantity at the intersection of the market supply and demand curves; at the equilibrium quantity, the quantity demanded equals the quantity supplied

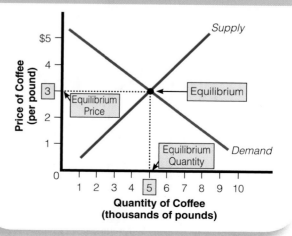

EXHIBIT 3.10 Market Equilibrium

fish brokers—sellers find buyers and buyers find sellers. Equilibrium is reached when the quantity demanded equals the quantity supplied. Only at the equilibrium price is the amount that sellers want to sell equal to the amount that buyers want to buy.

Shortages and Surpluses

What happens when the market price is not equal to the equilibrium price? If the price is not at the equilibrium level, buyers and sellers have an incentive to drive the price to equilibrium. Suppose the market price is above the equilibrium price, as seen in Exhibit 3.11(a). At $4 per pound, the quantity of coffee demanded would be 3,000 pounds, but the quantity supplied would be 7,000 pounds. At this price, a **surplus**, or excess quantity supplied, would exist. That is, at this price, growers would be willing to sell more coffee than consumers would be willing to buy. To get rid of the unwanted surplus, frustrated suppliers would have an incentive to cut their price to increase sales and rid themselves of storage costs and cut back on production. And as price falls, the quantity consumers would be willing to buy increases, ultimately eliminating the unsold surplus and returning the market to the equilibrium level. As long as the price is above the equilibrium level, some sellers will have unsold coffee and want to lower the price until it reaches equilibrium.

What would happen if the market price of coffee were below the equilibrium price? As seen in Exhibit 3.11(b), at $2 per pound, the yearly quantity demanded of 8,000 pounds would be greater than the 3,000 pounds that producers would be willing to supply at that low price. So at $2 per pound, a **shortage** or excess quantity

demanded of 5,000 pounds would exist. Some consumers are lucky enough to find coffee, but others are not able to find any sellers who are willing to sell them coffee at $2 per pound. Some frustrated consumers may offer to pay sellers more than $2. In addition, sellers noticing that there are disappointed consumers raise their prices. These actions by buyers and sellers cause the market price to rise. As the market price rises, the amount that sellers want to supply increases and the amount that buyers want to buy decreases. The upward pressure on price continues until equilibrium is reached at $3.

Scarcity and Shortages

People often confuse scarcity with shortages. Remember, most goods are scarce—desirable but limited. A shortage occurs when the quantity demanded is greater than the quantity supplied at the current price. We can eliminate shortages by increasing the price, but we cannot eliminate scarcity.

3-4b CHANGES IN EQUILIBRIUM PRICE AND QUANTITY

When one of the many determinants of demand or supply (input prices, prices of related products, number of suppliers, expectations, technology, and so on) changes, the demand and/or supply curves will shift, leading to changes in the equilibrium price and equilibrium quantity. We first consider a change in demand.

3-4c A CHANGE IN DEMAND

A shift in the demand curve—caused by a change in the price of a related good (substitutes or complements), income, the number of buyers, tastes, or expectations—results in a change in both equilibrium price and

---

EXHIBIT 3.11 Markets in Temporary Disequilibrium

a. Excess Quantity Supplied

b. Excess Quantity Demanded

© Cengage Learning 2014

equilibrium quantity, assuming the supply curve has not changed. But how and why does this relationship happen? The answer can be most clearly explained by means of an example. Suppose a new study claimed that two cups of coffee per day had significant health benefits. We would expect an increase in the demand for coffee. That is, at any given price, buyers want more coffee than before. At the original equilibrium, E_1, consumers want to buy Q_3 but sellers only want to sell Q_1, as seen in Exhibit 3.12. Market pressure drives the price up to a new equilibrium, E_2 at P_2. Both the equilibrium price and quantity rise because of the increase in demand. Notice that the *rightward shift in the demand curve causes a movement up along the supply curve*, causing an increase in quantity supplied.

3-4d A CHANGE IN SUPPLY

Like a shift in demand, a shift in the supply curve will also influence both equilibrium price and equilibrium quantity, assuming that demand for the product has not changed. For example, what impact would unfavorable weather conditions have in coffee-producing countries? Such conditions could cause a reduction in the supply of coffee. At any given price, sellers now want to sell less coffee. At the original equilibrium price of P_1, consumers still want to buy Q_1, but sellers are now only willing to supply Q_3. Thus, a shortage develops. Market pressure forces the price of coffee up until it reaches the new equilibrium at E_2, where the equilibrium price is P_2 and the equilibrium quantity is Q_2. A decrease in supply, *ceteris paribus*, will lead to a higher equilibrium price and a lower equilibrium quantity, as shown in Exhibit 3.13. Notice that the decrease in supply causes a *leftward shift in the supply curve resulting in a movement up along the demand curve*; a decrease in quantity demanded.

3-4e CHANGES IN BOTH SUPPLY AND DEMAND

We have discussed that, as part of the continual process of adjustment that occurs in the marketplace, supply and demand can each shift in response to many different factors, with the market then adjusting toward the new equilibrium. So far, we have considered only what happens when just one such change occurs at a time. In these cases, we learned that the results of the adjustments in supply and demand on the equilibrium price and quantity are predictable. However, both supply and demand will often shift in the same time period. Can we predict what will happen to equilibrium prices and equilibrium quantities in these situations?

As you will see, when supply and demand move at the same time, we can predict the change in one variable (price or quantity), but we are unable to predict the direction of the effect on the other variable with any certainty. The change in the second variable, then, is said to be *indeterminate*, because it cannot be determined without additional information about the size of the relative shifts in supply and demand. This concept will become clearer to you as we work through the following example.

An Increase in Supply and a Decrease in Demand

In Exhibit 3.14, shown on the next page, we have an increase in supply and a decrease in demand. These changes will clearly result in a decrease in the equilibrium price, because both the increase in supply and the decrease in demand work to push this price down. This drop in equilibrium price (from P_1 to P_2) is shown in the movement from E_1 to E_2 in Exhibit 3.14.

The effect of these changes on equilibrium price is clear, but how does the equilibrium quantity change?

EXHIBIT 3.12 An Increase in Demand

© Cengage Learning 2014

EXHIBIT 3.13 A Decrease in Supply

© Cengage Learning 2014

EXHIBIT 3.14 Shifts in Supply and Demand

a. A Small Increase in Supply and a Large Decrease in Demand

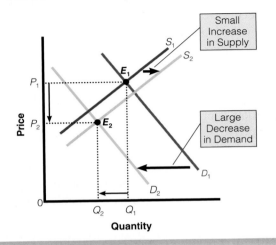

b. A Large Increase in Supply and a Small Decrease in Demand

The impact on equilibrium quantity is indeterminate because the increase in supply increases the equilibrium quantity and the decrease in demand decreases it. In this scenario, the change in the equilibrium quantity will vary depending on the relative changes in supply and demand. If, as shown in Exhibit 3.14(a), the decrease in demand is greater than the increase in supply, the equilibrium quantity will decrease. If, however, as shown in Exhibit 3.14(b), the increase in supply is greater than the decrease in demand, the equilibrium quantity will increase.

An Increase in Demand and Supply

It is also possible that both supply and demand will increase or decrease. This situation, for example, has happened with HD televisions (and with DVDs, laptops, cell phones, digital cameras, and other electronic equipment, too). As a result of technological breakthroughs and new factories manufacturing HD televisions, the supply curve for HD televisions shifted to the right. That is, at any given price, more HD televisions were offered than before. But with rising income and an increasing number of buyers in the market, the demand for HD televisions increased as well. As shown in Exhibit 3.15, both the increased demand and the increased supply caused an increase in the equilibrium quantity—more HD televisions were sold. The equilibrium price could have gone either up (because of increased demand) or down (because of increased supply), depending on the relative sizes of the demand and supply shifts. In this case, price is the indeterminate variable. However, in the case of HD televisions, we know that the supply curve shifted more than the demand curve, so that the effect of increased supply pushing prices down outweighed the effect of increased demand pushing prices

up. As a result, the equilibrium price of HD televisions has fallen (from P_1 to P_2) over time.

3-4f THE COMBINATIONS OF SUPPLY AND DEMAND

The possible changes in demand and/or supply shifts are presented in Exhibit 3.16, along with the resulting changes in equilibrium quantity and equilibrium price. While you could memorize the impact of the various possible changes in demand and supply, it would be better to draw a graph, whenever a situation of changing demand and/or supply arises. Give it a try.

EXHIBIT 3.15 An Increase in the Demand and Supply of HD Televisions

3-4g SUPPLY, DEMAND, AND THE MARKET ECONOMY

Supply and demand are at the very foundation of the market system. They determine the prices of goods and services and how our scarce resources are allocated. What is truly amazing is how producers respond to the complex wants of the population without having tremendous shortages or surpluses, despite the fact that in a "free market," no single individual or agency makes decisions about what to produce. The market system provides a way for millions of producers and consumers to allocate scarce resources. Buyers and sellers indicate their wants through their actions and inactions in the marketplace, and this collective "voice" determines how resources are allocated. But how is this information communicated? Market prices serve as the language of the market system.

We often say the decision is made by "the market" or "market forces," but this is of little help in pinpointing the name and the place of the decision maker. In fact, no single person makes decisions about the quantity and quality of television, cars, beds, or any other goods or services consumed in the economy. Literally millions of people, both producers and consumers, participate in the decision-making process. To paraphrase a statement made popular by the first great modern economist, Adam Smith, it is as if an invisible hand works to coordinate the efforts of millions of diverse participants in the complex process of producing and distributing goods and services.

Market prices communicate important information to both buyers and sellers. They reveal information about the relative availability of products to buyers and they provide sellers with critical information about the relative value that consumers place on those products. In effect, market prices provide a way for both buyers and sellers to communicate about the relative value of resources. This communication results in a shifting of resources from those uses that are less valued to those that are more valued.

EXHIBIT 3.16 The Impact of Supply and Demand Shifts on Price and Quantity

	Supply Unchanged	An Increase in Supply	A Decrease in Supply
Demand unchanged	P unchanged Q unchanged	P ↓ Q ↑	P ↑ Q ↓
An increase in demand	P ↑ Q ↑	P indeterminate* Q ↑	P ↑ Q indeterminate*
A decrease in demand	P ↓ Q ↓	P ↓ Q indeterminate*	P indeterminate* Q ↓

*Indeterminate means it may increase, decrease, or remain the same, depending on the size of the change in demand relative to the change in supply.

© Cengage Learning 2014

SECTION CHECK 4 ANSWERS

1. The intersection of the supply and demand curves shows the equilibrium price and equilibrium quantity in a market. This point is the market equilibrium point.

2. A surplus occurs when quantity supplied exceeds quantity demanded; a shortage occurs when quantity demanded exceeds quantity supplied.

3. Shifts in the demand or the supply curve will cause a corresponding change in the equilibrium price and/or quantity, *ceteris paribus*.

4. Supply and demand curves can shift simultaneously in response to changes in both supply and demand determinants.

5. When simultaneous shifts occur in both supply and demand curves, either the equilibrium price or the equilibrium quantity will be indeterminate without more information.

COLLEGE ENROLLMENT AND THE PRICE OF GOING TO COLLEGE

Q&A

Q: How is it possible that the price of a college education has increased significantly over the past 40 years, and yet many more students are attending college? Does this relationship defy the law of demand?

You can find the answer on the next page.

© iStockphoto.com/mattjeacock

COLLEGE ENROLLMENT AND THE PRICE OF GOING TO COLLEGE

Q&A

A: If we know the price of a college education (adjusted for inflation) and the number of students enrolled in college for the two years 1972 and 2012, we can tell a plausible story using the analysis of supply and demand. In exhibit (a) below suppose that we have data for points A and B, the price of a college education and the quantity (the number of college students enrolled in the respective years, 1972 and 2012). In exhibit (b), we connect the two points with supply and demand curves and see a decrease in supply and an increase in demand. Demand increased between 1972 and 2012 for at least two reasons: First, on the demand side, as the population grows, a greater number of buyers want a college education. Second, a college education is a normal good; as income increases, buyers increase their demand for a college education. Third, demand has increased because of the availability of relatively inexpensive government-backed student loans. On the supply side, several factors caused the supply curve for education to shift to the left: the cost of maintenance (hiring additional staff and increasing faculty salaries), new equipment (computers, lab equipment, and library supplies), and buildings (additional classrooms, labs, cafeteria expansions, and dormitory space).

This situation does not defy the law of demand that states that there is an inverse relationship between price and quantity demanded, *ceteris paribus.* The truth is that supply and demand curves are shifting constantly. In this case, the demand (increasing) and supply (decreasing) caused price and quantity to rise.

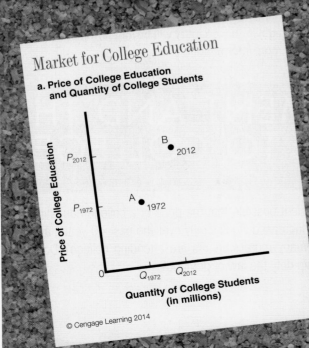

Market for College Education

a. Price of College Education and Quantity of College Students

© Cengage Learning 2014

b. Simultaneous Increase in Demand and Decrease in Supply

© Cengage Learning 2014

Chapter 3: Self-Review

Now that you are finished reading the chapter, review the questions below. You can write your answers in the space provided, then go online to see the answers at www.cengagebrain.com.

3-1 COMPETITIVE MARKETS

1. True or False: In a competitive market, buyers and sellers have significant market power.

3-2 DEMAND

2. What is the difference between an individual demand curve and a market demand curve?

3. If the price of zucchini increases, causing the demand for yellow squash to rise, what do we call the relationship between zucchini and yellow squash?

4. If plane travel is a normal good and bus travel is an inferior good, what will happen to the demand curves for plane and bus travel if people's incomes increase?

5. What would be the effects of each of the following on the demand for hamburger in Hilo, Hawaii? In each case, identify the responsible determinant of demand.
   a. The price of chicken falls.
   b. The price of hamburger buns doubles.
   c. Scientists find that eating hamburger prolongs life.
   d. The population of Hilo doubles.

3-3 SUPPLY

6. What are the two reasons that a supply curve is positively sloped?

7. If the price of corn rose,
   a. what would be the effect on the supply of corn?
   b. what would be the effect on the supply of wheat?

8. The following table shows the supply schedule for Rolling Rock Oil Co. Plot Rolling Rock's supply curve on a graph.

Price (dollars per barrel)	Quantity Supplied (barrels per month)
$5	10,000
10	15,000
15	20,000
20	25,000
25	30,000

Price (dollars per barrel)

0

Quantity Supplied (barrels per month)

3-4 MARKET EQUILIBRIUM PRICE AND QUANTITY

9. True or False: If the price charged is less than the equilibrium price, resulting in buyers wanting to buy more at that price than sellers are willing to sell, a shortage will occur.

10. When both supply and demand shift, what added information do we need to know in order to determine in which direction the indeterminate variable changes?

© Sam Hollenshead/Polaris.

When four floors of his building caved in,

killing three of his neighbors, Uttamchand K. Sojatwala, owner of a successful textile business, refused to leave his two bedroom, rent-controlled apartment in Mumbai, India. The city then cut off his electricity and water and threatened to arrest his wife, but he still wouldn't leave. In all, fifty-eight tenants refused to leave a rent-controlled apartment building that was considered too dangerous by city officials. Why did these residents take the risk? Cheap rent—$8.50 a month.

Rent controls can cause shortages and waiting lists, and landlords can lose the incentive to respond to their tenants' demands.

Test your Economics *street-smart* knowledge and see how you compare against other students! Scan here or visit CourseMate for Survey of ECON2.

4

Using Supply and Demand

I f a rock group increased the price it charges for concert tickets, what impact would that have on ticket sales? More precisely, would ticket sales fall a little or a lot? Would the group make more money by lowering the price or by raising the price? This chapter will allow you to answer these types of questions and more.

Elasticity is a measure of how much buyers and sellers respond to changes in prices. We now have a tool that can help us measure not just the direction of a change but the magnitude of a change when market conditions are altered. For example, will the quantity demanded of gasoline respond more in the short-run or the long-run. In this chapter, we will see the usefulness of the elasticity concept in many different applications.

Recall from Chapter 1 that the economist wears two hats—as the scientist that explains the world around him and as the policy maker who uses his theories to make the world a better place. In this chapter, we look at various government policies using supply and demand. But beware—policies often have unintended effects that the policy maker may not have anticipated. We will also see the importance of elasticity in determining the effects of taxes. If a tax is levied on the seller, will the seller pay all of the taxes? If the tax were levied on the buyer, will the buyer pay all of the taxes? We will see that elasticity, not who is legally required to pay the tax, is critical in the determination of tax burden. Elasticities will also help us to more fully understand many policy issues, such as luxury taxes. If Congress were to impose a large tax on yachts, what do you think would happen to yacht sales? What would happen to employment in the boat industry?

Finally, we will consider whether the price and output that result from the equilibrium of supply and demand are right from society's standpoint. Using the tools of consumer and producer surplus, we can demonstrate the efficiency of a competitive market. In other words, we can show that the equilibrium price and quantity in a competitive market maximize the economic welfare of consumers and producers. Maximizing total surplus (the sum of consumer and producer surplus) leads to an efficient allocation of resources. Efficiency makes the size of the economic pie as large as possible. How we distribute that economic pie (equity) is the subject of future chapters. Efficiency can be measured on objective, positive grounds, whereas equity involves normative analysis.

4-1 Price Elasticity of Demand

SECTION CHECK 1

Consider the following questions as you read through this section.

1. What is price elasticity of demand?

2. How do we measure consumers' responses to price changes?

3. What determines the price elasticity of demand?

In learning and applying the law of demand, we have established the basic fact that quantity demanded changes inversely with change in price, *ceteris paribus*. But how much does quantity demanded change? The extent to which a change in price affects quantity demanded may vary considerably from product to product and over the various price ranges for the same product. The **price elasticity of demand** measures the responsiveness of quantity demanded to a change in price. Specifically, price elasticity is defined as the percentage change in quantity demanded divided by the percentage change in price, or

$$\text{Price elasticity of demand } (E_D) = \frac{\text{Percentage change in quantity demand}}{\text{Percentage change in price}}$$

Note that, following the law of demand, price and quantity demanded show an inverse relationship. For this reason, the price elasticity of demand is, in theory, always negative. But in practice and for simplicity, this quantity is always expressed in absolute value terms—that is, as a positive number.

4-1a IS THE DEMAND CURVE ELASTIC OR INELASTIC?

It is important to understand the basic concepts behind elasticities. To do this, we must focus on the percentage changes in quantity demanded and price.

If the quantity demanded is responsive to even a small change in price, we call it elastic. On the other hand, if a huge change in price results in only a small change in quantity demanded, then the demand is said to be inelastic. For example, if a 10 percent increase in the price leads to a 50 percent reduction in the quantity demanded, we say that demand is elastic because the quantity demanded is sensitive to the price change.

$$E_D = \frac{\%\Delta Q_D}{\%\Delta P} = \frac{50\%}{10\%} = 5$$

Demand is elastic in this case because a 10 percent change in price led to a larger (50 percent) change in quantity demanded.

Alternatively, if a 10 percent increase in the price leads to a 1 percent reduction in quantity demanded, we say that demand is *inelastic* because the quantity demanded did not respond much to the price reduction.

$$E_D = \frac{\%\Delta Q_D}{\%\Delta P} = \frac{1\%}{10\%} = 0.10$$

Demand is inelastic in this case because a 10 percent change in price led to a smaller (1 percent) change in quantity demanded.

4-1b TYPES OF DEMAND CURVES

Economists refer to a variety of demand curves based on the magnitude of their elasticity. A demand curve, or a portion of a demand curve, can be elastic, inelastic, or unit elastic.

© Blue Jean Images/Alamy

Think of price elasticity like an elastic rubber band. When small price changes greatly affect, or "stretch," quantity demanded, the demand is elastic, much like a very stretchy rubber band. When large price changes cannot "stretch" demand, however, then demand is inelastic, more like a very stiff rubber band.

EXHIBIT 4.1 Elastic Demand

a. Elastic Demand ($E_D > 1$)

$$E_D = \frac{\%\Delta Q_D}{\%\Delta P} = \frac{0.20}{0.10} = 2$$

$10\%\Delta P$

$20\%\ \Delta Q_D$

Demand

b. Perfectly Elastic Demand ($E_D = \infty$)

Demand

© Cengage Learning 2014

elastic percentage change in quantity demanded is greater than the percentage change in price ($E_D > 1$)

inelastic percentage change in quantity demanded is less than the percentage change in price ($E_D < 1$)

unit elastic demand demand with a price elasticity of 1; the percentage change in quantity demanded is equal to the percentage change in price

Demand is **elastic** when the elasticity is greater than 1 ($E_D > 1$)—the quantity demanded changes proportionally more than the price changes. In this case, a given percentage increase in price, say 10 percent, leads to a larger percentage change in quantity demanded, say 20 percent, as seen in Exhibit 4.1(a). If the curve is *perfectly elastic*, the demand curve is horizontal. The elasticity coefficient is infinity because even the slightest change in price will lead to a huge change in quantity demanded—for example, a tiny increase in price will cause the quantity demanded to fall to zero. In Exhibit 4.1(b), a *perfectly elastic* demand curve (horizontal) is illustrated.

Demand is **inelastic** when the elasticity is less than 1; the quantity demanded changes proportionally less than the price changes. In this case, a given percentage change in price (for example 10 percent) is accompanied by a smaller reduction in quantity demanded (for example, 5 percent), as seen in Exhibit 4.2(a) on the next page. If the demand curve is *perfectly inelastic*, the quantity demanded is the same regardless of the price. The elasticity coefficient is zero because the quantity demanded does not respond to a change in price. This relationship is illustrated in Exhibit 4.2(b).

Goods for which E_D equals one ($E_D = 1$) are said to have **unit elastic demand**. In this case, the quantity demanded changes proportionately to price changes. For example, a 10 percent increase in price will lead to a 10 percent reduction in quantity demanded. This relationship is illustrated in Exhibit 4.3 on the next page.

The price elasticity of demand is closely related to the slope of the demand curve. Generally speaking, the flatter the demand curve passing through a given point, the more elastic the demand. The steeper the demand curve passing through a given point, the less elastic the demand.

4-1c THE DETERMINANTS OF THE PRICE ELASTICITY OF DEMAND

As you have learned, the elasticity of demand for a specific good refers to movements along its demand curve as its price changes. A lower price will increase quantity demanded, and a higher price will reduce quantity demanded. But what factors will influence the magnitude of the change in quantity demanded in response to a price change? That is, what will make the demand curve relatively more elastic, where Q_D is responsive to price changes, and what will make the demand curve relatively less elastic, where Q_D is less responsive to price changes?

For the most part, the price elasticity of demand depends on three factors: (1) the availability of close substitutes, (2) the proportion of income spent on the good, and (3) the amount of time that has elapsed since the price change.

PED depends on 3 factors:

• available substitutes

• income spent on good

• time since price change

© iStockphoto.com/subjug

EXHIBIT 4.2 Inelastic Demand

a. Inelastic Demand ($E_D < 1$)

$$E_D = \frac{\%\Delta Q_D}{\%\Delta P} = \frac{0.05}{0.10} = 0.5$$

10%ΔP

5% ΔQ_D

Demand

Q_2 Q_1

Price / Quantity

P_2 / P_1

b. Perfectly Inelastic Demand ($E_D = 0$)

Demand

20%ΔP

P_2 / P_1

$Q_1 = Q_2$

Price / Quantity

Availability of Close Substitutes

Goods *with* close substitutes tend to have more elastic demands. Why? Because if the price of such a good increases, consumers can easily switch to other now relatively lower-priced substitutes. In many examples, such as different brands of root beer or gasoline, the ease of substitution will make demand quite elastic for most individuals. Goods *without* close substitutes, such as insulin for diabetics, cigarettes for chain smokers, heroin for addicts, or emergency medical care for those with appendicitis or broken legs, tend to have inelastic demands. The demand for an antivenom shot after a rattlesnake bite is another example. Once

a person is bitten, that demand curve becomes extremely inelastic.

The degree of substitutability can also depend on whether the good is a necessity or a luxury. Goods that are necessities, such as food, have no ready substitutes and thus tend to have lower elasticities than do luxury items, such as jewelry.

When the good is broadly defined, it tends to be less elastic than when it is narrowly defined. For example, the elasticity of demand for food (a broad category) tends to be inelastic because few substitutes are available for food. But for a certain type of food, such as pizza (narrowly defined good), it is much easier to find a substitute—perhaps tacos, burgers, salads, burritos, or chili fries. That is, the demand for a particular type of food is more elastic because more and better substitutes are available than for food as an entire category.

Proportion of Income Spent on the Good

The smaller the proportion of income spent on a good, the lower its elasticity of demand. If the amount spent on a good relative to income is small, then the impact of a change in its price on one's budget will also be small. As a result, consumers will respond less to price changes for small-ticket items than for similar percentage changes in large-ticket items, where a price change could potentially have a large impact on the consumer's budget. For example, a 50 percent increase in the price of salt will have a much smaller impact on consumers' behavior than a similar percentage increase in the price of a new automobile. Similarly, a 50 percent increase in the cost of private university tuition will have a greater impact on students' (and sometimes parents') budgets than a 50 percent increase in textbook prices.

Time

For many goods, the more time that people have to adapt to a new price change, the greater the elasticity of demand. Immediately after a price change, consumers may be unable to locate good alternatives or easily

EXHIBIT 4.3 Unit Elastic Demand

$$E_D = \frac{\%\Delta Q_D}{\%\Delta P} = \frac{0.10}{0.10} = 1$$

10%ΔP

10% ΔQ_D

D

Q_2 Q_1

Price / Quantity

P_2 / P_1

change their consumption patterns. But as time passes, consumers have more time to find or develop suitable substitutes and to plan and implement changes in their patterns of consumption. For example, drivers may not respond immediately to an increase in gas prices, perhaps believing it to be temporary. However, if the price persists over a longer period, we would expect people to drive less, buy more fuel-efficient cars, move closer to work, carpool, take the bus, or even bike to work. So for many goods, especially nondurable goods (goods that do not last a long time), the short-run demand curve is generally less elastic than the long-run demand curve, as illustrated in Exhibit 4.4.

Estimated Price Elasticities of Demand

Because of shifts in supply and demand curves, researchers have a difficult task when trying to estimate empirically the price elasticity of demand for a particular good or service. Despite this difficulty, Exhibit 4.5 presents some estimates for the price elasticity of demand for certain goods. As you would expect, certain goods such as medical care, air travel, and gasoline are all relatively price inelastic in the short run because buyers have fewer substitutes. On the other hand, air travel in the long run is much more sensitive to price (elastic) because the available substitutes are much more plentiful. Exhibit 4.5 shows that the price elasticity of demand for air travel is 2.4, which means that a 1 percent increase in price will lead to a 2.4 percent reduction in quantity demanded. Notice, in each case where the data are available, the

EXHIBIT 4.5 Price Elasticities of Demand for Selected Goods

Good	Short Run	Long Run
Salt	—	0.1
Air travel	0.1	2.4
Gasoline	0.2	0.7
Medical care and hospitalization	0.3	0.9
Jewelry and watches	0.4	0.7
Physician services	0.6	—
Alcohol	0.9	3.6
Movies	0.9	3.7
China, glassware	1.5	2.6
Automobiles	1.9	2.2
Chevrolets	—	4.0

SOURCES: Adapted from Robert Archibald and Robert Gillingham, "An Analysis of the Short-Run Consumer Demand for Gasoline Using Household Survey Data," *Review of Economics and Statistics* 62 (November 1980): 622–628; Hendrik S. Houthakker and Lester D. Taylor, *Consumer Demand in the United States: Analyses and Projections* (Cambridge, Mass.: Harvard University Press, 1970), pp. 56–149; Richard Voith, "The Long-Run Elasticity of Demand for Commuter Rail Transportation," *Journal of Urban Economics* 30 (November 1991): 360–372.

estimates of the long-run price elasticities of demand are greater than the short-run price elasticities of demand. In short, the price elasticity of demand is greater when the price change persists over a longer time period.

SECTION CHECK 1 ANSWERS

1. Price elasticity of demand measures the percentage change in quantity demanded divided by the percentage change in price that caused it, moving along a demand curve.

2. If the demand for a good is price elastic in the relevant range, quantity demanded is very responsive to a price change. If the demand for a good is relatively price inelastic, quantity demanded is not very responsive to a price change.

3. The price elasticity of demand depends on: (1) the availability of close substitutes, (2) the proportion of income spent on the good, and (3) the amount of time that buyers have to respond to a price change.

EXHIBIT 4.4 Short-Run and Long-Run Demand Curves

© Cengage Learning 2014

4-2 Total Revenue and the Price Elasticity of Demand

SECTION CHECK 2

Keep the following questions in mind as you read through this section.

1. What is total revenue?

2. What is the relationship between total revenue and the price elasticity of demand?

3. Does the price elasticity of demand vary along a linear demand curve?

Now that we understand what price elasticity is, let's examine the relationship between it and total revenue.

4-2a HOW DOES THE PRICE ELASTICITY OF DEMAND IMPACT TOTAL REVENUE?

The price elasticity of demand for a good also has implications for total revenue. **Total revenue (TR)** is the amount sellers receive for a good or service. Total revenue is simply the price of the good (P) times the quantity of the good sold (Q): $TR = P \times Q$. The elasticity of demand will help to predict how changes in the price will impact total revenue earned by the producer for selling the good. Let's see how this works.

$$TR = P \times Q$$

total revenue (TR) the amount sellers receive for a good or service, calculated as the product price times the quantity sold

In Exhibit 4.6, we see that when the demand is price elastic ($E_D > 1$), total revenues will rise as the price declines, because the percentage

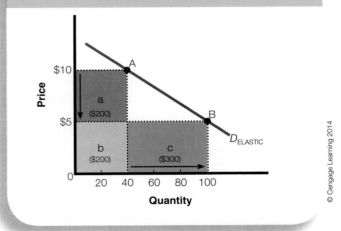

EXHIBIT 4.6 Elastic Demand and Total Revenue

© Cengage Learning 2014

increase in the quantity demanded is greater than the percentage reduction in price. For example, if the price of a good is cut in half (say from $10 to $5) and the quantity demanded more than doubles (say from 40 to 100), total revenue will rise from $400 ($10 × 40 = $400) to $500 ($5 × 100 = $500). Equivalently, if the price rises from $5 to $10 and the quantity demanded falls from 100 to 40 units, then total revenue will fall from $500 to $400. As this example illustrates, if the demand curve is relatively elastic, total revenue will vary inversely with a price change.

You can see from the following what happens to total revenue when demand is price elastic. (*Note:* The size of the price and quantity arrows represents the size of the percentage changes.)

When Demand Is Price Elastic

$$\downarrow TR = \uparrow P \times \downarrow Q$$

or

$$\uparrow TR = \downarrow P \times \uparrow Q$$

On the other hand, if demand for a good is relatively inelastic ($E_D < 1$), the total revenue will be lower at lower prices than at higher prices because a given price reduction will be accompanied by a proportionately smaller increase in quantity demanded. For example, as shown in Exhibit 4.7, if the price of a good is cut (say from $10 to $5) and the quantity demanded less than doubles (say it increases from 30 to 40), then total revenue will fall from $300 ($10 × 30 = $300) to $200 ($5 × 40 = $200). Equivalently, if the price increases from $5 to $10 and the quantity demanded falls from

EXHIBIT 4.7 Inelastic Demand and Total Revenue

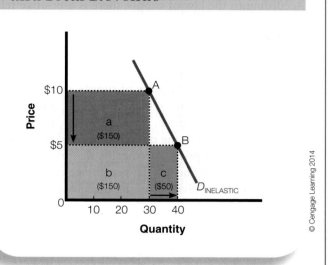

40 to 30, total revenue will increase from $200 to $300. To summarize, then: If the demand curve is inelastic, total revenue will vary directly with a price change.

When Demand Is Price Inelastic

$$\uparrow TR = \uparrow P \times \downarrow Q$$

or

$$\downarrow TR = \downarrow P \times \uparrow Q$$

In this case, the "net" effect on total revenue is reversed but easy to see. Again, the size of the price and quantity arrows represents the size of the percentage changes.

4-2b PRICE ELASTICITY CHANGES ALONG A LINEAR DEMAND CURVE

As we have just seen, the slopes of demand curves can be used to estimate their *relative* elasticities of demand: The steeper one demand curve is relative to another, the more inelastic it is relative to the other. However, except for the extreme cases of perfectly elastic and perfectly inelastic curves, great care must be taken when trying to estimate the degree of elasticity of one demand curve from its slope. In fact, as we will soon see, a straight-line demand curve with a constant slope will change elasticity continuously as you move up or down it. This is because the slope is the ratio of changes in the two variables (price and quantity), while the elasticity is the ratio of percentage changes in the two variables.

We can easily demonstrate that the elasticity of demand varies along a linear demand curve by using what we already know about the interrelationship between price and total revenue. Exhibit 4.8 shows a linear (constant slope) demand curve. In Exhibit 4.8(a), we see that when the price falls on the upper half of the demand curve from P_1 to P_2, and quantity demanded increases from Q_1 to Q_2, total revenue increases. That is, the new area of total revenue (area b + c) is larger than the old area of total revenue (area a + b). It is also true that if the price increased in this region (from P_2 to P_1), total revenue would fall, because b + c is greater than a + b. In this region of the demand curve, then, there is a negative relationship between price and total revenue. As we discussed earlier, this is characteristic of an elastic demand curve ($E_D > 1$).

EXHIBIT 4.8 Price Elasticity along a Linear Demand Curve

In 1974, the government imposed price ceilings on gasoline. The result was shortages. In some cities, such as Chicago, Portland, and New York, drivers waited over an hour to fill up their tanks. As you know, the value of your time has an opportunity cost.

unintended consequences the secondary effects of an action that may occur after the initial effects

you to buy a few gallons a day; when they ran out of gas, they closed for the day. Many gas stations were closed in the evenings and on weekends.

A number of government officials wanted to put the blame on OPEC, but if prices were allowed to rise to their equilibrium at E_2, shortages would have been avoided. Instead, it would have meant higher prices at P_2 and a greater quantity sold, Q_2 rather than Q_S. Of course, not everybody was unhappy with the price ceiling. Recall our discussion of opportunity cost in Chapter 2. People place different values on their time. People with a low opportunity cost of time but who cannot as easily afford the higher price per gallon (e.g., poor retired senior citizens) would be more likely to favor the controls. Surgeons, lawyers, and others who have high hourly wages and salaries would view the controls less favorably, because the time spent waiting in line would likely be worth more to them than paying the higher price for gasoline.

4-4e UNINTENDED CONSEQUENCES

When markets are altered for policy reasons, it is wise to remember that actions do not always have the results that were initially intended—in other words, actions can have **unintended consequences**. As economists, we must always look for the secondary effects of an action, which may occur along with the initial effects. For example, the government often has good intentions when it adopts price controls to help low-skilled workers or tenants in search of affordable housing, but such policies may also cause unintended consequences that could completely undermine the intended effects. Rent controls may have the immediate effect of lowering rents, but secondary effects may well include low vacancy rates, discrimination against low-income and large families, deterioration of the quality of rental units, and black markets. Similarly, a sizable increase in the minimum wage may help many low-skilled workers or apprentices but may also result in higher unemployment and/or a reduction in fringe benefits, such as vacations and discounts to employees. Society has to make tough decisions, and if the government subsidizes some programs or groups of people in one area, then something must always be given up somewhere else. The "law of scarcity" cannot be repealed!

4-4f ELASTICITIES AND TAXES: COMBINING SUPPLY AND DEMAND ELASTICITIES

Who pays the tax? Someone may be legally required to send the check to the government but that party is not necessarily the one who bears the burden of the tax.

The relative elasticity of supply and demand determines the distribution of the tax burden for a good. As we will see, if demand is relatively less elastic than supply in the relevant tax region, the largest portion of the tax is paid by the consumer. However, if demand is relatively more elastic than supply in the relevant tax region, the largest portion of the tax is paid by the producer.

In Exhibit 4.15(a) on the next page, the pre-tax equilibrium price is $1.00 and the pre-tax equilibrium quantity is Q_{BT}—the quantity before tax. If the government imposes a $0.50 tax on the seller, the supply curve shifts vertically by the amount of the tax (just as if an input price rose $0.50).

> As economists, we must always look for the secondary effects of an action, which may occur along with the initial effects.

When demand is relatively less elastic than supply in the relevant region, the consumer bears more of the burden of the tax. For example, in Exhibit 4.15(a), the demand curve is relatively less elastic than the supply curve. In response to the tax, the consumer pays $1.40 per unit, $0.40 more than the consumer paid before the tax increase. The producer, however, receives $0.90 per unit, which is $0.10 less than the producer received before the tax.

In Exhibit 4.15(b), demand is relatively more elastic than the supply in the relevant region. Here we see that

RENT CONTROL: NEW YORK'S SELF-DESTRUCTION

"Rent control appears to be the most efficient technique presently known to destroy a city—except for bombing," Swedish economist Assar Lindbeck observed in a 1972 book. Rent control is a big cause of New York City's chronic financial mess, a huge cause of its notorious housing scarcity and a neat illustration of its political unreality. Ending it would be a big step toward unleashing a construction boom and boosting its economy to offset destructive tax increases.

New York has maintained price controls on rent since World War II.... William Tucker, the writer who has studied the costs most closely, estimates the direct costs of rent control at $2 billion a year, exclusive of the effect of shrinking the property tax base.

Rent control ... has inhibited construction in the city. During the recession of 1990–91, the city actually lost more housing units than it gained....

The Manhattan Institute chartered an elaborate study by Henry O. Pollakowski, an MIT housing expert. He concluded, "tenants in low- and moderate-income areas receive little or no benefit from rent stabilization, while tenants in more affluent locations are effectively subsidized for a substantial portion of their rent."

Do tenants in low- and moderate-income areas reap the benefits of rent control?

SOURCE: Robert L. Bartley, "Rent Control: New York's Self-Destruction," *Wall Street Journal*, May 19, 2003, p. A17.

EXHIBIT 4.15 Elasticity and the Burden of Taxation

a. Demand Is Relatively Less Elastic Than Supply

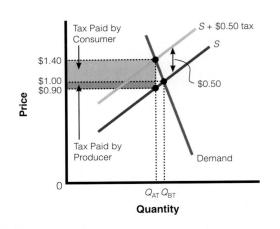

b. Demand Is Relatively More Elastic Than Supply

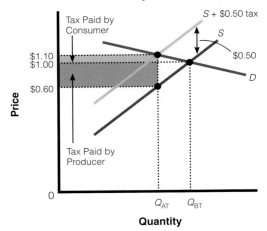

the greater burden of the same $0.50 tax falls on the producer. That is, the producer is now responsible for $0.40 of the tax, while the consumer only pays $0.10. In general, then, the tax burden falls on the side of the market that is relatively less elastic.

4-4g ELASTICITY APPLICATIONS: YACHTS, TAXES, AND ELASTICITIES

In 1991, Congress levied a 10 percent luxury tax. The tax applied to the "first retail sale" of luxury goods with sales prices above the following thresholds: automobiles, $30,000; boats, $100,000; private planes, $250,000; and furs and jewelry, $10,000. The Congressional Budget Office forecasted that the luxury tax would raise about $1.5 billion over five years. However, in 1991, the luxury tax raised less than $30 million in tax revenues. Why? People stopped buying items subject to the luxury tax.

Let's focus our attention on the luxury tax on yachts. Congress passed this tax thinking that the demand for yachts was relatively inelastic and that the tax would have only a small impact on the sale of new yachts. However, the people in the market for new boats had plenty of substitutes—used boats, boats from other countries, new houses, vacations, and so on. In short, the demand for new yachts was more elastic than Congress thought. Remember, when demand is relatively more elastic than supply, most of the tax is passed on to the seller—in this case, the boat industry (workers and retailers). And supply was relatively inelastic because boat factories are not easy to change in the short run. So sellers received

a lower price for their boats, and sales fell. In the first year after the tax, yacht retailers reported a 77 percent drop in sales, and approximately 25,000 workers were laid off. The point is that incorrectly predicting elasticities can lead to huge social, political, and economic problems. After intense lobbying by industry groups, Congress repealed the luxury tax on boats in 1993, and on January 1, 2003, the tax on cars finally expired.

SECTION CHECK 4 ANSWERS

1. Price controls involve government mandates to keep prices above or below the market-determined equilibrium price.

2. Price ceilings are government-imposed maximum prices. If price ceilings are set below the equilibrium price, shortages will result.

3. Price floors are government-imposed minimum prices. If price floors are set above the equilibrium price, surpluses will result.

4. The law of unintended consequences states that the results of certain actions may not always be as clear as they initially appear.

5. The relative elasticity of supply and demand determines the distribution of the tax burden for a good. If demand is more elastic than supply, producers bear the greater burden of the tax; if the supply is more elastic than the demand, consumers bear the greater burden.

DRUGS ACROSS THE BORDER

The United States spends billions of dollars a year to halt the importation of illegal drugs across the border. Although these efforts are clearly targeted at suppliers, who really pays the higher enforcement and evasion costs? The government crackdown has increased the probability of apprehension and conviction for drug smugglers. That increase in risk for suppliers increases their cost of doing business, raising the cost of importing and distributing illegal drugs. This would shift the supply curve for illegal drugs to the left, from S_1 to S_2, as seen in Exhibit 4.16. For most drug users—addicts, in particular—the price of drugs such as cocaine and heroin lies in the highly inelastic region of the demand curve. Because the demand for drugs is relatively inelastic in this region, the seller would be able to shift most of this cost onto the consumer (think of it as being similar to the tax shift just discussed). The buyer now has to pay a much higher price, P_B, and the seller receives a slightly lower price, P_S. That is, enforcement efforts increase the price of illegal drugs, but only a small reduction in quantity demanded results from this price increase. Increased enforcement efforts may have unintended consequences due to the fact that buyers bear the majority of the burden of this price increase. Tighter smuggling controls may, in fact, result in higher levels of burglary, muggings, and white-collar crime, as more cash-strapped buyers search for alternative ways of funding their increasingly expensive habit. In addition, with the huge financial rewards in the drug trade, tougher enforcement and higher illegal drug prices could lead to even greater corruption in law enforcement and the judicial system.

These possible reactions do not mean we should abandon our efforts against illegal drugs. Illegal drugs can impose huge personal and social costs—billions of dollars of lost productivity and immeasurable personal tragedy. However, solely targeting the supply side can have unintended consequences. Policy makers may get their best results by focusing on a reduction in demand—changing user preferences. For example, if drug education leads to a reduction in the demand for drugs, the demand curve will shift to the left—reducing the price and the quantity of illegal drugs exchanged, as shown in Exhibit 4.17. The remaining drug users, at Q_2, will now pay a lower price, P_2. This lower price for drugs will lead to fewer drug-related crimes, *ceteris paribus*.

It is also possible that the elasticity of demand for illegal drugs may be more elastic in the long run than in the short run. That is, in the short run, higher prices probably do not significantly affect drug use by established users and addicts. However, in the long run, the demand for illegal drugs may be more elastic; that is, the higher price may deter many younger, and poorer, people from experimenting with illegal drugs.

SOURCE: From Exploring Economics, 6e, by Robert L. Sexton, ISBN: 9781111970307

EXHIBIT 4.16 Government Effort to Reduce the Supply of Illegal Drugs

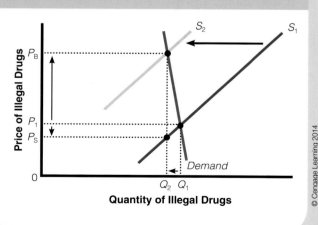

EXHIBIT 4.17 Drug Education Reduces Demand

OIL PRICES

One reason that small changes in supply (or demand) lead to large changes in oil prices and small changes in quantity is because of the inelasticity of demand (and supply) in the short run. Because bringing oil to market takes a long time, the elasticity of supply is relatively low—supply is inelastic. Few substitutes for oil products (e.g., gasoline) are available in the short run, as seen in Exhibit 4.18(a).

However, in the long run, demand and supply are more elastic. At higher prices, consumers will replace gas guzzlers with more fuel-efficient cars, and non-OPEC oil producers will expand exploration and production. Thus, in the long run, when supply and demand are much more elastic, the same size reduction in supply will have a smaller impact on price, as seen in Exhibit 4.18(b).

SOURCE: From Exploring Economics, 6e, by Robert L. Sexton, ISBN: 9781111970307

EXHIBIT 4.18 Oil Prices: Short Run vs. Long Run

a. Oil Prices in the Short Run

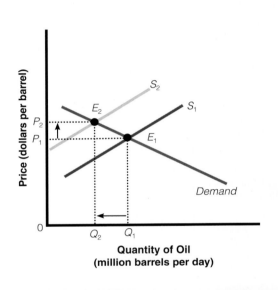

b. Oil Prices in the Long Run

© Cengage Learning 2014

4-5 Consumer Surplus, Producer Surplus, and the Efficiency of Markets

SECTION CHECK 5

Consider the following questions as you read through this section.

1. What is consumer surplus?

2. What is producer surplus?

3. How do we measure the total gains from trade?

While we have seen how market forces allocate society's scarce resources, we have not determined whether this is desirable. Let's consider how consumer and producer surpluses demonstrate the *efficiency* of a competitive market.

4-5a CONSUMER SURPLUS

In a competitive market, consumers and producers buy and sell at the market equilibrium price. However, some consumers will be willing and able to pay more for the good than they have to. But they would never knowingly buy something that is worth less to them. That is, what a consumer actually pays for a unit of a good is usually less than the amount she is *willing* to pay. For example, you would be willing and able to pay far more than the market price for a rope ladder to get out of a burning building. You would be willing to pay more than the market price for a tank of gasoline if you had run out of gas on a desolate highway in the desert. **Consumer surplus** is the monetary difference between the amount a consumer is willing and able to pay for an additional unit of a good and what the consumer actually pays—the market price. Consumer surplus for the whole market is the sum of all the individual consumer surpluses for those consumers who have purchased the good.

4-5b MARGINAL WILLINGNESS TO PAY FALLS AS MORE IS CONSUMED

Suppose it is a hot day and iced tea is going for $1 per glass, but Emma is willing to pay $4 for the first glass (point a), $2 for the second glass (point b), and $0.50 for the third glass (point c), reflecting the law of demand. How much consumer surplus will Emma receive? First, it is important to note the general fact that if the consumer is a buyer of several units of a good, the earlier units will have greater marginal value and therefore create more consumer surplus, because *marginal willingness to pay* falls as greater quantities are consumed in any period. In fact, you can think of the demand curve as a marginal benefit curve—the additional benefit derived from consuming one more unit. Notice in Exhibit 4.19 that Emma's demand curve for iced tea has a step-like shape. This is demonstrated by Emma's willingness to pay $4 and $2 successively for the first two glasses of iced tea. Thus, Emma will receive $3 of consumer surplus for the first glass ($4 – $1) and $1 of

consumer surplus for the second glass ($2 – $1), for a total consumer surplus of $4, as seen in Exhibit 4.19. Emma will not be willing to purchase the third glass, because her willingness to pay is less than its price ($0.50 versus $1.00).

> **consumer surplus** the difference between the price a consumer is willing and able to pay for an additional unit of a good and the price the consumer actually pays; for the whole market, it is the sum of all the individual consumer surpluses

In Exhibit 4.20, we can easily measure the consumer surplus in the market by using a market demand curve rather than an individual demand curve. In short, the market consumer surplus is the area under the market demand curve and above the market price (the shaded area in Exhibit 4.20). The market for chocolate contains millions of potential buyers, so we will get a smooth demand curve. Because the demand curve represents the *marginal benefits* consumers receive from consuming an additional unit, we can conclude that all buyers of chocolate receive at least some consumer surplus in the market because the marginal benefit is greater than the market price—the shaded area in Exhibit 4.20.

4-5c PRICE CHANGES AND CHANGES IN CONSUMER SURPLUS

Imagine that the price of your favorite beverage fell because of an increase in supply. Wouldn't you feel better off? An increase in supply and a lower price will increase your consumer surplus for each unit you

EXHIBIT 4.19 Emma's Consumer Surplus for Iced Tea

© Cengage Learning 2014

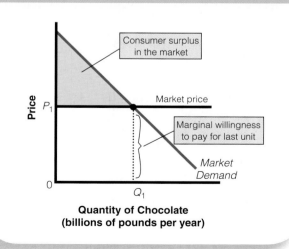

EXHIBIT 4.20 Consumer Surplus

© Cengage Learning 2014

Emma will receive $3 in consumer surplus for the first glass and $1 of consumer surplus for the second. She won't purchase a third, however, because the market price is higher than what she is willing to pay.

producer surplus the difference between what a producer is paid for a good and the cost of producing that unit of the good; for the market, it is the sum of all the individual sellers' producer surpluses—the area above the market supply curve and below the market price

were already consuming and will also increase your consumer surplus from additional purchases at the lower price. Conversely, a decrease in supply and an increase in price will lower your consumer surplus.

Exhibit 4.21 shows the gain in consumer

surplus associated with, say, a technological advance that shifts the supply curve to the right. As a result, equilibrium price falls (from P_1 to P_2) and quantity rises (from Q_1 to Q_2). Consumer surplus then increases from area P_1AB to area P_2AC, or a gain in consumer surplus of P_1BCP_2. The increase in consumer surplus has two parts. First, there is an increase in consumer surplus, because Q_1 can now be purchased at a lower price; this amount of additional consumer surplus is illustrated by area P_1BDP_2 in Exhibit 4.21. Second, the lower price makes it advantageous for buyers to expand their purchases from Q_1 to Q_2. The net benefit to buyers from expanding their consumption from Q_1 to Q_2 is illustrated by area BCD.

4-5d PRODUCER SURPLUS

As we have just seen, the difference between what a consumer would be willing and able to pay for a given quantity of a good and what a consumer actually has to pay is called consumer surplus. The parallel concept for producers is called producer surplus. **Producer surplus** is the difference between what a producer is paid for a good and the cost of producing one unit of that good. Producers would never knowingly sell a good that is worth more to them than the asking price. Imagine selling coffee for half of what it cost to produce—you won't be in business very long with that pricing strategy. The supply curve shows the minimum

EXHIBIT 4.21 Impact of an Increase in Supply on Consumer Surplus

© Cengage Learning 2014

EXHIBIT 4.22 A Firm's Producer Surplus

The firm's supply curve looks like a staircase. The marginal cost is under the stair and the producer surplus is above the red stair and below the market price for each unit.

© Cengage Learning 2014

amount that sellers must receive to be willing to supply any given quantity; that is, the supply curve reflects the marginal cost to sellers. The **marginal cost (MC)** is the cost of producing one more unit of a good. In other words, the supply curve is the marginal cost curve, just like the demand curve is the marginal benefit curve.

EXHIBIT 4.23 Market Producer Surplus

© Cengage Learning 2014

Because some units can be produced at a cost that is lower than the market price, the seller receives a surplus, or a net benefit, from producing those units. For example, in Exhibit 4.22, the market price is $4.50. Say the firm's marginal cost is $2 for the first unit, $3 for the second unit, $4 for the third unit, and $5 for the fourth unit. Because producer surplus for a particular unit is the difference between the market price and the seller's cost of producing that unit, producer surplus would be as follows: The first unit would yield $2.50; the second unit would yield $1.50; the third unit would yield $.50; and the fourth unit would add no more to producer surplus, because the market price equals the seller's cost.

> **marginal cost (MC)** the change in total costs resulting from a one-unit change in output

When there are a lot of producers, the supply curve is more or less smooth, like in Exhibit 4.23. Total producer surplus for the market is obtained by summing all the producer surpluses of all the sellers—the area above the market supply curve and below the market price up to the quantity actually produced—the shaded area in Exhibit 4.23. Producer surplus is a measurement of how much sellers gain from trading in the market.

Suppose an increase in market demand causes the market price to rise, say from P_1 to P_2; the seller now receives a higher price per unit, so additional producer surplus is generated. In Exhibit 4.24, we see the additions to producer surplus. Part of the added surplus (area P_2DBP_1) is due to a higher price for the quantity already being produced (up to Q_1) and part (area DCB)

EXHIBIT 4.24 Impact of an Increase in Demand on Producer Surplus

© Cengage Learning 2014

is due to the expansion of output made profitable by the higher price (from Q_1 to Q_2).

4-5e MARKET EFFICIENCY AND PRODUCER AND CONSUMER SURPLUS

With the tools of consumer and producer surplus, we can better analyze the total gains from exchange. The demand curve represents a collection of maximum prices that consumers are willing and able to pay for additional quantities of a good or service. It also shows the marginal benefits derived by consumers. The supply curve represents a collection of minimum prices that suppliers require to be willing and able to supply each additional unit of a good or service. It also shows the marginal cost of production. Both are shown in Exhibit 4.25. For example, for the first unit of output, the buyer is willing to pay up to $7, while the seller would have to receive at least $1 to produce that unit. However, the equilibrium price is $4, as indicated by the intersection of the supply and demand curves. It is clear that the two would gain from getting together and trading that unit, because the consumer would receive $3 of consumer

EXHIBIT 4.25 Consumer and Producer Surplus

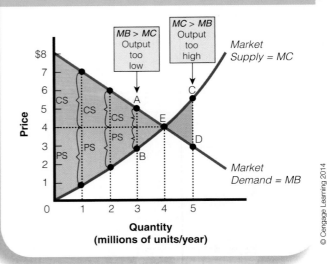

© Cengage Learning 2014

surplus ($7 – $4), and the producer would receive $3 of producer surplus ($4 – $1). Both would also benefit from trading the second and third units of output—in fact, both would benefit from trading every unit up to

In a competitive equilibrium, buyers value the last unit of output consumed by exactly the same amount that it cost to produce.

© iStockphoto.com/Orlando Rosu

the market equilibrium output. That is, the buyer purchases the good, except for the very last unit, for less than the maximum amount she would have been willing to pay; the seller receives for the good, except for the last unit, more than the minimum amount for which he would have been willing to supply the good. Once the equilibrium output is reached at the equilibrium price, all the mutually beneficial trade opportunities between the demander and supplier will have taken place, and the sum of consumer surplus and producer surplus is maximized. This is where the marginal benefit to buyers is equal to the marginal cost to producers. Both buyer and seller are better off from each of the units traded than they would have been if they had not exchanged them.

It is important to recognize that, in this case, the **total welfare gains** to the economy from trade in this good is the sum of the consumer and producer surpluses created. That is, consumers benefit from additional amounts of consumer surplus, and producers benefit from additional amounts of producer surplus. Improvements in welfare come from additions to both consumer and producer surpluses. In competitive markets with large numbers of buyers and sellers, at the market equilibrium price and quantity, the net gains to society are as large as possible.

Why would it be inefficient to produce only 3 million units? The demand curve in Exhibit 4.25 indicates that the buyer is willing to pay $5 for the 3 millionth unit. The supply curve shows that it only costs the seller $3 to produce that unit. That is, as long as the buyer values the extra output by more than it costs to produce that unit, total welfare would increase by expanding output. In fact, if output is expanded from 3 million units to 4 million units, total welfare (the sum of consumer and producer surpluses) will increase by area AEB in Exhibit 4.25.

What if 5 million units are produced? The demand curve shows that the buyer is only willing to pay $3 for the 5 millionth unit. However, the supply curve shows that it would cost about $5.50 to produce that 5 millionth unit. Thus, increasing output beyond equilibrium decreases total welfare, because the cost of producing this extra output is greater than the value the buyer places on it. If output is reduced from 5 million units to 4 million units, total welfare will increase by area ECD in Exhibit 4.25.

Not producing the efficient level of output, in this case 4 million units, leads to what economists call a **deadweight loss**. A deadweight loss is the reduction in both consumer and producer surpluses—it is the net loss of total surplus that results from the misallocation of resources.

In a competitive equilibrium, supply equals demand at the equilibrium. This means that the buyers value the last unit of output consumed by exactly the same amount that it cost to produce. If consumers valued the last unit by more than it cost to produce, welfare could be increased by expanding output. If consumers valued the last unit by less than it cost to produce, then welfare could be increased by producing less output.

In sum, *market efficiency* occurs when we have maximized the sum of consumer and producer surpluses, when the margin of benefits of the last unit consumed is equal to the marginal cost of productivity, $MB = MC$.

total welfare gains the sum of consumer and producer surpluses

deadweight loss net loss of total surplus that results from an action that alters a market equilibrium

4-5f EFFICIENCY AND TICKET SCALPING

The Super Bowl is a high-demand, limited-supply sports event. The face value on most Super Bowl tickets is in the $700 to $900 range. Many of the recipients of the tickets are corporate sponsors or are affiliated with the teams playing in the game. There are also some tickets that are allocated through a lottery. However, at the face value for the tickets at P_1, the quantity demanded far exceeds the quantity supplied as seen in Exhibit 4.26. In other words, the National Football League (NFL) has

EXHIBIT 4.26 The Market for Super Bowl Tickets

© Cengage Learning 2014

not priced their tickets equal to what the market will bear. Consequently, some fans are willing to pay much more, sometimes $6,000 to $7,000, for these tickets from scalpers, who buy the tickets at face value and try to sell them for a higher price. While ticket scalping is illegal in many states, scalpers will still descend on the host city to make a profit, even though the probability of arrest and conviction are substantial.

But is ticket scalping for athletic events and concerts really so objectionable? Could scalpers be transferring tickets into the hands of those who value them the most? The buyer must value attending the event more than the scalped price of the ticket or he would not buy the ticket. The seller would not sell her ticket unless she valued the money from the ticket more than attending the event. That is, scalpers may help markets achieve efficient outcomes by transferring tickets from those placing lower values on them to those placing higher values on them. Scalping is a voluntary activity that benefits both sellers and buyers.

The sponsors of the event are the losers, in the form of lost profits, for failing to charge the higher equilibrium market price. Why would the NFL not charge the higher price? Perhaps it sends a sign of goodwill to NFL fans, even if they have no appreciable chance of getting a ticket. That is, maybe the NFL is willing to take a hit on short-run profits to make sure they keep their base of fans (long-run profits).

SECTION CHECK 5 ANSWERS

1. The price elasticity of supply measures the relative change in the quantity supplied that results from a change in price. If the supply price elasticity is greater than 1, it is elastic; if it is less than 1, it is inelastic.

2. Supply tends to be more elastic in the long run than in the short run.

3. The relative elasticity of supply and demand determines the distribution of the tax burden for a good. If demand is more elastic than supply, producers bear the greater burden of the tax; if the supply is more elastic than the demand, consumers bear the greater burden.

© Win McNamee/Getty Images

Chapter 4: Self-Review

Now that you are finished reading the chapter, review the questions below. You can write your answers in the space provided, then go online to see the answers at www.cengagebrain.com.

4-1 PRICE ELASTICITY OF DEMAND

1. How is the price elasticity of demand calculated?

2. Why is the price elasticity of demand for products at a 24-hour convenience store likely to be lower at 2 A.M. than at 2 P.M.?

3. In each of the following cases, indicate which good you think has a relatively more price elastic demand and identify the most likely reason, in terms of the determinants of the elasticity of demand (more substitutes, greater share of the budget, or more time to adjust).
   a. cars or Chevrolets
   b. salt or housing
   c. going to a New York Mets game or a Cleveland Indians game
   d. natural gas this month or over the course of a year

4-2 TOTAL REVENUE AND THE PRICE ELASTICITY OF DEMAND

4. If taxi fares in a city rise, what will happen to the total revenue received by taxi operators? If the fares charged for subway rides, a substitute for taxi rides, do not change, what will happen to the total revenue earned by the subway as a result?

5. Why is a linear demand curve more price elastic at higher price ranges and more price inelastic at lower price ranges?

4-3 PRICE ELASTICITY OF SUPPLY

6. What does it mean to say the elasticity of supply for one good is greater than that for another?

7. True or False: Supply tends to be more elastic in the long run than in the short run.

4-4 SUPPLY, DEMAND, AND POLICIES OF GOVERNMENT

8. What predictable effects result from price ceilings such as rent control?

9. What predictable effects result from price floors such as the minimum wage?

10. True or False: The consumer bears more of the tax burden when demand is relatively more elastic than supply.

4-5 CONSUMER SURPLUS, PRODUCER SURPLUS, AND THE EFFICIENCY OF MARKETS

11. Why do the earlier units consumed at a given price add more consumer surplus than the later units consumed?

12. Why does a reduction in output below the efficient level create a deadweight loss?

13. Why is the efficient level of output in an industry defined as the output where the sum of consumer and producer surplus is maximized?

A4-1 Appendix— Using Supply and Demand in Health Care

The demand for health care has increased over the last several decades. The increase in demand for medical care has been particularly significant due to changes in income, insurance coverage, and population demographics. Consequently, the price of medical care has risen.

A4-1a INCOME

Rising U.S. real income has contributed to the increase in demand for medical services. Estimates of the income elasticity of health care vary but consistently indicate that most health care services are normal goods. (Evidence suggests that emergency care services, on the other hand, may be inferior because low-income uninsured individuals can often only gain access to physician services via the emergency room.)

Price Elasticity of Demand

Estimates of the price elasticity of demand for health care are as low as 0.2, indicating significant inelasticity of demand for medical services. That is, a 10 percent increase in price would reduce quantity demanded by only 2 percent. The quantity of medical care demanded appears to be quite insensitive to changes in price. For example, it is hard to imagine that anyone suffering a life-threatening injury would travel from emergency room to emergency room shopping for the lowest-priced care.

Health care is considered a necessity with few good substitutes, particularly when it comes to serious illness. Although vitamins and homeopathic therapies are available to treat minor ailments, few good alternatives to hospital- or physician-guided care are available to treat serious disease or injury. Additionally, many patients in the United States establish long-term relationships with primary care physicians and are reluctant to search for new physicians even if fees increase significantly. Physician services are, in this regard, "experience goods." Average consumers are "brand loyal," often preferring the physician they know and trust to an untried physician (even one with lower fees).

A4-1b INSURANCE AND THIRD-PARTY PAYERS

The health-services market differs from many others in that, because of insurance, the consumer often pays only a fraction of the direct cost of care. Third-party payers, such as insurance companies or health maintenance organizations, play significant roles in this industry. In fact, the structure of the health care payment system has important incentive effects and can alter the behavior of both patients and providers.

Approximately 85 percent of the U.S. population is covered by some kind of medical insurance policy. Most of that coverage (59.3 percent) is sponsored through employers. Despite the fact that the United States spends more on health care per capita than any other nation in the world, over 15 percent of the U.S. population remain uninsured. However, the health care system does provide a safety net whereby the cost of unreimbursed care is shifted to other health care payers. Many of the uninsured are able to receive some care, particularly from public hospitals and clinics.

As as result of third-party payments, both patients and physicians have a very limited incentive to keep health care costs down; patients only pay a small portion of the cost of the procedures. In addition, physicians order more tests and procedures because they are paid for each additional one. So no one has much incentive to keep costs down, but instead everyone has an incentive to allow them to rise. This is especially true when dealing with the terminally ill. In fact, almost one-third of Medicare expenditures are for patients in the last six months of their lives.

A4-1c DEMOGRAPHIC CHANGES

The aging of the U.S. population is an additional factor that explains the increase in demand for health care. More than 13 percent of the population is over 65. By 2035, that number is expected to reach 22 percent.

The elderly consume a disproportionate share of health care services (three to four times as much as the rest of the population). Illnesses that used to end life fairly quickly (infections, heart disease, and some cancers, for example) can now be treated effectively using expensive new procedures. Thus, the elderly are living longer, increasingly experiencing chronic disease (such as emphysema or Alzheimer's disease), and consuming larger total quantities of health care as a result. However, recent research shows that the aging U.S. population can only account for roughly 10 percent of the growth in health care spending.

A4-1d THE SUPPLY OF HEALTH CARE

The supply of health care has increased slowly since 1960 for several reasons: The number of providers has increased but has not kept up with the demand for medical services, the cost of medical education and training has increased, and the health industry began to use more high-cost technological equipment.

A4-1e DOCTORS AS GATEKEEPERS

Health care services may be provided through independent physicians, nonprofit hospitals, for-profit hospitals, health maintenance organizations, preferred provider organizations, nursing homes, hospices, home health providers, or other health care agents and agencies. Physicians are the primary suppliers of health care to ailing patients and are highly trained to perform diagnostic tests to identify and assess the seriousness of a patient's illness. Patients depend on their physicians' recommendations as to the appropriate courses of treatment, leading to a situation of asymmetric information: Doctors are better informed than their patients about health status and appropriate remedies. Primary care physicians act as gatekeepers, controlling access to prescription drugs, hospitals, surgeries, and other treatments. Acting in this capacity, physicians induce demand for additional medical services. If physicians are paid on a fee-for-service basis (as is common), incentives exist for doctors to err on the side of recommending too many services. The suppliers themselves help increase the demand for health care.

Traditional Insurance

Traditional health insurance in the United States provides **indemnity coverage** (security in the event of illness or injury) on a fee-for-service basis. Patients can freely choose physicians and treatment options in the event of illness. Individuals covered by fee-for-service plans typically pay an annual deductible and a small percentage of all health care costs incurred (called coinsurance) up to an annual limit.

Escalating health care costs over the past decade, however, led to a greater emphasis on cost containment. The result was a proliferation of organizations offering managed care, including health maintenance organizations and preferred provider organizations.

Health Maintenance Organizations

Health maintenance organizations (HMOs) combine two traditionally separated functions: the provision of comprehensive health care and its financing. HMOs seek to contain health care costs by exerting control over patients' treatment options. Patients are often limited to seeking treatment from plan doctors only, whose utilization of services is subject to review. Doctors are typically paid a salary and not reimbursed on a fee-for-service basis. Physicians are generally required to prescribe drugs from an approved list, or formulary, to encourage the substitution of cheaper alternatives for expensive branded products. In some instances, doctors are also provided with financial incentives to limit the utilization of plan services and thereby minimize costs.

Preferred Provider Organizations

A **preferred provider organization (PPO)** is a network of doctors who agree to provide services to a health plan's enrollees at discounted fees. Patients can choose from any of the doctors within the plan. Unlike those enrolled in an HMO, patients in a PPO can generally opt to see nonparticipating physicians, but they can do so only by incurring much higher out-of-pocket costs.

A4-1f EFFECTS OF HEALTH INSURANCE

The output level at the competitive equilibrium, Q_1, results in allocative efficiency—that is, there is no better use of the resources allocated to producing that level of health care output, as seen in Exhibit 4.27(a) on the next page. As we move down along the demand curve, the marginal benefit of an extra unit that customers receive falls. As we move up the supply curve, the marginal cost of producing an additional unit of health care rises. At equilibrium Q_1, $MB = MC$.

The availability of private and public health care insurance increases demand from D_1 to D_2 in Exhibit 4.27(b) on the next page. Roughly 80 percent of all health care is paid for by third parties. That is, at each possible price, consumers increase their demand for health care because insurance is picking up most of the bill. The increase in demand from D_1 to D_2 raises the price for health care to P_2, in Exhibit 4.27(b). However, with insurance, consumers do not pay price P_2; instead they only pay 20 percent of the new higher price, or P_3. Because this price is significantly less than the price without insurance, consumers increase their

indemnity coverage compensation toward the cost of medical services in the event of illness or injury

health maintenance organization (HMO) an organization that contracts with physicians, medical facilities, employers, and individuals to provide medical care to a group of individuals. Health care services are usually provided at a fixed price per patient. The cost of providing care is contained through the rationing of health care resources

preferred provider organization (PPO) is a network of doctors who agree to provide services to a health plan's enrollees at discounted fees

EXHIBIT 4.27 Supply and Demand for Health Care Services

a. No Health Insurance

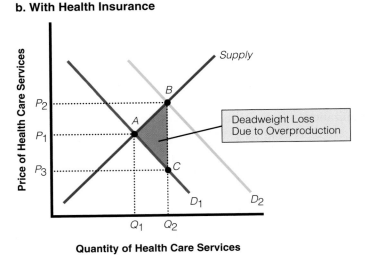

b. With Health Insurance

Deadweight Loss Due to Overproduction

© Cengage Learning 2014

consumption of health care to Q_2. At Q_2, the added consumption and production of health care is inefficient because the marginal cost of producing it (point B) is greater than the marginal benefit of consuming it (point C). This is measured using the before-insurance demand curve.

This leads to an efficiency versus equity dilemma. It is inefficient to produce more than Q_1 output because it leads to an overallocation of resources (deadweight loss). And the greater the availability of insurance, the greater the overallocation problem (deadweight loss); it would be even larger if health care was provided free under a national health program. The shaded area in Exhibit 4.27(b) represents the deadweight loss (the shaded triangle ABC). The fairness issue arises from the notion that all people should have access to basic health care. This is why the government created Medicare and Medicaid. It is also why federal money goes to subsidize private health insurance.

A4-1g TECHNOLOGICAL PROGRESS AND QUALITY OF CARE

Medical research and technological progress have vastly improved the quality of medical care. Innovative therapies help reduce disability, improve health, and prolong life. Some innovations undoubtedly reduce the overall cost of health care. For example, cholesterol-reducing

drugs can save thousands of dollars in surgical and hospitalization costs while reducing the likelihood of death from coronary heart disease. In addition, angioplasty and coronary bypass surgery has helped many patients with heart disease. Ulcers can now be treated with medication rather than surgery. Other innovations, however, significantly add to the cost of health care. For example, many cancer patients can now be saved through surgery, bone marrow transplants, radiation, and chemotherapy treatments. The availability of these treatment options (where previously little but comfort care would have been provided) adds many thousands of dollars per patient to the cost of treating disease.

Technological advances, through interaction with insurance, lead to a significant increase in the demand for medical care. Insured patients who bear a small fraction of health care costs naturally desire the best possible care, contributing to rising health care costs that far exceed the average level of inflation.

However, the news is not all good. While polio has been eradicated, other diseases like AIDS and breast cancer continue to take many lives despite the highest health care expenditures in the world. And diseases that had fallen off the radar, like tuberculosis, have reappeared. So while U.S. health care expenditures are the highest in the world, a number of countries have lower infant mortality rates and higher life expectancies.

A4-1h SHORTAGES

In Canada, where a national health care program controls prices and strictly rations care, conditions of excess demand for surgery prevail. In 2010, the total waiting time between referral from a general practitioner and delivery of elective treatment by a specialist, averaged across all 12 specialties and 10 provinces surveyed, had risen from 16.1 weeks in 2009 to 18.2 weeks in 2010. Consequently, some Canadians travel to the United States and pay for treatment themselves, rather than wait for insurance-covered care. Medical referral brokers help match frustrated Canadians with surgical providers in the United States (where fees can vary drastically). In addition, according to the *Canadian Medical Association Journal* (CMAJ), the extent of the doctor drain to the United States is a major concern. One in nine Canadian-trained doctors—including one in five specialists—is now practicing in the United States.

Likewise, shortages prevail in the market for organ transplants at zero price, as we can see in Exhibit 4.28. Ethical considerations leave policy makers reluctant to raise the price of organ transplantation or provide remuneration for organ donations. Trade in body parts is illegal, and few organs become available. Donated organs are rationed according to strict criteria.

A4-1i THE MARKET FOR HUMAN ORGANS

The demand curve for human organs is downward sloping, as seen in Exhibit 4.28. That is, the quantity demanded for human organs is lower at higher prices and higher at lower prices. Currently, the supply curve for human organs is perfectly inelastic (S' in Exhibit 4.28)—a fixed quantity of organs is available in the United States because all organs are required to be donated. Notice that in Exhibit 4.28, at a zero money price, P_0, for human organs, there will be a shortage—donors will supply Q_S organs per year but Q_D will be demanded, resulting in a shortage of $Q_S - Q_D$. That is, many people who want transplantable kidneys, livers, or hearts will not be able to obtain them because of lack of donors.

In 2005, roughly 28,000 organ transplants were made, but 100,000 people remained on the waiting lists. Shortages are so severe that thousands die each year waiting for needed organs. In 1998, 4,557 patients in the United States awaited lung transplants; 485 died. The same year, of the 17,983 U.S. patients waiting for a liver, 1,317 died. The average waiting period for an

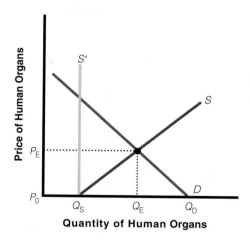

EXHIBIT 4.28 The Market for Human Organs

Under the current system, there is a transplantable organ shortage of $Q_S - Q_D$ at zero price. Under a market equilibrium, the price is P_E, and the quantity is Q_E. The demand for transplantable organs far exceeds the supply of organs available at the current price of transplantation services, zero. Because federal law prohibits the sale of organs, no upward pressure is exerted on the price of organs. The result is a persistent shortage of organs for transplant.

© Cengage Learning 2014

18- to 34-year-old needing a lung or a liver transplant in 1997 was 800 days or 273 days, respectively.

Advocates of allowing people to sell their own body parts argue that it would save roughly 6,000 lives a year. In addition, they argue that artificial legs, hips, joints, and hearts are sold, so why not live organs?

Suppose you signed a legal document stating that upon your death you would like to make your organs available for sale. Perhaps you could specify that the proceeds from the sale could go to a loved one, a charity, or a university. We would expect to see an upward-sloping supply curve for human organs—at higher prices, we would expect more people to allow their organs to be sold at death. In Exhibit 4.28, we present a hypothetical market where S is upward sloping, the market price rises to P_E and the quantity exchanged increases from Q_S to Q_E. In short, the price and quantity would rise, and the shortage would disappear. However, the sale of human organs has several problems. First, there may be an asymmetric information problem. When people receive money for their organs, they might hide "adverse" information about their health history. For example, a blood donor might not disclose a blood-borne infection such as hepatitis, AIDS, or some other virus. However, screening may resolve this problem. After all, there is a market for blood so the problem should not be insurmountable. However, it may be more difficult to detect disease-free kidneys, livers, and hearts. Second, there is the equity issue of allocating human organs on the basis of willingness to pay. Is it so wrong to sell kidneys if artificial limbs, hearts, and other body parts are already for sale legally? Third, it is also likely to increase health care spending as patients and insurance companies would have to pay a higher price. And increasing demand will only send that price even higher in the future.

Advocates of allowing the sale of human organs argue that the current system is just sending the market underground. Over $1 billion of body parts are purportedly exchanged in the global market. In November 2006, after years of denial, China acknowledged that most of the human organs used in China are taken from executed prisoners. According to rules adopted in 1984, a prisoner's organs can be taken if the relatives of the prisoner are unwilling to take the corpse or if the prisoner or his family agrees to the organ donation. Many of the recipients are foreigners (including those from the United States) who come to China, and pay a hefty sum to avoid the long wait in their home countries for organs.

A4-1j HEALTH CARE REFORM

In March of 2010, President Obama signed a law that provided health care reform. It is clear that the reforms will change coverage dramatically. But will it really reign in the underlying causes of health inflation? The United States has a large number of baby boomers who will be retiring soon. This will no doubt increase new health care spending.

Insurance companies will see a mixed bag. On the one hand, their costs will rise as they will be required to cover people with preexisting conditions and will no longer be allowed to place lifetime caps on coverage. On the other hand, insurance companies will benefit from the big expansion in the private insurance market as 32 million of the uninsured will be required to buy insurance.

One cost of the new program will undoubtedly be the large number of newly insured, who previously only used the emergency room and may now seek routine care. Of course, this could save money in the long run because, for example, taking statins (a cholesterol-lowering drug) is a lot less expensive than undergoing heart surgery. There will be both individual and employer mandates. Everyone in the United States must purchase health care coverage or pay a fine. Every firm with more than 50 employees must offer health care coverage or pay a fine. In addition, health insurance companies must cover everyone that applies, even if someone has a preexisting condition. With all the new, young, insured health care recipients, the moral hazard problem can only worsen. As the direct price for health care falls, the quantity demanded of health care services will rise. Since health care providers will be required to cover the costs, total expenditures on health care will rise.

So what about the young and healthy who are required to buy insurance? Unfortunately, they will not pay the low price that would reflect their risk. In the past, young people would pay roughly one-sixth of the premium it would cost an elderly customer. However, under the new federal laws, 60-year-old patients cannot be charged more than three times as much as 25-year-old patients. That is, young adults are going to be stuck with higher premiums. Health care reform is not going away anytime soon. As Princeton economist and Nobel laureate Paul Krugman states, "There is always a tunnel at the end of the tunnel." He thinks we will spend years, if not decades, dealing with this issue.

Drivers on congested "freeways" compete for limited space.

One way to internalize the externality is with a higher gasoline tax that would encourage people to drive less, carpool more, buy more fuel-efficient vehicles, and take public transportation. Some economists have estimated that in the United States the optimal corrective tax is at least 5 times higher than the current level.

Test your Economics *street-smart* knowledge and see how you compare against other students! Scan here or visit CourseMate for Survey of ECON2.

5

Market Failure and Public Choice

I n the previous chapter, we concluded that markets are efficient. But we made some assumptions about how markets work. If these assumptions do not hold, our conclusion about efficiency may be flawed. So, what are the assumptions?

First, in our model of supply and demand, we assumed that markets are perfectly competitive—many buyers and sellers exchanging similar goods in an environment where buyers and sellers can easily enter and exit the market. This is not always true. In some markets, few firms may have control over the market price. When firms can control the market price, we say that they have market power. This market power can cause inefficiency because it will lead to higher prices and lower quantities than the competitive solution.

Sometimes the market system fails to produce efficient outcomes because of side effects economists call *externalities*. With *positive externalities*, the private market supplies too little of the good in question (such as education). In the case of *negative externalities* (such as pollution), the market supplies too much.

Another possible source of market failure is that competitive markets provide less than the efficient quantity of public goods. A public good is a good or service that someone can consume simultaneously with everyone else even if he or she doesn't pay for it. For example, everyone enjoys the benefits of national defense and yet it would be difficult to exclude anyone from receiving these benefits. The problem is that if consumers know it is too difficult to exclude them, then they could avoid paying their share of the public good (take a free ride), and producers would find it unprofitable to provide the good. Therefore, the government provides important public goods such as national defense.

Many economists believe that asymmetric information can cause market failures. *Asymmetric information* is a situation in which some people know what other people don't know. This can lead to adverse selection, which occurs when an informed party benefits in an exchange by taking advantage of knowing more than the other party.

In the last section of this chapter, we will discuss public choice economics, the application of economic principles to politics.

5-1 Externalities

SECTION CHECK 1

Keep the following questions in mind as you read through this section.

1. What is a negative externality?
2. How are negative externalities internalized?
3. What is a positive externality?
4. How are positive externalities internalized?

Even if the economy is competitive, it is still possible that the market system fails to produce the efficient level of output because of side effects economists call **externalities**. With **positive externalities**, the private market supplies too little of the good in question, such as education. In the case of **negative externalities**, such as pollution, the market supplies too much. Both types of externalities are caused by economic agents—producers and consumers—receiving the wrong signals. That is, the free market works well in providing most goods but does less well without regulations, taxes, and subsidies in providing others.

5-1a NEGATIVE EXTERNALITIES IN PRODUCTION

The classic example of a negative externality in production is air pollution from a factory, such as a steel mill. If the firm uses clean air in production and returns dirty air to the atmosphere, it creates a negative externality. The polluted air "spills over" to outside parties. Now people in the neighboring communities may experience higher incidences of disease, dirtier houses, and other property damage. Such damages are real costs; but because no one owns the air, the firm does not have to pay for its use,

externality a benefit or cost from consumption or production that spills over onto those who are not consuming or producing the good

positive externality occurs when benefits spill over to an outside party who is not involved in producing or consuming the good

negative externality occurs when costs spill over to an outside party who is not involved in producing or consuming the good

unlike the other resources the firm uses in production. A steel mill pays for labor, capital, energy, and raw materials because it must compensate the owners of those inputs for their use. If a firm can avoid paying the costs it imposes on others—the external costs—it has lowered its own costs of production, but not the true costs to society.

Examples of negative externalities are numerous: the roommate who plays his stereo too loud at 2:00 A.M., the neighbor's dog that barks all night long or leaves "messages" on your front lawn, or the gardener who runs her leaf blower on full power at 7:00 A.M. on a Saturday. Driving our cars may be another area in which people don't bear the full costs of their choices. We pay the price to purchase cars, as well as to maintain, insure, and fuel them—those are the private costs. But do we pay for all of our external costs such as emissions, congestion, wear and tear on our highways, and the possible harm to those driving in cars smaller than ours?

Graphing Negative External Costs in Production

Let's take a look at the steel industry. In Exhibit 5.1, we see the market for steel. Notice that at each level of output, the first supply curve, $S_{PRIVATE}$, is lower than the second, S_{SOCIAL}. The reason is simple: $S_{PRIVATE}$ only includes the private costs to the firm—the capital, entrepreneurship, land, and labor for which it must pay. However, S_{SOCIAL} includes all of these costs plus the external costs that production imposes on others. If the firm could somehow be required to compensate society for the damage it causes, the cost of production for the firm would increase and would shift the supply curve to the left. That is, the true social cost of producing steel is represented by S_{SOCIAL} in Exhibit 5.1. The equilibrium at P_2 and Q_2 is efficient. The market equilibrium is not efficient because the true supply curve is above the demand curve at Q_1. At Q_1, the marginal benefits (point a) are less than the marginal cost (point b) and society would be better off if the firm produced less steel. The deadweight loss from overproduction is measured by the shaded area in Exhibit 5.1. From society's standpoint, Q_2 is the efficient level of output because it represents all the costs (private plus external costs) associated with the production of this good. If the suppliers of steel are not aware of or not responsible for the external costs, they will tend to produce too much. From society's standpoint, Q_1 and efficiency would be improved if less were produced.

5-1b WHAT CAN THE GOVERNMENT DO TO CORRECT FOR NEGATIVE EXTERNALITIES?

The government can intervene in market decisions in an attempt to take account of these negative externalities. It may do this by estimating the amount of those external costs and then taxing the manufacturer by that amount, forcing the manufacturer to internalize (bear) the costs.

Pollution Taxes

Pollution taxes are designed to internalize negative externalities. If government could impose a pollution tax equal to the exact size of the external cost, then the firm would produce the efficient level of output, Q_2.

That is, the tax would shift the supply curve for steel leftward to S_{SOCIAL} and would provide an incentive for the firm to produce at the socially optimum level of output. Additionally, tax revenues would be generated that could be used to compensate those who had suffered damage from the pollution or in some other productive way.

Regulation

Alternatively, the government could use regulation. The government might simply prohibit certain types of activities that cause pollution, or it might force firms to adopt a specific technology to reduce their emissions. However, regulators would have to know the best available technology for each and every industry. The purchase and use of new pollution-control devices would increase the cost of production and shift the supply curve to the left, from $S_{PRIVATE}$ to S_{SOCIAL}.

Which Is Better—Pollution Tax or Regulation?

Most economists agree that a pollution tax, or a corrective tax, is more efficient than regulation. The pollution tax is good because it gets rid of the externality and moves society closer to the efficient level of output. The tax also gives firms an incentive to find and apply new technology to further reduce pollution levels in their plant and consequently lower the tax they would have to pay. The higher the tax, the greater the reduction in pollution. In fact, if the tax is high enough, the plant may shut down. So the tax raises revenue and enhances economic efficiency. Under regulation, a firm has little

EXHIBIT 5.1 Negative Externalities in Production

Deadweight Loss Due to Overproduction

Efficient Equilibrium

S_{SOCIAL} (with external costs)

$S_{PRIVATE}$

Spillover Costs to Outside Parties

Market Equilibrium

P_2

P_1

b

a

$D_{PRIVATE}$

Price of Steel

0   Q_2 Q_1

Quantity of Steel

Many would consider that texting while driving creates a negative externality, as the dangers of multitasking behind the wheel are well documented. Of course, if you pull over to the side of the road and use your cell phone to report a crime or an accident, the use of the phone may provide a positive externality.

incentive to further reduce emissions once it reaches the predetermined level set by the regulated standard.

For example, a gas tax is a form of pollution tax: It helps reduce the externalities of pollution and congestion. The higher the tax, the fewer the vehicles on the road, the fewer miles driven, and the more fuel efficient vehicles purchased, each of which leads to less congestion and pollution. Therefore, the pollution tax, unlike other taxes, can enhance economic efficiency while generating revenue for the government.

5-1c POSITIVE EXTERNALITIES IN CONSUMPTION

Unlike negative externalities, positive externalities benefit others. For some goods, the individual consumer receives all the benefits. If you buy a hamburger, for example, you get all its benefits. On the other hand, consider education. This is a positive externality in consumption whose benefits extend beyond the individual consumer of education. Certainly, when you "buy" an education, you receive many of its benefits: greater future income, more choice of future occupations, and the consumption value of knowing more about life as a result of learning. However, these benefits, great as they may be, are not all the benefits associated with your education. You may be less likely to be unemployed or commit crimes; you may end up curing cancer or solving some other social problem. These nontrivial benefits are the positive external benefits of education.

The government frequently subsidizes education. Why? Presumably because the private market does not provide enough. It is argued that the education of a person benefits not only that person but all society, because a more informed citizenry can make more intelligent collective decisions, which benefits everyone.

Public health departments sometimes offer "free" inoculations against certain communicable diseases, such as influenza, because by protecting one group of citizens, everyone gets some protection; if one citizen is prevented from getting the disease, that person cannot pass it on to others. Many governmental efforts in the field of health and education are justified on the basis of positive externalities. Of course, because positive externalities are often difficult to measure, it is hard to demonstrate empirically whether many governmental education and health programs achieve their intended purposes.

In short, the presence of positive externalities interferes with reaching economic efficiency because of the tendency for the market to underallocate (produce too little) of this good.

Graphing Positive External Benefits of Consumption

Let's take the case of a new vaccine against the common cold. The market for the vaccine is shown in Exhibit 5.2. The demand curve, $D_{PRIVATE}$, represents the prices and quantities that buyers would be willing to pay in the private market to reduce their probability of catching the common cold. The supply curve shows the amounts that suppliers would offer for sale at different prices. However, at the equilibrium market output, Q_1, the output of vaccinations falls far short of the efficient level, Q_2. Why? Many people benefit from the vaccines, including those who do not have to pay for them; they are now less likely to be infected because others took the vaccine. If we could add the benefits derived by nonpaying consumers, the demand curve would shift to the right, from $D_{PRIVATE}$ to D_{SOCIAL}. The greater level of output, Q_2, that would result if D_{SOCIAL} were the observed demand reflects the efficient output level.

The market equilibrium at P_1 and Q_1 is not efficient because D_{SOCIAL} is above $D_{PRIVATE}$ for all levels of output between Q_1 and Q_2. That is, at Q_1 the marginal benefits (D_{SOCIAL}) at point b are greater than the marginal cost (S_{SOCIAL}) at point a. Consequently, a deadweight loss is associated with underproduction. In short, too little of the good is produced. Because producers are unable to collect payments from all those who benefit from the good or service, the market has a tendency to underproduce. In this case, the market is not producing enough

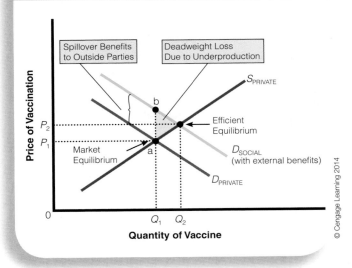

EXHIBIT 5.2 Positive Externalities in Consumption

vaccinations from society's standpoint and an *underallocation* of resources occurs.

Technology Spillover

Another potentially important positive externality is called a technology spillover. One firm's research and production can spill over to increase another firm's access to technological advances. For example, in technology industries like semiconductors, bioengineering, and software design, one firm's innovations are often imitated and improved on by other firms. The firm benefits from the new knowledge, but that knowledge also generates positive externalities that spill over to other firms. That is one reason why many technology firms are clustered together in California's Silicon Valley. That clustering allows workers to more easily share knowledge and collaborate in a rapidly changing industry. However, if other firms can easily imitate the developing firm's design, it can gain some of the developing firm's profits. This will cause firms to engage in less research and development, and therefore research and development will be underfunded in the market.

Should the government encourage firms with large spillovers by providing subsidies? The problem is that technology spillovers are difficult to measure. Patent protection is one way to deal with technology spillovers. Under the patent system, the firm that makes a technological breakthrough can capture most of the profits. The patent internalizes the externality and gives firms a greater incentive to invest in research and development.

5-1d WHAT CAN THE GOVERNMENT DO TO CORRECT FOR POSITIVE EXTERNALITIES?

How could society correct for this market failure? Two particular methods of achieving the higher preferred output are subsidies and regulation.

Subsidies

Government could provide a subsidy—either give refunds to individuals who receive an inoculation or provide an incentive for businesses to give their employees "free" inoculations at the office. If the subsidy was exactly equal to the external benefit of inoculation, the demand curve would shift from D_{PRIVATE} to D_{SOCIAL}, resulting in an efficient level of output, Q_2.

Regulation

The government could also pass a regulation requiring each person to get an inoculation. This approach would also shift the demand curve rightward toward the efficient level of output.

In summary, with positive externalities, the private market supplies too little of the good in question, such as education or inoculations for communicable diseases. In the case of negative externalities, the market supplies too much. In either case, buyers and sellers are receiving the wrong signals. The producers and consumers are not doing what they do because they are evil; rather, whether well-intentioned or ill-intentioned, they are behaving according to the incentives they face. The free market, then, works fine in providing most goods, but it functions less well without regulations, taxes, and subsidies in providing others.

Athletic superstars can have spillover benefits for the road team. For example, when David Beckham (British soccer star) joined the Los Angeles Galaxy in 2007, ticket sales soared. When the Galaxy played away, its opponents received the spillover benefits of his popularity through higher ticket sales.

5-1e NONGOVERNMENTAL SOLUTIONS TO EXTERNALITIES

Sometimes the externality problems can be handled by individuals without the intervention of government, and people may decide to take steps on their own to minimize negative externalities. Moral and social codes may prevent some people from littering, driving gas-guzzling cars, or using gas-powered mowers and log-burning fireplaces. The same self-regulation also applies to positive externalities. Philanthropists, for example, frequently donate money to public and private schools. In part, this must be because they view the positive externalities from education as a good buy for their charitable dollars.

5-1f WHY IS A CLEAN ENVIRONMENT NOT FREE?

In many respects, a clean environment is no different from any other desirable good. In a world of scarcity, we can increase our consumption of a clean environment only by giving up something else. The problem that we face is choosing the combination of goods that does the most to enhance human well-being. Few people would enjoy a perfectly clean environment if they were cold, hungry, and generally destitute. On the other hand, an individual choking to death in smog is hardly to be envied, no matter how great his or her material wealth.

Only by considering the additional cost as well as the additional benefit of increased consumption of all goods, including clean air and water, can decisions on the desirable combination of goods to consume be made properly.

> **public good** a good that is nonrival in consumption and nonexcludable
>
> **private good** a good that is rival in consumption and excludable

5-2 Public Goods

Now let us consider how public goods can cause market failure through resource misallocation.

5-2a PRIVATE GOODS VERSUS PUBLIC GOODS

Externalities are not the only culprit behind resource misallocation. A **public good** is another source of market failure. As used by economists, this term refers not to how these particular goods are purchased (i.e., by a government agency rather than some private economic agent) but to the properties that characterize them. In this section, we learn the difference between private goods, public goods, and common resources.

Private Goods

A **private good** such as a cheeseburger has two critical properties in this context: it is rival and excludable. First, a cheeseburger is rival in consumption because if one person eats a particular cheeseburger, nobody else can eat the same cheeseburger. Second, a cheeseburger is excludable. It is easy to keep someone from eating your cheeseburger by not giving it to him. Most goods in the economy, such as food, clothing, cars, and houses, are private goods that are rival and excludable.

Public Goods

The consumption of public goods, unlike private goods, is neither rival nor excludable. A public good is not rival because everyone can consume the good simultaneously; that is, one person's use of it does not diminish another's ability to use it. A public good is likewise *not excludable* because once the good is produced, it is prohibitively costly to exclude anyone from consuming the good. Consider national defense. Everyone enjoys the benefits of national defense (not rival) and it would be too costly to exclude anyone from those benefits (not excludable). That is, once the military has its defense in

Can skyscrapers be good for the environment? People who live in the city drive less, use more public transportation, and use less electricity and home heating because they tend to live in smaller living spaces compared to suburbanites. As a result, central city residents may emit less carbon into the atmosphere than suburbanites.

place, everyone is protected simultaneously (not rival) and it would be prohibitively costly to exclude anyone from consuming national defense (not excludable).

Another example of a public good is a flood control project. It would allow all the people who live in the flood plain area to enjoy the protection of the new program simultaneously (not rival). It would also be very difficult to exclude someone who lived in the middle of the project who said she did not want to pay (not excludable).

5-2b PUBLIC GOODS AND THE FREE-RIDER PROBLEM

The fact that a public good is not rival and not excludable makes the good difficult to produce privately. Some would know they could derive the benefits from the good without paying for it, because once it is produced, it is too difficult to exclude them. Some would try to take a *free ride*—derive benefits from something they did not pay for. Let's return to the example of national defense. Suppose the private protection of national defense is actually worth $100 to you. Assume that 100 million households in the United States are willing to make a $100 contribution for national defense. These contributions would add up to $10 billion. You might write a check for $100, or you might reason as

follows: "If I don't give $100 and everybody else does, I will be equally well protected plus derive the benefits of $100 in my pocket." Taking the latter course represents a rational attempt to be a **free rider**. The rub is that if everyone attempts to take a free ride, the ride will not exist.

The free-rider problem prevents the private market from supplying the efficient amounts of public goods. That is, no private firm would be willing to supply national defense because people can consume it without paying for it—the free-rider problem. Therefore, the government provides important public goods such as national defense.

5-2c THE GOVERNMENT AND BENEFIT-COST ANALYSIS

Everything the government provides has an opportunity cost. What is the best level of national defense? More national defense means less of something else that society may value more, such as health care or Social Security. To be efficient, additional goods from the public sector must also follow the rule of rational choice: pursue additional government activities if and only if the expected marginal benefits exceed the expected marginal costs. It all comes back to the adage "there are no free lunches."

In addition, there is the problem of assessing the value of these goods. Consider the case of a new highway. Before it builds the highway, the appropriate government agency will undertake a benefit-cost analysis of the situation. In this case, it must evaluate consumers' willingness to pay for the highway against the costs that will be incurred for construction and maintenance. However, those individuals who want the highway have an incentive to exaggerate their desire for it. At the same time, individuals who will be displaced or otherwise harmed by the highway have an incentive to exaggerate the harm that will be done to them. Together, these elements make it difficult for the government to accurately assess need. Ultimately, their evaluations are reduced to educated guesses about the net impact, weighing both positive and negative effects, of the highway on all parties concerned.

5-2d COMMON RESOURCES AND THE TRAGEDY OF THE COMMONS

In many cases, we do not have exclusive private property rights to things such as the air around us or the

Is busking, or street entertainment, a public good? The non-paying public benefits, so you have a free-rider problem. It is difficult to exclude someone from the pitch (where buskers play). However, if the street entertainers are really good, it is possible that local vendors will pay them because they might attract customers. Did you know busking has been around since the Roman Empire?

fish in the sea. They are common resources—goods that are owned by everyone and therefore not owned by anyone. When a good is not owned by anyone, individuals feel little incentive to conserve or use the resource efficiently.

A **common resource** is a rival good that is nonexcludable; that is, nonpayers cannot be easily excluded from consuming the good, and when one unit is consumed by one person, it means that it cannot be consumed by another. Fish in the vast ocean waters are a good example of a common resource. They are rival because fish are limited—a fish taken by one person is not available for others. They are nonexcludable because it is prohibitively costly to keep anyone from catching them—almost anyone with a boat and a fishing rod could catch one. Common resources can lead to tragedy—the tragedy of the commons. This is the case of private incentives failing to provide adequate maintenance of public resources.

Other examples of common resources to which individuals have relatively free access and that can be easily exploited are congested roads and the Internet.

"Free"way is a misnomer. No one owns the space on the freeway. Because there are no property rights to the freeway you cannot exclude others from driving on and sharing the freeway. When you occupy a part of the freeway you are keeping others from using that portion. So, all drivers compete for limited space causing a negative externality in the form of congestion.

common resource a rival good that is nonexcludable

The Internet poses a similar problem. If everyone attempts to access the same web site at the same time, overcrowding occurs and congestion can cause the site to slow down.

There are two possible solutions to the common property rights problem. First, the government, through taxes and fees, can attempt to internalize the externality. To prevent road congestion the government could charge drivers a toll—a corrective tax on congestion—or they could charge higher tolls on bridges during rush hour. A gasoline tax would be an inferior policy solution because although it would reduce driving, it would not necessarily reduce driving during peak periods. Similarly, the government can charge fees to reduce congestion in National Parks during peak periods. They can have restrictions through licensing on hunting and fishing to control animal populations.

Second, the government could assign private property rights to common resources. For example, private fish farms have become more profitable as overfishing depletes the stock of fish in open waters.

Poachers in Africa hunt elephants for their tusks. Where no one owns them, allowing owners to capture both the benefits and the costs from them, elephants roam free and are treated as a common resource. Poachers are numerous in those places and each poacher has an incentive to kill as many elephants as possible to get their tusks before someone else does. Kenya is one example, where the elephant population has fallen from 170,000 to 30,000 since 1975. On the other hand, the elephant population in Zimbabwe has increased from 20,000 to over 100,000 over the same period. Why? Zimbabwe allows safari hunting on private property, allowing effective ownership of the elephants on that property and providing the ability to protect its herds against poachers and the incentive to efficiently manage them.

SECTION CHECK 2 ANSWERS

1. A public good is both nonrival in consumption (one person's usage of it does not diminish another's ability to use it) and nonexclusive (no one can be excluded from using it).

2. A free rider is someone who attempts to enjoy the benefits of a good without paying for it. The free-rider problem prevents the private market from supplying the efficient amount of public goods.

3. A common resource good is rival in consumption but nonexcludable.

5-3 Asymmetric Information

SECTION CHECK 3

Keep the following questions in mind as you read through this section.

1. What is asymmetric information?
2. What is adverse selection?
3. What is moral hazard?

In this section, we will discuss the third potential cause of market failure—asymmetric information.

5-3a WHAT IS ASYMMETRIC INFORMATION?

When the available information is initially distributed in favor of one party relative to another, **asymmetric information** is said to exist. Suppose you bought a new car for $25,000 and about a month later you decide that you would be much happier with your old car and the money. So you call your salesperson and ask what your car is worth—perfect condition and less than 1,000 miles on the odometer. The salesperson tells you about $20,000. Why did your "new" car depreciate $5,000 in just one month? The problem is that a potential buyer is going to be skeptical. Why is that new car being sold? Is it a lemon?

Sellers are at an information advantage over potential buyers when selling a car because they have more information about the car than does the potential buyer. However, potential buyers know that sellers are more likely to sell a lemon. As a result, potential buyers will offer a lower price than they would if they could be certain of the quality. This is known as the lemon problem. Without incurring significant quality detection costs, such as having it inspected by a mechanic, the potential buyer is at an informational disadvantage relative to the seller. It is rational for the seller to claim that the car is in good shape and has no known defects, but the potential buyer cannot detect whether the car is a lemon or not without incurring costs. If the quality detection costs are sufficiently high, a solution is to price all used cars as if they are average quality. That is, used cars of the same year, make, and model generally will be offered at the same price, regardless of their known conditions. The seller of a lemon will then receive a payment that is more than the car is worth, and the seller of a relatively high-quality car will receive less than the car is worth. However, if a seller of a high-quality car does *not* receive what the car would sell for if the potential buyer knew its quality, the seller will rationally withdraw the offer to sell the car. Given the logical response of sellers of higher-than-average quality cars, the average quality of used cars on the market will fall, and consequently, many people will avoid buying in the used car market. In other words, the bad cars will drive the good cars out of the market. Thus, fewer used cars are bought and sold because fewer good cars are offered for sale. That is, information problems reduce economic efficiency. A situation where an informed party benefits in an exchange by taking advantage of knowing more than the other party is called **adverse selection**.

This distortion in the used car market resulting from adverse selection can be reduced by the buyer acquiring more information so that the buyer and seller have equal information. In the used car example, it might mean that an individual buyer would demand that an independent mechanic do a detailed inspection of the used car or that the dealership provide an extended warranty. A warranty provides a credible signal that this dealer is not selling lemons. In addition, new services such as carfax.com allow you to pay to find the history of a used car before you buy it. These services help in eliminating the adverse selection

asymmetric information occurs when the available information is initially distributed in favor of one party relative to another in an exchange

adverse selection a situation in which an informed party benefits in an exchange by taking advantage of knowing more than the other party

©iStockphoto.com/Brian Behunin

problem because buyers would have more information about the product they are buying.

The least-cost solution would have sellers reveal their superior information to potential buyers. The problem is that it is not individually rational for the seller to provide a truthful and complete disclosure, a point that is known by a potential buyer. Only if the seller is punished for not truthfully revealing exchange-relevant information will a potential buyer perceive the seller's disclosure as truthful.

Adverse selection also occurs in the insurance market. Imagine an auto insurance company that has a one-size-fits-all policy for their insurance premiums. Careful drivers would be charged the same premium as careless drivers. The company would assess the average risk of accidents for all drivers and then set the premium. Of course, this would be very appealing to careless drivers who are more likely to get in an accident, but not very appealing to careful drivers who have a much lower probability of getting in an accident. Under this pricing scheme, the bad drivers would drive the good drivers out of the market. Good drivers would be less likely to buy a policy, thinking that they are paying too much, since they are less likely to get in an accident than a careless driver. Many good drivers would exit the market, leaving a disproportionate share of bad drivers—exactly what the insurance companies do not want—people with a higher risk of getting in accidents. So what do they do?

Insurance companies set premiums according to the risk associated with particular groups of

drivers, so good drivers do not exit the market. One strategy they use for dealing with adverse selection is called *screening*, where they use observable information about people to reveal private information. For example, a 17-year-old male driving a sports car will be charged a much higher premium than a 40-year-old female driving a minivan, even if he is a careful driver. Or someone with a good driving record or good grades gets a discount on his insurance. Insurance companies have data on different types of drivers and the probability of those drivers being in accidents, and they use this data to set insurance premiums. They may be wrong on an individual case (the teenager may be accident-free for years), but they are likely to be correct on average.

Reputation and Standardization

Asymmetric information is also present in other markets, such as rare stamps, coins, paintings, and sports memorabilia, in which the dealer (seller) knows more about the product than does the potential buyer. Potential buyers want to be assured that these items are authentic, not counterfeits. Unless the seller can successfully provide evidence of the quality of the product, bad products will tend to drive good products out of the market, resulting in a market failure.

One method that sellers can use to convince potential buyers that their products are high quality is

You might normally prefer some other restaurant to a place like McDonald's, but when given the choice between that and someplace entirely unknown, you might be more inclined to choose the golden arches.

reputation. For example, if a supermarket has a reputation of selling fresh produce, you will be more likely to shop there. The same is true when you choose an electrician, plumber, or physician. In the used car market, the dealer might advertise how long he has been in business. This provides a signal that he has many satisfied customers. Therefore, he is likely to sell more used cars at a higher price. In short, if there is a reputation of high quality, it will minimize the market failure problem.

However, there may be cases in which it is difficult to develop a reputation. For example, take a restaurant or a motel on a desolate highway. These establishments may not receive repeat customers. Customers have little idea of the quality of food, the probability of bedbugs, and so on. In this case, *standardization* is important. A national restaurant or a motel chain provides standardization. While you may not frequent McDonald's when you are at home, when confronted with the choice between a little known restaurant and McDonald's, you may pick the McDonald's because of the standardized products backed by a large corporation.

Asymmetric Information and Job Market Signaling

Why does non–job-related schooling raise your income? Why would salaried workers work longer hours, putting in 60 to 70 hours a week? The reason is this behavior provides a useful signal to the employer about the person's intelligence and work ethic.

Signaling is important because it reduces information costs associated with asymmetric information; the seller of labor (potential employee) has more information about her work ethic and reliability than the buyer of labor (potential employer). Imagine how costly it would be to try out 150 potential employees for a job. In short, signals provide a measure that can help reduce asymmetric information and lower hiring costs.

There are strong signals and weak signals. Wearing a nice suit to work would be a weak signal because it does not necessarily distinguish a high-productivity worker from a low-productivity worker—a lazy worker can dress well, too. To provide a strong signal, it must be harder for a low-productivity worker to give the signal than it is for a high-productivity worker. Education is a strong signal in labor markets because it requires effort that many low-productivity workers may find too difficult to obtain. The education signal is also relatively easy to measure via years of education, grade-point average, highest degree attained, reputation of the university or college, rigor of courses attempted, and so on. Education can clearly improve a person's productivity;

even if it did not, however, it would be a useful signal because more productive people find it easier to obtain education than lazy people. Furthermore, productive people are more likely to attain more education in order to signal to their employer that they are productive. So it may not just be the knowledge obtained from a college education, it may be the effort that you are signaling—something you presumably already had before you entered college. So according to the signaling model, workers go to college not for the knowledge gained, but to send the important signal that they are highly productive.

Education sends an important signal, but it also provides knowledge, enhancing productivity. For example, many firms will not hire managers without an MBA because of the knowledge potential employees gained in courses such as finance and economics, but also because an MBA sends a powerful signal that the worker is disciplined and hard working.

Durable Goods, Signals, and Warranties

Why are people reluctant to buy durable goods such as televisions, refrigerators, and cameras without a warranty? Warranties are a signal. Honest and reliable firms find it less expensive to provide a warranty than do dishonest firms. The dilemma for consumers is that they are trying to distinguish the good brands from the bad brands. One way to do this is to see what kind of warranty the producer offers. Low-quality items would require more frequent and expensive servicing than high-quality items. Thus, producers of low-quality items will tend to not offer extensive warranties. In short, extensive warranties signal high quality, while items without extensive warranties signal poor quality. With this knowledge, consumers will pay more for high-quality products with good warranties.

5-3b WHAT IS MORAL HAZARD?

Another information problem is associated with the insurance market and is called moral hazard. If an individual is fully insured for fire, theft, auto, life, and so on, what incentives will this individual have to take additional precautions from risk? For example, a person with auto insurance may drive less cautiously than would a person without auto insurance.

Health insurance companies do, however, try to remedy the adverse selection problem by requiring regular checkups, offering discounts for nonsmokers, charging different deductibles and different rates for different age and occupational groups, and so on.

Additionally, those with health insurance may devote less effort and resources to staying healthy than those who are not covered. The problem, of course, is that if the insured are behaving more recklessly than they would if they were not insured, the result might be much higher insurance rates. The **moral hazard** arises from the fact that it is costly for the insurer to monitor the behaviors of the insured party. Suppose an individual knew that his car was protected with a "bumper to bumper" warranty. He might have less incentive to take care of the car, despite the manufacturer's contract specifying that the warranty was only valid under "normal wear and tear." It would be too costly for the manufacturer to detect if a product failure was the consequence of a manufacturing defect or abuse by the owner.

Adverse Selection versus Moral Hazard

Do not confuse adverse selection and moral hazard. Adverse selection is the phenomenon that occurs when one party in the exchange takes advantage of knowing more than the other party. Moral hazard involves the action taken *after* the exchange, such as if you were a nonsmoker who had just bought a life insurance policy and then started smoking heavily.

Winner's Curse

Suppose you and five other classmates were asked to bid on a jar of pennies. Nobody knows how many pennies are in the jar and you are not allowed to open the jar. The winner gets the jar of pennies. Let's say there are 500 pennies ($5) in the jar and you win by bidding $7. You are happy you won the bid until they count the pennies and you realize you just paid $7 for $5 worth of pennies. A common-value auction is where

© Jeffery Stone/Shutterstock

ADVERSE SELECTION

Q&A

Q: If individuals know a lot more about their health condition than an insurance company, do we have a case of adverse selection?

You can find the answer on the next page.

Who do you think knows more about this patient's health—the insurance company or the patient?

cork board: © iStockphoto.com/mattjeacock; Elder man; © Frank Siteman/Getty Images; Photo frame: © iStockphoto.com/U.P.images

ADVERSE SELECTION

Q&A

A: Yes. Even after a medical examination, individuals will know more about their health than the insurance company. That is, the buyers of health insurance have a better idea about their overall body conditions and nutritional habits than the seller, the insurance company. People with greater health problems tend to buy more health insurance than those who are healthy. This tendency drives up the price of health insurance to reflect the costs of sicker-than-average people, which drives people of average health out of the market. So the people who end up buying insurance will be the riskiest group.

the auctioned item has the same value than its worth for all buyers but the value is unknown prior to the bidding. We call this a **winner's curse** because in this case the "winner" is overly optimistic and bids more for an item than it is worth. Therefore, the winner could end up being worse off (cursed) than the loser.

The problem also occurs because value is subjective. In some cases, bidders have a difficult time establishing an item's value. Without complete information, participants with limited skill in establishing valuation may overpay for an item. Historically, we have seen this when speculative bubbles in the stock or real estate markets occur. Then, investors with little skill in valuation and incomplete information tend to push prices beyond their true value.

However, an actual overpayment will generally occur only if the winner fails to account for the winner's curse when bidding. So despite its dire-sounding name, the winner's curse does not necessarily have ill effects.

The severity of the winner's curse tends to increase with the number of bidders. This is because the more bidders there are, the more likely it is that some of them have overestimated the auctioned item's value. The more serious your error of overbidding, the more likely you are to win. However, if you win, you probably made a serious error. The best strategy may be to underbid. If the winner normally overestimates the true value by 20 percent, then you might offer 80 percent of what you think the item is worth. That way, if you happen to win by overbidding you won't "get taken to the cleaners." You might also choose not to participate in auctions likely to generate a winner's curse.

There is often confusion that the winner's curse applies to the winners of all auctions. However, it is worth repeating here that for auctions based on the private value someone places on a good (i.e., when the item is desired independent of its value in the market), the winner's curse does not arise.

> **winner's curse** a situation that arises in certain auctions in which the winner is worse off than the loser because of an overly optimistic value placed on the good

The winner's curse can also occur with underbidding, where people offer to do a job for less than other bidders. Imagine you need to hire a landscaper, so you get estimates from various landscapers. Who is likely to win? Probably the landscaper with the lowest estimate. However, he may not think he won if he underestimated the amount of work required in your yard.

SECTION CHECK 3 ANSWERS

1. Asymmetric information occurs when the available information is initially distributed in favor of one party relative to another in an exchange.

2. Adverse selection is a situation in which an informed party benefits in an exchange by taking advantage of knowing more about the good than the other party does.

3. Moral hazard occurs when one party to a contract passes on the cost of its behavior to the other party.

5-4 Public Choice

SECTION CHECK 4

Keep the following questions in mind as you read through this section.

1. What is public choice theory?
2. What is rational ignorance?
3. Why do special-interest groups arise?

When the market fails, as in the case of an externality or public good, it may be necessary for the government to intervene and make public choices. However, it is possible for government actions in response to externalities to make matters worse. That is, just because markets have failed to generate efficient results does not necessarily mean that government can do a better job—see Exhibit 5.3 below. One explanation for this outcome is presented by public choice theory.

5-4a WHAT IS PUBLIC CHOICE THEORY?

Public choice theory is the application of economic principles to politics. Public choice economists believe that government actions are an outgrowth of individual behavior. Specifically, they assume that the behavior of individuals in politics, as in the marketplace, will be influenced by self-interest. Bureaucrats, politicians, and voters make choices that they believe will yield them expected marginal benefits that will be greater than their expected marginal costs. Of course, the private sector and the public sector differ when it comes to the "rules of the game" that they must follow. The self-interest assumption is, however, central to the analysis of behavior in both arenas.

5-4b SCARCITY AND THE PUBLIC SECTOR

The self-interest assumption is not the only similarity between the market and public sectors. For example, scarcity is present in the public sector as well as in the private sector. Public schools and public libraries come at the expense of something else. Competition is also present in the public sector, as different government agencies compete for government funds and lobbyists compete with each other to get favored legislation through Congress.

5-4c THE INDIVIDUAL CONSUMPTION-PAYMENT LINK

In private markets, when a shopper goes to the supermarket to purchase groceries, the shopping cart is filled with many different goods that the consumer presumably wants and is willing to pay for; the shopping cart reflects the individual consumption-payment link. The link breaks down when an assortment of political goods is decided on by majority rule. These political goods might include such items as additional national defense, additional money for the space program, new museums, new public schools, increased foreign aid, and so on. Even though an individual may be willing to pay for some of these goods, it is unlikely that she will want to consume or pay for everything placed in the political shopping cart. However, if the majority decides that these political goods are important, the individual will have to purchase the goods through higher taxes, whether she values the goods or not.

EXHIBIT 5.3 Do People in Government Waste Tax Money? 1970–2008 (percent of population agreeing)

	'70	'72	'74	'76	'78	'80	'82	'84	'86	'88	'90	'92	'94	'96	'98	'00	'02	'04	'08
A Lot	69	66	74	74	77	78	66	65	**	63	67	67	70	59	61	59	48	61	72
Some	26	30	22	20	19	18	29	29	**	33	30	30	27	39	34	38	49	37	26
Not Very Much	4	2	1	3	2	2	2	4	**	2	2	2	2	1	4	3	3	2	1
Don't Know	1	2	2	3	2	2	3	2	**	2	1	1	1	0	1	1	0	1	1

**No data available for 1986 and 2006.

SOURCE: The American National Election Studies (www.electionstudies.org). THE ANES GUIDE TO PUBLIC OPINION AND ELECTORAL BEHAVIOR. Ann Arbor, MI: University of Michigan, Center for Political Studies [producer and distributor]. Table 5A.3. Available at http://www.electionstudies.org/nesguide/gd-index.htm#4, (accessed April, 16, 2010).

5-4d MAJORITY RULE AND THE MEDIAN VOTERS

In a two-party system, the candidate with the most votes wins the election. Because voters are likely to vote for the candidate who holds views similar to their own, candidates must pay close attention to the preferences of the majority of voters.

For example, in Exhibit 5.4 on the next page, we assume a normal distribution, with a continuum of voter preferences from the liberal left to the conservative right. We can see from the figure that only a few are extremely liberal or extremely conservative.

When you go shopping, you put the goods that you are willing to pay for in your cart. But what about political goods that people vote for like schools and foreign aid? How much are you willing to pay for these goods?

A successful campaign would have to address the concerns of the median voters (those in the middle of the distribution in Exhibit 5.4), resulting in moderate policies. For example, if one candidate ran a fairly conservative campaign, attracting voters at and to the right of V_1, an opponent could win by a landslide by taking a fairly conservative position just to the left of this candidate. Alternatively, if the candidate takes a liberal position, say V_2, then the opponent can win by campaigning just to the right of that position. In this case, it is easy to see that the candidate who takes the median position, V_M, is least likely to be defeated. Of course, the distribution does not have to be normal or symmetrical; it could be skewed to the right or left. Regardless of the distribution, however, the successful candidate will still seek out the median voters. In fact, the **median voter model** predicts a strong tendency for both candidates to choose a position in the middle of the distribution, and therefore the election will be close.

Of course, this model does not mean that all politicians will find or even attempt to find the median. For example, politicians may take different positions because they have arrived at different predictions of voter preferences or have merely misread public sentiment; or they may think they have the charisma to change voter preferences.

> **median voter model** a model that predicts candidates will choose a position in the middle of the distribution

5-4e VOTERS AND RATIONAL IGNORANCE

Representative democracy provides a successful mechanism for making social choices in many countries. But some important differences are evident in the way democracy is ideally supposed to work and how it actually works.

One of the keys to an efficiently working democracy is a concerned and informed electorate. Everyone is supposed to take time to study the issues and candidates and then carefully weigh the relevant information before deciding how to vote. Although an informed citizenry is desirable from a social point of view, it is not

EXHIBIT 5.4 The Median Voter

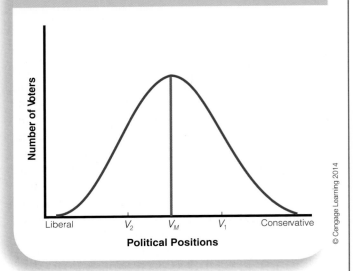

Number of Voters (vertical axis)

Liberal V_2 V_M V_1 Conservative

Political Positions

clear that individuals will find it personally desirable to become politically informed.

Obtaining detailed information about issues and candidates is costly. Many issues are complicated, and a great deal of technical knowledge and information is necessary to make an informed judgment on them. To find out what candidates are really going to do requires a lot more than listening to their campaign slogans. It requires studying their past voting records, reading a great deal that has been written either by or about them, and asking them questions at public meetings. Taking the time and trouble to do these things—and more—is the cost that each eligible voter has to pay personally for the benefits of being politically informed. These costs may help to explain why the majority of Americans cannot identify their congressional representatives and are unlikely to be acquainted with their representatives' views on Social Security, health care, tariffs, and agricultural policies.

For many people the costs of becoming politically informed are high, whereas the benefits are low. As a result, they limit their quest for political information to listening to the radio on the way to work, talking with friends, casual reading, and other things they would do anyway. Even though most people in society might be better off if everyone became more informed, it is not worth the cost for most individuals to make the requisite effort to become informed themselves.

Public choice economists refer to this lack of incentive to become informed as **rational ignorance**. People

rational ignorance lack of incentive to be informed

will generally make much more informed decisions as buyers than as voters. For example, you are likely to gather more information when making a decision on a car purchase than when you are deciding between candidates in an upcoming election. An uninformed decision on a car purchase will most likely affect your life much more than an uninformed decision on a candidate, especially when your vote will most likely not alter the outcome of the election.

The fact that one vote, especially in a state or national election, is highly unlikely to affect the outcome of the election may explain why some citizens choose not to vote. Many factors may determine the net benefits for voting, including candidates and issues on the ballot, weather, and distance to the polling booths. For example, we would certainly expect fewer voters to turn out at the polls on the day of a blizzard; the blizzard would change the net benefits. We would also expect more voters at the polls if the election were predicted to be a close one, with emotions running higher and voter perception that their individual vote is more significant.

If the cost of being an informed voter is high and the benefits low, why do people vote? Many people vote for reasons other than to affect the outcome of the election. They vote because they believe in the democratic process and because of civic pride. In other words, they perceive that the benefits they derive from being involved in the political process outweigh the costs.

Furthermore, rational ignorance does not imply that people should not vote; it is merely one explanation for why some people do not vote. The point that public choice economists are making is that some people will

Can we predict what would happen to voter turnout on a day like this? Some potential voters might rationally decide to stay home if they perceive the cost of going to the polls outweighed the benefit.

vote only if they think that their vote will make a difference; otherwise, they will not vote.

5-4f SPECIAL-INTEREST GROUPS

Even though many voters may be uninformed about specific issues, others may feel a strong need to be politically informed. Such individuals may be motivated to organize a **special-interest group**. These groups may have intense feelings about and a degree of interest in particular issues that is at variance with the general public. However, as a group these individuals are more likely to influence decision makers and have a far greater impact on the outcome of a political decision than they would with their individual votes.

If a special-interest group is successful in getting everyone else to pay for a project that benefits them, the cost will be spread over so large a number of taxpayers that the amount any one person will have to pay is negligible. Hence, the motivation for an individual citizen to spend the necessary time and effort to resist an interest group is minimal, even if she had a guarantee that this resistance would be effective.

Public choice economists believe that if government becomes a vehicle for promoting special interests, it fails in its primary responsibility of expanding opportunities for all. That is, instead of creating opportunities to benefit all through productive cooperation, government will have created the illusion that people can benefit at each others' expense. Public choice economists are not callously indifferent to the social benefits that government can provide. In fact, the difference between public choice economists and those who see every social ill as justification for expanding government is not a difference in moral vision. Instead, it is a difference in their interpretation of how government works. Public choice economists lean toward less government not because they want less from government, but because they, like many others, want less waste from government.

Politicians and Logrolling

Sometimes members of Congress engage in **logrolling.** Logrolling involves politicians trading votes for their legislation. For example, Representative A may tell Representative B that he will vote for her water bill if she votes for his new highway bill. Of course, if Representative B does not go along with Representative A's legislation, she runs the risk of not getting support for her legislation at a later date. Local projects such as federally funded dams, bridges, highways, housing projects, VA hospitals, job-training centers, and military bases are often pushed through Congress and state legislatures by logrolling.

The trading of votes could lead to an outcome where the majority of Congress supports the economic interests of the few at the economic expense of the many. This is especially true if the cost to the many is so low that they are rationally ignorant to the effects of rent-seeking behavior. Rent seeking occurs when individuals and firms use resources, like money and lobbyists, to influence government to grant them special privileges.

special-interest groups groups with an intense interest in particular voting issues that may be different from that of the general public

Why Is it Difficult to Reduce the Size of Government Programs?

It is very difficult politically to reduce government spending, even if the majority of voters favor such a reduction. When people argue for cutting government spending, they invariably have in mind government programs other than the ones they benefit from. So any attempt to reduce government spending by reducing one program at a time generally meets strong resistance from those benefitting from the program under review and receives little support from the millions of taxpayers who will save only a few dollars each if the program is eliminated.

The best hope for controlling spending is presenting a political package that calls for a simultaneous reduction in many programs. If government has grown to a point that people feel they are not getting their money's worth from their taxes, many groups may be willing to see their programs reduced if it means some savings on taxes paid to support everyone else's programs.

SECTION CHECK 4 ANSWERS

1. Public choice theory holds that the behavior of individuals in politics, as in the marketplace, is influenced by self-interest.

2. Rational ignorance is the condition in which voters tend to be relatively uninformed about political issues because of the high information costs and low benefits of being politically informed.

3. A special-interest group is a political pressure group formed by individuals with a common political objective.

Chapter 5: Self-Review

Now that you are finished reading the chapter, review the questions below. You can write your answers in the space provided, then go online to see the answers at www.cengagebrain.com.

5-1 EXTERNALITIES

1. Why are externalities also called spillover effects?

2. Indicate which of the following activities create a positive externality, a negative externality, or no externality at all:
   a. During a live theater performance, an audience member's cell phone loudly rings.
   b. You are given a flu shot.
   c. You purchase and drink a soda during a break from class.
   d. A college fraternity and sorority clean up trash along a two-mile stretch of the highway.
   e. A firm dumps chemical waste into a local water reservoir.
   f. The person down the hall in your dorm plays loud music while you are trying to sleep.

5-2 PUBLIC GOODS

3. Is a lighthouse a public good if it benefits many ship owners? What if it primarily benefits ships going to a port nearby?

4. In what way can government provision of public goods solve the free-rider problem?

5. True or False: Public goods are rival in consumption and nonexclusive.

6. For each of the following goods, indicate whether they are nonrival and/or nonexclusive. Indicate whether they are private or public goods.
   a. hot dogs
   b. cable TV
   c. broadcast TV
   d. automobiles
   e. national defense
   f. pollution control
   g. parking in a parking structure
   h. a sunset
   i. admission to a theme park

5-3 ASYMMETRIC INFORMATION

7. Why might withdrawals in several classes send a poor signal to potential employers?

8. Why is the winner's curse less likely for repeat-purchase items?

9. How would the adverse selection problem arise in the insurance market? How is it like the "lemon" used-car problem?

5-4 PUBLIC CHOICE

10. What principles does the public choice analysis of government behavior share with the economic analysis of market behavior?

11. Why is the tendency strong for candidates to choose positions in the middle of the distribution of voter preferences?

12. Why do you think news reporters are more informed than average citizens about public policy issues?

13. Fill-in-the-Blank: The _____ predicts that a candidate will choose a position in the middle of the distribution.

4LTR Press solutions are designed for today's learners through the continuous feedback of students like you. Tell us what you think about Survey of ECON and help us improve the learning experience for future students.

YOUR FEEDBACK MATTERS.

Complete the Speak Up survey in CourseMate at www.cengagebrain.com

 Follow us at www.facebook.com/4ltrpress

What questions

do you think Toyota had to ask when it decided to build this auto plant? Maybe how long it would take to get it up and running. What about the other possible uses of the building funds? Perhaps those could have been diverted to researching new engine technology. What if the economy slows down and Toyota finds it does not need the extra capacity anymore? Should it shut the plant down? What about all the money it already invested in the plant?

Test your Economics *street-smart* knowledge and see how you compare against other students! Scan here or visit CourseMate for Survey of ECON2.

6

Production and Costs

osts exist because resources are scarce and have competing uses—to produce more of one good means foregoing the production of another good. The cost of producing a good is measured by the worth of the most valuable alternative that was given up to obtain the resource, which is called the *opportunity cost*.

In Chapter 2, the production possibilities curve highlighted this trade-off. Recall that the opportunity cost of producing additional shelter was the food that had to be sacrificed. Other examples of opportunity costs abound: Paper used in this book could have been used in newspapers or magazines; steel used in the construction of a new building could have been used in the production of an automobile or a washing machine.

In this chapter, we examine the firm's costs in more detail—what really lies behind the firm's supply curve? A firm's costs are a key determinant in pricing and production decisions. As we will discover, the discussions in this chapter will prove to be very important building blocks for the theory of the firm.

6-1 Firms and Profits: Total Revenues Minus Total Costs

SECTION CHECK 1

Keep the following questions in mind as you read through this section.

1. What are explicit and implicit costs?
2. What are accounting profits?
3. What are economic profits?
4. What are sunk costs?

What exactly makes up a firm's cost of production? Let us begin by looking at the two distinct components of a firm's total cost: explicit costs and implicit costs.

6-1a EXPLICIT COSTS

Explicit costs are the input costs that require monetary payment—the out-of-pocket expenses that pay for labor services, raw materials, fuel, transportation, utilities, advertising, and so on. It is important to note that the explicit costs are opportunity costs to the firm. For example, money spent on electricity cannot be used for advertising. Remember that in a world of scarcity we are always giving up something to get something else. Trade-offs are pervasive. The costs discussed so far are relatively easy to measure, and an economist and an accountant would most likely arrive at the same figures. However, that will not always be the case.

If a company owns its own building in a growing urban area, can it protect itself from rising rents? Yes, but the company cannot avoid implicit costs. If the company owns the building and rents increase the opportunity cost of occupying his or her own building rise. By occupying its own building, the company is giving up the new, higher rents it could have received from renters if it had leased out the space.

6-1b IMPLICIT COSTS

Some of the firm's (opportunity) costs of production are implicit. **Implicit costs** do not require an outlay of money. Here is where the economist's and accountant's measures of costs diverge, because accountants do not include implicit costs. For example, what if you start your own yogurt shop? You give up the opportunity to make a salary working for someone else. And the money invested in your new business could have been invested elsewhere to earn interest. And what do you give up if you own the building where you have your new yogurt shop? The opportunity to rent it to someone else. These opportunity costs are less visible than explicit costs but are still part of the costs of doing business.

6-1c PROFITS

Economists generally assume that the ultimate goal of every firm is to maximize its **profits**. In other words, firms try to maximize the difference between what they give up for their inputs—their total costs (explicit and implicit)—and the amount they receive for their goods and services—their total revenues. Like revenues and costs, profits refer to flows over time. When we say that a firm earned $5 million in profit, we must specify the period in which the profit was earned—a week, month, year, and so on.

6-1d ARE ACCOUNTING PROFITS THE SAME AS ECONOMIC PROFITS?

A firm can make profits in the sense that the total revenues it receives exceed the explicit costs it incurs in the process of doing business. We call these profits **accounting profits**. Profits as accountants record them are based on total revenues and explicit costs and do not include implicit costs. An accountant's job is to keep track of money flows, which is why they measure explicit costs and usually ignore implicit costs.

Economists prefer an alternative way of measuring profits; they are interested in total revenues minus total costs (both explicit and implicit). Economists include the implicit costs as well as the explicit costs when calculating the total costs of the firm.

Summing up, measured in terms of accounting profits such as those reported in real-world financial statements, a firm has a profit if its total revenues exceed its explicit costs. In terms of **economic profits**,

explicit costs the opportunity costs of production that require monetary payment

implicit costs the opportunity costs of production that do not require monetary payment

profits the difference between total revenues and total costs

accounting profits total revenues minus total explicit costs

economic profits total revenues minus explicit and implicit costs a firm has profits if its total revenues exceed its total opportunity costs—both its explicit costs and implicit costs. Exhibit 6.1 on the next page illustrates the difference between accounting profits and economic profits.

6-1e A ZERO ECONOMIC PROFIT IS A NORMAL PROFIT

As we just discussed, an economic profit is less than an accounting profit because an economic profit includes implicit as well as explicit costs. In fact, an economist considers a zero economic profit a normal profit. A zero economic profit means that the firm is covering both explicit and implicit costs—the total opportunity costs of its resources. In other words, the firm's total revenues are sufficient to compensate for the time and money that owners put in the business. This is not as bad as it sounds. For example, suppose you become a farmer and make $80,000 a year. Initially you have to invest a $1 million to pay for the property, seed, and equipment. However, if you had put that money in the bank at say, a 3 percent interest rate, you would have made $30,000 a year; so you have an implicit cost of $30,000 per year in lost interest. In addition, you have an implicit cost of $50,000 a year because you did not take the job you were offered at the tractor dealership. So an accountant would have you making an economic profit of $80,000 but an economist would say you made zero economic profit, because your total revenue minus total costs

ACCOUNTING PROFITS AND ECONOMIC PROFITS

Q&A

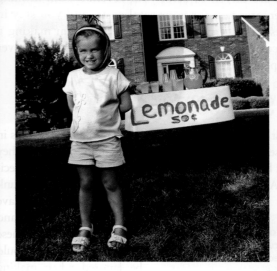

Q: Emily set up a lemonade stand in front of her house. One Saturday, she sold 50 cups of lemonade at 50 cents apiece to her friends, who were hot and thirsty from playing. These sales generated $25 in total revenues for Emily. Emily was pleased because she knew her total costs—for lemonade, mix, cups, and so on—were only $5. As she was closing up shop for the day, her neighbor, an accountant, stopped by to say hello. Emily told him about her successful day. He said, "What a great job! You made a $20 profit!" Excited, Emily rushed into the house to tell her mother, an economist, the great news. Will Emily's mother agree with the accountant's calculation of Emily's profits? If not, why?

A: No, Emily's mother will not agree with the accountant, because he forgot to include the implicit costs when calculating Emily's profits. That is, he neglected to take into account what Emily could have been doing with her time if she had not been selling lemonade. For example, she could have been playing with her friends, cleaning her room, or perhaps helping her friends make money at their garage sale. These lost opportunities are implicit costs that should be included in the calculation of Emily's economic profits.

result, the average fixed cost declines continuously.

It is often easier to understand these cost concepts by examining graphs that show the levels of the various costs at different output levels. The graph in Exhibit 6.6 shows the first three cost concepts: fixed, variable, and total costs. The total fixed cost (TFC) curve is always a horizontal line because, by definition, fixed costs are the same at all output levels—even at zero level of output. In Exhibit 6.6, notice that $TVC = 0$ when $Q = 0$; if no output is being produced, no variable costs are incurred.

The total cost (TC) curve is the summation of the total variable cost (TVC) and total fixed cost (TFC) curves. Because the total fixed cost curve is horizontal, the total cost curve lies above the total variable cost curve by a fixed (vertical) amount.

Exhibit 6.7 shows the average fixed cost curve, the average variable cost curve, the average total cost curve, and the associated marginal cost curve. In this exhibit, notice how the average fixed cost (AFC) curve constantly declines, approaching but never reaching zero. Remember, AFC is simply TFC/Q, so as output expands, AFC declines, because the total fixed cost is being spread over successively larger volumes of output. Also observe how the marginal cost (MC)

curve crosses the average variable cost (AVC) and average total cost (ATC) curves at their lowest points. At higher output levels, high marginal costs pull up the average variable cost and average total cost curves, while at low output levels, low marginal costs pull the curves down. In the next section, we will explain why the marginal cost curve intersects the average variable cost curve and the average total cost curve at their minimum points.

EXHIBIT 6.7 Average and Marginal Costs

A↔E = Average total cost
B↔E = Marginal cost
C↔E = Average variable cost
D↔E = Average fixed cost

© Cengage Learning 2014

EXHIBIT 6.6 Total and Fixed Costs

© Cengage Learning 2014

SECTION CHECK 3 ANSWERS

1. Fixed costs are costs that do not change with the level of output.

2. Variable costs are not fixed. Variable costs change as the level of output changes.

3. Marginal cost (MC) is the added cost of producing one more unit of output; it is the change in total cost associated with one more unit of output. Marginal cost is the cost relevant to decisions to produce more or less.

4. Average fixed cost (AFC) is fixed cost divided by output. Average variable cost (AVC) is variable cost divided by output. Average total cost (ATC) is total cost divided by output.

6-4 The Shape of the Short-Run Cost Curves

SECTION CHECK 4

Consider the following questions as you read through this section.

1. What is the relationship between marginal costs and marginal product?

2. Why is the average total cost curve U-shaped?

3. When marginal cost is greater than average cost, what happens to the average?

As we continue our discussion of costs in the short run, let us take a closer look at the various short-run cost curves.

6-4a THE RELATIONSHIP BETWEEN MARGINAL COSTS AND MARGINAL PRODUCT

The behavior of marginal costs bears a definite relationship to marginal product (MP). Say, for example, that the variable input is labor. Initially, as the firm adds more workers, the marginal product of labor tends to rise. When the marginal product of labor is rising, marginal costs are falling, because each additional worker adds more to the total output than the previous worker. Thus, the increase in total cost resulting from the production of another unit of output—marginal cost—falls. However, when marginal product of labor is declining, marginal costs are rising, because additional workers are adding less to total output. In sum, if an additional worker's marginal product is lower (higher) than that of previous workers, marginal costs increase (decrease), as seen in Exhibit 6.8. In area a of the two graphs in Exhibit 6.8, we see that as marginal product rises, marginal costs fall; in area b, we see that as marginal product falls, marginal costs rise. For example, if we are only producing a few bagels in our bagel shop, we have some idle resources such as toasters, cash registers, and so on. At this point, the marginal product of an extra worker is large and the marginal cost of producing one more bagel is small. However, when the bagel shop is crowded, producing many bagels with many workers using the equipment to capacity, the marginal product of hiring another worker is low. Why? Because the

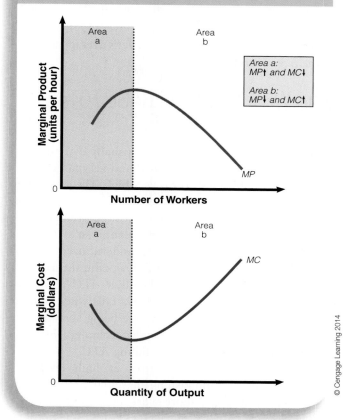

EXHIBIT 6.8 Marginal Product and Marginal Costs

Area a:
MP↑ and MC↓

Area b:
MP↓ and MC↑

© Cengage Learning 2014

new worker has to work in crowded conditions where she may be bumping into other workers as she waits to use the toasters and cash register. In short, when the number of bagels produced is high, the marginal product of another worker is low and the marginal cost of an additional bagel is large.

6-4b THE RELATIONSHIP BETWEEN MARGINAL AND AVERAGE AMOUNTS

The relationship between the marginal and the average is simply a matter of arithmetic; when a number (the marginal cost) being added into a series is smaller than the previous average of the series, the new average will be lower than the previous one. Likewise, when the marginal number is larger than the average, the average will rise. For example, if you have taken two economics exams and received a 90 percent on your first exam and an 80 percent on your second exam, you have an 85 percent average. If, after some serious studying, you get a 100 percent on the third exam (the marginal exam), what happens to your average? It rises to 90 percent.

Because the marginal is greater than the average, it "pulls" the average up. However, if the score on your third (marginal) exam is lower—a 70 percent—your average will fall to 80 percent, because the marginal is below the average. Similarly, a baseball or softball player will improve on his batting average if the next trip to the plate is a hit, and the player's average will fall if the player strikes out.

6-4c WHY IS THE AVERAGE TOTAL COST CURVE U-SHAPED?

Why is the average total cost curve usually U-shaped, as seen in Exhibit 6.9? At very small and very large levels of output, average total cost is very high. The reason for the high average total cost when the firm is producing a very small amount of output is the high average fixed cost—when the output rate of the plant is small relative to its capacity, the plant is being underutilized. But as the firm expands output beyond this point, the average total cost falls. Why? Remember that $ATC = AFC + AVC$, and average fixed cost always falls when output expands because the fixed costs are being spread over more units of output. Thus, it is the declining AFC that is primarily responsible for the falling ATC.

The average total cost rises at high levels of output because of diminishing marginal product. For example, as more and more workers are put to work using a fixed quantity of machines, the result may be crowded working conditions and/or increasing maintenance costs as equipment is used more intensively or as older, less-efficient machinery is called on to handle the greater output. In fact, diminishing marginal product sets in at the bottom of the marginal cost curve, as seen in Exhibit 6.9. That is, it is diminishing marginal product that causes marginal costs to increase, eventually causing the average variable cost and average total cost curves to rise. At large levels of output, relative to plant capacity, the fixed plant is overutilized, leading to high marginal costs that cause a high average total cost.

6-4d THE RELATIONSHIP BETWEEN MARGINAL COSTS AND AVERAGE VARIABLE AND AVERAGE TOTAL COSTS

Certain relationships exist between marginal costs and average variable and average total costs. For example, when the average variable cost is falling, marginal costs must be less than the average variable cost; and when the average variable cost is rising, marginal costs are greater than the average variable cost. Marginal costs are equal to the average variable cost at the lowest point of the average variable cost curve, as seen in Exhibit 6.10.

EXHIBIT 6.9 U-Shaped Average Total Cost Curve

© Cengage Learning 2014

EXHIBIT 6.10 Marginal Cost and Average Variable Cost

© Cengage Learning 2014

In the left-hand (shaded) portion of Exhibit 6.10, marginal costs are less than the average variable cost, and the average is falling. On the right side, marginal costs are greater than the average variable cost, and the average is rising. The same relationship holds for the marginal cost curve and the average total cost curve. In the left-hand (shaded) portion of Exhibit 6.11, marginal costs are less than the average total cost, and the average is falling. On the right side, marginal costs are greater than the average total cost, and the average is rising. So it is the marginal cost curve that determines the U shape of the *AVC* and *ATC* curves.

SECTION CHECK 4 ANSWERS

1. As marginal product rises, marginal cost falls. As marginal product falls, marginal cost rises.

2. Average total cost declines as output expands but then increases again as output expands still further beyond a certain point. Declining *AFC* is primarily responsible for the *ATC*. The *ATC* rises at high levels of output because of the diminishing marginal product.

3. When marginal costs are greater than the average variable cost, the average variable cost must be rising; when marginal costs are greater than the average total cost, the average total cost must be rising.

6-5 Cost Curves: Short-Run versus Long-Run

SECTION CHECK 5

Think about the following questions as you read through this section.

1. Why are long-run costs different than short-run costs?

2. What are economies of scale?

3. What are diseconomies of scale?

4. What are constant returns to scale?

In this section we will compare short-run cost curves to long-run cost curves.

6-5a WHY ARE LONG-RUN COST CURVES DIFFERENT FROM SHORT-RUN COST CURVES?

Over long enough periods, firms can vary all of their productive inputs. That is, time provides an opportunity to substitute lower-cost capital, such as larger plants or newer, more sophisticated equipment, for more expensive labor inputs. However, in the short

© Erik Dreyer/Getty Images

By having several screens in one complex, the cinema owners can cut down on advertising and employee costs as well as rent. Because of economies of scale, it may be less expensive to have eight screens in one building with one concession area, rather than eight separate theaters, each with one screen and a concession area.

economies of scale occur in an output range where *LRATC* falls as output increases

minimum efficient scale the output level where economies of scale are exhausted and constant returns to scale begin

diseconomies of scale occur in an output range where *LRATC* rises as output expands

constant returns to scale occur in an output range where *LRATC* does not change as output varies

run a firm cannot alter its plant size and equipment. These inputs are fixed in the short run, so the firm can only expand output by employing more variable inputs (e.g., workers and raw materials) in order to get extra output from the existing factory. If a company has to pay many workers overtime wages to expand output in the short run, over the long run firms may opt to invest in new equipment to conserve on expensive labor. That is, in the long run, the firm can expand its factories, build new ones, or shut down unproductive ones. Of course, the time it takes for a firm to get to the long run varies from firm to firm. For example, it may take only a couple of months to build a new coffee shop, while it may take a few years to build a new automobile plant.

In Exhibit 6.12, we see that the long-run average total cost (*LRATC*) curve lies equal to or below the short-run average total cost (*SRATC*) curves. The reason for the difference between the firm's long-run total cost curve and its short-run total cost curves is that in the long run, costs are lower because firms have greater flexibility in changing inputs that are fixed in the short run. Exhibit 6.12 presents three short-run average total cost curves, representing small, medium, and large plant sizes.

It also shows the long-run average total cost curve. In the *short run*, the firm is restricted to the current plant size, but in the long run it can choose the short-run cost curve for the level of production it is planning on producing. As the firm moves along the long-run average total cost curve, it is adjusting the size of the factory to the quantity of production.

For example, in Exhibit 6.12, if Apple wanted to expand output in the medium plant size from 1,000 computers per day to 1,200 computers per day, it would have no choice but to hire more workers in the short run, moving from point A to point B. Because of diminishing marginal product (adding more workers to fixed plant size), the short-run average total cost rises from $400 to $500. However, in the long run, Apple can expand its factory size and workforce and the average total cost returns to $400, moving from point A to point C.

6-5b WHAT ARE ECONOMIES OF SCALE?

By examining the long-run average total cost curve for a firm, we can see three possible production patterns. In Exhibit 6.12, we see that extremely small firms experience **economies of scale**, falling per-unit costs as output expands. These firms, then, are functioning inefficiently from a long-run perspective. The **minimum efficient scale** is the output level in which the economies of scale are exhausted and the long-run average total costs are minimized. Similarly, firms that expand beyond a certain point encounter **diseconomies of scale**; that is, they incur rising per-unit costs as their output grows. In more intermediate output ranges, firms of varying sizes can compete on a roughly equal basis as far as costs are concerned because they all exhibit approximately **constant returns to scale**. That is, their per-unit costs remain stable as output grows. In this example, Apple has economies of scale at low levels of output, constant returns to scale at intermediate levels of output, and diseconomies of very high levels of output.

EXHIBIT 6.12 Short- and Long-Run Average Total Costs

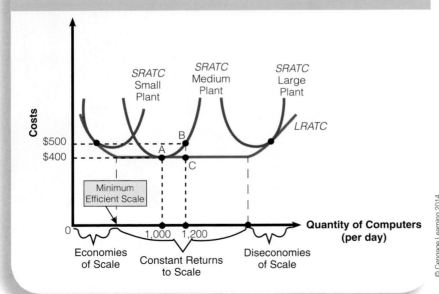

© Cengage Learning 2014

6-5c WHY DO ECONOMIES AND DISECONOMIES OF SCALE OCCUR?

As we have just seen, economies of scale exist when there is a reduction in the firm's long-run average costs as output expands. Firms may experience economies of scale for several reasons. First, if a firm operates on a larger scale, both workers and managers can become more specialized, allowing workers and managers to be more productive as output expands. Second, large initial set up costs in some industries, such as in some manufacturing sectors and in oil refining, means that high fixed costs are necessary to produce any output. That is, large firms can take advantage of highly efficient mass production techniques and equipment which are only economical if spread over a large output. Third, larger firms like Walmart may be able to purchase inputs at lower costs than smaller firms.

Recall that diseconomies of scale exist when there is an increase in the firm's long-run average costs as output expands. This may occur as the firm finds it increasingly difficult to handle the complexities of large-scale management. For example, information and coordination problems tend to increase when a firm becomes very large. This is why the *LRATC* is usually U-shaped. At low levels of output, firms generally benefit from increased size because they can take advantage of specialization. However, at high levels of output, the gains from specialization have already occurred, but coordination and bureaucratic problems increase.

SECTION CHECK 5 ANSWERS

1. Over longer time periods, firms can alter their production inputs in ways that are impossible in shorter periods. For instance, given enough time, a firm might be able to build new factories or purchase and install new equipment to improve their output. In the short run, however, a firm might have to pay workers overtime to improve output, resulting in higher costs.

2. At low output levels, when all inputs can be varied, some firms will experience economies of scale, where their per-unit costs decrease as output increases.

3. Firms that expand all inputs beyond a certain point will encounter diseconomies of scale, incurring rising per-unit costs as output grows in the long run.

4. In intermediate output ranges, firms may exhibit roughly constant returns to scale; in this range, their per-unit costs remain stable as output increases.

Chapter 6: Self-Review

Now that you are finished reading the chapter, review the questions below. You can write your answers in the space provided, then go online to see the answers at www.cengagebrain.com.

6-1 FIRMS AND PROFITS: TOTAL REVENUES MINUS TOTAL COSTS

1. If you turn down a job offer of $45,000 per year to work for yourself, what is the opportunity cost of working for yourself?

6-2 PRODUCTION IN THE SHORT RUN

2. True or False: All inputs vary in the long run.

3. What relationship does a production function represent?

4. Draw a typically shaped total output curve.

6-3 COSTS IN THE SHORT RUN

5. True or False: Average variable cost is the relevant cost to consider when a producer is deciding whether to produce more or less of a product.

6. If your season batting average going into a game was .300 (three hits per ten at bats) and you got two hits in five at bats during the game, would your season batting average rise or fall as a result?

7. A one-day ticket to visit the Screaming Coasters theme park costs $36, but you can also get a two-consecutive-day ticket for $40. What is the average cost per day for the two-day ticket? What is the marginal cost of the second consecutive day?

8. If your university pays lecture note takers $20 per hour to take notes in your economics class and then sells subscriptions for $15 per student, is the cost of the lecture note taker a fixed or variable cost of selling an additional subscription?

6-4 THE SHAPE OF THE SHORT-RUN COST CURVES

9. True or False: Average total cost rises as output expands over low-output ranges.

10. Why does the average total cost rise at some point as output expands further?

6-5 COST CURVES: SHORT-RUN VERSUS LONG-RUN

11. True or False: The *LRATC* curve has a shallower U shape than the *SRATC* because some inputs are fixed in the long run.

12. What may cause economies or diseconomies of scale?

At the Chicago Board of Trade (CBOT),

prices are set by thousands of buyers interacting with thousands of sellers. The goods in question are typically standardized, and information is readily available. Every buyer and seller knows the price, the quantity, and the quality of the goods. Transaction costs are negligible. Here we can see a pretty close approximation of a perfectly competitive market.

Test your Economics *street-smart* knowledge and see how you compare against other students! Scan here or visit CourseMate for Survey of ECON2.

© Jon Arnold Images Ltd/Alamy

7

Firms in Perfectly Competitive Markets

A firm must answer two critical questions: What price should we charge for the goods and services we sell, and how much should we produce? The answers to these two questions will depend on the market structure.

The behavior of firms will depend on the number of firms in the market, the ease with which firms can enter and exit the market, and the ability of firms to differentiate their products from those of other firms. There is no typical industry. An industry might include one firm that dominates the market, or it might consist of thousands of smaller firms that each produce a small fraction of the market supply. Between these two end points are many other industries. However, because we cannot examine each industry individually, we break them into four main categories: perfect competition, monopoly, monopolistic competition, and oligopoly.

In a perfectly competitive market, the market price is the critical piece of information that a firm needs to know. A firm in a perfectly competitive market can sell all it wants at the market price. A firm in a perfectly competitive market is said to be a price taker, because it cannot appreciably affect the market price for its output or the market price for its inputs. For example, suppose a Washington apple grower decides that he wants to get out of the family business and go to work for Microsoft. Because he may be one of 50,000 apple growers in the United States, his decision will not appreciably change the price of the apples, the production of apples, or the price of inputs.

7-1 A Perfectly Competitive Market

SECTION CHECK 1

Keep the following questions in mind as you read through this section.

1. What are the characteristics of a firm in a perfectly competitive market?

2. What is a price taker?

perfect competition a market structure characterized by many buyers and sellers, identical (homogeneous) products, and easy market entry and exit

price taker a perfectly competitive firm that takes the price it is given by the intersection of the market demand and market supply curves

This chapter examines **perfect competition**, a market structure characterized by (1) many buyers and sellers, (2) identical (homogeneous) products, and (3) easy market entry and exit. Let us examine these characteristics in greater detail.

3 Characteristics of Perfect Competition
- many buyers and sellers
- identical products
- easy entry and exit

© iStockphoto.com/subjug

7-1a MANY BUYERS AND SELLERS

In a perfectly competitive market, there are *many buyers and sellers*—perhaps thousands or conceivably millions. Because each firm is so small in relation to the industry, its production decisions have no impact on the market; each regards price as something over which it has no control. For this reason, perfectly competitive firms are called **price takers**: They must take the price given by the market because their influence on price is insignificant. If the price of wheat in the wheat market is $5 a bushel, then individual wheat farmers will receive $5 a bushel for their wheat. Similarly, no single buyer of wheat can influence the price of wheat, because each buyer purchases only a small amount of the wheat traded. We will see how this relationship works in more detail in the next section.

7-1b IDENTICAL (HOMOGENEOUS) PRODUCTS

Consumers believe that all firms in perfectly competitive markets *sell identical (or homogeneous) products*. For example, in the wheat market, we are assuming it is not possible to determine any significant and consistent qualitative differences in the wheat produced by different farmers. Wheat produced by Farmer Jones looks, feels, smells, and tastes like that produced by Farmer Smith. In short, a bushel of wheat is a bushel of wheat. The products of all the firms are considered to be perfect substitutes.

7-1c EASY ENTRY AND EXIT

Product markets characterized by perfect competition *have no significant barriers to entry or exit*. Therefore it is fairly easy for entrepreneurs to become suppliers of the product or, if they are already producers, to stop supplying the product. "Fairly easy" does not mean that any person on the street can instantly enter the business but rather that the financial, legal, educational, and other barriers to entering the business are modest, enabling large numbers of people to overcome the barriers and enter the business, if they so desire, in any given period. If buyers can easily switch from one seller to another and sellers can easily enter or exit the industry, then they have met the perfectly competitive condition of easy entry and exit. Because of this easy market entry, perfectly competitive markets generally consist of a large number of small suppliers.

A perfectly competitive market is approximated most closely in highly organized markets for securities and agricultural commodities, such as the New York Stock Exchange or the Chicago Board of Trade. Wheat, corn, soybeans, cotton, and many other agricultural products are sold in perfectly competitive markets. Although all the criteria for a perfectly competitive market are rarely met, a number of markets come close to satisfying them. Even when all the assumptions do not hold, it is important to note that studying the model of perfect competition is useful because many markets resemble perfect competition—that is, markets in which firms face highly elastic (flat) demand curves and relatively easy entry and exit. The model also gives us a standard of comparison. In other words, we can make comparisons with the perfectly competitive model to help us evaluate what is going on in the real world.

SECTION CHECK 1 ANSWERS

1. A perfectly competitive market is characterized by many buyers and sellers, an identical (homogeneous) product, and easy market entry and exit.

2. In markets with so many buyers and so many sellers, neither buyers nor sellers have any control over price in perfect competition. They must take the going price and hence are called price takers.

7-2 An Individual Price Taker's Demand Curve

SECTION CHECK 2

Keep the following questions in mind as you read through this section.

1. Why individual price takers will not raise or lower their prices?

2. Will the position of individual price takers' demand curves change when market price changes?

In this section, we will discuss how perfectly competitive firms are price takers and how a change in the market price affects the perfectly competitive firm's demand curve.

7-2a AN INDIVIDUAL FIRM'S DEMAND CURVE

The market price and output are determined by the intersection of the market supply and demand curves, as seen in Exhibit 7.1(b). As we stated earlier, perfectly competitive markets have many buyers and sellers and the goods offered for sale are essentially identical. Consequently, no buyer or seller can influence the market price. They take the market price as given.

For example, no single consumer of wheat can influence the market price of wheat because each buyer purchases such a small percentage of the total amount sold in the wheat market. Likewise, each wheat farmer sells relatively small amounts of almost identical wheat, so the farmer has little control over wheat prices. Individual wheat farmers know that they cannot dispose of their wheat at any figure higher than the current market price; if they attempt to charge a higher price, potential buyers will simply make their purchases from other wheat farmers. Further, the farmers certainly would not knowingly charge a lower price, because they could sell all they want at the market price.

Likewise, in a perfectly competitive market, individual sellers can change their outputs, and it will not alter the market price. The large number of sellers who are selling identical products make this situation possible. Each producer provides such a small fraction of the total supply that a change in the amount he offers does *not* have a noticeable effect on market equilibrium price. In a perfectly competitive market, then, an individual firm can sell as much as it wishes to place on the market at the prevailing price; the demand, as seen by the seller, is perfectly elastic.

It is easy to construct the demand curve for an individual seller in a perfectly competitive market. Remember, she will not charge more than the market

EXHIBIT 7.1 Market and Individual Firm Demand Curves in a Perfectly Competitive Market

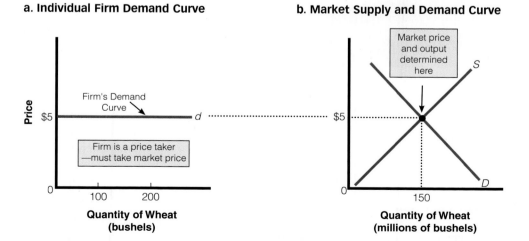

a. Individual Firm Demand Curve

Firm's Demand Curve

Firm is a price taker —must take market price

Price / $5 / d

0 / 100 / 200

Quantity of Wheat (bushels)

b. Market Supply and Demand Curve

Market price and output determined here

S

$5

0 / 150

D

Quantity of Wheat (millions of bushels)

© Cengage Learning 2014

price because no one will buy it, and she will not charge less because she can sell all she wants at the market price. Thus, the farmer's demand curve is horizontal over the entire range of output that she could possibly produce. If the prevailing market price of the product is $5, the farmer's demand curve will be represented graphically by a horizontal line at the market price of $5, as shown in Exhibit 7.1(a).

7-2b A CHANGE IN MARKET PRICE AND THE FIRM'S DEMAND CURVE

To say that producers under perfect competition regard price as a given is not to say that price is constant. The *position* of the firm's demand curve varies with every change in the market price. In Exhibit 7.2, we see that when the market price for wheat increases, say as a result of an increase in market demand, the price-taking firm will receive a higher price for all its output. Or when the market price decreases, say as a result of a decrease in market demand, the price-taking firm will receive a lower price for all its output.

In effect, sellers are provided with current information about market demand and supply conditions as a result of price changes. It is an essential aspect of the perfectly competitive model that sellers respond to the signals provided by such price movements, so they must alter their behavior over time in the light of actual experience, revising their production decisions to reflect changes in market price. In this respect, the perfectly competitive model is straightforward; it does

not assume any knowledge on the part of individual buyers and sellers about market demand and supply— they only have to know the price of the good they sell.

7-3 Profit Maximization

The objective of the firm is to maximize profits. To maximize profits, the firm wants to produce the amount that maximizes the difference between its total revenues and total costs. In this section, we will examine the different ways to look at revenue in a perfectly competitive market: total revenue, average revenue, and marginal revenue.

7-3a TOTAL REVENUE

Total revenue (TR) is the revenue that the firm receives from the sale of its products. Total revenue from a product equals the price of the good

EXHIBIT 7.2 Market Prices and the Position of a Firm's Demand Curve

© Cengage Learning 2014

Total Revenue (TR)

$$TR = P \times q$$

Average Revenue (AR)

$$AR = TR \div q = (P \times q) \div q$$

Marginal Revenue (MR)

$$MR = \Delta TR \div \Delta q$$

average revenue (AR)
the total revenue divided by the number of units sold

marginal revenue (MR)
the increase in total revenue resulting from a one-unit increase in sales

(P) times the quantity (q) of units sold ($TR = P \times q$). For example, if a farmer sells 10 bushels of wheat a day for $5 a bushel, his total revenue is $50 ($5 × 10 bushels). (*Note:* We will use the lowercase letter q to denote the single firm's output and reserve the uppercase letter Q for the output of the entire market. For example, q would be used to represent the output of one lettuce grower, while Q would be used to represent the output of all lettuce growers in the lettuce market.)

7-3b AVERAGE REVENUE AND MARGINAL REVENUE

Average revenue (AR) equals total revenue divided by the number of units of the product sold ($TR \div q$, or $[P \times q] \div q$). For example, if the farmer sells 10 bushels at $5 a bushel, total revenue is $50 and average revenue is $5 per bushel ($50 ÷ 10 bushels). Thus, in perfect competition, average revenue is equal to the price of the good.

Marginal revenue (MR) is the additional revenue derived from the production of one more unit of the good. In other words, marginal revenue represents the increase in total revenue that results from the sale of one more unit ($MR = \Delta TR \div \Delta q$). In a perfectly competitive market, because additional units of output can be sold without reducing the price of the product, marginal revenue is constant at all outputs and equal

to average revenue. For example, if the price of wheat per bushel is $5, the marginal revenue is $5. Because total revenue is equal to price multiplied by quantity ($TR = P \times q$), as we add one additional unit of output, total revenue will always increase by the amount of the product price, $5. Marginal revenue facing a perfectly competitive firm is equal to the price of the good.

In perfect competition, then, we know that marginal revenue, average revenue, and price are all equal: $P = MR = AR$. These relationships are clearly illustrated in the calculations presented in Exhibit 7.3.

7-3c HOW DO FIRMS MAXIMIZE PROFITS?

Now that we have discussed the firm's cost curves (in Chapter 6)

If the price of wheat per bushel is $5, the marginal revenue is $5.

EXHIBIT 7.3 Revenues for a Perfectly Competitive Firm

Quantity (q)	Price (P)	Total Revenue (TR = P × q)	Average Revenue (AR = TR ÷ q)	Marginal Revenue (MR = ΔTR ÷ Δq)
1	$5	$5	$5	
2	5	10	5	$5
3	5	15	5	5
4	5	20	5	5
5	5	25	5	5

and its revenues, we are ready to see how a firm maximizes its profits. A firm's profits equal its total revenues minus its total costs. However, at what output level must a firm produce and sell to maximize profits? In all types of market environments, the firm will maximize its profits at the level of output that maximizes the difference between total revenue and total cost, which is at the same output level at which marginal revenue equals marginal cost.

7-3d EQUATING MARGINAL REVENUE AND MARGINAL COST

The importance of equating marginal revenue and marginal cost is seen in Exhibit 7.4. As output expands beyond zero up to q^*, the marginal revenue derived from each unit of the expanded output exceeds the marginal cost of that unit of output; so the expansion of output creates additional profits. This addition to profit is shown as the leftmost shaded section in Exhibit 7.4. As long as marginal revenue exceeds marginal cost, profits continue to grow. For example, if the firm decides to produce q_1, the firm sacrifices potential profits, because the marginal revenue from producing more output is greater than the marginal cost. Only at q^*, where $MR = MC$, is the output level just right (not too large, not too small). Further expansion of output beyond q^* will lead to losses on the additional output (i.e., decrease the firm's overall profits), because $MC > MR$. For example, if the firm produces q_2, the firm incurs losses on the output produced beyond q^*; the firm should reduce its output. Only at output q^*, where $MR = MC$, can we find the **profit-maximizing level of output**.

Be careful to avoid making the mistake of focusing on profit per unit rather than total profit. That is, you might think that at q_1, if MR is much greater than MC, the firm should not produce more because the profit per unit is high at this point. However, that would be a mistake because a firm can add to

Be careful to avoid making the mistake of focusing on profit per unit rather than total profit.

EXHIBIT 7.4 Finding the Profit-Maximizing Level of Output

A firm maximizes profits by producing the quantity where $MR = MC$ at q^*.

Lost profit $q_1 < q^*$

Lost profit $q_2 > q^*$

MC

$d (P = MR)$

Price

$5

0 q_1 q^* q_2

Quantity of Wheat (bushels per year)

its total profits as long as $MR > MC$—that is, all the way to q^*.

The Marginal Approach

We can use the data from the table in Exhibit 7.5 to find Farmer Jones's profit-maximizing position. Columns 5 and 6 show the marginal revenue and marginal cost, respectively. The first bushel of wheat that Farmer Jones produces has a marginal revenue of $5 and a marginal cost of $2; so producing that bushel of wheat increases profits by $3 ($5 − $2). The second bushel of wheat produced has a marginal revenue of $5 and a marginal cost of $3; so producing that bushel of wheat increases profits by $2 ($5 − $3). Farmer Jones wants to produce those units and more. That is, as long as marginal revenue exceeds marginal cost, producing and selling those units add more to revenues than to costs; in other words, they add to profits. However, once he expands production beyond four units of output, Farmer Jones's costs are less than his marginal revenues, and his profits begin to fall. Clearly, Farmer Jones should not produce beyond 4 bushels of wheat.

Let us take another look at profit maximization using the table in Exhibit 7.5. Comparing columns 2 and 3—the calculations of total revenue and total cost, respectively—we see that Farmer Jones maximizes his profits at output levels of 3 or 4 bushels, where he will make profits of $4. In column 4—profit—you can see that there is no higher level of profit at any of the

EXHIBIT 7.5 Cost and Revenue Calculations for a Perfectly Competitive Firm

Quantity (1)	Total Revenue (2)	Total Cost (3)	Profit (TR − TC) (4)	Marginal Revenue ($\Delta TR \div \Delta q$) (5)	Marginal Cost ($\Delta TC \div \Delta q$) (6)	Change in Profit (MR − MC) (7)
0	$0	$2	$−2			
				$5	$2	$3
1	5	4	1			
				5	3	2
2	10	7	3			
				5	4	1
3	15	11	4			
				5	5	0
4	20	16	4			
				5	6	−1
5	25	22	3			

© Cengage Learning 2014

other output levels. Producing 5 bushels would reduce profits by $1, because marginal revenue, $5, is less than the marginal cost, $6. Consequently, Farmer Jones would not produce this bushel of output. If $MR > MC$, Farmer Jones should increase production; if $MR < MC$, he should decrease production.

In the next section, we will use the profit-maximizing output rule to see what happens when changes in the market cause the price to fall below average total cost and even below average variable cost. We will introduce the three-step method to determine whether the firm is making an economic profit, is minimizing its losses, or should be temporarily shut down.

SECTION CHECK 3 ANSWERS

1. Total revenue is price times the quantity sold ($TR = P \times q$).

2. Average revenue is total revenue divided by the quantity sold ($AR = TR \div q = P$, or $[P \times q] \div q$).

3. Marginal revenue is the change in total revenue from the sale of an additional unit of output ($MR = \Delta TR \div \Delta q$). In a competitive industry, the price of the good equals both the average revenue and the marginal revenue.

4. As long as the marginal revenue exceeds marginal cost, the seller should expand production, because producing and selling those units adds more to revenues than to costs; that is, it increases profits. However, if the marginal revenue is less than the marginal cost, the seller should decrease production.

7-4 Short-Run Profits and Losses

SECTION CHECK 4

Keep the following questions in mind as you read through this section.

1. How do we determine whether a firm is generating an economic profit?

2. How do we determine whether a firm is experiencing an economic loss?

3. How do we determine whether a firm is making zero economic profits?

4. Why does a firm not produce when price is below average variable cost?

In the previous section, we discussed how to determine the profit-maximizing output level for a perfectly competitive firm. So how do we know whether a firm is actually making economic profits or losses?

7-4a THE THREE-STEP METHOD

Determining whether a firm is generating economic profits, economic losses, or zero economic profits at the profit-maximizing level of output, q^*, can be done in three easy steps. First, we will walk through these steps, and then we will apply the method to three situations for a hypothetical firm in the short run in Exhibit 7.6.

1. Find where marginal revenue equals marginal cost and proceed straight down to the horizontal quantity axis to find q^*, the profit-maximizing output level.

2. At q^*, go straight up to the demand curve and then to the left to find the market price, P^*. Once you have identified P^* and q^*, you can find total revenue at the profit-maximizing output level, because $TR = P \times q$.

3. The last step is to find the total cost. Again, go straight up from q^* to the average total cost (ATC) curve and then left to the vertical axis to compute the average total cost *per unit*. If we multiply average total cost by the output level, we can find the total cost ($TC = ATC \times q$).

Total Economic Profit = $(P^* - ATC) \times q^*$

If total revenue is greater than total cost at q^*, the firm is generating economic profits. If total revenue is less than total cost at q^*, the firm is generating economic losses. If total revenue is equal to total cost at q^*, there are zero economic profits (or a normal rate of return).

Alternatively, to find total economic profits, we can take the product price at P^* and subtract the average total cost at q^*. This will give us per-unit profit. If we multiply this by output, we will arrive at total economic profit. $(P^* - ATC) \times q^* =$ Total economic profit.

Remember, the cost curves include implicit and explicit costs—that is, we are covering the opportunity costs of our resources. Therefore, even with zero economic profits, no tears should be shed, because the firm is covering both its implicit and explicit costs. Because firms are also covering their implicit costs, or what they could be producing with these resources in another endeavor, economists sometimes call this zero economic

profit a *normal rate of return*. That is, the owners are doing as well as they could elsewhere, in that they are getting the normal rate of return on the resources they invested in the firm.

The Three-Step Method in Action

Exhibit 7.6 shows three different short-run equilibrium positions; in each case, the firm is producing at a level where marginal revenue equals marginal cost. Each of these alternatives shows that the firm is maximizing profits or minimizing losses in the short run.

Assume that three alternative prices—$6, $5, and $4—are available for a firm with given costs. In Exhibit 7.6(a), the firm receives $6 per unit at an equilibrium level of output ($MR = MC$) of 120 units. Total revenue ($P \times q^*$) is $6 × 120, or $720. The average total cost at 120 units of output is $5, and the total cost ($ATC \times q^*$) is $600. Following the three-step method, we can calculate that this firm is earning a total economic profit of $120. Or we can calculate total economic profit by using the following equation: $(P^* - ATC) \times q^* = (\$6 - \$5) \times 120 = \$120$.

In Exhibit 7.6(b), the market price has fallen to $4 per unit. At the equilibrium level of output, the firm is now producing 80 units of output at an average total cost of $5 per unit. The total revenue is now $320 ($4 × 80), and the total cost is $400 ($5 × 80). We can see that the firm is now incurring a total economic loss of $80. Or we can calculate total economic profit by using the following equation: $(P^* - ATC) \times q^* = (\$4 - \$5) \times 80 = -\$80$.

In Exhibit 7.6(c), the firm is earning zero economic profits, or a normal rate of return. The market price

EXHIBIT 7.6 Short-Run Profits, Losses, and Zero Economic Profits

a. Economic Profit — (Profit-Maximizing Output)

b. Economic Loss — (Loss-Minimizing Output)

c. Zero Economic Profits — (Profit-Maximizing Output)

is \$4.90, and the average total cost is \$4.90 per unit for 100 units of output. In this case, economic profits are zero, because total revenue, \$490, minus total cost, \$490, is equal to zero. This firm is just covering all its costs, both implicit and explicit. Or we can calculate total economic profit by using the following equation: $(P^* - ATC) \times q^* = (\$4.90 - \$4.90) \times 100 = \$0$.

7-4b EVALUATING ECONOMIC LOSSES IN THE SHORT RUN

A firm generating an economic loss faces a tough choice: Should it continue to produce or should it shut down its operation? To make this decision, we need to add another variable to our discussion of economic profits and losses: average variable cost. Variable costs are costs that vary with output—for example, wages, raw material, transportation, and electricity. If a firm cannot generate enough revenues to cover its variable costs, it will have larger losses if it operates than if it shuts down (when losses are equal to fixed costs). That is, the firm will shut down if its total revenue ($P \times q$) is less than its variable costs (VC). If we divide $P \times q$ by q we get P, and if we divide VC by q we get AVC, so if $P < AVC$, a profit-maximizing firm will shut down. Thus, a firm will not produce at all unless the price is greater than its average variable cost.

Operating at a Loss

At price levels greater than or equal to the average variable cost, a firm may continue to operate in the short run even if its average total cost—variable and fixed costs—is not completely covered. That is, the firm may continue to operate even though it is experiencing an economic loss. Why? Because fixed costs continue whether the firm produces or not; it is better to earn enough to cover a portion of fixed costs than to earn nothing at all. For example, a restaurant may decide to stay open for lunch if its revenues can cover variable costs. Many of a restaurant's costs are fixed—rent, insurance, kitchen appliances, pots, pans, tableware, and so on. These are sunk costs in the short run and shutting down for lunch would not reduce these costs. The restaurant's lunch decision hinges on whether or not the revenue from the few lunchtime customers can cover the variable costs like staff and extra food. If the restaurant owner cannot cover the variable costs at lunchtime, she shuts it down for lunch.

Similarly, a grocery store may stay open all night even if it anticipates only a few customers. To the person on the street, this may look unprofitable. However, the relevant question to the store owner is not whether all the cost can be covered, but whether the additional sales from staying open all night cover the variable costs of electricity, staff, and extra food. Many businesses that are "failing" may continue to operate so they can at least cover part of their fixed costs, like rent.

In Exhibit 7.7, price is less than average total cost but more than average variable cost. In this case, the firm produces in the short run, but at a loss. To shut down would make this firm worse off, because it can cover at least some of its fixed costs with the excess of revenue over its variable costs.

Why might a restaurant stay open at lunch even though there are only a few customers?

EXHIBIT 7.7 Short-Run Losses: Price above *AVC* but below *ATC*

The Decision to Shut Down

Exhibit 7.8 illustrates a situation in which the price a firm is able to obtain for its product is below its average variable cost at all ranges of output. In this case, the firm is unable to cover even its variable costs in the short run. Because the firm is losing even more than the fixed costs it would lose if it shut down, it is more logical for the firm to cease operations. Hence, if *P* < *AVC*, the firm can cut its losses by shutting down. For example, because the demand for a summer camp will be lower during the off season, it is likely that revenues may be too low for the camp to cover its variable costs and the owner will choose to shut down. And by shutting down during the off season the owner will at least not have to pay the variable costs like salaries for the camp staff, food, and electricity. Similarly, an auto plant may respond to a reduction in demand for their automobiles by temporarily shutting down one of their plants. However, remember these firms cannot escape their fixed costs by shutting down. When demand picks up, and the firm can cover its variable costs, production will resume.

The Short-Run Supply Curve

As we have just seen, at all prices above the minimum *AVC*, a firm produces in the short run even if average total cost (*ATC*) is not completely covered; and at all prices below the minimum *AVC*, the firm shuts down. The firm produces above the minimum *AVC* even if it is incurring economic losses because it can still earn enough in total revenues to cover all its average variable cost and a portion of its fixed costs, which is better than not producing and earning nothing at all.

In graphical terms, the **short-run supply curve** of an individual competitive seller is identical to the portion of the *MC* curve that lies above the minimum of the *AVC* curve. As a cost relation, this curve shows the marginal cost of producing any given output; as a supply curve, it shows the equilibrium output that the firm will supply at various prices in the short run. The solid red line in Exhibit 7.9 is the firm's supply curve—the portion of *MC* above its intersection with *AVC*. The declining portion of the *MC* curve has no significance for supply, because if the price falls below the average variable cost, the firm is better off shutting down—producing no output. The shutdown point is at the minimum point on the average variable cost curve where the output level is q_{SHUTDOWN}. Beyond the point of lowest *AVC*, the marginal costs of successively larger amounts of output are progressively greater, so the firm will supply larger and larger amounts only at higher prices.

EXHIBIT 7.8 Short-Run Losses: Price below *AVC*

7-4c DERIVING THE SHORT-RUN MARKET SUPPLY CURVE

The **short-run market supply curve** is the summation of all the individual firms' supply curves (that is, the portion of the firms' *MC* above *AVC*) in the market. Because the short run is too brief for new firms to enter the market, the market supply curve is the summation of *existing* firms. For example, in Exhibit 7.11, at P_1, each of the 1,000 identical firms in the industry produces 500 bushels of wheat per day at point a in Exhibit 7.11(a); and the quantity supplied in the market is 500,000 bushels of wheat, point A, in Exhibit 7.11(b). We can again sum horizontally at P_2; the quantity supplied for each of the

EXHIBIT 7.9 The Firm's Short-Run Supply Curve

1,000 identical firms is 800 bushels of wheat per day at point b in Exhibit 7.11(a), so the quantity supplied for the industry is 800,000 bushels of wheat per day, point B in Exhibit 7.11(b). Continuing this process gives us the market supply curve for the wheat market. In a market of 1,000 identical wheat farmers, the market supply curve is 1,000 times the quantity supplied by each firm, as long as the price is above AVC.

EVALUATING SHORT-RUN ECONOMIC LOSSES

Q&A

Q: Lei-ann is one of many florists in a medium-size urban area. That is, we assume that she works in a market similar to a perfectly competitive market and operates, of course, in the short run. Lei-ann's cost and revenue information is shown in the accompanying table. Based on this information, what should Lei-ann do in the short run and why?

A: Fixed costs are unavoidable unless the firm goes out of business. Lei-ann really has two choices in the short run—either to operate or to shut down temporarily. In the table of Lei-ann's daily revenue and cost schedule, we saw that Lei-ann makes $2,000 a day in total revenue, but her daily costs (fixed and variable) are $2,500. She has to pay her workers, pay for fresh flowers, and pay for the fuel used by her drivers in picking up and delivering flowers. She must also pay the electricity bill to heat her shop and keep her refrigerators going to protect her flowers. That is, every day, poor Lei-ann is losing $500; but she still might want to operate the shop despite the loss. Why? Lei-ann's average variable cost (comprised of flow-ers, transportation, fuel, daily wage earners, and so on) amounts to $1,500 a day; her fixed costs (insurance, property taxes, rent for the building, and refrigerator payments) are $1,000 a day. Now, if Lei-ann does not operate, she will save on her variable cost—$1,500 a day—but she will be out the $2,000 a day she makes in revenue from selling her flowers. Thus, every day she operates, she is better off than if she had not operated at all. That is, if the firm can cover the average variable cost, it is better off operating than not operating. But suppose Lei-ann's VC were $2,100 a day. Then Lei-ann should not operate, because every day she does, she is $100 worse off than if she shut down altogether. In short, a firm will shut down if $TR < VC$ or $(P \times q) < VC$. If we divide both sides by q, the firm will shut down if $P < AVC$ or $(P \times q) \div q < VC \div q$.

Why does Lei-ann even bother operating if she is making a loss? Perhaps the economy is in a recession and the demand for flowers is temporarily down, but Lei-ann thinks things will pick up again in the next few months. If Lei-ann is right and demand picks up, her prices and marginal revenue will rise, and she may have a chance to make short-run economic profits.

EXHIBIT 7.10 Lei-ann's Daily Revenue and Cost Schedule

Total Revenue	$2,000
Total Costs	2,500
Variable Costs	1,500
Fixed Costs	1,000

EXHIBIT 7.11 Deriving the Short-Run Market Supply Curve

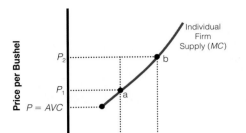

a. Individual Firm Supply Curve for Wheat

b. Market Supply Curve for Wheat

Reviewing the Short-Run Output Decision

Exhibit 7.12 shows the firm's short-run output at these various market prices: P_1, P_2, P_3, and P_4.

At the market price of P_1, the firm would not cover its average variable cost—the firm would produce zero output, because the firm's losses would be smaller if it shut down and stopped producing. At the market price of P_2, the firm would produce at the loss-minimizing output of q_2 units. It would operate rather than shut down, because it could cover all its average variable costs and some of its fixed costs. At the market price of P_3, the firm would produce q_3 units of output and make zero economic profit (a normal rate of return). At the market price of P_4, the firm would produce q_4 units of output and be making short-run economic profits.

SOURCE: From Exploring Economics, 6e, by Robert L. Sexton, ISBN: 9781111970307

EXHIBIT 7.12 The Short-Run Output Decision

SECTION CHECK 4 ANSWERS

1. The profit-maximizing output level is found by equating MR to MC at q^*. If at that output the firm's price is greater than its average total costs, it is making an economic profit.

2. If at the profit-maximizing output level, q^*, the price is less than the average total cost, the firm is incurring an economic loss.

3. If at the profit-maximizing output level, q^*, the price is equal to average total cost, the firm is making zero

SECTION CHECK 4 CONTINUED

economic profits; that is, the firm is covering both its implicit and explicit costs (making a normal rate of return).

4. If the price falls below the average variable cost, the firm is better off shutting down rather than operating in the short run, because it would incur greater losses from operating than from shutting down.

7-5 Long-Run Equilibrium

SECTION CHECK 5

Keep the following questions in mind as you read through this section.

1. When an industry is earning profits, will it encourage the entry of new firms?

2. What happens when an industry experiences economic loss?

3. Why do perfectly competitive firms make zero economic profits in the long run?

Now Let us consider how firms will behave in the long run.

7-5a ECONOMIC PROFITS AND LOSSES DISAPPEAR IN THE LONG RUN

If farmers are able to make economic profits producing wheat, what will their response be in the long run? Farmers will increase the resources that they devote to the lucrative business of producing wheat. Suppose Farmer Jones is making an economic profit (he is earning an above-normal rate of return) producing wheat. To make even more profits, he may take land away from other crops to plant more wheat. Other farmers or people who are holding land for speculative purposes may also decide to plant wheat on their land.

As word gets out that wheat production is proving profitable, it will cause a supply response—the market supply curve will shift to the right as more firms enter the industry and existing firms expand, as shown in Exhibit 7.13(b). With this shift, the quantity of wheat supplied at any given price is greater than before. It may take a year or even longer, of course, for the complete supply response to take place, simply because it takes some time for information on profit opportunities to spread and still more time to plant, grow, and harvest the wheat. Note that the effect of increasing supply, *ceteris paribus,* is a reduction in the equilibrium price of wheat.

Suppose that, as a result of the supply response, the price of wheat falls from P_1 to P_2. The impact of the change in the market price of wheat, over which Farmer Jones has absolutely no control, is simple. If his costs do not change, he moves from making a profit ($P_1 > ATC$) to zero economic profits ($P_2 = ATC$), as shown in Exhibit 7.13(a). In long-run equilibrium, perfectly competitive firms make zero economic profits. Remember, a zero economic profit means that the firm actually earns a normal return on the use of its capital. A zero economic profit is an equilibrium or stable situation because any positive economic (above-normal) profit signals resources into the industry, beating down prices and therefore revenues to the firm.

EXHIBIT 7.13 Profits Disappear with Entry

a. Individual Firm

b. Market

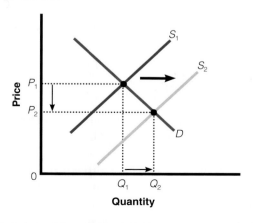

© Cengage Learning 2014

EXHIBIT 7.14 Losses Disappear with Exit

a. Individual Firm

b. Market

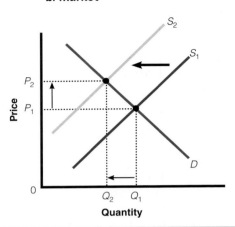

© Cengage Learning 2014

For example, in the late 1990s when the organic food industry was in its infancy, an organic apple grower could sell its apples at a much higher price than regular apples, a price that covered more than its cost of production—an economic profit. Today, there are many organic farmers, increasing market supply and decreasing the market price and moving firms toward zero economic profits—a normal rate of return.

Any economic losses signal resources to leave the industry, causing supply reductions that lead to increased prices and higher firm revenues for the remaining firms. For example, in Exhibit 7.14 we see a firm that continues to operate despite its losses—ATC is greater than P_1 at q_1. With losses, however, some firms will exit the industry, causing the market supply curve to shift from S_1 to S_2 and driving up the market price to P_2. This price increase reduces the losses for the firms remaining in the industry, until the losses are completely eliminated at P_2. The remaining firms will maximize profits by producing at q_2 units of output, where profits and losses are zero. Only at zero economic profits is there no tendency for firms to either enter or leave the industry.

7-5b THE LONG-RUN EQUILIBRIUM FOR THE COMPETITIVE FIRM

The long-run competitive equilibrium for a perfectly competitive firm is illustrated graphically in Exhibit 7.15. At the equilibrium point e, where $MC = MR$, short-run and long-run average total costs are also equal. The average total cost curves touch the marginal cost and marginal revenue (demand) curves at the equilibrium output point. Because the marginal revenue curve is also the average revenue curve, average revenue and average total cost are equal at the equilibrium point. The long-run equilibrium in perfect competition depicted in Exhibit 7.15 has an interesting feature. Note that the equilibrium output occurs at the lowest point on the average total cost curve. As you may recall, this occurs because the marginal cost curve must intersect the average total cost curve at the latter curve's lowest point. Hence, the equilibrium condition in the long run in perfect competition is for each firm to produce at the output that minimizes average total cost. At this long-run equilibrium, all firms in the industry earn zero economic profits consequently, new firms have no incentive to enter the market and existing firms have no incentive to exit the market.

EXHIBIT 7.15 The Long-Run Competitive Equilibrium

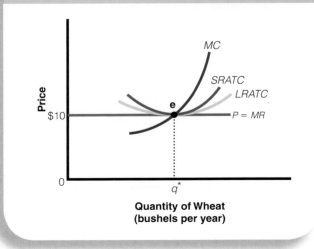

© Cengage Learning 2014

7-6 Long-Run Supply

SECTION CHECK 6

Keep the following questions in mind as you read through this section.

1. What are constant-cost industries?
2. What are increasing-cost industries?
3. What are decreasing-cost industries?
4. What is productive efficiency?
5. What is allocative efficiency?

The preceding sections considered the costs for an individual, perfectly competitive firm as it varies output, on the assumption that the prices it pays for inputs (costs) are given. However, when the output of an entire industry changes, the likelihood is greater that changes in costs will occur. How will the changes in the number of firms in an industry affect the input costs of individual firms? In this section, we develop the long-run supply (LRS) curve. As we will see, the shape of the

© iStockphoto.com/Wendell and Carolyn

long-run supply curve depends on the extent to which input costs change with the entry or exit of firms in the industry. We will look at three possible types of industries, when considering long-run supply: constant-cost industries, increasing-cost industries, and decreasing-cost industries.

7-6a A CONSTANT-COST INDUSTRY

In a **constant-cost industry**, the prices of inputs do not change as output is expanded. The industry may not use inputs in sufficient quantities to affect input prices. For example, say the firms in the industry use a lot of unskilled labor, but the industry is small. In such a case, as output expands, the increase in demand for unskilled labor will not cause the market wage for unskilled labor to rise. Similarly, suppose a paper clip maker decides to double its output. It is highly unlikely that its demand for steel will have an impact on steel prices, because its demand for the input is so small.

Once long-run adjustments are complete, by necessity each firm operates at the point of lowest long-run average total cost, because supply shifts with entry and exit, eliminating profits. Therefore, each firm supplies the market with the quantity of output that it can produce at the lowest possible long-run average total cost.

In Exhibit 7.16, we can see the impact of an unexpected increase in market demand. Suppose that recent reports show that blueberries can lower cholesterol, lower blood pressure, and significantly reduce the risk of all cancers. The increase in market demand for blueberries leads to a price increase from P_1 to P_2 as the firm increases output from q_1 to q_2, and blueberry industry output increases from Q_1 to Q_2, as seen in Exhibit 7.16(b). The increase in market demand generates a higher price and positive profits for existing firms in the short run. The existence of economic profits will attract new firms into the industry, causing the short-run supply curve to shift from S_1 to S_2 and lowering price until excess profits are zero. This shift results in a new equilibrium, point C in Exhibit 7.16(c). Because the industry is one with constant costs, industry expansion does not alter firms' cost curves, and the industry long-run supply curve is horizontal. That is, the long-run equilibrium price is at the same level that prevailed before demand increased; the only long-run effect of the increase in demand is an increase in industry output, as more firms enter that are just like existing firms

EXHIBIT 7.16 Demand Increase in a Constant-Cost Industry

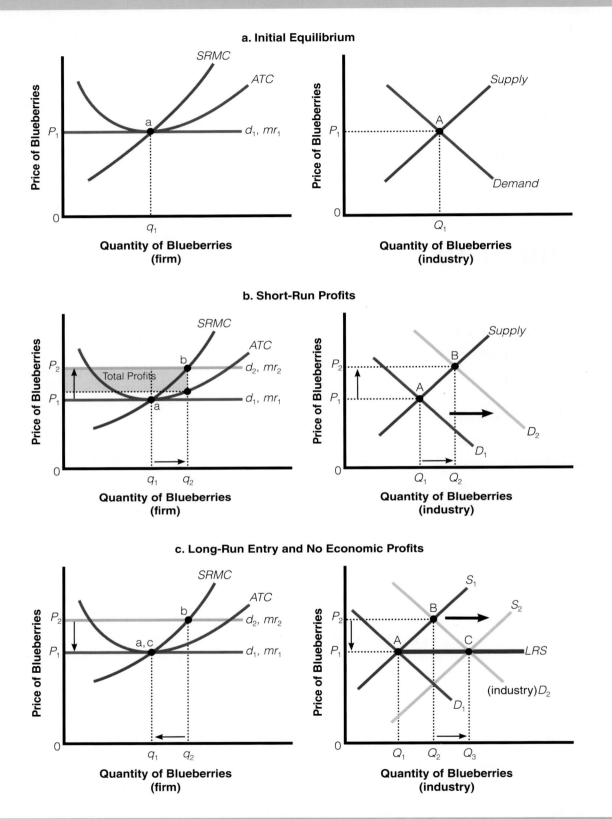

a. Initial Equilibrium

b. Short-Run Profits

c. Long-Run Entry and No Economic Profits

(shown in Exhibit 7.16[c]). The long-run supply curve is horizontal when the market has free entry and exit, there are a large number of firms with identical costs, and input prices are constant. Because these strong assumptions do not generally hold, we will now discuss when the long-run supply curve has a positive or negative slope.

Growth in the airline industry results in more congestion of airports and airspace—external diseconomies of scale.

increasing-cost industry an industry in which input prices rise (and cost curves rise) as industry output rises

7-6b AN INCREASING-COST INDUSTRY

In an **increasing-cost industry**, a more common scenario, the cost curves of individual firms rise as the total output of the industry increases. Increases in input prices, shown as upward shifts in cost curves, occur as larger quantities of factors are employed in the industry. When an industry utilizes a large portion of an input, input prices will rise when the industry uses more of the input.

Increasing cost conditions are typical of *extractive* industries, such as agriculture, fishing, mining, and lumber, which utilize large portions of the total supply of specialized natural resources such as land or mineral deposits. As the output of such an industry expands, the increased demand for the resources raises the prices that must be paid for their use. Because additional resources of a given quality cannot be produced, greater supplies can be obtained only by luring them away from other industries, or by using lower-quality (and less-productive, thus higher-cost) resources.

As the output of an increasing cost industry expands, the increased demand for the resources raises the prices that must be paid for their use.

Wheat production is a typical example of an increasing-cost industry. As the output of wheat increases, the demand for land suitable for the production of wheat rises, and thus the price paid for the use of land of any given quality increases.

If there were a construction boom in a fully employed economy, would it be more costly to get additional resources such as skilled workers and raw materials? Yes; if this is an increasing-cost industry, the industry can only produce more output if it gets a higher price because the firm's costs of production rise as output expands. As new firms enter and output expands, the increase in demand for inputs causes the price of inputs to rise—the cost curves of all construction firms shift upward as the industry expands. Or consider a downtown building boom in which the supply of workers who are willing to work on tall skyscrapers is very inelastic (a very steep supply of labor curve). The high demand for these few workers causes their wages to rise sharply and the cost of skyscrapers to rise. The industry can produce more output but only at a price increased enough to compensate the firm for the higher input costs. In an increasing-cost industry, the long-run supply curve is upward sloping.

Another example is provided by the airlines. Growth in the airline industry results in more congestion of airports and airspace. That is, as the output of the airline industry increases, the firm's cost increases, *ceteris paribus*. This situation of an upward-sloping long-run industry supply curve is what economists call *external diseconomies of scale*—factors that are beyond the firm's control (that is, external) raise the firm's costs as industry output expands. In contrast, recall the discussion of diseconomies of scale in the previous chapter: the costs were internal to the firm—the costs were higher due to managing a larger firm.

7-6c A DECREASING-COST INDUSTRY

It is also possible that an expansion in the output of an industry can lead to a reduction in input costs and shift the *MC* and *ATC* curves downward, and the market price falls because of *external economies of scale*. We use the

decreasing-cost industry an industry in which input prices fall (and cost curves fall) as industry output rises

productive efficiency where a good or service is produced at the lowest possible cost

allocative efficiency where $P = MC$ and production will be allocated to reflect consumer preferences

term *external* because the cost decreases are external to the firm; no one firm can gain by its own expansion. That is, the gain occurs when the total industry's output expands. The new long-run market equilibrium has more output at a lower price—that is, the long-run supply curve for a **decreasing-cost industry** is downward sloping (not shown).

Consider a new mining region developed in an area remote from railroad facilities back in the days before motor vehicles. So long as the total output of the mines was small, the ore was hauled by wagon, an extremely expensive form of transportation. But when the number of mines increased and the total output of the region rose substantially, it became feasible to construct a railroad to serve the area. The railroad lowered transportation costs and reduced the costs of all firms in the industry. As a practical matter, decreasing-cost industries are rarely encountered, at least over a large range of output. However, some industries may operate under decreasing-cost conditions in the short intervals of output expansion when continued growth makes possible the supply of materials or services at reduced cost. A larger industry might benefit from improved transportation or financial services, for example.

This situation might occur in the computer industry. The firms in the industry may be able to acquire computer chips at a lower price as the industry's demand for computer chips rises. Why? Perhaps it is because the computer chip industry can employ cost-saving techniques that become more economical at higher levels of output. That is, the marginal and average costs of the firm fall as input prices fall because of expanded output in the industry.

7-6d PERFECT COMPETITION AND ECONOMIC EFFICIENCY

In this chapter, we have seen that a firm in a perfectly competitive market produces at the minimum point of the *ATC* curve in the long run and charges a price equal to that cost. Because competitive firms are producing using the least-cost method, the minimum value of resources is being used to produce a given level of output. This leads to lower product prices for consumers. In short, **productive efficiency** requires that firms produce goods and services in the least costly way, where $P = $ minimum *ATC*, as seen in Exhibit 7.15 on page 152. However, productive efficiency alone does not guarantee that markets are operating efficiently—society must also produce the goods and services that society wants most. This leads us to what economists call **allocative efficiency**.

We say that the output that results from equilibrium conditions of market demand and market supply in perfectly competitive markets achieve an efficient allocation of resources.

At the intersection of market supply and market demand, we find the competitive equilibrium price, P^*,

---

EXHIBIT 7.17 Allocative Efficiency and Perfect Competition

a. Producing Less Than the Competitive Level of Output Lowers Welfare

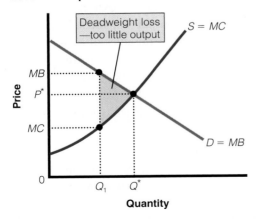

b. Producing More Than the Competitive Level of Output Lowers Welfare

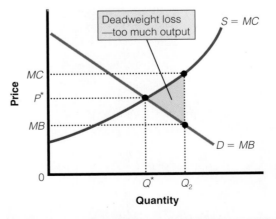

and the competitive equilibrium output, Q^*. In competitive markets, market supply equals market demand, and $P = MC$. When $P = MC$, buyers value the last unit of output by the same amount that it cost sellers to produce it. If buyers value the last unit by more than the marginal cost of production, resources are not being allocated efficiently, as at Q_1 in Exhibit 7.17(a). Think of the demand curve as the marginal benefit curve ($D = MB$) and the supply curve as the marginal cost curve ($S = MC$). According to the rule of rational choice, we should pursue an activity as long as the expected marginal benefits are greater than the expected marginal costs. For example, in Exhibit 7.17(a), if Q_1 is produced, then the marginal benefits from producing additional units are greater than the marginal costs. The shaded area is deadweight loss. That is, at Q_1, resources are not being allocated efficiently, and output should be expanded.

We can also produce too much output. For example, if output is expanded beyond Q^* in Exhibit 7.17(b), the cost to sellers for producing the good is greater than the marginal benefit to consumers. The shaded area is deadweight loss. Society would gain from a reduction in output back to Q^*. Once the competitive equilibrium is reached, the buyers' marginal benefit equals the sellers' marginal cost. That is, in a competitive market, producers efficiently use their scarce resources (labor, machinery, and other inputs) to produce what consumers want. In this sense, perfect competition achieves allocative efficiency.

SECTION CHECK 6 ANSWERS

1. In constant-cost industries, the cost curves of the firm are not affected by changes in the output of the entire industry. Such industries must be small demanders of resources in the market.

2. In an increasing-cost industry, the cost curves of the individual firms rise as total output increases. This case is the most common.

3. A decreasing-cost industry has a downward-sloping long-run supply curve. Firms experience lower costs as the industry expands.

4. Productive efficiency occurs in perfect competition because the firm produces at the minimum point of the *ATC* curve.

5. Allocative efficiency occurs when $P = MC$; production is allocated to reflect consumers' wants.

Chapter 7: Self-Review

Now that you are finished reading the chapter, review the questions below. You can write your answers in the space provided, then go online to see the answers at www.cengagebrain.com.

7-1 A PERFECTLY COMPETITIVE MARKET

1. Why do firms in perfectly competitive markets involve homogeneous goods?

2. Which of the following are most likely to be perfectly competitive?
   a. Chicago Board of Trade
   b. fast-food industry
   c. computer software industry
   d. New York Stock Exchange
   e. clothing industry

7-2 AN INDIVIDUAL PRICE TAKER'S DEMAND CURVE

3. True or False: The demand curve of a perfectly competitive firm can be represented as perfectly elastic (horizontal) at the market price.

4. How does an individual perfectly competitive firm's demand curve change when the market price changes?

7-3 PROFIT MAXIMIZATION

5. True or False: For a perfectly competitive firm, marginal revenue is always greater than the price.

7-4 SHORT-RUN PROFITS AND LOSSES

6. How is the profit-maximizing output quantity determined?

7. If a profit-maximizing perfectly competitive firm is earning a profit because total revenue exceeds total cost, why must the market price exceed average total cost?

8. Complete the following table and identify the profit-maximizing output.

Quantity	Price	Total Revenue	Marginal Revenue	Marginal Cost	Total Profit
10	$12	$120	$12	$8	$25
11	12			9	
12	12			11	
13	12			12	
14	12			14	

7-5 LONG-RUN EQUILIBRIUM

9. Why does entry eliminate positive economic profits in a perfectly competitive industry?

10. True or False: A situation of zero economic profits is a stable long-run equilibrium situation for a perfectly competitive industry.

7-6 LONG-RUN SUPPLY

11. What must be true about input costs as industry output expands for a constant-cost industry?

12. What must be true about input costs as industry output expands for an increasing-cost industry?

ONE APPROACH.
70 UNIQUE SOLUTIONS.

Richard Branson, the owner of Virgin Atlantic Airlines,

currently has a monopoly on commercial space travel. Book your place in space now and join around 340 Virgin Galactic astronauts who will venture into space. Tickets cost $200,000 and deposits start at $20,000.

Test your Economics *street-smart* knowledge and see how you compare against other students! Scan here or visit CourseMate for Survey of ECON2.

© Europics/News.com

8

Monopoly

Monopoly is at the other end of the spectrum from perfect competition. A pure monopoly is a market with a single seller. Because it is the sole supplier, a monopoly faces the market demand curve for its product.

Consequently, the monopolist has control over the market price—it is a price maker. The monopolist can choose any combination of price and quantity along its market demand curve. But do not confuse ability with incentive. The monopolist, just like the perfectly competitive firm, will maximize profits (or minimize losses) by producing at the output level where $MR = MC$.

A pure monopoly is rare in the real world. But situations in which a few firms compete with each other are quite common. For example, Microsoft's Windows operating system, certain patented prescription drugs, and your cable company are all examples of near monopolies. All of these firms have some monopoly power—control over prices and output.

In this chapter, we will see how a monopolist determines the profit-maximizing price and output. We will also compare monopoly and perfect competition to see which is more efficient. Does the monopoly equilibrium solution lead to higher prices and lower output levels than does the perfectly competitive equilibrium solution? If so, what can the government do about it?

8-1 Monopoly: The Price Maker

SECTION CHECK 1

Keep the following questions in mind as you read through this section.

1. What is a monopoly?
2. Why is pure monopoly rare?
3. What are the sources of monopoly power?
4. What is a natural monopoly?

monopoly the single supplier of a product that has no close substitute

natural monopoly a firm that can produce at a lower cost than a number of smaller firms can

What is a monopoly? A **monopoly** exists when a market consists of only one seller of a product with no close substitute and natural or legal barriers to prevent entry competition. The reason a monopoly is the only firm in the market is because other firms cannot enter—there are barriers to entry. In monopoly, "the firm" and "the industry" are one and the same. Consequently, the firm sets the price of the good, because the firm faces the industry demand curve and can pick the most profitable point on that demand curve. Monopolists are price makers (rather than price takers) that try to pick the price that will maximize their profits.

8-1a PURE MONOPOLY IS A RARITY

Few goods and services truly have only one producer. One might think of a small community with a single bank, a single newspaper, or even a single grocery store. Even in these situations, however, most people can bank out of town, use a substitute financial institution, buy out-of-town newspapers or read them on the Web, go to a nearby town to buy groceries, and so on. Near-monopoly conditions exist, but absolutely pure monopoly is unusual.

One market in which there is typically only one producer of goods and services within an area is public utilities. In any given market, usually only one company provides natural gas or supplies water. Moreover, governments themselves provide many services for which they are often the sole provider, such as sewer services, fire and police protection, and military protection. Most of these situations resemble a pure monopoly. However, for most of these goods and services, substitute goods and services are available. People heating their homes with natural gas can switch to electric heat (or vice versa). In some areas, residents can even substitute home-collected rainwater or well water for what the local water company provides.

Even though the purist may correctly deny the existence of monopoly, the number of situations where monopoly conditions are closely approximated is numerous enough to make the study of monopoly more than a theoretical abstraction; moreover, the study of monopoly is useful in clarifying certain desirable aspects of perfect competition.

8-1b BARRIERS TO ENTRY

A monopolist can use several ways to make it virtually impossible for other firms to overcome barriers to entry.

For example, a monopolist might prevent potential rivals from entering the market by establishing legal barriers, taking advantage of economies of scale, or controlling important inputs.

Legal Barriers

In the case of legal barriers, the government might franchise only one firm to operate an industry, as is the case for postal services in most countries. The government can also provide licensing designed to ensure a certain level of quality and competence. Workers in many trade industries—hair stylists, bartenders, contractors, electricians, and plumbers, for instance—must obtain government licensing.

Also, the government could award patents that encourage inventive activity. It can cost millions of dollars to develop a new drug or computer chip, for example, and without a patent to recoup some of the costs, a company would certainly be less motivated to pursue inventive activity. As long as the patent is in effect, the company has the potential to enjoy monopoly profits for many years. After all, why would a firm engage in costly research if any company could take a free ride on their discovery and produce and sell the new drug or computer chip?

Economies of Scale

The situation in which one large firm can provide the output of the market at a lower cost than two or more smaller firms is called a **natural monopoly**. With a natural monopoly, it is more efficient to have one firm produce the good. The reason for the cost advantage is economies of scale; that is, *ATC* falls as output expands throughout the relevant output range, as seen in Exhibit 8.1. Public utilities, such as water, gas, and

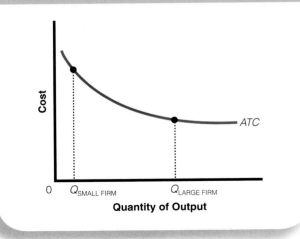

EXHIBIT 8.1 Economies of Scale

© Cengage Learning 2014

electricity, are examples of natural monopoly. It is less costly for one firm to lay down pipes and distribute water than for competing firms to lay down a maze of competing pipes. That is, a single water company can supply the town water more efficiently than a large number of competing firms.

Control Over an Important Input

Another barrier to entry could exist if a firm had control over an important input. For example, from the late nineteenth century to the early 1940s, the Aluminum Company of America (Alcoa) had a monopoly in the production of aluminum. Its monopoly power was guaranteed because of its control over an important ingredient in the production of aluminum—bauxite. Similarly, the De Beers diamond company of South Africa had monopoly power because it controlled roughly 80 percent of the world's output of diamonds.

However, today De Beers accounts for less than 40 percent of diamond production. Increased competition and the discovery of new diamond deposits has finally broken the monopoly in the diamond industry. A number of producers from countries such as Russia, Canada, and Australia chose to start distributing diamonds outside of the De Beers channel, thus effectively ending the monopoly. To keep their share of the market from falling further, De Beers differentiated their diamonds by branding them with a mark only visible under a microscope, and many other diamond firms have followed suit. By branding diamonds, sellers are assuring their customers of the quality of their diamonds and that the customers are not buying "blood" diamonds that have been exported from war-ravaged areas of Africa, where the revenues are used to fund military efforts. De Beers's new strategy has been effective; they are now more profitable today with a 40 percent market share than when they maintained an 80 percent market share.[1]

However, the ownership of key resources is rarely the source of monopoly power. Many goods are traded internationally and resources are owned by many different people around the world. It is uncommon that a firm would control a resource where there was not a close substitute.

[1]Cockburn, A., (2002) Diamonds: The Real Story. *National Geographic*, vol. 201, no. 3, March 2002, pp. 2–35.

SECTION CHECK 1 ANSWERS

1. A pure monopoly exists in a market with only one seller of a product for which no close substitute is available.

2. Pure monopolies are rare because few goods and services have only one existing producer.

3. Sources of monopoly power include legal barriers, economies of scale, and control over important inputs.

4. A natural monopoly occurs when one firm can provide the good or service at a lower cost than two or more smaller firms.

8-2 Demand and Marginal Revenue in Monopoly

SECTION CHECK 2

Keep the following questions in mind as you read through this section.

1. How does the demand curve for a monopolist differ from that for a perfectly competitive firm?

2. Why is marginal revenue less than price in monopoly?

In monopoly, the market demand curve may be regarded as the demand curve for the firm's product because the monopoly firm is the market for that particular product. The demand curve indicates the quantities that the firm can sell at various possible prices. In monopoly, the demand curve for the firm's product declines as additional units are placed on the market—the demand curve is downward sloping. In monopoly, the firm cannot set both its price and the quantity it sells. That is, the monopolist would love to sell a larger quantity at a high price, but cannot. If the monopolist raises the price, the amount sold will fall; if the monopolist lowers the price, the amount sold will rise.

Recall that in perfect competition, many buyers and sellers of homogeneous goods (resulting in a perfectly elastic demand curve) mean that competitive firms can sell all they want at the market price. They face a horizontal demand curve. The firm takes the price of its output as determined by the market forces of supply and demand. Monopolists, and all other firms that are price makers, face a downward-sloping demand curve.

EXHIBIT 8.2 Comparing Demand Curves: Perfect Competition versus Monopoly

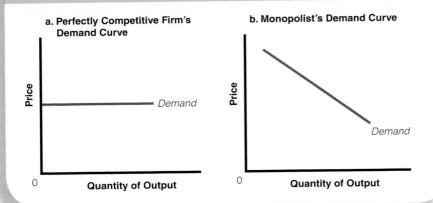

a. Perfectly Competitive Firm's Demand Curve

Price — Demand

0   Quantity of Output

b. Monopolist's Demand Curve

Price

Demand

0   Quantity of Output

If the monopolist raises its price, it will lose some—but not all—of its customers. The two demand curves are displayed side by side in Exhibit 8.2.

In Exhibit 8.3 below, we see the price of the good, the quantity of the good, the *total revenue* (which is the quantity sold times the price [$TR = P \times Q$]), and the average revenue, that is, the amount of revenue the firm receives per unit sold ($AR = TR \div Q$). The average revenue is simply the price per unit sold, which is exactly equal to the market demand curve, and the *marginal revenue (MR)*—the amount of revenue the firm receives from selling an additional unit—is equal to $\Delta TR \div \Delta Q$.

Taking the information from Exhibit 8.3, we can create the demand and marginal revenue curves as seen in Exhibit 8.4. We see that the marginal revenue is always less than the price of the good. To understand why, suppose the firm cuts its price from $4 to $3.

To induce a third daily customer to purchase the good, the firm must cut its price to $3. In doing so, it gains $3 in revenue from the newest customer—the output effect. However, it loses $2 in revenue because each of the first two customers are now paying $1 less than

previously—the price effect. The marginal revenue is $1 ($3 − $2), which is less than the price of the good ($3).

Exhibit 8.4 graphs the relationship between the demand curve and the marginal revenue curve for a monopolist. Because *a monopolist's marginal revenue is always less than the price*, the marginal revenue curve will always lie below the demand curve, as shown in Exhibit 8.4. Recall that in perfect competition, the firm could sell all it wanted at the market price, and the price was equal to marginal revenue. However, in monopoly, if the seller wants to expand output, it will have to lower the price on *all* units; the monopolist receives additional revenue from the new unit sold (the output effect) but will receive less revenue on all the units it was previously selling (the price effect). Thus, when the monopolist cuts the price to attract new customers, the old customers benefit.

In Exhibit 8.5, we can compare marginal revenue for the competitive firm with marginal revenue for the monopolist. The firm in perfect competition can sell another unit of output without lowering its price; hence, the marginal revenue from selling its last unit of output is the market price. However, the monopolist has a downward-sloping demand curve. To sell an extra unit of output, the price falls from P_1 to P_2, and the monopolist loses area c in Exhibit 8.5(b).

It is important to note that even though a monopolist can set its price anywhere it wants, it will not set its price as high as possible—be careful not to confuse ability with incentive. As we will see in the next section, some prices along the demand curve will not be profitable for a firm. In other words, the monopolist can enhance profits by either lowering the price or raising it, depending on the circumstances.

EXHIBIT 8.3 Total, Marginal, and Average Revenue

Price	Quantity	Total Revenue (TR = P × Q)	Average Revenue (AR = TR/Q)	Marginal Revenue (MR = ΔTR/ΔQ)
$6	0	—	—	
				$5
5	1	$5	$5	
				3
4	2	8	4	
				1
3	3	9	3	
				−1
2	4	8	2	
				−3
1	5	5	1	

EXHIBIT 8.4 Demand and Marginal Revenue for the Monopolist

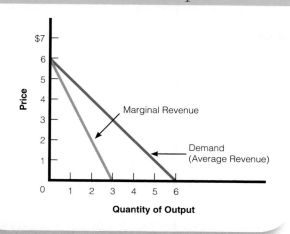

8-2a THE MONOPOLIST'S PRICE IN THE ELASTIC PORTION OF THE DEMAND CURVE

The relationships between the elasticity of demand and the marginal and total revenue are shown in Exhibit 8.6. In Exhibit 8.6(a), elasticity varies along a linear demand curve. Recall from Chapter 4 that above the midpoint, the demand curve is elastic ($E_D > 1$); below the midpoint, it is inelastic ($E_D < 1$); and at the midpoint, it is unit elastic ($E_D = 1$). How does elasticity relate to total and marginal revenue? In the elastic portion of

EXHIBIT 8.6 The Relationship between the Elasticity of Demand and Total and Marginal Revenue

a. Demand and Marginal Revenue

b. Total Revenue

the curve shown in Exhibit 8.6(b), when the price falls, total revenue rises and marginal revenue is positive. In the inelastic region of the demand curve, when the price falls, total revenue falls, and marginal revenue is negative. At the midpoint of the linear demand curve in Exhibit 8.6(b), the total revenue curve reaches its highest point and $MR = 0$.

For example, suppose the price falls on the top half of the demand curve in Exhibit 8.6(a) from $90 to $80; total revenue increases from $90 ($90 × 1) to $160 ($80 × 2), and marginal revenue is positive at $70. Because a reduction in price leads

EXHIBIT 8.5 Marginal Revenue—Competitive Firm versus Monopolist

a. Perfect Competitive Firm's Demand Curve

b. Monopolist's Demand Curve

to an increase in total revenue, the demand curve is elastic in this region. Now suppose the price falls from $20 to $10 on the lower portion of the demand curve; total revenue falls from $160 ($20 × 8) to $90 ($10 × 9), and marginal revenue is negative at −$70. Because a reduction in price leads to a decrease in total revenue, the demand curve is inelastic in this region.

A monopolist will never knowingly operate on the inelastic portion of its demand curve, because increased output will lead to lower total revenue in this region. Not only are total revenues falling, but total costs will rise as the monopolist produces more output. Similarly, if the monopolist were to lower its output, it could increase its total revenue and lower its total costs (because it costs less to produce fewer units), leading to greater economic profits.

DEMAND AND MARGINAL REVENUE

Q&A

Q: Using the concepts of total revenue and marginal revenue, show why marginal revenue is less than price in a monopoly situation. Suppose a monopolist wants to expand output from one unit to two units. To sell two units rather than one, the monopolist must lower its price from $10 to $8, as shown in Exhibit 8.7. Will the marginal revenue be less than the price?

A: In Exhibit 8.7, we see that to sell two units, the monopolist will have to lower the price on both units to $8. That is, the seller doesn't receive $10 for unit one and $8 for unit two but receives $8 for both units. Therefore, what happens to marginal revenue? This answer involves two parts: First, a loss in revenue, $2, occurs from selling the first unit at $8 instead of $10. Second, the gain in revenue

from the additional output—the second unit—is $8. Thus, the marginal revenue is $6 ($8 − $2), which is less than the price of the good, $8. The monopolist's marginal revenue will always be less than the price of the downward-sloping demand curve.

SOURCE: From SEXTON, Exploring Economics, 6E. © 2013 Cengage Learning.

EXHIBIT 8.7 The Demand and Marginal Revenue Curve

Price	Quantity	Total Revenue	Marginal Revenue
$10	1	$10	
8	2	16	$6
6	3	18	2

© Cengage Learning 2014

© iStockphoto.com/mattjeacock

8-3 The Monopolist's Equilibrium

Keep the following questions in mind as you read through this section.

1. How does the monopolist decide what output to produce?

2. How does the monopolist decide what price to charge?

3. How do we know whether the monopolist is making a profit or incurring a loss?

4. Can the monopolist's economic profits last into the long run?

So how does the monopolist determine the profit-maximizing output? In the preceding section, we saw how a monopolist could choose any point along a demand curve. However, the monopolist's decision as to what level of output to produce depends on more than the marginal revenue derived at various outputs. The firm faces production costs; and the monopolist, like the perfect competitor, will maximize profits at that output where $MR = MC$. This point is demonstrated graphically in Exhibit 8.8.

As you can see in Exhibit 8.8, at output level Q_1, the marginal revenue exceeds the marginal cost of production, so it is profitable for the monopolist to expand output. Profits continue to grow until output Q_M is reached. Beyond that output, say at Q_2, the

marginal cost of production exceeds the marginal revenue from production, so profits decline. The monopolist should cut production back to Q_M. Therefore, the equilibrium output is Q_M. At this output, marginal cost and marginal revenue are equal.

> The monopolist's three-step method
> —Find the profit-maximizing output level.
> —Find total revenue at the profit-maximizing output level.
> —Find total cost.

8-3a THE THREE-STEP METHOD FOR THE MONOPOLIST

Let us return to the three-step method we used in Chapter 7. Determining whether a firm is generating positive economic profits, economic losses, or zero economic profits at the profit-maximizing level of output, Q_M, can be done in three easy steps.

1. Find where marginal revenue equals marginal cost and proceed straight down to the horizontal (quantity) axis to find Q_M, the profit-maximizing output level for the monopolist.

2. At Q_M, go straight up to the demand curve and then to the left to find the market price, P_M. Once you have identified P_M and Q_M, you can find total revenue at the profit-maximizing output level, because $TR = P \times Q$.

3. The last step is to find total cost. Again, go straight up from Q_M to the average total cost (ATC) curve and then left to the vertical axis to compute the average total cost at Q_M. If we multiply average total cost by the output level, we can find the total cost ($TC = ATC \times Q$).

8-3b PROFITS FOR THE MONOPOLIST

Exhibit 8.8 does not show what profits, if any, the monopolist is actually making. This missing information is found in Exhibit 8.9 on the next page which shows the equilibrium position for a monopolist, this time adding an average total cost (ATC) curve. As we just discussed, the firm produces where $MC = MR$, at output Q_M. At output Q_M (100) and price P_M ($6) the firm's total revenue is equal to DAQ_M0, which is $P_M \times Q_M$ ($600). At output Q_M, the firm's total cost is CBQ_M0, which is $ATC \times Q_M$ ($400). In Exhibit 8.9, we see that total revenue is greater than total cost, so the firm has a total profit of area DABC. Or, $P_M - ATC$

EXHIBIT 8.8 Equilibrium Output and Price for a Monopolist

Lost total profits from producing too little output; $MR > MC$

Marginal Cost

The demand curve shows the price, P_M, consistent with the profit-maximizing output, Q_M

$MR = MC$ determines the profit-maximizing output, Q_M

Marginal Revenue

Lost total profits from producing too much output; $MC > MR$

Price

P_M

0 Q_1 Q_M Q_2

Quantity

D

© Cengage Learning 2014

© iStockphoto.com/subjug

EXHIBIT 8.9 A Monopolist's Profits

© Cengage Learning 2014

EXHIBIT 8.10 A Monopolist's Losses

© Cengage Learning 2014

(price minus average total cost) is the per-unit profit, $2. The width of the box (segment CB) is the quantity sold (0 to Q_M), 100 units. Hence, the area of the box is the monopoly firm's total profit, $200 (per-unit profit × quantity sold).

In perfect competition, profits in an economic sense will persist only in the short run. In the long run, new firms will enter the industry and increase industry supply, thereby driving down the price of the good and eliminating profits. In monopoly, however, profits are not eliminated, because one of the conditions for monopoly is that barriers to entry exist. Other firms cannot enter, so economic profits persist in the long run.

8-3c LOSSES FOR THE MONOPOLIST

It is easy to imagine a monopolist ripping off consumers by charging prices that result in long-run economic profits. However, many companies with monopoly power have gone out of business. Imagine that you received a patent on a bad idea such as a roof ejection seat for a helicopter, or that you had the sole rights to turn an economics textbook into a screenplay for a motion picture. Although you may be the sole supplier of a product, you are not guaranteed that consumers will demand your product. Even without a close substitute for your product, you will always face competition for the consumer dollar, and other goods may provide greater satisfaction.

Exhibit 8.10 illustrates loss in a monopoly situation. In this graph, notice that the demand curve is below the average total cost curve. In this case, the monopolist will incur a loss because of insufficient

demand to cover the average total cost at any price and output combination along the demand curve. At Q_M, total cost, CBQ_M0, is greater than total revenue, DAQ_M0, so the firm incurs a total loss of CBAD. Or, total revenue is $600 ($P_M \times Q_M = \$6 \times 100$) and total cost is $700 ($ATC \times Q_M = \$7 \times 100$), for an economic loss of $100. Notice that the total revenue is great enough to cover the variable costs of $400 ($TVC = \$4 \times 100$). That is, the firm can reduce its losses by operating rather than shutting down in the short run. However, in monopoly as in perfect competition, a firm will go out of business in the long run if it cannot generate enough revenue to cover its total costs.

In summary, if total revenue is greater than total cost at Q_M, the firm generates a total economic profit; and if total revenue is less than total cost at Q_M, the firm generates a total economic loss. If total revenue is equal to total cost at Q_M, the firm earns zero economic profit. Remember, the cost curves include implicit and explicit costs, so in this case, the monopolist is covering the total opportunity costs of its resources and earning a normal profit or rate of return.

8-3d PATENTS

Governments confer one form of monopoly power through patents and copyrights. A patent puts the government's police power behind the patent-holder's exclusive right to make a product for a specified period (up to 20 years) without anyone else being able to make an identical product. As Exhibit 8.11 suggests, the patent gives the supplier at least temporary monopoly power over that good or service. The firm with the patent can then price its product well above marginal

EXHIBIT 8.11 Impact of Patent Protection on Equilibrium Price and Quantity

© Cengage Learning 2014

costs, at P_M. Notice that the marginal cost curve is flat. The reason is that most of the cost of many products under patent, such as prescription drugs, is in the development stage. Once the drug is available for the market, the marginal costs are close to constant (flat). When the patent expires, the price of the patented good or service usually falls substantially with the entry of competing firms into the market. The price will fall toward the perfectly competitive price P_{PC}, and the output will increase toward Q_{PC}. However, if the company's patent expires, it does not lose all of its monopoly power. Some of its loyal customers will continue to pay slightly more than

© iStockphoto.com/Alan Crawford

Some drugs cost millions of dollars for research and development. Without the protection of a patent, the firm might not have been able to make profits from its inventive activity for very long, which is why the government issues patents that last up to 20 years. However, after the patent expires, many popular drugs lose their protection and prices can then fall by 30 percent or more.

the competitive price because of their concern that the generic product is not a perfect substitute for the drug they had been taking for years.

Why does the government give inventors this limited monopoly power, raising the prices of pharmaceutical drugs and other "vital" goods? The rationale is simple. Without patents, inventors would have little incentive to incur millions of dollars in research and development expenses to create new products (e.g., lifesaving drugs), because others could immediately copy the idea and manufacture the products without incurring the research expenses. Similarly, copyrights stimulate creative activity of other kinds, giving writers the incentive to write books that earn royalties and are not merely copied for free. The enormous number of computer programs written for home computers reflects the fact that program writers receive royalties from the sale of each copy sold; that is why they and the firms they work for vehemently oppose unauthorized copying of their work.

SECTION CHECK 3 ANSWERS

1. The monopolist, like the perfect competitor, maximizes profits at that output where marginal revenue equals marginal cost.

2. The monopolist sets the price according to the demand for the product at the profit-maximizing output.

3. Monopoly profits can be found by comparing the price per unit and average total cost per unit at Q^*. If $P > ATC$, a firm realizes economic profits. If $P < ATC$, it has economic losses.

4. Monopolists' profits can last into the long run because of a monopoly's barriers to entry.

8-4 Monopoly and Welfare Loss

SECTION CHECK 4

Keep the following questions in mind as you read through this section.

1. How does monopoly lead to inefficiencies?

2. What is the welfare loss in monopoly?

3. Does monopoly retard innovation?

Is monopoly a good or bad thing? In this section, we will consider various arguments as to the effects a monopoly might have on the market.

8-4a DOES MONOPOLY PROMOTE INEFFICIENCY?

Monopoly is often considered to be bad. Two main objections form the basis for concerns about the establishment of monopoly power. First, on equity grounds, many people feel that it is not "fair" for monopoly owners to have persistent economic profits when they work no harder than other firms. However, to most economists, the more serious objection is that monopolies result in market inefficiencies. That is, monopoly leads to a lower output and higher prices than would exist under perfect competition. Exhibit 8.12 demonstrates why. In monopoly, the firm produces output Q_M and charges price P_M. Suppose, however, that perfect competition exists and the industry is characterized by many small firms that could produce output with the same efficiency (at the same cost) as one large firm. Then the marginal cost curve shown in Exhibit 8.12 is the sum of all the individual marginal cost curves of the individual firms, which is the industry supply curve.

In the perfectly competitive market, the equilibrium price and quantity would be determined where the marginal cost (or supply) curve intersects with the demand curve, at output Q_{PC} and price P_{PC}. Thus, the competitive equilibrium solution provides for more output and lower prices than the solution prevailing in monopoly, which leads to the major efficiency objection to monopoly: Monopolists charge higher prices and produce less output. This situation may also be viewed as "unfair," in that consumers are burdened more than under the alternative competitive arrangement.

Welfare Loss in Monopoly

In addition to the monopolist producing lower levels of output at higher prices, notice that the monopolist produces at an output where the price (P_M) is greater than the marginal cost (MC_M). Because $P > MC$, the value to society from the last unit produced is greater than its costs (MC_M). That is, the monopoly is not producing enough of the good from society's perspective. We call the area c + e in Exhibit 8.12 the welfare or deadweight loss due to monopoly. In perfect competition, the equilibrium is P_{PC} and the equilibrium quantity is Q_{PC}. Consumer surplus is area a + b + c, and the product surplus is area d + e + f. In monopoly, the equilibrium price is higher at P_M and the equilibrium

EXHIBIT 8.12 Perfect Competition versus Monopoly

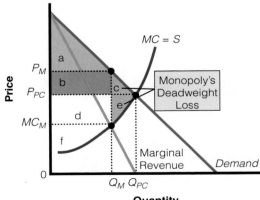

	Perfect Competition	Monopoly	Change
Consumer Surplus	a + b + c	a	– b – c
Producer Surplus	d + e + f	b + d + f	b – e
Welfare	a + b + c + d + e + f	a + b + d + f	– c – e

© Cengage Learning 2014

quantity is lower at Q_M. Under monopoly, consumer surplus is area a, producer surplus is area b + d + f, and lost welfare or the deadweight loss of monopoly is c + e.

The actual amount of the welfare loss in monopoly is of considerable debate among economists. Estimates vary from between one-tenth of 1 percent to 6 percent of national income. The variation depends on the researchers' estimates of elasticity of demand, whether firm or industry data were used, whether adjustments for profits were made (for the inclusion of royalties and intangibles), and whether the researcher included some proxy for scarce resources used in attempting to create the monopoly.

8-4b DOES MONOPOLY RETARD INNOVATION?

Another argument against monopoly is that a lack of competition tends to retard technological advancement. Monopolists become comfortable reaping their monopolistic profits, so they do not work hard at product improvement, technical advances designed to promote efficiency, and so forth. The American railroad is sometimes cited as an example of this situation. Early in the last century, railroads had strong monopoly power, but they did not spend much on research or development; they did not aggressively try to improve rail transport. Consequently, technical advances in substitute modes of transportation—such as cars, trucks, and airplanes—led to a loss of monopoly power for the railroads.

However, the notion that monopoly retards all innovation can be disputed. Many near-monopolists are, in fact, important innovators. Companies such as Microsoft, International Business Machines (IBM), Polaroid, and Xerox have all, at one time or another, had strong market positions, in some instances approaching monopoly secured by patent protection, but they were also important innovators. Indeed, innovation helps firms initially obtain a degree of monopoly status, because patents can give a monopoly to new products and/or cost-saving technology. Even the monopolist wants more profits, and any innovation that lowers costs or expands revenues creates profits for the monopolist. In addition, because patents expire, a monopolist may be expected to innovate in order to obtain additional patents and preserve its monopoly power. Therefore, the incentive to innovate might well exist in monopolistic market structures.

8-5 Monopoly Policy

Because monopolies pose certain problems with respect to efficiency, equity, and power, the public, through its governments, must decide how to deal with the phenomenon. Two major approaches to dealing with such problems are commonly employed: antitrust policies and regulation. It should be pointed out that in these discussions, the word *monopoly* is sometimes used in a loose, general sense to refer to imperfectly competitive markets, not just to "pure" monopoly.

8-5a ANTITRUST POLICIES

Perhaps the most obvious way to deal with monopoly is to make it illegal. The government can bring civil lawsuits or even criminal actions against businesspeople or corporations engaged in monopolistic practices. By imposing costs on monopolists that can be either monetary or nonmonetary (such as the fear of lawsuits or even jail sentences), antitrust policies reduce the profitability of monopoly.

The Compromise: Average Cost Pricing

A compromise between monopoly pricing and marginal cost pricing is found at point B in Exhibit 8.13, at output Q_{AC}, which is somewhere between the excessively low output and high prices of an unregulated monopoly and the excessively high output and low prices achieved when prices are equated with marginal cost pricing. At point B, price equals average total cost. The monopolist is permitted to price the product where economic profit is zero, earning a normal economic profit or rate of return, such as firms experience in perfect competition in the long run. This compromise is called **average cost pricing**.

In the real world, regulators often permit utilities to receive a "fair and reasonable" return that is a rough approximation to that suggested by average cost pricing, at point B. Point B would seem "fair" in that the monopolist is receiving rewards equal to those that a perfect competitor would ordinarily receive—no more, no less. Point B permits more output at a significantly lower price than is possible at point A, where the monopolist is unregulated, even though output is still somewhat less and price somewhat more than that suggested by point C, the socially optimum or best position.

8-5e DIFFICULTIES IN AVERAGE COST PRICING

Several difficulties arise in trying to implement an average cost pricing strategy. These include inaccuracies in cost calculations, a lack of incentives to keep costs down, and the influence of special interest groups.

Inaccurate Calculations of Costs

The actual implementation of a rate (price) that permits a "fair and reasonable" return is more difficult than the analysis suggests. The calculations of costs and values are difficult. In reality, the firm may not know exactly what its demand and cost curves look like, which forces regulatory agencies to use profits, another somewhat ambiguous target, as a guide. If profits are "too high," lower the price; if profits are "too low," raise the price. In addition, what if the regulated firm has more information than the regulators about its firm, workers, and technology (asymmetric information)? If the firm can persuade regulators that its average cost is higher than it actually is, the regulated price could be set higher, closer to the monopoly price.

No Incentives to Keep Costs Down

Another problem is that average cost pricing offers the monopolist no incentive to reduce costs. That is, if the firm's costs rise from ATC_1 to ATC_2 as shown in Exhibit 8.14, the price will rise from P_1 to P_2. If costs fall, the firm's price will fall. In either scenario, the firm will still be earning a normal rate of return. In other words, if the regulatory agency sets the price at any point where the ATC curve intersects the demand curve, the firm will earn a normal rate of return. Thus, if the agency is going to set the price wherever ATC intersects the demand curve, the firm might just think, "Why not let average costs rise? Why not let employees fly first class and dine in the finest restaurants? Why not buy concert tickets and season tickets to sporting events?" And if the regulated monopolist knows that the regulators will reduce prices if costs fall, the regulated monopolist does not benefit from lower costs. Regulators have tackled this problem by allowing the regulated firm to keep some of the profits that come from lower costs; that is, they do not adhere strictly to average cost pricing.

Special-Interest Groups

In the real world, consumer groups are constantly battling for lower utility rates, while the utility companies themselves are lobbying for higher rates so they can approach the monopoly profits indicated by point A in Exhibit 8.13, Decisions are not always made in a calm, objective, dispassionate atmosphere free from outside involvement. It is precisely the political economy of rate setting that disturbs some critics of this approach to dealing with the monopoly problem. For example, a rate-making commissioner could become friendly with a utility company, believing that he could obtain a nice job after his tenure as a regulator expires. The temptation would be great for the commissioner to be generous to the utility company.

EXHIBIT 8.14 Changes in Average Costs

© Cengage Learning 2014

On the other hand, the tendency might be for regulators to bow to pressure from consumer groups. A politician who wants to win votes can almost always succeed by attacking utility rates and promising rate "reform" (lower rates). If zealous rate regulators listen too closely to consumer groups and push rates down to a level indicated by point C in Exhibit 8.13, the industry might be too unstable to attract capital for expansion.

In recent years, we have seen a trend away from regulation toward competition; for example, after AT&T was broken up by the courts in 1982, the long-distance market became very competitive, and local telephone service is much more competitive now than in the past. Technological advances now allow us to separate the production of electric power or natural gas from the distributor, which will ultimately lead to greater competition in these markets. Some states have already started to deregulate the electricity market.

SECTION CHECK 5 ANSWERS

1. Antitrust policies are government policies to reduce the profitability of a monopoly and push production closer to the social optimum.

2. Under government regulation, a monopolist might be allowed to continue operation but with certain price limits imposed on it.

3. Average cost pricing sets price equal to average total cost, where the demand curve intersects average total costs.

8-6 Price Discrimination

SECTION CHECK 6

Keep the following questions in mind as you read through this section.

1. What is price discrimination?

2. Why does price discrimination exist?

3. Does price discrimination work when reselling is easy?

Sometimes sellers will charge different customers different prices for the same good or service when the cost of providing that good or service does not differ among customers. This practice is called **price discrimination**. Under certain conditions, the monopolist finds it profitable to discriminate among various buyers, charging higher prices to those who are more willing to pay and lower prices to those who are less willing to pay.

8-6a CONDITIONS FOR PRICE DISCRIMINATION

The ability to practice price discrimination is not available to all sellers. To practice price discrimination, the three conditions listed below must hold.

PRICE DISCRIMINATION OVER TIME

Q&A

Q: Why do people pay a lot more for a hardcover book than a paperback book?

You can find the answer on the next page.

cork board: © iStockphoto.com/mattjeacock; Books: © DAVID GRAY/Reuters/Landov

Market Power

Price discrimination is possible only with market power. A monopoly, an oligopoly, a monopolistically competitive firm, or a cartel may be able to price discriminate. In cases with a large number of competing firms, discrimination is less likely because competitors tend to undercut the high prices charged by the firms that are engaging in price discrimination.

Market Segregation

Price discrimination can only occur if the demand curves for markets, groups, or individuals are different. If the demand curves are not different, a profit-maximizing monopolist would charge the same price in both markets. Price discrimination requires the ability to separate customers according to their willingness to pay. That is, consumers must differ in their sensitivity to price (elasticity of demand) and firms must be able to identify how consumers differ in their sensitivities to price.

No Resale

For price discrimination to work, the person buying the product at a discount must have difficulty in reselling the product to customers being charged more.

Otherwise, those getting the items cheaply would want to buy extra amounts of the product at the discounted price and sell it at a profit to others. Price differentials between groups erode if reselling is easy.

8-6b WHY DOES PRICE DISCRIMINATION EXIST?

Price discrimination results from the profit-maximization motive. Our graphical analysis of monopoly described the demand curve for the product and the corresponding marginal revenue curve. Sometimes, however, different groups of people have different demand curves and therefore react differently to price changes. A producer can make more money by charging these different buyers different prices. For example, if the price of a movie ticket is increased from $7 to $10, many kids who would attend at $7 may have to stay home at $10, as they (and perhaps their parents) balk at paying the higher price. The impact of raising prices on attendance may be less, however, for adults, who have higher incomes in the first place and for whom the ticket price may represent a smaller part of the expenses of an evening out.

Thus, a different demand curve applies for those, say, under 2, as opposed to those who are older.

PRICE DISCRIMINATION OVER TIME

Q&A

A: Sometimes firms engage in price discrimination over time to increase their profits. Although a hardcover book is only slightly more expensive to publish, the real reason for the price differential between hardcover and paperback books is the price elasticity of demand. Some people are willing to pay a higher price to be among the first to read a book; the demand curve is relatively inelastic for these devoted fans. Other individuals have a more elastic demand curve for these goods and are willing to wait for the book to come out in paperback. Other customers, such as libraries, find that paperbacks are not durable enough to be good substitutes for hardbacks. Sellers are able to profit from this difference in elasticities of demand by charging more to those who are more willing to pay and charging a lower price to those who are less willing to pay. Thus, book publishers are able to profit.

Specifically, the elasticity of demand with respect to price is greater for children than for adults, meaning that the demand and marginal revenue curves for children are different from the curves for adults. Assume, for simplicity, that the marginal cost is constant. The profit-maximizing movie theater owner will price where the constant marginal costs equal marginal revenue for each group. As you can see in Exhibit 8.15(a), the demand curve for children is relatively elastic—firms will charge these customers a lower price. The adult demand curve, shown in Exhibit 8.15(b), is less elastic; firms will charge adult customers a higher price. But in order for price discrimination to be feasible, the seller must be able to successfully distinguish members of targeted groups.

8-6c EXAMPLES OF PRICE DISCRIMINATION

Other examples of price discrimination in the United States are plentiful. Here are just a few.

Airline Tickets

Seats on airplanes usually go for different prices. Airlines sell high-priced, no-strings-attached fares, and they sell restricted fares—tickets that require Saturday night layovers or must be purchased weeks in advance. This airline pricing strategy allows the airlines to discriminate against business travelers, who usually have little advance warning, travel on the weekdays, and are not as willing to spend their weekends away from home and family. Because business travelers have a high willingness to pay (a relatively inelastic demand curve), the airlines can charge them

higher prices. If the airlines were to cut prices for these clients, their revenues would fall. On the other hand, the personal traveler (perhaps a vacationer) can choose among many substitutes, such as other modes of transportation and different times. In short, the personal traveler has a lower willingness to pay (a relatively elastic demand curve). Thus, the airlines can clearly make more money by charging a higher price to those who have a higher willingness to pay (less elastic demand) and a lower price to those who have a lower willingness to pay (more elastic demand)—those who are willing to book in advance and stay over on Saturday nights. If the airlines charged a higher single price to everyone, those with a lower willingness to pay would not travel; if they charged a lower single price to everyone, they would lose profits by receiving less revenue from those who were willing to pay more.

Coupons

The key to price discrimination is observing the difference in demand curves for different customers. The coupon cutter, who spends an hour looking through the Sunday paper for coupons, will probably have a relatively more elastic demand curve than, say, a busy and wealthy physician or executive. Consequently, firms charge a lower price to customers with a lower willingness to pay (more elastic demand)—the coupon cutter—and a higher price to those who do not use coupons (less elastic demand).

College and University Tuition

Another example of price discrimination is the financial aid packages given by many colleges and universities. That is, even though colleges do not charge different tuitions to different students, they do offer different financial aid packages. Furthermore, to receive financial aid, parents must disclose their family income and wealth. In short, students who are well off financially tend to pay more for their education than do students who are less well off.

EXHIBIT 8.15 Price Discrimination in Movie Ticket Prices

a. Demand Curve for Children

b. Demand Curve for Adults

© Cengage Learning 2014

You can go to a TKTS booth on the day of a Broadway play and often get a substantial discount on theater tickets. This is a form of price discrimination where once producers know how many empty seats they have, they offer discounts to fill the rest. Once the show starts, an empty seat brings in no revenue. By offering tickets at a heavy discount to those who are willing to wait in line, the theatre is able to increase attendance and raise revenue.

Quantity Discounts

Another form of price discrimination occurs when customers buy in large quantities, as with public utilities and wholesalers. But even stores will sell a six-pack of soda for less than six single cans. For example, the local bagel shop might sell you a baker's dozen, where you get 13 bagels for the price of 12. This type of price discrimination allows the producer to charge a higher price for the first unit than for, say, the 20th. This form of price discrimination is effective because a buyer's willingness to pay declines as additional units are purchased.

SECTION CHECK 6 ANSWERS

1. When producers charge different prices for the same good or service when no cost difference exists, it is called price discrimination.

2. Price discrimination occurs if demand differs among buyers and the seller can successfully identify group members, because producers can make profits by charging different prices to each group.

3. Price discrimination would not work well if the person buying the product could easily resell the product to another customer at a higher profitable price.

Chapter 8: Self-Review

Now that you are finished reading the chapter, review the questions below. You can write your answers in the space provided, then go online to see the answers at www.cengagebrain.com.

8-1 MONOPOLY: THE PRICE MAKER

1. Why does monopoly depend on the existence of barriers to entry?

2. Why is a pure monopoly a rarity?

3. Which of the following could be considered a monopoly?
   a. Kate Hudson (an actress)
   b. De Beers diamond company
   c. the only doctor in a small town
   d. Ford Motor Company

8-2 DEMAND AND MARGINAL REVENUE IN MONOPOLY

4. Fill-in-the-Blank: The market and firm demand curves are _____ for a monopolist.

5. Why is a monopoly a price maker, but a perfectly competitive firm a price taker?

6. True or False: Marginal revenue is less than price for a profit-maximizing monopolist.

8-3 THE MONOPOLIST'S EQUILIBRIUM

7. How do you find the profit-maximizing price for a monopolist?

8. True or False: A monopolist cannot earn positive economic profits in the long run.

8-4 MONOPOLY AND WELFARE LOSS

9. How is the welfare cost of monopoly measured?

10. How can economies of scale lead to monopoly?

8-5 MONOPOLY POLICY

11. True or False: Antitrust laws promote greater price competition.

12. What are some difficulties encountered when regulators try to implement average cost pricing for natural monopolies?

8-6 PRICE DISCRIMINATION

13. Why is it generally easier to price discriminate for services than for goods?

14. How can offering quantity discounts increase a producer's profits?

What kind of market do you think

the coffee market is in which McDonald's and Starbucks compete? Obviously these firms are not the only coffee sellers out there. And McDonald's had little difficulty getting into the market when it introduced its new McCafé coffee line. Sounds like a competitive market, right? But are they really selling the same product? Think about their prices. And what about the atmosphere of their stores? Do you associate the same ideas with their different brands? Perhaps this market does not quite fit the perfectly competitive mold.

Test your Economics *street-smart* knowledge and see how you compare against other students! Scan here or visit CourseMate for Survey of ECON2.

9

Monopolistic Competition and Oligopoly

Restaurants, clothing stores, beauty salons, video stores, hardware stores, and coffee houses have elements of both competitive and monopoly markets. Recall that the perfectly competitive model includes many buyers and sellers; coffee houses can be found in almost every town in the country. You can even find Starbucks in Barnes & Noble bookstores and in grocery stores. In addition, the barriers to entry of owning an individual coffee shop are relatively low. However, monopolistically competitive firms sell a differentiated product and thus each firm has an element of monopoly power. Each coffee store is different. It might be different because of its location or décor. It might be different because of its products. It might be different because of the service it provides. Monopolistically competitive markets are common in the real world. They are the topic of this chapter.

9-1 Monopolistic Competition

SECTION CHECK 1

Keep the following questions in mind as you read through this section.

1. What are the distinguishing features of monopolistic competition?

2. How can a firm differentiate its product?

Monopolistic competition is a market structure in which many producers of somewhat different products compete with one another. For example, a restaurant is a monopoly in the sense that it has a unique name, menu, quality of service, location, and so on; but it also has many competitors—others selling prepared meals. That is, monopolistic competition has features in common with both monopoly and perfect competition, even though

monopolistic competition a market structure with many firms selling differentiated products this explanation may sound like an oxymoron—like "jumbo shrimp" or "civil war." As with monopoly, individual sellers in monopolistic competition believe that they have some market power. But monopolistic competition is probably closer to competition than monopoly. Entry into and exit out of the industry is unrestricted, and consequently, the industry has many independent sellers. By virtue of the relatively free entry of new firms, the long-run price and output behavior, and zero long-run economic profits, monopolistic competition is similar to perfect competition. However, the monopolistically competitive firm produces a product that is different (that is, *differentiated* rather than identical or homogeneous) from others, which leads to some degree of monopoly power. In a sense, sellers in a monopolistically competitive market may be regarded as "monopolists" of their own particular brands; but unlike firms with a true monopoly, competition occurs among the many firms selling similar (but not identical) brands. For example, a buyer living in a city of moderate size and in the market for books, CDs, toothpaste, furniture, shampoo, video rentals, restaurants, eyeglasses, running shoes, movie theaters, supermarkets, and music lessons has many competing sellers from which to choose.

9-1a THE THREE BASIC CHARACTERISTICS OF MONOPOLISTIC COMPETITION

The theory of monopolistic competition is based on three characteristics: (1) product differentiation, (2) many sellers, and (3) free entry.

Product Differentiation

One characteristic of monopolistic competition is **product differentiation**—the accentuation of unique product qualities, real or perceived, to develop a specific product identity.

The significant feature of differentiation is the buyer's belief that various sellers' products are not the same, whether the products are actually different or not. Aspirin and some brands of over-the-counter cold medicines are examples of products that are similar or identical but have different brand names. Product differentiation leads to preferences among buyers dealing with or purchasing the products of particular sellers.

product differentiation
goods or services that are slightly different, or perceived to be different, from one another

Characteristics of Monopolistic Competition
1) product differentiation
2) many sellers
3) free entry

© iStockphoto.com/subjug

Physical Differences Physical differences constitute a primary source of product differentiation. For example, brands of ice cream (such as Dreyer's and Breyers), running shoes (such as Nike and Asics), or fast-food Mexican restaurants (such as Taco Bell and Del Taco) differ significantly in taste to many buyers.

Prestige Prestige considerations also differentiate products to a significant degree. Many people prefer to be seen using the currently popular brand, while others prefer the "off" brand. Prestige considerations are particularly important with gifts—Cuban cigars, Montblanc pens, beluga caviar, Godiva chocolates, Dom Perignon champagne, Rolex watches, and so on.

Location Location is a major differentiating factor in retailing. Shoppers are not willing to travel long distances to purchase similar items, which is one reason for the large number of convenience stores and service station mini-marts. Most buyers realize brands of gasoline do not differ significantly, which means the location of a gas station might influence their choice of gasoline. Location is also important for restaurants. Some restaurants can differentiate their products with beautiful views of the city lights, ocean, or mountains.

Service Service considerations are likewise significant for product differentiation. Speedy and friendly service or lenient return policies are important to many people. Likewise, speed and quality of service may significantly influence a person's choice of restaurants.

The Impact of Many Sellers

When many firms compete for the same customers, any particular firm has little control over or interest in what other firms do. That is, a restaurant may change prices or improve service without a retaliatory move on the part of other competing restaurants, because the time and effort necessary to learn about such changes may have marginal costs that are greater than the marginal benefits.

The Significance of Free Entry

Entry in monopolistic competition is relatively unrestricted in the sense that new firms may easily start the production of close substitutes for existing products, as happens with restaurants, styling salons, barber shops, and many forms of retail activity. Because of relatively free entry, economic profits tend to be eliminated in the long run, as is the case with perfect competition.

9-2 Price and Output Determination in Monopolistic Competition

SECTION CHECK 2

Keep the following questions in mind as you read through this section.

1. How are short-run economic profits and losses determined?

2. How is long-run equilibrium determined?

In this section we will discuss the factors that determine price and output in monopolistic competition. We will begin by looking at short-run equilibrium.

9-2a DETERMINING SHORT-RUN EQUILIBRIUM

Because monopolistically competitive sellers are price makers rather than price takers, they do not regard price as a given by market conditions as perfectly competitive firms do.

The cost and revenue curves of a typical seller are shown in Exhibit 9.1; the intersection of the marginal revenue and marginal cost curves indicates that the short-run profit-maximizing output will be q^*. Now, by observing how much will be demanded at that output level, we find our profit-maximizing price, P^*. That is, at the equilibrium quantity, q^*, we go vertically to the demand curve and read the corresponding price on the vertical axis, P^*.

Three-Step Method for Monopolistic Competition

Let us return to the same three-step method we used in Chapters 7 and 8. Determining whether a firm is generating economic profits, economic losses, or zero economic profits at the profit-maximizing level of output, q^*, can be done in three easy steps.

1. Find where marginal revenues equal marginal costs and proceed straight down to the horizontal quantity axis to find q^*, the profit-maximizing output level.

2. At q^*, go straight up to the demand curve then to the left to find the market price, P^*. Once you have identified P^* and q^*, you can find total revenue at the profit-maximizing output level, because $TR = P \times q$.

EXHIBIT 9.1 Short-Run Equilibrium in Monopolistic Competition

a. Determining Profits

(Profit-Maximizing Output)
Quantity

b. Determining Losses

(Loss-Minimizing Output)
Quantity

© Cengage Learning 2014

3. The last step is to find total costs. Again, go straight up from q^* to the average total cost (ATC) curve and then left to the vertical axis to compute the average total cost *per unit*. If we multiply average total costs by the output level, we can find the total costs ($TC = ATC \times q$).

If total revenue is greater than total costs at q^*, the firm is generating total economic profits. And if total revenue is less than total costs at q^*, the firm is generating total economic losses.

Or, if we take the product price at P^* and subtract the average cost at q^*, this will give us per-unit profit. If we multiply this by output, we will arrive at total economic profit, that is, $(P^* - ATC) \times q^* =$ total profit.

Remember, the cost curves include implicit and explicit costs—that is, even at zero economic profits the firm is covering the total opportunity costs of its resources and earning a normal profit or rate of return.

9-2b SHORT-RUN PROFITS AND LOSSES IN MONOPOLISTIC COMPETITION

Exhibit 9.1(a) shows the equilibrium position of a monopolistically competitive firm. As we just discussed, the firm produces where $MC = MR$, or output q^*. At output q^* and price P^*, the firm's total revenue is equal to $P^* \times q^*$, or $800. At output q^*, the firm's total cost is $ATC \times q^*$, or $700. In Exhibit 9.1(a), we see that total revenue is greater than total cost so the firm has a total economic profit. That is, $TR - TC$ ($800 - $700) or $P^* - ATC \times q^*$ ([$8 - $7] \times 100$) = total economic profit ($100).

In Exhibit 9.1(b), at q^*, price is below average total cost, so the firm is minimizing its economic loss. At q^*, total cost ($800) is greater than total revenue ($700). So the firm incurs a total loss ($100) or $(P^* - ATC) \times q^*$ = total economic losses ([$7 - $8] \times 100 = -$100$).

9-2c DETERMINING LONG-RUN EQUILIBRIUM

The short-run equilibrium situation, whether involving profits or losses, will probably not last long, because entry and exit occur in the long run. If market entry and exit are sufficiently free, new firms will have an incentive to enter the market when there are economic profits, and exit when there are economic losses.

EXHIBIT 9.2 Long-Run Equilibrium for a Monopolistically Competitive Firm

© Cengage Learning 2014

9-2d ACHIEVING LONG-RUN EQUILIBRIUM

The process of entry and exit will continue until all firms in the industry are making zero economic profits. When the market reaches this long-run equilibrium, no firms have an incentive to enter or exit.

Once entry and exit have driven profits to zero, the demand curve and average total cost curve will

Costco's liberal return policy is legendary and differentiates its product from many others. Internet stories include attempts to return 10-year-old ping-pong tables and a woman who kept bringing back her fresh-cut flowers because they would lose their color after two weeks. Costco did have to change its return policy for electronics because customers would repeatedly turn in computers or televisions and upgrade to newer models—sometimes getting a better and less expensive television or computer.

© iStockphoto.com/slobo

be tangent to each other, as seen in Exhibit 9.2. At the profit-maximizing output level, q^*, the firm earns zero economic profits.

In short, the monopolistically competitive producers are a lot like monopolists; they face a downward-sloping demand curve and set marginal revenue to marginal cost to determine the profit-maximizing output level. However, the difference is that at this profit-maximizing level of output, the monopolistically competitive firm cannot make economic profits in the long run because the barriers to entry and exit in this market are assumed to be zero.

SECTION CHECK 2 ANSWERS

1. A monopolistically competitive firm is making short-run economic profits when the equilibrium price is greater than average total costs at the equilibrium output; when equilibrium price is below average total cost at the equilibrium output, the firm is minimizing its economic loss.

2. In the long run, equilibrium price equals average total costs. With that, economic profits are zero, eliminating incentives for firms to either enter or exit the industry.

9-3 Monopolistic Competition versus Perfect Competition

SECTION CHECK 3

Keep the following questions in mind as you read through this section.

1. What are the differences and similarities between monopolistic competition and perfect competition?

2. Why does the monopolistically competitive firm fail to meet productive efficiency?

3. Why does the monopolistically competitive firm fail to meet allocative efficiency?

We have seen that both monopolistic competition and perfect competition have many buyers and sellers and relatively free entry. However, product differentiation enables a monopolistic competitor to have some influence over price. Consequently, a monopolistically competitive firm has a downward-sloping demand curve, but because of the large number of good substitutes for its product, the curve tends to be much more elastic than the demand curve for a monopolist.

excess capacity occurs when the firm produces below the level at which average total cost is minimized

9-3a THE SIGNIFICANCE OF EXCESS CAPACITY

Because the demand curve is downward sloping in monopolistic competition, its point of tangency with the *ATC* curve will not and cannot be at the lowest level of average cost. What does this statement mean? It means that even when long-run adjustments are complete, firms are not operating at a level that permits the lowest average cost of production—the efficient scale of the firm. The existing plant, even though optimal for the equilibrium volume of output, is not used to capacity; that is, **excess capacity** exists at that level of output. Excess capacity occurs when the firm produces below the level where average total cost is minimized.

9-3b FAILING TO ACHIEVE PRODUCTIVE EFFICIENCY

Unlike a perfectly competitive firm, a monopolistically competitive firm could increase output and lower its average total cost, as shown in Exhibit 9.3(a) on the next page. However, any attempt to increase output to attain lower average cost would be unprofitable, because the price reduction necessary to sell the greater output would cause marginal revenue to fall below the marginal cost of the increased output. As we can see in Exhibit 9.3(a), to the right of q^*, marginal cost is greater than marginal revenue. Consequently, in monopolistic competition, the tendency is too many firms in the industry, each producing a volume of output less than what would allow lowest cost. Economists call this tendency a failure to reach productive efficiency. For example, the market may have too many grocery stores or too many service stations, in the sense that if the total volume of business were concentrated in a smaller number of sellers, average cost, and thus price, could in principle be less.

EXHIBIT 9.3 Comparing Long-Run Perfect Competition and Monopolistic Competition

a. Monopolistically Competitive Firm

b. Perfectly Competitive Firm

9-3c FAILING TO MEET ALLOCATIVE EFFICIENCY, TOO

Productive inefficiency is not the only problem with a monopolistically competitive firm. Exhibit 9.3(a) shows a firm that is not operating where price is equal to marginal costs. In the monopolistically competitive model, at the intersection of the MC and MR curves (q^*), we can clearly see that price is greater than marginal cost. Society is willing to pay more for the product (the price, P^*) than it costs society to produce it (MC at q^*). In this case, the firm is failing to reach allocative efficiency, where price equals marginal cost. Because the price is greater than the marginal cost, it would be profitable for the monopolistically competitive firm to sell to another customer. If it were a perfectly competitive firm, it would not care because price is equal to marginal cost and the extra profit from another customer would be zero.

In short, firms are not producing at the minimum point of ATC, failing to meet productive efficiency; and they are not charging a price equal to marginal cost, failing to meet allocative efficiency. Note that in Exhibit 9.3(b), the perfectly competitive firm has reached both productive efficiency ($P = ATC$ at the minimum point on the ATC curve) and allocative efficiency ($P = MC$).

However, in defense of monopolistic competition, the higher average cost and the slightly higher price and lower output may simply be the price firms pay for differentiated products—variety. That is, just because monopolistically competitive firms have not met the conditions for productive and allocative efficiency, it is not obvious that society is not better off.

9-3d WHAT ARE THE REAL COSTS OF MONOPOLISTIC COMPETITION?

We just argued that perfect competition meets the tests of allocative and productive efficiency and that monopolistic competition does not. Can we "fix" a monopolistically competitive firm to look more like an efficient, perfectly competitive firm? One remedy might entail using government regulation, as in the case of a natural monopoly. However, this process would be costly because a monopolistically competitive firm makes no economic profits in the long run. Therefore, asking monopolistically competitive firms to equate price and marginal cost would lead to economic losses, because long-run average total cost would be greater than price at $P = MC$. Consequently, the government would have to subsidize the firm. Living with the inefficiencies in monopolistically competitive markets might be easier than coping with the difficulties entailed by regulations and the cost of the necessary subsidies.

We argued that the monopolistically competitive firm does not operate at the minimum point of the ATC curve, whereas the perfectly competitive firm does. However, is this comparison fair? A monopolistic competition involves differentiated goods and services, whereas a perfect competition does not. In other words, the excess capacity that exists in monopolistic competition is the price we pay for product differentiation. Have you ever thought about the many restaurants, movies, and gasoline stations that have "excess capacity"? Can you imagine a world where all firms were working at full capacity? After all, choice is a good, and most of us value some choice.

In short, the inefficiency of monopolistic competition is a result of product differentiation. Because consumers value variety—the ability to choose from competing products and brands—the loss in efficiency must be weighed against the gain in increased product variety. The gains from product diversity can be large and may easily outweigh the inefficiency associated with a downward-sloping demand curve. Remember, firms differentiate their products to meet consumers' demand.

In addition, in most monopolistically competitive markets, many of the firms compete and products are substitutable. No single firm has substantial monopoly power. Consequently, the size of the deadweight loss will be small. Also, the firm's demand curve will be relatively elastic so the firm will be much closer to minimizing ATC than a monopoly.

Remember this little caveat: The theory of the firm is like a road map that does not detail every gully, creek, and hill, but does give directions to get from one geographic point to another. Any particular theory of the firm may not tell precisely how an individual firm will operate, but it does provide valuable insight into the ways firms will tend to react to changing economic conditions such as entry, demand, and cost changes.

SECTION CHECK 3 ANSWERS

1. Both the competitive firm and the monopolistically competitive firm may earn short-run economic profits, but these profits will be eliminated in the long run.

2. Because monopolistically competitive firms face a downward-sloping demand curve, average total cost is not minimized in the long run, after entry and exit have eliminated profits. Monopolistically competitive firms fail to reach productive efficiency, producing at output levels less than the efficient output.

3. The monopolistically competitive firm does not achieve allocative efficiency, because it does not operate where the price is equal to marginal costs, which means that society is willing to pay more for additional output than it costs society to produce additional output.

9-4 Oligopoly

SECTION CHECK 4

Keep the following questions in mind as you read through this section.

1. What is oligopoly?

2. What is mutual interdependence?

3. Are economies of scale a major barrier to entry?

Oligopolies exist, by definition, where relatively few firms control all or most of the production and sale of a product ("oligopoly" = few sellers). The products may be homogeneous or differentiated, but the barriers to entry are often high, which makes it difficult for firms to enter into the industry. Consequently, long-run economic profits may be earned by firms in the industry.

Did you know that four companies—Apple, Dell, Hewlett-Packard, and Acer—account for more than 75 percent of all the laptops and desktop computers sold in the United States? This is what economists call a highly concentrated market. When a market is made up of a few sellers, it is called an

oligopoly a market structure in which relatively few firms control all or most of the production and sale of a product

mutual interdependence
when a firm shapes its policy with an eye to the policies of competing firms

oligopoly. Why are there so few competitors in industries such as computers, breakfast cereals, discount stores, and cigarettes? The answer is that barriers to entry are high, primarily due to economies of scale.

Other examples of oligopolistic markets include commercial airlines, oil, automobiles, steel, and sports drinks. In all of these instances, the market is dominated by anywhere from a few to several big companies, although they may have many different brands (e.g., General Motors, General Foods, and Apple Computers). In this chapter, we will learn about the unique characteristics of firms in this industry.

9-4a MUTUAL INTERDEPENDENCE

Oligopoly is characterized by **mutual interdependence** among firms; that is, each firm shapes its policy with an eye to the policies of competing firms. Oligopolists must strategize, much like good chess or bridge players who are constantly observing and anticipating the moves of their rivals. Oligopoly is likely to occur whenever the number of firms in an industry is so small that any change in output or price by one firm appreciably impacts the sales of competing firms. In this situation, it is almost inevitable that competitors will respond directly to these actions in determining their own policies.

9-4b WHY DO OLIGOPOLIES EXIST?

Primarily, oligopoly is a result of the relationship between the technological conditions of production and potential sales volume. For many products, a firm cannot obtain a reasonably low cost of production unless it is producing a large fraction of the market output. In other words, substantial economies of scale are present in oligopoly markets. Automobile and steel production are classic examples of this. Because of legal concerns such as patents, large start-up costs, and the presence of pronounced economies of scale, the barriers to entry are quite high in oligopoly.

9-4c MEASURING INDUSTRY CONCENTRATION

The extent of oligopoly power in various industries can be measured by means of concentration ratios.

EXHIBIT 9.4 Four-Firm Concentration Ratios, U.S. Manufacturing

Industry	Share of Value of Shipments by the Top Four Firms (%)
Cigarettes	95
Household laundry equipment	93
Breweries	91
Electric lightbulbs	89
Refrigerators and freezers	85
Small arms ammunition	83
Aluminum production	83
Breakfast cereals	82
Motor vehicles	81
Aircraft	81
Vacuum cleaners	78
Tires	76
Computers	75
Motorcycles and bicycles	72
Soaps, detergents	61

SOURCE: U.S. Census Bureau

A concentration ratio indicates the proportion of total industry shipments (sales) of goods produced by a specified number of the largest firms in the industry, or the proportion of total industry assets held by these largest firms. We can use four-firm or eight-firm concentration ratios; most often, concentration ratios are for the four largest firms.

The extent of oligopoly power is indicated by the four-firm concentration ratio for the United States shown in Exhibit 9.4. Note that for breakfast cereals, to take an example, the four largest firms produce 87 percent of all breakfast cereals produced in the United States. Concentration ratios of 70 to 100 percent are common in oligopolies. That is, a high concentration ratio means that a few sellers dominate the market.

Concentration ratios, however, are not a perfect guide to industry concentration. One problem is that they do not take into consideration foreign competition. For example, the U.S. auto industry is highly concentrated but faces stiff competition from foreign automobile producers. The same is true for motorcycles and bicycles.

9-4d ECONOMIES OF SCALE AS A BARRIER TO ENTRY

Economies of large-scale production make operation on a small scale during a new firm's early years extremely unprofitable. A firm cannot build up a large market overnight; in the interim, average total cost is so high that losses are heavy. Recognition of this fact discourages new firms from entering the market, as illustrated in Exhibit 9.5. We can see that if an automobile company produces quantity Q_{LARGE} rather than Q_{SMALL}, it will be able to produce cars at a significantly lower cost. If the average total cost to a potential entrant is equivalent to point A on the ATC curve and the price of automobiles is less than P_1, a new firm would be deterred from entering the industry.

9-4e EQUILIBRIUM PRICE AND QUANTITY IN OLIGOPOLY

It is difficult to predict how firms will react in situations of mutual interdependence. No firm knows what its demand curve looks like with any degree of certainty, and therefore it has a limited knowledge of its marginal revenue curve. To know anything about its demand curve, the firm must know how other firms will react to its prices and other policies. In the absence of additional assumptions, then, equating marginal revenue and expected marginal cost is relegated to guesswork. Thus, it is difficult for an oligopolist to determine its profit-maximizing price and output.

The barriers to entry in the auto industry are formidable. A new entrant would have to start out as a large producer investing billions of dollars in plants, equipment, and advertising to compete with existing firms.

© J van der Wolf/Shutterstock.com

SECTION CHECK 4 ANSWERS

1. Oligopolies exist where relatively few firms control all or most of the production and sale of a product. The products may be homogeneous or differentiated, but the barriers to entry are often very high and, consequently, they may be able to realize long-run economic profits.

2. When firms are mutually interdependent, each firm shapes its policy with an eye to the policies of competing firms.

3. Economies of large-scale production make operation on a small scale extremely unprofitable. Recognition of this fact discourages new firms from entering the market.

EXHIBIT 9.5 Economies of Scale as a Barrier to Entry

© Cengage Learning 2014

9-5 Collusion and Cartels

SECTION CHECK 5

Consider the following questions as you read through this section.

1. Why do firms collude?

2. Why does collusion break down?

3. How can existing firms deter potential entrants?

9-5a UNCERTAINTY AND PRICING DECISIONS

The uncertainties of pricing decisions are substantial in oligopoly. The implications of misjudging the behavior of competitors could prove to be disastrous. An executive who makes the wrong pricing move may force the firm to lose sales or, at a minimum, be forced himself to back down in an embarrassing fashion from an announced price increase. Because of this uncertainty, some believe that oligopolists change their prices less frequently than perfect competitors, whose prices may change almost continually. The empirical evidence, however, does not clearly indicate that prices are in fact always slow to change in oligopoly situations.

9-5b COLLUSION

Because the actions and profits of oligopolists are so dominated by mutual interdependence, the temptation is great for firms to collude—to get together and agree to act jointly in pricing and other matters. If firms believe they can increase their profits by coordinating their actions, they will be tempted to collude. **Collusion** reduces uncertainty and increases the potential for economic profits. From society's point of view, collusion creates a situation in which goods very likely become overpriced and underproduced, with consumers losing out as the result of a misallocation of resources.

9-5c JOINT PROFIT MAXIMIZATION

Agreements between or among firms on sales, pricing, and other decisions are usually referred to as cartel agreements. A **cartel** is a collection of firms making an agreement.

Cartels may lead to what economists call **joint profit maximization**: Price is based on the marginal revenue function, which is derived from the product's total (or market) demand schedule and the various firms' marginal cost schedules, as shown in Exhibit 9.6. With outright agreements—necessarily secret because of antitrust laws (in the United States, at least)—firms that make up the market will attempt to estimate demand and cost schedules and then set optimum price and output levels accordingly.

collusion when firms act together to restrict competition

cartel a collection of firms that agree on sales, pricing, and other decisions

joint profit maximization determination of price based on the marginal revenue derived from the market demand schedule and marginal cost schedule of the firms in the industry

Equilibrium price and quantity for a collusive oligopoly are determined according to the intersection of the marginal revenue curve (derived from the market demand curve) and the horizontal sum of the short-run marginal cost curves for the oligopolists. As shown in Exhibit 9.6, the resulting equilibrium quantity is Q^* and the equilibrium price is P^*. Collusion facilitates joint profit maximization for the oligopoly. If the oligopoly is maintained in the long run, it charges a higher price, produces less output, and fails to maximize social welfare, relative to perfect competition, because $P^* > MC$ at Q^*.

The manner in which total profits are shared among firms in the industry depends in part on the relative costs and sales of the various firms. Firms with low costs and large supply capabilities will obtain the largest profits, because they have greater bargaining power. Sales, in turn, may depend in large measure on consumer preferences for various brands if there is product differentiation. With outright collusion, firms may agree on market shares and the division of profits. The division of total profits will depend on the relative bargaining strength of each firm, influenced by its relative financial strength, ability to inflict damage (through price wars) on other firms if an agreement is not reached, ability to withstand similar actions on the part of other firms, relative costs, consumer preferences, and bargaining skills.

Recent examples of collusion (price fixing) have occurred in a wide range of industries, from art auctions to tomatoes, paint to vitamins, and cars to LCD panels.

EXHIBIT 9.6 Collusion in Oligopoly

© Cengage Learning 2014

9-5d WHY ARE MOST COLLUSIVE OLIGOPOLIES SHORT LIVED?

Collusive oligopolies are potentially highly profitable for participants but detrimental to society. Fortunately, most strong collusive oligopolies are rather short lived for two reasons. First, in the United States and in some other nations, collusive oligopolies are strictly illegal under antitrust laws. Second, for collusion to work, firms must agree to restrict output to a level that will support the profit-maximizing price. At that price, firms can earn positive economic profits. Yet a great temptation is for firms to cheat on the agreement of the collusive oligopoly; and because collusive agreements are illegal, the other parties have no way to punish the offender. Why do they have a strong incentive to cheat? Because any individual firm could lower its price slightly and thereby increase sales and profits, as long as it goes undetected. Undetected price cuts could bring in new customers, including rivals' customers. In addition, nonprice methods of defection include better credit terms, rebates, prompt delivery service, and so on.

The OPEC Cartel

The most spectacularly successful example of a collusive oligopoly able to earn monopoly-type profits is the Organization of Petroleum Exporting Countries (OPEC) cartel. Although organized in 1960, it only became successful as a collusive oligopoly in 1973.

OPEC began acting as a cartel in part because of political concern over U.S. support for Israel. For 20 years before 1973, the price of crude oil had hovered around $2 a barrel. In 1973, OPEC members agreed to quadruple oil prices in nine months; later price increases pushed the cost of a barrel of oil to more than $20. OPEC's share of total world oil output steadily increased, from around 20 percent of total world output in the early 1940s to about 70 percent by 1973, when OPEC became an effective cartel. Prices then stabilized, falling in real terms (adjusted for inflation) between 1973 and 1978 as OPEC sought the profit-maximizing price and politics remained relatively calm. By the early 1980s, however, prices were approaching $40 per barrel. From the mid-1980s to the mid-1990s, OPEC oil prices hovered around $20 per barrel because of increases in non-OPEC production and the uncertain willingness of key suppliers (such as Saudi Arabia) to restrict supply. Recall that members in a cartel are trying to raise the price of oil through a coordinated effort at reducing the quantity produced.

The problem is that collectively, OPEC members would like to maintain a high price, but individually each country would like to increase its production to increase its profits. Many OPEC members have cheated on their agreements.

This means OPEC now controls 75 percent of the world's proven oil reserves (but it only produces about 40 percent of the crude oil each year), giving it some clout as a cartel. However, it is not just OPEC. High oil prices emerge because of growing world demand and the political instability in the Middle East. By July 2006, oil prices had reached $78 per barrel. Between 2004 and 2008, oil prices rose sharply because of growing world demand (in part due to increased demand from the fast-growing economies of China and India) and political instability in the Middle East. In early 2008, oil hit a record high of around $140 a barrel, but by the end of 2008, in the midst of a worldwide recession, the price of oil fell below $40, despite OPEC's attempts to keep prices higher.

However, by 2012, with an increase in worldwide demand and fears of Middle East supply disruptions, oil increased to over $100 a barrel.

9-5e PRICE LEADERSHIP

Over time, an implied understanding may develop in an oligopoly market that a large firm is the **price leader**, sending a signal to competitors, perhaps through a press release, that they have increased their prices. This approach is not outright collusion because no formal

> **price leader** a large firm in an oligopoly that unilaterally makes changes in its product prices that competitors tend to follow

price follower a competitor in an oligopoly that goes along with the pricing decision of the price leader

price leadership when a dominant firm that produces a large portion of the industry's output sets a price that maximizes its profits, and other firms follow

cartel arrangement or formal meetings are used to determine price and output, but this is what is called tacit collusion. Any competitor that goes along with the pricing decision of the price leader is called a **price follower**.

Price leadership is most likely to develop when one firm, the so-called dominant firm, produces a large portion of the total output. The dominant firm sets the price that maximizes its profits, and the smaller firms, which would have little influence over price anyway, act as if they are perfect competitors and sell all they want at that price. In the past, a number of firms have been price leaders: U.S. Steel and Bethlehem Steel, RJ Reynolds (tobacco), General Motors (automobiles), Kellogg's (breakfast cereals), and Goodyear (tires). In the banking industry, various dominant banks have taken turns being the dominant firm in announcing changes in the prime interest rate—the interest rate that banks charge large corporate clients. Because the prime rate is widely cited in newspapers, it makes it easy for other banks to follow the lead and avoid frequent changes and competitive warfare.

9-5f WHAT HAPPENS IN THE LONG RUN IF ENTRY IS EASY?

Mutual interdependence is, in itself, no guarantee of economic profits, even if the firms in the industry succeed in maximizing joint profits. The extent to which economic profits disappear depends on the ease with which new firms can enter the industry. When entry is easy, excess profits attract newcomers. New firms may break down existing price agreements by undercutting

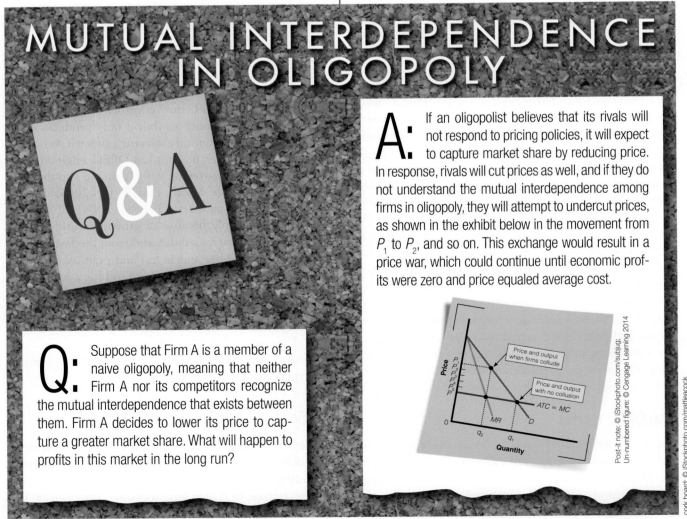

MUTUAL INTERDEPENDENCE IN OLIGOPOLY

Q&A

Q: Suppose that Firm A is a member of a naive oligopoly, meaning that neither Firm A nor its competitors recognize the mutual interdependence that exists between them. Firm A decides to lower its price to capture a greater market share. What will happen to profits in this market in the long run?

A: If an oligopolist believes that its rivals will not respond to pricing policies, it will expect to capture market share by reducing price. In response, rivals will cut prices as well, and if they do not understand the mutual interdependence among firms in oligopoly, they will attempt to undercut prices, as shown in the exhibit below in the movement from P_1 to P_2, and so on. This exchange would result in a price war, which could continue until economic profits were zero and price equaled average cost.

EXHIBIT 9.7 Long-Run Equilibrium and Deterring Entry

© Cengage Learning 2014

prices in an attempt to establish themselves in the industry. In response, older firms may reduce prices to avoid excessive sales losses; as a result, the general level of prices will begin to approach average total cost.

9-5g HOW DO OLIGOPOLISTS DETER MARKET ENTRY?

If most firms reach a scale of plant and firm size great enough to allow lowest-cost operation, their long-run positions will be similar to that shown in Exhibit 9.7. To simplify, we have drawn MC and ATC constant. The equilibrium, or profit-maximizing, price in an established oligopoly is represented by P^*. Typically, the rate of profit in these industries is high, which would encourage entry. However, empirical research indicates that oligopolists often initiate pricing policies that reduce the entry incentive for new firms. Established firms may deliberately hold prices below the maximum profit point at P^*, charging a price of, say, P_1. This lower-than-profit-maximizing price may discourage newcomers from entering. Because new firms would likely have higher costs than existing firms, the lower price may not be high enough to cover their costs. However, once the threat of entry subsides, the market price may return to the profit-maximizing price, P^*.

9-5h ANTITRUST AND MERGERS

In the beginning of this chapter, we introduced a method for determining

an industry's market structure called a concentration ratio. However, the Justice Department and the Federal Trade Commission (FTC) both prefer to use a measure called the Herfindahl-Hirschman Index (HHI). The HHI is measured by taking the square for each firm's share of market sales summed over the firms in the industry. For example, if the industry has three firms and their market share is 50 percent, 30 percent, and 20 percent, respectively, the HHI would be:

$$HHI = 50^2 + 30^2 + 20^2 = 3,800$$

By squaring, the HHI produces a much larger number when the industry is dominated by a few firms. According to the Justice Department, an HHI below 1,000 is very competitive, an HHI between 1,000 and 1,800 is somewhat competitive, and an HHI over 1,800 indicates an oligopoly. The HHI takes into account the relative size and distribution of the firms in a market. The HHI is lowest when a market consists of a large number of firms of relatively equal size. The HHI increases both as the number of firms in the market decreases and as the disparity in size between those firms increases.

A potential merger resulting in an HHI over 1,000 will receive close scrutiny. In 2007, for example, Whole Foods made a takeover bid for Wild Oats. Both were organic grocery stores. The FTC argued that the takeover would increase prices and limit competition in the organic food market. Whole Foods argued that it competes with many grocery stores that carry healthy food and organic products. The merger was eventually completed in August 2007, when a federal appeals court refused to block the deal.

Three Types of Mergers

There are three different types of mergers.

1. A *horizontal merger* combines firms that sell similar products; for example, if Motel 6 merges with Holiday Inn or GM merges with Chrysler.
2. A *vertical merger* combines firms at different stages of production; for example, Pepsi merged with Pizza Hut and Taco Bell. Similarly, a hotel chain may merge with a mattress company.
3. A *conglomerate merger* combines firms in different industries. For example, an automobile company might merge with a pharmaceutical company.

Since vertical mergers are not often a threat to competition, they are not usually subject to antitrust probes. They do

Three Types of Mergers
1) horizontal
2) vertical
3) conglomerate

© iStockphoto.com/subjug

not reduce competition in other markets. This is also true of conglomerate mergers—when an auto company merges with a pharmaceutical company, neither increases market share. Most of the antitrust issues occur with horizontal mergers. For example, an attempted merger between Office Depot and Staples was blocked.

9-5i ANTITRUST AND PRICING STRATEGIES

Most economists agree that price fixing should be illegal. However, there are antitrust laws that forbid other types of activities of which the effects are not as obvious: predatory pricing, price discrimination, and tying.

Predatory Pricing

If the price is deliberately kept low (below average variable cost) to drive a competitor out of the market, it is called **predatory pricing**. However, both economists and the courts have a difficult time deciding whether or not a price is truly predatory. Even if the price is driven down below average variable cost (recall from Chapter 7 that when price is below *AVC*, it is the shutdown point of a firm), the courts still have to determine whether the low price destroyed the rival and kept it out of business and whether the firm raised its price to the monopoly level once the rival had been driven out of the industry. Microsoft, American Airlines, and other companies have been accused of predatory pricing, but none of them were convicted because it is so difficult to distinguish predatory pricing from vigorous competition.

Price Discrimination

Price discrimination, as we studied in Chapter 8, is a common pricing strategy for many businesses. It generally does not reduce competition unless it is part of a strategy to block entry or force a competitor out of the market; therefore, it is not normally challenged by antitrust authorities. However, it can be challenged under the Robinson-Patman Act, which places restrictions on allowable price discrimination.

Tying

Tie-in-sales *require* that a customer who buys one product (the tying good) must also buy another product (the tied good) that the customer needs in order to use the first product. Two companies that followed this

practice were Xerox and IBM. When Xerox was the largest photocopier producer, they required companies that rented their machines to also buy paper from them. Similarly, IBM required that users of its computers buy IBM computer cards. IBM charged more for the computer cards than other firms would have charged.

Antitrust authorities look for dominant firms that use these types of pricing discrimination policies. For example, the Supreme Court ruled that studios could not force theaters to buy an entire package of films in order to get the rights to show a blockbuster movie. That is, tying a blockbuster movie together with a package of not-so-good B movies could allow studios to expand their market power. To economists, the "jury" is still out on whether various forms of price discrimination really impede competition.

SECTION CHECK 5 ANSWERS

1. The mutual interdependence of oligopolists tempts them to collude in order to reduce uncertainty and increase potential for economic profits.

2. Most strong collusive oligopolies are rather short lived for primarily two reasons: (1) Collusive oligopolies are strictly illegal under U.S. antitrust laws, and (2) there is a great temptation for firms to cheat on the agreement of the collusive oligopoly.

3. Firms in an oligopoly may deliberately hold prices below the short-run profit-maximizing point in order to discourage newcomers from entering the market.

9-6 Game Theory and Strategic Behavior

SECTION CHECK 6

Consider the following questions as you read through this section.

1. What is game theory?
2. What is a dominant strategy?
3. What is Nash equilibrium?

In some respects, noncollusive oligopoly resembles a military campaign or a poker game. Firms take certain actions not because they are necessarily advantageous in themselves but because they improve the position of the oligopolist relative to its competitors and may ultimately improve its financial position. For example, a firm may deliberately cut prices, sacrificing profits either to drive competitors out of business or to discourage them from undertaking actions contrary to the interests of other firms.

9-6a WHAT IS GAME THEORY?

Some economists have suggested that the entire approach to oligopoly equilibrium price and output should be recast. They replace the analysis that assumes that firms attempt to maximize profits with one that examines firm behavior in terms of a strategic game. This point of view, called **game theory**, stresses the tendency of various parties in such circumstances to act in a way that minimizes damage from opponents. This approach involves a set of alternative actions (with respect to price and output levels, for example); the action that would be taken in a particular case depends on the specific policies followed by each firm. The firm may try to figure out its competitors' most likely countermoves to its own policies and then formulate alternative defense measures.

Each firm will react to the price, quantity, and quality of rival firms. Because each firm is interdependent, each must observe the moves of its rivals.

Cooperative and Noncooperative Games

Games, in interactions between oligopolists, can either be cooperative or noncooperative. An example of a **cooperative game** would be two firms that decide to collude in order to improve their profit-maximization position. However, as we discussed earlier, enforcement costs are usually too high to keep all firms from cheating on collusive agreements. Consequently, most games are **noncooperative games**, in which each firm sets its own price without consulting other firms. The primary difference between cooperative and noncooperative games is the contract. For example, players in a cooperative game can talk and set binding contracts, while those in noncooperative games are assumed to act independently, with no communication and no binding contracts. Because antitrust laws forbid firms to collude, we will assume that most strategic behavior in the marketplace is noncooperative.

9-6b THE PRISONERS' DILEMMA

A firm's decision makers must map out a pricing strategy based on a wide range of information. They must also decide whether their strategy will be effective and whether it will be affected by competitors' actions. A strategy that will be optimal regardless of the opponents' actions is called a **dominant strategy**. A famous game that has a dominant strategy and demonstrates the basic problem confronting noncolluding oligopolists is known as the **prisoners' dilemma**.

Imagine that a bank robbery occurs and two suspects are caught. The suspects are placed in separate cells in the county jail and are not allowed to talk with each other. Four results are possible in this situation: both prisoners confess, neither confesses, Prisoner A confesses but Prisoner B does not, or Prisoner B confesses but Prisoner A does not. In Exhibit 9.8 on the next page, we see the **payoff matrix**, which summarizes the possible outcomes from the various strategies. Looking at the payoff matrix, we can see that if both prisoners confess to the crime, each will serve six years in jail. However, if neither confesses, each prisoner may only

game theory firms attempt to maximize profits by acting in ways that minimize damage from competitors

cooperative game collusion by two firms in order to improve their profit maximizations

noncooperative game each firm sets its own price without consulting other firms

dominant strategy strategy that will be optimal regardless of opponents' actions

prisoners' dilemma the basic problem facing noncolluding oligopolists in maximizing their own profits

payoff matrix a summary of the possible outcomes of various strategies

EXHIBIT 9.12 Characteristics of the Four Major Market Structures

Characteristic	Perfect Competition	Monopoly	Monopolistic Competition	Oligopoly
Number of firms	Very many	One	Many	A few
Firm role in determining price	No role; price taker	Major role; price maker	Some role	Some role
Long-run economic profits possible	No	Yes	No	Yes
Barriers to entry or exit from industry	No substantial ones	Extremely great	Minor barriers	Considerable barriers
Type of product	Homogeneous	Homogeneous	Differentiated	Homogeneous or differentiated
Key characteristic	Firms are price takers	Only one firm	Product differentiation	Mutual interdependence

© Cengage Learning 2014

they stick to the plan rather than cheat—that is, fail to cooperate. Many cartels appear to employ the tit-for-tat strategy. In short, the most effective strategy to promote cooperation is tit-for-tat.

9-6e THE FOUR MAJOR MARKET STRUCTURES REVISITED

You might legitimately ask the question: If perfectly competitive and monopolistic firms are rare and monopolistically competitive and oligopoly firms are common, why did we study the former first? What we learned from the perfectly competitive model about costs, entry, exit, and efficiency are still important concepts for imperfectly competitive firms. In addition, the applications of oligopoly and monopolistic competition theory are still somewhat controversial among economists—so we started with what we know best. Exhibit 9.12 provides an overview of the various types of market structures.

Chapter 9: Self-Review

Now that you are finished reading the chapter, review the questions below. You can write your answers in the space provided, then go online to see the answers at www.cengagebrain.com.

9-1 MONOPOLISTIC COMPETITION

1. How is monopolistic competition a mixture of monopoly and perfect competition?

2. Why is free entry necessary for monopolistic competition?

3. List three ways in which a grocery store might differentiate itself from its competitors.

9-2 PRICE AND OUTPUT DETERMINATION IN MONOPOLISTIC COMPETITION

4. What is the short-run profit-maximizing policy of a monopolistically competitive firm?

5. How is the long-run equilibrium of monopolistic competition like that of perfect competition?

9-3 MONOPOLISTIC COMPETITION VERSUS PERFECT COMPETITION

6. True or False: A monopolistic competitor's demand curve is downward sloping and relatively inelastic.

7. What is the price we pay for differentiated goods under monopolistic competition?

9-4 OLIGOPOLY

8. True or False: Concentration ratios indicate the fraction of total industry labor supply accounted for by the largest firms in the industry.

9. How do economies of scale result in barriers to entry in oligopoly models?

9-5 COLLUSION AND CARTELS

10. True or False: Barriers to entry are necessary for successful, ongoing collusion.

11. Why do horizontal mergers tend to concern antitrust authorities more than vertical or conglomerate mergers?

9-6 GAME THEORY AND STRATEGIC BEHAVIOR

12. True or False: Noncooperative games are those in which actions are taken independently.

13. In the prisoners' dilemma, if each prisoner believed that the other prisoner would deny the crime, would each choose to deny the crime?

© WALT DISNEY/THE KOBAL COLLECTION

Actor Johnny Depp gets paid a lot of money

per film because he controls scarce resources: his talent and his name recognition. People's talents that are in limited supply relative to demand will command and receive higher salaries.

Test your Economics *street-smart* knowledge and see how you compare against other students! Scan here or visit CourseMate for Survey of ECON2.

10

Labor Markets, Income Distribution, and Poverty

Approximately 75 percent of national income goes to wages and salaries for labor services. So, how are salary levels among the individuals who supply those services determined? After laborers take their share, the remaining 25 percent of national income is compensation received by the owners of land and capital and the entrepreneurs who employ these resources to produce valued goods and services.

In labor markets, actor Johnny Depp can make more than $20 million acting in one film. Baseball player Alex Rodriguez of the New York Yankees makes $25 million a year. Singer Lady Gaga's income is many times larger than that of the average college professor or medical doctor. Female models make more than male models, yet male basketball players make more than female basketball players. Why do these differences occur? To understand the reasons for the wide variation in compensation workers receive for their labors, we must focus on the workings of supply and demand in the labor market.

In this chapter, we will also study the relationship between productivity and wages, labor unions, income distribution, and poverty.

SECTIONS IN CHAPTER 10

10-1 Input Markets

SECTION CHECK 1

Keep the following questions in mind as you read through this section.

1. How is income distributed among workers, landowners, and the owners of capital?

2. What is derived demand?

Let us begin by looking at derived demand and how it affects production in input markets.

10-1a DETERMINING THE PRICE OF A PRODUCTIVE FACTOR: DERIVED DEMAND

Input markets are the markets for the factors of production used to produce output. Output (goods and services) markets and input markets have one major difference. In input or factor markets, the demand for an input derived from consumers' demand for the good or service produced with that input is called a **derived demand**. That is, the demand for an input such as labor is derived from the demand for the good or service. Thus, consumers do *not* demand the labor directly—it is the goods and services the labor produces that consumers demand. For example, the chef at a restaurant is paid and her skills are in demand because she produces what customers want—great-tasting meals. The "price" of any productive factor is directly related to consumer demand for the final good or service.

SECTION CHECK 1 ANSWERS

1. Supply and demand determine the prices paid to workers, landowners, and capital owners.

2. In factor or input markets, demand is derived from consumers' demand for the final good or service that the input produces.

10-2 Supply and Demand in the Labor Market

SECTION CHECK 2

Keep the following questions in mind as you read through this section.

1. What is the marginal revenue product for an input?

2. Why is the demand curve for labor downward sloping?

3. What is the relationship between the wage rate and the quantity of labor supplied?

Because firms are trying to maximize their profits, they try (by definition) to make the *difference* between total revenue and total cost as large as possible. An input's attractiveness, then, varies with what the input can add to the firm's revenues relative to what the input adds to costs.

10-2a WILL HIRING THAT INPUT ADD MORE TO REVENUE THAN COSTS?

In a competitive labor market, the demand for labor is determined by its **marginal revenue product (MRP)**, which is the additional revenue that a firm obtains from one more unit of input. Why? Suppose a worker adds $500 per week to a firm's sales by his productivity; he produces 100 units that add $5 each to firm revenue. To determine whether the worker adds to the firm's profits, we would need to calculate the marginal resource cost associated with the worker. The **marginal resource cost (MRC)** is the amount that an extra input adds to the firm's total costs. In this case, the marginal resource cost is the wage the employer has to pay to entice an extra worker. Assume that the marginal resource cost of the worker, the market wage, is $350 per worker per week. In our example, the firm would find its profits growing by adding one more worker, because the marginal benefit (MRP) associated with the worker, $500, would exceed the marginal cost (MRC) of the worker, $350. So we can see that just by adding another worker to its labor force, the firm would increase its weekly profits by $150 ($500 − $350). Even if the market wage was $490 per week, the firm could slightly increase its profits by hiring the employee, because the marginal revenue product, $500, is greater than the added labor cost, $490. At wage payments greater than $500, however, the firm would not be interested in the worker, because the marginal resource cost would exceed the marginal revenue product, making additional hiring unprofitable.

10-2b THE DEMAND CURVE FOR LABOR SLOPES DOWNWARD

The downward-sloping demand curve for labor indicates a negative relationship between wage and the quantity of labor demanded. Higher wages will decrease the quantity of labor demanded, whereas lower wages will increase the quantity of labor demanded. But why does this relationship exist?

The major reason for the downward-sloping demand curve for labor (illustrated in Exhibit 10.1) is

EXHIBIT 10.1 The Marginal Revenue Product of Labor

Marginal Revenue Product (demand curve for labor)

the law of diminishing marginal product. Remember that the law of diminishing marginal product states that as increasing quantities of some variable input (say, labor) are added to fixed quantities of another input (say, land or capital), output will rise, but at some point it will increase by diminishing amounts.

Consider a farmer who owns a given amount of land. Suppose the farmer is producing wheat, and the relationship between output and labor force requirements is that indicated in Exhibit 10.2. Output expands as more workers are hired to cultivate the land, but the growth in output steadily slows, meaning that the added output associated with one more

EXHIBIT 10.2 Diminishing Marginal Productivity on a Hypothetical Farm

Units of Labor Input (workers)	Total Wheat Output (bushels per year)	Marginal Product of Labor (bushels per year)
0	—	
		3,000
1	3,000	
		2,500
2	5,500	
		1,500
3	7,000	
		1,000
4	8,000	
		500
5	8,500	
		300
6	8,800	
		200
7	9,000	

worker declines as more workers are added. For example, in Exhibit 10.2, when a third worker is hired, total wheat output increases from 5,500 bushels to 7,000 bushels, an increase of 1,500 bushels in terms of marginal product. However, when a fourth worker is added, total wheat output only increases from 7,000 bushels to 8,000 bushels, or a marginal increase of 1,000 bushels. Note that the reason for the decline in marginal product is *not* that the workers being added are steadily inferior in terms of ability or quality relative to the first workers. Indeed, for simplicity, we assume that each worker has exactly the same skills and productive capacity. But as more workers are added, each additional worker has fewer of the fixed resources with which to work, and marginal product falls. For example, the fifth worker might merely cultivate the same land more intensively. The work of the fifth worker, then, might only slightly improve output. That is, the **marginal product (MP)**—the number of physical units of added output from the addition of one additional unit of input—falls.

> **marginal product (MP)** the change in total output of a good that results from a one-unit change in input

As we discussed earlier, the marginal revenue product (MRP) is the change in total revenue associated with an additional unit of input. The marginal revenue product is equal to the marginal product (that is, the units of output added by a worker) multiplied by marginal revenue (MR) (that is, the price of the output):

$$MRP = MP \times MR$$

The MRP curve takes on different characteristics depending on whether the output market is competitive or imperfectly competitive. In this chapter, we assume the product, or output markets, are competitive. Recall from Chapter 7 that in perfectly competitive markets, the firm will sell all its output at the market price. Consequently, the marginal revenue from the sale of an additional unit is also equal to the market price. Therefore, when output markets are perfectly competitive, the marginal revenue product of a factor is equal to the marginal product times the price of the product the firm is selling:

$$MRP = MP \times P$$

For example, if an additional worker adds 10 bushels of wheat per day (marginal product) and each of these 10 bushels sells for $10 (price of the product), then the worker's marginal revenue product is $100 per day.

EXHIBIT 10.3 Marginal Revenue Product, Output, and Labor Inputs

Quantity of Labor	Total Output (bushels per week)	Marginal Product of Labor (bushels per week)	Product Price (dollars per bushel)	Marginal Revenue Product of Labor	Wage Rate (MRC) (dollars per week)	Marginal Profit (MRP – W)
0	0					
		100	$10	$1,000	$550	$450
1	100					
		90	10	900	550	350
2	190					
		80	10	800	550	250
3	270					
		70	10	700	550	150
4	340					
		60	10	600	550	50
5	400					
		50	10	500	550	−50
6	450					
		40	10	400	550	−150
7	490					
		30	10	300	550	−250
8	520					

© Cengage Learning 2014

The marginal revenue product of labor declines because of the diminishing marginal product of labor when additional workers are added. This decline in MRP is illustrated in Exhibit 10.3, which shows various output and revenue levels for a wheat farmer using different quantities of labor. We see in Exhibit 10.3 that the marginal product, or the added physical volume of output, declines as the number of workers grows, because of diminishing marginal product. Thus, the fifth worker adds only 60 bushels of wheat per week compared with 100 bushels for the first worker.

10-2c HOW MANY WORKERS WILL AN EMPLOYER HIRE?

Profits are maximized if the firm hires only to the point at which the wage equals the expected marginal revenue product; that is, the firm will hire up to the last unit of input for which the marginal revenue product is expected to exceed the wage. Because the demand curve for labor and the value of the marginal revenue product show the quantity of labor that a firm demands at a given wage in a competitive market, we say that the marginal revenue product (MRP) is the same as the demand curve for labor for a competitive firm.

Using the data in Exhibit 10.3, if the market wage is $550 per week, it would pay for the wheat farmer to employ five workers. The fifth worker's marginal revenue product ($600) exceeds the wage, so profits are increased $50 by adding the worker. Adding a sixth worker would be unprofitable, however, as that worker's marginal revenue product of $500 is less than the wage of $550. Hiring the sixth worker would reduce profits by $50.

But what if the market wage increases from $550 to $650? In this case, hiring the fifth worker becomes unprofitable, because the marginal resource cost, $650, is now greater than the marginal revenue product of $600. That is, a higher wage rate, *ceteris paribus*, lowers the employment levels of individual firms.

In a competitive labor market, many firms are competing for workers, and no single firm is big enough by itself to have any significant effect on the level of wages. The intersection of the market supply of labor and the market demand for labor determines the competitive market wage, as shown in Exhibit 10.4(a). The firm's ability to hire all the workers it wishes at the prevailing wage is analogous to perfect competition in output markets, where a firm can sell all it wants at the going price.

In Exhibit 10.4(b), when the firm hires less than q^* workers, the marginal revenue product exceeds the market wage, so adding workers expands profits. With more than q^* workers, however, the "going wage" exceeds marginal revenue product, and hiring additional workers lowers profits. With q^* workers, profits are maximized.

In this chapter, we assume that labor markets are competitive, with many buyers and sellers of labor, and no individual worker having an impact on wages. It is generally a realistic assumption because in most labor markets firms compete with each other to attract workers, and workers can choose from many possible employers.

EXHIBIT 10.4 The Competitive Firm's Hiring Decision

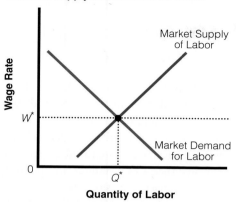

a. Market Supply and Demand for Labor

Market Supply of Labor

Wage Rate

W^*

Market Demand for Labor

0   Q^*

Quantity of Labor

b. Firm's Supply and Demand for Labor

Wage Rate

W^*

Firm's Labor Supply (*MRC*)

Marginal Revenue Product (demand curve for labor)

0   q^*

Quantity of Labor

© Cengage Learning 2014

10-2d THE MARKET LABOR SUPPLY CURVE

How much work effort individuals are collectively willing and able to supply in the marketplace is the essence of the market supply curve. Just as was the case in our earlier discussion of the law of supply, a positive relationship exists between the wage rate and the quantity of labor supplied. As the wage rate rises, the quantity of labor supplied increases, *ceteris paribus*; as the wage rate falls, the quantity of labor supplied falls, *ceteris paribus*. This positive relationship is consistent with the evidence that the total quantity of labor supplied by *all* workers increases as the wage rate increases, as shown in Exhibit 10.5.

EXHIBIT 10.5 The Market Supply Curve of Labor

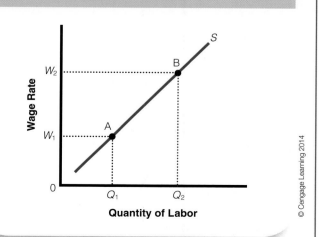

S

W_2 B

Wage Rate

W_1 A

0   Q_1 Q_2

Quantity of Labor

© Cengage Learning 2014

10-3 Labor Market Equilibrium

SECTION CHECK 3

Keep the following questions in mind as you read through this section.

1. How are the equilibrium wage and employment determined in labor markets?

2. What shifts the labor demand curve?

3. What shifts the labor supply curve?

EXHIBIT 10.6 Supply and Demand in the Competitive Labor Market

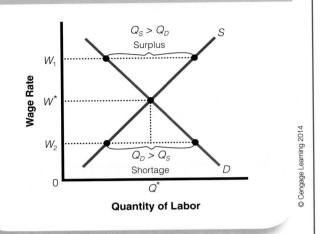

The equilibrium wage and quantity in competitive markets for labor is determined by the intersection of labor demand and labor supply. As shown in Exhibit 10.6, the equilibrium wage, W^*, and equilibrium employment level, Q^*, are found at that point where the quantity of labor demanded equals the quantity of labor supplied. At any wage higher than W^*—at W_1, for example—the quantity of labor supplied exceeds the quantity of labor demanded, resulting in a surplus of labor. In this situation, unemployed workers are willing to undercut the established wage in order to get jobs, pushing the wage down and returning the market to equilibrium. At a wage below the equilibrium level—at W_2, for example—quantity demanded exceeds quantity supplied, resulting in a labor shortage. In this situation, employers are forced to offer higher wages in order to

hire as many workers as they would like. Note that only at the equilibrium wage are both suppliers and demanders able to exchange the quantity of labor they desire.

10-3a SHIFTS IN THE LABOR DEMAND CURVE

In Chapter 3, we demonstrated that the determinants of demand can shift the demand curve for a good or service. In the case of an input such as labor, two important factors can shift the demand curve: increases in labor productivity—caused by technological advances, for instance—or changes in the output price of the good—caused by, say, an increased demand for the firm's product. Exhibit 10.7 highlights the impact of these changes.

Changes in Labor Productivity

Workers can increase productivity if they have more capital or land with which to work, if technological improvements occur, or if they acquire additional skills or experience (human capital). This increase in productivity will increase the marginal product of the labor and shift the demand curve for labor to the right from D_1 to D_2, as in Exhibit 10.7(a). However, if labor productivity falls, then marginal product will fall, and the demand curve for labor will shift to the left [see Exhibit 10.7(b)].

Changes in the Demand for the Firm's Product

The greater the demand for the firm's product, the greater the firm's demand for labor or any other variable input (the *derived demand* discussed earlier). The

EXHIBIT 10.7 Shifts in the Labor Demand Curve

a. Increase in Labor Demand

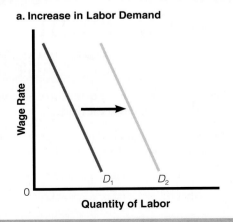

b. Decrease in Labor Demand

reason for this is that the higher demand for the firm's product increases the firm's marginal revenue, which increases marginal revenue product. That is, the greater demand for the product causes prices to rise, and the price of the product is part of the value of the labor to the firm ($MRP = MP \times P$). Therefore, the rising product price shifts the labor demand curve to the right. Of course, if demand for the firm's product falls, the labor demand curve will shift to the left as marginal revenue product falls.

10-3b SHIFTING THE LABOR SUPPLY CURVE

In Chapter 3, we learned that changes in the determinants of supply can shift the supply curve for goods and services to the right or left. Likewise, several factors can cause the labor supply curve to shift. These factors include immigration and population growth, the number of hours workers are willing to work at a given wage (worker tastes or preferences), nonwage income, and amenities. Exhibit 10.8 on page 211 illustrates the impact of these factors on the labor supply curve.

Immigration and Population Growth

If new workers enter the labor force, the labor supply curve will shift to the right—from S_1 to S_2 in Exhibit 10.8(a). Of course, if workers leave the country—and thus the labor force—or the relevant population declines, the supply curve will shift to the left, as shown in Exhibit 10.8(b).

Number of Hours People Are Willing to Work (Worker Preferences)

If people become willing to work more hours at a given wage (due to changes in worker tastes or preferences), the labor supply curve will shift to the right, as shown in the movement from S_1 to S_2 in Exhibit 10.8(a). If they become willing to work fewer hours at a given wage, the labor supply curve will shift to the left, as shown in Exhibit 10.8(b).

Nonwage Income

Increases in income from other sources than employment can cause the labor supply curve to shift to the left. For example, if you just won $20 million in your state's Super Lotto, you might decide to take yourself out of the labor force. Likewise, a decrease in nonwage income might push a person back into the labor force, thus shifting the labor supply curve to the right.

Amenities

Amenities associated with a job or location—such as good fringe benefits, safe and friendly working conditions, a child-care center, and so on—will make for a more desirable work environment, *ceteris paribus*. These amenities will cause an increase in the supply of labor, resulting in a rightward shift of the labor supply curve—from S_1 to S_2 in Exhibit 10.8(a). If job conditions deteriorate, the labor supply will decrease, shifting the labor supply curve to the left, as shown in Exhibit 10.8(b).

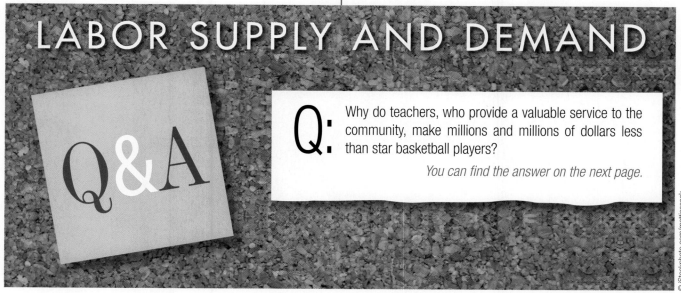

LABOR SUPPLY AND DEMAND

Q&A

Q: Why do teachers, who provide a valuable service to the community, make millions and millions of dollars less than star basketball players?

You can find the answer on the next page.

© iStockphoto.com/mattjeacock

LABOR SUPPLY AND DEMAND

Q&A

A: It is the marginal revenue product of additional teachers and the supply of teachers that determine the market wage (regardless of how important we consider the job). A teacher's marginal revenue product is likely to be well below $5 million a year. Most people probably think that teachers are more important than star basketball players, yet teachers make a lot less money. Of course, the reason for this is simple supply and demand. A lot of people enjoy watching star basketball players, but only a few individuals have the skill to perform at that level. Although demand for teachers is large, the number of potential suppliers is also relatively large. As shown in the accompanying exhibits, this relationship between supply and demand translates into a much lower wage for teachers than for star basketball players.

a. Labor Market for Star Basketball Players

Wage Rate

W_B

S

D

0   Q_B

Quantity of Star Basketball Players (hundreds)

© Cengage Learning 2014

b. Labor Market for Teachers

Wage Rate

S

W_T

D

0   Q_T

Quantity of Teachers (millions)

© Cengage Learning 2014

EXHIBIT 10.8 Shifts in the Labor Supply Curve

 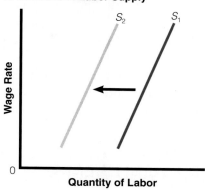

a. Increase in Labor Supply

Wage Rate / *Quantity of Labor* — S_1, S_2

b. Decrease in Labor Supply

Wage Rate / *Quantity of Labor* — S_2, S_1

© Cengage Learning 2014

Angelina Jolie: © Helga Esteb/Shutterstock.com; Marilyn Monroe: © 20TH CENTURY FOX/THE KOBAL COLLECTION

Why does Angelina Jolie make so much more money than Marilyn Monroe did, even after indexing for inflation? With cable TV, Internet, and so on, movie studios can generate more revenue from stars than they could in the past, so studios are willing to pay their stars larger salaries.

SECTION CHECK 3 ANSWERS

1. The intersection of the labor demand curve and the labor supply curve determines equilibrium wages and employment levels in the labor market.

2. The labor demand curve can shift when a change in productivity or a change in the demand for the final product occurs.

3. The labor supply curve can shift when changes in immigration or population growth, workers' preferences, nonwage income, or amenities occur.

10-4 Labor Unions

SECTION CHECK 4

Consider the following questions as you read through this section.

1. Why do labor unions exist?

2. What is the impact of unions on wages?

3. Can unions increase productivity?

While the percentage of workers in labor unions in the U.S. has fallen sharply over the last 60 years, unions can still exert a significant influence on markets. In this section we will examine what labor unions are, why they exist, and their relationship to various markets.

10-4a WHY ARE THERE LABOR UNIONS?

The supply and demand curves for labor can help us better understand the impact of labor unions. Labor unions such as the United Auto Workers (UAW) and the United Farm Workers (UFW) were formed to increase their members' wages and to improve working conditions. On behalf of its members, the union negotiates with firms through a process called **collective bargaining**—discussions between representatives of employers and unions focused on balancing what is best for workers and employers. Why is collective bargaining necessary? The argument is that when economies begin to industrialize and urbanize, firms become larger, and often the "boss" becomes more distant from the workers. In small shops or on farms, workers usually have a close relationship with an owner/employer; but in larger enterprises, the workers may only know a supervisor and have no direct contact with either the owner or upper management. Workers realize that acting together as a union of workers they have more power in the collective bargaining process than they would acting individually.

10-4b UNION IMPACT ON LABOR SUPPLY AND WAGES

Labor unions influence the quantity of union labor hired and the wages at which they are hired, primarily through their ability to alter the supply of labor services from what would exist if workers acted independently. One way of influencing supply, of course, is by raising barriers to entry into a given occupation. For example, by restricting membership, unions can reduce the quantity of labor supplied to industry employers from what it otherwise would be. As a result, wages in that occupation will increase, as shown in Exhibit 10.9(a), from W_1 to W_2. As you can see in the shift from Q_1 to Q_2, some union workers will consequently receive higher wages, but others will become unemployed.

Unions raise wages above what would prevail in a competitive labor market, causing (1) some workers to be unemployed and (2) lower wages in the non-union sector. Many economists believe that this relationship explains why wages are approximately 15 percent higher in union jobs, even when nonunion workers have comparable skills. Of course, the unions will appropriate some of these gains through dues, initiation fees, and the like, so the workers themselves will not receive the full benefit.

10-4c WAGE DIFFERENCES FOR SIMILARLY SKILLED WORKERS

Suppose you have two labor sectors: the union sector and the nonunion sector. If unions are successful in obtaining higher wages, either through bargaining or threatening to strike or by restricting membership, wages will rise and employment will fall in the union sector, as shown in Exhibit 10.9(a). With a downward-sloping demand curve for labor, higher wages mean that less labor will be demanded in the union sector. Workers who are equally skilled but unable to find union work will seek nonunion work, thus increasing supply and, in turn, lowering wages in the nonunion sector. This effect is shown in Exhibit 10.9(b). Thus, comparably skilled workers will experience higher wages in the union sector (W_1) than in the nonunion sector (W_2).

10-4d CAN UNIONS LEAD TO INCREASED PRODUCTIVITY?

Harvard economists Richard Freeman and James Medoff argue that unions might actually increase worker productivity by increasing marginal productivity. Their argument is that unions provide a collective voice that workers can use to communicate their discontents more effectively, thereby lowering the number of union workers who quit their jobs. Resignations can be

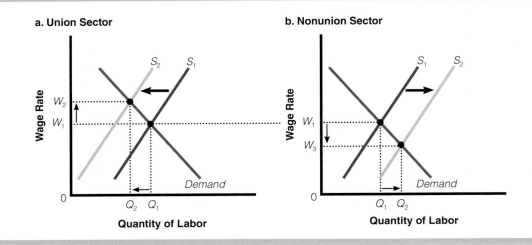

EXHIBIT 10.9 The Effect of Unions on Wages

a. Union Sector

b. Nonunion Sector

© Cengage Learning 2014

particularly costly for firms that invest in training their employees in job-specific skills. In addition, by handling workers' grievances, unions may increase worker motivation and morale. The combined impact of fewer resignations and improved morale could boost productivity.

However, this improvement in worker productivity in the labor sector should show up on the bottom line—the profit statement of the firm. Although the evidence is still preliminary, it appears that unions tend to lower the profitability of firms, not raise it.

In sum, there is disagreement on the impact of unions on the economy. Like many other institutions, there are benefits and costs to unions.

SECTION CHECK 4 ANSWERS

1. Workers form labor unions because they realize that acting together gives them collective bargaining power.

2. Labor unions try to increase their members' wages. Through restrictive membership, a union can reduce the labor supply in the market for union workers, thus reducing employment and raising wages. This union "restriction" increases the supply of workers in the nonunion sector and shifts supply to the right, lowering wages for nonunion workers.

3. Some argue that unions can help reduce job turnover, thus reducing the need for repeated investment in job-specific skills training, and improve morale by handling worker grievances. However, what evidence exists suggests that unions tend to lower the profitability of firms. Obviously there are both benefits and costs to unions.

10-5 Income Distribution

SECTION CHECK 5

Consider the following questions as you read through this section.

1. What has happened to income distribution since 1935?

2. Are income distribution statistics accurate?

3. How significant is income mobility?

4. How much income inequality exists in other countries?

In many economies, some individuals will have high income and others will have low income. How unequal is the U.S. income distribution? And why do some individuals earn more than others? We will address these and other questions regarding income distribution and poverty in this section.

10-5a MEASURING INCOME INEQUALITY

Exhibit 10.10 shows a breakdown of average annual family income by groups of five (or quintiles): the bottom fifth, the second fifth, the third fifth, the fourth fifth, the top fifth and the top 5 percent.

Exhibit 10.11 on the next page illustrates the changing distribution of measured income in the United States since 1935. As you can see in this table, the proportion of income received by the richest Americans (top 5 percent) declined sharply after 1935 but has been edging back up since the 1980s. The proportion received by the poorest Americans (the lowest 20 percent) has remained virtually unchanged since 1935. Most of the observed changes occurred between 1935 and 1950, probably reflecting the impact of the Great Depression and new government programs in the 1930s, as well as World War II. From 1950 to 1980, there was little change in the overall distribution of income. Two significant changes have occurred since the 1980s: The lowest one-fifth of families have seen their share of measured income fall from 5.3 percent to 3.8 percent of all income, and the top one-fifth of families have seen their share of measured income rise from 41.1 to 47.8 percent of all income.

EXHIBIT 10.10 Income Distribution of the United States, 2010

Group	Annual Family Income
Bottom Fifth	Under $26,685
Second Fifth	$26,685–$48,000
Third Fifth	$48,000–$74,144
Fourth Fifth	$74,144–$113,744
Top Fifth	$113,774 and over
Top 5 percent	$200,254 and over

SOURCE: U.S. Census Bureau

EXHIBIT 10.11 Income Inequality in the United States

Year	Lowest Fifth	Second Fifth	Third Fifth	Fourth Fifth	Highest Fifth	Highest 5%
1935	4.1%	9.2%	14.1%	20.9%	51.7%	26.5%
1950	4.5	12.0	17.4	23.4	42.7	17.3
1960	4.8	12.2	17.8	24.0	41.3	15.9
1970	5.4	12.2	17.6	23.8	40.9	15.6
1980	5.3	11.6	17.6	24.4	41.1	14.6
1990	4.6	10.8	16.6	23.8	44.3	17.4
2000	4.3	9.8	15.5	22.8	47.4	20.8
2005	4.0	9.6	15.3	22.9	48.1	21.1
2010	3.8	9.5	15.4	23.5	47.8	20.0

SOURCE: U.S. Census Bureau

10-5b ARE WE OVERSTATING THE DISPARITY IN THE DISTRIBUTION OF INCOME?

Failing to take into consideration differences in age, certain demographic factors, institutional factors, and government redistributive activities have all been identified as elements that influence income distribution data and may suggest that we might be overstating inequality.

Differences in Age

At any moment in time, middle-age people tend to have higher incomes than both younger and older people. Middle age is when most people are at their peak in terms of productivity and participate in the labor force to a greater extent than do the very old or very young. Put differently, if every individual earned exactly the same total income over his or her lifetime, we would still observe some inequality at any given moment in time simply because people usually earn more in middle age.

Inequality resulting from this demographic difference overstates the true inequality in the lifetime earnings of people. A typical 50-year-old male earns nearly twice the income of a male in his early 20s and nearly one-third more than workers over 65. Since 1950, the proportion of individuals who are either very young or very old has grown, meaning that in a relative sense, more people are in lower-income age groups.

Other Demographic Trends

Other demographic trends, such as the increased number of divorced couples and the rise of two-income

families, also cause the measured distribution of income (which is measured in terms of household income) to appear more unequal. For example, in the 1950s, the overwhelming majority of families had single incomes. Today, many households have two breadwinners instead of one. Suppose their incomes rise from $50,000 a year to roughly $100,000; thus, these households move into a higher-income quintile and create greater apparent income inequality. At the same time, divorces create two households instead of one, lowering income per household for divorced couples; thus, they move into lower-income quintiles, also creating greater apparent income inequality.

> In short, high-income and low-income earners will always be with us, but more than likely they will be different people.

Government Activities

Some economists argue that the impact of increased government activity should be considered in evaluating the measured income distribution. Government-imposed taxes burden different income groups in different ways. Also, government programs benefit some groups of income recipients more than others. For example, state-subsidized higher education seems to benefit the high- and middle-income groups more than the poor (because far more students from the higher-income groups go to college), as have such things as government subsidies to airports and airlines, operas, and art museums. Some programs, though, clearly aid the poor more than the rich. Food stamps, school lunch programs, housing subsidies, Medicaid, and several other programs provide recipients with **in-kind transfers**. In-kind transfers are given in the form of goods and services rather than money. When in-kind transfers are included in income distribution data, many economists conclude that they have served to reduce levels of inequality significantly from the levels suggested by aggregate income statistics.

On balance, the evidence suggests that inequality of money income in the United States declined from 1935 to 1950 and then remained rather stable until 1980. Since then, the distribution of income has become less equal. However, if we consider age distribution, institutional factors, and in-kind transfer programs, it is safe to say that the income distribution is more equal than it appears in Exhibit 10.11.

10-5c HOW MUCH MOVEMENT HAPPENS ON THE ECONOMIC LADDER?

A study of income mobility during the decade of 1995–2005 found that 50 percent of individuals who began in the poorest quintile ended up in a higher quintile by 2005. In addition, 5 percent of those in the lower quintile made it to the top quintile and 25 percent made it to the middle fifth. And many of those in the top quintile in 1995 were not there in 2005; almost 60 percent had dropped out of the highest quintile. In short, the distribution of income is much more equal when one looks over a time period longer than one year. Most Americans experience significant fluctuations in their economic well-being from one year to the next.

Generational studies also suggest considerable income mobility—that is, incomes of fathers and sons tend to be only slightly positively correlated. If a father had lifetime income earnings 20 percent above his generation, his son could expect to earn income about 8 percent above his generation. Virtually no positive correlation could be made between the earnings of

grandchildren and grandparents. In short, high-income and low-income earners will always be with us, but more than likely they will be different people.

10-5d WHY DO SOME EARN MORE THAN OTHERS?

Many reasons explain why some people earn more income than others. Some reasons for income differences include differences in age, skill, human capital (education and training), and preferences toward risk and leisure.

Age

The amount of income people earn varies over their lifetimes. Younger people with few skills tend to make little income when they begin their working careers. Income rises as workers gain experience and on-the-job training. As productivity increases, workers can command higher wages. These wage earnings generally increase up to the age of 50 and fall dramatically at retirement age, around 65.

Skills and Human Capital

Some workers are just more productive than others and therefore earn higher wages. Greater productivity can be a result of innate skills or of improvements in human capital, such as training and education. In Exhibit 10.12 on the next page, we see that college graduates' average earnings are much greater than high school graduates. Their unemployment rates are much lower, too. The financial rewards for attending college are higher than ever. Why is the gap widening between skilled and unskilled workers? One possibility is that increasing international trade over the last 30 years prompted an increase in domestic demand for skilled workers and a decrease in demand for domestic unskilled workers (unskilled workers are relatively cheap and plentiful in developing countries). That is, the United States tends to import goods produced with unskilled workers and export goods produced with skilled workers. In addition, technological changes to more sophisticated equipment can lead to an increase in demand for skilled workers. Other workers, such as star athletes and rock stars, have specialized talents that are in huge demand, so they make more money than those with fewer skills or with skills that are in less demand.

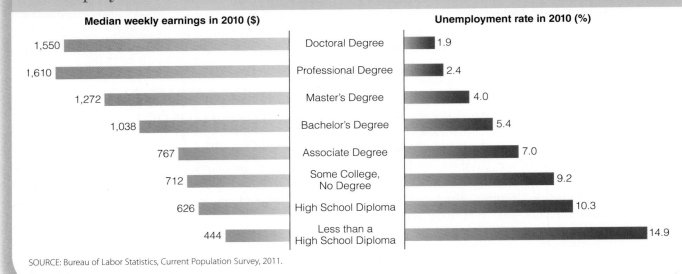

EXHIBIT 10.12 Education Pays in Higher Earnings and Lower Unemployment Rates

Median weekly earnings in 2010 ($)		Unemployment rate in 2010 (%)
1,550	Doctoral Degree	1.9
1,610	Professional Degree	2.4
1,272	Master's Degree	4.0
1,038	Bachelor's Degree	5.4
767	Associate Degree	7.0
712	Some College, No Degree	9.2
626	High School Diploma	10.3
444	Less than a High School Diploma	14.9

SOURCE: Bureau of Labor Statistics, Current Population Survey, 2011.

Worker Preferences

Aside from differences in age, skills, education, and training, people have different attitudes about and preferences regarding their work. Because workaholics (by definition) work longer hours, they earn more than others with comparable skills. Some workers earn more because they work more intensely than others. Still others may choose jobs that pay less but have more amenities—flexible hours, favorable job locations, generous benefit programs, child care, and so on. Some people choose to work less and spend more time pursuing leisure activities, such as traveling, hobbies, or spending time with family and friends. It is not for us to say that one preference is better than another but simply to recognize that these choices lead to differences in earnings.

Job Preferences

Finally, some of the differences in income are the result of the risks or undesirable features of some occupations. Police officers and firefighters are paid higher wages because of the dangers associated with their jobs. The same would be true for window washers on skyscrapers and painters on the Golden Gate bridge. Coal miners and garbage collectors are paid more than other workers with comparable skill levels because of the unpleasantness of the jobs. In short, some workers have higher earnings because they are

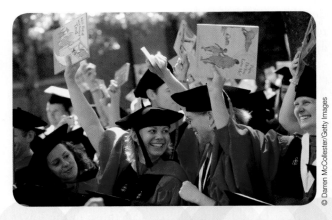

The number of women being admitted to top-flight MBA programs is rising. At Harvard, roughly 40 percent of the graduating class of 2013 will be females. Pennsylvania's Wharton School has a class closer to 45 percent female. Women have represented over 57 percent of enrollments on undergraduate campuses since 2000.

compensated for the difficult, risky, or unappealing nature of their jobs.

10-5e INCOME DISTRIBUTION IN OTHER COUNTRIES

Is the United States typical of advanced, industrial nations with respect to the distribution of income among its population? This question is difficult to answer with absolute certainty, given international differences in defining income, difficulties in measuring the impact of taxes, the problem of nonmonetary payments, and so on. Despite these hurdles, international comparisons of income distribution have been made.

Exhibit 10.13, constructed with data from the World Bank, shows that income inequality is greater in the United States and the United Kingdom than in Sweden and Japan. Japan's ratio of 4.5 means that the richest 10 percent of the population makes 4.5 times as much income as the bottom ten percent. In Brazil, the richest ten percent of the population makes 51.3 times as much income as the bottom 10 percent. The table shows that some of the greatest disparities in income are found in developing countries such as Mexico, South Africa, and Brazil.

Although income in equality within nations is often substantial, it is far less than income in equality among nations. A majority of income inequality on Earth reflects differences in living standards among countries rather than disparities within nations. This conclusion is borne out by statistics.

EXHIBIT 10.13 Global Income Inequalities

Income Inequality	Country	Gap between Rich and Poor (Ratio)
Most Equal	Japan	4.5
	Sweden	6.2
	Germany	6.9
	India	8.6
	France	9.1
	Canada	9.4
	Russia	11.0
	China	13.2
	United Kingdom	13.8
	United States	15.9
	Nigeria	16.3
	Mexico	21.0
	Chile	26.2
	Argentina	31.6
	South Africa	35.1
Least Equal	Brazil	40.6

NOTE: The ratio of the richest 10% to the poorest 10% gives us the gap between rich and poor. The smaller the ratio, the greater the equality.

SOURCE: World Bank

10-6 Poverty

SECTION CHECK 6

Consider the following questions as you read through this section.

1. How do we define poverty?

2. How many people live in poverty?

3. What is a negative income tax?

At several points in the previous discussion, the words *rich* and *poor* were used without being defined. Of particular interest is the question of poverty. Our concern over income distribution largely arises because most people believe that those with low incomes have lower satisfaction than those with higher incomes. Thus, the "poor" people are those who, in a material sense, suffer relative to other people. It is desirable, therefore, to define and measure the extent of poverty in the United States.

10-6a DEFINING POVERTY

The federal government measures poverty by using a set of money income thresholds that vary by family size. If the family's total income is less than the established family threshold, then that family, and every individual in it, is considered poor. The poverty thresholds are

poverty rate the percentage of the population who fall below the poverty line

poverty line a set of money income thresholds, established by the federal government, that vary by family size and are used to detect who is poor; if a family's total income is less than the established family threshold, then that family, and every individual in it, is considered poor

adjusted annually for inflation. The **poverty rate** is the percentage of the population that falls below this absolute level, called the **poverty line**. The official poverty rate for the United States is currently set at three times the cost of providing a nutritionally adequate diet—roughly $20,000 for a family of four. The official poverty definition may overstate the level of poverty because it does not include noncash benefits (such as public housing, Medicaid, and food stamps).

The amount of poverty fell steadily in the 1960s, was steady in the 1970s, and rose during the recession in the early 1980s. The poverty rate then fell slightly during the rest of the 1980s and rose again during the recessions of 1990–1991 and the recessions of 2001 and 2008–2009. As you would expect, when the economy is in a recession, unemployment rises and poverty tends to increase. Exhibit 10.14 provides some statistics on the U.S. poverty rate.

Poverty rates vary considerably among different races. Exhibit 10.15 shows that poverty rates for blacks and Hispanics were much higher than for whites. However, poverty rates fell markedly for blacks and Hispanics during the 1990s. Household status also influences poverty. A family headed by a female with

EXHIBIT 10.15 Poverty among Different Groups, 2010

Group	Below Poverty Rate
Female household, no husband present	31.6
Black	27.4
Hispanic	26.6
Children (under age 18)	22.0
Male household, no wife present	15.8
All persons	15.1
Asian	12.1
Elderly (over age 65)	9.9
White, not Hispanic	9.0
Married-couple families	6.2

SOURCE: U.S. Census Bureau

no husband present is about five times more likely to experience poverty than a family headed by a married couple. Children are also more likely than average to be members of poor families—see Exhibit 10.15.

10-6b INCOME REDISTRIBUTION

A variety of programs are designed to reduce poverty and redistribute income. We examine several of them here.

EXHIBIT 10.14 Poverty Rate: 1959 to 2010

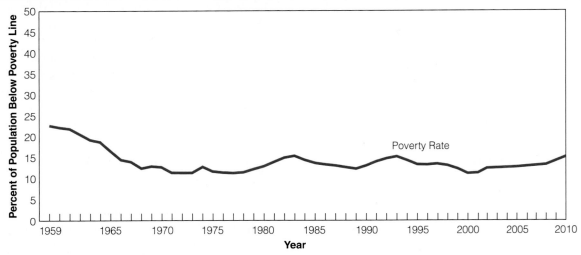

SOURCE: U.S. Census Bureau, Current Population Survey, 2011.

Taxes

One way to redistribute income to reduce disparities among individuals is through federal income tax. The federal income tax is designed to be a **progressive tax system**—one that imposes higher marginal tax rates on higher incomes. For example in 2011, if individuals made less than $34,500, their marginal tax rate was 15 percent. Income in excess of $34,500 but less than $83,600 was taxed at a marginal tax rate of 25 percent; income between $83,600 and $174,400 was taxed at a marginal tax rate of 28 percent; and income in the range of $174,400 to $379,150 was taxed at a marginal tax rate of 33 percent. Any income earned by an individual over $379,150 was taxed at a marginal tax rate of 35 percent.

Transfer Payments

A second means by which income redistribution can be carried out by the government is through direct transfer payments to the lower part of the income distribution. Transfer payments are payments made to individuals, for which goods or services are exchanged. They come in the form of in-kind transfers—direct transfers of goods or services such as food stamps, housing subsidies, and Medicaid—and **cash transfers** of direct cash payments such as welfare, Social Security, and unemployment compensation.

Social Security, Medicare, and Unemployment Compensation Social Security is a cash transfer program that provides income primarily to older persons. Social Security accounts for almost 45 percent of all federal transfer payments. Medicare is an in-kind transfer—a health insurance subsidy program that pays many of the doctor and hospital bills for those over the age of 65. Neither of these programs are considered welfare programs because one does not have to be poor to receive benefits. These two programs, Social Security and Medicare, account for almost 70 percent of all transfer payments. Benefits for the unemployed in the form of unemployment compensation are also a social insurance form of transfer payments. All three of these social insurance programs are event based—they are received upon job loss, old age, or disability.

Welfare Programs

The social insurance programs (Social Security, Medicare, and unemployment compensation) are different from welfare programs, for which a person or a family must prove they have a low enough income to qualify. Medicaid, a program designed to give health care to the poor, and the food stamp program are examples. Other welfare programs include **Supplemental Security Income (SSI)**, a program designed for the most needy, elderly, disabled, and blind, and **Temporary Assistance for Needy Families (TANF)**, designed to help families that have few financial resources. The **Earned Income Tax Credit (EITC)** is a program that allows the working poor to receive income refunds that can be greater than the taxes they paid during the last year. It is a **means-tested income transfer program** (eligibility is dependent on low income) like food stamps, Medicaid, and housing subsidies.

progressive tax system tax system that imposes higher marginal tax rates on higher incomes; the federal income tax is designed to be a progressive tax system

cash transfers direct cash payments such as welfare, Social Security, and unemployment compensation

Supplemental Security Income (SSI) a welfare program designed for the most needy, elderly, disabled, and blind

Temporary Assistance for Needy Families (TANF) a welfare program designed to help families that have few financial resources

Earned Income Tax Credit (EITC) a welfare program that allows the working poor to receive income refunds that can be greater than the taxes they paid during the last year

means-tested income transfer program program in which eligibility is dependent on low income; food stamps, Medicaid, and housing subsidies are examples of means-tested income transfer programs

Negative Income Tax

A negative income tax collects taxes from high-income families and gives subsidies to low-income families. Thus, it is a tax and transfer program. It uses the personal income tax system to set up a series of payments to citizens and tax receipts by the U.S. Treasury according to a schedule based on family size and actual income earned. The plan would not require setting up a new system. It could be an extension of the fully computerized system that already exists.

How Does it Work? High-income families would pay a tax; low-income families would receive a subsidy. For example, suppose the government formula for a negative tax is Tax = (25 percent × income) − $10,000. So, if a family earned $100,000 a year, it would pay $15,000 in taxes (0.25 × $100,000 = $25,000 − $10,000 = $15,000). A family that earned $40,000 a year would pay $0.00 in taxes (0.25 × $40,000 = $10,000 − $10,000 = $0). And a family that earned $20,000 would owe −$5,000 (0.25 × $20,000 = $5,000 − $10,000 = −$5,000). That is, this family would get $5,000 in return.

The Case for a Negative Income Tax Many economists favor a negative income tax. They point out that it would not require the massive bureaucracy that now exists for administering public assistance, food stamps, and other programs. Hence, many of the resources now spent for this huge bureaucracy could be spent on other priorities, or used to provide the negative tax (the government payment) to needy families. No one would have to demonstrate need. It would not encourage illegitimate births, family break-ups, or many claims the current welfare system does.

Negative income tax: Pros
- no bureaucracy

The Case Against a Negative Income Tax On the other hand, many economists oppose a negative income tax, pointing out that it might cost "too much." In particular, if for political reasons such current welfare programs as food stamps and subsidized housing cannot be dismantled, then the negative income tax would just be one more facet of the welfare system.

Negative income tax: Cons
- the work disincentive effect

They also contend that any effective negative income tax would have a *work disincentive effect*. That is, the payoff for returning to work would be smaller with an effective negative income tax program, so that many who could work might nevertheless decide not to do so. There is also concern that cash assistance, rather than in-kind welfare (food stamps, housing subsidies, etc.) would lead to poor consumption choices—perhaps drugs and alcohol. However, recipients would substitute food stamps for cash purchases, allowing them to buy whatever they wanted. And some critics say while it subsidizes the unfortunate, it also subsidizes the lazy and undeserving.

Government Subsidies

A third way that governments can help the less affluent is by using government revenues to provide low-cost public services. Inexpensive public housing, subsidized public transport, and even public parks are services that probably serve the poor to a greater extent than the rich. "Free" public education is viewed by many as an equalizing force in that it opens up opportunities

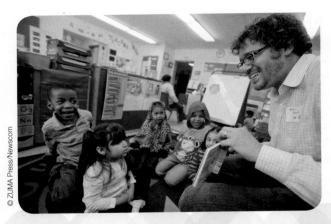

Early childhood education for high-risk kids could have potentially large payoffs. Many studies have confirmed that early years of learning are critical to cognitive development. Participants from early childhood programs are more likely to graduate from high school, more likely to earn more, and less likely to be on welfare or commit crimes. And that helps all of us.

for children of less prosperous members of society to obtain employment that could improve their economic status. Of course, not all government programs benefit the relatively poor at the expense of the rich. For example, federal government subsidies to commuter railroads primarily lower the cost to affluent suburbanites of getting to work in the central city. Support for public universities may help the middle- or even upper-income groups more than the poor. In addition, agricultural subsidies often provide large benefits to farmers who already have large incomes.

SECTION CHECK 6 ANSWERS

1. One method of defining poverty is to determine an absolute income level that is necessary to provide the basic necessities of life in minimum quantities. The poverty rate, then, would be the proportion for persons who fail to earn the minimum income standard.

2. The poverty level fell steadily in the 1960s, remained steady during the 1970s, and rose during the early 1980s. After falling again in the late 1980s, the poverty rate rose during the recessions of 1990–1991, 2001, and 2008–2009. The poverty rate can vary widely between different segments of the population.

3. A negative income tax is a tax and transfer program the collects taxes from higher income families and gives subsidies to lower income families.

Chapter 10: Self-Review

Now that you are finished reading the chapter, review the questions below. You can write your answers in the space provided, then go online to see the answers at www.cengagebrain.com.

10-1 INPUT MARKETS

1. Why is the demand for tractors and fertilizer derived from the demand for agricultural products?

10-2 SUPPLY AND DEMAND IN THE LABOR MARKET

2. True or False: A firm will hire another worker if the marginal revenue product of labor exceeds the market wage rate.

3. Why does the marginal product of labor eventually fall?

10-3 LABOR MARKET EQUILIBRIUM

4. True or False: If wages were above their equilibrium level, they would tend to fall toward the equilibrium level.

5. Why do increases in technology or increases in the amounts of capital or other complementary inputs increase the demand for labor?

10-4 LABOR UNIONS

6. Why are service industries harder to unionize than are manufacturing industries?

7. How do union restrictions on membership or other barriers to entry affect the wages of members?

10-5 INCOME DISTRIBUTION

8. How does the growth of both two-earner families and divorced couples increase measured income inequality?

9. How might each of the following affect the distribution of income in the near term?
   a. There is a massive influx of low-skilled immigrants.
   b. A new baby boom occurs.
   c. The new baby boomers enter their 20s.
   d. The new baby boomers reach age 65 or older.
   e. There is an increase in cash transfer payments, such as Supplemental Security Income.
   f. There is an increase in in-kind transfer payments, such as food stamps.

10-6 POVERTY

10. What are some of the programs designed to reduce poverty and redistribute income?

During the Great Depression,

U.S. unemployment levels reached historic highs—nearly 25%. Unemployment levels remained in the double-digits through 1941. Keeping high levels of employment, price stability, and high rates of economic growth are the major goals of macroeconomic policy. We will discuss unemployment and other macroeconomic issues in this chapter.

Test your Economics *street-smart* knowledge and see how you compare against other students! Scan here or visit CourseMate for Survey of ECON2.

11

Introduction to Macroeconomics: Unemployment, Inflation, and Economic Fluctuations

Now we focus our attention on macroeconomics and, in particular, on two key concepts that are at the heart of macroeconomics and economic policy making: unemployment and inflation.

To those who have just lost a job, unemployment ranks high on the stress meter. To an elderly person who is living on a fixed income, inflation and the loss of purchasing power may be just as threatening.

In this chapter, we see how economists define unemployment and inflation and consider the problems associated with each. In the last section of this chapter, we examine the short-run fluctuations in the economy—the so-called business cycle.

11-1 Macroeconomic Goals

SECTION CHECK 1

Keep the following questions in mind as you read through this section.

1. What are the most important macroeconomic goals in the United States?

2. How has the United States shown its commitment to these goals?

Recall from Chapter 1 that macroeconomics is the study of the whole economy—the study of the forest, not the trees. Let us begin by looking at some of the major issues that ultimately drive macroeconomic decisions.

11-1a THREE MAJOR MACROECONOMIC GOALS

Nearly every society has been interested in three major macroeconomic goals: (1) maintaining employment of human resources at relatively high levels, meaning that jobs are relatively plentiful and financial suffering from lack of work and income is relatively uncommon;

SECTIONS IN CHAPTER 11

223

3 Major Macroeconomic Goals

1) High employment

2) Stable price levels

3) High econominc growth levels

© iStockphoto.com/subjug

(2) maintaining prices at a relatively stable level so that consumers and producers can make better decisions; and (3) achieving a high rate of economic growth, meaning a growth in output per person over time. We use the term **real gross domestic product (RGDP)** to measure output or production. The term *real* is used to indicate that the output is adjusted for the general increase in prices over time. Technically, gross domestic product (GDP) is defined as the total value of all final goods and services produced in a given period of time, such as a year or a quarter. Accomplishing smooth, rapid economic growth in an environment of stable prices and low unemployment is no easy task. Sometimes the cure for one problem comes at the expense of another. In the coming chapters we will discuss the causes and possible remedies for high inflation, high unemployment, and sluggish economic growth.

11-1b ACKNOWLEDGING OUR GOALS: THE EMPLOYMENT ACT OF 1946

Many economic problems—particularly those involving unemployment, price instability, and economic stagnation—are pressing concerns for the U.S. government. The **Employment Act of 1946** and the Full Employment and Balanced Growth Act of 1978 (the Humphrey–Hawkins Act) commit the U.S. government to pursuing unemployment policies that are also consistent with price stability. This legislation was the first formal acknowledgment of these primary macroeconomic goals.

SECTION CHECK 1 ANSWERS

1. The most important U.S. macroeconomic goals are full employment, price stability, and economic growth.

2. The Employment Act of 1946 and the Full Employment and Balanced Growth Act of 1978 (the Humphrey–Hawkins Act) demonstrated the United States' commitment to the major macroeconomic goals.

11-2 Employment and Unemployment

SECTION CHECK 2

Keep the following questions in mind as you read through this section.

1. What are the consequences of unemployment?

2. What is the unemployment rate?

3. Does unemployment affect everyone equally?

4. How long are people typically unemployed?

In this section, we will discuss the issues surrounding unemployment and how it affects the economy.

11-2a THE CONSEQUENCES OF HIGH UNEMPLOYMENT

Unemployment figures are reported by the U.S. Department of Labor on a monthly basis. The news of lower unemployment usually sends stock prices higher; and the news of higher unemployment usually sends stock prices lower. Politicians are also concerned about the unemployment figures because elections often hinge precariously on whether unemployment has been rising or falling.

Nearly everyone agrees that it is unfortunate when a person who wants a job cannot find one. A loss of a job can mean financial insecurity and a great deal of anxiety. High rates of unemployment in a society can increase tensions and despair. A family without income from work undergoes great suffering; as a family's savings fade, family members wonder where they are going to obtain the means to survive. Society loses some potential output of goods when some of its productive resources—human or nonhuman—remain idle, and potential consumption is reduced. Clearly, then, a loss in efficiency occurs when people willing to work and equipment able to produce remain idle. That is, other things being equal, relatively high rates of unemployment are viewed almost universally as undesirable.

11-2b WHAT IS THE UNEMPLOYMENT RATE?

When discussing unemployment, economists and politicians refer to the **unemployment rate**. To calculate the unemployment rate, you must first understand another

EXHIBIT 11.1 The U.S. Labor Force, 2012

Labor Force (Employed + Unemployed)

(155.01 million)

| Civilians Employed **(142.29 million)** | Unemployed **(12.72 million)** | Out of Labor Force **(87.96 million)** |

Total Adult Population

(242.97 million)

SOURCE: Bureau of Labor Statistics

important concept—the **labor force**. The labor force is the number of people aged 16 and older who are available for employment, as shown in Exhibit 11.1. The civilian labor force figure excludes people in the armed services and those in prisons or mental hospitals. Other people regarded as outside the labor force include homemakers, retirees, and full-time students. These groups are excluded from the labor force because they are not considered currently available for employment.

When we say that the unemployment rate is 5 percent, we mean that 5 percent of the population aged 16 and older who are willing and able to work are unable to get jobs. This 5 percent means that 5 out of 100 people in the total labor force are unemployed. To calculate the unemployment rate, we simply divide the number of unemployed by the number in the civilian labor force:

$$\frac{Unemployment}{rate} = \frac{Number\ of\ unemployed}{Civilian\ labor\ force} \times 100$$

In May 2012, the number of civilians unemployed in the United States was 12.72 million, and the civilian labor force totaled 155.07 million. Using these data, we can calculate that the unemployment rate in February 2012 was 8.2 percent:

$$Unemployment\ rate = \frac{12.72\ million}{155.01\ million} \times 100$$

$$= 0.082 \times 100 = 8.2\ percent$$

11-2c THE WORST CASE OF U.S. UNEMPLOYMENT

By far, the worst employment downturn in U.S. history occurred during the Great Depression, which

began in late 1929 and continued until 1941. Unemployment rose from only 3.2 percent of the labor force in 1929 to more than 20 percent in the early 1930s, and double-digit unemployment persisted through 1941. The debilitating impact of having millions of productive people out of work led Americans (and people in other countries as well) to say, "Never again." Some economists would argue that modern macroeconomics, with its emphasis on the determinants of unemployment and its elimination, truly began in the 1930s.

labor force the number of people aged 16 and older who are available for employment

11-2d VARIATIONS IN THE UNEMPLOYMENT RATE

Exhibit 11.2 on the next page shows U.S. unemployment rates over the last 50 years. Unemployment since 1960 ranged from a low of 3.5 percent in 1969 to a high of 10.8 percent in 1982. The financial crisis of 2008 led to unemployment rates of 9.8 percent by early 2010. Unemployment in the worst years is two or more times what it is in good years. Before 1960, variations in unemployment were more pronounced.

11-2e ARE UNEMPLOYMENT STATISTICS ACCURATE REFLECTIONS OF THE LABOR MARKET?

In periods of prolonged recession, some individuals think that the chances of landing a job are so bleak that they

EXHIBIT 11.2 U.S. Unemployment Rates, 1960–2012

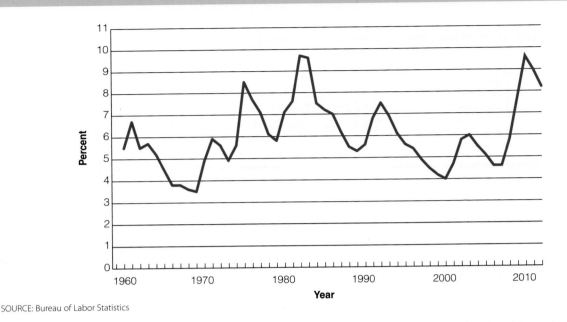

SOURCE: Bureau of Labor Statistics

---

discouraged worker an individual who has left the labor force because he or she could not find a job

quit looking. These people are called **discouraged workers**. Individuals who have not actively sought work for four weeks are not counted as unemployed; instead, they fall out of the labor force. Also, people looking for full-time work who grudgingly settle for part-time jobs are counted as "fully" employed, even though they are only "partly" employed. At least partially balancing these two biases in government employment statistics, however, is the number of people who are overemployed—that is, working overtime or at more than one job. Also, a number of jobs in the underground economy (e.g., drug dealing, prostitution, gambling, and so on) are not reported. In addition, many people may claim they are seeking work when, in fact, they may just be going through the motions so they can continue to collect unemployment compensation or receive other government benefits.

11-2f WHO ARE THE UNEMPLOYED?

Unemployment usually varies greatly across different segments of the population and over time.

Education as a Factor in Unemployment

According to the Bureau of Labor Statistics, the unemployment rate across the sexes and races among college graduates is significantly lower than for those who do not complete high school. In May 2012, the unemployment rate for individuals without high school diplomas was 13 percent, compared with 3.9 percent for those with bachelor's degrees and higher. Further, college graduates have lower unemployment rates than people who have some college education but did not complete their bachelor's degrees (7.9 percent).

Age, Sex, and Race as Factors in Unemployment

The incidence of unemployment varies widely among the population. Unemployment tends to be greater among the very young, among blacks and other minorities, and among workers with few skills. The unemployment rate for adult females tends to be higher than that for adult males.

Considering the great variations in unemployment for different groups in the population, we calculate separate unemployment rates for groups classified by sex, age, race, family status, and type of occupation. Exhibit 11.3 shows unemployment rates for various groups. Note that the variation around the average unemployment rate for the total population of 8.2 percent was considerable. The unemployment rate for blacks was much higher than the rate for whites, a phenomenon that has persisted throughout the post–World War II period. Unemployment among teenagers was

EXHIBIT 11.3 Unemployment in the United States by Age, Sex, and Race

a. U.S. Unemployment, by Sex and Age

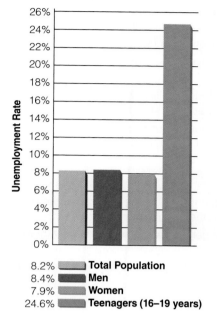

8.2%	**Total Population**
8.4%	**Men**
7.9%	**Women**
24.6%	**Teenagers (16–19 years)**

b. U.S. Unemployment, by Race or Ethnic Group

8.2%	**Total Population**
7.4%	**White**
13.6%	**Black**
11.0 %	**Hispanic**

SOURCE: Bureau of Labor Statistics

much higher than adult unemployment, at 24.6 percent. Some would regard teenage unemployment a lesser evil than unemployment among adults, because most teenagers have parents or guardians on whom they can rely for subsistence.

11-2g CATEGORIES OF UNEMPLOYED WORKERS

According to the Bureau of Labor Statistics, the four main categories of unemployed workers are **job losers** (those who have been temporarily laid off or fired), **job leavers** (those who have quit their jobs), **reentrants** (those who worked before and are reentering the labor force), and **new entrants** (those entering the labor force for the first time—primarily teenagers). It is a common misconception that most workers are unemployed because they have lost their jobs. Although job losers may typically account for 50–60 percent of the unemployed, a sizable fraction is due to job leavers, new entrants, and reentrants, as seen in Exhibit 11.4 on the next page.

11-2h HOW MUCH UNEMPLOYMENT?

Even though unemployment is painful to those who have no source of income, reducing unemployment is not costless. In the short run, a reduction in unemployment may come at the expense of a higher rate of inflation, especially if the economy is close to full capacity, where resources are almost fully employed. Moreover, trying to match employees with jobs can quickly lead to significant inefficiencies because of mismatches between a worker's skill level and the level of skill required for a job. For example, the economy would be wasting resources subsidizing education if people with PhDs in biochemistry were driving taxis or tending bars. That is, the skills of the employee may be higher than those necessary for the job, resulting in what economists

job loser an individual who has been temporarily laid off or fired

job leaver a person who quits his or her job

reentrant an individual who worked before and is now reentering the labor force

new entrant an individual who has not held a job before but is now seeking employment

EXHIBIT 11.4 Alternative Measures of Labor Underutilization

Measure and Description	Rate
U-1 Persons unemployed 15 weeks or longer, as a percent of the civilian labor force	4.6
U-2 Job losers and persons who completed temporary jobs, as a percent of the civilian labor force	4.6
U-3 Total unemployed, as a percent of the civilian labor force (official unemployment rate)	8.2
U-4 Total unemployed plus discouraged workers, as a percent of the civilian labor force plus discouraged workers	8.7
U-5 Total unemployed, plus discouraged workers, plus all other persons marginally attached to the labor force, as a percent of the civilian labor force plus all persons marginally attached to the labor force	9.7
U-6 Total unemployed, plus all persons marginally attached to the labor force, plus total employed part time for economic reasons, as a percent of the civilian labor force plus all persons marginally attached to the labor force	14.9

Bureau of Labor Statistics definitions:

Marginally attached workers: persons who currently are neither working nor looking for work but indicate that they want and are available for a job and have looked for work sometime in the past 12 months.

Discouraged workers: a subset of the marginally attached. These are persons who have given a job-market-related reason for not currently looking for work.

Persons employed part time for economic reasons: those who want and are available for full-time work but have had to settle for a part-time schedule.

SOURCE: U.S. Bureau of Labor Statistics, June 2012.

---

underemployment a situation in which a worker's skill level is higher than necessary for a job

call **underemployment.** Another source of inefficiencies is placing employees in jobs beyond their abilities. Because of the problems associated with accurately measuring the unemployment rate, the Bureau of Labor Statistics (BLS) calculates alternative measures of labor underutilization, as shown in Exhibit 11.4.

11-2i HOW LONG ARE PEOPLE USUALLY UNEMPLOYED?

The duration of unemployment is equally as important as the amount of unemployment. The financial consequences of a head of household's being unemployed for four or five weeks are usually not extremely serious, particularly if the individual is covered by an unemployment compensation system. The impact becomes much more serious if that person is unemployed for several months. Therefore, it is useful to look at the average duration of unemployment to discover what percentage of the labor force is unemployed longer than a certain period, say 15 weeks. Exhibit 11.6 presents

EXHIBIT 11.5 Reasons for Unemployment

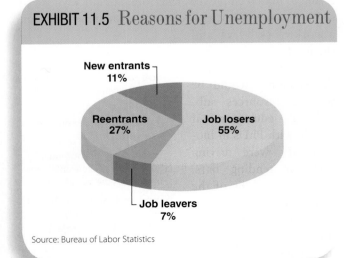

New entrants 11%
Reentrants 27%
Job losers 55%
Job leavers 7%

Source: Bureau of Labor Statistics

EXHIBIT 11.6 Duration of Unemployment

Duration	Percent Unemployed
Less than 5 weeks	20
5 to 14 weeks	24
15 to 26 weeks	13
27 weeks and over	43

SOURCE: Bureau of Labor Statistics

EXHIBIT 11.7 Labor Force Participation Rates for Men and Women

	1950	1960	1970	1980	1990	2000	2010
Total	59.2%	59.4%	60.4%	63.8%	66.5%	67.1%	64.7%
Men	86.4%	83.3%	79.7%	77.4%	76.4%	74.8%	71.2%
Women	33.9%	37.7%	43.3%	51.5%	57.5%	59.9%	58.6%

SOURCE: Bureau of Labor Statistics

data on the duration of unemployment. As you can see in this table, 20 percent of the unemployed were out of work less than five weeks, and 43 percent of the total unemployed were out of work for more than six months. The duration of unemployment tends to be greater when the amount of unemployment is high and smaller when the amount of unemployment is low. Unemployment of any duration, of course, means a potential loss of output. This loss of current output is permanent; it is not made up when unemployment starts falling again.

11-2j LABOR FORCE PARTICIPATION RATE

The percentage of the working age (aged 16 and older) population that is in the labor force is what economists call the **labor force participation rate**. Since 1950, the labor force participation rate increased from 59.2 percent to 64.7 percent today. During this time, the gender makeup of the labor force participation rate has changed significantly. For example, the number of women working shifted dramatically, reflecting the changing role of women in the workforce. Some factors contributing to this dramatic change are technological advances in household appliances and the decline in average household size. In Exhibit 11.7, we see that in 1950, less than 34 percent of women were working or looking for work. At the start of 2010 that figure was roughly 59 percent. In 1950, more than 85 percent of men were working or looking for work. In 2010 the labor force participation rate for men fell to 71 percent, as many men stay in school longer, retire earlier, and live longer. In addition, as more women become employed, more men become stay-at-home dads. Full-time students, stay-at-home dads, and retirees mean that more men are now out of the labor force.

SECTION CHECK 2 ANSWERS

1. The consequences of unemployment for society include a reduction in potential output and consumption—a decrease in efficiency.

2. The unemployment rate is found by taking the number of people officially unemployed and dividing by the number in the civilian labor force.

3. Unemployment rates are highest for minorities, the young, and less-skilled workers.

4. The duration of unemployment tends to be greater (smaller) when the amount of unemployment is high (low).

11-3 Types of Unemployment

SECTION CHECK 3

Keep the following questions in mind as you read through this section.

1. What is frictional unemployment?

2. What is structural unemployment?

3. What is cyclical unemployment?

4. What is the natural rate of unemployment?

In examining the status of and changes in the unemployment rate, it is important to recognize that unemployment can take several forms.

labor force participation rate the percentage of the working age population in the labor force

In this section, we will examine the three types of unemployment—frictional, structural, and cyclical—and evaluate the relative effects of each on the overall unemployment rate.

11-3a FRICTIONAL UNEMPLOYMENT

In a dynamic economy in which people are constantly losing or leaving their jobs, some frictional unemployment is always present. **Frictional unemployment** is the temporary unemployment that results from the search time that occurs when people are searching for suitable jobs and firms are looking for suitable workers. People seeking work do not usually take the first job offered to them. Likewise, firms do not usually take the first person they interview. People and firms engage in a search to match up skills and interests. While the unemployed are looking, they are frictionally unemployed.

For example, consider an advertising executive who was fired in Chicago and is now actively looking for similar work in San Francisco. Of course, not all unemployed workers were fired; some may have voluntarily quit their jobs. In either case, frictional unemployment is short term and results from normal turnover in the labor market, as when people change from one job to another.

11-3b SEASONAL UNEMPLOYMENT

Some unemployment occurs because certain types of jobs are seasonal in nature. This type of unemployment is called **seasonal unemployment**. For example, a ski instructor in Aspen might become seasonally unemployed at the end of April when ski season is over. Or a roofer in Minnesota may become seasonally unemployed during the harsh winter months. In agricultural areas, employment increases during harvest season and falls after the season is over. Even a forest firefighter in a national park might only be employed during the summer and fall, when forest fires peak. Occupations that experience either sharp seasonal shifts in demand or are subject to changing weather conditions may lead to seasonal unemployment—like in agriculture where employment increases during harvest season. Because this type of unemployment can make the unemployment rate higher in the off-season and lower during

frictional unemployment the unemployment that results from workers searching for suitable jobs and firms looking for suitable workers

seasonal unemployment unemployment that occurs because of seasonal factors such as weather or fluctuations in the demand for some goods or services during different times of the year

What type of unemployment would occur if these coal miners lost their jobs as a result of a permanent reduction in demand for coal and needed retraining to find other employment? Usually, structural unemployment occurs because of workers' lack of skills or long-term changes in demand. Consequently, it generally lasts for a longer period than does frictional unemployment.

the in-season, the Bureau of Labor Statistics (BLS) publishes a seasonally adjusted unemployment rate as well. These figures are more accurate because they take into account the effects of seasonal unemployment.

11-3c SHOULD WE WORRY ABOUT FRICTIONAL UNEMPLOYMENT?

Geographic and occupational mobility are considered good for the economy because they generally lead human resources to go from activities of relatively low productivity or value to areas of higher productivity, increasing output in society as well as the wage income of the mover. Indeed, some of this frictional unemployment involving searches by firms and workers to find *more* suitable matchups is obviously beneficial to the economy. Even though the amount of frictional unemployment varies somewhat over time, it is unusual for it to be much less than 2 percent of the labor force. Actually, frictional unemployment tends to be somewhat greater in periods of low unemployment, when job opportunities are plentiful. This high level of job opportunity stimulates mobility, which, in turn, creates some frictional unemployment.

11-3d STRUCTURAL UNEMPLOYMENT

A second type of unemployment is structural unemployment. Like frictional unemployment, structural unemployment is related to occupational movement or mobility—in this case, to a lack of mobility. Structural unemployment occurs when workers lack the necessary skills for jobs that are available or have particular skills that are no longer in demand. For example, if a machine operator in a manufacturing plant loses his job, he could still remain unemployed despite the openings for computer programmers in his community. The quantity of unemployed workers conceivably could equal the number of job vacancies, with the unemployment persisting because the unemployed lack the appropriate skills. Given the existence of structural unemployment, it is wise to look at both unemployment and job vacancy statistics in assessing labor market conditions. Structural unemployment, like frictional unemployment, reflects the dynamic dimension of a changing economy. Over time, new jobs open up that require new skills, while old jobs that required different skills disappear. It is not surprising, then, that many people advocate government-subsidized retraining programs as a means of reducing structural unemployment.

Another reason for structural unemployment is that low-skilled workers are frequently unable to find desirable long-term employment. Some of these low-skilled jobs do not last long and involve little job training, so a worker may soon be looking for a new job. Because they acquired no new skill from the old job, they may be stuck without long-term secure work. That is, structural workers cannot be said to be "in-between jobs" like those who are frictionally unemployed. Structural unemployment is more long term and serious than frictional unemployment because these workers do not have marketable skills.

The dimensions of structural unemployment are debatable, in part because of the difficulty in precisely defining the term in an operational sense. Structural unemployment varies considerably—sometimes it is low and at other times, as in the 1970s and early 1980s, it is high. To some extent, in the latter period, jobs in the traditional sectors, such as automobile manufacturing and oil production, were giving way to jobs in the computer and biotechnology sectors. Consequently, structural unemployment was higher.

11-3e SOME UNEMPLOYMENT IS UNAVOIDABLE

Some unemployment is actually normal and important to the economy. Frictional and structural unemployment are simply unavoidable in a vibrant economy. To a considerable extent, we can view both frictional and structural unemployment as phenomena resulting from imperfections in the labor market. For example, if individuals seeking jobs and employers seeking workers had better information about each other, the amount of frictional unemployment would be considerably less. It takes time for suppliers of labor to find the demanders of labor services, and it takes time and money for labor resources to acquire the necessary skills. But because information and job searches are costly, bringing together demanders and suppliers of labor services does not occur instantaneously.

11-3f CYCLICAL UNEMPLOYMENT

Often, unemployment is composed of more than just frictional and structural unemployment. In years of relatively high unemployment, some joblessness may result from short-term cyclical fluctuations in the economy. We call this **cyclical unemployment**. Whenever the unemployment rate is greater than normal, such as during a recession, it is due to cyclical unemployment. Most attempts to solve the cyclical unemployment problem emphasized increasing aggregate demand to counter recession.

The Cost of Cyclical Unemployment

When the unemployment rate is high, numerous economic and social hardships result. The economic costs are the forgone output when the economy is not producing at its potential level. According to Okun's Law (really, a rule of thumb), a 1 percent increase in cyclical unemployment reduces output by 2 percentage points. Thus, we can actually estimate the economic costs of not producing at our potential output. The costs are particularly high for those groups with the least skills—the poorly educated and teenagers with little work experience.

11-3g THE NATURAL RATE OF UNEMPLOYMENT

It is interesting to observe that over the period in which annual unemployment data are available, the median, or "typical," annual unemployment rate has been at or slightly above 5 percent. Some economists call this typical unemployment rate the **natural rate of unemployment**. When unemployment rises well

structural unemployment the unemployment that results from workers not having the skills to obtain long-term employment

cyclical unemployment unemployment due to short-term cyclical fluctuations in the economy

natural rate of unemployment the median, or "typical," unemployment rate, equal to the sum of frictional and structural unemployment when they are at a maximum

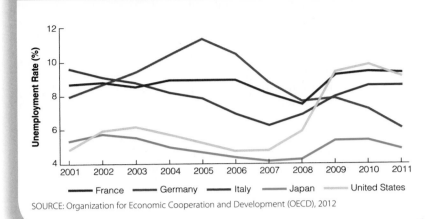

EXHIBIT 11.8 Unemployment Rates of Five Industrialized Nations, 2001–2011

SOURCE: Organization for Economic Cooperation and Development (OECD), 2012

Full Employment and Potential Output

When all the resources of an economy—labor, land, and capital—are fully employed, the economy is said to be producing its **potential output**. Literally, *full employment of labor* means that the economy is providing employment for all who are willing and able to work with no cyclical unemployment. It also means that capital and land are fully employed. That is, at the natural rate of unemployment, all resources are fully employed, the economy is producing its potential output, and no cyclical unemployment is present. It does not mean the economy will always be producing at its potential output of resources. For example, when the economy is experiencing cyclical unemployment, the unemployment rate is greater than the natural rate. It is also possible for the economy to temporarily exceed the natural rate, as workers put in overtime or moonlight by taking on extra employment.

In Exhibit 11.8, we see the unemployment rates for the United States are lower than for Italy, France and Germany but higher than Japan. In fact, European unemployment rates have been, on average, two percentage points higher than the United States over the last few decades. Why? Many economists believe the answer lies in differences in unemployment benefits and labor market regulations. In Europe, unemployment benefits are higher and last longer. Consequently, incentives for the unemployed to look for or accept work are reduced. Also, labor regulations in Europe make it difficult to fire employees, which makes employers more reluctant to hire new workers. Japan has lower unemployment rates because many companies give workers job security for life. Labor laws and social norms have also led to fewer layoffs.

above 5 percent, we have abnormally high unemployment; when it falls well below 5 percent, we have abnormally low unemployment. The natural rate of unemployment of approximately 5 percent roughly equals the sum of frictional and structural unemployment when they are at their maximums. Thus, we can view unemployment rates below the natural rate as reflecting the existence of below-average levels of frictional and structural unemployment. When unemployment rises above the natural rate, however, it reflects the existence of cyclical unemployment. In short, the natural rate of unemployment is the unemployment rate that occurs when the economy is experiencing neither a recession nor a boom. The natural rate of unemployment is also called the *full employment rate of unemployment*.

The natural rate of unemployment can change over time as technological, demographic, institutional, and other conditions vary. For example, as baby boomers age, the natural rate falls because middle-aged workers generally experience lower unemployment rates than do younger workers. In addition, the Internet and job placement agencies have improved access to employment information and allowed workers to find jobs more quickly. Also, the new work requirements of the welfare laws increased the number of people with jobs. Thus, the natural rate is not fixed, because it can change with demographic changes over time.

potential output the amount of real output the economy would produce if its labor and other resources were fully employed, that is, at the natural rate of unemployment

SECTION CHECK 3 ANSWERS

1. Frictional unemployment results when workers move from one job to another as workers search for suitable jobs and firms look for suitable workers.

2. Structural unemployment results when people who are looking for jobs lack the required skills for the jobs that are available if a long-term change in demand occurs.

3. Cyclical unemployment is caused by recession.

4. The natural rate of unemployment is achieved when cyclical unemployment is almost completely eliminated.

11-4 Reasons for Unemployment

SECTION CHECK 4

Keep the following questions in mind as you read through this section.

1. How does a higher minimum wage lead to greater unemployment among the young and unskilled?

2. How does an efficiency wage cause a higher rate of unemployment?

3. Does unemployment insurance increase the unemployment rate?

In this section, we will look at the causes of frictional and structural unemployment. In later chapters, we will discuss the causes of cyclical unemployment.

11-4a WHY DOES UNEMPLOYMENT EXIST?

In many markets, prices adjust to the market equilibrium price and quantity, and no prolonged periods of shortage or surplus occur. However, in labor markets, obstacles prevent wages from adjusting and balancing the quantity of labor supplied and the quantity of labor demanded. In Exhibit 11.9, we see that W_1 is higher than the market equilibrium wage that equates the quantity demanded of labor with the quantity supplied of labor. At W_1, the quantity of labor supplied is greater than

EXHIBIT 11.9 Wages above Equilibrium Lead to Greater Unemployment

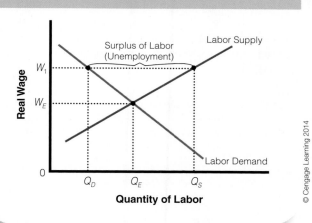

© Cengage Learning 2014

the quantity of labor demanded, resulting in an excess quantity supplied of labor—unemployment. That is, more people want to work at the going (non-equilibrium) wage than employers want to hire, and those who are not able to find work are "unemployed." Why? Economists cite three reasons for the failure of wages to balance the labor demand and labor supply equilibrium—minimum wages, unions, and the efficiency wage theory.

11-4b MINIMUM WAGES AND UNEMPLOYMENT

Many different types of labor markets exist for different types of workers. The labor market for workers with little experience and job skills is called the unskilled labor market. Suppose the government decided to establish a **minimum wage rate** (an hourly wage floor) for unskilled workers above the equilibrium wage, W_E. At the minimum wage, the quantity of labor supplied grows because more people are willing to work at a higher wage. However, the quantity of labor demanded falls because some employers would find it unprofitable to hire low-skilled workers at the higher wage. At W_1, a gap exists between the quantity of labor demanded and the quantity supplied, representing a surplus of unskilled workers—unemployment, as seen in Exhibit 11.9.

Because minimum wage earners, a majority of whom are 25 years or younger, are a small portion of the labor force, most economists believe the effect of minimum wage on unemployment is small.

11-4c THE IMPACT OF UNIONS ON THE UNEMPLOYMENT RATE

Unions negotiate their wages and benefits collectively through their union officials, a process called collective bargaining. If, through this process of collective bargaining, union officials are able to increase wages, then unemployment will rise in the union sector. If the bargaining raises the union wage above the equilibrium level, the quantity of union labor demanded will decrease, and the quantity of union labor supplied will increase—that is, union workers will be unemployed. The union workers who still have their jobs will be better off, but some who are equally skilled will be unemployed and will either seek nonunion work or wait to be recalled in the union sector. Many economists believe that is why wages are approximately 15 percent higher

efficiency wage model
a theory stating that higher wages lead to greater productivity

in union jobs, even when nonunion workers have comparable skills. On the other hand, even though wages in the union sector are typically higher than the market wage, the presence of unions does not necessarily lead to greater unemployment, because workers can find jobs in the nonunion sector. Less than 10 percent of private sector jobs are unionized.

11-4d EFFICIENCY WAGE

In economics, it is generally assumed that as productivity rises, wages rise, and workers can raise their productivity through investments in human capital such as education and on-the-job training. However, some economists follow the **efficiency wage model**, which is based on the belief that *higher wages lead to greater productivity*.

In the efficiency wage model, employers pay their employees more than the equilibrium wage to be more efficient. Proponents of this theory suggest that it may lead to attracting the most productive workers, fewer job turnovers, and higher morale, which in turn can lead to lower hiring and training costs. In addition, higher-paid workers may be healthier (better diets) and therefore more productive. This is particularly true in developing countries. In Exhibit 11.9, suppose workers are paid W_E. Why wouldn't they shirk at their current job if someone else will hire them almost immediately at the same wage? In short, there are few adverse consequences to shirking. One option for firms is to pay an efficiency wage. However, if all firms pay an efficiency wage, like W_1 in Exhibit 11.9, then why can't they just shirk and if fired, find another firm that will pay them W_1? The reason is because at W_1, firms are paying higher than the equilibrium wage reducing the number of jobs, so fired workers might face a prolonged period of unemployment.

THE JOB MARKET

While the job market is improving slightly, one particular challenge faces labor markets: long-term unemployment. Long-term unemployment has reached nearly every segment of the population, but some groups have been hit particularly hard. The typical long-term unemployed worker is a white man with a high school education or less. Older unemployed workers also tend to be out of work longer. "The longer folks are out of a job, the longer it takes them to find a new one." What is particularly troubling for the long-term unemployed is that their skill levels deteriorate. Consequently, they are more likely to stop looking—becoming discouraged workers.

Education has not been a cure-all. More college graduates have become long-term unemployed. They represent 15.9 percent of the long-term jobless, compared with 14.9 percent of all unemployed workers. Those with high school degrees who haven't been to college comprise 40.7 percent of long-term unemployed, compared with 37.8 percent of all unemployed workers.

Worker mobility has fallen sharply. That is, the number of job seekers who successfully relocate for new positions has hit historically low levels. "What's unique in this job cycle is hires and fires are very low, and fewer people are quitting jobs," says Jeffrey Cleveland, senior economist at the investment firm Payden & Rygel. In addition, taking jobs in other cities is harder in this housing market, as more and more people decide to keep their homes. In short, employers are frequently finding that job candidates don't have the right skills to match the jobs they have to offer.

One reason why corporations aren't hiring is the absence of clarity about the costs of financial and health care regulations and the weakness of global growth. Austan Goolsbee, former White House Council of Economic Advisers chair, stated: "We've got to rely on government policies that are trying to leverage the private sector and give incentives to the private sector to be doing the growth." University of Chicago economist Raghuram Rajan says, "The truth is, there aren't many short-term fixes. The real answers to the jobs problem will take more time." And that means chronically high unemployment may persist.

The silver lining is that chronically high joblessness won't last forever. As incomes and wages in emerging markets rise, demand will rise, leading globally focused companies to begin increasing hiring in the United States.

SOURCES: Roya Wolverson, "Why Is Chronic Joblessness on the Rise?" *Time*, June 8, 2011. "http://curiouscapitalist.blogs.time.com/2011/06/08/is-chronic-joblessness-here-to-stay/".

Ben Tracy, "Chronic Unemployment Highest Since Great Depression," June 5, 2011, *CBS News*. http://www.cbsnews.com/stories/2011/06/05/eveningnews/main20069136.shtml.

Sara Murray, "Chronic Joblessness Bites Deep: Long-Term Unemployment Hits New High, Cuts Across Income Levels, Demographics," *The Wall Street Journal*, June 2, 2010. http://online.wsj.com/article/SB10001424052748703961204575280753219161046.html?mod=WSJ_hpp_MIDDLENexttoWhatsNewsThird.

In 1914, Henry Ford increased his workers' wages from $3 to $5 per day—roughly twice the going wage rate for unskilled workers. This wage rate led to long lines of workers seeking jobs at the Ford plant—that is, quantity supplied greatly exceeded quantity demanded at the efficiency wage rate. Ford knew that assembly-line work was boring, and to overcome the problem he was having with morale and absenteeism, he decided to increase daily wages to $5 a day. At the time, many business leaders were skeptical because this put Ford's labor costs at nearly twice that of his rivals. However, Ford's profits continued to mount. Historical records suggest that the efficiency wage led to lower turnover, less absenteeism, better hires, and less shirking—in short, greater worker productivity. Even though the higher wages led to higher labor costs, the costs were more than offset by the increase in worker productivity.

Some scholars have argued that the positive effects of the efficiency wage are unique to assembly-line production and its high degree of worker interdependence. However, it is costly for firms to pay an efficiency wage. Consequently, firms must monitor their workers' efforts. If enough firms resort to paying the efficiency wage rate, it leads to a surplus of workers who want jobs and cannot find them. This, like a binding minimum wage, leads to unemployment.

11-4e JOB SEARCH

Another reason for unemployment has to do with the nature of labor markets. Because of frictional unemployment, some unemployment would exist even if labor supply and labor demand were balanced. Different firms offer different compensation packages (i.e., salary, fringe benefits, and working conditions), and workers are sometimes unaware of these packages when they seek the "best" job available. It takes time and money to locate the best available opportunities. Also, not all job seekers are the same: They have different tastes and preferences about types of jobs and job locations. Sometimes it is difficult to get the information about particular jobs to the right job candidate. These search activities prolong the duration of unemployment. However, the search goes on because the job seeker hopes to find a better offer.

The labor demand and supply curves are constantly shifting. That is, labor markets are constantly in flux—there are always people losing jobs, leaving jobs, and reentering jobs. In a growing and dynamic economy, jobs are constantly being destroyed and created, leading to temporary unemployment as workers search for the best jobs for their skills.

11-4f UNEMPLOYMENT INSURANCE

Losing a job can lead to considerable hardships, and unemployment insurance is designed to partially offset the severity of the unemployment problem. The program does not cover those who were fired or quit their jobs. To qualify, recipients must have worked a certain length of time and lost their jobs because the employer no longer needed their skills. The typical compensation is half salary for 26 weeks. Although the program is intended to ease the pain of unemployment, it also leads to prolonged periods of unemployment, as job seekers stay unemployed for longer periods searching for new jobs.

For example, some unemployed people may show little drive in seeking new employment, because unemployment insurance lowers the opportunity cost of being unemployed. Say a worker making $400 a week when employed receives $220 in compensation when unemployed; as a result, the cost of losing the job is not $400 a week in forgone income but only $180. It has been estimated that the existence of unemployment compensation programs may raise overall unemployment rates by as much as 1 percent.

Without unemployment insurance, a job seeker would be more likely to take the first job offered, even if the job did not match the job seeker's preferences or skill levels. A longer job search might mean a better match, but it comes at the expense of lost production and greater amounts of tax dollars.

Of course, that does not mean that unemployment insurance is necessarily a bad program. It still serves its desired goal of reducing income uncertainty. Workers who turn down unattractive jobs have an opportunity to find better jobs that may be better suited for their tastes and skills. In summary, most economists believe that eliminating unemployment insurance could reduce unemployment, but they disagree on whether economic well-being is reduced or enhanced by a change in the policy.

11-4g DOES NEW TECHNOLOGY LEAD TO GREATER UNEMPLOYMENT?

The widespread belief that technological advances inevitably result in the displacement of workers is not necessarily true. Generally, new inventions are cost saving, and these cost savings usually generate higher incomes for producers and lower prices and better products for consumers—benefits that ultimately result in the growth of other industries. If the new equipment is a substitute for labor, it might displace workers. For example, many

EXHIBIT 11.10 Skill-Biased Technical Change and Wage Inequality

a. Skilled Workers

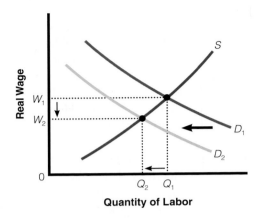

b. Unskilled Workers

© Cengage Learning 2014

fast-food restaurants installed self-service beverage bars to replace workers. However, new capital equipment requires new workers to manufacture and repair the new equipment. The most famous example of this trade-off is the computer, which was supposed to displace thousands of workers. Instead, the computer generated a whole new growth industry that created jobs. The problem is that it is easy to see only the initial effect of technological advances (displaced workers) but difficult to recognize the implications of that invention throughout the whole economy over time.

Some economists believe that some of the real-wage differentials between skilled and unskilled workers in the last couple of decades are due to technical changes that are biased toward skilled workers. New machines, with highly sophisticated computerization, require highly skilled workers. Consequently, the new machines make these workers more productive and therefore they receive higher real wages. In Exhibit 11.10(a), we graph the labor market for skilled workers. Because of the

increase in demand for skilled labor—skilled workers can produce more with the new machines—their real wages and employment are higher. At the same time, the demand is lower for workers who do not have the technical training to work with specialized machinery, and the demand for unskilled workers falls, as seen in Exhibit 11.10(b). As a result of the decrease in demand for unskilled workers, real wages and employment fall. Thus, skill-biased technical change tends to create even greater disparities between the wages of skilled and unskilled workers. The message: stay in school (vocational or traditional).

> It has been estimated that the **existence of unemployment compensation programs** may raise overall unemployment rates by as much as 1 percent.

SECTION CHECK 4 ANSWERS

1. At the minimum wage, the quantity of labor supplied grows. However, the quantity of labor demanded falls because some employers would find it unprofitable to hire low-skilled workers at the higher wage. Thus a higher minimum wage can lead to higher unemployment—particularly among unskilled teenage workers.

2. If the efficiency wage rate is greater than the equilibrium wage rate, the quantity of labor supplied is greater than the quantity of labor demanded, resulting in greater amounts of unemployment.

3. Some unemployed persons may show little drive in seeking new employment, given the existence of unemployment compensation. Unemployment compensation lowers the opportunity cost of being unemployed.

11-5 Inflation

SECTION CHECK 5

Keep the following questions in mind as you read through this section.

1. What is the purpose of a price-level index?
2. Who are the winners and losers during inflation?
3. Can wage earners avoid the consequences of inflation?

11-5a STABLE PRICE LEVEL AS A DESIRABLE GOAL

Just as full employment brings about one kind of economic security, an overall stable **price level** increases another form of economic security. Most prices in the U.S. economy tend to rise over time. The continuing rise in the *overall* price level is called **inflation**. Even when the level of prices is stable, some prices will be rising while others are falling. However, when inflation is present, the goods and services with rising prices will outweigh the goods and services with lower prices. Without stability in the price level, consumers and producers will experience more difficulty in coordinating their plans and decisions. When the *overall* price level is falling, it is called **deflation**. The average price level in the U.S. economy fell throughout the late nineteenth century.

A reduction in the rate of inflation is called *disinflation*. In the United States, we saw disinflation from 1981–1986, 1991–1994, and 2001–2003. It is difficult and costly to bring the inflation rate down once it has become expected. Most economists believe that the inflation rates of the 1970s were finally brought under control by the 1980–1981 recession, when the unemployment rate reached 10.7 percent. Thus, most believe the best policy is to not let inflation get out of control in the first place—one of the primary jobs of the Federal Reserve System.

In general, the only thing that can cause a *sustained* increase in the rate of inflation is a high rate of growth in money, a topic we will discuss further in upcoming chapters.

11-5b MEASURING INFLATION

We often use the term *purchasing power* when we discuss how much a dollar can buy of goods and services. In times of inflation, a dollar cannot buy as many goods and services. Thus, the higher the inflation rate, the greater the rate of decline in purchasing power.

In periods of high and variable inflation, households and firms have a difficult time distinguishing between changes in the **relative price** of individual goods and services (the price of a specific good compared to the prices of other goods) and changes in the general price level of all goods and services. Suppose the price of milk rises by 5 percent between 2012 and 2013, but the overall price level (inflation rate) increases by only 2 percent during that period. Then we could say that between 2012 and 2013, the relative price of milk rose only 3 percent (5 percent – 2 percent). The next year, the price of milk might increase 5 percent again, but the general inflation rate might be 6 percent. That is, between 2013 and 2014, the relative price of milk might actually fall by 1 percent (5 percent – 6 percent). Remember, the relative price is the price of a good relative to all other goods and services. Because of this difficulty in establishing relative prices, inflation distorts the information that flows from price signals. Does the good have a higher price because it has become relatively more scarce and therefore more valuable relative to other goods, or did the price rise along with all other prices because of inflation? This muddying of price information undermines good decision making.

Thus, we need a method to measure inflation. We adjust for the changing purchasing power of the dollar by constructing a price index. Essentially, a **price index** attempts to provide a measure of the prices paid for a certain bundle of goods and services over time.

11-5c THE CONSUMER PRICE INDEX AND THE GDP DEFLATOR

There are many different types of price indices. The most well-known index, the **consumer price index (CPI)**, measures the trend in the prices of certain goods and services purchased for consumption purposes. It attempts to weight these goods and services by how much consumers buy of each of item shown, as in Exhibit 11.11.

price level the average level of prices in the economy

inflation a rise in the overall price level, which decreases the purchasing power of money

deflation a decrease in the overall price level, which increases the purchasing power of money

relative price the price of a specific good compared to the price of other goods

price index a measure of the trend in prices paid for a certain bundle of goods and services over a given period

consumer price index (CPI) a measure of the cost of a market basket that represents the consumption of a typical household

GDP deflator a price index that helps measure the average price level of all final consumer goods and services produced

The CPI may be most relevant to households trying to evaluate their changing financial positions over time.

The **GDP deflator** corrects for changing prices in even broader terms. The GDP deflator measures the average level of prices of all final goods and services produced in the economy.

11-5d HOW IS A PRICE INDEX CREATED?

Constructing a price index is complicated. First, literally thousands of goods and services are in our economy; attempting to include all of them in an index would be cumbersome and make the index expensive to compute, and it would take a long time to gather the necessary data. Therefore, a "bundle" or "basket" of representative goods and services is selected by the index calculators (the Bureau of Labor Statistics of the U.S. Department of Labor for consumer and wholesale price indices and the Office of Business Economics of the Department of Commerce for the GDP deflator).

Calculating a Simple Price Index

Suppose a consumer typically buys 24 loaves of bread and 12 gallons of milk in a year. The table that follows lists the prices of bread and milk and the cost of the consumer's typical market basket in the years 2010–2012.

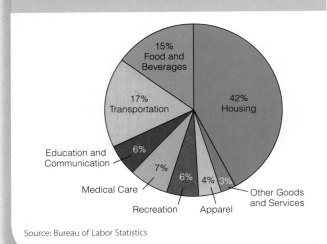

EXHIBIT 11.11 The Typical CPI Shopping Basket of Goods and Services

15% Food and Beverages
17% Transportation
42% Housing
6% Education and Communication
7% Medical Care
6% Recreation
4% Apparel
3% Other Goods and Services

Source: Bureau of Labor Statistics

Year	Price of Bread	Price of Milk	Cost of Market Basket
2010	$1.00	$2.00	(24 × $1.00) + (12 × $2.00) = $48.00
2011	$1.15	$2.10	(24 × $1.15) + (12 × $2.10) = $52.80
2012	$1.40	$2.20	(24 × $1.40) + (12 × $2.20) = $60.00

Using the numbers from the table above and the following formula, we can calculate a price index to measure the inflation rate.

$$Price\ index = \frac{Cost\ of\ market\ basket\ in\ current\ year}{Cost\ of\ market\ basket\ in\ base\ year} \times 100$$

The year 2010 is designated as the base year, so its value is set equal to 100.

Year	Price Index
2010	$48/$48 × 100 = 100
2011	$52.80/$48 × 100 = 110
2012	$60/$48 × 100 = 125

A comparison of the price indices shows that between 2010 and 2011, prices increased an average of 10 percent. In addition, between 2010 and 2012, 25 percent inflation occurred.

$$Price\ index = \frac{Cost\ of\ market\ basket\ in\ 2012}{Cost\ of\ market\ basket\ in\ 2010} \times 100$$

$$= \frac{\$60}{\$48} \times 100 = 125$$

That is, the price index for 2012 compared with 2010 is 125. Therefore, using the price index formula, we can say that prices are 25 percent higher in 2012 than they were in 2010, the base year.

Unfortunately, not all prices move by the same amount or in the same direction. Consequently, we need to calculate an average of the many price changes. This calculation is complicated by several factors. First, goods and services change in quality over time, so the observed price change may, in reality, reflect a quality change in the product rather than the purchasing power of the dollar. A $300 television set today is dramatically better than a television set in 1950. Second, new products come on the market and old products occasionally disappear. For example, color TV sets did not exist in 1950 but are a major consumer item now. How can we calculate changes in prices over time when some products did not even exist in the earlier period? Clearly, calculating a price index is not a simple, direct process, and many factors can potentially distort the CPI.

11-5e PROBLEMS WITH CPI

It is very difficult to measure changes in the price level. Since 1995, the Bureau of Labor Statistics (BLS) has been eliminating or reducing biases that cause the index to overstate inflation. Many economists believe that the BLS improvements have cut the inflationary bias in half and it is now estimated to be less than 1 percent per year.

It is important that the CPI measure inflation accurately or that the degree of bias be known. If the CPI does not measure inflation correctly, cost-of-living adjustments for wages, social security benefits, and even alimony and child support will be distorted. It is estimated that 30 percent of federal outlays are tied to the CPI. So a 1 percent correction in the upward bias of CPI could amount to saving billions of dollars a year. The are four biases that cause changes in the CPI to overstate the true inflation rate.

The Substitution Bias

Substitution bias occurs because the CPI measures the price changes of a fixed basket of goods and services. That is, it assumes that consumers purchase the same amount of each product in the basket. Thus, it does not capture the savings that households enjoy when they change their spending in response to relative price changes. When prices change from year to year, they do not change proportionately. Some prices rise more than others. Consumers respond to incentives; they buy less of those goods that have increased a large amount and buy more of those goods that have risen just a little or fallen. If the basket is fixed, it misses people substituting away from the high-priced goods, and the CPI overstates the increased cost of living.

The Quality Bias

This bias arises because some of any increase in the price of an item may be due to an improvement in quality, rather than being a pure price increase. For example, take the personal computer, where greater speeds and more features have become available without substantial increases in price. If the CPI only looks at the price of a computer, they will miss the quality changes from these features. Quality improvements in many areas—such as medical care—are difficult to measure, so the quality bias is more likely to occur. And features of a product that become mandatory—such as seat belts, which buyers are forced to purchase—are particularly difficult to handle.

The New Outlet Bias

This type of bias is similar to substitution bias, but refers to where households shop rather than to what they purchase. Over the past 15 years, for example, the growth of discount stores like Costco and Sam's Club has helped consumers lower their expenditures. A similar problem arises with online shopping, which now accounts for a significant fraction of sales. However, when the BLS collects data on the same or similar products from full-price retail stores, the CPI overstates the prices some buyers actually paid.

The New Product Bias

This bias occurs because new products, such as iPhones or iPads, are not introduced into the index until they are commonplace items. This means that the substantial price decreases and quality increases that occur during the early years following introduction are not captured by the index.

11-5f GDP DEFLATOR VERSUS CPI

Is the CPI or the GDP deflator a better indicator of inflation? Or does it not really matter which one we use? The two measures tend to move in the same direction but the CPI tends to be much more volatile—it bounces around more than the GDP deflator. However, both measures probably overstate the inflation rate. One important difference between them that can yield different results is that the GDP deflator measures the price of all goods and services that are *produced domestically*, while the CPI measures the goods and services *bought by consumers*. For example, a Porsche produced in Stuttgart, Germany, will show up in the CPI, but it will not show up in the GDP deflator because it was not produced in the U.S. economy. More important, the same is true for the price of oil, because much of U.S. oil is imported. Consequently, oil price increases are fully captured in the CPI but only partially captured in the GDP deflator—partially captured because those increases do add to the cost of production.

However, suppose the price of an airplane or aircraft carrier being produced domestically for the military increases. Because it is produced domestically, its price will show up in the GDP deflator but not in the typical consumer basket—the CPI.

11-5g THE PRICE LEVEL OVER THE YEARS

Unanticipated and sharp changes in the price level are almost universally considered to be "bad" and to require a policy remedy. What is the historical record

EXHIBIT 11.12 Inflation in the United States, 1913–2011

Consumer Price Index

All Urban Consumers (CPI-U), Annual Percentage Change

SOURCE: Bureau of Labor Statistics, *Consumer Price Index*, Table Containing History of CPI-US. All Items Indexes and Annual Percent Changes From 1913 to Present. Washington, D.C.

of changes in the overall U.S. price level? Exhibit 11.12 shows changes in the consumer price index (CPI), the standard measure of inflation, from 1913 to 2011. Can you believe that in 1940, stamps were 3 cents per letter, postcards were a penny, the median price of a house was $2,900, and the price of a new car was $650? However, the problem with comparing prices today with prices in the past is that it focuses on the number of dollars it takes to buy something, rather than the purchasing power of the dollar. For example, if prices and wages both doubled overnight, raising the price of a quart of

milk from $1 to $2, you would be no worse off because you would still work the same number of minutes to buy a quart of milk.

In Exhibit 11.13, we can see that inflation rates in the US are similar to Europe since 2001—not extraordinarily high, not extraordinarily low. Inflation rates in Japan are consistently lower. Inflation rates declined in 2009 as a result of the reduction in demand from the global recession. Inflation rates rebounded in 2010 and 2011 as the global economy began to recover.

EXHIBIT 11.13 Inflation Rates of Five Industrialized Nations, 2001–2011

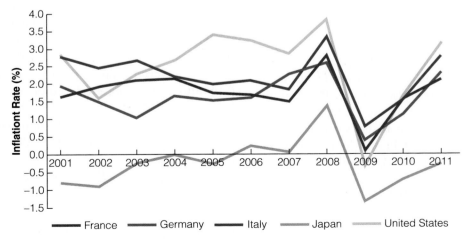

SOURCE: Organization For Economic Cooperation and Development (OECD), 2012

11-5h WHO LOSES WITH INFLATION?

Inflation brings about changes in peoples' purchasing power, and these changes may be either desirable or undesirable. Suppose you retire on a fixed pension of $2,000 per month. Over time, that $2,000 will buy less and less if prices generally rise. Your real income—your income adjusted to reflect changes in purchasing power—falls. Inflation lowers income in real terms for people on fixed-dollar incomes. Likewise, inflation can hurt creditors. For example, suppose a bank loaned someone money for a house at a 4 percent fixed rate for 20 years, in the early 1960s (a period of low inflation). However, the 1970s was a period of high inflation rates (roughly 10 percent per year). Under this scenario, because the lender did not correctly anticipate the higher rate of inflation, the lender is the victim of unanticipated inflation. That is, the borrower is paying back with dollars that have much less purchasing power than those dollars they borrowed in the early 1960s. Another group that sometimes loses from inflation, at least temporarily, comprises people whose incomes are tied to long-term contracts. If inflation begins shortly after a labor union signs a three-year wage agreement, it may completely eat up the wage gains provided by the contract. The same applies to businesses that agree to sell quantities of one thing, say coal, for a fixed price for a given number of years.

If some people lose because of changing prices, others must gain. Debtors pay back dollars worth less in purchasing power than those borrowed. Corporations that can quickly raise the prices on their goods may have revenue gains greater than their increases in costs, providing additional profits. Wage earners sometimes lose from inflation because wages may rise at a slower rate than the price level. The redistributional impact of inflation is not the result of conscious public policy; it just happens. Some economists believe that significant costs are incurred when individuals and firms devote resources to protecting themselves against expected future inflation. This could include working out long-term contracts with automatic adjustments for employment or purchases of raw materials and other goods.

The uncertainty that inflation creates can also discourage investment and economic growth. When inflation rates are high, they also tend to vary considerably, which creates a lot of uncertainty. This uncertainty complicates planning for businesses and households, which is vital to capital formation, as well as adding an inflation risk premium to long-term interest rates.

Moreover, inflation can raise one nation's price level relative to price levels in other countries. In turn, this shift can make financing the purchase of foreign goods difficult, or it can decrease the value of the national currency relative to that of other countries.

hyperinflation extremely high rates of inflation for sustained periods of time

Costs of High Inflation

Predictably low rates of inflation, while still a problem, are considerably better than high and variable inflation rates. A slow predictable rate of inflation makes predicting future price increases relatively easy. Consequently, setting interest rates will be an easier task and the redistribution effects of inflation will be minimized. In addition, high and variable inflation rates make it almost impossible to set long-term contracts because prices and interest rates may be changing by the day, or even by the hour in the case of **hyperinflation**—extremely high rates of inflation for sustained periods of time.

In its extreme form, inflation can lead to a complete erosion of faith in the value of the pieces of paper we commonly call money. In Germany, after both world wars, prices rose so fast that people in some cases finally refused to take paper money, insisting instead on payment in goods or metals, whose prices tend to move predictably with inflation. Unchecked inflation can feed on itself and may ultimately lead

© World History Archive/Alamy

German woman using money as fuel in her wood-burning stove. During the 1923–24 hyperinflation in Germany, it took less paper money to generate needed heat in the stove by burning the money than it did to use it to buy wood to burn.

to hyperinflation of 300 percent or more per year. We saw these rapid rates of inflation in Argentina in the 1980s and Brazil in the 1990s. Most economists believe we can live quite well in an environment of low, steady inflation, but no economist believes we can prosper with high, variable inflation.

11-5i UNANTICIPATED INFLATION DISTORTS PRICE SIGNALS

We often use the term *purchasing power* when we discuss how many goods and services a dollar can buy. In times of inflation, a dollar buys fewer goods and services. Thus, the higher the inflation rate, the greater the rate of decline in purchasing power. In periods of high and variable inflation, households and firms have a difficult time distinguishing between changes in the relative prices of individual goods and services and changes in the general price level.

11-5j OTHER COSTS OF ANTICIPATED AND UNANTICIPATED INFLATION

Whether inflation is perfectly anticipated or not, firms incur costs as a result of the need to change prices more frequently. For example, a restaurant might have to print new menus, or a department or mail-order store may have to print new catalogs, to reflect the new higher prices. These costs are called **menu costs**; they are the costs of changing posted prices. In some South American economies in the 1980s, inflation increased at more than 300 percent per year, with prices changing on a daily, or even hourly, basis in some cases. Imagine how large the menu costs could be in an economy such as that! Another problem with inflation is that, even when inflation is fully anticipated, some people will experience a cost from holding money. Firms and households have to hold some money for daily transactions. People holding on to money will find its purchasing power is eroded each year by the the rate of inflation.

The **shoe-leather cost** of inflation is the cost of going to and from the bank to check on your assets (so often that you wear out the leather on your shoes). Specifically, high rates of inflation erode the value of a

INFLATION AND CAPITAL GAINS TAXES

In an environment of inflation, the tax code can distort market signals and may lead to a reduction in saving, lending, and investment. To many economists, the problem stems from capital gains tax (a tax on a person's assets) being taxed in nominal terms rather than in real terms (adjusted for inflation). For example, suppose you sold a stock in 1980 for $50,000 that you bought in 1970 for $40,000. In real terms, adjusted for inflation, you would have lost money because the 25 percent increase in the stock price would be less than the percentage change in the inflation rate (over 100%). In fact, inflation was so high in the 1970s you would have lost money on your stock in real terms and then have to pay capital gains tax on the nominal gains—$10,000 ($50,000 – $40,000)—ouch! Thus, many economists believe capital gains should be taxed on real gains. In this case, you could write off capital losses because you actually lost money on your investment in real terms. These costs are not just a redistribution cost but can impact economic growth if the taxes are discouraging saving and investment.

From SEXTON, Exploring Economics, 6E. © 2013 Cengage Learning.

currency, which means that people will want to hold less currency—perhaps going to the ATM once a week rather than twice a month. That is, the higher inflation rates lead to higher nominal interest rates, which may induce more individuals to put money in the bank rather than allowing it to depreciate in their pockets. So, the cost is really the time and convenience sacrificed to keep less money on hand than you would if inflation were not a factor. The effects of shoe-leather costs of inflation, like those of menu costs, are modest in countries with low inflation rates but can be quite large in countries where inflation is substantial.

11-5k INFLATION AND INTEREST RATES

The interest rate is usually reported as the **nominal interest rate**, which means it is not adjusted for inflation. We determine the **real interest rate** by taking the nominal rate of interest and subtracting the inflation rate:

Real interest rate = Nominal interest rate − Inflation rate

For example, if the nominal interest rate was 5 percent, and the inflation rate was 3 percent, the real interest rate would be 2 percent.

If people can correctly anticipate inflation, they will behave in a manner that will largely protect them against loss. However, if the inflation is not correctly anticipated (it is not an easy task to predict inflation), inflation will still redistribute income. Consider the creditor who believes that the overall price level will rise 6 percent a year, based on experience in the immediate past. Would that creditor lend money to someone at a 5 percent rate of interest? No. A 5 percent rate of interest means that a person borrowing $1,000 now will pay back $1,050 ($1,000 plus 5 percent of $1,000) one year from now. But if prices go up 6 percent, it will take $1,060 to buy what $1,000 does today ($1,060 is 6 percent more than $1,000). Thus, the creditor lending at 5 percent will get paid back an amount ($1,050) less than the purchasing power of the original loan ($1,060) at the time it was paid back. The real interest rate would actually be negative. To protect themselves, creditors will demand a rate of interest large enough to compensate for the deteriorating value of money.

Understanding the difference between nominal and real interest rates is critical. In most economic decisions, it is the real rate of interest that matters because it is this rate that shows how much borrowers pay and lenders receive in terms of purchasing power—goods and services money can buy. Investors and lenders will do best when the real interest rates are high.

When the nominal interest rate is high, the inflation rate tends to be high; and when the nominal interest rate is low, the inflation rate tends to be low. Why? When inflation is high, borrowers offer and lenders demand higher nominal interest rates to compensate for the falling value of money in the future. When the inflation rate is low, borrowers offer and lenders demand lower nominal interest rates because the value of money (purchasing power) is falling less quickly. Therefore, the tendency is for nominal interest rates and inflation rates to move together—high inflation rates mean high nominal interest rates, and low inflation rates mean low nominal interest rates.

11-5l DO CREDITORS ALWAYS LOSE DURING INFLATION?

Usually, lenders are able to anticipate inflation with reasonable accuracy. For example, in the late 1970s, when the inflation rate was more than 10 percent a year,

nominal interest rates on a 90-day Treasury bill were relatively high. In 2002, with low inflation rates, the nominal interest rate was relatively low. If the inflation rate is anticipated accurately, new creditors will not lose nor will debtors gain from a change in the inflation rate. However, nominal interest rates and real interest rates do not always run together. For example, in periods of high *unexpected* inflation, the nominal interest rates can be high when the real interest rates are low or even negative.

11-5m PROTECTING OURSELVES FROM INFLATION

Increasingly, groups try to protect themselves from inflation by means of cost of living clauses in contracts. Many long-term contracts between firms and unions include a cost-of-living allowance (COLA) that automatically increases when the consumer price index (CPI) increases. With these clauses, laborers automatically get wage increases that reflect rising prices. The same is true of many pensioners, including those on Social Security. Personal income taxes likewise are now indexed (adjusted) for inflation. However, some of the tax code is still not indexed for inflation. These factors affect the incentives to work, save, and invest. Also, adjustable mortgage rates adjust to market conditions, reducing the chance that there will be winners and losers with changes in the unanticipated inflation rate.

SECTION CHECK 5 ANSWERS

1. A price-level index allows us to compare prices paid for goods and services over time by creating a measure of how many dollars it would take to maintain a constant purchasing power over time.

2. Inflation generally hurts creditors and those on fixed incomes and pensions; debtors generally benefit from inflation.

3. Wage earners attempt to keep pace with inflation by demanding higher wages each year or by indexing their annual wage to inflation.

11-6 Economic Fluctuations

SECTION CHECK 6

Keep the following questions in mind as you read through this section.

1. What are short-term economic fluctuations?

2. What are the four stages of a business cycle?

3. What is the difference between a recession and a depression?

The aggregate amount of economic activity in the United States and most other nations has increased markedly over time, even on a per capita basis, indicating economic growth. Short-term fluctuations in the level of economic activity also occur.

11-6a SHORT-TERM FLUCTUATIONS IN ECONOMIC GROWTH

We sometimes call the short-term fluctuations in economic activity **business cycles**. Exhibit 11.14 illustrates the distinction between long-term economic growth and short-term economic fluctuations. Over a long period, the line representing economic activity slopes upward, indicating increasing real output. Over short periods, however, both upward and downward output changes occur. Business cycles refer to the short-term ups and downs in economic activity, not to the long-term trend in output, which in modern times has been upward.

business cycles short-term fluctuations in the economy relative to the long-term trend in output

expansion when output (real GDP) is rising significantly—the period between the trough of a recession and the next peak

peak the point in time when expansion comes to an end, that is, when output is at the highest point in the cycle

contraction when the economy is slowing down—measured from the peak to the trough

trough the point in time when output stops declining, that is, when business activity is at its lowest point in the cycle

recession a period of significant decline in output and employment

11-6b THE PHASES OF A BUSINESS CYCLE

A business cycle has four phases—expansion, peak, contraction, and trough—as illustrated in Exhibit 11.15. The period

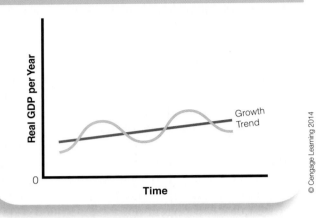

EXHIBIT 11.14 Business Cycles and Economic Growth

© Cengage Learning 2014

of **expansion** is when output (real GDP) is rising significantly. Usually, during the expansion phase, unemployment is falling and both consumer and business confidence are high. Thus, investment is rising, as are expenditures for expensive durable consumer goods, such as automobiles and household appliances. The **peak** is the point in time when the expansion comes to an end, when output is at the highest point in the cycle. The **contraction** is a period of falling real output and is usually accompanied by rising unemployment and declining business and consumer confidence. The contraction phase is measured from the peak to the **trough**—the point in time when output stops declining and business activity is at its lowest point in the cycle. Investment spending and expenditures on consumer durable goods fall sharply in a typical contraction. The contraction phase is also called **recession**, a period of significant decline in output and employment (lasting

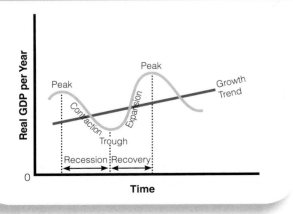

EXHIBIT 11.15 Four Phases of a Business Cycle

© Cengage Learning 2014

more than a few months). Unemployment is relatively high at the trough, although the actual maximum amount of unemployment may not occur exactly at the trough. Often, unemployment remains fairly high well into the expansion phase. The expansion phase is measured from the trough to the peak.

11-6c HOW LONG DOES A BUSINESS CYCLE LAST?

The length of any given business cycle is not uniform. Because it does not have the regularity that the term *cycle* implies, economists often use the term *economic fluctuation* rather than *business cycle*. In addition, economic fluctuations are almost impossible to predict. In both the 1980s and the 1990s, expansions were quite long by historical standards. The contraction phase is one of recession, a decline in business activity. A severe recession is called a **depression**. Likewise, a prolonged expansion in economic activity is sometimes called a **boom**. Exhibit 11.16 shows the record of U.S. business cycles since 1920. Notice that contractions seem to be getting shorter

over time. The National Bureau of Economic Research (NBER) Business Cycle Dating Committee determined that a recession began in March 2001, ending an expansion that lasted from March 1991 to March 2001. The attacks of September 11, 2001, clearly deepened the contraction and may have been instrumental in turning a contraction into a recession. The committee met in November of 2008 and determined that the economy peaked in December 2007, marking the end of a 73-month expansion and the beginning of an 18-month recession that ended in June of 2009. There is a delay before the NBER announces the beginning or end of a recession, because of the complexities involved in gathering and evaluating the data. So the official beginning and end dates of a recession are not known until many months later.

depression severe recession or contraction in output

boom period of prolonged economic expansion

11-6d SEASONAL FLUCTUATIONS AFFECT ECONOMIC ACTIVITY

The determinants of cyclical fluctuations in the economy are the major thrust of the next several chapters, and some fluctuation in economic activity reflects seasonal patterns. Business activity, whether measured by production or by the sale of goods, tends to be high in the two months before the winter holidays and somewhat lower in summertime, when many families are on vacation. Within individual industries, of course, seasonal fluctuations in output often are extremely pronounced, agriculture being the best example. Often, key

EXHIBIT 11.16 A Historical Record of U.S. Recessions, 1920–2011

Peak	Trough	Length of Recession (months)
January 1920	July 1921	18
May 1923	July 1924	14
October 1926	November 1927	13
August 1929	March 1933	43
May 1937	June 1938	13
February 1945	October 1945	8
November 1948	October 1949	11
July 1953	May 1954	10
August 1957	April 1958	8
April 1960	February 1961	10
December 1969	November 1970	11
November 1973	March 1975	16
January 1980	July 1980	6
July 1981	November 1982	16
July 1990	March 1991	8
March 2001	November 2001	8
December 2007	June 2009	18

SOURCES: National Bureau of Economic Research, Inc., *Business Cycle Expansions and Contractions,* U.S. Department of Commerce. Washington, D.C., December 1, 2008. Available at http://www.nber.org/cycles.html (accessed March 18, 2010).

© Artostock.com/Alamy

economic statistics, such as unemployment rates, are seasonally adjusted, meaning the numbers are modified to account for normal seasonal fluctuations. Thus, seasonally adjusted unemployment rates in summer months are below actual unemployment rates, because employment is normally high in summertime due to the inflow of school-age workers into the labor force.

11-6e FORECASTING CYCLICAL CHANGES

The farmer and the aviator rely heavily on weather forecasters for information on climatic conditions in planning their activities. Similarly, businesses, government agencies, and, to a lesser extent, consumers rely on economic forecasts to learn of forthcoming developments in the business cycle. If it looks as if the economy will continue in an expansionary phase, businesses may expand production to meet a perceived forthcoming need; if it looks as if contraction is coming, businesses may decide to be more cautious.

Forecasting Models

Using theoretical models, which will be discussed in later chapters, economists gather statistics on economic activity in the immediate past, including, for example, consumer expenditures, business inventories, the supply of money, governmental expenditures, tax revenues, and so on. Using past historical relationships between these factors and the overall level of economic activity (which form the basis of the economic theories), they formulate *econometric models*. Statistics from the immediate past are plugged into the model, and forecasts are made. Because human behavior changes, and our assumptions about certain future developments may not be correct, our numbers are imperfect, and our econometric models are not always accurate. But like the weather forecasts, although the econometric models are not perfect, they are helpful.

Economic Indicators

The media also publish data on business cycle indicators that fall into three main categories: **leading economic indicators**, coincident economic indicators, and lagging economic indicators.

The index of leading economic indicators are designed to predict activity in the U.S. economy six to nine months into the future and can be useful as short-term predictors of the economy. The stock market, measured by the S&P

500 index, is one of the leading economic indicators. For example, the stock market often turns downward before a recession and usually begins to improve before the economy recovers from a slump. Another leading indicator is new consumer goods orders; often consumers reduce their spending on big-ticket items like homes and automobiles before a recession begins. Interest rates are also an important economic indicator because they have strong effects on consumer and business spending. Other leading economic indicators include the length of the average workweek, initial claims for unemployment, new building permits, new orders for plant and equipment, the extent of delayed deliveries, and the money supply (M2). The Department of Commerce combines all these into an index of leading indicators. If the index rises sharply for two or three months, it is likely (but not certain) that increases in the overall level of activity will follow.

However, using leading economic indicators to predict future trends can be unreliable. For example, if the federal government responds with policies to combat the recession as soon as the leading economic indicators begin predicting it, then a recession that would have occurred may fail to materialize. On the other hand, a self-fulfilling prophecy may result if businesses respond with cutbacks in orders for plants and equipment as soon as the leading economic indicators begin predicting a recession.

In addition to leading economic indicators, there are coincident economic indicators, which help to predict peaks and troughs. In other words, they change with real GDP. For example, as real GDP increases we would expect an increase in total employment, personal income, industrial production, and sales.

Lagging economic indicators follow economic activity. That is, they change after real GDP changes. For example, the duration of unemployment is a lagging economic indicator. As real GDP rises and the economy begins to recover, it may take many months before the average time unemployed workers remain unemployed falls. Other lagging indicators include interest rates, the unemployment rate, and the consumer price index.

SECTION CHECK 6 ANSWERS

1. Business cycles (or economic fluctuations) are short-term fluctuations in the amount of economic activity, relative to the long-term growth trend in output.

2. The four stages of a business cycle are expansion, peak, contraction, and trough.

3. Recessions occur during the contraction phase of a business cycle. Severe long-term recessions are called depressions.

Chapter 11: Self-Review

Now that you are finished reading the chapter, review the questions below. You can write your answers in the space provided, then go online to see the answers at www.cengagebrain.com.

11-1 MACROECONOMIC GOALS

1. What is the Employment Act of 1946?

11-2 EMPLOYMENT AND UNEMPLOYMENT

2. Fill-in-the-Blanks: The unemployment rate _____ as the number of unemployed people increases and it _____ when the labor force grows, *ceteris paribus*.

3. Why might the fraction of the unemployed who are job leavers be higher in a period of strong labor demand?

4. Suppose you live in a community of 100 people. If 80 people are aged 16 and older and 72 people are willing and able to work, what is the unemployment rate in this community?

11-3 TYPES OF UNEMPLOYMENT

5. True or False: Frictional unemployment occurs when the unemployment rate is greater than normal.

6. What is the traditional government policy "cure" for cyclical unemployment?

7. True or False: At full employment (at the natural rate of unemployment), only frictional unemployment is present.

11-4 REASONS FOR UNEMPLOYMENT

8. What is an efficiency wage?

9. True or False: New technology increases unemployment.

10. In a severe recession, what would tend to happen to the people in the following categories:
    a. job losers
    b. job leavers
    c. reentrants
    d. new entrants

11-5 INFLATION

11. Say you owe money to Big River Bank. Will you gain or lose from an unanticipated decrease in inflation?

12. How could inflation make people turn to exchange by barter?

11-6 ECONOMIC FLUCTUATIONS

13. True or False: Unemployment will fall during an economy's expansionary phase and rise during a contractionary phase.

Are you richer than Andrew Carnegie?

Carnegie, a steel magnate at the turn of the 20th century, was one of the wealthiest Americans ever to live, with a net worth valued at $100 billion in today's dollars. However, despite all his wealth, Carnegie could not buy many of the things you can today. When his business was at its height, he could not travel by air or by car, he had no AC for hot and humid days, and he could not watch television in high definition, surf the Internet, call or text friends on his cell phone, or listen to music from iTunes. The medical care he had access to was nowhere near as advanced as what you can find. All of these things have been made possible for you because of the increases in productivity and economic growth that America has experienced since Carnegie's day.

Test your Economics *street-smart* knowledge and see how you compare against other students! Scan here or visit CourseMate for Survey of ECON2.

12

Economic Growth

John Maynard Keynes, one of the most influential economic thinkers of all time, once said that "in the long run, we are all dead." He made this statement because he was primarily concerned with explaining and reducing short-term fluctuations in the level of business activity. He wanted to smooth out the business cycle, largely because of the implications that cyclical fluctuations had for buyers and sellers in terms of unemployment and price instability. No one would deny that Keynes's concerns were important and legitimate.

At the same time, however, Keynes's flippant remark about the long run discounts the fact that human welfare is greatly influenced by long-term changes in a nation's capacity to produce goods and services. Emphasis on short-run economic fluctuations ignores the longer-term dynamic changes that affect output, leisure, real income, and lifestyle.

What are the determinants of long-run economic change in our ability to produce goods and services? What are some of the consequences of rapid economic change? Why are some nations rich, whereas others are poor? Does growth in output improve our economic welfare? We will explore these questions in this chapter.

12-1 Economic Growth

SECTION CHECK 1

Keep the following questions in mind as you read through this section.

1. What is economic growth?
2. What is the Rule of 70?
3. What is productivity?

Economic growth is usually measured by the annual percentage change

economic growth an upward trend in the real per capita output of goods and services

249

in real output of goods and services per capita (real GDP per capita), reflecting the expansion of the economy over time. We focus on per capita because we want to isolate the effect of increased population on economic growth. That is, an increase in population, *ceteris paribus,* will lower the standard of living because more people will be sharing a fixed real GDP. It is also important to note that our economic growth rate does not say anything about the distribution of output and income. For example, a country could have extraordinary growth in per capita output and yet the poor might make little or no improvement in their standard of living. That is, it is possible that income group made little or no gain.

In Chapter 2, we introduced the production possibilities curve. Along the production possibilities curve, the economy is producing at its potential output. How much the economy will produce at its potential output, sometimes called its *natural rate of output,* depends on the quantity and quality of its resources, including labor, capital (factories, machinery, tools, productive skills, etc.), and natural resources (land, coal, timber, oil, iron, etc.). In addition, technology can increase the economy's production capabilities. As shown in Exhibit 12.1, improvements in and greater stocks of land, labor, capital, and entrepreneurial activity will shift the production possibilities curve outward. Another way of saying that economic growth has shifted the production possibilities curve outward is to say that it has increased potential output.

12-1a THE RULE OF 70

If Nation A and Nation B start off with the same population and the same level of real GDP, will a slight difference in their growth rates over a long period of time make much of a difference? Yes. In the first year or two, the difference will be small; but even over a decade the difference will be large, and after 50 to 100 years it will be huge. The final effect will be a much higher standard of living in the nation with the greater economic growth, *ceteris paribus.*

A simple formula called the Rule of 70 shows how long it will take a nation to double its output at various growth rates. If you take a nation's growth rate and divide it into 70, you will have the approximate time it will take to double the income level. For example, if a nation grows at 3.5 percent per year, then the economy will double every 20 years (70/3.5). However, if an economy only grows at 2 percent per year, the economy will double every 35 years (70/2); and at a 1 percent annual growth rate, it will take 70 years to double income (70/1). So even a small change in the growth rate of a nation will have a large impact over a lengthy period.

In Exhibit 12.2, we see the growth rates in real GDP for the United States since 1790. The exhibit shows U.S. real GDP per capita (measured in year 2005 dollars) grew from $1,025 in 1790 to $42,671 in 2011. Compared to in the depth of the Great Depression in 1932, Americans today, on average, can purchase almost 7 times the amount of goods and services.

In Exhibit 12.3, we see a comparison of selected industrial countries. Because of differences in growth rates, some countries will become richer than others over time. With relatively slower economic growth, today's richest countries will not be the richest for very long. On the other hand, with even slight improvements in economic growth, today's poorest countries will not remain poor for long. China and India have both experienced spectacular economic growth over the past 20 years. Because of this economic growth, much of the world is now poorer than these two heavily populated countries. Other countries, such as Ireland, once one of the poorest countries in Western Europe, is now one of the richest. Disappointing growth rates over the past 30 years have left Argentina's economy and standard of living unchanged for a quarter of a century.

Because of past economic growth, the "richest" or "most-developed" countries today have many times the market output of the "poorest" or "least-developed" countries. Put differently, the most-developed countries produce and market more output in a day than the least-developed countries do in a year. The international differences in income, output, and wealth are indeed striking and have caused a great

EXHIBIT 12.1 Economic Growth and the Shifting Production Possibilities Curve

Capital Goods

Consumption Goods

0

© Cengage Learning 2014

EXHIBIT 12.2 U.S. Real GDP per Capita (2005 dollars)

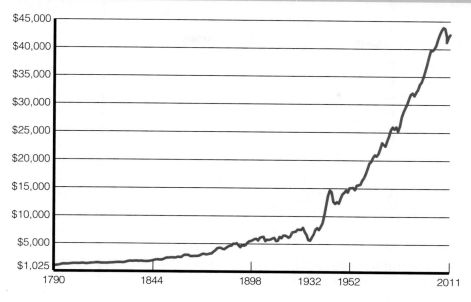

SOURCE: http://www.measuringworth.com

deal of friction between developed and less-developed countries. The United States and the nations of the European Union experienced sizable increases in real output over the past two centuries; but even in 1800, most of these nations were better off in terms of market output than many impoverished present-day countries such as Ethiopia, India, and Nepal. See the U.S. real GDP per capita growth from 1790–1860 in Exhibit 12.2.

China and India

Both China and India have per capita real GDP levels that are far less than the United States. The power of compound interest could well change this ranking in the future. As Nobel laureate Robert Lucas once said, "Once one starts to think about differences in growth rates among countries, it is hard to think about anything else." But the current rate of economic growth in these two countries will change things in the future. India experienced an average annual growth rate of almost 9 percent per year from 2003–2008. The economic growth rate slowed in 2008–2009 as India felt the effect of the global financial crisis. India has a highly educated English-speaking population and is a major exporter of software services and software workers.

China is growing at about 10 percent per year. Foreign investment in China has helped spur output of both domestic and export goods. China only grew

EXHIBIT 12.3 Growth in Real GDP per Capita in Selected Industrial Countries

	2003–2012
United States	1.5%
Japan	0.6
Germany	0.4
France	1.4
Italy	0.5
United Kingdom	1.1
Canada	2.9

SOURCE: International Monetary Fund

at 9 percent annually in 2008, its slowest growth rate since 2001. The global financial crisis had a larger impact on China than India because China's economy is more heavily reliant on exports. Exports account for about one-third of China's GDP. Since economic liberalization began in 1978, China's investment and export-led economy has grown 70 times bigger and is the fastest-growing major economy in the world. China has the world's third largest nominal GDP, although its per capita income is still low, behind roughly a hundred countries.

The rapid economic growth in both countries has pulled millions out of poverty. However, both countries are still relatively poor compared to the United States, many European countries, and Japan because these countries started the process toward long-run economic growth many decades, or even centuries, ago.

12-1b PRODUCTIVITY: THE KEY TO A HIGHER STANDARD OF LIVING

Will the standard of living in the United States rise, level off, or decline over time? For a large part, the answer depends on productivity growth. **Productivity** is the amount of goods and services a worker can produce per hour. Productivity is especially important because it determines a country's standard of living. That is, sustained economic growth occurs when workers' productivity rises. For example, slow growth of capital investment can lead to lower labor productivity and, consequently, lower wages. On the other hand, increases in productivity and higher wages can occur as a result of carefully crafted economic policies, such as tax policies that stimulate investment or programs that encourage research and development.

The link between productivity and the standard of living may be understood most easily by recalling the circular flow model where we show that aggregate expenditures are equal to aggregate income. In other words, the aggregate value of all goods and services produced in the economy must equal the payments made to the factors of production—the wages and salaries paid to workers, the rental payment to capital, the profits, and so on. That is, the only way an economy can increase its rate of consumption in the long run is by increasing the amount it produces. But why are some countries so much better than others at producing goods and services? We will answer this question in the next section, as we examine the determinants of productivity—physical capital, human capital, natural resources, and technology.

© Mike Blank/Getty Images

How could these workers increase their productivity? New plant equipment, additional training, and advancements in technology could all increase the productivity of each worker. Greater productivity could then lead to higher wages and in turn a higher standard of living.

12-2 Determinants of Long-Run Economic Growth

SECTION CHECK 2

Keep the following questions in mind as you read through this section.

1. What factors contribute to long-run economic growth?

2. What is human capital?

Why are there vastly different standards of living around the world? The answer can be found in a single concept: labor productivity. Real GDP per capita depends on increases in labor productivity. **Labor productivity** is defined as output per unit of worker. Sustained economic growth can only occur if the amount of output by the average worker increases. As we explained earlier, a nation's standard of living ultimately depends on its ability to produce goods and services.

12-2a FACTORS THAT CONTRIBUTE TO PRODUCTIVITY GROWTH

We will look at four major factors that contribute to growth in productivity. These include physical capital, human capital, natural resources,

Four factors in productivity growth

1) Physical capital
2) Human capital
3) Natural resources
3) Technology

and technology. Today's workers generally produce more output than workers in the past.

labor productivity
output per unit of worker

Of today's workers, those in some countries, like the United States, generally produce more output than do workers in most other countries. Workers with higher productivity usually have more physical capital like buildings and computers, are more educated than their counterparts, and have benefited from tremendous technological advancements.

Now that we know how productivity leads to long-run economic growth, let us look at the factors that lead to greater productivity.

Physical Capital

Recall that physical capital includes goods such as tools, machinery, and factories that have already been produced and are now producing other goods and services. Combining workers with more capital makes workers more productive. Thus, capital investment can lead to increases in labor productivity.

Even in primitive economies, workers usually have some rudimentary tools to further their productive activity. Consider the farmer who needs to dig a ditch to improve drainage in his fields. If he used just his bare hands, it might take a lifetime to complete the job. If he used a shovel, he could dig the ditch in hours or days. But with a big earth-moving machine, he could do it in minutes. Most economists agree that capital formation has played a significant role in the economic development of nations. Physical capital, like human capital, increases labor productivity.

Per-Worker Production Function

In Chapter 2, we found that by increasing the rate of saving, we can produce a greater amount of new capital goods and increase the stock of productive capital for the future. Because resources are scarce, in order to invest in new capital, society must sacrifice some current consumption. To save more now, we need to consume less now. Ultimately, this will allow society to consume more in the future.

In Exhibit 12.4 on the next page, we see how the amount of capital per worker influences the amount of output per worker. This positively sloped curve is called the per-worker production function. Holding the other determinants of output constant (human capital, natural resources and technology), we see that, moving up along the production function,

© iStockphoto.com/subjug

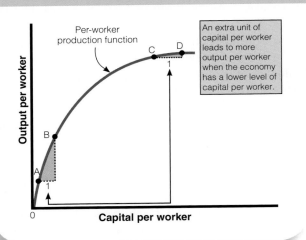

EXHIBIT 12.4 Per-Worker Production Function

Per-worker production function

An extra unit of capital per worker leads to more output per worker when the economy has a lower level of capital per worker.

Output per worker

Capital per worker

© Cengage Learning 2014

when the quantity of capital per worker rises, so does the amount of output per worker, but at a diminishing rate—the curve eventually becomes flatter as more capital per worker is added. That is, capital is subject to diminishing marginal returns. If the economy has a very low level of capital, an extra unit of capital leads to a relatively large increase in output—a movement from point A to point B in Exhibit 12.4. If the economy already has a great deal of capital, an extra unit of capital leads to a relatively smaller increase in output—a movement from point C to point D in Exhibit 12.4. Imagine that you owned a small store and you had 10 employees and one computer. As you added more computers, output per worker rose, but only up to a point. What if you added 20 computers to your work force of 10? Adding more computers (capital) still adds to output but by smaller and smaller additional amounts. This is what is called diminishing marginal returns to capital. Thus, in the long run, other things being equal, the benefits of a higher saving rate and additional capital stock become smaller and the rate of growth slows.

Some economists believe diminishing marginal returns to capital can help explain the variation in growth rates between rich and poor countries. In poor countries, where there is little capital, small increases in capital investment can lead to relatively large increases in productivity. In rich countries, where workers already have large amounts of capital, increases in capital investment may have a very small additional effect on productivity. Economists call this the catch up effect.

innovation applications of new knowledge that create new products or improve existing products

Human Capital

When workers acquire qualitative improvements (learning new skills, for example), output increases. Workers with a large stock of human capital are more productive than those with small stocks of human capital. Indeed, it has become popular to view labor skills as human capital that can be augmented or improved by education and on-the-job training. Like physical capital, human capital must be produced, usually by means of teachers, schoolrooms, libraries, computer labs, and time devoted to studying. Human capital may be more important than physical capital as a determinant of labor productivity. Human capital also includes improvements in health. Better health conditions allow workers to be more productive. In fact, University of Chicago economist and Nobel laureate Robert Fogel has shown that improved health from better nutrition has a significant impact on long-run economic growth.

Natural Resources

An abundance of natural resources, such as fertile soil, and other raw materials, such as timber and oil, can enhance output. Many scholars cite the abundance of natural resources in the United States as one reason for its historical success. Canada and Australia are endowed with a large natural resource base and high per capita incomes. Resources are, however, not the whole story; for example, Japan and Hong Kong have had tremendous economic success despite having relatively few natural resources. In addition, Kuwait and Saudi Arabia are rich because they sit on top of large pools of oil. On the other hand, Brazil has a large and varied natural resource base, yet its income per capita is relatively low compared with that of many developed countries. It appears that a natural resource base can affect the initial development process, but sustained growth is influenced by other factors. However, most economists would agree that a limited resource base does pose an important obstacle to economic growth.

Technology

Most economists believe that it is the progress in technology that drives productivity. It is technology that allows workers to produce more even with the same amount of physical and human capital. Technological change can lead to better machinery and equipment, increases in capital, and better organization and production methods. Technological advances stem from human ingenuity and creativity in developing new ways of combining the factors of production to enhance the amount of output from a given quantity of resources. The process of technological advance involves invention and innovation. **Innovation** is the adoption of the product or process. For example, in the United States, the invention and innovation of the cotton gin, the Bessemer steel-making process, and the railroad were important stimuli to economic growth. New technology, however, must be introduced into productive use by managers or entrepreneurs who weigh the perceived estimates of benefits of the new technology against estimates of costs. Thus, the entrepreneur is also an important economic factor in the growth process.

Technological advances permit us to economize on one or more inputs used in the production process. They can permit savings of labor. For example, when a new machine does the work of many workers, technology is said to be embodied in capital and to be labor saving. Technology, however, can also be land (natural resource) saving or even capital saving. For example, nuclear fission has permitted us to build power plants that economize on the use of coal, a natural resource. The reduction in transportation time that accompanied the invention and innovation of the railroad allowed businesses to reduce the capital they needed in the form of inventories. Because goods could be obtained more quickly, businesses could reduce the stock kept on their shelves.

And inventions can come in all sizes. Obviously, the semiconductor chip made a huge impact on productivity and growth, but so did the Post-it note that was introduced in the early 1980s, the laptop computer, and barcode scanners that were first introduced in Wal Mart stores. We have also seen huge advances in communication (the Internet) and medicines.

Bar codes are scanned more than 10 billion times a day. Before bar codes, grocery stores and retail stores would have to shut down and inventory every item on the shelves. This was an expensive and cumbersome job.

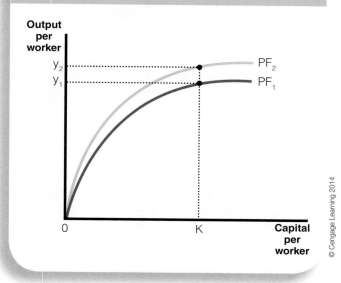

EXHIBIT 12.5 Technological Change and the Per-Worker Production Function

© Cengage Learning 2014

In short, better methods of organization and production can lead to increases in labor productivity. When fewer workers are needed in a grocery store or a department store due to better methods of organization or new machinery and equipment, labor productivity rises.

In Exhibit 12.5, we see that technological change can shift the per-worker production curve upward, producing more output per worker with the same amount of capital per worker.

Technological change allows the economy to escape the full impact of diminishing marginal returns to capital. Thus, in the long run, *ceteris paribus,* an economy must experience technological advance in order to improve its standard of living and overcome the diminishing marginal returns to capital.

12-2b NEW GROWTH THEORY

The greater the reward for new technology, the more research and technology will occur. According to Paul Romer, a new growth economist, economic growth can continue unimpeded, as long as we keep coming up with new ideas. And there is a role for government, too—encouraging the creation of new ideas. While the market is a great engine for economic growth, it can be "turbocharged" with strong institutional support for education and science. Romer believes that it is ideas that drive economic growth. To Romer, economic growth comes from increases in value—rearranging fixed amounts of matter and making new combinations that are more valuable. "There are zillions of combinations that we can use to make new goods and services we value."

SECTION CHECK 2 ANSWERS

1. The factors that contribute to economic growth are increased quantity and quality of labor, natural resources, physical capital, and technological advances.

2. Labor, or human capital, can be improved through investment in human capital—that is, education, on-the-job training, and experience can improve the quality of labor.

12-3 Public Policy and Economic Growth

SECTION CHECK 3

Keep the following questions in mind as you read through this section.

1. Why is the saving rate so important for increasing economic growth?

2. Why is research and development so important for economic growth?

3. Why are property rights so important for increasing economic growth?

4. Why is education so important for economic growth?

Economic growth means more than an increase in the real income (output) of the population. A number of other important changes accompany changes in output. Claims that economic growth stimulates political freedom or democracy have even been made, but evidence for that correlation is far from conclusive. Even though some democratic societies are rich and some

authoritarian ones are poor, the opposite also holds. That is, some features of democracy, such as majority voting and special interest groups, may actually be growth retarding. For example, if the majority decides to vote for large land reforms and wealth transfers, the consequences will be higher taxes and market distortions that will reduce incentives for work, investment, and ultimately economic growth. However, a nation can pursue a number of policies that will increase economic growth.

12-3a SAVING RATES, INVESTMENT, CAPITAL STOCK, AND ECONOMIC GROWTH

One of the most important determinants of economic growth is the saving rate. To consume more in the future, we must save more now. Generally, higher levels of saving will lead to higher rates of investment and capital formation and, therefore, greater economic growth. Individuals can either consume or save their income. If individuals choose to consume all their income, they will have nothing left for saving, which businesses could use for investment purposes to build new plants or replace worn-out or obsolete equipment. With little investment in capital stock, there will be little economic growth. Capital can also increase as a result of injections of capital from abroad (foreign direct investments), but the role of national saving rates in economic growth is of particular importance.

Sustained rapid economic growth is associated with high rates of saving and investment around the world. However, investment alone does not guarantee economic growth. Economic growth hinges on the quality and type of investment as well as on investments in human capital and improvements in technology.

12-3b INFRASTRUCTURE

Infrastructure (e.g., highways, ports, bridges, power lines, airports, and information technology) is critical to economic coordination and activity. Some infrastructure is private and some is public. In the past several decades, the amount of government investment in U.S. infrastructure has fallen. Some economists argue that improvements in infrastructure could lead to higher productivity. Others argue the causality runs in the other direction—that higher productivity leads to greater infrastructure. In addition, a special interest problem concerns favored districts with political clout that end up as the recipients of improved infrastructure, which may not be an efficient solution. Most would agree, however, that poor infrastructure is a major deterrent to economic growth.

12-3c RESEARCH AND DEVELOPMENT

Some scholars believe that the importance of **research and development (R&D)** is understated. Research and development consists of the activities undertaken to create new products and processes that will lead to technological progress. The concept of R&D is broad indeed—it can include new products, management improvements, production innovations, or simply learning by doing. However, it is clear that investing in R&D and rewarding innovators with patents have paid big dividends in the past 50 to 60 years. Some would argue that even larger rewards for research and development would spur even more rapid economic growth. Some types of scientific research may have far-reaching benefits that cannot be captured by a private firm. Such a case presents a compelling argument for government support of basic research. GPS satellite systems in cars, for example, were originally designed for military purposes. In addition, an important link exists between R&D and capital investment. As already noted, when capital depreciates over time, it is replaced with new equipment that embodies the latest technology. Consequently, R&D may work hand-in-hand with investment to improve growth and productivity. Lastly, R&D may benefit foreigners as they import goods from technologically advanced countries to make their firms more efficient.

12-3d THE PROTECTION OF PROPERTY RIGHTS IMPACTS ECONOMIC GROWTH

Economic growth rates tend to be higher in countries where the government enforces property rights. Property rights give owners the legal right to keep or sell their properties—land, labor, or capital. Without property rights, life would be a huge "free-for-all," where people could take whatever they wanted. Economists call the government's ability to protect private property rights and enforce contracts the *rule of law.*

> **research and development (R&D)** activities undertaken to create new products and processes that will lead to technological progress

In most developed countries, property rights are effectively protected by the government. However, in developing countries, such protection is not usually the case. If the government does not enforce property rights, the private sector must respond in costly ways that stifle economic growth. For example, an unreliable judiciary system means that entrepreneurs must often rely on informal agreements that are difficult to enforce. As a result, they may have to pay bribes to get things done, and even then, they may not get the promised services. Individuals may have to buy private security or pay "organized crime" for protection against crime and corruption. In addition, landowners and business owners may be fearful of coups or takeovers from a new government, which might confiscate their property altogether. In short, if government is not adequately protecting property rights, the incentive to invest will be hindered, and political instability, corruption, and lower rates of economic growth will be likely. However, it may well be a two-way street. In the words of former U.N. Secretary-General Kofi Annan, "There will be no development without security and no security without development."

According to Professor Daron Acemoglu of MIT, the reason some nations succeed and others don't comes down to the soundness and transparency of their government institutions—the ability of a nation's citizens to own property, freely elect representatives, and live without fear of crime and corruption.

12-3e FREE TRADE AND ECONOMIC GROWTH

Allowing free trade can also lead to greater output because of the principle of comparative advantage. Essentially, the principle of comparative advantage suggests that if two nations or individuals with different resource endowments and production capabilities specialize in producing a smaller number of goods and services and engage in trade, both parties will benefit. Total output will rise.

12-3f EDUCATION

Education, investment in human capital, may be just as important as improvements in physical capital. At any given time, an individual has a choice between current work and investment activities such as education that can increase future earning power. An individual will usually accept reduction in current income to devote effort to education and training. In turn, a certain return on the investment is expected because in later years, the individual will earn a higher wage rate (the amount of the increase depending on the nature of the education and training as well as natural ability). For example, in the United States, a person with a college education can be expected to earn almost twice as much per year as a high school graduate.

One argument for government subsidizing education is that the investment can increase the skill level of the population and raise the standard of living. However, even if the individual does not benefit financially from increased education, society may benefit culturally and in other respects from having its members highly educated. For example, more education can lead to lower crime rates, new ideas that may benefit society, and more informed voters.

With economic growth, illiteracy rates fall and formal education grows. The correlation between per capita output and the proportion of the population that is able to read or write is striking. Improvements in literacy stimulate economic growth by reducing barriers to the flow of information; when information costs are high, out of ignorance, many resources flow to

Policy: Institutional Economics

Douglass C. North, an economic historian, was the recipient of the Nobel Prize in Economics in 1993. One of North's contributions is his analysis of the linkage between institutional changes and economic growth. According to North, "The sources of sustained economic growth and the determinants of income distribution are to be found in the institutional structure of a society. Economic historians can no longer write good economic history without explicitly taking into account the institutional structure of the system, both economic and political. We cannot avoid the political aspect because decisions made outside the marketplace have had, and will continue to have, a fundamental influence upon growth and welfare."

Institutions matter because they affect the choices open to people, shape incentives, and are an important determinant of human action. The institutional structure of a society (or the "rules of the game," as Mr. North calls it) includes formal rules (such as constitutions, property rights, laws of contract), informal constraints (conventions, customs, codes of conduct), and the means of enforcing both formal and informal standards of behavior (courts, social ostracism, personal beliefs). As in sports, the way the game is played and its outcome depend on the nature of the rules, the character of the players, and the fairness (impartiality) of the referee. Moreover, the choice of the rules and the enforcement mechanisms will be affected by prevailing ideology and culture.

According to North, rules must be credible if they are to be effective. That is, they must be enforced. Private enforcement is possible, but as economic life becomes more complex, political institutions become the major instrument for defining and enforcing property rights. The history of economic performance cannot be separated from the history of political performance. The New Institutional Economics studies both.

North has shown that those countries that (1) adopt a rule of law, one which limits the power of government over economic life and protects the rights of persons and property and (2) maintain open markets and freedom of contract are more likely to achieve long-run economic prosperity than those that do not.

According to North, economic change is "path dependent": The future depends on the past and present choices. History is not predetermined or based on some grand design; it is the sum of human actions. How we act will depend on the rules we inherit and formulate, as well as on our cultural and moral heritage. But ultimately, it is individuals who must choose.

SOURCES: Douglass C. North, *Growth and Welfare in the American Past*, 2nd ed. (Englewood Cliffs, NJ: Prentice Hall, 1974); and James Dorn, "North Wins Nobel for New Institutional Economics," *The Margin* (Spring 1994), 56.

or remain in uses that are unproductive. Moreover, education imparts skills that are directly useful in raising labor productivity, whether it is mathematics taught to a sales clerk, engineering techniques taught to a college graduate, or just good ideas that facilitate production and design.

Many economists believe that the tremendous growth in East Asia (South Korea, Taiwan, Hong Kong, and Singapore) in the last half of the twentieth century was a result of good basic education for many of their citizens. This reason was one of many factors that contributed to growth, including high rates of saving and a large increase in labor force participation.

However, in poorer developing countries, the higher opportunity costs of education present an obstacle. Children in developing countries are an important part of the labor force starting at a young age. If they attend school, children cannot help in the fields—planting, harvesting, fence building, and participating in many other tasks—which many households depend on in the rural areas of developing countries. A child's labor contribution to the family is far less important in a developed country. Thus, the higher opportunity cost of education in developing countries is one of the reasons that school enrollments are lower.

Education may also be a consequence of economic growth, because as incomes rise, people's tendency to consume education increases. People increasingly look to education for more than the acquisition of immediately applicable skills. Education becomes a consumption good as well as a means of investing in human capital. There are also a number of factors that can lead to slower economic growth. Countries that fail to enforce the rule of law, experience wars and revolutions, and have poor education and health systems and low rates of saving and investment are not likely to grow very rapidly.

Do Economies Converge?

Many economists believe that, holding other things equal, countries with lower real GDP per capita will grow faster than countries with higher real GDP per capita. However, other things—including infrastructure, the extent to which the rule of law is followed, and the level of education—are not equal. Adjusting for such additional variables, there is a tendency for poorer countries to grow faster. This has certainly been true of South Korea, Taiwan, and Singapore, which have invested in technology and human resources, but many poor countries of Africa and Latin America continue to be poor. So, there is no guarantee that being poorer leads to greater economic growth.

Why is it easier for developing countries to grow faster than advanced ones? First, they can adopt existing technology from developed countries. Second, developed economies may be subject to diminishing marginal returns to capital—a concept we discussed earlier in the chapter. Third, population growth is higher in developing counties, leading to lower levels of per capita consumption for a given level of economic output. For example, in Western Europe and the United States, population growth rates are currently about 1 percent per year, while in some of the poorer African countries, they can approach 3 percent per year or more. In addition, while technology is portable, the ability to use that technology is not. With low literacy rates and educational attainment, as in sub-Saharan African nations, countries can lack the human capital to adopt and use the new technology.

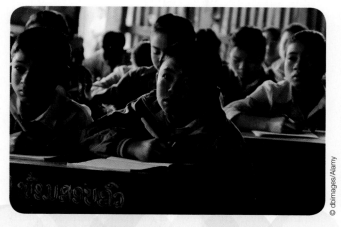

Many economists believe that the recent growth in East Asian countries is a result of improved basic education.

© dbimages/Alamy

SECTION CHECK 3 ANSWERS

1. Generally, higher levels of saving will lead to higher rates of investment and capital formation and, therefore, to greater economic growth.

2. Innovations resulting from investments in research and development have the potential to accelerate economic growth even further.

3. Economic growth rates tend to be higher in countries where the government enforces property rights more vigorously.

4. Education, investment of human capital, is important to improving standards of living and economic growth.

12-4 Measuring Economic Growth and Its Components

SECTION CHECK 4

Keep the following questions in mind as you read through this section.

1. What is gross domestic product?
2. Why must expenditures equal income?

Now let us take a look at how we measure economic growth.

12-4a WHAT IS GROSS DOMESTIC PRODUCT?

The measure of aggregate economic performance that gets the most attention in the popular media is **gross domestic product (GDP)**, which is defined as the value of all final goods and services produced within a country during a given period. By convention, that period is almost always one year. But let's examine the rest of this definition. What is meant by "final good or service" and "value"?

Measuring the Value of Goods and Services

Value is determined by the market prices at which goods and services sell. Underlying the calculations, then, are the various equilibrium prices and quantities for the multitude of goods and services produced.

What Is a Final Good or Service?

gross domestic product (GDP) the measure of economic performance based on the value of all final goods and services produced within a country during a given period

double counting adding the value of a good or service twice by mistakenly counting the intermediate goods and services in GDP

The word *final* means that the good is ready for its designated ultimate use. Many goods and services are intermediate goods or services—that is, used in the production of other goods. For example, suppose U.S. Steel Corporation produces some steel that it sells to Ford for use in making an automobile. If we counted the value of steel used in making the car as well as the full value of the finished auto in the GDP, we would be engaging in **double counting**—adding the value of the steel in twice, first in its raw form and second in its final form, the automobile.

12-4b PRODUCTION, INCOME, AND THE CIRCULAR FLOW MODEL

When we calculate GDP in the economy, we are measuring the value of total production—our total expenditures on the economy's output of goods and services. However, we are also measuring the value of total income. Why? It is because every dollar of spending by some buyer ends up being a dollar of income for some seller. In short, expenditures, (spending) must equal income. And this is true whether it is a household, firm, or the government that buys the good or service. The main point is that when we spend (the value of total expenditure), it ends up as someone's income (the value of total income). Buyers have sellers.

In Exhibit 12.6, we reintroduce the circular flow model to show the flow of money in the economy. For example, households use some of their income to buy domestic goods and services and some to buy foreign goods and services (imports). Households also use some of their income to pay taxes and invest in financial markets (stocks, bonds, saving accounts, and other financial assets). When income flows into the financial system as saving, it makes it possible for consumers, firms, and government to borrow. This market for saving and borrowing is vital to a well-functioning economy.

Firms sell their goods and services to domestic and foreign consumers and foreign firms and government. Firms use their factors of production (labor, land, capital, and entrepreneurship) to produce goods and services. Firms pay wages to workers, interest for the use of capital, and rent for land. Profits are the return to entrepreneurs for taking the risk of producing the goods and services. Wages, rent, interest, and profit comprise aggregate income in the economy. Government provides transfer payments such as Social Security and unemployment insurance payments. Whether we add up the aggregate expenditure on final goods and services or the value of aggregate income (wages, rent, interest, and profit), we get the same GDP. For an economy as a whole, expenditures and income are the same. Actually, while the two should be exactly the same, there may be a slight variation because of data issues.

EXHIBIT 12.6 The Expanded Circular Flow Model

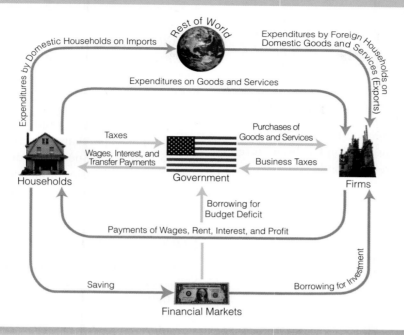

SECTION CHECK 4 ANSWERS

1. Gross domestic product (GDP) is the value of all final goods and services produced within a country during a given time period.

2. All of our spending (the value of total expenditure) ends up as someone's income (the value of total income). Every buyer has a seller.

12-5 Measuring Total Production

SECTION CHECK 5

Keep the following questions in mind as you read through this section.

1. What are the four categories of purchases included in the expenditure approach?
2. How are net exports calculated?
3. How is national income calculated?
4. What does personal income measure?

One approach to measuring GDP is the **expenditure approach**.

12-5a THE EXPENDITURE APPROACH TO MEASURING GDP

With the expenditure approach, GDP is calculated by adding how much market participants spend on final goods and services over a specific period of time. For convenience and for analytical purposes, economists usually group spending into four categories: consumption, designated by the letter C; investment, I; government purchases, G; and net exports, which equals exports (X) minus imports (M), or $X - M$. According to the expenditure method, then,

Four spending categories
1) Consumption (C)
2) Investment (I)
3) Government purchases (G)
4) Net exports (X – M)

$$GDP = C + I + G + (X - M)$$

Consumption (C)

Consumption refers to the purchase of consumer goods and services by households.

expenditure approach calculation of GDP by adding the expenditures by market participants on final goods and services over a given period

consumption purchases of final goods and services

investment the creation of capital goods to augment future production

For most of us, a large percentage of our income in a given year goes for consumer goods and services. The consumption category does not include purchases by business or government. As Exhibit 12.7 indicates, in 2012, U.S. consumption expenditures totaled more than $9 trillion ($9,545.6 billion). This figure was 71 percent of GDP. In this respect, the 2012 data were fairly typical. In every year since 1929, when GDP accounts began to be calculated annually, consumption has been more than half of total expenditures on goods and services (even during World War II).

Investment (*I*)

Investment, according to economists, refers to the creation of capital goods—inputs such as machines and tools whose purpose it is to produce other goods.

How Stable Are Investment Expenditures? In recent years, investment expenditures generally hovered around 15 percent of gross domestic product. Investment spending is the most volatile category of GDP, however, and tends to fluctuate considerably with changing business conditions. When the economy is booming, investment purchases tend to increase dramatically. In downturns, the reverse happens. In the first year of the Great Depression, investment purchases declined by 37 percent. In recent years, expenditures on capital goods have been a smaller proportion of GDP in the United States than in many other developed nations. This fact worries some people who are concerned about GDP growth in the United States compared to that in other countries, because investment in capital goods is directly tied to a nation's future production capabilities.

Government Purchases (*G*)

The portion of government purchases included in GDP is expenditures on goods and services. For example, a government must pay the salaries of its employees, and it must also make payments to the private firms with which it contracts to provide various goods and services, such as highway construction companies and weapons manufacturers. All these payments would be included in GDP. However, *transfer payments* (such as Social Security, farm subsidies, and welfare) are not included in government purchases, because this spending does not go to purchase newly produced goods or services but is merely a transfer of income among the country's citizens (which is why such expenditures are called transfer payments).

Exports (*X – M*)

Some of the goods and services produced in the United States are exported for use in other countries. The fact that these goods and services were made in the United States means that they should be included in a measure of U.S. production. Thus, we include the value of exports when calculating GDP. At the same time, however, some of our expenditures in other categories (consumption and investment, in particular) were for foreign-produced goods and services. These imports must be excluded from GDP to obtain an accurate measure of U.S. production. Thus, GDP calculations measure net exports, which equals total exports (X) minus total imports (M). Net exports are a small proportion of GDP and are often negative for the United States.

12-5b OTHER MEASURES OF TOTAL PRODUCTION AND TOTAL INCOME

In addition to computing the gross domestic product, the Bureau of Economic Analysis (BEA) also computes

EXHIBIT 12.7 GDP: The Expenditure Approach

Category	Amount (billions of current dollars)	Percent of GDP
Consumption (*C*)	$10,726	71%
Investment (*I*)	1,916	13
Government purchases (*G*)	3,031	20
Net exports of goods and services (*X – M*)	−579	−4
Gross domestic product	$15,094	100%

SOURCE: Bureau of Economic Analysis

five additional measures of production and income: gross national product, net national product, national income, personal income, and disposable personal income.

Incomes received by people providing goods and services are actually payments to the owners of productive resources. These payments are sometimes called **factor payments**. Factor payments include wages for the use of labor services, rent for land, payments for the use of capital goods in the form of interest, and profits for entrepreneurs who put labor, land, and capital together. Before we can measure national income, we must make three adjustments to GDP. First, we must look at the net income of foreigners—that is, we add any income earned abroad by U.S. citizens or firms and we subtract any income earned in the United States by foreign firms and citizens. This difference between net income of foreigners and GDP is called **gross national product (GNP)**. For example, we would add to GDP the profits sent back to the United States from Wal Mart stores in Canada and Mexico. However, the profits Toyota earns in the United States are sent back to Japan and are subtracted from U.S. GDP, so GNP becomes the income earned worldwide by U.S. firms and residents. In the United States, the difference between GDP and GNP is small because net income of foreigners is a small percentage of GDP.

The second adjustment we make to find national income is to deduct depreciation from GNP. **Depreciation** payments are annual allowances set aside for the replacement of worn-out plant and equipment. After we subtract depreciation, we have **net national product (NNP)**.

The final adjustment is to subtract **indirect business taxes**. The best example of an indirect business tax is a sales tax. For example, a DVD might cost $14.95 plus a tax of $1.20 for a total of $16.15. The retail distributor, DVD producer, and others will share $14.95 in proceeds, even though the actual equilibrium price is $16.15. In other words, the output (DVD) is valued at $16.15, even though recipients get only $14.95 in income. Besides sales taxes, other important indirect business taxes include excise taxes (e.g., taxes on cigarettes, automobiles, and liquor) and gasoline taxes.

Five measures of production and income
- Gross national product
- Net national product
- National income
- Personal income
- Disposable personal income

© iStockphoto.com/subjug

Now we can measure **national income (NI)**, which is a measure of the income earned by owners of resources—factor payments. Accordingly, national income includes payments for labor services (wages, salaries, and fringe benefits), payments for use of land and buildings (rent), money lent to finance economic activity (interest), and payments for use of capital resources (profits). To obtain GDP, we add indirect business taxes, depreciation, and net income of foreigners.

We should keep in mind that not all income can be used by those who earn it. **Personal income (PI)** measures the amount of income received by households (including transfer payments) before income taxes. **Disposable personal income** is the personal income available to individuals after taxes.

factor payments wages (salaries), rent, interest payments, and profits paid to the owners of productive resources

gross national product (GNP) the difference between net income of foreigners and GDP

depreciation annual allowance set aside to replace worn-out capital

net national product (NNP) GNP minus depreciation

indirect business taxes taxes, such as sales tax, levied on goods and services sold

national income (NI) a measure of income earned by owners of the factors of production

personal income (PI) the amount of income received by households before personal taxes

disposable personal income the personal income available after personal taxes

SECTION CHECK 5 ANSWERS

1. Four categories of spending are used in the GDP calculation: consumption (C), investment (I), government purchases (G), and net exports ($X - M$).

2. Net exports are calculated by subtracting total imports from total exports.

3. National income (NI) is measured by adding together the payments to the factors of production—wages, rent, interest, and profit.

4. Personal income (PI) measures the amount of income received by households (including transfer payments) before personal taxes.

12-6 Problems in Calculating an Accurate GDP

SECTION CHECK 6

Keep the following questions in mind as you read through this section.

1. What are the problems with using GDP to measure output?

2. What is per capita GDP?

The primary problem in calculating accurate GDP statistics becomes evident when attempts are made to compare the GDP over time. Between 1970 and 1978, a period of relatively high inflation, GDP in the United States rose more than 100 percent. What great progress! Unfortunately, however, the "yardstick" used in adding the values of different products, the U.S. dollar, also changed in value over this period. A dollar in 1979, for example, would certainly not buy as much as a dollar in 1970, because the *overall* price level for goods and services increased.

12-6a HOW DO WE SOLVE THIS PROBLEM?

One solution to this problem would be to use physical units of output—which, unlike the dollar, do not change in value from year to year—as the measure of total economic activity. The major problem with this approach is that different products have different units of measurement. How can anyone add tons of steel to bushels of wheat, kilowatts of electricity, gallons of paint, cubic feet of natural gas, miles of air passenger travel, and number of magazines sold? To compare GDP values over time, the calculations must use a common, or standardized, unit of measure, which only money can provide.

A Price-Level Index

The dollar, then, is the yardstick of value we can use to correct the inflation-induced distortion of the GDP. We must adjust for the changing purchasing power of the dollar by using a price index. As we discussed in the last chapter, a price index attempts to provide a measure of the prices

real gross domestic product per capita real output of goods and services per person

paid for a certain bundle of goods and services over time. The price index can be used to deflate the nominal or current dollar GDP values to a real GDP expressed in dollars of constant purchasing power.

12-6b REAL GDP

Once the price index has been calculated, the actual procedure for adjusting nominal, or current dollar, GDP to get real GDP is not complicated. For convenience, an index number of 100 is assigned to some base year. The base year is arbitrarily chosen—it can be any year. The Bureau of Economic Analysis (BEA) currently uses 2005 as a base year.

The formula for converting any year's nominal GDP into real GDP (in base year dollars) is as follows:

$$Real\ GDP = \frac{Nominal\ GDP}{Price\ index} \times 100$$

Suppose the GDP deflator (price index) was expressed in terms of 2005 prices (2005 = 100), and the GDP price deflator for 2010 is 110.992, as seen in Exhibit 12.8. The increase in the figure means that prices were roughly 11 percent higher in 2010 than they were in 2005.

To correct the 2011 nominal GDP, we take the nominal GDP figure for 2010—$14,526.5 billion—and divide it by the GDP deflator 110.992, which results in a quotient of 130.88 billion. We then multiply this number by 100, giving us $13,088 billion, which would be the 2010 GDP in 2005 dollars (that is, 2010 real GDP, in terms of the 2005 base year). Or to correct the 2000 nominal GDP into real GDP, take the nominal GDP figure for 2000, $9,951.5 billion, and divide it by the GDP deflator (88.723), which results in a quotient of 112.164 billion. We then multiply this number by 100, giving us $11,216.4 billion, which would be the 2000 GDP in 2005 dollars (that is, 2000 real GDP, in terms of the 2005 base year).

In Exhibit 12.9, notice that in the years after the base year (2005), real GDP is greater than nominal GDP. This means the price level has risen since 2005, lowering the purchasing power of the dollar. Prior to 2005, nominal GDP was less than real GDP; the purchasing power of the dollar was higher relative to the base year (2005). Also, notice that nominal GDP rises more rapidly than real GDP because inflation is included in the nominal GDP figures.

12-6c IS REAL GDP ALWAYS LESS THAN NOMINAL GDP?

In modern times, inflation has been prevalent. For many readers of this book, the price level (as measured by the consumer price index and the GDP deflator) has risen in

EXHIBIT 12.8 Real GDP: Correcting GDP for Price Index Changes 2000–2010

| (1) | (2) | (3) | (4) [(2) ÷ (3)] × 100 |
Year	Nominal GDP (billions of dollars per year)	GDP Deflator (2005 = 100)	Real GDP (billions of dollars per year, 2005 dollars)
2000	$ 9,951.5	88.723	$11,216.4
2001	10,286.2	90.727	11,337.5
2002	10,642.3	92.196	11,543.1
2003	11,142.2	94.135	11,836.4
2004	11,853.3	96.786	12,246.9
2005	12,623.0	100	12,623.0
2006	13,377.2	103.231	12,958.5
2007	14,028.7	106.227	13,206.4
2008	14,291.5	108.552	13,165.6
2009	13,939.0	109.727	12,703.1
2010	14,526.5	110.992	13,088.0

SOURCE: U.S. Bureau of Economic Analysis, 2011.

every year of their lifetime, because the last year with a declining price level was 1955. Therefore, the adjustment of nominal (money) GDP to real GDP will tend to reduce the growth in GDP suggested by nominal GDP figures. Given the distortions introduced by inflation, most news reports about GDP today speak of real GDP changes, although this distinction is not always made explicit.

12-6d REAL GDP PER CAPITA

The measure of economic well-being, or standard of living, most often used is **real gross domestic product per capita**. We use a measure of real GDP for reasons already cited. To calculate real GDP per capita, we divide the real GDP by the total population to get the

EXHIBIT 12.9 Nominal and Real GDP 1950–2011 (2005 base year)

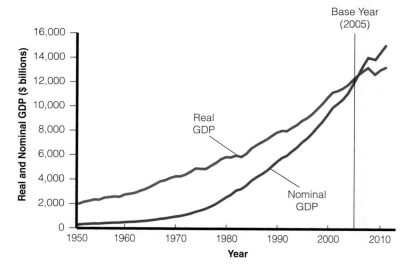

Source: Louis D. Johnston and Samuel H. Williamson, "What Was the U.S. GDP Then?" *MeasuringWorth*, 2008. Available at http://www.measuringworth.org/usgdp/

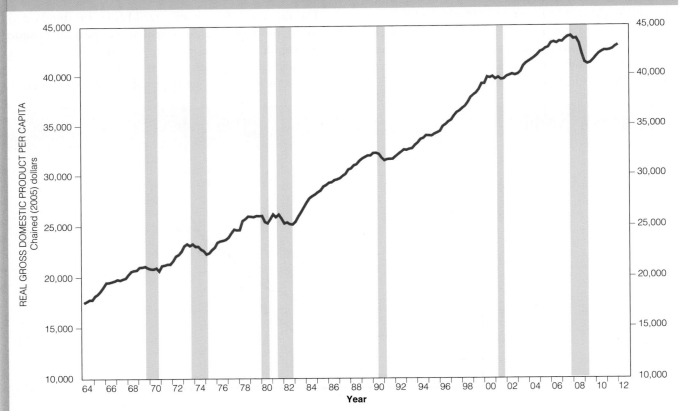

value of real output of final goods and services per person. *Ceteris paribus*, people prefer more goods to fewer, so a higher GDP per capita would seemingly make people better off, improving their standard of living. Economic growth, then, is usually considered to have occurred anytime the real GDP per capita has risen. In Exhibit 12.10, we see that in the United States the real gross domestic product per capita has grown sharply from 1958 to 2008. Real GDP per capita is almost three times larger in 2008 than it was in 1958. However, the growth in real GDP per capita is not steady, as seen by the shaded areas that represent recessions in Exhibit 12.10. Falling real GDP per capita can bring on many human hardships, such as rising unemployment, lower profits, stock market losses, and bankruptcies.

How is it that, between 1997 and 2007, Venezuela's nominal GDP was one of the most rapid in the world yet its real GDP growth was similar to other countries, at around 3 percent per year? The answer is that most of the growth in its nominal GDP came from high inflation.

© Alexander Chaikin/Shutterstock.com

EXHIBIT 12.10 Real GDP per Capita

NOTE: Shaded areas represent recessions.

SOURCE: Bureau of Economic Analysis, *Survey of Current Business*, Selected NIPA Tables. 90(3) Washington, D.C., May 2012. D-57. Available at http://www.bea.gov/scb/(accessed July 25, 2012). http://www.bea.gov/scb/pdf/2012/05%20May/D%20pages/0512dpg_d.pdf

12-6e WHY IS THE MEASURE OF PER CAPITA GDP SO IMPORTANT?

Because one purpose of using GDP as a crude welfare measure is to relate output to human desires, we need to adjust for population change. If we do not take population growth into account, we can be misled by changes in real GDP values. For example, in some less-developed countries in some periods, real GDP has risen perhaps 2 percent a year, but the population has grown just as fast. In these cases, the real output of goods and services per person has remained virtually unchanged, but this would not be apparent in an examination of real GDP trends alone.

> If we do not take **population growth** into account, we can be misled by changes in real GDP values.

SECTION CHECK 6 ANSWERS

1. It is difficult to compare real GDP over time because of the changing value of money over time.

2. Per capita real GDP is real output of goods and services per person. In some cases, real GDP may increase, but per capita real GDP may actually drop as a result of population growth.

12-7 Problems with GDP as a Measure of Economic Welfare

SECTION CHECK 7

Keep the following questions in mind as you read through this section.

1. What are some of the deficiencies of GDP as a measure of economic welfare?

2. What are nonmarket transactions?

3. What is the underground economy?

Real GDP is often used as a measure of the economic welfare of a nation. The accuracy of this measure for that purpose is questionable, however, because several important factors are excluded from its calculation. These factors include nonmarket transactions, the underground economy, leisure, externalities, and the quality of the goods purchased.

12-7a NONMARKET TRANSACTIONS

Nonmarket transactions include the provision of goods and services outside traditional markets for which no money is exchanged. We simply do not have reliable enough information on this output to include it in the GDP. The most important single nonmarket transaction omitted from the GDP is the services of house-wives (or househusbands). These services are not sold in any market, so they are not entered into the GDP; but they are nonetheless performed. For example, if a single woman hires a tax accountant, those payments enter into the calculation of GDP. Suppose, though, that the woman marries her tax accountant. Now the woman no longer pays her husband for his accounting services. Reported GDP falls after the marriage, although output does not change.

In less-developed countries, where a significant amount of food and clothing output is produced in the home, the failure to include nonmarket economic activity in GDP is a serious deficiency. Even in the United States, homemade meals, housework, and the vegetables and flowers produced in home gardens are excluded, even though they clearly represent an output of goods and services.

12-7b THE UNDERGROUND ECONOMY

It is impossible to know for sure the magnitude of the underground economy, which includes unreported income from both legal and illegal sources. For example, illegal gambling and prostitution are not included in the GDP, leading to underreporting of an unknown magnitude. The reason these activities are excluded, however, has nothing to do with the morality of the services performed; rather, the cause of the exclusion is that most payments made for these services neither are reported to government authorities nor go through normal credit channels. Likewise, cash payments made to employees "under the table" slip through the GDP net. Estimates of the size of the underground economy vary from less than 4 percent to more than 20 percent of GDP. It also appears that a significant portion of this unreported income comes from legal sources, such as self-employment.

12-7c MEASURING THE VALUE OF LEISURE

The value that individuals place on leisure is omitted in calculating GDP. Most of us could probably get a part-time job if we wanted to, earning some additional money by working in the evening or on weekends. Yet we choose not to do so. Why? The opportunity cost is too high—we would have to forgo some leisure. If you work on Saturday nights, you cannot see your friends, go to parties, attend concerts, watch television, or go to the movies. The opportunity cost of leisure is the income forgone by not working. For example, if people start taking more three-day weekends, GDP will surely fall, but can we necessarily say that the standard of living will fall? GDP will fall, but economic well-being may rise.

Leisure, then, has a positive value that does not show up in the GDP accounts. To put leisure in the proper perspective, ask yourself whether you would rather live in Country A, which has a per capita GDP of $25,000 a year and a 30-hour work week, or Country B, with a $25,000 per capita GDP and a 50-hour work week. Most people would choose Country A. The problem posed by this omission in GDP can be fairly significant in international comparisons or observations of one nation over time.

12-7d GDP AND EXTERNALITIES

As we have discussed in earlier chapters, positive and negative externalities may result from the production of some goods and services. As a result of these externalities, the equilibrium prices of these goods and services—the figures used in GDP calculations—do not reflect their true values to society (unless, of course, the externalities have been internalized). For example, if a steel mill produces 100,000 more tons of steel, GDP increases; GDP does not, however, decrease to reflect damages from the air pollution that results from the production of that additional steel. Likewise, additional production of a vaccine would be reflected in the GDP, but the positive benefit to members of society—other than the purchaser—would not be included in the calculation. In other words, while GDP measures the goods and services produced, it does not adequately measure the "goods" and "bads" that result from the production processes.

GDP doesn't measure everything that contributes to or detracts from our well-being; it is difficult to measure the value of those effects. Environmentalists believe that national income accounts should adjust for changes in the environment. But this leads to many conceptual problems, such as how to measure the marginal values of goods and services not sold in markets and how to adjust for geographical differences in environmental damage. The critical issue is whether important trends in "uncounted" goods and services result in questionable conclusions about whether we are becoming better or worse off.

Growing Underground

Underground economies are large and growing rapidly in most countries. High taxes and labor market regulations are the reasons why 17 percent of economic activity goes unreported in OECD [Organization for Economic Co-operation and Development] countries, while corruption explains the large black market in some developing ones.

By definition, national income statistics capture economic activity reported by individuals and corporations. A large and growing portion of economic activity, however, goes unrecorded in most countries. This "underground" economy consists of legal activities that are concealed, mainly for reasons of tax evasion. Underground activity grew during the 1970s, when government became pervasive in national economies. As tax rates were raised to finance public spending programs, an increasing number of individuals risked dodging taxes. It is only since the 1980s that economists have attempted to estimate the size of underground economies. This task is inherently difficult.

Nevertheless, it is important to estimate the size and growth of all economic activity, not only the reported kind. For one thing, cross-country comparisons of per capita income depend on it. By one account, Italy would be one of the richest European countries if its large black market were included alongside reported income. More importantly, GDP growth figures and unemployment rates may be severely distorted if a sudden increase in taxes pushes more people underground. Accurate statistics about overall economic activity and true unemployment are essential for effective economic policy decisions.

An article in the *Journal of Economic Literature* takes a closer look at the size, causes, and consequences of underground economies. Its authors, Friedrich Schneider of the University of Linz and Dominick Enste of the University of Cologne, claim that no cross-country comparison of underground economies has yet been undertaken. In their research, the authors compare the relative size of underground economies for 76 countries and track their growth over time. They point out that even though estimates of underground economies are naturally inexact, economists generally agree that they are growing in most countries. Moreover, underground economies vary significantly in size, from a small fraction of "official" GDP (Switzerland), to nearly three-quarters of economic output (Nigeria, Egypt, and Thailand).

But first, what drives people underground? The authors argue that underground activity grows when tax rates rise. This is most noticeable in Scandinavian countries where governments have created some of the most generous public programs over the past few decades, and have consequently witnessed a substantial rise in their underground economies. This unsurprising claim is substantiated by the data. Norway, for example, has seen its underground economy grow from a negligible 1.5 percent of GNP in 1960 to a staggering 18 percent in 1995 (based on the currency demand approach). The high fiscal burden in other Scandinavian countries has led to a similar growth in their underground economies. In contrast, countries with relatively small public sectors—such as Switzerland and the United States—have developed much smaller underground markets.

The study shows that underground economies have grown in all OECD countries over the past few decades, representing an alarming 17 percent of reported GDP by 1997. In countries such as Spain, Portugal, Italy, Belgium, and Greece, the estimated size of unreported economic activity stood at 22 to 30 percent. "In the European Union at least 20 million workers and in OECD countries about 35 million work in the unofficial economy. Moreover, the amount doubled within 20 years."

The authors find evidence that fewer regulations (that are properly enforced), lower tax rates, and a better rule of law lead to smaller underground economies, and consequently generate higher tax revenues. These factors are absent in many countries of Latin America, where underground economies amount to one-quarter to one-third of official GNP, and in the former Soviet Union, where underground economies stand at more than one-third of reported income.

SOURCE: Author's discussion of Friedrich Schneider and Dominick H. Enste, "Shadow Economies: Size, Causes and Consequences," *Journal of Economic Literature* (March 2000), and *Economic Intuition* (Summer 2000).

12-7e QUALITY OF GOODS

GDP can also miss important changes in the improvements in the *quality* of goods and services. For example, the quality of a computer bought today differs significantly from one that was bought 10 years ago, but it will not lead to an increase in measured GDP. The same is true of many other goods, from cellular phones to automobiles to medical care.

12-7f OTHER MEASURES OF ECONOMIC WELL-BEING

Even if we included some of these statistics that are difficult to measure, such as nonmarket transactions, the underground economy, leisure, externalities, and the quality of products, GDP would still not be a precise measure of economic well-being. Many other indices of well-being should be considered: life expectancies, infant mortality rates, education and environmental quality, levels of discrimination and fairness, health care, low crime rates, and minimum traffic congestion, just to name a few. GDP is a measure of economic production, not a measure of economic well-being. However, greater levels of GDP can lead to improvements in economic well-being, because society will now be able to afford better education and health care and a cleaner, safer environment.

SECTION CHECK 7 ANSWERS

1. Factors making it difficult to use GDP as a welfare indicator include nonmarket transactions, the underground economy, leisure, externalities, and the quality of goods.

2. Nonmarket transactions are the exchanges of goods and services that do not occur in traditional markets and for which no money is exchanged.

3. The underground economy is the unreported production and income that come from legal and illegal activities.

Chapter 12: Self-Review

Now that you are finished reading the chapter, review the questions below. You can write your answers in the space provided, then go online to see the answers at www.cengagebrain.com.

12-1 ECONOMIC GROWTH

1. Why does the production possibilities curve shift outward with economic growth?

2. Fill-in-the-Blank: When the Dutch "created" new land with their system of dikes, their production possibilities curve shifted _____.

12-2 DETERMINANTS OF LONG-RUN ECONOMIC GROWTH

3. True or False: No single factor is capable of completely explaining economic growth patterns.

4. Fill-in-the-Blank: Countries with relatively _____ labor would be leaders in labor-saving innovations.

12-3 PUBLIC POLICY AND ECONOMIC GROWTH

5. What impact will free trade have on economic growth?

6. True or False: Increasing the capital stock will lead to economic growth.

12-4 MEASURING ECONOMIC GROWTH AND ITS COMPONENTS

7. True or False: GDP measures all goods or services produced.

12-5 MEASURING TOTAL PRODUCTION

8. If Mary received a welfare check this year, would that transfer payment be included in this year's GDP? Why or why not?

9. True or False: Inventory investment and net exports can be negative.

12-6 PROBLEMS IN CALCULATING AN ACCURATE GDP

10. Fill-in-the-Blank: If we overestimated inflation over time, our calculations of real GDP growth would be _____-estimated.

11. Why would the growth in real GDP overstate the growth of output per person in a country with a growing population?

12-7 PROBLEMS WITH GDP AS A MEASURE OF ECONOMIC WELFARE

12. True or False: GDP measures include nonmarket transactions.

13. How do pollution and crime affect GDP? How do pollution- and crime-control expenditures impact GDP?

is downward sloping and why the short-run aggregate supply curve is upward sloping.

13-1a HOW IS THE QUANTITY OF REAL GDP DEMANDED AFFECTED BY THE PRICE LEVEL?

The aggregate demand curve slopes downward, which means an inverse (or opposite) relationship exists between the price level and real gross domestic product (RGDP) demanded. Exhibit 13.1 illustrates this relationship, where the quantity of RGDP demanded is measured on the horizontal axis and the overall price level is measured on the vertical axis. As we move from point A to point B on the aggregate demand curve, we see that an increase in the price level causes RGDP demanded to fall. Conversely, if a reduction in the price level occurs—a movement from B to A—RGDP demanded increases. Why do purchasers in the economy demand less real output when the price level rises and more real output when the price level falls?

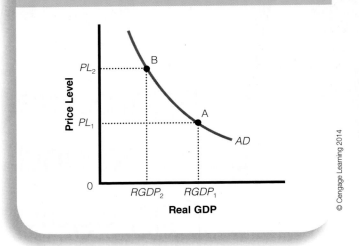

EXHIBIT 13.1 The Aggregate Demand Curve

© Cengage Learning 2014

13-1b WHY IS THE AGGREGATE DEMAND CURVE NEGATIVELY SLOPED?

Three complementary explanations exist for the negative slope of the aggregate demand curve: the real wealth effect, the interest rate effect, and the open economy effect.

The Wealth Effect: Changes in Consumer Spending

If you had $1,000 in cash stashed under your bed while the economy suffered a serious bout of inflation, the purchasing power of your cash would be eroded by the extent of the inflation. That is, an increase in the price level reduces the real value of money and makes consumers poorer, encouraging them to spend less. A decrease in consumer spending means a decrease in quantity of RGDP demanded.

In the event that the price level falls, the reverse would hold true. A falling price level increases the real value of money and makes consumers wealthier, encouraging them to spend more. An increase in consumer spending means an increase in the quantity of RGDP demanded. This is called the wealth effect of a change in the price level. Because of the wealth effect, consumer spending, C, falls (rises) when the price level increases (decreases).

The Interest Rate Effect: A Change in Investment

If the price level falls, households and firms will need to hold less money to conduct their day-to-day activities.

© Zigy Kaluzny/Getty Images

Firms will need to hold less money for such inputs as wages and taxes; households will need to hold less money for such purchases as food, rent, and clothing. At a lower price level, households and firms will shift their "excess" money into interest-earning assets such as bonds or savings accounts. This will increase the supply of funds to the loanable funds market, leading to lower interest rates. As interest rates fall, households and firms will borrow more and buy more goods and services—thus, the quantity of RGDP demanded will increase.

If the price level rises, households and firms will need to hold more money to buy goods and services and conduct their daily activities. Households and firms will need to borrow money, and this increased demand for loanable funds will result in higher interest rates. At higher interest rates, consumers may give up plans to buy new cars or houses, and firms may delay investments in plant and equipment.

In sum, a higher price level raises the interest rate and discourages investment spending and decreases the quantity of RGDP demanded. A lower price level reduces the interest rate and encourages investment spending causing RGDP demanded to rise.

The Open Economy Effect

Many goods and services are bought and sold in global markets. If the price level in the United States rises relative to the price level in other countries, U.S. exports will become relatively more expensive and foreign imports will become relatively less expensive. Some U.S. consumers will shift from buying domestic goods to buying foreign goods (imports). Some foreign consumers will stop buying U.S. goods. U.S. exports will fall and U.S. imports will rise. Thus, net exports will fall, thereby reducing the amount of RGDP purchased in the United States. A lower price level makes U.S. exports less expensive and foreign imports more expensive. So U.S. consumers will buy more domestic goods, and foreign consumers will buy more U.S. goods. This will increase net exports, thereby increasing the amount of RGDP purchased in the United States.

SECTION CHECK 1 ANSWERS

1. An aggregate demand curve shows the inverse relationship between the total amounts of real goods and services (RGDP) that are demanded at each possible price level.

2. The aggregate demand curve is downward sloping because of the real wealth effect, the interest rate effect, and the open economy effect.

13-2 Shifts in the Aggregate Demand Curve

SECTION CHECK 2

Keep the following questions in mind as you read through this section.

1. What is the difference between a movement along and a shift in the aggregate demand curve?

2. What variables shift the aggregate demand curve to the right?

3. What variables shift the aggregate demand curve to the left?

Like the supply and demand curves described in Chapter 3, the aggregate demand curve may experience both shifts and movements.

13-2a SHIFTS VERSUS MOVEMENTS ALONG THE AGGREGATE DEMAND CURVE

In the previous section, we discussed three factors—the wealth effect, the interest rate effect, and the open economy effect—that result in the downward slope of the aggregate demand curve. Each of these factors, then, generates a movement *along* the aggregate demand curve, in reaction to changes in the general price level. In this section, we will discuss some of the many factors that can cause the aggregate demand curve to shift to the right or left.

The whole aggregate demand curve can shift to the right or left, as shown in Exhibit 13.2 on the next page. Put simply, if some non-price level determinant causes total spending to increase, the aggregate demand curve will shift to the right. If a non-price level determinant causes the level of total spending to decline, the aggregate demand curve will shift to the left. Let us look at some specific factors that could cause the aggregate demand curve to shift.

13-2b AGGREGATE DEMAND CURVE SHIFTERS

Anything that changes the amount of total spending in the economy (holding price levels constant) will

EXHIBIT 13.2 Shifts in the Aggregate Demand Curve

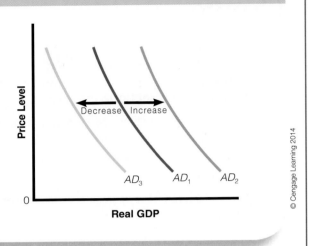

© Cengage Learning 2014

may also cause some consumers to put off additional spending. In fact, some economists believe that part of the 1990–1992 recession was due to consumer debt that had built up during the 1980s. In addition to maxing out their credit cards, some individuals lost equity in their homes and, consequently, experienced reductions in their wealth and purchasing power—again shifting aggregate demand to the left.

Changing Investment (*I*)

Investment is also an important determinant of aggregate demand. Increases in the demand for investment goods occur for a variety of reasons. For example, if business confidence increases or real interest rates fall, business investment will increase and aggregate demand will shift to the right. A reduction in business taxes would also shift the aggregate demand curve to the right, because businesses would now retain more of their profits to invest. However, if interest rates or business taxes rise, we would expect to see a leftward shift in aggregate demand.

Changing Government Purchases (*G*)

Government purchases are another part of total spending and therefore must have an impact on aggregate demand. An increase in government purchases, *ceteris paribus*, shifts the aggregate demand curve to the right, whereas a reduction shifts aggregate demand to the left.

Changing Net Exports (*X* – *M*)

Global markets are also important in a domestic economy. For example, when major trading partners experience economic slowdowns (as did the Asian market in the late 1990s), they will demand fewer U.S. imports. This causes U.S. net exports ($X - M$) to fall, shifting aggregate demand to the left. Alternatively a boom in the economies of major trading partners may lead to an increase in our exports to them, causing net exports ($X - M$) to rise and aggregate demand to increase.

affect the aggregate demand curve. An increase in any component of GDP (*C, I, G,* or *X – M*) will cause the aggregate demand curve to shift rightward. Conversely, decreases in *C, I, G,* or *X – M* will shift aggregate demand leftward.

Changing Consumption (*C*)

A whole host of changes could alter consumption patterns. For example, an increase in consumer confidence, an increase in wealth, or a tax cut can increase consumption and shift the aggregate demand curve to the right. An increase in population will also increase the aggregate demand because more consumers will be spending more money on goods and services.

Of course, the aggregate demand curve could shift to the left as a result of decreases in consumption demand. For example, if consumers sense that the economy is headed for a recession or if the government imposes a tax increase, the result will be a leftward shift of the aggregate demand curve. Because consuming less is saving more, an increase in saving, *ceteris paribus*, will shift aggregate demand to the left. Consumer debt

© iStockphoto.com/Mark Evans

13-3 The Aggregate Supply Curve

SECTION CHECK 3

Keep the following questions in mind as you read through this section.

1. What does the aggregate supply curve represent?

2. Why do producers supply more as the price level increases in the short run?

3. Why is the long-run aggregate supply curve vertical at the natural rate of output?

The **aggregate supply (AS) curve** is the relationship between the total quantity of final goods and services that suppliers are *willing* and *able* to produce and the overall price level. The aggregate supply curve represents how much RGDP suppliers are willing to produce at different price levels. In fact, the two aggregate supply curves are a **short-run aggregate supply (SRAS) curve** and a **long-run aggregate supply (LRAS) curve**. The short-run relationship refers to a period when output can change in response to supply and demand, but input prices have not yet been able to adjust. For example, nominal wages are assumed to adjust slowly in the short run. The long-run relationship refers to a period long enough for the prices of outputs and all inputs to fully adjust to changes in the economy.

13-3a WHY IS THE SHORT-RUN AGGREGATE SUPPLY CURVE POSITIVELY SLOPED?

In the short run, the aggregate supply curve is upward sloping, as shown in Exhibit 13.3. At a higher price level, then, producers are willing to supply more real output, and at lower price levels, they are willing to supply less real output. Why would producers be willing to supply more output just because the price level increases? Two possible explanations are the profit effect and the misperception effect.

The Profit Effect

For many firms, input costs—wages and rents, for example—are relatively constant in the short run. Workers and other material input suppliers often enter into long-term contracts with firms at prearranged prices. Thus, the slow adjustments of input prices are due to contracts that do not adjust quickly to output price level changes. So when the price level rises, output

> **aggregate supply (AS) curve** the total quantity of final goods and services suppliers are willing and able to supply at a given price level
>
> **short-run aggregate supply (SRAS) curve** the graphical relationship between RGDP and the price level when output prices can change but input prices are unable to adjust
>
> **long-run aggregate supply (LRAS) curve** the graphical relationship between RGDP and the price level when output prices and input prices can fully adjust to economic changes

EXHIBIT 13.3 The Short-Run Aggregate Supply Curve

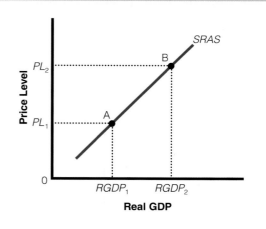

© Cengage Learning 2014

prices rise relative to input prices (costs), raising producers' short-run profit margins. With this short-run profit effect, the increased profit margins make it in producers' self-interest to expand production and sales at higher price levels. If the price level falls, output prices fall and producers' profits tend to fall. That is, a lower price level leads to a lower profit per unit of output and lower RGDP supplied because wages and other input prices can be slow to adjust in the short run. Again, this is because many input costs, such as wages and other contracted costs, are relatively constant in the short run. When output price levels fall, producers find it more difficult to cover their input costs and, consequently, reduce their levels of output.

The Misperception Effect

The second explanation for the upward-sloping short-run aggregate supply curve is that producers can be fooled by price changes in the short run. That is, changes in the overall price level can temporarily mislead producers about what is taking place in their particular market. For example, suppose a wheat farmer sees the price of wheat rising. Thinking that the *relative price* of wheat is rising (i.e., that wheat is becoming more valuable in real terms), the wheat farmer supplies more. Suppose, however, that wheat was not the only thing for which prices were rising. What if the prices of many other goods and services that the farmer consumes were rising at the same time as a result of an increase in the price level? The relative price of wheat, then, was not actually rising, although it appeared so in the short run. In this case, the farmer was fooled into supplying more based on his *short-run misperception* of relative prices. In other words, producers can be fooled into thinking that the relative prices of the items they are producing are rising and mistakenly increase production.

Similarly, if the overall price level falls, many wheat farmers may mistakenly believe the relative price of wheat has fallen. This could fool these farmers into temporarily producing less wheat.

Workers can also be fooled. If the price level is rising, the first thing they may notice is that their nominal wages—expressed in current dollars—are rising. So they may mistakenly believe that the reward for working has risen and increase the quantity of labor they supply. Only later do they realize that the price of the goods and services they buy is also rising; that is, their real wages (wages that are adjusted for inflation) have not risen. They have been fooled into supplying more of their labor into the market.

The key in all of these cases is that their short-run misperceptions about relative prices temporarily fools

the supplier into producing more as the overall price level rises and producing less as the overall price level falls. This leads to an upward-sloping short-run aggregate supply curve.

13-3b WHY IS THE LONG-RUN AGGREGATE SUPPLY CURVE VERTICAL?

Along the short-run aggregate supply curve, we assume that wages and other input prices are constant. This assumption is not the case in the long run, which is a period long enough for the price of all inputs to fully adjust to changes in the economy. When we move along the long-run supply curve, we are looking at the relationship between RGDP produced and the price level, once input prices have been able to respond to changes in output prices. Along the long-run aggregate supply ($LRAS$) curve, two sets of prices are changing: the price of outputs and the price of inputs. That is, along the $LRAS$ curve, a 10 percent increase in the price of goods and services is matched by a 10 percent increase in the price of inputs. The long-run aggregate supply curve is thus insensitive to the price level. As we can see in Exhibit 13.4, the $LRAS$ curve is drawn as perfectly vertical, reflecting the fact that the level of RGDP producers are willing to supply is not affected by changes in the price level. Note that the vertical long-run aggregate supply curve will always be positioned at the natural rate of output, where all resources are fully employed ($RGDP_{NR}$). That is, in the long run, firms will always produce at the maximum level allowed by their

EXHIBIT 13.4 The Long-Run Aggregate Supply Curve

A change in the price level does not change the amount of RGDP supplied in the long run.

© Cengage Learning 2014

capital, labor, and technological inputs, regardless of the price level.

The long-run equilibrium level is where the economy will settle when undisturbed and when all resources are fully employed. Remember that the economy will always be at the intersection of aggregate supply and aggregate demand; but that point will not always be at the natural rate of output, $RGDP_{NR}$. Long-run equilibrium will only occur where the aggregate supply and aggregate demand curves intersect along the long-run aggregate supply curve at the natural, or potential, rate of output.

SECTION CHECK 3 ANSWERS

1. The short-run aggregate supply curve measures how much RGDP suppliers are willing to produce at different price levels.

2. In the short run, producers supply more as the price level increases because wages and other input prices tend to change more slowly than output prices. For this reason, producers can make a profit by expanding production when the price level rises.

3. In the long run, input prices change proportionally with output prices. The position of the *LRAS* curve is determined by the level of capital, land, labor, and technology at the natural rate of output, $RGDP_{NR}$.

13-4 Shifts in the Aggregate Supply Curve

SECTION CHECK 4

Keep the following questions in mind as you read through this section.

1. Which factors of production affect the short-run and long-run aggregate supply curves?

2. What factors shift the short-run aggregate supply curve exclusively?

We will now examine the determinants that can shift the short-run and long-run aggregate supply curves, as shown in Exhibit 13.5.

EXHIBIT 13.5 Shifts in Both Short-Run and Long-Run Aggregate Supply

© Cengage Learning 2014

13-4a SHIFTING SHORT-RUN AND LONG-RUN SUPPLY CURVES

Any change in the quantity of any factor of production available—capital, land, labor, or technology—can cause a shift in both the long-run and short-run aggregate supply curves. We will now see how these factors can change the positions of both types of aggregate supply curves.

How Capital Affects Aggregate Supply

Changes in the stock of capital will alter the amount of goods and services the economy can produce. Investing in capital improves the quantity and quality of the capital stock, which lowers the cost of production in the short run. This change in turn shifts the short-run aggregate supply curve rightward and firms will supply more output at every price level. It also allows output to be permanently greater than before, shifting the long-run aggregate supply curve rightward, *ceteris paribus*.

Changes in human capital can also alter the aggregate supply curve. Investments in human capital include educational or vocational programs and on-the-job training. All these investments in human capital cause productivity to rise. As a result, the short-run aggregate supply curve shifts to the right, because a more skilled workforce lowers the cost of production. The *LRAS* curve also shifts to the right, because greater output is achievable on a permanent, or sustainable, basis, *ceteris paribus*.

Under CEO Larry Ellison's guidance, Oracle became a leading supplier in the market for database software. Oracle's software has helped many firms access, store, organize, and retrieve information in more efficient ways.

Land (Natural Resources)

Remember that, in economics, *land* has an all-encompassing definition that includes all natural resources. An increase in natural resources, such as successful oil exploration, would presumably lower the costs of production and expand the economy's sustainable rate of output, shifting both the short-run and long-run aggregate supply curves to the right. Likewise, a decrease in available natural resources would result in a leftward shift of both the short-run and long-run aggregate supply curves. For example, in the 1970s and early 1980s, when the OPEC cartel was strong and effective at raising world oil prices, both short-run and long-run aggregate supply curves shifted to the left, as the members of the cartel deliberately reduced the production of oil.

The Labor Force

The addition of workers to the labor force, *ceteris paribus*, can increase aggregate supply. For example, during the 1960s, women and baby boomers entered the labor force in large numbers. This increase tended to depress wages and increase short-run aggregate supply, *ceteris paribus*. The expanded labor force also increased the economy's potential output, increasing long-run aggregate supply. Japan's aging population has been causing a decrease in the labor force in recent years—a leftward shift in the long-run aggregate supply curve, *ceteris paribus*.

Technology and Entrepreneurship

Bill Gates of Microsoft, the late Steve Jobs of Apple Computer, and Larry Ellison of Oracle are just a few examples of entrepreneurs who, through inventive activity, developed innovative technology. Computers and specialized software led to many cost savings—ATMs, bar-code

scanners, biotechnology, and increased productivity across the board. These activities shifted both the short-run and long-run aggregate supply curves rightward by lowering costs and expanding real output possibilities.

Government Regulations

Increases in government regulations can make it more costly for producers. This increase in production costs results in a leftward shift of the short-run aggregate supply curve, and a reduction in society's potential output shifts the long-run aggregate supply curve to the left as well.

Likewise, a reduction in government regulations on businesses would lower the costs of production and expand potential real output, causing both the *SRAS* and *LRAS* curves to shift to the right.

13-4b WHAT FACTORS SHIFT SHORT-RUN AGGREGATE SUPPLY ONLY?

Some factors shift the short-run aggregate supply curve but do not change the long-run aggregate supply curve. The most important of these factors are wages and other input prices, productivity, and unexpected supply shocks. Exhibit 13.6 illustrates the effect of these factors on short-run aggregate supply.

Wages and Other Input Prices

The price of factors, or inputs, that go into producing outputs will affect only the short-run aggregate supply curve if they do not reflect permanent changes in the supplies of some factors of production. For example, if money

EXHIBIT 13.6 Shifts in Short-Run Aggregate Supply but Not Long-Run Aggregate Supply

SHIFTS IN THE SHORT-RUN AGGREGATE SUPPLY CURVE

Q&A

Q: Why do wage increases (and other input prices) affect the short-run aggregate supply but not the long-run aggregate supply?

A: Remember, in the short run, wages and other input prices are assumed to be constant along the *SRAS* curve. If the firm has to pay more for its workers or any other input, its costs will rise. That is, the *SRAS* curve will shift to the left. This shift from $SRAS_1$ to $SRAS_2$ is shown in Exhibit 13.7. The reason the *LRAS* curve will not shift is that unless these input prices reflect permanent changes in input supply, those changes will only be temporary, and output will not be permanently or sustainedly different as a result. Other things being equal, if an input price is to be permanently higher, relative to other goods, its supply must have decreased; but that would mean that potential real output, and hence long-run aggregate supply, would also shift left.

or nominal wages increase without a corresponding increase in labor productivity, it will become more costly (less profitable) for suppliers to produce goods and services at every price level, causing the *SRAS* curve to shift to the left. As Exhibit 13.7 shows, long-run aggregate supply will not shift because, with the same supply of labor as before, potential output does not change.

Nonlabor Input Prices

A decrease in the price of a nonlabor input, like oil, will lower production costs (making firms more profitable), and they will be more willing to increase supply at every given price level, shifting the SRAS curve to the right. If the price of steel or oil rises, automobile producers will find it more expensive to do business because their production costs will rise, resulting in a leftward shift in the short-run aggregate supply curve. The *LRAS* curve will not shift, however, as long as the capacity to make steel has not been reduced.

EXHIBIT 13.7 Supply Shifts

Along *LRAS*, price level and input prices rise by the same percentage.

An increase in input prices shifts the *SRAS*.

Along *SRAS*, price level changes but input prices do not.

$RGDP_{NR}$

Real GDP

Price Level

© Cengage Learning 2014

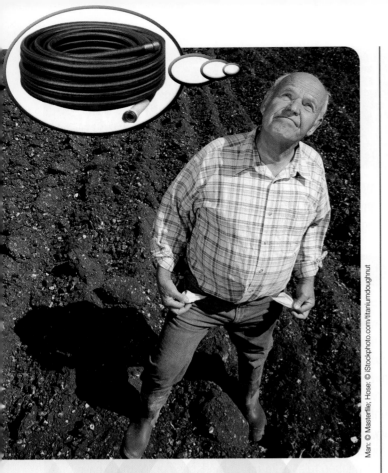

Natural disasters such as droughts can temporarily increase the costs of production. This farmer would have to pay extra to bring water in from somewhere else.

Changes in the Expected Future Price Level

If workers and firms believe that the price level is going to increase in the near future, they will try to adjust their wages and other input prices to compensate for the price level increase. For example, labor unions might fight to get a 3 percent increase in wages for their members if they anticipate the price level to rise 3 percent next year. If they are successful in getting the wage increase for their members, this will cause the short-run aggregate supply curve to shift to the left. Of course, firms and workers can make incorrect predictions about the future price level. For example, if workers expect a small increase in the price level and it turns out to be much larger, they will negotiate for even higher wages in the next contract—this will shift the *SRAS* curve leftward. The higher wages will increase the firm's costs, and it will need higher prices now to produce the same level of output. If most firms and workers are making the adjustment to a higher than expected price level, then the *SRAS* curve will shift left. If they are adjusting to the price level being lower than expected, then the *SRAS* curve will shift right.

supply shocks unexpected temporary events that can either increase or decrease aggregate supply

Supply Shocks

Supply shocks are unexpected temporary events that can either increase or decrease the short-run aggregate supply. For example, negative supply shocks like major widespread flooding, earthquakes, droughts, and other natural disasters can increase the costs of production, causing the short-run aggregate supply curve to shift to the left, *ceteris paribus*. However, once the temporary effects of these disasters have been felt, no appreciable change in the economy's productive capacity has occurred, so the long-run aggregate supply doesn't shift as a result. Other temporary supply shocks, such as disruptions in trade due to war or labor strikes, will have similar effects on short-run aggregate supply. However, positive supply shocks such as favorable weather conditions or temporary price reductions of imported resources like oil can lower production costs and shift the short-run aggregate supply curve rightward. During the mid- to late 1990s, the United States experienced a positive supply shock as the Internet, and information technology in general, gave a huge boost to productivity.

SECTION CHECK 4 ANSWERS

1. Any increase in the quantity of any of the factors of production—capital, land, labor, or technology—that are available will cause both the long-run and short-run aggregate supply curves to shift to the right. A decrease in any of these factors will shift both of the aggregate supply curves to the left.

2. Changes in the input price and temporary supply shocks will shift the short-run aggregate supply curve but will not affect the long-run aggregate supply curve.

13-5 Macroeconomic Equilibrium

SECTION CHECK 5

Keep the following questions in mind as you read through this section.

1. What is short-run macroeconomic equilibrium?
2. What is the long-run macroeconomic equilibrium?
3. What are recessionary and inflationary gaps?
4. What is wage and price inflexibility?

EXHIBIT 13.8 Long-Run Macroeconomic Equilibrium

The short-run equilibrium level of real output and the price level are given by the intersection of the aggregate demand curve and the short-run aggregate supply curve. When this equilibrium occurs at the potential output level, the economy is operating at full employment on the long-run aggregate supply curve, as shown in Exhibit 13.8.

Only a short-run equilibrium that is at potential output is also a long-run equilibrium. Short-run equilibrium can change when the aggregate demand curve or the short-run aggregate supply curve shifts rightward or leftward; but the long-run equilibrium level of RGDP only changes when the *LRAS* curve shifts. Sometimes, these supply or demand changes are anticipated; at other times, however, the shifts occur unexpectedly. Economists call these unexpected shifts *shocks*.

The economy can be either at a point where actual and potential *RGDP* are equal at $RGDP_{NR}$ or the economy can be at a point where the potential *RGDP* and actual *RGDP* are not equal. In Exhibit 13.9, we see that it is rare that actual and potential *RGDP* are equal. In other words, the economy can be in a boom, where actual *RGDP* is greater than potential *RGDP*, or in a recession, where actual *RGDP* is less than potential *RGDP*. However, notice that the economy does not often stray too far from potential *RGDP*—of course, the recent exception is the financial crisis of 2008.

13-5a RECESSIONARY AND INFLATIONARY GAPS

As we have just seen, equilibrium will not always occur at full employment. In fact, equilibrium can occur at less than the potential output of the economy, $RGDP_{NR}$

EXHIBIT 13.9 Actual and Potential Real GDP from 1989 to 2011

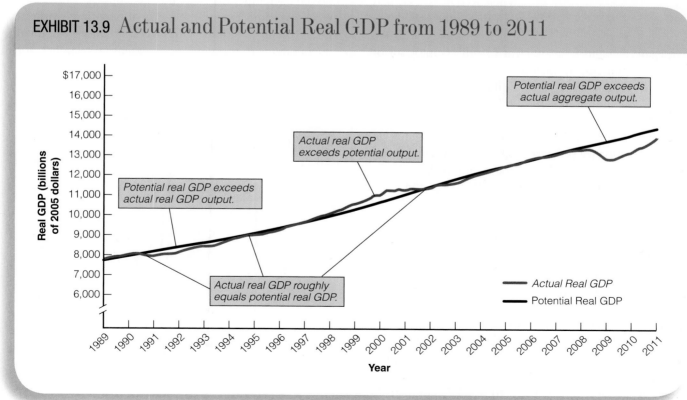

EXHIBIT 13.10 Recessionary and Inflationary Gaps

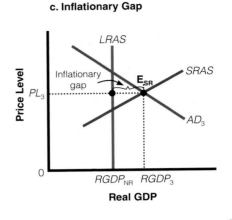

a. Recessionary Gap

b. Long-Run Equilibrium

c. Inflationary Gap

© Cengage Learning 2014

recessionary gap the output gap that occurs when the actual output is less than the potential output

inflationary gap the output gap that occurs when the actual output is greater than the potential output

demand-pull inflation a price-level increase due to an increase in aggregate demand

(a **recessionary gap**), temporarily beyond $RGDP_{NR}$ (an **inflationary gap**), or at potential GDP. Exhibit 13.10 shows these three possibilities. In (a), we have a recessionary gap at the short-run equilibrium, E_{SR}, at $RGDP_1$. When RGDP is less than $RGDP_{NR}$, the result is a recessionary gap— aggregate demand is insufficient to fully employ all of society's resources, so unemployment will be above the normal rate. In (c), we have an inflationary gap at the short-run equilibrium, E_{SR}, at $RGDP_3$, where aggregate demand is so high that the economy is temporarily operating beyond full capacity ($RGDP_{NR}$); this gap will lead to inflationary pressure, and unemployment will be below the normal rate. In (b), the economy is just right where AD_2 and $SRAS$ intersect at $RGDP_{NR}$—the long-run equilibrium position.

13-5b DEMAND-PULL INFLATION

Demand-pull inflation occurs when the price level rises as a result of an increase in aggregate demand. Consider the case in which an increase in consumer optimism results in a corresponding increase in aggregate demand. Exhibit 13.11 shows that an increase in aggregate demand causes an increase in the price level and an increase in real output. The movement is along the $SRAS$ curve from point E_1 to point E_2 and causes

an inflationary gap. Recall that an increase in output occurs as a result of the increase in the price level in the short run, because firms have an incentive to increase real output when the prices of the goods they are selling are rising faster than the costs of the inputs they use in production.

Note that E_2 in Exhibit 13.11 is positioned beyond $RGDP_{NR}$—an inflationary gap. It seems strange that the economy can operate beyond its potential, but it is possible—temporarily—as firms encourage workers to work overtime, extend the hours of part-time workers, hire recently retired employees, reduce frictional unemployment through more extensive searches for employees, and so on. However, this level of output and employment *cannot* be sustained in the long run.

EXHIBIT 13.11 Demand-Pull Inflation

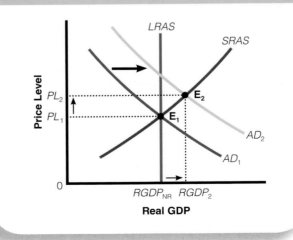

© Cengage Learning 2014

13-5c COST-PUSH INFLATION

The 1970s and early 1980s witnessed a phenomenon known as **stagflation**, where lower growth and higher prices occurred together. Some economists believe that this situation was caused by a leftward shift in the short-run aggregate supply curve, as shown in Exhibit 13.12. If the aggregate demand curve did not increase significantly but the price level did, then the inflation was caused by supply-side forces, which is called **cost-push inflation**.

The increase in oil prices was the primary culprit responsible for the leftward shift in the aggregate supply curve. As we discussed in the previous section, an increase in input prices can cause the short-run aggregate supply curve to shift to the left; and this spelled big trouble for the U.S. economy—higher price levels, lower output, and higher rates of unemployment. The impact of cost-push inflation is illustrated in Exhibit 13.12.

In Exhibit 13.12, we see that the economy is initially at full-employment equilibrium at point E_1. A sudden increase in input prices, such as an increase in the price of oil, shifts the $SRAS$ curve to the left—from $SRAS_1$ to $SRAS_2$. As a result of the shift in short-run aggregate supply, the price level rises to PL_2, and real output falls from $RGDP_{NR}$ to $RGDP_2$ (point E_2). Firms demand fewer workers as a result of higher input costs that cannot be passed on to consumers. This lower demand, in turn, leads to higher prices, lower real output, and more unemployment—and a recessionary gap. In the United States, these negative supply shocks occurred in 1974, 1979, 1990, 2005, and 2007–2008. These supply shocks can change real GDP significantly, but temporarily, away from potential aggregate output at $RGDP_{NR}$. In 2007, the price of many raw materials shot up globally—a global negative supply shock. Many countries around the world felt the effects of the negative supply shock.

However, recessions are not all bad—they can at least slow the rate of inflation. Two periods of serious inflation, 1974–1975 and 1979–1981, were followed by recessions and a slower rate of inflation.

What Helped the United States Recover in the 1980s?

As far as energy prices are concerned, oil prices fell during the 1980s when OPEC lost some of its clout because of internal problems. In addition, many non-OPEC oil producers increased production. The net result in the short run was a rightward shift in the aggregate supply curve. Holding aggregate demand constant, this rightward shift in the aggregate supply curve leads to a lower price level, greater output, and lower rates of unemployment—moving the economy back toward E_1 in Exhibit 13.12.

13-5d A DECREASE IN AGGREGATE DEMAND AND RECESSIONS

Just as cost-push inflation may cause a recessionary gap, so may a decrease in aggregate demand. For example, consider the case in which consumer confidence plunges and the stock market "tanks." As a result, aggregate demand falls, shown in Exhibit 13.13 on the next page as the shift from AD_1 to AD_2, leaving the economy in a new short-run equilibrium at point E_2. Households, firms, and governments buy fewer goods and services at every price level. In response to this drop in demand, output falls from $RGDP_{NR}$ to $RGDP_2$, and the price level falls from PL_1 to PL_2. Therefore, in the short run, this fall in aggregate demand causes higher unemployment and a reduction in output—and it, too, can lead to a recessionary gap.

The recession of 2001 and the slow recovery that followed can be attributed to three shocks that affected aggregate demand: the end of the stock market boom, the terrorist attacks of September 11 (this event had an impact on both stock market wealth and consumer confidence), and a series of corporate scandals that rocked the stock market. Corrective stabilizing measures were taken following these events to prevent even further damage. For example, the Federal Reserve continued to lower interest rates. Lower interest rates stimulate the economy by encouraging investment and consumption spending. Other stabilizing measures included a tax cut passed by Congress in 2001 and increased government

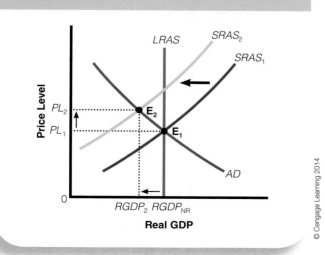

EXHIBIT 13.12 Cost-Push Inflation

© Cengage Learning 2014

EXHIBIT 13.13 Short-Run Decrease in Aggregate Demand

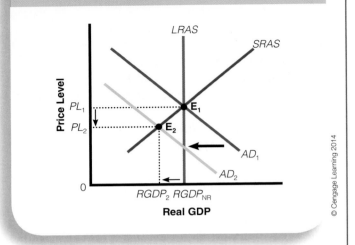

© Cengage Learning 2014

spending to help rebuild New York City and provide financial assistance to the ailing airline industry. Both the 2001 tax cut and the war on terrorism led to an increase in government spending. Both of these policies shifted the aggregate demand curve to the right, reducing the magnitude of the 2001 recession. The recovery did not pick up steam until 2003.

Most of the post-war recessions have been caused by negative demand shocks. Negative supply shocks have been relatively few, but quite severe, in terms of unemployment rates. The 2007–2008 recession appears to be the product of both negative demand and supply shocks.

During the financial crisis of 2008, both consumers and firms reduced their spending, and this caused the aggregate demand curve to shift to the left, in turn

Increases in military spending can increase aggregate demand, other things being equal.

© Reuters/CORBIS

leading to a recessionary gap. In short, real estate and financial market wealth decreased, precautionary saving by consumers increased as confidence fell, obtaining credit became more difficult, and both households and firms adopted a wait-and-see attitude. The rate of inflation slowed and GDP fell over 2 percent in a year. It began with a boom-to-bust story in the housing market and then rippled into the stock market. In order to prop up aggregate demand, the Federal Reserve increased the money supply and lowered interest rates. In addition, Congress enacted a number of measures to stimulate consumption, investment, and government spending. This helped to shift the aggregate demand curve to the right and RGDP and the price level rose by the end of 2009. We will discuss this in much more detail in our chapters on monetary and fiscal policy.

13-5e ADJUSTING TO A RECESSIONARY GAP

Many recoveries from a recessionary gap occur because of increases in aggregate demand—perhaps consumer and business confidence picks up, or the government lowers taxes and/or lowers interest rates to stimulate the economy. That is, an eventual rightward shift in the aggregate demand curve takes the economy back to potential output—$RGDP_{NR}$.

However, it is possible for the economy to *self-correct* through declining wages and prices. In Exhibit 13.14, at point E_2, the intersection of PL_2 and $RGDP_2$, the economy is in a recessionary gap—that is, the economy is producing less than its potential output. At this lower level of output, firms lay off workers to avoid inventory accumulation. In addition, firms may cut prices

EXHIBIT 13.14 Adjusting to a Recessionary Gap

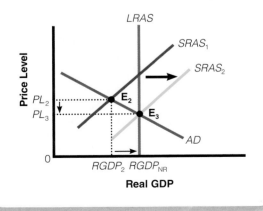

© Cengage Learning 2014

to increase demand for their products. Unemployed workers and other input suppliers may also bid down wages and prices. That is, laborers and other input suppliers are now willing to accept lower wages and prices for the use of their resources, and the resulting reduction in production costs shifts the short-run supply curve from $SRAS_1$ to $SRAS_2$. Eventually, the economy returns to a long-run equilibrium at point E_3, the intersection of $RGDP_{NR}$ and a lower price level, PL_3.

13-5f SLOW ADJUSTMENTS TO A RECESSIONARY GAP

Many economists believe that wages and prices may be slow to adjust, especially downward. This downward **wage and price inflexibility** may prolong the duration of a recessionary gap.

For example, in Exhibit 13.14 we see that the economy is in a recession at E_2 and $RGDP_2$. The economy will eventually self-correct to $RGDP_{NR}$ at E_3, as workers and other input owners accept lower wages and prices for their inputs, shifting the $SRAS$ curve to the right from $SRAS_1$ to $SRAS_2$. However, if wages and other input prices are sticky, the economy's adjustment mechanism might take many months to totally self-correct.

Japan witnessed several recessionary gaps in the 1990s and even experienced deflation as the self-adjustment mechanism predicts. However, the adjustment out of the recessionary gap was slow and painful.

13-5g WHAT CAUSES WAGES AND PRICES TO BE STICKY DOWNWARD?

Empirical evidence supports several explanations for the downward stickiness of wages and prices. Firms may not be able to legally cut wages because of long-term labor contracts (particularly with union workers) or a legal minimum wage. Efficiency wages may also limit a firm's ability to lower wage rates. Menu costs may cause price inflexibility as well.

Efficiency Wages

In economics, it is generally assumed that as productivity rises, wages will rise, and that workers can raise their productivity through investments in human capital such as education and on-the-job

training. However, some economists believe that in some cases, *higher wages will lead to greater productivity*.

In the efficiency wage model, employers pay their employees more than the equilibrium wage as a means to increase efficiency. Proponents of this theory suggest that higher-than-equilibrium wages might attract the most productive workers, lower job turnover and training costs, and improve morale. Because the efficiency wage rate is greater than the equilibrium wage rate, the quantity of labor that would be willingly supplied is greater than the quantity of labor demanded, resulting in greater amounts of unemployment.

However, aside from creating some additional unemployment, the efficiency wage could also cause wages to be inflexible downward. For example, if aggregate demand decreases, firms that pay efficiency wages may be reluctant to cut wages, fearing that cuts could lead to lower morale, greater absenteeism, and general productivity losses. In short, if firms are paying efficiency wages, they may be reluctant to lower wages in a recession, leading to downward wage inflexibility.

Menu Costs

Some costs are associated with changing prices in an inflationary environment. Thus, the higher price level in an inflationary environment is often reflected slowly, as restaurants, mail-order houses, and department stores change their prices gradually so as to incur fewer *menu costs* (the costs of changing posted prices) in printing new catalogs, new mailers, new advertisements, and so on. Because businesses are not likely to change all their prices immediately, we can say that some prices are sticky, or slow to change. For example, many outputs, such as steel, are inputs in the production of other products, such as automobiles. As a result, these prices are slow to change.

> **wage and price inflexibility** the tendency for prices and wages to only adjust slowly downward to changes in the economy

Today's Special — higher menu costs

© iStockphoto.com/Scott Stanley

Suppose aggregate demand unexpectedly decreases. This change could lower the price level. Some firms may adjust to the change quickly. Others, however, may move more slowly because of menu costs, causing their prices to become too high (above equilibrium). Ultimately, the sales and outputs will fall, potentially causing a recession. Firms not responding quickly to changes in demand fail to do so for a reason; and to some economists, menu costs are at least part of that reason.

13-5h ADJUSTING TO AN INFLATIONARY GAP

In Exhibit 13.15, the economy is in an inflationary gap at E_2, where $RGDP_2$ is greater than $RGDP_{NR}$. Because the price level, PL_2, is higher than the one workers anticipated, PL_1, workers become disgruntled with wages that have not adjusted to the new price level (if prices have risen but wages have not risen as much, real wages have fallen). Recall that along the SRAS curve, wages and other input prices are assumed to be constant. Therefore, workers' and input suppliers' purchasing power falls as output prices rise. Real (adjusted for inflation) wages have fallen. Consequently, workers and other suppliers demand higher prices if they are to be willing to supply their inputs. As input prices respond to the higher level of output prices, the short-run aggregate supply curve shifts to the left, from $SRAS_1$ to $SRAS_2$. Suppliers will continue to seek higher prices for their inputs until they reach the long-run equilibrium, at point E_3 in Exhibit 13.15. At point E_3, input suppliers' purchasing power is restored at the long-run equilibrium, at $RGDP_{NR}$ and a new higher price level, PL_3.

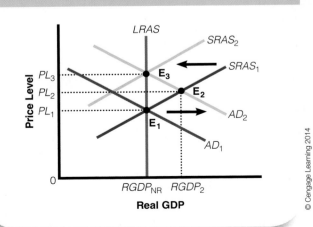

EXHIBIT 13.15 Adjusting to an Inflationary Gap

© Cengage Learning 2014

13-5i PRICE LEVEL AND RGDP OVER TIME

In Exhibit 13.16, we traced out the pattern of RGDP versus the price level. According to the Bureau of Economic Analysis, both the price level and RGDP have been rising over the last 36 years. So what is responsible for the changes? The answer is both aggregate demand and aggregate supply. Aggregate demand has risen because of growing population (which impacts consumption and investment spending), rising income, increases in government purchases, and increases in the money supply. Aggregate supply has been generally increasing as well, including increases in the labor force and improvements in labor productivity and technology.

SECTION CHECK 5 ANSWERS

1. Short-run macroeconomic equilibrium occurs at the intersection of the aggregate demand curve and the short-run aggregate supply curve.

2. A short-run equilibrium is also a long-run equilibrium only if it is at potential output on the long-run aggregate supply curve.

3. If short-run equilibrium occurs at less than the potential output of the economy, $RGDP_{NR}$, the result is a recessionary gap. If the short-run equilibrium temporarily occurs beyond $RGDP_{NR}$, the result is an inflationary gap.

4. Wages and other input prices may be slow to adjust, especially downward. This downward wage and price inflexibility may lead to prolonged periods of recession.

13-6 The Classical and the Keynesian Macroeconomic Models

SECTION CHECK 6

Keep the following questions in mind as you read through this section.

1. What is Say's law?

2. What was Keynes's criticism of the classical school?

3. What is the full-employment classical school model?

EXHIBIT 13.16 U.S. Price Level and RGDP

NOTE: In 2009 both the price level and real GDP declined from those figures of the previous year.

SOURCE: Bureau of Economic Analysis, National Economic Accounts, Current-dollar and "real" GDP. Washington, D.C., February 26, 2010. Available at http://bea.gov/national/index.htm#gdp (accessed February 26, 2010).

Historically, the two primary approaches to macroeconomics have been the classical school and the Keynesian school. Let us begin with the classical school. The classical school of thought believed that wages and prices adjust quickly to changes in supply and demand.

13-6a THE CLASSICAL SCHOOL AND SAY'S LAW

Writing at the beginning of the nineteenth century, the French economist Jean Baptiste Say formulated a notion, since dubbed Say's law, which in its simplest form states that "supply creates its own demand." More precisely, the production of goods and services creates income for owners of inputs (land, labor, capital, and entrepreneurship) used in production, which in turn creates a demand for goods. According to Say's law, we need not worry about output not being utilized; production creates income, which creates demand for goods, which leads to still more production. That is, Say's law establishes that full employment can be maintained because total spending will be great enough for firms to sell all

the output a fully employed economy can produce. Say's ideas were incorporated into the teachings of classical economists of the late nineteenth century.

Before the 1930s, the problem of unemployment was considered one that could be analyzed using microeconomic analysis; indeed, macroeconomics as we know it today did not exist. The theory that evolved to analyze unemployment suggested that joblessness could be eliminated by market forces, in the same way that shortages and surpluses of goods and services are eliminated by movement in the relative prices of those goods.

The Full-Employment Classical School Model

The macroeconomic models presented in this text draw from both schools of thought and emphasize the commonality between the two schools. The classical school focuses on the economy at full employment, because both schools agree that in the long run both wages and prices adjust freely to changes in demand and supply and the economy moves back naturally to its potential, full-employment output level. That is, eventually (in the

JEAN BAPTISTE SAY

long run) all markets adjust to their equilibrium values. Recall that full employment does not mean zero unemployment; rather, it refers to zero cyclical unemployment. Some structural and frictional unemployment occurs naturally in a dynamic and vibrant economy.

The actual output that the economy produces need not be the same as potential output—what the economy can produce without leading to inflation. If the economy is producing at less than its potential output, unemployment is greater than the natural rate; if the economy is producing at greater than its potential output, unemployment is less than the natural rate, causing inflationary pressures. That is, it is possible on the peak of a business cycle that actual real GDP can exceed potential real GDP, but only for a short period of time. The problem is that the causal observer often confuses potential and actual output. When the economy is accelerating at a fast clip, some observers believe we are on a new growth trajectory. And when the economy slows, some observers confuse this change with doom and gloom.

Earlier in this chapter we discussed monetary and fiscal policy, using the *AS/AD* model to examine business cycles and short-run policy prescriptions that involve government intervention to help the economy get back to its long-run growth trajectory.

Changes in Aggregate Demand in the Classical Model

In Exhibit 13.17, we see the impact of either an increase or a decrease in aggregate demand in the classical model. According to Say's law, prolonged unemployment is impossible in the long-run classical model. Prices, wages, and interest rates all adjust quickly, which keeps workers and resources fully employed at the natural rate of real output, $RGDP_{NR}$. The classical school made very little distinction between the short run and the long run, so the only aggregate supply curve is the vertical long-run aggregate supply curve, *LRAS* in Exhibit 13.17. That is, there is no separate short-run aggregate supply curve in the classical model. Prices and wages adjust so quickly that the economy seldom remains far from $RGDP_{NR}$.

EXHIBIT 13.17 Changes in Aggregate Demand in the Classical Model

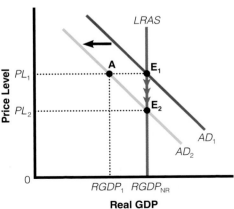

a. An Increase in Aggregate Demand

b. A Decrease in Aggregate Demand

In Exhibit 13.17(a), if prices, wages, and interest rates were not completely and quickly flexible, an increase in aggregate demand from AD_1 to AD_2 might cause the economy to move toward point A beyond $RGDP_{AD}$. However, when the price level rises, input suppliers bid up input prices and the economy quickly adjusts to the new price level at PL_2, moving along the $LRAS$.

In Exhibit 13.17(b), there is a decrease in aggregate demand that could cause the economy to move toward point A, where resources (labor, factories, and other inputs) would be unemployed. However, because input suppliers will compete against each other, it will drive input prices down. If this occurs quickly, as predicted in the classical model, the economy will not experience prolonged unemployment and will adjust to the new price level, PL_2, along the $LRAS$.

13-6b KEYNES'S CRITICISM OF THE CLASSICAL SCHOOL

In 1936, John Maynard Keynes's book, *The General Theory of Employment, Interest and Money*, was published. Along with Adam Smith's *The Wealth of Nations* in the eighteenth century, *The General Theory of Employment, Interest and Money* was one of the most influential books in economics. In his book, Keynes attacked the classical economic theory. He pointed out the naiveté of Say's law: Not all income generated from output need be used to buy goods and services; it can also be saved, hoarded, or taxed away. Supply does not automatically create an adequate demand. Keynes's severest attacks were against classical ideas about unemployment. With unemployment rates at that time in the double digits, where did the classicists go wrong?

To begin with, when a recession begins, wages rarely fall quickly to a new equilibrium level consistent with full employment. Long-term labor contracts with unions, minimum wage laws, and other factors often prevent wages from falling as quickly as the classical model suggests. Thus, wage inflexibility prevents the market solution from working rapidly enough to avert a prolonged recession.

The Keynesian Short-Run Aggregate Supply Curve—Sticky Prices and Wages

Keynes and his followers argued that wages and prices are inflexible downward. As we just discussed, wage stickiness can arise as a result of long-term labor and raw material contracts, unions, and minimum wage laws. If wages and prices are sticky and the economy

> Long-term labor contracts with unions, minimum wage laws, and other factors often prevent wages from falling as quickly as the classical model suggests.

has sufficient excess capacity, then the short-run aggregate supply curve is flat, because full employment of all resources is not reached until $RGDP_{NR}$. That is, with so many resources idle, producers will not have to compete with each other for machinery or labor, and input prices will tend to stay flat.

In Exhibit 13.18(a) on the next page, we see the Keynesian aggregate supply curve. When RGDP is well below potential output, an increase or decrease in aggregate demand has no impact on the price level but considerable impact on RGDP and employment.

However, most macroeconomists now believe that price and wages are not completely inflexible downward. Wages and prices tend to be less flexible when excess capacity is available—the slope of the $SRAS$ is flatter the further it is below full employment. When the economy is temporarily operating beyond $RGDP_{NR}$, the $SRAS$ is steep because higher output prices are necessary if firms are expanding output in this unsustainable region beyond full employment. That is, the firm can increase output by working labor and

When a recession begins, wages rarely fall quickly to a new equilibrium level consistent with full employment.

EXHIBIT 13.18 The Keynesian Aggregate Supply Curve

a. The Keynesian Short-Run Aggregate Supply

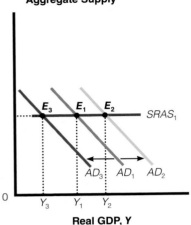

b. The Shape of The Aggregate Supply Curve

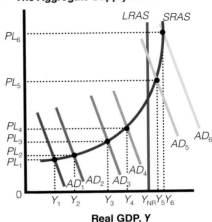

capital more intensively. When resources are idle, output will be more responsive to changes in AD, and the price

> Wage inflexibility prevents the market solution from working rapidly enough to avert a prolonged recession.

level will not be as responsive—the $SRAS$ is flatter—as it moves from AD_1 to AD_2 in Exhibit 13.18(b). And when resources are at full capacity, output is less responsive to changes in AD and the price level is highly responsive— the $SRAS$ is steeper—as it moves from AD_5 to AD_6, as seen in Exhibit 13.18(b). That is, the steeper the $SRAS$ curve, the greater the price level effect and the smaller the RGDP effect.

Economists continue to debate the actual shape of the short-run aggregate supply curve because the shape of the $SRAS$ has important implications for changes in aggregate demand, as seen in Exhibit 13.18(b). Over the flatter range of the short-run aggregate supply curve, a change in aggregate demand leads to a small change in the price level and a large change in Real GDP(Y)—AD_1 to AD_2. In the middle range, a change in aggregate demand leads to an appreciable change in both the price level and RGDP(Y)—AD_3 to AD_4. In the steep portion of the $SRAS$ curve, very little

additional output can be produced as the economy is at, or temporarily beyond, full capacity—AD_5 to AD_6. Any change in aggregate demand in this steep range will lead to sharp changes in the price level and little or no change in RGDP(Y). In the chapters to come we will see that when the government uses expansionary monetary or fiscal policy to stimulate aggregate demand, it must be careful to assess where it is on the $SRAS$ curve. If the economy is on the flat portion of the $SRAS$ curve, stimulus works better than on the steep part.

SECTION CHECK 6 ANSWERS

1. Say's law stated that "supply creates its own demand." It also argued that full employment could be maintained in an economy.

2. Keynes rejected Say's law because, in addition to spending income from production of goods and services, it can go toward saving, hoarding, or taxes.

3. Potential real output is the level of real output the economy can produce without leading to inflation. If the economy is producing less than potential output, unemployment is greater than its natural rate. If the economy is temporarily producing more than potential output, unemployment is less than its natural rate.

Chapter 13: Self-Review

Now that you are finished reading the chapter, review the questions below. You can write your answers in the space provided, then go online to see the answers at www.cengagebrain.com.

13-1 THE AGGREGATE DEMAND CURVE

1. **True or False: An increased price level reduces the quantities of investment goods and consumer durables demanded.**

2. **What is the open economy effect?**

13-2 SHIFTS IN THE AGGREGATE DEMAND CURVE

3. **Fill-in-the-Blank: An increase in the demand for consumption goods results in a(n) _____ in aggregate demand.**

4. **Fill-in-the-Blank: A falling demand for investment goods results in a(n) _____ in aggregate demand.**

5. **True or False: An increase in the money supply tends to decrease expenditures on consumption and investment, *ceteris paribus*.**

13-3 THE AGGREGATE SUPPLY CURVE

6. **What relationship does the short-run aggregate supply curve represent?**

13-4 SHIFTS IN THE AGGREGATE SUPPLY CURVE

7. **Fill-in-the-Blank: Lower input costs _____ the level of RGDP supplied at any given price level.**

8. **What would happen to short- and long-run aggregate supply if unusually good weather led to bumper crops of most agricultural produce?**

13-5 MACROECONOMIC EQUILIBRIUM

9. **What is demand-pull inflation?**

10. **True or False: Cost-push inflation is caused by a rightward shift in the short-run aggregate supply curve.**

11. **Fill-in-the-Blank: The economy self-corrects for a short-run recession through _____ wages and prices.**

13-6 THE CLASSICAL AND KEYNESIAN MACROECONOMIC MODELS

12. **Fill-in-the-Blank: The _____ school of thought emphasized that markets can rapidly adjust to changes.**

13. **What would keep wages from falling quickly in a recession?**

14. **Fill-in-the-Blank: If wages are sticky downward, a decrease in aggregate demand will primarily _____ real output.**

PART **3**

Every year, the President delivers

a budget proposal like this one, the proposed budget for 2012, for approval by congress. The President's budget details proposed government spending for the coming fiscal year, which begins on October 1. The Congressional budget committees will then begin drafting budget resolutions to pass along to the House and Senate.

Test your Economics *street-smart* knowledge and see how you compare against other students! Scan here or visit CourseMate for Survey of ECON2.

14
Fiscal Policy

I n earlier chapters, we discussed how an economy can face a recessionary gap when aggregate demand is deficient or an inflationary gap when there is excessive aggregate demand.

In this chapter, we will see how the government can employ fiscal policy—the use of government purchases, transfers, and/or taxes—to combat recessions or curb inflationary pressures. We will see how the government obtains revenues through taxation and examine the different types of taxation. We will also see that a number of problems are associated with successfully enacting and applying fiscal policy to stabilize an economy. Finally, we will examine the supply-side effects of taxes.

14-1 Fiscal Policy

SECTION CHECK 1

Keep the following questions in mind as you read through this section.

1. What is fiscal policy?

2. How does expansionary fiscal policy affect the government's budget?

3. How does contractionary fiscal policy affect the government's budget?

Fiscal policy is the use of government purchases, taxes, and transfer payments to alter RGDP and the price level. Government spending takes two forms: government purchases of goods and services such as national defense and education, and transfer payments such as Social Security, Medicare, and Medicaid. So government expenditures (spending) equals the sum of government purchases and government transfer payments. The government takes in the bulk of its tax revenues from three taxes: personal income taxes, corporate income taxes, and payroll taxes (like Social Security and Medicare).

fiscal policy use of government purchases, taxes, and transfer payments to alter equilibrium output and the price level

The government may use fiscal policy to stimulate the economy during a contraction (or recession) or to try to curb an economic expansion in order to bring inflation under control. In the early 1980s, large tax cuts helped the U.S. economy out of a recession. In the 1990s, Japan used large government spending programs to try to spend itself out of a recessionary slump. In 2001, a large tax cut was implemented to combat an economic slowdown and to promote long-term economic growth in the United States. And the fiscal stimulus package that the Obama administration enacted in 2009 to combat the recession was the largest fiscal stimulus since World War II. But that was small compared to the $2.5 trillion spent on the financial system. When the government should use such policies and how well they work are just a couple of the questions we will address in this chapter.

14-1a FISCAL STIMULUS AFFECTS THE BUDGET

Government spending (for purchases of goods and services and transfer payments) that exceeds tax revenues causes a **budget deficit**. When tax revenues are greater than government spending, a **budget surplus** exists. A balanced budget, where government expenditures equal tax revenues, seldom occurs unless efforts are made to deliberately balance the budget as a matter of public policy.

14-1b THE GOVERNMENT AND TOTAL SPENDING

In a previous chapter, we learned that the aggregate demand is equal to consumer spending, investment spending, government purchases, and net exports: $AD = C + I + G + (X - M)$. The government directly controls government purchases, but government can also indirectly affect aggregate demand through taxes and transfer programs. For example, an increase in taxes and/or a reduction in transfer payments can reduce disposable income and decrease consumer spending. Similarly, a decrease in taxes and/or an increase in transfer payment can increase disposable income and lead to an increase in consumer

budget deficit occurs when government spending exceeds tax revenues for a given fiscal year

budget surplus occurs when tax revenues are greater than government expenditures for a given fiscal year

JAPAN'S FISCAL POLICY EXPERIMENT

Prior to the 1990s, Japan experienced several decades of rapid economic growth with only a mild recession in 1974. However, the 1990s were a different story—the exuberant bubble burst, as the stock market made a major correction and land values plunged. Consequently, consumption and investment spending—two major components of aggregate demand—fell.

In the decade of the 1990s, Japan grew at an unusually slow rate—1.2 percent per year—almost 3 percentage points below the average growth rate of the previous decade. In order to combat the recession, the Japanese launched a fiscal policy stimulus package of unprecedented tax cuts and spending increases. Government expenditures rose from slightly over 30 percent of GDP to almost 40 percent of GDP. The Japanese government spent well over a trillion dollars during the decade to heal their ailing economy. Because of the tax cuts, government tax revenues fell from 34 percent to 31 percent of GDP. And the continued fiscal efforts, financed with lower taxes and higher government spending, led to a growing debt problem. (The debt-to-GDP ratio almost doubled in the decade of the 1990s—from 0.58 in 1991 to 1.1 in 2000.)

The results of the fiscal policy are mixed. The fiscal policy clearly did not bring about a full recovery. However, some economists argue that without the spending and tax cuts, the Japanese would have suffered a depression rather than a sustained period of slow economic growth. Other economists argue that the wasteful nature of government spending was the reason that fiscal policy was not more successful. The Japanese built bridges, railroad lines, tunnels, and highways to sparsely populated areas. It is safe to say that none of these projects would have been undertaken by the private sector. Thus, a better-designed fiscal policy might have been more effective.

SOURCE: John H. Makin, "Japan's lost decade: Lessons for America," *American Enterprise Institute for Public Policy Research*, February 2001. Available at http://www.aei.org/outlook/12375 (accessed July 8, 2010).

spending. The government can also influence investment spending through business taxes. For example, a tax cut for firms may increase investment spending and shift the aggregate demand curve to the right. Thus, the government can change aggregate demand in a number of ways.

14-2 Government Spending and Taxation

In this section, we will see how the government obtains revenues through taxation to provide public goods and services, and we will examine the different types of taxes the government can enforce.

14-2a GROWTH IN GOVERNMENT

Government plays a large role in the economy, and its role increased markedly during World War II. From 1950–1975, government expenditures grew from about 25 percent of GDP to 33 percent of GDP. However, government expenditures increased sharply with the recession that began in 2008. By 2009, government expenditures reached a peacetime record of 39 percent of GDP, as seen in Exhibit 14.1 on the next page.

National defense spending fluctuates with international tension. The aftermath of the terrorist attacks of September 11, 2001, and the wars in Iraq and Afghanistan, led to increases in defense spending. Consequently, defense spending, as a percentage of total federal spending, rose from 17 percent in 2001 to 20 percent in 2011. Terrorism is probably not going away any time soon, so defense expenditures will most likely remain high. The global recession of 2007–2009 also expanded the size of government further. In addition, the Obama administration has created a greater role for government in the health care and energy sectors. Finally, as baby boomers age, there will be an even greater demand on public pensions and health care. Government spending will probably not be shrinking soon.

Areas of government growth can be identified at least in part by looking at statistics on the types of federal government spending. Exhibit 14.2 on the next page shows that 37 percent of federal government spending in 2011 went to Social Security and income security programs. Another 24 percent was spent on health care and Medicare (for the elderly). The remaining federal expenditures were national defense, 20 percent; interest on the national debt, 6 percent; and miscellaneous items such as foreign aid, agriculture, transportation, and housing, 13 percent.

14-2b GENERATING GOVERNMENT REVENUE

Governments have to pay their bills like any person or institution that spends money. But how do they obtain revenue? In most years, a large majority of government activity is financed by taxation. What kinds of taxes are levied on the American population?

At the federal level, most taxes or levies are on income. Exhibit 14.3 on page 299 shows that 83 percent of tax revenues come in the form of income taxes on individuals and social insurance taxes (payroll taxes to fund Social Security and Medicare). Payroll taxes as a share of federal revenue have grown from 10 percent in 1950 to 36 percent in 2012. Payroll taxes are split between employees and employers. The Social Security share of federal taxes has steadily risen as the proportion of the population over age 65 has grown and as Social Security benefits have been increased. Consequently, payroll taxes have risen significantly in recent years. Other taxes on such items as gasoline, liquor, and tobacco products, provide for a small proportion of government revenues, as do customs duties, estate and gift taxes, and some minor miscellaneous taxes and user charges.

The U.S. federal government relies more heavily on income-based taxes than nearly any other government in the world. Most other governments rely more heavily on sales taxes, excise taxes, and customs duties.

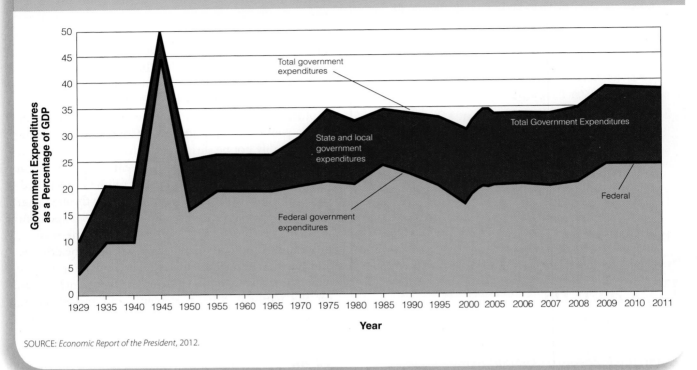

SOURCE: *Economic Report of the President*, 2012.

14-2c SOCIAL SECURITY: HOW CAN WE SAVE IT?

What are the options for saving Social Security?

1. Increase the payroll taxes to a rate closer to 15 percent. It is currently 10.4 percent.

2. Increase the age of full-time benefits to age 70. The problem is that seniors already have a difficult time finding employment and may not be able to do the physical work expected of them.

3. Implement "means testing." Means testing would reduce the benefits to retirees who have "sufficient means" for retirement.

4. Increase the return to Social Security funds. The government might be interested in investing part of Social Security in the stock market. Historical returns are much greater in the stock market.

   The real rate of return (indexed for inflation) has been roughly 7 percent in the stock market compared with only 2 percent for government bonds. However, one of the drawbacks of government

EXHIBIT 14.2 Federal Government Expenditure 2011

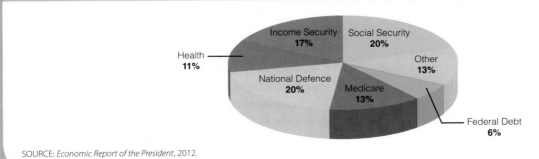

SOURCE: *Economic Report of the President*, 2012.

EXHIBIT 14.3 Federal Tax Revenues

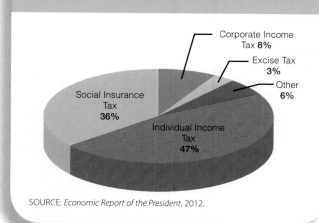

- Corporate Income Tax **8%**
- Excise Tax **3%**
- Other **6%**
- Social Insurance Tax **36%**
- Individual Income Tax **47%**

SOURCE: *Economic Report of the President, 2012.*

investment in the stock market is the potential for political abuse. With such a large amount of funds, the temptation emerges for the government to favor some firms and punish others.

5. Put some of the payroll tax in an individual retirement plan and let individuals manage their own funds—perhaps choosing from a list of mutual funds.

6. Let individuals choose to continue with the current Social Security system or contribute a minimum of, say, 10 percent or 20 percent of their wages to a private investment fund. This option has been tried in a number of Central and South American countries. In Chile, almost 90 percent of workers choose to leave the government Social Security program to invest privately.

Critics of the private plan argue that it is risky, individuals might make poor investment decisions, and the government might ultimately have to pay for their mistakes. That is, the stock market may have a good long-term track record, but it is still inherently uncertain and risky because of economic fluctuations. This is not consistent with a guaranteed stream of retirement income.

A Progressive Tax

One effect of substantial taxes on income is that the "take home" income of Americans is significantly altered by the tax system. **Progressive taxes**, of which the federal income tax is one example, are designed so that those with higher incomes pay a greater proportion of their income in taxes. A progressive tax is one tool that the government can use to redistribute income. It should be noted, however, that certain types of income are excluded from income for taxation purposes, such as interest on municipal bonds and income

in kind—food stamps or Medicare, for example.

A Regressive Tax

Payroll taxes, the second most important source of income for the federal government, are actually **regressive taxes**; that is, they take a greater proportion of the income of lower-income groups than of higher-income groups. The reasons for this are simple. Social Security contributions, for example, are imposed as a fixed proportion (usually 6.2 percent on employees and an equal amount on employers) of wage and salary income up to $110,100 as of 2012. The self-employed pay the entire amount. Also, wealthy persons have relatively more income from sources such as dividends and interest that are not subject to payroll taxes, and earnings above a certain level are not subject to some payroll taxes.

At first glance it appears that employers and employees split the burden of Social Security tax (called the Federal Insurance Contribution Act, or FICA). However, recall our discussion of elasticity and its burden of taxation. Most labor economists believe the labor supply curve is relatively inelastic compared to the

© AP Photo/The Oakland Press, Jose Juarez

If a person who earns $20,000 a year spends $2,000 of it on lottery tickets, she will spend 10 percent of her income. If a person who earns $200,000 a year spends $2,000 of it on lottery tickets, she will only pay 1 percent. They both have the same chance of winning.

But if people in different income brackets spend the same amount on the lottery, then the lottery acts as a regressive tax because it places a heavier burden on the poor than the rich. Studies show that lottery sales tend to be higher in zip codes where per capita income is lower. Thus, non-winning lottery tickets may act like a regressive tax for the state.

demand curve for labor, so employers will pass on most of the tax in the form of lower wages to employees. So, if workers are relatively unresponsive to a decrease in the wage rate (they have a relatively inelastic labor supply curve), then employers can pass most of the tax on in the form of lower wages, as seen in Exhibit 14.4. Congress may have intended an even split on the payroll tax between workers and firms. That is, half is paid out of the firm's revenue and half is deducted from the paychecks of workers. However, we have learned that the burden of the tax does not depend on whether it is levied on the buyer or the seller but rather it depends on the price elasticity of supply and demand.

An Excise Tax

Some consider an **excise tax**—a sales tax on individual products such as alcohol, tobacco, and gasoline—to be the most unfair type of tax because it is generally the most regressive. Excise taxes on specific items impose a far greater burden, as a percentage of income, on the poor and middle classes than on the wealthy, because low-income families generally spend a greater proportion of their income on these items than do high-income families.

In addition, excise taxes may lead to economic inefficiencies. By isolating a few products and subjecting them to discriminatory taxation, excise taxes subject economic choices to political manipulation, which leads to inefficiency.

14-2d FINANCING STATE AND LOCAL GOVERNMENT ACTIVITIES

Historically, the primary source of state and local revenue has been property taxes. In recent decades, state and local governments have relied increasingly on sales and income taxes for revenues. Today, sales taxes account for roughly 19 percent of revenues, property taxes account for 16 percent, and personal and corporate income taxes account for another 15 percent. Approximately 20 percent of state and local revenues come from the federal government as grants. The remaining share of revenues comes from license fees and user charges (e.g., payment for utilities, occupational license fees, tuition fees) and other taxes.

14-2e SHOULD WE HAVE A FLAT TAX?

Some politicians and individuals believe that we should scrap the current progressive income tax and replace it with a **flat tax**. A flat tax, also called a proportional tax, is designed so that everybody would be charged the same percentage of their income. How would a flat tax work? What do you think would be the advantages and disadvantages of a flat tax?

With a flat tax, a household could simply report its income, multiply it by the tax rate, and send in the money. Because no deductions are involved, the form could be a single page! But most flat tax proposals call for exempting income to a certain level—say, the poverty line.

Actually, if the flat tax plan allowed individuals to deduct a standard allowance of, say, $20,000 from their wages, the tax would still be progressive. Here is how it would work: If you were earning less than $20,000 a year, you would not have to pay any income taxes. However, if you earned $50,000 a year, and the flat tax rate was 15 percent, after subtracting your $20,000 allowance you would be paying taxes on $30,000. In this system, you would have to pay $4,500 in taxes (0.15 × $30,000) and your average tax rate would be 9 percent ($4,500/$50,000 = 0.09). Now, say you made $100,000 a year. After taking your $20,000 allowance, you would have to pay a 15 percent tax on $80,000, and you would owe the government $12,000. Notice,

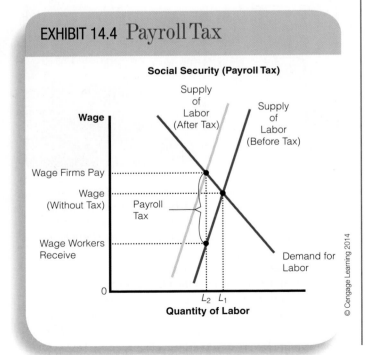

EXHIBIT 14.4 Payroll Tax

Social Security (Payroll Tax)

Wage

Supply of Labor (After Tax)

Supply of Labor (Before Tax)

Wage Firms Pay

Wage (Without Tax)

Payroll Tax

Wage Workers Receive

Demand for Labor

0   L_2 L_1

Quantity of Labor

© Cengage Learning 2014

however, that your average tax rate would be higher: 12 percent ($12,000/$100,000 = 0.12) as opposed to 9 percent. So if the flat tax system allows individual taxpayers to take a standard allowance, like most flat tax proposals, then the tax is actually progressive. That is, lower- and middle-income families will pay, on average, a smaller average tax rate, even though everyone has the same tax rate over the stipulated allowance.

The advantages of the flat tax are that all of the traditional exemptions, such as entertainment deductions, mortgage interest deductions, business travel expenses, and charitable contribution deductions, would be out the door, along with the possibilities of abuses and misrepresentations that go with tax deductions. Taxpayers could fill out tax returns in the way they did in the old days, in a space about the size of a postcard. Advocates argue that the government could collect the same amount of tax revenues, but the tax would be much more efficient, as many productive resources would be released from looking for tax loopholes to doing something productive from society's standpoint.

Of course, some versions of the flat tax will hurt certain groups. Not surprisingly, realtors and home owners, who like the mortgage interest deductions, and tax accountants, who make billions every year preparing tax returns, will not be supportive of a flat tax with no deductions. And, of course, many legitimate questions would inevitably arise, such as: What would happen to the size of charitable contributions if the charitable contribution deduction was eliminated? And how much will the housing sector be hurt if the mortgage interest deduction was eliminated or phased out? After all, the government's intent of the tax break was to increase home ownership. And the deductions for hybrid cars are intended to get drivers into cleaner, more fuel-efficient cars. These deductions could be gone in most flat tax proposals. In addition, the critics of the flat tax believe that the tax is not progressive enough to eliminate the inequities in income and are skeptical of the tax-revenue–raising capabilities of a flat tax.

Some flat-tax proposals exclude taxing income from saving and investment such as interest, dividends, and capital gains. This exemption is intended to encourage investment, saving and economic growth. However, it raises some equity issues. Under this proposal, a family earning $70,000 a year would have to pay taxes while a wealthy retiree, living on his or her interest and dividends, might pay zero taxes. Is that fair?

In short, many people like the appeal of a flat tax but may not like the particulars. For example, think of

middle-income households who would lose their mortgage interest deduction. Eliminating this exemption could lead to falling home values. Reworking the tax code might provide a better alternative.

> **ability to pay principle** belief that those with the greatest ability to pay taxes should pay more than those with less ability to pay
>
> **vertical equity** different treatment based on level of income and the ability to pay principle

14-2f TAXES: EFFICIENCY AND EQUITY

In Part 1 of this textbook, we talked about efficiency—getting the most out of our scarce resources. However, taxes for the most part are not efficient (except for internalizing externalities and providing public goods) because they change incentives and distort the values that buyers and sellers place on goods and services. That is, decisions made by buyers and sellers are different from what they would be without the tax. Taxes can be inefficient because they may lead to less work, less saving, less investment, and lower output.

Economists spend a lot of time on issues of efficiency, but policymakers (and economists) are also concerned about other goals, such as fairness. Income redistribution through taxation may also lead to greater productivity for low-income workers through improvements in health and education. Even though what is fair to one person may not be fair to another, most people would agree that we should have a fair tax system based on either ability to pay or benefits received.

Ability to Pay Principle and Vertical Equity

The **ability to pay principle** is simply that those with the greatest ability to pay taxes (richer people) should pay more than those with the least ability to pay taxes (poorer people). This concept is known as **vertical equity**—people with different levels of income should be treated differently. The federal income tax is a good example of the ability to pay principle, because the rich pay a larger percentage of their income in taxes. That is, high-income individuals will pay a higher percentage of their income in taxes than low-income individuals. The richest 20 percent of households in the United States make slightly more than 60 percent of the income but pay roughly 85 percent of the federal income tax; the poorest 40 percent actually have a negative tax (many in the group receive tax credits). When you add payroll taxes (Social Security) and Medicare, the tax system

benefits received principle the belief that those receiving the benefits from taxes are those who should pay for them

becomes less progressive than the federal income tax: 40 percent of the low-income taxpayers pay about 3 percent and the top 20 percent of income earners pay slightly less than 70 percent. Sales taxes are not a good example of the ability to pay principle, because low-income individuals pay a larger percentage of their income in such taxes.

Benefits Received Principle

The **benefits received principle** means that the individuals receiving the benefits are those who pay for them. Take the gasoline tax: the more miles one drives on the highway, the more gasoline used and the more taxes collected. The tax revenues are then used to maintain the highways. Or those who benefit from a new airport or an opera house should be the ones who pay for such public spending. Although this principle may work for some private goods, it does not work well for public goods such as national defense and the judicial system. Because we collectively consume national defense, it is not possible to find out who benefits and by exactly how much.

Administration Burden of Taxation

The administration burden of the income tax also leads to another deadweight loss. Imagine if everyone filled out a one-page tax form that took no more than 5 minutes. Instead the opportunity cost of the hours of time and services used in tax preparation is in the billions of dollars. The government also spends a great deal to enforce these taxes. A simplified tax system would reduce the deadweight loss.

Social Policy of Taxes

Taxes and subsidies can be efficiency enhancing when used to correct for externalities. For example, the government may view it as good social policy to subsidize cleaner, more efficient hybrid vehicles. Or they may want to put a high tax on cigarettes in an attempt to reduce teen smoking. In other words, taxes on alcohol and cigarettes may be used to discourage these activities—sometimes we call these "sin taxes."

The Burden of the Corporate Income Tax

Corporate income taxes are generally popular among voters because they think the tax comes from the corporation. But corporations don't pay taxes; people pay taxes. Indeed, the corporation does write the check to the IRS, but that does not mean that the corporation (and its stockholders) bears the burden of the tax. Some of the tax burden (perhaps a great deal) is passed on to consumers in the form of higher prices. It will also affect investors' rates of return.

Less investment leads to less capital for workers, which lowers workers' productivity and real wages. The key here is to be careful to distinguish between who legally pays the tax and who incurs the burden of the tax.

SECTION CHECK 2 ANSWERS

1. Over a third of federal spending goes toward pensions and income security programs.

2. A progressive tax takes a greater proportion of the income of higher-income groups than of lower-income groups. A regressive tax takes a greater proportion of the income of lower-income groups than of higher-income groups.

3. A flat tax charges all income earners the same percentage of their income.

4. The ability to pay principle is the belief that those with the greatest ability to pay taxes should pay more than those with less ability.

5. The benefits received principle means that individuals receiving the benefits are those who pay for them.

14-3 Fiscal Policy and the *AD/AS* Model

SECTION CHECK 3

Keep the following questions in mind as you read through this section.

1. How can government stimulus of aggregate demand reduce unemployment?

2. How can government reduction of aggregate demand reduce inflation?

The primary tools of fiscal policy, government purchases, taxes, and transfer payments, can be presented in the context of the aggregate supply and demand

EXHIBIT 14.5 Expansionary Fiscal Policy to Close a Recessionary Gap

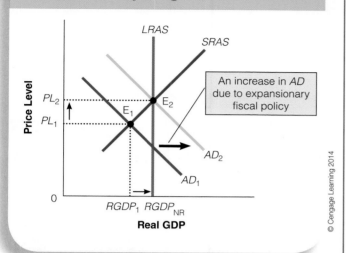

model. In Exhibit 14.5, we have used the *AD/AS* model to show how the government can use fiscal policy as either an expansionary or contractionary tool to help close a recessionary or an inflationary gap.

14-3a EXPANSIONARY FISCAL POLICY TO CLOSE A RECESSIONARY GAP

If the government decides to purchase more, cut taxes, and/or increase transfer payments, *ceteris paribus,* total purchases will rise. That is, increased government purchases, tax cuts, or transfer payment increases can increase consumption, investment, and government purchases, shifting the aggregate demand curve to the right. The effect of this increase in aggregate demand depends on the position of the macroeconomic equilibrium before the government stimulus. For example, in Exhibit 14.5, the initial equilibrium is at E_1, a recession scenario, with real output below potential RGDP. Starting at this point and moving along the short-run aggregate supply curve, an increase in government purchases, a tax cut, and/or an increase in transfer payments would lead to an increase in aggregate demand, ideally from AD_1 to AD_2. The result of such a change would be an increase in the price level, from PL_1 to PL_2, and an increase in RGDP, from $RGDP_1$ to $RGDP_{NR}$. If the policy change is of the right

magnitude and timed appropriately, the expansionary fiscal policy might stimulate the economy, pull it out of the contraction and/or recession, and result in full employment at $RGDP_{NR}$. The recessionary gap is then closed.

14-3b CONTRACTIONARY FISCAL POLICY TO CLOSE AN INFLATIONARY GAP

Suppose that the price level is at PL_1 and that short-run equilibrium is at E_1, as shown in Exhibit 14.6. Say that the government decides to reduce its purchases, increase taxes, or reduce transfer payments. A government purchase change may directly affect aggregate demand.

A tax increase on consumers or a decrease in transfer payments will reduce households' disposable incomes, reducing purchases of consumption goods and services, and higher business taxes will reduce investment purchases. The reductions in consumption, investment, and/or government purchases will shift the aggregate demand curve leftward, ideally from AD_1 to AD_2. This lowers the price level from PL_1 to PL_2 and brings RGDP back to the full-employment level at $RGDP_{NR}$, resulting in a new short- and long-run equilibrium at E_2, and the inflationary gap is closed.

Exhibit 14.7 on the next page summarizes the preceding discussion of the tools available to the government for enacting fiscal policy.

EXHIBIT 14.6 Contractionary Fiscal Policy to Close an Inflationary Gap

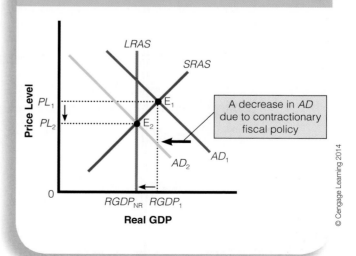

EXHIBIT 14.7 Summary of Fiscal Policy Tools

Macroeconomic Problem	Fiscal Policy Prescription	Fiscal Policy Tools
Unemployment (Slow or negative RGDP growth rate—below $RGDP_{NR}$)	Expansionary fiscal policy to increase aggregate demand	Cut taxes Increase government purchases Increase government transfer payments
Inflation (Rapid RGDP growth rate—beyond $RGDP_{NR}$)	Contractionary fiscal policy to decrease aggregate demand	Raise taxes Decrease government purchases Decrease government transfer payments

Global Tax: Revenues and Government Spending as a Percentage of GDP

In the table below, we see tax burdens for several major countries. Notice that the United States is in the middle of the pack. In fact, the U.S. tax burden is low compared to many European countries. Also, notice that some of the developing countries have lower tax burdens, like Chile, Mexico, and India. This is consistent with the history of the United States. That is, as the population of a country grows wealthier, the government often takes a larger share of income in taxes.

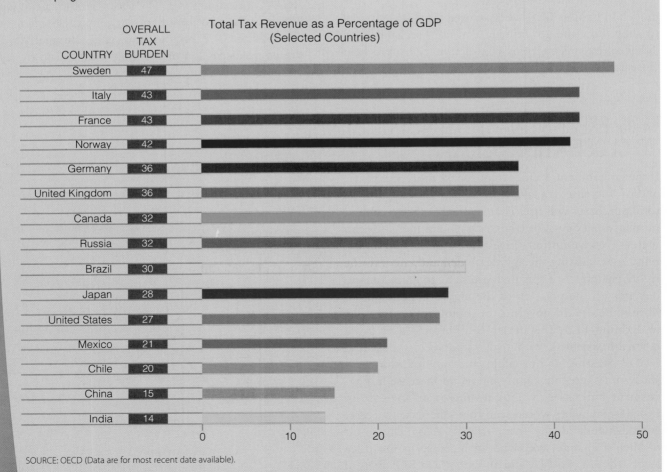

Total Tax Revenue as a Percentage of GDP (Selected Countries)

COUNTRY	OVERALL TAX BURDEN
Sweden	47
Italy	43
France	43
Norway	42
Germany	36
United Kingdom	36
Canada	32
Russia	32
Brazil	30
Japan	28
United States	27
Mexico	21
Chile	20
China	15
India	14

SOURCE: OECD (Data are for most recent date available).

14-4 The Multiplier Effect

Any one of the major spending components of aggregate demand (C, I, G, or $X - M$) can initiate changes in aggregate demand, thereby producing a new short-run equilibrium. If policymakers are unhappy with the present short-run equilibrium GDP, perhaps they consider unemployment too high because of a current aggregate demand shortfall. If government were to increase its purchases of jet fighters, highways, and schools, this increased spending would lead to an increase in aggregate demand. That is, they can deliberately manipulate the level of government purchases to obtain a new short-run equilibrium value. But how much new additional government purchasing is necessary?

14-4a WHAT IS THE MULTIPLIER EFFECT?

Usually, when an increase in purchases of goods or services occurs, the ultimate increase in total purchases tends to be greater than the initial increase, which is known as the **multiplier effect**. But how does this effect work? Suppose the government increases its defense budget by $10 billion to buy aircraft carriers. When the government purchases the aircraft carriers, not only does it add to the total demand for goods and services directly, but it also provides $10 billion in added income to the companies that actually construct the aircraft carriers. These companies will then hire more workers and buy more capital equipment and other inputs to produce the new output. The owners of these inputs therefore receive more income because of the increase in government purchases. What will they do with this additional income? Although behavior will vary somewhat among individuals, collectively they will probably spend a substantial part of the additional income on additional consumption purchases, pay some additional taxes incurred because of the income, and save a bit of it as well. The **marginal propensity to consume (MPC)** is the fraction of additional disposable (after-tax) income that a household consumes rather than saves. That is, MPC is equal to the *change* in consumption spending (ΔC) divided by the change in disposable income (ΔDY).

$$MPC = \Delta C / \Delta DY$$

For example, suppose you won a lottery prize of $1,000. You might decide to spend $750 of your winnings today and save $250. In this example, your marginal propensity to consume is 0.75 (or 75 percent), because out of the extra $1,000, you decided to spend 75 percent of it ($0.75 \times \$1,000 = \$750$). The term *marginal propensity to consume* has two parts: (1) *marginal* refers to the fact that you received an *extra* amount of disposable income—an addition to your income, not your total income; and (2) *propensity to consume* refers to how much you tend to spend on consumer goods and services out of your additional income.

The flip side of the marginal propensity to consume is the **marginal propensity to save (MPS)**, which is the proportion of an addition to your income that you would save, or not spend on goods and services today. That is, MPS is equal to the change in savings (ΔS) divided by the change in disposable income (ΔDY).

$$MPS = \Delta S / \Delta DY$$

In the lottery example, your marginal propensity to save is 0.25, or 25 percent, because you decided to save 25 percent of your additional disposable income

multiplier effect a chain reaction of additional income and purchases that results in total purchases that are greater than the initial increase in purchases

marginal propensity to consume (MPC) the additional consumption resulting from an additional dollar of disposable income

marginal propensity to save (MPS) the change in savings divided by the change in disposable income

(0.25 × $1,000 = $250). Because your additional disposable income must be either consumed or saved, the marginal propensity to consume plus the marginal propensity to save must add up to 1, or 100 percent.

14-4b THE MULTIPLIER EFFECT AT WORK

Suppose that out of every dollar in *added* disposable income generated by increased investment purchases, individuals collectively spend two-thirds, or 67 cents, on consumption purchases. In other words, the MPC is 2/3. The initial $10 billion increase in government purchases causes both a $10 billion increase in aggregate demand and an income increase of $10 billion to suppliers of the inputs used to produce aircraft carriers; the owners of those inputs, in turn, will spend an additional $6.67 billion (2/3 of $10 billion) on additional consumption purchases. A chain reaction has been started. The added $6.67 billion in consumption purchases by those deriving income from the initial investment brings a $6.67 billion increase in aggregate demand and in new income to suppliers of the inputs that produced the goods and services. These persons, in turn, will spend some two-thirds of their additional $6.67 billion in income, or $4.44 billion, on consumption purchases. This $4.44 billion becomes aggregate demand and income to still another group of people, who will then proceed to spend two-thirds of that amount, or $2.96 billion, on consumption purchases.

The chain reaction continues, with each new round of purchases providing income to a new group of people who in turn increase their purchases. As successive changes in consumption purchases occur, the feedback becomes smaller and smaller. The added income generated and the number of resulting consumer purchases get smaller because some of the increase in income goes to savings and tax payments that do not immediately flow into greater investment or government spending. As indicated in Exhibit 14.8, the fifth change in consumption is indeed much smaller than the first change in consumption.

What is the total impact of the initial increase in government purchases on additional consumption and

Save

Consume

What is your marginal propensity to save?

© Brand X Pictures/Getty Images

EXHIBIT 14.8 The Multiplier Process

Change in government purchases	$10.00 billion—direct effect on *AD*
First change in consumption purchases	6.67 billion (2/3 of 10)
Second change in consumption purchases	4.44 billion (2/3 of 6.67)
Third change in consumption purchases	2.96 billion (2/3 of 4.44)
Fourth change in consumption purchases	1.98 billion (2/3 of 2.96)
Fifth change in consumption purchases	1.32 billion (2/3 of 1.98)

The sum of the indirect effect on *AD*, through induced additional consumption purchases, is equal to $20 billion.

$30 billion = Total change in aggregate demand

© Cengage Learning 2014

income? We can find the answer by using the multiplier formula, calculated as follows:

$$Multiplier = 1/(1 - MPC)$$

In this case,

$$Multiplier = 1/(1 - 2/3) = 1/(1/3) = 3$$

An initial increase in government purchases of $10 billion will increase total purchases by $30 billion ($10 billion × 3), as the initial $10 billion in government purchases also generates an additional $20 billion in consumption.

14-4c CHANGES IN THE MPC AFFECT THE MULTIPLIER PROCESS

Note that the larger the marginal propensity to consume, the larger the multiplier effect, because relatively more additional consumption purchases out of any given income increase generates relatively larger secondary and tertiary income effects in successive rounds of the process. For example, if the MPC is 3/4, the multiplier is 4:

$$Multiplier = 1/(1 - 3/4) = 1/(1/4) = 4$$

If the MPC is only 1/2, however, the multiplier is 2:

$$Multiplier = 1/(1 - 1/2) = 1/(1/2) = 2$$

14-4d THE MULTIPLIER AND THE AGGREGATE DEMAND CURVE

As we discussed earlier, when the federal Department of Defense decides to buy additional aircraft carriers, it affects aggregate demand. It increases the incomes of owners of inputs used to make the aircraft carriers, including profits that go to the owners of the firms involved. That is the initial effect. The secondary effect—the greater income that results—will lead to increased consumer purchases. In addition, the higher profits for the firms involved in carrier construction may lead them to increase their investment purchases. So the initial effect of the government's purchases will tend to have a multiplied effect on the economy. In Exhibit 14.9, we can see that the initial impact of a $10 billion additional purchase by the government directly shifts the aggregate demand curve from AD_1 to AD_2. The multiplier effect then causes the aggregate demand to shift out $20 billion further, to AD_3. If MPC is 2/3, the total effect on aggregate demand of a $10 billion increase in government purchases is therefore $30 billion.

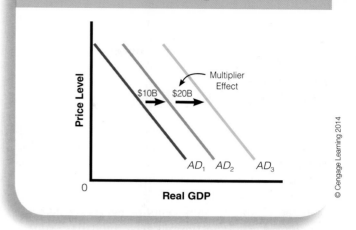

EXHIBIT 14.9 The Multiplier Effect

14-4e TAX CUTS AND THE MULTIPLIER

If the government finds that it needs to use fiscal stimulus to move the economy to the natural rate, increased government spending is only one alternative. The government can also stimulate business and consumer spending through tax cuts. Both Japan (1999) and the United States (2001 and 2003) have recently employed tax cuts to stimulate their economies.

How much of an AD shift do we get from a change in taxes? As in the case of government spending, it depends on the marginal propensity to consume. However, the tax multiplier is smaller than the government spending multiplier because government spending has a direct impact on aggregate demand, whereas a tax cut has only an indirect impact on aggregate demand. Why? Because consumers will save some of their income from the tax cut. So if the MPC is 3/4, then when their disposable income rises by $1,000, households will increase their consumption by $750 while saving $250 of the added income.

To compare the multiplier effect of a tax cut with an increase in government purchases, suppose there were a $10 billion tax cut and that the MPC is 2/3. The initial increase in consumption spending from the tax cut would be 2/3 × $10 billion (MPC × tax cut) = $6.67 billion. Because in this case people would save one-third of their tax cut income, the effect on aggregate demand of the change in taxes would be smaller than that of a change of equal size in government purchases. The cumulative change in spending (the increase in AD) due to the $10 billion tax cut is found by plugging the initial effect of the changed consumption spending into our earlier formula: 1/(1 − MPC) × $6.67 billion, which is 3 × $6.67 = $20 billion. So the initial tax cut of $10 billion leads to a stimulus of $20 billion in consumer spending. Although this amount is less than the $30 billion from government purchases, it is easy to see why tax cuts and government purchases are both attractive policy prescriptions for a slow economy.

14-4f TAXES AND INVESTMENT SPENDING

Taxes can also stimulate investment spending. For example, if a cut in corporate-profit taxes leads to expectations of greater after-tax profits, it could fuel additional investment spending. That is, tax cuts designed for consumers and investors can stimulate both the C and I components of aggregate demand. A number of administrations have used this strategy to stimulate aggregate spending and shift the aggregate demand curve to the right, including Kennedy (1963), Reagan (1981), and Bush (2001 and 2003).

14-4g A REDUCTION IN GOVERNMENT PURCHASES AND TAX INCREASES

A reduction in government purchases and tax increases are magnified by the multiplier effect, too. Suppose the government made cutbacks in the space program. Not only would it decrease government purchases directly, but aerospace workers would be laid off and unemployed workers would cut back on their consumption spending; this initial cutback would have a multiplying effect through the economy, leading to an even greater reduction in aggregate demand. Similarly, tax hikes would leave consumers with less disposable income, so they would cut back on their consumption, which would lower aggregate demand and set off the multiplier process, leading to an even larger cumulative effect on aggregate demand.

14-4h TIME LAGS, SAVING, AND IMPORTS REDUCE THE SIZE OF THE MULTIPLIER

The multiplier process is not instantaneous. If you get an additional $100 in income today, you may spend two-thirds of that on consumption purchases eventually, but you may wait six months or even longer to do it. Such time lags mean that the ultimate increase in purchases resulting from an initial increase in purchases may not be achieved for a year or more. The extent of the multiplier effect visible within a short time will be less than the total effect indicated by the multiplier formula. In addition, saving and money spent on import goods (which are not part of aggregate demand for domestically produced goods and services) will reduce the size of the multiplier, because each of them reduces the fraction of a given increase in income that will go to additional purchases of domestically produced consumption goods.

It is also important to note that the multiplier effect is not restricted to changes in government purchases and taxes. The multiplier effect can apply to changes that alter spending in any of the components of aggregate demand: consumption, investment, government purchases, or net exports.

Some have argued that the multiplier effect of a new sports stadium, for example, will lead to additional local spending that will be three or four times the amount of the initial investment. However, this outcome is unlikely. It is important to remember that money spent on the stadium (taxpayer dollars) could also have been spent on food, clothing, entertainment, recreation, and many other goods and services. So the expenditures on the stadium come at the expense of other consumer expenditures. In addition, the multiplier is most effective when it brings idle resources into production. If all resources are fully employed, the expansion in demand and the multiplier effect will lead to a higher price level, not increases in employment and RGDP.

14-4i THE 2007–2009 RECESSION

The 2007–2009 recession will probably end up being the worst recession since the Great Depression. It has lead to the largest peacetime fiscal expansion in history. Many countries around the world have been increasing the size of their budget deficits by cutting taxes and increasing government spending. There is debate among economists on the effectiveness of fiscal policy to stimulate the economy and much of that debate depends on the size of the multiplier. A multiplier of 1 means that an increase in government purchases of $1 billion would increase aggregate demand and lead to an increase of $1 billion of RGDP. The economy could now have new highways, bridges, fighter jets, and aircraft carriers without sacrificing other components of aggregate demand such as private consumption and investment. How is this possible? The answer is that these are idle resources that are now being put to use. If the multiplier is greater than 1 it is even more magical; RGDP rises by more than the increase in government purchases.

The Obama administration's economists believed the multiplier for government purchases was close to 1.5 (a $1 billion increase in government purchases will increase a country's GDP by $1.5 billion). Other economists believed that the multiplier for government purchases is much smaller, closer to 0.8. So there was considerable debate on the size of the government purchases multiplier. The Congressional Budget Office (CBO) estimates the tax multiplier to be between 0.6–1.5 for a two-year tax cut for lower-and middle-income people and between 0.2–0.6 for a one-year tax cut for higher-income people.

However, economists do agree that the multiplier is very small—close to zero—when the economy is at or near full employment and that the effectiveness of fiscal policy depends on the type of action that is taken. For example, the short-run effect of government spending on infrastructure such as highways and bridges tends to be greater than, say, that of a tax cut by which individuals will save a large portion of their tax windfall. Tax cuts for poorer people may be more effective than those for richer, because the poor tend to spend a larger proportion of their additional (marginal) income. Economists also agree that tax multipliers are much higher when taxes are permanent than when they are temporary and that fiscal multipliers will be lower in heavily indebted economies than in prudent ones.

In the words of macroeconomist Robert Barro, "Do not use the cover of fiscal policy to undertake massive public works programs that do not pass muster from the perspective of cost-benefit analysis ... it is wrong now to think that added government spending is free."[1]

© Dwight Smith/Shutterstock

> The short-run effect of government spending on infrastructure such as highways and bridges tends to be greater than, say, that of a tax cut by which individuals will save a large portion of their tax windfall.

14-4j FISCAL POLICY DURING THE GREAT RECESSION

In the spring of 2008, Congress cut taxes by $95 billion through a rebate program. Because it was just a one-time, temporary tax cut, we would expect a smaller stimulus effect. And it looks like that is what happened. According to the CBO (Congressional Budget Office), it appears that taxpayers spent only 35 percent of their rebates. Presumably a more permanent tax cut would have led to greater consumption spending.

What About Government Spending?

Congress passed the American Recovery and Reinvestment Act of 2009. This was a $860 billion package of both spending increases and tax cuts. About $240 billion was for tax cuts including a reduction in the payroll tax for Social Security. Over $200 billion went to health care, social service, and education. Other sectors that received substantial funding included transportation, aid to states, research into alternative energy, and transportation—highways, bridges, and airports.

Was the Fiscal Stimulus Successful?

It is difficult to say with certainty, because it is difficult to hold other things constant. The CBO, a non-partisan organization, estimates that without the stimulus package, the unemployment rate would have been approximately 1 or 2 percent higher. And RGDP rose almost 4.5 percent from early 2009 to the end of 2010. So the fiscal stimulus package probably did reduce the severity of the recession, but did not come close to bringing the economy back to full employment at the natural rate.

---

[1] Robert J. Barro, "Voodoo multipliers," *Economists' Voice*, February 2009, available at www.bepress.com/ev (accessed July 13, 2010).

14-5 Supply-Side Effects of Tax Cuts

SECTION CHECK 5

Keep the following questions in mind as you read through this section.

1. What is supply-side fiscal policy?

2. How do supply-side policies affect long-run aggregate supply?

3. What do its critics say about supply-side ideas?

The debate over short-run stabilization policies has been going on for some time, with no sign that it is close to being settled. When policymakers discuss methods of stabilizing the economy, the focus since the 1930s has been on managing the economy through demand-side policies. But one group of economists believes that we should be focusing on the supply side of the economy as well, especially in the long run, rather than just on the demand side. In particular, they believe that individuals will save less, work less, and provide less capital when taxes, government transfer payments (such as welfare), and regulations are too burdensome on productive activities. In other words, they believe that fiscal policy can work on the supply side of the economy as well as the demand side.

14-5a IMPACT OF SUPPLY-SIDE POLICIES

Supply-siders would encourage the government to reduce individual and business taxes, deregulate, and increase spending on research and development. Supply-siders believe that these types of government policies could generate greater long-term economic growth by stimulating personal income, savings, and capital formation.

The Laffer Curve

High marginal income tax rates could conceivably reduce work and investment incentives and increase tax evasion to the point that government revenues are lower than they would be at some lower marginal income tax rate. Economist Arthur Laffer argued that point graphically in what has been called the Laffer curve, depicted in Exhibit 14.10. When marginal income tax rates are low, increasing the federal marginal tax rate will increase federal tax revenues, as shown by the movement from point B to point C in Exhibit 14.10. However, at higher federal marginal tax rates, disincentive effects and increased tax evasion may actually reduce federal tax revenue. Over this range of marginal income tax rates, lowering taxes may actually increase federal tax revenue. This relationship is shown by the movement from point D to point C in Exhibit 14.10. A high marginal income tax rate on the rich might reduce the incentive to work, save, and invest, and perhaps as important, it might produce illegal shifts in transactions to what has been termed the underground economy, meaning that people make cash and barter transactions that are difficult for any tax collector to observe. If tax evasion becomes common, the equity and revenue-raising efficiency of the tax system suffers, as does general respect for the law.

Although all economists believe that incentives matter, disagreement exists as to the shape of the Laffer curve and where the economy actually is on the Laffer curve. That is, many economists believe that tax cuts increase incentives to work and invest, but current U.S. tax levels do not appear to be on the downward side of the Laffer curve. There is also no evidence that prior to the Reagan cuts of the 1980s, the average marginal tax rate was high enough that a cut in tax rates would result in larger overall tax revenues. However, it is possible that taxpayers in the high-income group were on that portion of the curve. Other studies have shown that maximum tax revenues occurred in Sweden between 70 to 80 percent marginal income tax rates. So there may actually be a point where the marginal income tax rates of a country may be so high that tax revenues will fall. Some economists believe that France might also be close to that point.

From Exploring Economics, 6e, by Robert L. Sexton, ISBN: 9781111970307

EXHIBIT 14.10 The Laffer Curve

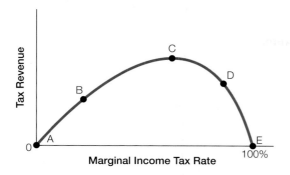

If the marginal income tax rate is set at 100 percent, at point E, citizens will have no incentive to work or invest and tax revenues will be zero. Tax revenues will also be zero if the tax rate is zero, at point A. If the economy has a relatively high marginal income tax rate, at point D, tax revenues could be increased by lowering the marginal income tax rate, a move toward point C. However, as marginal income tax rates are lowered beyond point C, the tax revenues fall. Moving in the other direction, from point B to point C, we see that tax revenues would increase with higher marginal income tax rates up to point C. At higher marginal income tax rates beyond point C, tax revenues would fall.

EXHIBIT 14.11 The Impact of Supply-Side Policies on Short-Run and Long-Run Aggregate Supply

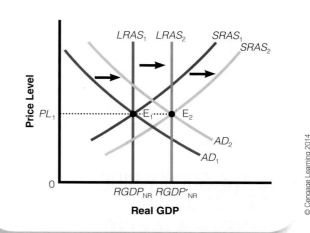

It also depends on the type of taxes. With regard to capital taxes, the United States and many developed countries may be on the left side of the Laffer curve. However, one study shows that Denmark and Sweden may be to the right of the peak on capital taxes. That is, cutting taxes might improve their budgetary situation.

Research and Development and the Supply Side of the Economy

Some economists believe that investment in research and development will have long-run benefits for the economy. In particular, greater research and development will lead to new technology and knowledge, which will permanently shift the short- and long-run aggregate supply curves to the right. The government could encourage investments in research and development by giving tax breaks or subsidies to firms. The challenge, of course, is to produce *productive* research and development.

How Do Supply-Side Policies Affect Long-Run Aggregate Supply?

We see in Exhibit 14.11 that rather than being primarily concerned with short-run economic stabilization, supply-side policies are aimed at increasing both the short-run and long-run aggregate supply curves. If these policies are successful and maintained, output and employment will increase in the long run, as reflected in the shift from $RGDP_{NR}$ to $RGDP'_{NR}$. Both short- and long-run aggregate supply will increase over time, as the effects of deregulation and major structural changes in plants and equipment work their way through the economy. It takes workers some time to fully respond to improved work incentives.

14-5b CRITICS OF SUPPLY-SIDE ECONOMICS

Of course, those who believe in supply-side economics have their critics. These critics are skeptical about the magnitude of the impact of lower taxes on work effort and the impact of deregulation on productivity. Critics claim that the tax cuts of the 1980s led to moderate real output growth but only through a reduction in real tax revenues, inflation, and large budget deficits.

Although real economic growth followed the tax cuts, supply-side critics say that it came as a result of a policy makers with another option in the event of a severe downturn. The use of fiscal policy can reassure investors and consumers that the government realizes it has the potential to make up for insufficient demand, especially if the economy is far from its potential output.

SECTION CHECK 6 ANSWERS

1. Automatic stabilizers are changes in government transfer payments or tax collections that happen automatically and with effects that vary inversely with business cycles.

2. The tax system is the most important automatic stabilizer; it has the greatest ability to smooth out swings in GDP during business cycles. Other automatic stabilizers are unemployment compensation and welfare payments.

14-7 The National Debt

SECTION CHECK 7

Keep the following questions in mind as you read through this section.

1. How is a budget deficit financed?

2. What impact does a budget deficit have on the interest rate?

3. What impact does a budget surplus have on the interest rate?

When government spending exceeds tax revenues, a budget deficit results. When tax revenues are greater than government spending, a budget surplus exists. A balanced budget occurs through deliberate efforts that are a matter of public policy.

The national debt (also called *public debt*) is the federal government's indebtedness at a moment in time. It is a result of previous budget deficits and surpluses. That is, the government accumulates debt by running deficits and it reduces debt by running surpluses.

Budget Deficit:
Government Spending > Tax Revenues

Budget Surplus:
Tax Revenues > Government Spending

14-7a HOW GOVERNMENT FINANCES THE NATIONAL DEBT

For many years, the U.S. government has run budget deficits and built up a large national debt. How does it pay for those budget deficits? After all, it has to have some means of paying out the funds necessary to support government expenditures that are in excess of the funds derived from tax payments. One thing the government can do is simply print money—dollar bills. This approach was used to finance much of the Civil War budget deficit, both in the North and in the Confederate states. However, printing money to finance activities is highly inflationary and also undermines confidence in the government. Typically, the budget deficit is financed by issuing debt. The federal government in effect borrows an amount necessary to cover the deficit by issuing bonds, or IOUs, payable typically at some maturity date.

So the government finances the deficit by borrowing from the public. It sells debt to investors in the private sector here and abroad. When the government runs a surplus, it uses the receipts to reduce its outstanding debt.

14-7b WHY RUN A BUDGET DEFICIT?

From 1960 through 1997, the federal budget was in deficit every year except one—in 1969, the government ran a small budget surplus. Budget deficits can be important because they provide the federal government with the flexibility to respond appropriately to changing economic circumstances. For example, the government may run deficits during special emergencies such as military involvements, earthquakes, fires, or floods. The government may also use a budget deficit to avert an economic downturn.

Historically, the largest budget deficits and a growing government debt occur during war years, when defense spending escalates and taxes typically do not rise as rapidly as spending. When the war is over, government spending declines and the public debt as a percentage of GDP falls. There are a couple of good reasons why debt financing is the appropriate policy for war financing. One, it keeps taxes smooth over time. It would be inefficient to raise taxes sharply during a war. Two, debt financing of a war passes on part of the cost to future generations. This may be fair on grounds that the country is now safer for future generations.

The federal government will also typically run budget deficits during recessions, as taxes are cut and government spending increases. However, in the 1980s, deficits and debt soared in a relatively peaceful and prosperous time. In 1980, President Reagan ran a platform of lowering taxes and reducing the size of government. Although the tax cuts occurred, the reduction in the growth of government spending did not. The result was huge peacetime budget deficits and a growing national debt that continued through the early 1990s, as shown in Exhibit 14.13.

However, when President Clinton took office in 1993, he set a goal to reduce the budget deficit. This goal was a high priority for both Democrats and Republicans. And after nearly a decade of uninterrupted economic growth, the deficit eventually turned into a budget surplus. In 2001 the budget surplus slipped into a deficit for three primary reasons: (1) the 2001 tax cut that President Bush promised in his presidential campaign; (2) the war on terrorism and wars in Iraq and Afghanistan; and (3) the 2001 recession that led to less tax revenue and greater government spending.

As a result of the financial crisis of 2007–2009, the federal deficit relative to GDP rose to levels not seen since World War II. The recession reduced revenues and increased spending. The American Recovery and Reinvestment Act added over $860 billion to the deficit. The deficit for fiscal year 2011 was $1.3 trillion, the second largest shortfall in history. The U.S. ran a larger deficit in 2009, when the government provided a huge bailout to bolster financial markets. The nation's deficit that year was $1.412 trillion. Large deficits are also projected for the next decade.

The primary reason for the growth in the budget deficit was the deep, wide, and long recession of 2007–2009. Recessions lead to increases in government spending and reductions in tax revenues, which is a recipe for a growing budget deficit.

As life expectancies rise and elderly people become a greater percentage of the population, there will be increases in government spending for both Social Security and Medicare. This, combined with the trend toward smaller family sizes, will lead to fewer taxpayers to support government benefits for the growing elderly population.

Health care costs (Medicare and Medicaid) will continue to rise because new and better health care costs more. Some economists believe we will have to raise taxes significantly to cover these costs. Other economists believe that higher taxes would impose too high a cost on workers. Instead, they believe that policy makers should devise programs to decrease benefits to the elderly and encourage people to take a greater role in taking care of themselves.

Reducing the budget deficit will be one of the greatest challenges of the coming decades. The CBO projects the federal budget deficit will total $7 trillion over the next decade if current laws remain unchanged. Furthermore, the office states that if certain policies that are scheduled to expire under current law are extended instead, deficits may be much larger. Its report also mentions that the aging of the U.S. population and rising health care

EXHIBIT 14.13 Federal Budget (Percentage of GDP)

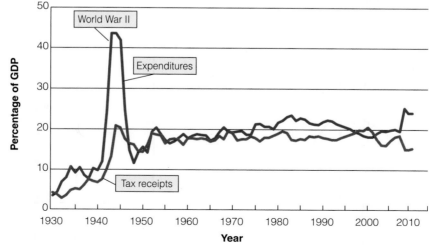

SOURCE: Office of Management and Budget, *Historical Tables*.

costs will put increasing pressure on the budget. Their prognosis is that if the federal debt continues to expand faster than the economy—as it has since 2007—the growth of people's income will slow, the share of federal spending devoted to paying interest on the debt will rise, and the risk of a fiscal crisis will increase.

14-7c AN INCREASE IN THE BUDGET DEFICIT: SHORT-RUN AND LONG-RUN EFFECTS

In the short run, running a larger deficit is the same as running expansionary fiscal policy; either tax cuts and/or increases in government purchases will shift the aggregate demand curve to the right, from AD_1 to AD_2, resulting in a higher price level and higher RGDP, as seen in Exhibit 14.14. That is, in the short run, an aggressive program of deficit spending can avert a recession.

In the long run, however, the story is different. When the government borrows to finance a budget deficit, it causes the real interest rate to rise. The higher real interest rate will "crowd out" private investment by households and firms (more on the crowding out effect in Chapter 17). Higher private investment and increases in capital formation are critical in a growing economy. Thus, increasing the budget deficit leads to a higher real interest rate, which decreases private investment, reduces the growth in the nation's capital stock, and retards the growth rate of potential GDP, as seen in Exhibit 14.15.

So were the the large budget deficits of 2008–2010 worth it? Some economists would argue that some of the increase in the deficit was important for short-run stimulus. However, as the economy begins to recover, the huge deficits will eventually cause capital stock to grow more slowly and retard potential growth in the long run. And almost all economists agree that that the long-run deficit is a real problem.

14-7d THE BURDEN OF NATIONAL DEBT

The "burden" of the debt is a topic that has long interested economists, particularly whether it falls on present or future generations. Exhibit 14.16 shows the burden as a percentage of GDP from 1900 to 2012. Recall that the national debt rises whenever the government runs a budget deficit. In Exhibit 14.16 we see large deficits occurred during both World Wars, the Great Depression, and the Great Recession of 2007–2009. All of these events increased the ratio of debt to GDP. Notice that the budget surplus of 1998–2001 caused the debt-to-GDP ratio to fall. However, with the return to deficits in 2002 it continued its upward movement.

Arguments can be made that the generation of taxpayers living at the time that the debt is issued shoulders the true cost of the debt, because the debt permits the government to take command of resources that might be available for other, private uses. In a sense, the resources it takes to purchase government bonds

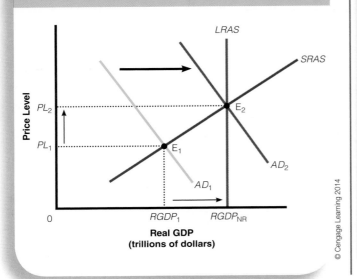

EXHIBIT 14.14 A Larger Budget Deficit—The Short-Run Effects

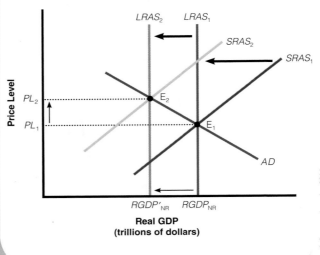

EXHIBIT 14.15 A Larger Budget Deficit—The Long-Run Effects

EXHIBIT 14.16 Federal Government Debt 1900–2012

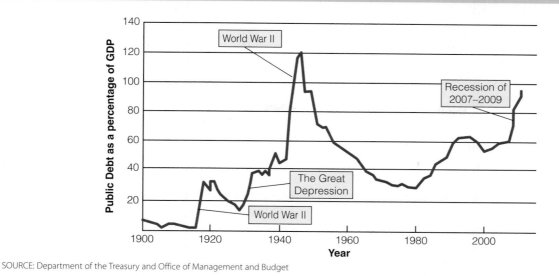

SOURCE: Department of the Treasury and Office of Management and Budget

might take away from private activities, such as private investment financed by private debt. No economist can deny, however, that the issuance of debt does involve some intergenerational transfer of incomes. Long after national debt is issued, a new generation of taxpayers is making interest payments to people of the generation that bought the bonds issued to finance that debt.

If the national debt is created intelligently, however, the "burden" of the debt should be less than the benefits derived from the resources acquired as a result, particularly when the debt allows for an expansion in real economic activity or for the development of vital infrastructure for the future. The opportunity cost of expanded public activity may be small in terms of private activity that must be forgone to finance the public activity if unemployed resources are put to work. The real issue of importance is whether the government's activities have benefits that are greater than their costs; whether it is done through raising taxes, printing money, or running deficits, it is, for the most part, a "financing issue." It is also possible that parents can offset some of the intergenerational debt by leaving larger bequests.

14-7e A BALANCED BUDGET AMENDMENT?

What are the arguments for and against requiring a balanced budget? If we had a balanced budget, how could we allow the government to run deficits during emergencies? Some individuals believe that we must control the deficits through responsible fiscal restraint—a belief that has prompted a drive to add a balanced budget amendment to the U.S. Constitution.

But the possibility that the spending activities of the federal government may be constitutionally restricted is terrifying to some. Opponents' arguments can be summarized as follows:

First, at best, a balanced budget amendment would be ineffective because it is impossible to guarantee that revenues and expenditures will always match up on an annual basis. Second, at worst, a balanced budget amendment would reduce the fiscal flexibility of the federal government, thereby making it more difficult to respond appropriately to changing economic circumstances. Furthermore, if the public would support the government balancing its budget, our elected representatives already have the power to respond to this desire. Third, it could be counterproductive to balance the budget every year. What would the government have to do to balance the budget during a recession? Raise taxes and cut government spending. But these actions would just deepen the recession. In short, to balance the budget every year, the government might have to take actions that would destabilize the economy.

No amendment to the Constitution can ensure that the budget will ever be perfectly balanced. No one can exactly predict revenues or expenditures over a specified interval. And in some circumstances, budget flexibility can be justified. Finally, it is true that Congress has the control over the taxing and spending needed to eliminate chronic deficits if it chooses to do so. Given all these factors, why should we clutter up the Constitution with a balanced budget amendment?

Proponents of a balanced budget amendment argue that, in the absence of fiscal restraints, excessive government spending will occur because of the private advantages that each of us realizes from spending on "our" government programs that are paid for almost entirely by other taxpayers. Of course, each of us suffers from having to pay for the programs of others, and most of us would be willing to reduce our special-interest demands if others would do the same. But we all recognize that as long as we continue to pay for the programs of others, we enjoy no advantage from reducing our individual demands on the government treasury. In this uncontrolled setting, we are in a spending free-for-all, with penalties for the fiscally responsible and rewards for the fiscally irresponsible.

Of course, a balanced budget amendment could be written that would allow the government to run deficits in times of special emergencies such as military involvement, earthquakes, financial crises, fires, or floods. In addition, the voters might adopt a plan that would allow for a two-thirds vote to increase the deficit or that would opt for a balanced budget over the business cycle instead of balancing the budget every year. Any of these proposals could work toward controlling runaway federal spending to some degree. A balanced budget would mean greater national saving, investment, and economic growth. A smaller debt would also lead to less of a burden on future generations of taxpayers. Inheriting this debt will lower future standards of living, other things being equal. However, what if the deficit is reduced by cutting back on spending in education? With less education, future generations could be less productive with lower incomes. If the deficit became so large that financing the debt (sometimes called monetizing the debt) became problematic, then there might be a temptation to turn to inflation to finance the debt. In addition, parents and grandparents could offset some of this problem to the extent that they save more now and bequeath larger inheritances to their children.

The most important issue of all might be at what level of spending the budget should be balanced. Some have argued that a constitutional amendment linking the growth of government spending with the growth in GDP may yield the best results. Stanford economist, John Taylor, advocates holding spending to 19½ percent of GDP. He argues that with the current tax system, federal tax revenues and federal spending would be in balance, on average, at 19½ percent. It would also allow for revenue-neutral tax reforms. Taylor says this plan would allow for higher tax revenue through economic growth, not from higher tax rates. Many would prefer deficits in a smaller budget to a much larger, but balanced, budget. However, the real issue, as always, is: Are we getting government goods and services with benefits that are greater than costs?

SECTION CHECK 7 ANSWERS

1. A budget deficit is financed by issuing debt.

2. When the government borrows to finance a budget deficit, it causes the interest rate to rise.

3. When the government runs a budget surplus, it adds to national saving, lowers the interest rate, and stimulates private investment and capital formation.

Chapter 14: Self-Review

Now that you are finished reading the chapter, review the questions below. You can write your answers in the space provided, then go online to see the answers at www.cengagebrain.com.

14-1 FISCAL POLICY

1. Fill-in-the-Blank: If the federal government decreases its purchases of goods and services, the budget deficit _____.

2. True or False: If the federal government increases taxes and/or decreases transfer payments, it is employing a contractionary fiscal policy.

14-2 GOVERNMENT SPENDING AND TAXATION

3. What finances the majority of federal government spending?

4. True or False: Excise taxes on items such as alcohol, tobacco, and gasoline are considered flat taxes.

5. Fill-in-the-Blank: The federal income tax is an example of the _____ principle.

14-3 FISCAL POLICY AND THE *AD/AS* MODEL

6. What is a recessionary gap?

7. Fill-in-the-Blank: The appropriate fiscal policy to combat a recessionary gap is _____.

14-4 THE MULTIPLIER EFFECT

8. What would the multiplier be if the marginal propensity to consume was:
   a. 1/3
   b. 1/2
   c. 3/4

9. True or False: The marginal propensity to consume is always less than one.

14-5 SUPPLY-SIDE EFFECTS OF TAX CUTS

10. True or False: Supply-side economics is more concerned with short-run economic stabilization than long-run economic growth.

11. Why could you say that supply-side economics is really more about after-tax wages and after-tax returns on investment than it is about tax rates?

14-6 AUTOMATIC STABILIZERS

12. True or False: Automatic stabilizers are affected by a time lag.

13. How do automatic stabilizers affect budget deficits and surpluses?

14-7 THE NATIONAL DEBT

14. What will happen to the interest rate when a budget surplus occurs?

PART **3**

What is money?

When we talk about money, we usually think of bills and coins, like these pennies that are about to be stamped at the mint. Hard currency, however, is not the only form of money that we use. While mints will create money by printing and stamping coins and bills, there is another way that money can be created, namely through banks creating loans. We will discuss this money creation process in Section 15-3.

Test your Economics *street-smart* **knowledge and see how you compare against other students! Scan here or visit CourseMate for Survey of ECON2.**

15

Monetary Institutions

Money is very important to the economy. Recall the circular flow model in which households trade money for the goods and services they buy in product markets, and firms exchange money for inputs they buy to produce the goods and services they sell in factor markets. In this chapter, we will discuss the different forms of money, the different functions of money, and how banks create money. We will learn how the Federal Reserve works to keep banks safe. At the end of the chapter, we will examine some periods of bank failure in the twentieth century.

15-1 What Is Money?

SECTION CHECK 1

Keep the following questions in mind as you read through this section.

1. What is money?

2. How does money lower the costs of making transactions?

3. How does money serve as a store of value?

Money is anything that is generally accepted in exchange for goods and services. In colonial times, commodities such as tobacco and wampum (Native American beads made from shells) were sometimes used as money. At some times and in some places, even cigarettes and whiskey have been used as money. Using commodities as money has several disadvantages, however, the most important of which is that many commodities deteriorate easily after a few trades. Precious metal coins have been used for money for millennia, partly because of their durability.

15-1a THE FUNCTIONS OF MONEY

Money has four important functions in the economy: as a medium of exchange, a unit of account, a store

money anything generally accepted in exchange for goods or services

Four functions of money
1) *Medium of exchange*
2) *Unit of account*
3) *Store of value*
4) *Means of deferred payment*

of value, and a means of deferred payment. Let's examine the four important functions of money and see how they are different than other assets in the economy such as stocks, bonds, art, real estate, and a comic book collection.

Money as a Medium of Exchange

The primary function of money is to serve as a **medium of exchange**, to facilitate transactions, and to lower transaction costs. That is, sellers will accept it as payment in a transaction. However, money is not the only medium of exchange; rather, it is the only medium that is generally accepted for most transactions. How would people trade with one another in the absence of money? They would **barter** for goods and services that they desire.

The Barter System Is Inefficient Under a barter system, individuals pay for goods or services by offering other goods and services in exchange. Suppose you are a farmer who needs some salt. You go to the merchant selling salt and offer her 30 pounds

Tobacco was once used as money in colonial America—in particular, in Virginia and Maryland. Tobacco was used rather than other commodities because it was resistant to spoilage.

of wheat for 2 pounds of salt. The wheat that you use to buy the salt is not money, because the salt merchant may not want wheat and therefore may not accept it as payment. This issue is one of the major disadvantages of barter: The buyer may not have appropriate items of value to the seller. The salt merchant may reluctantly take the wheat that she does not want, later bartering it away to another customer for something that she does want. In any case, barter is inefficient because several trades may be necessary to receive the desired goods. That is, the problem with barter is that it requires a double coincidence of wants—both traders must be willing to trade their products with each other. Money solves the problem of double coincidence of wants because people will accept money for the items they sell.

Moreover, barter is extremely expensive over long distances. What would it cost me, living in California, to send wheat to Maine in return for an item in the L.L. Bean catalog? It is much cheaper to mail a check. Finally, barter is time-consuming because of difficulties in determining the value of the product that is being offered for barter. For example, the person selling the salt may wish to inspect the wheat first to make sure that it is pure and not contaminated with dirt or insects. Barter, in short, is expensive and inefficient, and it generally prevails only where limited trade is carried out over short distances, which generally means in relatively primitive economies. The more complex the economy (e.g., the higher the real GDP per capita), the greater the economic interactions between people, and consequently, the greater the need for one or more universally accepted assets serving as money. Only in a Robinson Crusoe economy, where people live in isolated settlements and are generally self-sufficient, is the use of money unnecessary.

Money as a Unit of Account

Besides serving as a medium of exchange, money is also a unit of account. With a barter system, one does not know precisely what 30 pounds of wheat are worth relative to 2 pounds of salt. With money, a common "yardstick" exists, so people can precisely compare the values of diverse goods and services. Thus, if wheat costs 50 cents a pound and salt costs $1 a pound, we can say that a pound of salt is valued at precisely two times as much as a pound of wheat ($1/$0.50 = 2). By providing a universally understood unit of account, money serves to lower the information costs involved in making transactions. Without money, a person might not know what a good price for salt is, because so many different commodities can be bartered for it. With money, only one price for salt is necessary, and that price is readily available as information to the potential consumer. We use money as a unit of account when we measure and record economic value.

Money as a Store of Value

Money also serves as a store of value. It can provide a means of saving or "storing" things of value in an efficient manner. A farmer in a barter society who wants to save for retirement might accumulate enormous inventories of wheat, which he would then gradually trade away for other goods in his old age. This approach is a terribly inefficient way to save. The farmer would have to construct storage buildings to hold all his wheat; and the interest payments he would earn on the wheat would actually be negative, because it is quite likely that rats would eat part of it or it would otherwise deteriorate. Most important, physical goods of value would be tied up in unproductive use for many years. With money, the farmer saves pieces of paper that can be used to purchase goods and services in his old age. It is both cheaper and safer to store paper rather than wheat.

Money as a Means of Deferred Payment

Finally, money is a **means of deferred payment**. Money makes it much easier to borrow and to repay loans. With barter, lending is cumbersome and subject to an

> By providing a universally understood unit of account, money serves to lower the information costs involved in making transactions.

added problem. What if a wheat farmer borrows some wheat and agrees to pay it back in wheat next year, but the value of wheat soars because of a poor crop resulting from drought? The debt will be paid back in wheat that is far more valuable than that borrowed, creating a problem for the borrower. Of course, fluctuations in the value of money can also occur; indeed, inflation has been a major problem in our recent past and continues to be a problem in many countries. But the value of money fluctuates far less than the value of many individual commodities, so lending in money imposes fewer risks on buyers and sellers than lending in commodities.

SECTION CHECK 1 ANSWERS

1. Money is anything that is generally accepted in exchange for goods and services.

2. By providing a universally understood unit of account, money serves to lower the information costs involved in making transactions.

3. Money is both cheaper and easier to store than other goods.

15-2 Measuring Money

SECTION CHECK 2

Keep the following questions in mind as you read through this section.

1. What is currency?

2. What is liquidity?

3. What is included in the money supply?

Currency consists of coins and/or paper that some institution or government has created to be used in the trading of goods and services and the payment of debts. Currency in the form of metal coins is still used as money throughout the world today. But metal currency has a disadvantage: It is bulky. Also, certain types of metals traditionally used in coins, such as gold and silver, are not available in sufficient quantities to meet our demands for a monetary instrument. For these reasons, metal coins have for centuries been supplemented by paper currency, often in the form of bank notes. In the United States, the Federal Reserve System (the Fed) issues Federal Reserve notes in various denominations, and this paper currency, along with coins, provides the basis for most transactions of relatively modest size in the United States today. (The Federal Reserve System will be discussed further in the next chapter.)

means of deferred payment the attribute of money that makes it easier to borrow and to repay loans

currency coins and/or paper created to facilitate the trade of goods and services and the payment of debts

15-2a CURRENCY AS LEGAL TENDER

In the United States and most other nations of the world, metallic coins and paper currency are the only forms of **legal tender**. In other words, coins and paper money have been officially declared to be money—to be acceptable for the settlement of debts incurred in financial transactions. In effect, the government says, "We declare these instruments to be money, and citizens are expected to accept them as a medium of exchange." Legal tender is **fiat money**—a means of exchange that has been established not by custom and tradition or because of the value of the metal in a coin but by government fiat, or declaration.

15-2b DEMAND DEPOSITS AND OTHER CHECKABLE DEPOSITS

Most of the money that we use for day-to-day transactions, however, is not official legal tender. Rather, it is a monetary instrument that has become "generally accepted" in exchange over the years and has now, by custom and tradition, become money. What is this instrument? It is balances in checking accounts in banks, more formally called **demand deposits**.

Demand deposits are defined as balances in bank accounts that depositors can access on demand by simply writing checks. Some other forms of accounts in financial institutions also have virtually all the attributes of demand deposits. For example, other checkable deposits earn interest but have some restrictions, such as higher monthly fees or minimum balance requirements. These interest-earning checking accounts effectively permit the depositors to write "orders" similar to checks and assign the rights to the deposit to other persons, just as we write checks to other parties. Practically speaking, funds in these accounts are the equivalent of demand deposits and have become an important component in the supply of money. Both these types of accounts are forms of **transaction deposits** because they can be easily converted into currency or used to buy goods and services directly. **Traveler's checks**, like currency and demand deposits, are also easily converted into currency or used directly as a means of payment.

15-2c THE POPULARITY OF DEMAND DEPOSITS AND OTHER CHECKABLE DEPOSITS

Demand deposits and other checkable deposits have replaced paper and metallic currency as the major source of money used for larger transactions in the United States and in most other relatively well-developed nations for several reasons, including the ease and safety of transactions, lower transaction costs, and transaction records.

Ease and Safety of Transactions

Paying for goods and services with checks is easier (meaning cheaper) and less risky than paying with paper money. Paper money is readily transferable: If someone takes a $20 bill from you, it is gone, and the thief can use it to buy goods with no difficulty. If, however, someone steals a check that you have written to the telephone company to pay a monthly bill, that person will probably have great difficulty using it to buy goods and services because he has to be able to identify himself as a representative of the telephone company. If someone steals your checkbook, the thief can use your checks as money only if he can successfully forge your signature and provide some identification. Hence, transacting business by check is much less risky than using legal tender; an element of insurance or safety exists in the use of transaction deposits instead of currency.

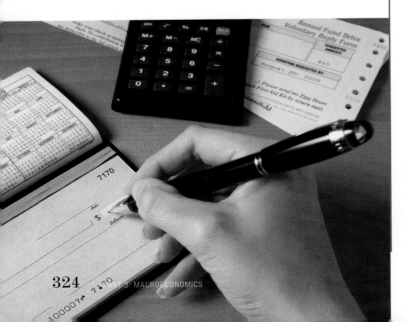

© jwohlfeil/Shutterstock

Lower Transaction Costs

Suppose you decide that you want to buy a sweater that costs $81.28 from the current Urban Outfitters mail-order catalog. It is much cheaper, easier, and safer for you to send a check for $81.28 rather than four $20 bills, a $1 bill, a quarter, and three pennies. Transaction deposits are popular precisely because they lower transaction costs compared with the use of metal or paper currency. In small transactions, the gains in safety and convenience of checks are outweighed by the time and cost required to write and process them; in these cases, transaction costs are lower with paper and metallic currency. Therefore, it is unlikely that the use of paper or metallic currency will disappear entirely.

15-2d CREDIT AND DEBIT CARDS

A credit card is "generally acceptable in exchange for goods and services." At the same time, however, a credit card payment is actually a guaranteed loan available on demand to the cardholder, which merely defers the cardholder's payment for a transaction using a demand deposit. After all, the word "credit" means that you are receiving money today with a promise to pay it back in the future—it really is a short-term loan. Ultimately, an item purchased with a credit card must be paid for with a check; monthly payments on credit card accounts are required to continue using the card. A credit card, then, is not money but rather a convenient tool for carrying out transactions that minimizes the physical transfer of checks or currency. In this sense, it is a substitute for the use of money in exchange and allows the cardholder to use any given amount of money in future exchanges.

A debit card is a card that lets you access your money via your checking account, but the card is not money. They are called debit cards because they reduce or debit your bank account directly when you use them. People often prefer to use debit cards because no checkbook is required. They are a convenient way to access a checking account. They may be safer than credit cards because debit cards require a personal identification number (PIN). However, there is no grace period, and the transaction immediately reduces the amount of money in your bank account. Consequently, consumers have less leverage when disputing a purchase; with a check, you can stop payment, and with a credit card you have a grace period between purchase and payment.

15-2e SAVINGS ACCOUNTS

Economists are not completely in agreement on what constitutes money for all purposes. They agree, nearly universally, that coins, paper currency, demand and other checkable deposits, and traveler's checks are certainly forms of money, because all are accepted as direct means of payment for goods and services. Some economists, however, argue that for some purposes *money* should be more broadly defined to include **nontransaction deposits**. Nontransaction deposits are fund accounts against which the depositor *cannot* directly write checks, hence the name. If these funds cannot be used directly as a means of payment but must first be converted into money, why do people hold such accounts? People use these accounts primarily because they generally pay higher interest rates than transaction deposits.

The two primary types of nontransaction deposits that exist are savings accounts and time deposits (sometimes referred to as certificates of deposit, or CDs). Most purists would argue that nontransaction deposits are **near money** assets but not money itself. Why? Savings accounts and time deposits cannot be used directly to purchase a good or service. They are not a direct medium of exchange. For example, you cannot go into a supermarket, pick out groceries, and give the clerk the passbook to your savings account. You must convert funds from your savings account into currency or demand deposits before you can buy goods and services. Thus, strictly speaking, nontransaction deposits do not satisfy the formal definition of money. At the same time, however, savings accounts are assets that can be quickly converted into money at the face value of the account. In the jargon of finance, savings accounts are highly liquid assets. True, under federal law commercial banks legally can require depositors to request withdrawal of funds in writing and then defer making payment for several weeks. But

> **nontransaction deposits** funds that cannot be used for payment directly but must be converted into currency for general use
>
> **near money** nontransaction deposits that are not money but can be quickly converted into money

> [Economists are not completely in agreement on what constitutes money for all purposes.]

in practice no bank prohibits immediate withdrawal, although early withdrawal from some time deposits, especially certificates of deposit, may require the depositor to forgo some interest income as a penalty.

15-2f MONEY MARKET MUTUAL FUNDS

Money market mutual funds are interest-earning accounts provided by brokers who pool funds into investments such as Treasury bills. These funds are invested in short-term securities, and depositors are allowed to write checks against their accounts subject to certain limitations. This type of fund experienced tremendous growth over the last 20 years. Money market mutual funds are highly liquid assets. They are considered to be near money because they are relatively easy to convert into money for the purchases of goods and services.

15-2g STOCKS AND BONDS

Virtually everyone agrees that many other forms of financial assets, such as stocks and bonds, are not money. Suppose you buy 1,000 shares of common stock in Microsoft at $30 per share, for a total of $30,000. The stock is traded daily on the New York Stock Exchange and elsewhere; you can readily sell the stock and get paid in legal tender or a demand deposit. Why, then, is this stock not considered money? First, it will take a few days for you to receive payment for the sale of stock; you cannot turn the asset into cash as quickly as you can a savings deposit in a financial institution. Second, and more importantly, the value of the stock fluctuates over time, and as the owner of the asset, you have no guarantee that you will be able to obtain its original nominal value at any time. Thus, stocks and bonds are not generally considered to be money.

15-2h LIQUIDITY

Money is an asset that we generally use to buy goods or services. In fact, it is so easy to convert money into goods and services that we say it is the most liquid of assets. When we speak of **liquidity**, we are referring to the ease with which one asset can be converted into another asset or

money market mutual funds interest-earning accounts provided by brokers who pool funds into such investments as Treasury bills

liquidity the ease with which one asset can be converted into another asset or into goods and services

M1 the narrowest definition of money; includes currency, checkable deposits, and traveler's checks

M2 a broader definition of money that includes M1 plus savings deposits, time deposits, and noninstitutional money market mutual fund shares

goods and services. For example, to convert a stock into goods and services would prove to be somewhat more difficult—contacting your broker or going online, determining at what price to sell your stock, paying the commission for the service, and waiting for the completion of the transaction. Clearly, stocks are not as liquid an asset as money. But other assets are even less liquid—for example, converting your painting collection or your baseball cards or Barbie dolls into other goods and services.

15-2i THE MONEY SUPPLY

Because a good case can be made either for including or for excluding savings accounts, certificates of deposit (CDs), and money market mutual funds from an operational definition of the money supply depending on its intended purpose, we will compromise and do both. Economists call the narrow definition of money—currency, checkable deposits, and traveler's checks—**M1**. The broader definition of money, encompassing M1 plus savings deposits, time deposits (except for some large-denomination certificates of deposit), and noninstitutional money market mutual fund shares, is called **M2**.

The difference between M1 and M2 is striking, as evidenced by the different sizes of the total stock of money depending on which definition is used. As Exhibit 15.1 shows, M2 is more than four times the

EXHIBIT 15.1 Two Definitions of the Money Supply: M1 and M2

M2

M1

Currency = $1048.6 billion

Currency + Checkable deposits + Traveler's checks = $2,256.1 billion

M1 + Savings deposits + Small-denomination time deposits + Noninstitutional money market mutual fund shares + Money market deposit accounts = $9,943.7 billion

SOURCE: Federal Reserve, *Federal Reserve Statistical Release*, H.6 Money Stock Measures, Tables 1 and 3. Washington, D.C., March 25, 2010. Available at http://www.federalreserve.gov/releases/h6/Current/ (accessed July 13, 2012.)

magnitude of M1. In other words, people strongly prefer to keep the bulk of their liquid assets in the form of savings accounts of various kinds.

15-2j HOW WAS MONEY "BACKED"?

Until fairly recently, coins in most nations were largely made from precious metals, usually gold or silver. These metals had a considerable intrinsic worth: If the coins were melted down, the metal would be valuable for use in jewelry, industrial applications, dentistry, and so forth. Until 1933, the United States was on an internal **gold standard**, meaning that the dollar was defined as equivalent in value to a certain amount of gold, and paper currency or demand deposits could be freely converted to gold coin. The United States abandoned the gold standard, however, eventually phasing out gold currency. Some silver coins and paper money convertible into silver remained; but by the end of the 1960s, even this tie between the monetary system and precious metals was gone—in part because the price of silver soared so high that the metal in coins had an intrinsic worth greater than its face value, leading people to hoard coins or even melt them down. When two forms of money are available, people prefer to spend the form of money that is less valuable. This tendency is a manifestation of **Gresham's Law**: "Cheap money drives out dear money."

15-2k WHAT REALLY BACKS OUR MONEY NOW?

Consequently, today no meaningful precious metal "backing" gives our money value. Why, then, do people accept dollar bills in exchange for goods? After all, a dollar bill is a piece of generally wrinkled paper about 6 inches by 2.5 inches in size, with virtually no inherent utility or worth. Do we accept these bills because it states on the front of the bills, "This note is legal tender for all debts, public and private"? Perhaps, but we accept some forms of currency and money in the form of demand deposits without that statement.

The true backing behind money in the United States is faith that people will take it in exchange for goods and services. People accept with great eagerness these small pieces of green paper with pictures of long-deceased people with funny-looking hair simply because we believe that they will be exchangeable for goods and services with an intrinsic value. If you were to drop two pieces of paper of equal size on the floor in front of 100 students, one a blank piece of paper and the other a $100 bill, and then leave the room, most of the group would probably start scrambling for the $100 bill, while the blank piece of paper would be ignored. Such is our faith in the green paper's practical value that some will even fight over it. As long as people have confidence in something's convertibility into goods and services, "money" will exist and no further backing is necessary.

Because governments represent the collective will of the people, they are the institutional force that traditionally defines money in the legal sense. People are

Money: © LUCAS JACKSON/Reuters/Landov; Gold: © C Squared Studios/Getty Images

PAWN SHOPS AND LIQUIDITY

Q&A

Q: What do pawn shops sell?

A: The typical response is that they sell used goods. In fact, they sell few used goods. However, they do sell something that is even more important to their clientele. They sell liquidity. When individuals hock their wares at pawn shops, they are usually desperate and are willing to pledge their watches, rings, or whatever as collateral. The pawn shop will allow you to buy your pawned item back in some specified time period for a higher price (that is, an interest charge). In this sense, pawn shops are like banks and will lend you money for a specified period of time if you are willing to pay the interest. But even if individuals don't buy their pawned item back, this behavior of selling and taking a lower price than could be obtained through the classifieds in order to get the money now, demonstrates that buyers are willing to pay for liquidity.

© iStockphoto.com/mattjeacock

willing to accept pieces of paper as money only because of their faith in the government. When people lose faith in the exchangeability of pieces of paper that the government decrees as money, even legal tender loses its status as meaningful money. Something is money only if people will generally accept it. Governments play a key role in defining money, but much of its value is actually created by private businesses in the pursuit of profit. A majority of U.S. money, whether M1 or M2, is in the form of deposits at privately owned financial institutions.

People who hold money, then, must have faith not only in their government but also in banks and other financial institutions. If you accept a check drawn on a regional bank, you believe that bank or, for that matter, any bank will be willing to convert that check into legal tender (currency), enabling you to buy goods or services that you want to have. Thus, you have faith in the bank as well. In short, our money is money because of the confidence we have in private financial institutions and our government.

SECTION CHECK 2 ANSWERS

1. Currency consists of coins and/or paper created to facilitate the trade of goods and services and the payment of debts.

2. The ease with which one asset can be converted into another asset or goods and services is called liquidity.

3. M1 is made up of currency, checkable deposits, and traveler's checks. M2 is made up of M1, plus savings accounts, time deposits, and money market mutual funds.

15-3 How Banks Create Money

SECTION CHECK 3

Keep the following questions in mind as you read through this section.

1. How is money created?
2. What is a reserve requirement?
3. How do reserve requirements affect how much money can be created?

The biggest players in the banking industry are **commercial banks**. Commercial banks are financial institutions organized to handle everyday financial transactions of businesses and households through demand deposit accounts and savings accounts and by making short-term commercial and consumer loans. These banks account for more than two-thirds of all the deposits in the banking industry; they maintain almost all the demand deposits and close to half the savings accounts.

Nearly 1,000 commercial banks operate in the United States. This number is in marked contrast to most other nations, where the leading banks operate throughout the country and where a large proportion of total bank assets are held in a handful of banks. Until recently, federal law restricted banks from operating in more than one state. This law has changed, and the structure of banking as we know it will inevitably change with the emergence of interstate banking, mergers, and "hostile" takeovers.

Aside from commercial banks, the banking system includes two other important financial institutions: **savings and loan associations** and **credit unions**. Savings and loan associations provide many of the same services as commercial banks, including checkable deposits, a variety of time deposits, and money market deposit accounts. The almost 2,000 members of savings and loan associations have typically invested most of their savings deposits in home mortgages. Credit unions are cooperatives made up of depositors with some common affiliation, such as the same employer or union.

15-3a THE FUNCTIONS OF FINANCIAL INSTITUTIONS

Financial institutions offer a large number of financial functions. For example, they often will pay an individual's monthly bills by automatic withdrawals, administer estates, and rent safe-deposit boxes, among other things. Most important, though, they are depositories for savings and liquid assets that are used by individuals and firms for transaction purposes. They can create money by making loans. In making loans, financial institutions act as intermediaries (the middle persons) between savers who supply funds and borrowers seeking funds to invest.

commercial banks financial institutions organized to handle everyday financial transactions of businesses and households through demand deposit accounts and savings accounts and by making short-term commercial and consumer loans

savings and loan association financial institution organized as cooperative associations that holds demand deposits and savings of members in the form of dividend-bearing shares and makes loans, especially home mortgages loans

credit unions financial cooperatives made up of depositors with a common affiliation

15-3b HOW DO BANKS CREATE MONEY?

As we have already learned, most money, narrowly defined, is in the form of transaction deposits assets that can be directly used to buy goods and services. But how did the balance in, say, a checking account get there in the first place? Perhaps it was through a loan made by a commercial bank. When a bank lends to a person, it does not typically give the borrower cash (paper and metallic currency). Rather, it gives the borrower the funds by issuing a check or by adding funds to an existing checking account. If you go into a bank and borrow $1,000, the bank probably will add $1,000 to your checking account at the bank, creating a new checkable deposit money.

15-3c HOW DO BANKS MAKE PROFITS?

Banks make loans and create checkable deposits to make profits. How do they make their profits? By collecting higher interest payments on the loans they make than they pay their depositors for those funds. If you borrow $1,000 from Bank One, the interest payment you make, less the expenses the bank incurs in making the loan, including their costs of acquiring the funds, represents profit to the bank.

15-3d RESERVE REQUIREMENTS

Because the way to make more profit is to make more loans, banks want to make a large volume of loans. Stockholders of banks want the largest profits possible; so what keeps

reserve requirements
holdings of assets at the bank or at the Federal Reserve Bank as mandated by the Fed

fractional reserve system a system that requires banks to hold reserves equal to some fraction of their checkable deposits

secondary reserves highly liquid, interest-paying assets held by the bank

banks from making nearly infinite quantities of loans? Primarily, government regulatory authorities limit the loan issuance of banks by imposing **reserve requirements**. Banks are required to keep on hand a quantity of cash or reserve accounts with the Federal Reserve equal to a prescribed proportion of their checkable deposits.

15-3e FRACTIONAL RESERVE SYSTEM

Even in the absence of regulations restricting the creation of checkable deposits, a prudent bank would put some limit on their loan (and therefore deposit) volume. Why? For people to accept checkable deposits as money, the checks written must be generally accepted in exchange for goods and services. People will accept checks only if they know that they are quickly convertible at par (face value) into legal tender. For this reason, banks must have adequate cash reserves on hand (including reserves at the Fed that can be almost immediately converted to currency, if necessary) to meet the needs of customers who wish to convert their checkable deposits into currency or spend them on goods or services.

Our banking system is sometimes called a **fractional reserve system**, because banks, by law as well as by choice, find it necessary to keep cash on hand and reserves at the Federal Reserve equal to some fraction of their checkable deposits. If a bank were to create $100 in demand deposits for every $1 in cash reserves that it

had, the bank might well find itself in difficulty before too long. Why? Consider a bank with $10,000,000 in demand and time deposits and $100,000 in cash reserves. Suppose a couple of large companies with big accounts decide to withdraw $120,000 in cash on the same day. The bank would be unable to convert into legal tender all the funds requested. The word would then spread that the bank's checks are not convertible into lawful money, possibly causing a "run on the bank." The bank would have to quickly convert some of its other assets into currency, or it would be unable to meet its obligations to convert its deposits into currency and it would have to close.

Therefore, even in the absence of reserve regulations, few banks would risk maintaining fewer reserves on hand than they thought prudent for their amount of deposits (particularly demand deposits). Reserve requirements exist primarily to control the amount of demand and time deposits and thus the size of the money supply; they do not exist simply to prevent bank failures.

While banks must meet their reserve requirements, they do not want to keep any more of their funds as additional reserves than necessary for safety, because cash assets do not earn any interest. To protect themselves but also earn some interest income, banks usually keep some of their assets in highly liquid investments, such as U.S. government bonds. These types of highly liquid, interest-paying assets are often called **secondary reserves**.

15-3f A BALANCE SHEET

Earlier in this chapter, we learned that money is created when banks make loans. We will now look more closely at the process of bank lending and its impact on the stock of money. In doing so, we will examine the structure and behavior of our hypothetical bank, Bank One. To get a

This scene from It's a Wonderful Life shows a run on a savings and loan that demonstrates the power of the fractional reserve banking system. George's bank almost had to close because it did not have enough cash on hand to cover the high volume of withdrawals.

Movie stills: © Hulton Archive/Getty Images; Filmstrip: © iStockphoto.com/belterz good picture of the size of the bank, what it owns, and what it owes, we look at its **balance sheet**, which is like a financial "photograph" of the bank at a single moment. Exhibit 15.2 presents a balance sheet for Bank One.

Assets

The assets of a bank are the items of value that the bank owns (e.g., cash, reserves at the Federal Reserve, bonds, and its buildings), including contractual obligations of individuals and firms to pay funds to the bank (loans). The largest asset item for most banks is loans. Banks maintain most of their assets in the form of loans because interest payments on loans are the primary means by which they earn revenue. Some assets are kept in the form of non-interest-bearing cash and reserve accounts at the Federal Reserve to meet legal reserve requirements (and to meet the cash demands of customers). Typically, relatively little of a bank's reserves, or cash assets, is physically kept in the form of paper currency in the bank's vault or at tellers' windows. Most banks keep the majority of their reserves as reserve accounts at the Federal Reserve. As previously indicated, banks usually also keep some assets in the form of bonds that are quickly convertible into cash if necessary (secondary reserves).

Liabilities

All banks have substantial liabilities, which are financial obligations that the bank has to other people. The predominant liability of virtually all banks is deposits. If you have money in a demand deposit account, you have the right to demand cash for that deposit at any time. Basically, the bank owes you the amount in your checking account. Time deposits similarly constitute a liability of banks.

Capital Stock

For a bank to be healthy and solvent, its assets, or what it owns, must exceed its liabilities, or what it owes others. In other words, if the bank were liquidated and all the assets converted into cash and all the obligations to others (liabilities) paid off, some cash would still be left to distribute to the owners of the bank, that is, its stockholders. This difference between a bank's assets and its liabilities constitutes the bank's capital. Note that this definition of capital differs from the earlier definition, which described capital as goods used to further production of other goods (machines, structures, tools, etc.). In this case, the capital stock is the equity owned by shareholders both in and out of the community. As you can see in Exhibit 15.2, capital is included on the right side of the balance sheet, so that both sides (assets and liabilities plus capital) are equal in amount. Any time the aggregate amount of bank assets changes, the aggregate amount of liabilities and capital must also change by the same amount, by definition.

balance sheet a financial record that indicates the balance between a bank's assets and its liabilities plus capital

required reserve ratio the percentage of deposits that a bank must hold at the Federal Reserve Bank or in bank vaults

excess reserves reserve levels held above that required by the Fed

15-3g THE REQUIRED RESERVE RATIO

Suppose for simplicity that Bank One faces a reserve requirement of 10 percent on all deposits. This percentage is often called the required reserve ratio. But what does a **required reserve ratio** of 10 percent mean? It means that the bank must keep cash on hand or at the Federal Reserve Bank equal to one-tenth (10 percent) of its deposits. For example, if the required reserve ratio is 10 percent, banks are required to hold $100,000 in required reserves for every $1 million in deposits. The remaining 90 percent of cash is called **excess reserves**.

Reserves in the form of cash and reserves at the Federal Reserve earn no revenue for the bank; no profit is made from holding cash. Whenever excess reserves

EXHIBIT 15.2 Balance Sheet, Bank One

Assets		Liabilities and Capital	
Cash (reserves)	$ 2,000,000	Transaction deposits (checking deposits)	$ 5,000,000
Loans	6,100,000	Savings and time deposits	4,000,000
Bonds (U.S. government and municipal)	1,500,000	Total liabilities	$ 9,000,000
Bank building, equipment, fixtures	400,000	Capital	1,000,000
Total Assets	**$10,000,000**	**Total Liabilities and Capital**	**$10,000,000**

© Cengage Learning 2014

appear, banks will invest the excess reserves in interest-earning assets—sometimes bonds, but usually loans.

15-3h LOANING EXCESS RESERVES

Let's see what happens when someone deposits $100,000 at Bank One. We will continue to assume that the required reserve ratio is 10 percent. That is, the bank is required to hold $10,000 in required reserves for this new deposit of $100,000. The remaining 90 percent, or $90,000, becomes excess reserves, most of which will likely become available for loans for individuals and businesses.

However, the story doesn't end here. Let's say that the bank loans all its new excess reserves of $90,000 to an individual who is remodeling her home. At the time the bank makes the loan, its money supply increases by $90,000. Specifically, no one has less money—the original depositor still has $100,000, and the bank adds $90,000 to the

People do not usually borrow money and sit on it. They take out loans to make purchases.

borrower's checking account (demand deposit). A new demand deposit, or checking account, of $90,000 has been created. *Because demand deposits are money, the issuers of the new loan have created money.*

Furthermore, borrowers are not likely to keep borrowed money in their checking accounts for long, because they usually take out loans to make purchases. If a loan is used for remodeling, the borrower pays the construction company; the owner of the construction company, in turn, will likely deposit the money into his account at another bank to add even more funds for additional money expansion. This whole process is summarized in Exhibit 15.3.

Now suppose that Bank One faces a reserve requirement of 20 percent. The bank must keep cash on hand or at the Federal Reserve Bank equal to one-fifth (20%) of its deposits. If the

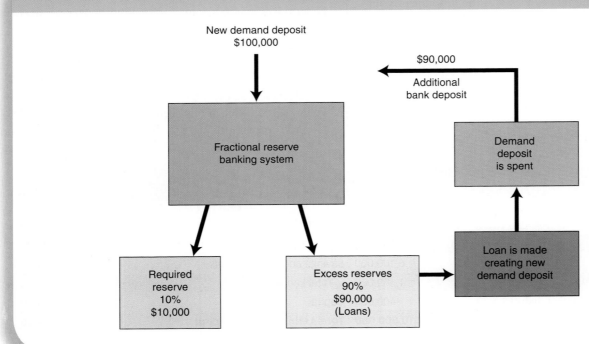

EXHIBIT 15.3 Fractional Reserve Banking System

New demand deposit $100,000

Fractional reserve banking system

Required reserve 10% $10,000

Excess reserves 90% $90,000 (Loans)

Loan is made creating new demand deposit

Demand deposit is spent

$90,000 Additional bank deposit

© Cengage Learning 2014

bank's deposits (demand and time) sum to $9,000,000, required reserves are calculated as follows:

$$\text{Deposits} \times \text{Reserve ratio} = \$9,000,000 \times 0.20$$
$$= \$1,800,000$$

The bank then is required to maintain $1,800,000 in cash. Bank One, however, actually has $2 million in cash, meaning that it has excess reserves, or $200,000.

$$\text{Excess reserves} = \text{Actual reserves} - \text{Required reserves}$$
$$= \$2,000,000 - \$1,800,000$$
$$= \$200,000$$

Suppose Bank One decided to make loans with its $200,000 in excess reserves. For simplicity's sake, let us suppose it makes one loan of $200,000 to a manufacturer for an addition to its chocolate factory. What will be the bank's balance sheet after it makes the loan? As Exhibit 15.4 indicates, both assets and liabilities rise by $200,000. The bank simply gives the borrower a checking account with $200,000 in it, a new deposit liability of the bank. In return, the borrower gives the bank an IOU agreeing to pay back the $200,000 plus interest at some future date. Thus, loans rise by $200,000 over the level on the initial balance sheet.

Note that in making the loan, Bank One did not have to reduce its cash reserves. It did not give the borrower cash; it simply created new money by giving the borrower $200,000 in a checking account. Therefore, even after making a loan equal to its initial excess reserves of $200,000, the bank still has some excess reserves. The bank's deposits rose to $9,200,000; 20 percent of that is $1,840,000. Yet the bank has $2,000,000 in actual reserves. Excess reserves are still $160,000 ($2,000,000 − $1,840,000 = $160,000).

If it still has some excess reserves, should the bank make still more loans? No. Why? Because when the chocolate manufacturer borrowed $200,000, it did so in order to expand the factory. Few people borrow money and simply let the money sit in a checking account while they pay interest on the loan. It is reasonable to assume that the chocolate maker will shortly take all or part of the $200,000 out of the checking account, probably in the form of a check to a construction company for $200,000. What will the construction company do with the check? Put it in its bank. With many different banks in the United States, it is likely that the construction company has its checking account in another bank. Suppose its account is in Bank Two. Bank Two credits the account of the construction company with $200,000 in demand deposits, then takes the check and uses the facilities of the Federal Reserve System or a bank clearinghouse to present the check to Bank One for payment. Bank One will then have to pay Bank Two $200,000 in cash.

Therefore, Bank One will eventually (depending on how long it takes the chocolate manufacturer to spend the $200,000 it borrowed) face losing cash reserves equal to the loan. After Bank Two presents the check that was written by the chocolate manufacturer to Bank One for payment, Bank One's balance sheet changes again, as indicated in Exhibit 15.5 on the next page.

As the chocolate maker spends the $200,000, demand deposits fall by that amount, so that the bank's liabilities also decline by $200,000. The bank transfers $200,000 in cash to Bank Two. Incidentally, rarely is cash actually physically moved, given the expense and risk. Typically, the local Federal Reserve Bank simply reduces the cash reserves of Bank One by $200,000 and increases Bank Two's by $200,000.

When the smoke clears, the chocolate manufacturer has its factory addition, and Bank One has an interest-paying IOU equal to $200,000. Bank One's cash reserves have fallen, however, to an amount ($1,800,000) exactly equal to its required reserves. Had the bank initially loaned out more than its $200,000 in excess reserves, the bank would have found its reserves below the required level as soon as the borrower spent the loan, assuming that the receiver of the funds had his or her bank account in another bank. Therefore, one important rule of thumb in banking is that a single bank in a banking system of many banks can safely make loans only equal to the amount of its excess reserves.

EXHIBIT 15.4 Balance Sheet for Bank One after Loan

Assets		Liabilities and Capital	
Cash (reserves)	$ 2,000,000	Demand deposits	$ 5,200,000
Loans	6,300,000	Time deposits	4,000,000
Bonds (U.S. government and municipal)	1,500,000	Total liabilities	$ 9,200,000
Bank building, equipment, fixtures	400,000	Capital	1,000,000
Total Assets	**$10,200,000**	**Total Liabilities and Capital**	**$10,200,000**

© Cengage Learning 2014

EXHIBIT 15.5 Balance Sheet for Bank One after Loan Funds Are Spent

Assets		Liabilities and Capital	
Cash (reserves)	$ 1,800,000	Demand deposits	$ 5,000,000
Loans	6,300,000	Time deposits	4,000,000
Bonds (U.S. government and municipal)	1,500,000	Total liabilities	$ 9,000,000
Bank building, equipment, fixtures	400,000	Capital	1,000,000
Total Assets	$10,000,000	Total Liabilities and Capital	$10,000,000

© Cengage Learning 2014

15-3i IS MORE MONEY MORE WEALTH?

When banks create more money by putting their excess reserves to work, they make the economy more liquid. Clearly, more money is in the economy after the loan, but is the borrower any wealthier? The answer is no. Even though borrowers have more money to buy goods and services, they are not any richer, because the new liability, the loan, has to be repaid.

In short, banks create money when they increase demand deposits through the process of creating loans. However, the process does not stop here. In the next section, we will see how the process of loans and deposits has a multiplying effect throughout the banking industry.

> One important **rule of thumb in banking** is that a single bank in a banking system of many banks can safely make loans only equal to the amount of its excess reserves.

15-4 The Money Multiplier

We just learned that banks can create money (demand deposits) by making loans and that the monetary expansion of an individual bank is limited to its excess reserves. Let us now take a look at the multiple expansion effect created by these loans.

15-4a THE MULTIPLE EXPANSION EFFECT

The individual bank's limits in making loans ignores the further effects of a new loan and the accompanying expansion in the money supply. New loans create new money directly, but they also create excess reserves in other banks, which leads to still further increases in both loans and the money supply. With this multiple expansion effect, a given volume of bank reserves creates a multiplied amount of money.

New Loans and Multiple Expansions

To see how the process of multiple expansion works, consider what happens when Bank One receives a new cash deposit of $100,000. For convenience, say the bank is only required to keep new cash reserves equal to one-tenth (10 percent) of new deposits. Thus, Bank One is only required to hold $10,000 of the $100,000 deposit for required reserves. The bank therefore has $90,000 in excess reserves as a consequence of the new cash deposit.

Bank One will probably put its newly acquired excess reserves to work in some fashion earning income in the form of interest. Most likely, it will make one or more new loans totaling $90,000.

When the borrowers from Bank One get their loans, the borrowed money will almost certainly be spent on something new—machinery, a new house, a new car, or greater store inventories. The new money will lead to new spending.

The $90,000 spent by people borrowing from Bank One will likely end up in bank accounts in still other banks, such as Bank Two in Exhibit 15.6 on the next page. Bank Two now has a new deposit of $90,000 with which to make more loans and create still more money. So Bank Two's statement of changes in assets and liabilities, called a *T-account*, now looks like this:

Bank Two

Assets		Liabilities	
Reserves	$ 9,000	Checking	
Loans	$81,000	deposits	$90,000

After the deposits, Bank Two has liabilities of $90,000. Thus, Bank Two creates $81,000 of money. Now if the money deposited in Bank Two is made available for a loan and is then deposited in Bank Three, the T-account for Bank Three will be:

Bank Three

Assets		Liabilities	
Reserves	$ 8,100	Checking	
Loans	$72,900	deposits	$81,000

This process continues with Bank Three, Bank Four, Bank Five, and others. The initial cash deposit made by Bank One thus has a chain-reaction effect that ultimately involves many banks and a total monetary impact that is far greater than would be suggested by the size of the original deposit of $100,000. That is, every new loan gives rise to excess reserves, which lead to still further lending and deposit creation. Of course, each round of lending is smaller than the preceding one, because some (we are assuming 10 percent) of the new money created must be kept as required reserves.

15-4b THE MONEY MULTIPLIER

The **money multiplier** measures the potential amount of money that the banking system generates with each dollar of reserves. The following formula can be used to measure the total maximum potential impact on the supply of money:

Potential money creation = Initial deposit × Money multiplier

To find the size of the money multiplier, we simply divide 1 by the reserve requirement $(1/R)$. The larger the reserve requirement, the smaller the money multiplier. Thus, a reserve requirement of 25 percent, or one-fourth, means a money multiplier of 4. Likewise, a reserve requirement of 10 percent, or one-tenth, means a money multiplier of 10.

In the example given in Exhibit 15.6, where Bank One (facing a 10% reserve requirement) receives a new $100,000 cash deposit, the initial deposit equals $100,000. Potential money creation, then, equals $100,000 (initial deposit) multiplied by 10 (the money multiplier), or $1,000,000. Using the money multiplier, we can calculate that the total potential impact of the initial $100,000 deposit is some $1,000,000 in money being created. In other words, the final monetary impact is 10 times as great as the initial deposit. Most of this increase, $900,000, has been created by the increase in demand deposits generated when banks make loans; the remaining $100,000 is from the initial deposit.

Why Is it Only "Potential" Money Creation?

Note that the expression "potential money creation" was used in describing the impact of creating loans and deposits out of excess reserves. Why "potential"? Some banks could choose not to lend all their excess reserves. Some banks might be extremely conservative and keep some extra newly acquired cash assets in that form. When they do, the chain reaction effect is reduced by the amount of excess reserves not loaned out.

Moreover, some borrowers may not spend all their newly acquired bank deposits, or they may wait a considerable period before doing so. Others may put their borrowed funds into time deposits rather than checkable deposits, which would reduce the M1 expansion process but not the M2 expansion process. Still others

money multiplier
measures the potential amount of money that the banking system generates with each dollar of reserves

EXHIBIT 15.6 The Multiple Expansion Process

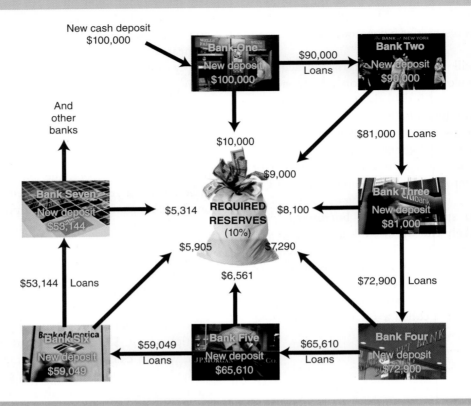

New cash deposit $100,000

Bank One
New deposit
$100,000

$90,000 Loans

Bank Two
New deposit
$90,000

$81,000 Loans

$10,000

$9,000

REQUIRED RESERVES (10%)

$8,100

Bank Three
New deposit
$81,000

And other banks

Bank Seven
New deposit
$53,144

$5,314

$5,905

$7,290

$72,900 Loans

Bank Four
New deposit
$72,900

$53,144 Loans

$6,561

Bank of America
Bank Six
New deposit
$59,049

$59,049 Loans

Bank Five
New deposit
$65,610

$65,610 Loans

may choose to keep some of their loans as currency in their pockets. Such leakages and time lags in the bank money expansion process usually mean that the actual monetary impact of an initial deposit created out of excess reserves within a short time is less than that indicated by the money multiplier. Still, the multiplier principle does work, and a multiple expansion of deposits will generally occur in a banking system that is characterized by fractional reserve requirements.

SECTION CHECK 4 ANSWERS

1. New loans mean new money (demand deposits), which can increase spending as well as the money supply.

2. The banking system as a whole can potentially create money equal to several times the amount of total reserves or new money equal to several times the amount of excess reserves; the exact amount may be determined by the money multiplier, which is equal to one divided by the reserve requirement.

15-5 The Collapse of America's Banking System, 1920–1933

SECTION CHECK 5

Keep the following questions in mind as you read through this section.

1. What caused the collapse of the banking system between 1920 and 1933?

2. How are bank failures avoided today?

Perhaps the most famous utterance from Franklin D. Roosevelt, the president of the United States from 1933 to 1945, was made on the day he assumed office, when he declared, "The only thing we have to fear is fear itself." These 10 words succinctly summarize the problems that led the world's leading economic power to a near total collapse in its system of commercial banking and, with that, to an abrupt and unprecedented decline in the money supply. The decline in the money supply, in turn, contributed to an economic downturn that had dire consequences for many, especially for the one-fourth of the labor force unemployed at the time of Roosevelt's first inaugural address.

15-5a WHAT HAPPENED TO THE BANKING INDUSTRY?

In 1920, 30,000 banks were operating in the United States; by 1933, the number declined to about 15,000. What happened? In some cases, bank failure reflected imprudent management or even criminal activity on the part of bank officers (stealing from the bank). More often, though, banks in rural areas closed as a consequence of having large sums of assets tied up in loans to farmers who, because of low farm prices, were not in a position to pay off the loans when they came due. Rumors spread that a bank was in trouble, and those rumors, even if false, became self-fulfilling prophecies. Bank "runs" developed, and even conservatively managed banks with cash equal to 15 percent or 20 percent of their deposit liabilities found themselves with insufficient cash reserves to meet the withdrawal requests of panicky depositors.

The bank failures of the 1920s, while numerous, were generally scattered around small towns in the country. In general, confidence in banks actually increased during that decade; and by the fall of 1929, there were $11 in bank deposits for every $1 of currency in circulation.

The first year following the stock market crash of 1929 saw little dramatic change in the banking system; but in late 1930, a bank with the unfortunately awesome-sounding name of the Bank of the United States failed—the largest bank failure in the country up to that time. This failure had a ripple effect. More runs on banks occurred as depositors became jittery. Banks, fearing runs, stopped lending their excess reserves, thereby aggravating a fall in the money supply and reducing business investment.

As depositors converted their deposits to currency, bank reserves fell, as did the ability of banks to support deposits. The situation improved a bit in 1932, when a newly created government agency, the Reconstruction Finance Corporation (RFC), made loans to distressed banks. By early 1933, however, the decline in depositor confidence had reached the point that the entire banking system was in jeopardy. On March 4, newly inaugurated President Roosevelt declared a national bank holiday, closing every bank in the country for nearly two weeks. Then, only the "good" banks were allowed to reopen, an action that increased confidence.

By this time, the deposit-currency ratio had fallen from 11 to 1 (in 1929) to 4 to 1. Passage of federal deposit insurance in mid-1933 greatly strengthened depositor confidence and led to money reentering the banks. The recovery process began.

15-5b WHAT CAUSED THE COLLAPSE?

The collapse occurred for several reasons. First, the nation had thousands of relatively small banks. Customers believed that depositor withdrawals could force a bank to close, and the mere fear of bank runs made them a reality. Canada, with relatively few banks, most of them large with many branches, had no bank runs. Second, governmental attempts to stem the growing distress were weak and too late. Financial aid to banks was nonexistent; the Federal Reserve System and other governmental efforts began only in 1932—well into the decline. Third, deposit insurance, which would have bolstered customer confidence, did not exist. The financial consequences of bank failures were correctly perceived by the public to be dire. Fourth, growing depositor fear was enhanced by the fact that the economy was in a continuous downward spiral, eroding the basis for any optimism that bank loans would be safely repaid.

15-5c BANK FAILURES TODAY

The combination of the Federal Deposit Insurance Corporation (FDIC) and the government's greater willingness to assist distressed banks has reduced the number of bank failures in recent times. Now, when a bank runs into financial difficulty, the FDIC may assist another bank in taking over the assets and liabilities of the troubled bank so that no depositor loses a cent. We do not see depositors run on banks because the FDIC will make good on deposits. There are costs and benefits of insuring deposits. On the cost side is that bankers whose deposits are insured may take greater risks. On the benefit side, deposit insurance means that, changes in the money supply due to a loss of deposits from failed banks are no longer a big problem. Better bank stability means a greater stability in the money supply, which means, as will be more explicitly demonstrated in the next chapter, a greater level of economic stability.

However, in the 1980s, a savings and loan crisis occurred, one of the worst financial crises since the Great Depression. The inflation of the 1970s had created a problem for many savings and loans. They had made a large number of real estate loans in the early

1970s, when the inflation rate was relatively low at about 5 percent. Then, during most of the rest of that decade, inflation rates rose rapidly and nominal interest rates soared. The savings and loans were in a squeeze—they had to pay high interest rates to attract depositors but were earning low interest rates on their real estate loans from the early 1970s. This disastrous combination for the savings and loans caused many of them to go belly up.

Unfortunately, interest rates were not the only problem. The government eased regulations to make it easier for savings and loans to compete for deposits with other financial institutions in the national market. Deregulation, coupled with deposit insurance, put savings and loans in a gambling mood. Many savings and loans poured money into high-risk real estate projects and other risky ventures. Depositors had little incentive to monitor their banks because they knew they would be protected up to $100,000 on their accounts by the government. Eventually, more than a thousand thrift institutions went bankrupt. Depositors were saved, but taxpayers were not. Taxpayers ended up paying the bill

for much of the savings and loan debacle—the bailout for the financial losses has been estimated to be more than $150 billion. The Thrift Bailout Bill of 1989 provided funds for the bailout and new, stricter provisions for banks.

Financial crises are a little like earthquakes. We know that they will happen but we do not know exactly when and with what magnitude. For example, not many economists forecasted the financial crisis of 2007–2009.

SECTION CHECK 5 ANSWERS

1. The banking collapse of 1920–1933 occurred because of customers' fears and the weakness of the government's attempts to correct the problem.

2. The creation of the Federal Deposit Insurance Corporation has largely eliminated bank runs in recent times.

Chapter 15: Self-Review

Now that you are finished reading the chapter, review the questions below. You can write your answers in the space provided, then go online to see the answers at www.cengagebrain.com.

15-1 WHAT IS MONEY?

1. True or False: Using money is better than barter.

2. Why do virtually all societies create something to function as money?

15-2 MEASURING MONEY

3. True or False: Our money is currently backed by gold.

4. Which one of each of the following pairs of assets is most liquid?
   a. Microsoft stock or a traveler's check
   b. a 30-year bond or a six-month Treasury bill
   c. a certificate of deposit or a demand deposit
   d. a savings account or 10 acres of real estate

5. True are False: Credit cards are a form of money.

6. Fill-in-the-Blank: M2 is a _____ definition of money than M1.

15-3 HOW BANKS CREATE MONEY

7. If a bank had reserves of $30,000 and demand deposits of $200,000 (and no other deposits), how much could it lend out if it faced a required reserve ratio of:
   a. 10 percent?
   b. 15 percent?
   c. 20 percent?

8. Is a demand deposit an asset or a liability?

9. Fill-in-the-Blank: Legal reserve deposit regulations _____ bank profits.

15-4 THE MONEY MULTIPLIER

10. Calculate the magnitude of the money multiplier if banks were to hold 100 percent of deposits in reserve.

11. True or False: The supply of money and the volume of bank loans both increase or decrease at the same time.

15-5 THE COLLAPSE OF AMERICA'S BANKING SYSTEM, 1920–1933

12. How did the combination of increased holding of excess reserves by banks and currency by the public lead to bank failures in the 1930s?

13. What are the four reasons cited in the text for the collapse of the U.S. banking system in this period?

14. True or False: The creation of the FDIC increased bank stability.

The Federal Reserve

has been chaired by three men over the last 30 years. Paul Volcker (top middle) served as chair from 1979–1987. He was succeeded by Alan Greenspan (bottom left), who chaired the Fed until 2006. Greenspan was then followed by the current chairman, Ben Bernanke (bottom right).

Test your Economics *street-smart* knowledge and see how you compare against other students! Scan here or visit CourseMate for Survey of ECON2.

16

The Federal Reserve and Monetary Policy

The chairperson of the Federal Reserve System is one of the most important policymakers in the country. The importance of the Federal Reserve System and monetary policy cannot be overestimated. In this chapter, we will see how deliberate changes in the money supply can affect aggregate demand and lead to short-run changes in the output of goods and services as well as the price level. That is, monetary policy can be an effective tool for helping to achieve and maintain price stability, full employment, and economic growth. We will also see that monetary-policy tools, just like fiscal-policy tools, have problems of implementation.

16-1 The Federal Reserve System

SECTION CHECK 1

Keep the following questions in mind as you read through this section.

1. What is the most important function of a central bank?
2. Who controls the Federal Reserve System?
3. How is the Fed tied to Congress and the executive branch?

In most countries of the world, the job of manipulating the supply of money belongs to the "central bank."

16-1a THE FUNCTIONS OF A CENTRAL BANK

A central bank performs many functions. First, the central bank is a "banker's bank." It is the bank where commercial banks maintain their own cash deposits—their reserves. Second, the central bank performs a number of service functions for commercial banks, such as transferring funds and checks between various commercial banks in the banking system. Third, the central bank typically serves as the primary bank for the central government, handling, for example, its payroll accounts. Fourth, the central bank buys and sells foreign currencies and generally assists in the completion of financial transactions with other countries. Fifth, it serves as the "lender of last resort," helping banking institutions in financial distress. Sixth, the central bank is concerned with the stability of the banking system and the money supply, which, as we have already seen, results from the loan decisions of banks. The central bank can and does impose regulations on private commercial banks; it thereby regulates the size of the money supply and influences the level of economic activity. The central bank also implements monetary policy, which, along with fiscal policy, forms the basis of efforts to direct the economy to perform in accordance with macroeconomic goals.

> **The Six Functions of the Fed**
>
> 1) Banker's bank
> 2) Service functions for commercial banks
> 3) Bank for the government
> 4) Manages transactions with other countries
> 5) Lender of last resort
> 6) Maintains banking system stability

© iStockphoto.com/subjug

16-1b LOCATION OF THE FEDERAL RESERVE SYSTEM

In most countries, the central bank is a single bank; for example, the central bank of Great Britain, the Bank of England, is a single institution located in London. In the United States, however, the central bank is 12 institutions, closely tied together and collectively called the Federal Reserve System. The Federal Reserve System, or Fed, as it is nicknamed, comprises separate banks in Boston, New York, Philadelphia, Richmond, Atlanta, Dallas, Cleveland, Chicago, St. Louis, Minneapolis–St. Paul, Kansas City, and San Francisco. As Exhibit 16.1 shows, these banks and their branches are spread all over the country, but they are most heavily concentrated in the eastern states.

Each of the 12 banks has branches in key cities in its district. For example, the Federal Reserve Bank of Cleveland serves the fourth Federal Reserve district and has branches in Pittsburgh, Cincinnati, and Columbus. Each Federal Reserve Bank has its own board of directors and, to a limited extent, can set its own policies. Effectively, however, the 12 banks act in unison on major policy issues, with control of major policy decisions resting with the Board of Governors and the Federal Open Market Committee, headquartered in Washington, D.C. The Chairman of the Federal Reserve Board of Governors (currently Ben Bernanke) is generally regarded as one of the most important and powerful economic policymakers in the country.

16-1c THE FED'S RELATIONSHIP TO THE FEDERAL GOVERNMENT

The Federal Reserve System was created in 1913 because the U.S. banking system had so little stability and no central direction. Technically, the Fed is privately owned by the banks that "belong" to it. Banks are not required to belong to the Fed; however, since the passage of new legislation in 1980, virtually no difference exists between the requirements for member and nonmember banks.

The private ownership of the Fed is essentially meaningless, because the Federal Reserve Board of Governors, which controls major policy decisions, is appointed by the president of the United States, not by the stockholders. The owners of the Fed have relatively little control over its operations and receive only small fixed dividends on their modest financial stake in the system. Again, the feature of private ownership but public control was a compromise made to appease commercial banks opposed to direct public (government) regulation.

The Fed's Ties to the Executive Branch

An important aspect of the Fed's operation is that, historically, it has enjoyed a considerable amount of independence from both the executive and legislative branches of government. In fact, central banks with greater degrees of independence appear to have a lower annual inflation rate. True, the president appoints the seven members of the Board of Governors, subject to Senate approval; but the term of appointment is 14 years. No member of the Federal Reserve Board will face reappointment from the president who initially made the appointment, because presidential tenure is limited to two four-year terms. Moreover, the terms of board members are staggered, so a new appointment is made only every two years. It is practically impossible for a single president to appoint a majority of the members of the board; and even if it were possible, members have little fear of losing their jobs as a result of presidential wrath. The chair of the Federal Reserve Board is a member of the Board of Governors and serves a four-year term. The chair is truly the chief executive officer of the system and effectively runs it, with considerable help from the presidents of the 12 regional banks.

16-1d FED OPERATIONS

Many of the key policy decisions of the Federal Reserve are actually made by its Federal Open Market Committee (FOMC), which consists of the seven members of the Board of Governors; the president of the New York Federal Reserve Bank; and four other presidents of Federal Reserve Banks, who serve on the

EXHIBIT 16.1 Boundaries of Federal Reserve Districts and Their Branch Territories

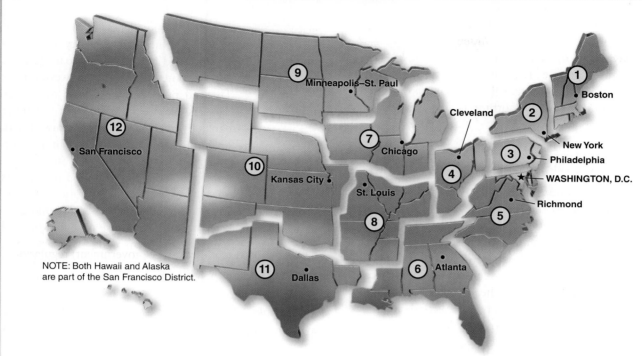

NOTE: Both Hawaii and Alaska are part of the San Francisco District.

SOURCE: Board of Governors of the Federal Reserve System, *95th Annual Report*, 2008, Maps of the Federal Reserve System. Federal Reserve. Washington, D.C. June 2009. Available at http://federalreserve.gov/boarddocs/rptcongress/annual08/default.htm (accessed March 27, 2010).

committee on a rotating basis. The FOMC makes most of the key decisions influencing the direction and size of changes in the money supply; and their regular, closed meetings are accordingly considered important by the business community, news media, and government.

SECTION CHECK 1 ANSWERS

1. Of the six major functions of a central bank, the most important is its role in regulating the money supply.

2. The Federal Reserve System consists of 12 Federal Reserve banks. Although these banks are independent institutions, they act largely in unison on major policy decisions. The Federal Reserve Board of Governors and the Federal Open Market Committee are the prime decision makers for U.S. monetary policy.

3. The President of the United States appoints members of the Federal Reserve Board of Governors to a 14-year term, with only one appointment made every two years. The president also selects the Chair of the Federal Reserve Board, who serves a four-year term. The only other government intervention in the Fed can come from legislation passed in congress.

16-2 How Does the Federal Reserve Change the Money Supply?

SECTION CHECK 2

Keep the following questions in mind as you read through this section.

1. What are the three major tools of the Fed?

2. How can the Fed stimulate the economy?

3. How can the Fed restrain the economy?

As noted previously, the Federal Reserve Board of Governors and the FOMC are the prime decision makers for U.S. monetary policy. They decide whether to expand the money supply and, it is hoped, the real level of economic activity, or to contract the money supply, hoping to cool inflationary pressures. How does the Fed control the money supply, particularly when it is the privately owned commercial banks that actually create and destroy money by making loans, as we discussed earlier?

The Fed has three major methods by which to control the supply of money: It can engage in open market operations, change reserve requirements, or change its discount rate. Of these three, by far the most important is open market operations.

16-2a OPEN MARKET OPERATIONS

Open market operations involve the purchase and sale of government bonds by the Federal Reserve System. At its regular meetings, the FOMC decides to buy or sell government bonds. Open market operations are the most important method the Fed uses to influence the money supply for several reasons. First, it is a device that can be implemented quickly and cheaply—the Fed merely calls an agent who buys or sells bonds. Second, it can be done quietly, without a lot of political debate or a public announcement. Third, it is a rather powerful tool, as any given purchase or sale of bonds has an ultimate impact several times the amount of the initial transaction. Fourth, the Fed can use this tool to change the money supply by a small or large amount on any given day.

The trading desk at the Federal Reserve Bank in New York is responsible for buying and selling government bonds. When the Fed wants to increase the money supply, the FOMC tells the trading desk at the Federal Reserve Bank in New York to buy U.S. government bonds from the public in the nation's bond market. The seller of the bonds will likely deposit their new funds in the bank, increasing excess reserves. The new reserves would lead to new loans and checking account deposits, putting the money multiplier in motion and ultimately increasing the money supply.

If the Fed wanted to decrease the money supply, the FOMC would tell the trading desk to sell government bonds to the public in the nation's bond market. The buyers would pay with checks drawn from their bank. The reserves at their bank would fall. The decrease in reserves would lead to fewer loans and checkable account deposits, setting the money multiplier in motion in reverse, leading to a reduction in the money supply.

In short, if the Fed believes the economy needs to be stimulated, it will buy government bonds. If the Fed wishes to slow the economy down, it will sell government bonds.

open market operations purchase and sale of government securities by the Federal Reserve System

16-2b THE RESERVE REQUIREMENT

Even though open market operations are the most important and widely utilized tool for achieving monetary objectives that the Fed has at its disposal, they are not its potentially most powerful tool. The Fed possesses the power to change the reserve requirements of member banks by altering the reserve ratio. It can have an immediate and significant impact on the ability of member banks to create money. Suppose the banking system as a whole has $500 billion in deposits and $60 billion in reserves, with a reserve ratio of 12 percent. Because $60 billion is 12 percent of $500 billion, the system has no excess reserves. Suppose now that the Fed lowers reserve requirements by changing the reserve ratio to 10 percent. Banks then are required to keep only $50 billion in reserves ($500 billion $\times$ 0.10), but they still have $60 billion. Thus, the lowering of the reserve requirement gives banks $10 billion in excess reserves. The banking system as a whole can expand deposits and the money stock by a multiple of this amount, in this case 10 (10% equals 1/10; the banking multiplier is the reciprocal of this, or 10). The lowering of the reserve requirement in this case, then, would permit an expansion in deposits of $100 billion, which represents a 20 percent increase in the stock of money, from $500 to $600 billion.

When Does the Fed Use This Tool?

Relatively small reserve requirement changes can thus have a big impact on the potential supply of money. This tool is so potent, in fact, that it is seldom used. In other words, the power of the reserve requirement is not only its advantage but also its disadvantage, because a small reduction in the reserve requirement can make a huge change in the number of dollars that are in excess reserves in banks all over the country. Such huge changes in required reserves and excess reserves have the potential to disrupt the economy.

Frequent changes in the reserve requirement would make it difficult for banks to plan. For example, a banker might worry that if she makes loans now and then the Fed raises the reserve requirement, she would not have enough reserves to meet the new reserve requirements. However, if she does not make loans and the Fed leaves the reserve requirement alone, she loses the opportunity to earn income on those loans.

Carpenters don't use sledgehammers to hammer small nails or tacks; the tool is too big and powerful to use effectively. For the same reason, the Fed changes reserve requirements rather infrequently. For example, between 1970 and 1980, the Fed changed the reserve requirement only twice, and less than 1 percent on each occasion. Furthermore, changes in the reserve requirement, because they are so powerful, are a sign that monetary policy has swung strongly in a new direction.

Fed Now Pays Interest on Reserves

In October of 2008, the Fed began to pay interest on reserves held with the Fed—both required reserves and excess reserves. This provides the Fed with a new tool. If the Fed raised the interest rate it paid on reserves, we would expect banks to hold more in excess reserves, decreasing the size of the money multiplier and reducing the money supply. If the Fed wanted to increase the money supply, it could decrease the interest rate it pays on reserves, lowering holdings of excess reserves and increasing the money multiplier.

16-2c THE DISCOUNT RATE

Banks having trouble meeting their reserve requirement can borrow funds directly from the Fed at its discount window. A bank might borrow from the Fed when it has too few reserves to meet the reserve requirement or has recently experienced an unexpectedly high amount of withdrawals. The interest rate the Fed charges on these borrowed reserves is called the **discount rate**. The Fed can control the money supply by altering the discount rate. If the Fed raises the discount rate, it discourages banks from borrowing reserves from the Fed. This reduces the quantity of reserves in the banking system, which leads to a reduction in the money supply. That is, if the Fed wants to contract the money supply, it will raise the dis-

> **discount rate** interest rate that the Fed charges commercial banks for the loans it extends to them

A lower discount rate will encourage banks to borrow from the Fed, increasing the quantity of reserves and the money supply.

count rate, making it more costly for banks to borrow reserves.

If the Fed is promoting an expansion of money and credit, it will lower the discount rate, making it cheaper for banks to borrow reserves. Thus, a lower discount rate will encourage banks to borrow from the Fed, increasing the quantity of reserves and the money supply.

The discount rate sometimes changes fairly frequently, often several times a year. Sometimes the rate will be moved several times in the same direction within a single year, which has a substantial cumulative effect.

The Significance of the Discount Rate

The discount rate is a relatively unimportant tool, mainly because member banks do not rely heavily on the Fed for borrowed funds and often the Fed would not lend them all they want to borrow. It is something most of them believe should be reserved for real emergencies. In October of 1987, when the stock market crashed, Fed chair Alan Greenspan used discount lending to help financial institutions that were in trouble. Many Wall Street brokerage firms needed temporary funds to finance the high volume of stock trades. The Fed was there to help. Also, in the financial crisis of 2008, the collapse of the housing market coupled with mortgage defaults meant that many financial institutions were in trouble. The Fed provided loans to many of these financial institutions that were in trouble.

© Rubberball/Getty Images

When banks have short-term needs for cash to meet reserve requirements, they are more likely to take a short-term (often overnight) loan from another bank in the federal funds market. For that reason, many people pay a lot of attention to the interest rate on federal funds.

In recent years, the Federal Reserve has increased its focus on the federal funds rate as the primary indicator of its stance on monetary policy. The Fed announces a federal funds rate target at each FOMC meeting. This rate is watched closely, because it affects all the interest rates throughout the economy—auto loans, mortgages, and so on.

Normally the discount rate is set 1.0 percentage point above the federal funds rate target. Setting the discount rate above the fund rate is designed to keep banks from turning to this source. Thus, most discount lending is small.

The Fed could use the discount rate by altering the discount rate relative to the federal funds rate. However, the discount rate's main significance is that changes in the rate are commonly viewed as a signal of the Fed's intentions with respect to monetary policy. Discount rate changes are widely publicized, unlike open market operations, which are carried out in private and announced several weeks later in the minutes of the FOMC.

However, in response to the financial crisis, there was a considerable amount of lending through the discount window beginning in the fall of 2008. The Fed reduced the spread between the discount rate and the federal funds rate; by the spring of 2008, the discount rate was only 0.25 percentage point above the federal funds rate, when it had usually been a full percentage point higher.

16-2d HOW THE FED REDUCES THE MONEY SUPPLY

The Fed can do three things to reduce the money supply or reduce the rate of growth in the money supply: (1) sell bonds, (2) raise reserve requirements, or (3) raise the discount rate. Of course, the Fed could also opt to

use a combination of these three tools in its approach. These moves tend to decrease aggregate demand.

16-2e HOW THE FED INCREASES THE MONEY SUPPLY

If the Fed is concerned about underutilizing resources (e.g., unemployment), it can engage in precisely the opposite policies: (1) buy bonds, (2) lower reserve requirements, or (3) lower the discount rate. The Fed can also use a combination of these three approaches. These moves tend to increase aggregate demand.

16-2f DIFFICULTIES IN CONTROLLING THE MONEY SUPPLY

In a fractional reserve banking system, the Fed cannot precisely control the money supply because of two problems: people and banks.

The Fed cannot precisely control the amount of money that people want to hold as currency in circulation versus as deposits in their financial institutions. The more cash people put in the bank, the more excess reserves the bank has for lending purposes and the more money created. Alternatively, if people are concerned about the health of the financial system and choose to take money out of the bank in order to hold more currency, it would reduce banks' excess reserves, reducing lending and the supply of money. Either change can alter the money supply without any action from the Fed.

Banks can also choose to not lend out all of their excess reserves. When banks keep more excess reserves, the Fed has less control over the money supply because banks rather than Fed policy dictates how much will be lent out. If banks make money by making loans, why would they keep excess reserves? Banks may choose to become more cautious because of the current economic climate; to avoid risk they may choose to hold on to more excess reserves. Consequently, the banking system would create less money with a given level of reserves than it normally would and the money supply would fall.

This may not be a huge problem because the Fed keeps massive amounts of data on the behavior of banks and their depositors. As a result, changes in currency

Tools for reducing the money supply
1) Sell bonds
2) Raise reserve requirements
3) Raise the discount rate

Tools for increasing the money supply
1) Buy bonds
2) Lower reserve requirements
3) Lower the discount rate

© iStockphoto.com/subjug

QE2 to the Rescue?

In the fall of 2010, the Federal Reserve announced a plan to resume monetary easing by purchasing $600 billion in long-term Treasuries. The plan, which expired in June of 2011, was quantitative easing, number 2 (QE2). It was called number 2 because the Fed had already used asset purchases earlier, during the financial crisis. Japan used a similar policy in the 1990s, when its interest rates were also near zero.

Despite potential risks, the Federal Reserve's plans to buy $600 billion in U.S. Treasury bonds by June of next year will expand the money supply and should stimulate the economy, according to National Center for Policy Analysis Distinguished Fellow Bob McTeer, former president of the Federal Reserve Bank of Dallas and member of the Federal Open Market Committee (FOMC).

According to McTeer, "Banks aren't exactly hoarding cash, but they're not lending enough either, that's because holding extra cash reserves has been prudent during these turbulent times. By providing more reserves through the purchase of Treasuries, however, there will be fewer benefits to holding additional cash and it will increasingly be in bankers' interests to put their excess reserves to work through loans and investments."

McTeer acknowledged that the magnitude of quantitative easing—$600 billion by June 2011—is "large but all of it may not be needed." "The fear, of course, is inflation," McTeer warned. However, "some measures of inflation are below one percent and there is a great deal of slack in the economy; capacity utilization is low and unemployment is high. So the Fed believes that under these conditions it can stimulate growth in the money supply without a high risk of inflation."

A number of economists are also concerned that quantitative easing could depreciate the value of the dollar in foreign exchange markets. McTeer states, "More dollars created might depress it in foreign exchange markets but, if the monetary surge works, a healthier U.S. economy might strengthen it. In any case, flexible exchange rates are intended to reconcile whatever domestic policies are appropriate for domestic conditions with the rest of the world. Internal policies may have external circumstances, but charges that the intent is to spur the domestic economy through currency depreciation are way off base."

The QE2 program has increased bank reserves, but banks have added to their excess reserves rather than creating large amounts of money through lending and investing. There has been no multiple expansion of the money supply, as would be the case if the banking system kept very few excess reserves.

Monetary Easing versus Blockage

From Exploring Economics, 6e, by Robert L. Sexton, ISBN: 9781111970307

circulation or excess reserve holdings by banks can be remedied with offsetting policies the Fed can control.

16-3 Money, Interest Rates, and Aggregate Demand

SECTION CHECK 3

Keep the following questions in mind as you read through this section.

1. How do changes in income change the money market equilibrium?

2. How does the Fed's buying and selling of bonds affect RGDP in the short run?

3. How are the real and nominal interest rates connected in the short run?

The Federal Reserve's policies with respect to the money supply have a direct effect on short-run nominal interest rates and, accordingly, on the components of aggregate demand.

16-3a THE MONEY MARKET

money market market in which money demand and money supply determine the equilibrium interest rate

The **money market** is the market in which money demand and money supply determine the equilibrium *nominal* interest rate.

When the Fed acts to change the money supply by changing one of its policy variables, it alters the money market equilibrium.

Money has several functions, but why would people hold money instead of other financial assets? That is, what is responsible for the demand for money? Transaction purposes, precautionary reasons, and asset purposes are at least some of the determinants of the demand for money.

Transactions Demand for Money

First, the primary reason that money is demanded is for transaction purposes—to facilitate exchange. Workers are generally paid by the week or month. However, most people want to hold on to money so they can buy goods and services on a continual basis, not just on payday. They want to keep money for everyday predictable expenses. For example, nobody would want to buy pizza with stocks and bonds. How costly would it be to convert less liquid assets like stocks or bonds into goods and services? Those costs would include the loss of interest and possible withdrawal penalties. In addition, the higher a person's income, the more transactions that person is likely to make (because consumption is income related); the greater will be GDP; and the greater will be the demand for money for transaction purposes, *ceteris paribus*.

Precautionary Demand for Money

Second, people like to have money on hand for precautionary reasons—so called "mattress money." If unexpected medical or other expenses require an unusual outlay of cash, people want to be prepared. The extent to which an individual holds cash for precautionary reasons depends partly on that person's income and partly on the opportunity cost of holding money, which is determined by market rates of interest. The higher the market interest rates, the higher the opportunity cost of holding money; and so people will hold less of their financial wealth as money.

Asset Demand for Money

Third, money has a trait—liquidity—that makes it a desirable asset. Other things being equal, people prefer assets that are more liquid to those that are less liquid. That is, people want to be able to easily convert some of their money into goods and services. For this reason, most people wish to have some of their portfolio in the form of money. At higher interest rates on other assets, the amount of money desired for this purpose will be smaller, because the opportunity cost of holding money will have risen.

16-3b THE DEMAND FOR MONEY AND THE NOMINAL INTEREST RATE

The quantity of money demanded varies inversely with the nominal interest rate. When interest rates are higher, the opportunity cost—in terms of the interest income on alternative assets—of holding monetary assets is higher, and persons will want to hold less money. At the same time, the demand for money, particularly for transaction purposes, is highly dependent on income levels, because the transaction volume varies directly with income. Finally, the demand for money depends on the price level. If the price level increases, buyers will need more money to purchase their goods and services. If the price level falls, buyers will need less money to purchase their goods and services.

The demand curve for money is presented in Exhibit 16.2. At lower interest rates, the quantity of money demanded is greater, illustrated by a movement from A to B. That is, the lower the interest rate, the lower the opportunity cost of holding money. An increase in income will lead to an increase in the demand for money, depicted by a rightward shift in the money demand (MD) curve, a movement from A to C.

16-3c WHY IS THE SUPPLY OF MONEY RELATIVELY INELASTIC?

The supply of money is largely governed by the regulatory policies of the central bank. Whether interest rates are 4 percent or 14 percent, banks seeking to maximize profits will increase lending as long as they have reserves above their desired level. Even a 4 percent return on loans provides more profit than maintaining those assets in non-interest-bearing cash or reserve accounts at the Fed, which currently earn very low interest rate from the Fed. Given this fact, the money supply is effectively almost perfectly inelastic with respect to interest rates over their plausible range. Therefore, we draw the money supply (MS) curve as vertical, *ceteris paribus*, in Exhibit 16.3, with changes

EXHIBIT 16.2 Money Demand, Interest Rates, and Income

A → B = Increase in the quantity of money demanded
A → C = Increase in the demand for money

© Cengage Learning 2014

in Federal Reserve policies acting to shift the money supply curve.

16-3d THE MONEY MARKET

Equilibrium in the money market is found by combining the money demand and money supply curves, as shown in Exhibit 16.3. Money market equilibrium occurs at that *nominal* interest rate where the quantity of money demanded equals the quantity of

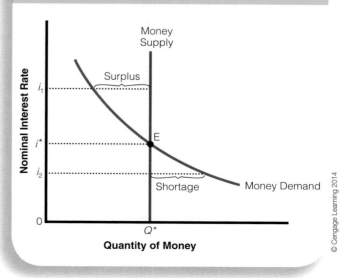

EXHIBIT 16.3 Money Market Equilibrium

© Cengage Learning 2014

money supplied. Initially, the money market is in equilibrium at i^* in Exhibit 16.3.

Money Market Equilibrium

In Exhibit 16.3, we see that equilibrium occurs at point E, where the quantity of money demanded by the public is equal to the quantity of the money supplied by the banking system, given the policies adopted by the Fed. At i_2, below the equilibrium interest rate, the quantity of money that people want to hold is greater than the quantity that is available from the banking system—there is a shortage at i_2. Consequently, people will try to increase their holdings of money by reducing their holdings of bonds or other interest-bearing assets. Because many people are trying to rid themselves of bonds, bond sellers realize they must increase interest on bonds to attract buyers. Thus, the interest rate rises to the equilibrium level, i^*.

At i_1, the interest rate is above the equilibrium level, the quantity of money people want to hold is less than the quantity that is available from the banking system; there is a surplus of money at i_1. Those that are holding the surplus of money (cash and checkable deposits) will try to exchange money for other assets such as bonds. As the demand for bonds rises, bond sellers can pay less interest but still attract enough buyers. As the interest rate falls, people become more willing to hold money, until the interest rate reaches equilibrium at i^*, where people are content holding the money the banking system has supplied.

The Money Market and the Aggregate Demand Curve

Recall the interest rate effect that moved us along the aggregate demand curve when the price level changed. We now look at that relationship in more detail. Specifically, when the price level rises from PL_1 to PL_2 in Exhibit 16.4, people demand more money and the money demand curve shifts from MD_1 to MD_2. That is, at the new higher price level, PL_2, many goods and services will have higher prices, so people will want to hold more money, MD_2 rather than MD_1.

How does an increase in the demand for money affect the money market? The increase in the demand for money, coupled with a fixed money supply (controlled by the Fed), will cause the interest rate to increase from i_1 to i_2. At the higher interest rate, the cost of borrowing and the return to saving are higher. In short, fewer households will be borrowing for houses and cars, and fewer firms will be investing in new factories and equipment. Thus, the quantity of RGDP demanded falls from $RGDP_1$ to $RGDP_2$.

Of course, the reverse is true as well. A lower price level leads to a decrease in the demand for money because, on average, goods and services have lower price tags. The reduction in the demand for money causes a reduction in the interest rate, which encourages consumption and investment that increases RGDP demanded. Hence, this leads to the downward sloping aggregate demand curve—a lower price level leads to an increase in RGDP demanded.

EXHIBIT 16.4 The Money Market and the Aggregate Demand Curve

a. Money Market

b. Aggregate Demand Curve

© Cengage Learning 2014

How Do Income Changes Affect the Equilibrium Position?

Rising national income increases the demand for money, shifting the money demand curve to the right from MD_1 to MD_2 and leading to a new higher equilibrium interest rate.

How Would an Increase in the Money Supply Affect Equilibrium Interest Rates and Aggregate Demand?

A Federal Reserve policy change that increased the money supply would be depicted by a shift in the money supply curve to the right. As a result of this shift, the equilibrium quantity of money demanded increases as equilibrium interest rates fall. The immediate impact of expansionary monetary policy is to decrease the interest rate. Because the money demand curve has not changed, the interest rate falls to the new equilibrium at E_2. The interest rate falls to induce people to hold the additional money supplied by the banking system, MS_2. The lower interest rate, or the fall in the cost of borrowing money, then leads to an increase in aggregate demand for goods and services at the current price level. The lower interest rate will increase home sales, car sales, business investments, and so on. That is, an increase in the money supply will lead to lower interest rates and an increase in aggregate demand, as seen in Exhibit 16.5. Thus, when the Fed changes policy to increase the money supply, the interest rate falls. This increases RGDP demanded at each and every price level. If the Fed changes policy to reduce the money supply, the interest rate would rise, which would lower RGDP demanded at each and every price level.

16-3e DOES THE FED TARGET THE MONEY SUPPLY OR INTEREST RATES?

Some economists believe that the Fed should try to control interest rates. Other economists believe that the Fed should try to control the money supply. Unfortunately, the Fed cannot do both—it must pick one or the other.

Recall that the Fed controls the money supply but not the money demand. The demand for money is determined by households and firms. In Exhibit 16.6 on the next page, the economy is initially at point A, where the interest rate is i_1 and the quantity of money is at Q_1. Now, suppose the demand for money were to increase because of an increase in national income, an increase in the price level, or because people desire to hold more money. As a result, the demand curve for money shifts to the right, from MD_1 to MD_2. If the Fed decides it does not want the money supply to increase, it can pursue a policy of no monetary growth, which leads to an increase in the interest rate to i_2 at point C. The Fed could also try to keep the interest rate stable at i_1, but it can only do so by increasing the growth in the money supply through expansionary monetary policy. The Fed cannot simultaneously pursue policies of no monetary growth and monetary expansion; it must choose a higher interest rate, a greater money supply, or some combination of both. The Fed cannot completely control both the growth in the money supply and the interest rate. If it attempts to keep the interest rate steady in the face of increased money demand, it must increase the growth in the money supply. If it tries to keep the growth of the money supply in check in the face of increased money demand, the interest rate will rise.

EXHIBIT 16.5 The Impact of an Increase in the Supply of Money

a. Impact on the Money Market

b. Impact on Aggregate Demand

© Cengage Learning 2014

EXHIBIT 16.6 Fed Targeting Money Supply versus the Interest Rate

In short, monetary policy can be applied in terms of the money supply or the interest rate (the federal funds rate). When FOMC sets a federal funds rate target, the Fed's bond traders are told to do whatever is necessary to get the equilibrium interest rate to the target level. To lower the federal funds rate, Fed bond traders buy government bonds. This increases the money supply and lowers the interest rate. If FOMC raises the target for the federal funds rate, its bond traders sell government bonds. This decreases the money supply and raises the interest rate.

The Problem

The problem with targeting the money supply is that the demand for money fluctuates considerably in the short run. Focusing on the growth in the money supply when the demand for money is changing unpredictably leads to large fluctuations in interest rates, as occurred in the U.S. economy during the late 1970s and early 1980s. These erratic changes in interest rates could seriously disrupt the investment climate.

Keeping interest rates in check also creates problems. For example, when the economy grows, the demand for money also grows, so the Fed has to increase the money supply to keep interest rates from rising. If the economy is in a recession, the demand for money falls, and the Fed has to contract the money supply to keep interest rates from falling. This approach leads to the wrong policy prescription—expanding the money supply during a boom eventually leads

to inflation, and contracting the money supply during a recession makes the recession even worse.

16-3f WHICH INTEREST RATE DOES THE FED TARGET?

The Fed targets the federal funds rate. Remember the federal funds rate is the interest rate that banks charge each other for short-term loans. A bank that may be short of reserves might borrow from another bank that has excess reserves. The Fed has been targeting the federal funds rate since about 1965. At the close of the meetings of the FOMC, the Fed usually announces whether the federal funds rate target will be increased, decreased, or left alone as shown in Exhibit 16.7.

Monetary policy decisions may be enacted either through the money supply or through the interest rate. That is, if the Fed wants to pursue a contractionary monetary policy (a reduction in aggregate demand), this policy can take the form of a reduction in the money supply or a higher interest rate. If the Fed wants to pursue an expansionary monetary policy (an increase in aggregate demand), this policy can take the form of an increase in the money supply or a lower interest rate. So why is the interest rate used? First, many economists believe that the primary effects of monetary policy are felt through the interest rate. Second, the money supply is difficult to measure accurately. Third, as we mentioned earlier, changes in the demand for money may complicate money supply targets. Last, people are more familiar with changes in the interest rate than with changes in the money supply.

16-3g DOES THE FED INFLUENCE THE REAL INTEREST RATE IN THE SHORT RUN?

Most economists believe that in the short run the Fed can control the nominal interest rate and the real

EXHIBIT 16.7 Federal Funds Rate

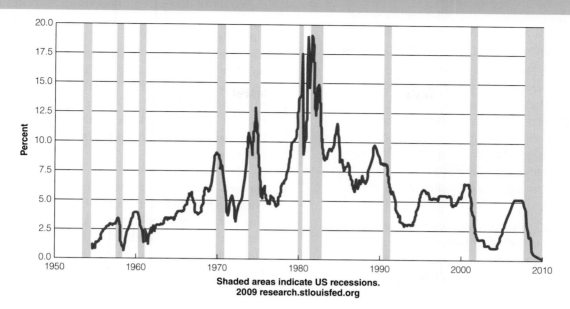

Shaded areas indicate US recessions.
2009 research.stlouisfed.org

SOURCES: Federal Reserve, *Federal Reserve Statistical Release*, Historical Data: Federal Funds (effective) Annual, Washington, D. C. March 26, 2010. Available at http://www.federalreserve.gov/releases/h15/data.htm (accessed March 27, 2010); National Bureau of Economic Research, Inc., Business Cycle Expansions and Contractions, U.S. Department of Commerce. Washington, D.C., December 1, 2008. Available at http://www.nber .org/cycles.html (accessed March 18, 2010).

interest rate. Recall that the real interest rate is equal to the nominal interest rate minus the expected inflation rate. Therefore, a change in the nominal interest rate tends to change the real interest rate by the same amount, because the expected inflation rate is slow to change in the short run. That is, if the expected inflation rate does not change, the relationship between the nominal and real interest rates is a direct relationship: A 1 percent reduction in the nominal interest rate will generally lead to a 1 percent reduction in the real interest rate in the short run. However, for the long run—several years after the inflation rate has adjusted—the equilibrium real interest rate will be given by the intersection of the demand and supply of loanable funds curves.

Exhibit 16.8 summarizes the preceding discussion of the tools available to the Fed for enacting monetary policy.

EXHIBIT 16.8 Summary of Fed Tools for Monetary Policy

Macroeconomic Problem	Monetary Policy Prescription	Fed Policy Tools
Unemployment (Slow or negative RGDP growth rate—below $RGDP_{NR}$)	Expansionary monetary policy to increase aggregate demand	Buy bonds Lower discount rate Lower reserve requirement
Inflation (Rapid RGDP growth rate—beyond $RGDP_{NR}$)	Contractionary monetary policy to decrease aggregate demand	Sell bonds Raise discount rate Raise reserve requirement

© Cengage Learning 2014

16-4 Expansionary and Contractionary Monetary Policy

SECTION CHECK 4

Keep the following questions in mind as you read through this section.

1. What is expansionary monetary policy?
2. What is contractionary monetary policy?
3. How does monetary policy impact real GDP and the price level?

Let us take a look at how the Fed might use its monetary policy to regulate economic growth.

16-4a EXPANSIONARY MONETARY POLICY IN A RECESSIONARY GAP

If the Fed engages in expansionary monetary policy to combat a recessionary gap, the increase in the money supply will lower the interest rate. The lower interest rate reduces the cost of borrowing and the return to saving. Therefore, firms invest in new plants and equipment, while households increase their investment in

housing at the lower interest rate. In short, when the Fed increases the money supply, interest rates fall, and the quantity demanded of goods and services increases at each and every price level. The aggregate demand curve shifts from AD_1 to AD_2, as seen in Exhibit 16.9. The result is greater RGDP growth at a higher price level at E_2. In this case, the Fed has eliminated the recession, and RGDP is equal to the potential level of output at $RGDP_{NR}$. During the recession of 2001, the Fed aggressively lowered the federal funds rate to stimulate aggregate demand when it was faced with a recessionary gap.

For example, in the first half of 2001, the Fed slashed interest rates to their lowest levels since August 1994. Between January 2001 and August 2001, the Fed cut the federal funds rate target by 3 percentage points, clearly demonstrating that it was concerned that the economy was dangerously close to falling into a recession. Then came the events of September 11 and the corporate scandals. By the end of the year, the federal funds rate, which began at 6.5 percent, was at 1.75 percent, the lowest it had been since 1961. With the slow recovery, the Fed pushed the rate down further, to 1.25 percent in November 2002. The Fed's actions were aimed at increasing consumer confidence, restoring stock market wealth, and stimulating investment. That is, the Fed's move was designed to increase aggregate demand in an effort to increase output and employment to long-run equilibrium at E_2.

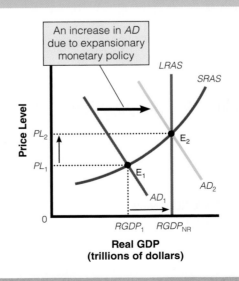

EXHIBIT 16.9 Expansionary Monetary Policy in a Recessionary Gap

© Cengage Learning 2014

16-4b CONTRACTIONARY MONETARY POLICY IN AN INFLATIONARY GAP

The Fed may engage in contractionary monetary policy if the economy faces an inflationary gap. Suppose the economy is at initial short-run equilibrium, E_1, in Exhibit 16.10. In order to combat inflation, suppose the Fed engages in an open market sale of bonds. This would lead to a decrease in the money supply, causing the interest rate to rise. The higher interest rate means that borrowing is more expensive, and the return to saving is higher. Consequently, firms find it more costly to invest in plants and equipment, and households find it more costly to finance new homes. In short, when the Fed decreases the money supply, it raises the interest rate and decreases the quantity of goods and services demanded at every price level. That is, the aggregate demand curve shifts leftward from AD_1 to AD_2 in Exhibit 16.10. The result is a lower RGDP and a lower price level, at E_2. The economy is now at $RGDP_{NR}$ where RGDP equals the potential level of output.

16-4c MONETARY POLICY IN THE OPEN ECONOMY

For simplicity, we have assumed that the global economy does not affect domestic monetary policy. This assumption is incorrect. Suppose the Fed decides to pursue an expansionary policy by buying bonds on the open market. As we have seen, when the Fed buys bonds on the open market, the immediate effect is that the money supply increases and interest rates fall. With lower domestic interest rates, some domestic investors will invest funds in foreign markets, exchanging dollars for foreign currency, which leads to a deprecia- tion of the dollar (a decrease in the value of the dollar). The depreciation of the dollar makes the U.S. market more attractive to for- eign buyers and foreign markets relatively less attractive to domestic buyers. That is, this shift means an increase in net exports— fewer imports and greater exports—and an increase in RGDP in the short run.

Similarly, the Fed may pursue a contractionary mon- etary policy by selling bonds on the open market. When

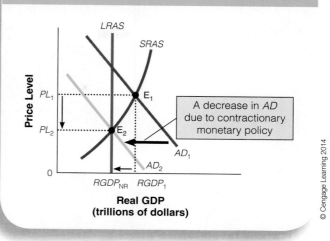

EXHIBIT 16.10 Contractionary Monetary Policy in an Inflationary Gap

A decrease in AD due to contractionary monetary policy

© Cengage Learning 2014

the Fed sells bonds on the open market, the immediate effect is it reduces the money supply and causes interest rates to rise; foreign investors will convert their curren- cies to dollars to take advantage of the relatively higher interest rates. These purchases will lead to an appreciation of the dollar (an increase in the value of a currency), which will make U.S. goods and services relatively more expensive—foreigners will import less and domestic consumers will buy more exports. The result is a decrease in net exports and a reduction in RGDP in the short run.

Corporate scandals and the September 11 terrorist attacks ex- acerbated the economic downturn of 2001. In its efforts to fight off a recession, the Fed cut rates from a high of 6.5 percent all the way down to 1.75 percent.

© Greg Smith/CORBIS

1400 Smith Street

MONEY AND THE ADIAS MODEL

Q&A

Q: During the Great Depression in the United States, the price level fell, the money wage rate fell, real GDP fell, and unemployment reached 25 percent. Investment fell, and as banks failed, the money supply fell dramatically. Can you show the effect of these changes from a vibrant 1929 economy to a battered 1932 economy using the *AD/AS* model?

A: The 1929 economy was at PL_{1929} and $RGDP_{NR}$, as you can see in the accompanying exhibit. The lack of consumer confidence coupled with the large reduction in the money supply, wealth lost in the stock market crash, and falling investment sent the aggregate demand curve reeling. As a result, the aggregate demand curve fell from AD_{1929} to AD_{1932}, real GDP fell to $RGDP_{1932}$, and the price level fell to PL_{1932}.

16-5 Money and Inflation

SECTION CHECK 5

Keep the following questions in mind as you read through this section.

1. What is the equation of exchange?
2. What is the velocity of money?
3. What is the quantity theory of money and prices?

For many centuries, scholars have known that there is a positive relationship between the money supply, the price level, the growth in the money supply, and the inflation rate. In the 1500s, there was a huge influx of gold and silver that flowed into Europe following the Spanish conquest in the New World. The influx of precious metals almost tripled the money supply of Europe. Too many coins were chasing what goods were available, and prices rose steadily in the sixteenth century.

16-5a THE INFLATION RATE AND THE GROWTH IN THE MONEY SUPPLY

One of the major reasons that the control of the money supply is so important is that, in the long run, the amount of money in circulation and the overall price level are closely linked. It is virtually impossible for a country to have sustained inflation without a rapid growth in the money supply. The inflation rate tends to be greater in periods of rapid monetary expansion than in periods of slower growth in the money supply. In Exhibit 16.11 on the next page, we see that international data supports the relationship between higher money growth and a higher inflation rate.

velocity of money a measure of how frequently money is turned over

16-5b THE EQUATION OF EXCHANGE

In the early twentieth century, Yale economist Irving Fisher formalized the relationship between money and the price level with the equation of exchange. The equation of exchange (or quantity equation) can be written as:

$$M \times V = P \times Q$$

where M is the money supply, however defined (usually M_1 or M_2), V is the velocity of money, P is the price level, and Q is real output (RGDP).

The **velocity of money** refers to its "turnover" rate, or the intensity with which money is used. Specifically, V represents the average number of times that each dollar is used in purchasing final goods or services in a one-year period. For example, a $20 bill may travel from you to the delicatessen owner, who passes it on to a doctor for the co-payment on medical services, who passes it on to a car dealership as part of a down payment for a new car. The faster money circulates, the higher the velocity.

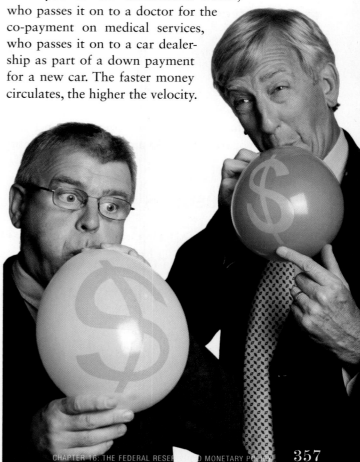

© Digital Vision/Getty Images

EXHIBIT 16.11 Money Supply Growth and Inflation Rates in Selected Countries, 1980–2002

SOURCE: *International Financial Statistics*, International Monetary Fund, Washington, D.C., 2008, Volume LXI, pp. 51–53 and pp. 79–81.

quantity theory of money and prices a theory of the connection between the money supply and the price level when the velocity of money is constant

Velocity is defined as the nominal or current dollar value of output divided by the money supply, or:

$$V = \text{Nominal GDP} / M$$

Suppose we have a simple economy that only produces frozen yogurt. The economy produces 200 quarts of frozen yogurt per year. The frozen yogurt sells for $5 a quart and the quantity

That is, the people in the economy spend $1,000 per year on frozen yogurt. If there is only $100 of money in the economy, each dollar must change hands on average 10 times per year. Thus, the velocity is 10.

The Quantity Theory of Money and Prices

If we make certain assumptions about the variables in the equation of exchange, we can clearly see the relationship between the money supply and the price level. This relationship is called the **quantity theory of money and prices**. If velocity (V) and real GDP (Q) both remain constant, then a 10 percent increase in the money supply will lead to a 10 percent increase in the price level—that is, the money supply and the price level change by the same proportion. We can then extend this equation to link the growth rates of these four variables. Using the *growth version*

V **represents** the average number of times that each dollar is used in purchasing final goods or services in a one-year period.

of money in the economy is $100. Plugging the numbers into our equation, we get:

$$V = \text{Nominal GDP} / M$$
$$= (P \times Q) / M$$
$$= (\$5 \times 200) / \$100 = 10$$

of the quantity equation, we can transform $M \times V = P \times Q$ into:

Growth rate of the money supply + Growth rate of velocity = Growth rate of the price level (inflation rate) + Growth rate of real output

This makes it easier to see the effects of the money supply on the inflation rate. Suppose money growth is 5 percent per year, the growth of real output is 3 percent per year, and velocity has not changed at all—its growth rate is 0 percent. What is the inflation rate? The growth rate of M (5 percent) + the growth rate of V (0 percent) = the growth rate of prices _____ + the growth rate of Q (3 percent). In this situation, the growth rate of prices (the inflation rate) is equal to 2 percent. We can also extend the analysis to predict the inflation rate when real GDP and velocity also vary. For example, if velocity grew at 1 percent annually rather than at zero percent in our example, the inflation rate would be 3 percent rather than 2 percent.

If velocity remains constant, then the growth rate of velocity (the percentage change from one year to the next) will be zero. Then we can simplify our equation once more:

Inflation rate = Growth rate of the money supply − Growth rate of real GDP

If this is the case, there are three possible scenarios:

1. If money supply grows at a faster rate than real GDP, then there will be inflation.
2. If money supply grows at a slower rate than real GDP, then there will be deflation.
3. If money supply grows at the same rate as real GDP, the price level will be stable.

Economists once expected they could treat the velocity of money as a given, because the determinants of velocity they focused on would change only very slowly. We now know that velocity is not constant, but often moves in a fairly predictable pattern. Historically, the velocity of money has been quite stable over a long period of time, particularly when using the M2 definition of money. Thus, the connection between money supply and the price level is still fairly predictable, especially during periods of high inflation.

If an increase in the money supply leads to inflation in the long run, why do countries allow the growth rate of their money supply to increase so rapidly? There are several possible reasons. For instance, due to war or political instability, countries' spending may exceed what they can raise through borrowing from the public or taxation, so they create more money to pay their bills. The more money they create, the larger amount of inflation they will experience.

Hyperinflation

The relationship between the growth rate of the money supply and the inflation rate is particularly strong when there is very rapid inflation, called hyperinflation. One of the most famous cases of hyperinflation was in Germany in the 1920s—inflation rose to roughly 300 percent *per month* for over a year. The German government had incurred large amounts of debt as a result of World War I and could not raise enough money to pay its expenses, so it printed huge amounts of money. The inflation rate increased so quickly that store owners would change their prices in the middle of the day, firms had to pay workers several times a week, and many resorted to barter. Recently, Zimbabwe, Brazil, Argentina, and Russia have all experienced hyperinflation. The cause of hyperinflation is simply excessive money growth.

SECTION CHECK 5 ANSWERS

1. The equation of exchange is expressed as $M \times V = P \times Q$, where M is the money supply, V is the velocity of money, P is the average level of prices of final goods and services, and Q is real GDP in a given year.

2. The velocity of money (V) represents the average number of times that a dollar is used in purchasing final goods or services in a one-year period.

3. The equation of exchange is a particularly useful tool when analyzing the effects of a change in the money supply on the price level or inflation rate in the aggregate economy.

During the 1920s, hyperinflation in Germany got so bad that workers, such as those pictured, used laundry baskets to carry out their pay packets.

© Popperfoto/Getty Images

Chapter 16: Self-Review

Now that you are finished reading the chapter, review the questions below. You can write your answers in the space provided, then go online to see the answers at www.cengagebrain.com.

16-1 THE FEDERAL RESERVE SYSTEM

1. What are the six primary functions of a central bank?
   1)
   2)
   3)
   4)
   5)
   6)

16-2 HOW DOES THE FEDERAL RESERVE CHANGE THE MONEY SUPPLY?

2. True or False: An open market sale of government securities (bonds) would be a tactic of expansionary monetary policy.

3. True or False: An increase in the discount rate would be a tactic of contractionary policy.

4. Fill-in-the-Blank: The money supply _____ if the Fed made an open market purchase of government bonds, *ceteris paribus*.

16-3 MONEY, INTEREST RATES, AND AGGREGATE DEMAND

5. What are the three primary reasons for the demand for money?

6. Fill-in-the-Blank: An _____ relationship exists between the interest rate and the price of bonds.

7. True or False: The Fed signals its intended monetary policy through the federal funds rate target it sets.

8. True or False: If the earnings available on other financial assets rose, you would want to hold less money.

16-4 EXPANSIONARY AND CONTRACTIONARY MONETARY POLICY

9. In which direction would the money supply change if:
   a. the Fed raised the reserve requirement?
   b. the Fed conducted an open market sale of government bonds?
   c. the Fed raised the discount rate?
   d. the Fed conducted an open market sale of government bonds and raised the discount rate?
   e. the Fed conducted an open market purchase of government bonds and raised reserve requirements?

16-5 MONEY AND INFLATION

10. If nominal GDP is $200 billion and the money supply is $50 billion, what must velocity be?

11. True or False: If the money supply increases and velocity does not change, nominal GDP will increase.

12. Fill-in-the-Blank: The equation of exchange is _____.

13. True or False: In the equation of exchange, if *V* doubled, nominal GDP would triple.

The passing of the American Recovery

and Reinvestment Act of 2009 was not without controversy. In an effort to bolster the economy in the face of the financial crisis, the bill offered a wide range of provisions, including tax cuts, spending on welfare programs, and various infrastructure projects. Many questions arose, however, at the time of its passing: How much money should be spent, and on what? When will these initiatives come into effect? Should the government even be getting involved? Beyond the bill itself, further questions arose as to how the fiscal policy of the government fit in with the monetary policy of the Fed. As you can see, fiscal and monetary policy are not easy to implement. We will discuss many of these issues in this chapter.

Test your Economics *street-smart* knowledge and see how you compare against other students! Scan here or visit CourseMate for Survey of ECON2.

17

Issues in Macroeconomic Theory and Policy

We begin this chapter by discussing the problems that exist in implementing fiscal and monetary policy. We discuss the problems with crowding out, time lags, imperfect information, and coordination. Can human behavior counteract government policy? What if the expansionary policy is anticipated? What if it is unanticipated? Or what if the anticipated expansionary policy is greater than the actual policy? Should policy makers even use expansionary and contractionary monetary and fiscal policies? Are they effective? Or should policy makers allow the economy to self-correct? What are the policy difficulties of dealing with supply shocks? Should the Fed use inflation targeting? And if so, should they target inflation at zero? Macroeconomists do not completely agree on the preceding questions. These are topics we will discuss throughout this chapter. In the final section, we will discuss the financial crisis of 2007–2009.

17-1 Problems in Implementing Fiscal and Monetary Policy

SECTION CHECK 1

Keep the following questions in mind as you read through this section.

1. What problems exist in implementing fiscal policy?
2. What problems exist in implementing monetary policy?
3. What problems exist in coordinating monetary and fiscal policies?

In this section we will examine the problems that policy makers encounter when implementing fiscal and monetary policy. First, we will look at fiscal policy and monetary policy. Then we will discuss coordination issues and step back to get a look at the overall difficulties of macroeconomic policymaking.

17-1a POSSIBLE OBSTACLES TO EFFECTIVE FISCAL POLICY

Let's begin our discussion with the problems that fiscal policy makers must consider.

The Crowding-Out Effect

Some economists believe that fiscal policy is not as potent as we described earlier because of the crowding-out effect. This occurs when household consumption and investment spending decrease as a result of financing a budget deficit. There are direct effects. For example, if the government spent more on school lunch programs, individuals might buy fewer groceries. There are also indirect effects. If the government spends more on defense and social programs without raising taxes for those programs, the deficit will rise.

Let's see how more spending on government purchases can lead to less investment spending. The multiplier effect of an increase in government purchases implies that the increase in aggregate demand will tend to be greater than the initial fiscal stimulus, other things being equal. However, because all other things will not tend to stay equal in this case, the multiplier effect may

not hold true. For example, an increase in government purchases stimulates aggregate demand. As the new spending takes place, income and real GDP will rise, which will cause households and firms to increase their demand for money to accommodate increased buying and selling. The increase in the demand for money will cause the interest rate to rise. As a result of the higher interest rate, consumers may decide against buying a car, a home, or other interest-sensitive goods, and businesses may cancel or scale back plans to expand or buy new capital equipment. In short, the higher interest rate will choke off some private spending on goods and services, and as a result, the impact of the increase in government purchases may be smaller than first assumed. Economists call this the **crowding-out effect**.

In Exhibit 17.1, suppose government purchases initially increased by $10 billion. This change by itself would shift aggregate demand to the right by $10 billion times the multiplier, from AD_1 to AD_2. However, when the government increases its purchases of goods and services, it leads to an increase in income. The increase in income leads to an increase in the demand for money and a higher interest rate. The higher interest rate crowds out investment spending, causing the aggregate demand curve to shift left, from AD_2 to AD_3. Because both these processes are taking place at the same time, the net effect is an increase in aggregate demand from AD_1 to AD_3 rather than to AD_2.

The multiplier and crowding-out effect can also affect the size of the shift in aggregate demand from a tax change. Recall that when tax cuts stimulate consumer spending, earnings and profits rise, which further stimulates consumer spending—the multiplier effect. But the higher income leads to an increase in the demand for

With the crowding-out effect, the increase in government spending can drive away private spending on goods and services.

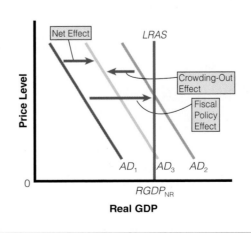

EXHIBIT 17.1 The Crowding-Out Effect

money, which tends to lead to higher interest rates. The higher interest rates make borrowing more costly and reduce investment spending—the crowding-out effect. Also, remember that if households view tax cuts as permanent, they are more likely to increase spending by a larger amount than if they view the tax as temporary.

The Crowding-Out Effect in the Open Economy

Another form of crowding out can take place in international markets. For example, say the government increases spending, this increase in demand raises incomes for workers and owners, which leads to an increase in the demand for money to pay for the spending and drives up the interest rate (assuming the money supply is unchanged). The higher U.S. interest rate will attract funds from abroad. To invest in the U.S. economy, foreigners will first have to convert their currencies into dollars. The increase in the demand for dollars relative to other currencies will cause the dollar to appreciate in value, making foreign imports relatively cheaper in the United States and U.S. exports relatively more expensive in other countries. This change will cause net exports $(X - M)$ to fall for two reasons. One, because of the higher relative price of the dollar, foreign imports will become cheaper for those in the United States, and imports will increase. Two, because of the higher relative price of the dollar, U.S.-made goods will become more expensive to foreigners, and exports will decrease. The increase in imports and the decrease in exports will cause a reduction in net exports and a fall in aggregate demand. The net effect will be that fiscal policy will have a smaller effect on aggregate demand than it would otherwise.

Time Lags in Fiscal Policy Implementation

It is important to recognize that in a democratic country, fiscal policy is implemented through the political process, and that process takes time. Often, the lag between the time that a fiscal response is desired, the time an appropriate policy is implemented, and the time its effects are felt is considerable. Sometimes a fiscal policy designed to deal with a contracting economy may actually take effect during a period of economic expansion, or vice versa, resulting in a stabilization policy that actually destabilizes the economy.

The Recognition Lag
Government tax or spending changes require both congressional and presidential approval. Suppose the economy is beginning a downturn. It may take two or three months before enough data are gathered to indicate the actual presence of a downturn. This time span is called the *recognition lag*. Sometimes a future downturn can be forecast through econometric models or by looking at the index of leading indicators,

but usually decision makers are hesitant to plan policy on the basis of forecasts that are not always accurate.

The Implementation Lag
At some point, however, policy makers may decide that some policy change is necessary. At this point, experts are consulted, and congressional committees hold hearings and listen to testimony on possible policy approaches. During the consultation phase, many decisions have to be made. If, for example, a tax cut is recommended, what form should the cut take, and how large should it be? Across-the-board income tax reductions? Reductions in corporate taxes? More generous exemptions and deductions from the income tax (e.g., for child care, casualty losses, education of children)? In other words, who should get the benefits of lower taxes? Likewise, if the decision is made to increase government expenditures, which programs should be expanded or initiated, and by how much? Because these questions have profound political consequences, reaching decisions is seldom easy and usually involves substantial compromise and a great deal of time.

Finally, once the House and Senate have completed their separate deliberations and have arrived at a final version of the fiscal policy bill, it is presented to Congress for approval. After congressional approval is secured, the bill then goes to the president for approval or veto. These steps are all part of what is called the *implementation lag*.

From 1990 to 1991, the actual output of the economy was less than the potential output of the economy—a recessionary gap. Because automatic stabilizers resulted in lower taxes and larger transfer payments, consumption did not fall as far as it might have.

However, before President Clinton began his term in 1993, he believed that more was needed, so he put together a stimulus package of additional government spending and tax cuts. But by the time the bill reached the floor of Congress, the recession was over, illustrating how difficult it is to time fiscal stimulus. When the economy went into recession in March of 2001, it was not until a year later that the stimulus package was signed into law. Another example is when President John F. Kennedy thought the economy was operating below its potential in 1962; Congress finally passed a tax cut in 1964.

The Impact Lag
Even after legislation is signed into law, it takes time to bring about the actual fiscal stimulus desired. If the legislation provides for a reduction in withholding taxes, for example, it might take a few months before the changes show up in workers' paychecks. With respect to changes in government purchases, the delay is usually much longer. If the government increases spending for public works projects such as sewer systems, new highways, or urban renewal,

it takes time to draw up plans and get permissions, to advertise for bids from contractors, to get contracts, and then to begin work. Further delays might occur because of government regulations. For example, an environmental impact statement must be completed before most public works projects can begin, a process that often takes many months or even years, called the *impact lag*.

17-1b PROBLEMS IN CONDUCTING MONETARY POLICY

The lag problem inherent in adopting fiscal policy changes is less acute for monetary policy, largely because the decisions are not slowed by the same budgetary process. That is, the implementation lag is longer for fiscal policy. The FOMC of the Federal Reserve, for example, can act quickly (in emergencies almost instantly, by conference call) and even secretly to buy or sell government bonds, the key day-to-day operating tool of monetary policy. However, the length and variability of the lag before its effects on output and employment are felt are still significant, and the time before the full price-level effects are felt is even longer and more variable. According to the Federal Reserve Bank of San Francisco, the major effects of a change in policy on growth in the overall production of goods and services usually are felt within three months to two years; the effects on inflation tend to involve even longer lags, one to three years or more.

How Do Commercial Banks Implement the Fed's Monetary Policies?

One limitation of monetary policy is that it ultimately must be carried out through the commercial banking system. The central bank (the Federal Reserve System in the United States) can change the environment in which banks act, but the banks themselves must take the steps necessary to increase or decrease the money supply. Usually, when the Fed is trying to constrain monetary expansion, it has no difficulty in getting banks to make appropriate responses. Banks must meet their reserve requirements; and if the Fed raises bank reserve requirements, sells bonds, and/or raises the discount rate, banks must obtain the necessary cash or reserve deposits at the Fed to meet their reserve requirements. In response, banks will call in loans that are due for collection, sell secondary reserves, and so on in order to obtain the necessary reserves. In the process of collecting loans, the banks decrease the money supply.

When the Federal Reserve wants to induce monetary expansion, however, it can provide banks with excess reserves (e.g., by lowering reserve requirements or buying government bonds), but it cannot force the banks to make loans, thereby creating new money. Ordinarily, of course, banks want to convert their excess reserves to interest-earning income by making loans. But in a deep recession or depression, banks might be hesitant to make enough loans to put all those reserves to work, fearing that they will not be repaid. Their pessimism might lead them to perceive that the risks of making loans to many normally creditworthy borrowers outweigh any potential interest earnings (particularly at the low real interest rates that are characteristic of depressed times). Some have argued that banks maintaining excess reserves rather than loaning them out was, in fact, one of the monetary policy problems that arose in the Great Depression.

Banks that Are Not Part of the Federal Reserve System and Policy Implementation

A second problem with monetary policy relates to the fact that the Fed can control deposit expansion at member banks, but it has no control over global and nonbank institutions that also issue credit (loan money) but are not subject to reserve requirement limitations; examples are pension funds and insurance companies. Therefore, while the Fed may be able to predict the impact of its monetary policies on loans issued by member banks, global and nonbanking institutions can alter the impact of monetary policies adopted by the Fed. Hence, the real question is how precisely the Fed can control the short-run real interest rates and the money supply through its monetary policy instruments.

17-1c FISCAL AND MONETARY COORDINATION PROBLEMS

Another problem that may arise out of existing institutional policy-making arrangements is the coordination of fiscal and monetary policy. Congress and the president make fiscal policy decisions, whereas monetary policy making is in the hands of the Federal Reserve System. A macroeconomic problem arises if the federal government's fiscal decision makers differ with the Fed's monetary decision makers on policy objectives or targets. For example, the Fed may be more concerned about keeping inflation low, while fiscal policy makers may be more concerned about keeping unemployment low.

Alleviating Coordination Problems

In recognition of potential macroeconomic policy coordination problems, the chairman of the Federal Reserve Board has participated for several years in meetings with top economic advisers of the president. An attempt is made in these meetings to reach a consensus on the

© Blend Images/Getty Images

the $SRAS$ leftward from $SRAS_1$ to $SRAS_2$ and to the new long-run equilibrium at E_4.

Imperfect Information

In addition, the problem of imperfect information enters the picture. For example, in order to know how much to stimulate the economy, policy makers must know the size of the multiplier and by how much RGDP should increase. But some economists disagree on the natural rate of real output ($RGDP_{NR}$), and it may be difficult to know where RGDP is at any given moment in time; government estimates are approximations and are often corrected at a later period. The government must also know the exact MPC. If the estimate is too low, the multiplier will be less than expected and the stimulus will be too small. If the estimate of MPC is too high, the multiplier will be more than expected and the stimulus will be too large.

appropriate policy responses, both monetary and fiscal. Still, they sometimes disagree, and the Fed occasionally works to partly offset or even neutralize the effects of fiscal policies that it views as inappropriate. Some people believe that monetary policy should be more directly controlled by the president and Congress, so that all macroeconomic policy will be determined more directly by the political process. Also, it is argued that such a move would enhance coordination considerably. Others, however, argue that it is dangerous to turn over control of the nation's money supply to politicians, rather than allowing decisions to be made by technically competent administrators who are more focused on price stability and more insulated from political pressures applied by the public and special interest groups.

Timing Is Critical

The timing of fiscal policy and monetary policy is crucial. Because of the significant lags before the fiscal and monetary policy has its impact, the increase in aggregate demand may occur at the wrong time. For example, imagine that we are initially at AD_1 in Exhibit 17.2. The economy is currently suffering from low levels of output and high rates of unemployment. In response, policy makers decide to increase government purchases and implement a tax cut, or alternatively they could have increased the money supply. But from the time when the policy makers recognize the problem to the time when the policies have a chance to work themselves through the economy, business and consumer confidence both increase, shifting the aggregate demand curve rightward from AD_1 to AD_2—increasing RGDP and employment. When the fiscal policy takes hold, the policies will have the undesired effect of causing inflation, with little permanent effect on output and employment. This effect may be seen in Exhibit 17.2, as the aggregate demand curve shifts from AD_2 to AD_3. At E_3, input owners will require higher input prices, shifting

17-1d OVERALL PROBLEMS WITH MONETARY AND FISCAL POLICY

Much of macroeconomic policy in this country is driven by the idea that the federal government can counteract economic fluctuations: stimulating the economy (with increased government spending, tax cuts, and easy money) when it is weak and restraining

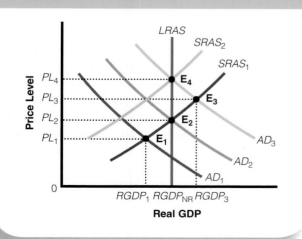

EXHIBIT 17.2 Timing Expansionary Policy

© Cengage Learning 2014

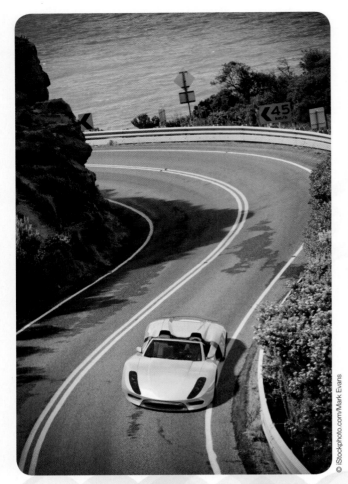

Some economists believe that fine-tuning the economy is like driving a car with an unpredictable steering lag on a winding road, or driving while looking only through the sideview mirror.

But let us assume that economists can outperform astrologers at forecasting. Indeed, let us be completely unrealistic and assume that economists can provide completely accurate economic forecasts of what will happen if macroeconomic policies are unchanged. Even then, they cannot be certain of how best to promote stable economic growth.

If economists knew, for example, that the economy was going to dip into another recession in six months, they would then need to know exactly how much each possible policy would spur activity to keep the economy stable. But such precision is unattainable, given the complexity of economic forecasting. Furthermore, despite assurances to the contrary, economists are not always certain what effect a policy will have on the economy. Will an increase in government purchases quicken economic growth? It is widely assumed so; but how much? Moreover, increasing government purchases increases the budget deficit, which could send a frightening signal to the bond markets. The result might be to drive up interest rates and choke off economic activity. Thus, even when policymakers know in which direction to nudge the economy, they cannot be sure which policy levers to pull, or how hard to pull them, in order to fine-tune the economy to stable economic growth.

But let us further assume that policy makers know when the economy will need a boost and which policy will provide the right boost. A third crucial consideration is how long it will take a policy before it has its effect on the economy. The trouble is that, even when increased government purchases or an expansionary monetary policy does give the economy a boost, no one knows precisely how long it will take to do so. The boost may come quickly or it may come many months (even years) in the future, when it may add inflationary pressures to an economy already overheating rather than help the economy to recover from a recession.

Macroeconomic policymaking is rather like driving down a twisting road in a car with an unpredictable lag and degree of response in the steering mechanism. If you turn the wheel to the right; the car will eventually veer to the right, but you don't know exactly when or how much. In short, severe practical difficulties are inherent in trying to fine-tune the economy. Even the best forecasting models and methods are far from perfect. Economists are not exactly sure where the economy is or where or how fast it is going, making it difficult to prescribe an effective policy. Even if we do know where the economy is headed, we cannot be sure how large a policy's effect will be or when it will take effect.

it when it is overheating. However, policy makers must adopt the right policies in the right amounts at the right time for such "stabilization" to do more good than harm; and to do this, government policy makers need far more accurate and timely information than experts can give them.

First, economists must know not only which way the economy is heading but also how rapidly it is changing. Even the most current data on key variables such as employment, growth, productivity, and so on, reflect conditions in the past, not the present. The unvarnished truth is that in our incredibly complicated world, no one knows exactly what the economy will do, no matter how sophisticated the econometric models used; our models are only approximations. It has often been said, and not completely in jest, that the purpose of economic forecasting is to make astrology look respectable.

17-2 Rational Expectations

SECTION CHECK 2

Keep the following questions in mind as you read through this section.

1. What is the rational expectations theory?

2. What do critics say about the rational expectations theory?

Can human behavior counteract government policy? Is it possible that people can anticipate the plans of policy makers and alter their behavior quickly to neutralize the intended impact of government action? For example, if workers see that the government is allowing the money supply to expand rapidly, they may quickly demand higher money wages to offset the anticipated inflation. In the extreme form, if people could instantly recognize and respond to government policy changes, it might be impossible to alter real output or unemployment levels through policy actions, because government policy makers could no longer surprise households and firms. An increasing number of economists believe that there is at least some truth to this point of view. At a minimum, most economists accept the notion that real output and the unemployment rate cannot be altered with the ease that was earlier believed; some believe that the unemployment rate can seldom be influenced by fiscal and monetary policies.

theory of rational expectations belief that workers and consumers incorporate the likely consequences of government policy changes into their expectations by quickly adjusting wages and prices

17-2a THE RATIONAL EXPECTATIONS THEORY

The relatively new extension of economic theory that leads to this rather pessimistic conclusion regarding macroeconomic policy's ability to achieve our economic goals is called the **theory of rational expectations**. The notion that expectations or anticipations of future events are relevant to economic theory is not new; for decades, economists have incorporated expectations into models analyzing many forms of economic behavior. Only in the recent past, however, has a theory evolved that tries to incorporate expectations as a central factor in the analysis of the entire economy.

The interest in rational expectations has grown rapidly in the last decade. Acknowledged pioneers in the development of the theory include Professor Robert Lucas of the University of Chicago and Professor Thomas Sargent of the University of Minnesota. In 1995, Professor Lucas won the Nobel Prize for his work in rational expectations.

Rational expectations economists believe that wages and prices are flexible and that households and firms incorporate the likely consequences of government policy changes quickly into their expectations. In addition, rational expectations economists believe that the economy is inherently stable after macroeconomic shocks and that tinkering with fiscal and monetary policy cannot have the desired effect unless households and firms are caught "off guard" (and catching them off guard gets harder the more you try to do it).

Rational Expectations and the Consequences of Government Macroeconomic Policies

Rational expectations theory, then, suggests that government economic policies designed to alter aggregate demand to meet macroeconomic goals are of limited effectiveness. When policy targets become public, it is argued, people will alter their own behavior from what it would otherwise have been to maximize their own utility, and in so doing, they largely negate the intended impact of policy changes. If government policy seems tilted toward permitting more inflation to try to reduce unemployment, people start spending their money faster than before, become more adamant in their demands for wages and other input prices, and so on. In the process of quickly altering their behavior to reflect the likely consequences of policy changes, they make it more difficult (costly) for government authorities to meet their macroeconomic objectives. Rather than fooling people into changing real wages, and therefore unemployment, with inflation "surprises," changes in inflation are quickly reflected into expectations with little or no effect on unemployment or real output even in the short run. As a consequence, policies intended to reduce unemployment through stimulating aggregate demand will often fail to have the intended effect. Fiscal and monetary policy, according to this view, will work only if the people are caught off guard or are fooled by policies and thus do not modify their behavior in a way that reduces policy effectiveness.

Anticipation of an Expansionary Monetary Policy

Consider the case in which an increase in aggregate demand is a result of an expansionary monetary policy. This increase is reflected in Exhibit 17.3 in the shift from AD_1 to AD_2. Because of the predictable inflationary consequences of that expansionary policy, prices immediately adjust to a new level at PL_2. Consumers, producers, workers, and lenders who *anticipated* the effects of the expansionary policy simply build the higher inflation rates into their product prices, wages, and interest rates. That is, households and firms realize that expansionary monetary policy can cause inflation if the economy is working close to capacity. Consequently, in an effort to protect themselves from the higher anticipated inflation, workers ask for higher wages, suppliers increase input prices, and producers raise their product prices. Because wages, prices, and interest rates are assumed to be flexible, the adjustments take place immediately. This increase in input costs for wages, interest, and raw materials causes the aggregate supply curve to shift up or leftward, shown as the movement from $SRAS_1$ to $SRAS_2$ in Exhibit 17.3. So the desired policy effect of greater real output and reduced unemployment from a shift in the aggregate demand curve is offset by an upward or leftward shift in the aggregate supply curve caused by an increase in input costs.

Unanticipated Expansionary Policy

Again, consider the case of an increase in aggregate demand that results from an expansionary monetary policy. However, this time it is *unanticipated*. The increase

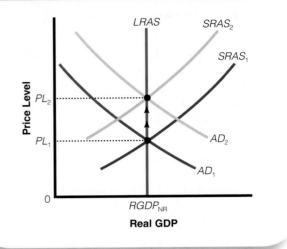

EXHIBIT 17.3 Rational Expectations and the *AD/AS* Model

© Cengage Learning 2014

in the money supply is reflected in Exhibit 17.4 in the shift from AD_1 to AD_2. This unanticipated change in monetary policy stimulates output and employment in the short run, as the equilibrium moves from point A to point B. At the new short-run equilibrium, the output is at $RGDP_2$ and the price level is at PL_2. This output is beyond $RGDP_{NR}$, so it is not sustainable in the long run. Because it is unanticipated, workers and other input owners are expecting the price level to remain at PL_1, rather than PL_2. However, when input owners

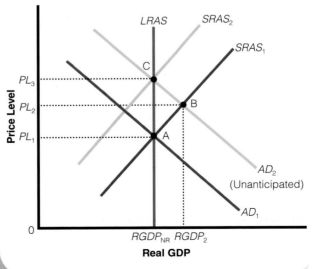

EXHIBIT 17.4 An Expansionary Policy that Is Unanticipated

© Cengage Learning 2014

eventually realize that the actual price level has changed, they will require higher input prices, shifting the $SRAS$ from $SRAS_1$ to $SRAS_2$. At point C, we see that output has returned to $RGDP_{NR}$ but at a higher price level, PL_3.

Therefore, when the expansionary policy is unanticipated, it leads to a short-run expansion in output and employment. But in the long run, the only impact of the change in monetary policy is a higher price level—inflation. In short, when the change is correctly anticipated, expansionary monetary (or fiscal) policy does not result in a change in real output. However, if the expansionary monetary (fiscal) policy is unanticipated, the result is a short-run increase in RGDP and employment, but in the long run, it just means a higher price level.

In fact, the only way that monetary or fiscal policy can change output in the rational expectations model is with a surprise—an unanticipated change. For example, on April 18, 2001, between regularly scheduled meetings of the Federal Open Market Committee, the Fed surprised financial markets with an aggressive half-point cut in the interest rate. The Fed was trying to boost consumer confidence and impact falling stock market wealth. The surprise reduction in the interest rate sent the stock market soaring as the Dow posted one of its largest single-day point gains, and the NASDAQ had its fourth largest percentage gain. Former Fed Chairman Greenspan hoped that this move would shift the AD curve rightward, leading to higher levels of output.

Critics of Rational Expectations Theory

Of course, rational expectations theory does have its critics. Critics want to know whether households and firms are completely informed about the impact that, say, an increase in money supply will have on the economy. In general, all citizens will not be completely informed, but key players such as corporations, financial institutions, and labor organizations may well be informed about the impact of these policy changes. But other problems arise. For example, are wages and other input prices really that flexible? That is, even if decision makers could anticipate the eventual effect of policy changes on prices, those prices may still be slow to adapt (e.g., what if you had just signed a three-year labor or supply contract when the new policy was implemented?).

Most economists reject the extreme rational expectations model of complete wage and price flexibility. In fact, most economists still believe a short-run trade-off between inflation and unemployment results because some input prices are slow to adjust to changes in the price level. However, in the long run, the expected inflation rate adjusts to changes in the actual inflation rate at the natural rate of unemployment, $RGDP_{NR}$.

17-3 Controversies in Macroeconomic Policy

SECTION CHECK 3

Keep the following questions in mind as you read through this section.

1. Are fiscal and monetary policies effective?

2. Should central banks target inflation?

3. Could indexing reduce the costs of inflation?

Economies tend to fluctuate. Consumer or business pessimism leads to a reduction in aggregate demand. As aggregate demand falls, so does output and employment. The rising unemployment and the fall in income cause additional damage to the economy. The economy is now operating to the left of the $LRAS$ (or inside its production possibilities curve); resources are not being used efficiently when actual output is less than potential output. Many economists believe that in the short run, policy makers have the ability to alter aggregate demand. If the aggregate demand is insufficient, policy makers can stimulate aggregate demand by increasing government spending, cutting taxes, and increasing the growth rate of the money supply. If aggregate demand is excessive, policy makers can reduce aggregate demand by decreasing government spending, increasing taxes, and reducing the growth rate of the money supply.

These macroeconomists are called *activists*, and they believe that in the short run, discretionary monetary and fiscal policy can stimulate the economy that is in a recessionary gap or dampen the economy that is in an inflationary boom with aggregate demand management. However, other economists believe that aggregate demand stimulus cannot *keep* the rate of unemployment below the natural rate. Most economists accept the basic notion of the natural rate hypothesis that suggests the unemployment rate will be close to the natural rate in the long run. Other economists, *rational expectations theorists*, believe that government economic policies designed to alter aggregate demand are not all that effective because households and firms form expectations to economic policy causing prices and wages to adjust quickly, leaving the output roughly the same but at a higher price level. To these economists, monetary and fiscal policy will only work if it comes as a surprise to the public.

However, most economists do not accept the notion that households and firms have rational expectations and that wages and prices adjust quickly because of wage and other input contracts. Even if households and firms formed rational expectations, if prices and wages adjusted slowly, expansionary monetary policy could lead to a lower unemployment level.

Most macroeconomists believe both that monetary and fiscal policy can shift the aggregate demand and that the intervention can be counterproductive. Recall our discussion in the previous chapter about the lags associated with both fiscal and monetary policies. The long and uncertain lags may lead to policies that are counterproductive. In other words, the policies aimed at closing a recessionary gap may cause an inflationary gap if the stimulus occurs at the wrong time. Or policies aimed at closing an inflationary gap may overshoot the goal and cause a recessionary gap. The problem is that we do not operate with a clear crystal ball. For policy makers, timing and the exact size of the stimulus are essential for effective stabilization policies.

Other economists believe that the potency of expansionary fiscal policy will be diminished by the crowding-out effect. That is, expansionary fiscal policy increases the real interest rate when it borrows money to finance its deficit, which crowds out private investment. It is also possible that the economy is stimulated with fiscal or monetary policy in the short run for political gains that will only be inflationary in the long run. Recall that expansionary monetary policy lowers the real interest rate and stimulates private investment.

Other questions the policy makers will have to answer are: What are the output effects of the fiscal or monetary policy? What is the marginal propensity to consume (MPC) of the tax cut? How much will the central bank have to change the real interest rate to get the desired change in residential and commercial spending?

For most economists, monetary policy is the preferred tool for stabilization because the inside lags (the time from when a policy is needed to the time it is implemented) are much shorter. Recall that the federal open market committee (FOMC) meets eight times a year. Fiscal policy requires Congress to convene and debate the tax cuts or expenditure increases. However, fiscal policy may be used in special circumstances when monetary policy alone cannot do the job. Automatic stabilizers (e.g., taxes that impact disposable income and unemployment compensation) are an important part of fiscal policy and have a much smaller lag because they are implemented automatically.

17-3a POLICY DIFFICULTIES WITH SUPPLY SHOCKS

Recall that a negative supply shock, like those the United States experienced in the 1970s, leads to an increase in the price level and a reduction in real aggregate output ($RGDP$), as seen in Exhibit 17.5. The recession of 1990–1991 began when Iraq invaded Kuwait and both oil-exporting countries took their oil off the world market. Crude oil prices more than doubled in roughly five months, from an average of $15 a barrel in June 1990 to $33 a barrel in October 1990. The higher oil prices shifted the SRAS curve to the left as seen in Exhibit 17.5, causing an increase in the price level and a reduction in RGDP.

After a negative demand shock (not shown but a leftward shift in the *AD* curve from, say, point A), policy makers can employ expansionary fiscal and/or monetary policy which can help shift the economy back to its original position. However, this is not the case with a negative

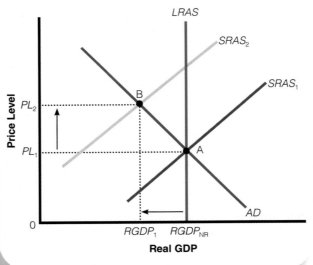

EXHIBIT 17.5 A Negative Supply Shock

EXHIBIT 17.6 Policy Response to a Supply Shock

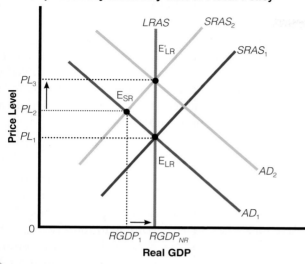

a. Expansionary Monetary and/or Fiscal Policy

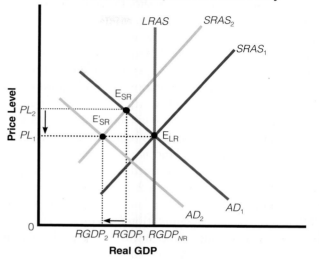

b. Contractionary Monetary and/or Fiscal Policy

© Cengage Learning 2014

supply shock. For example, suppose policy makers choose to use expansionary fiscal and/or monetary policy as a response to the recession caused by the supply shock; this increase in aggregate demand causes an increase in aggregate output ($RGDP$) but leads to even greater inflation, as seen in Exhibit 17.6(a). Or if policy makers choose to use contractionary fiscal and/or monetary policy to control inflation, this decrease in aggregate demand leads to a lower price level but causes an even lower level of aggregate output with higher rates of unemployment, as seen in Exhibit 17.6(b). In short, stagflation caused by a supply shock makes economic policy making very difficult.

17-3b WHAT SHOULD THE CENTRAL BANK DO?

Most economists believe that monetary policy should take the lead in stabilization policy and that the central bank should be independent and insulated from political pressure to avoid political business cycles. Political business cycles may occur if central banks ally themselves with an incumbent party and pursue expansionary monetary policy prior to an election. Even though the short-run impact may be increased output, employment, and a victory for the incumbent party in the election, the long-run impact will be inflation. So, faced with these potential problems, how should the central bank set its monetary policy?

Some macroeconomists believe that the central bank should adopt rules, such as a constant growth rate in the money supply. According to the rule advocates, if

the money supply were only allowed to increase by, say, 3–5 percent per year (enough to accommodate new economic growth), the result would be less uncertainty and greater economic stability. In other words, if the fixed rule is followed and the growth rate is 3 percent per year and the monetary growth rate is 3 percent per year, the average rate of inflation is zero. This situation seldom occurs, but the point here is that it would add credibility to the Federal Reserve as being tough on inflation. It would make it clear that what the Fed says it is going to do is consistent with what it actually does.

© Jamie Farrant/iStockphoto.com

Without proper timing or the right stimulus, it is easy for policy makers to miss their target.

17-3c INFLATION TARGETING

Some macroeconomists believe that we can do better than targeting the growth rate of monetary aggregates. These economists believe we should target the inflation rate. Targeting the inflation rate would require the central bank to attempt to stay in a certain band of inflation for a specified period of time—say 2–3 percent. The key to targeting is that it enhances credibility and could help to "anchor" inflationary expectations and lead to greater price stability. After all, successful monetary policy hinges critically on the ability to manage expectations. Several countries have inflation targets in place: The Bank of England is at 2 percent, the Bank of Canada is at 2 percent, Brazil is at 4.5 percent, and Chile is at the range between 2 percent and 4 percent. Empirical studies show a tendency for inflation rates to fall in countries that use inflation targeting.

Critics of inflation targeting will argue that central banks need flexibility. Good leaders, like Volcker and Greenspan, proved that they can handle the job without set rules or targets. In other words, the United States has kept inflation low without rules or targeting, so those opposed to targets say, "If it ain't broke, don't fix it." Others argue that it may cause banks to focus too much attention on inflation at the expense of other goals such as output and employment. For example, a recessionary gap will normally cause the central bank to lower the interest rate to stimulate spending, output, and employment rather than just focus on inflation. Some might ask: If the Fed is going to put a target band on inflation, why not put one on unemployment and long-term interest rates too?

Targeting Inflation at Zero

So, if central banks are targeting low inflation rates of 2 percent, why not target inflation rates at 0 percent? After all, we have seen the costs to inflation: shoe leather costs, menu costs, changes in tax liabilities, changes in the distribution of income—and it leads to a distortion of the price system. However, these costs are probably small if inflation rates are low and expected to stay low. The other problem associated with a zero inflation rate is that it would be difficult to precisely hit the target all the time, and it could lead to deflation (the average price level of goods and services are falling), as it did in Japan in the 1990s. Also, some macroeconomists worry that if the inflation rate is targeted at zero the interest rate may fall to zero in a recession and render expansionary macroeconomic policy powerless. Other problems are unanticipated shocks and unanticipated financial crises. Monetary authorities need the flexibility to respond to these shocks by temporarily going outside the target range. For instance, the Federal Reserve was there to respond to the stock market crash of October 19, 1987—when stock prices fell by more than 20 percent in a single day (the biggest ever one-day decline)—and to the shock created by the terrorist attacks on September 11, 2001, when the Federal Reserve made massive discount loans to banks to avoid a financial crisis.

Critics of targeting a zero inflation rate believe that achieving zero inflation is almost impossible and the costs are too high. The costs of disinflation (lowering the rate of inflation) can be high. Reducing the inflation rate by 1 percent may reduce output by as much as 5 percent. Disinflation is not painless.

The Taylor Rule

A variant of monetary rules and inflation targeting is the Taylor rule. It is a hybrid—part rule, part discretion. Taylor's formula uses a rule to decide when to use discretionary decisions. According to John Taylor, "The federal funds rate is increased or decreased according to what is happening to both real GDP and inflation. In particular, if real GDP rises 1 percent above potential GDP the federal funds rate should be raised, relative to the current inflation rate, by .5 percent. And if inflation rises by 1 percent above its target of 2 percent, then

In 1985, Bolivia had an inflation rate approaching 12,000 percent per year, and the government decided to put the brakes on the money supply. The resulting hyperinflation was over in a month, no output was lost, and credibility was restored. The public must believe the government's anti-inflation policy or it will not work.

the federal funds rate should be raised by .5 percent relative to the inflation rate. When real GDP is equal to potential GDP and inflation is equal to its target of 2 percent, then the federal funds rate should remain at about 4 percent, which would imply a real interest rate of 2 percent on average. The policy rule was purposely chosen to be simple. Clearly, the equal weights on inflation and the GDP gap are an approximation reflecting the finding that neither variable should be given a negligible weight." If the central bank used this rule, market participants could easily predict central bank behavior, creating greater stability and certainty.

Asset Price Inflation

Some economists believe that the Fed should be concerned about asset pricing—especially housing and stock market prices. The period of 1999–2004 saw inflation at a low rate of about 2.5 percent per year, yet housing prices were rising 25 percent and higher in some markets. In some countries, such as Australia and Great Britain, the central banks are paying closer attention to the growth in asset prices even when consumer price inflation is low. Others believe that the central bank should not concern itself with the value that consumers place on stocks and housing. If the bubble bursts, the Fed can lower interest rates to bolster the economy.

Of course, as we found out during the financial crisis of 2007–2009, there are several questions that must be answered. One of the most important is: Can you identify housing or stock bubbles when they are appearing? The extent of monetary policy intervention may depend on the bubble. In the recession of 2007–2009, the housing bubble spread throughout the economy quickly and violently, before interest rate policy could be used to offset the damaging effects.

17-3d INDEXING AND REDUCING THE COSTS OF INFLATION

Another approach to some of the problems posed by inflation is **indexing**. As you recall, inflation poses substantial equity and distributional problems only when it is unanticipated or unexpected. One means of protecting parties against unanticipated price increases is to write contracts that automatically change the prices of goods or services whenever the overall price level changes, effectively rewriting agreements

in terms of dollars of constant purchasing power. Wages, loans, and mortgage payments—everything possible—would be changed every month or so by an amount equal to the percentage change in some broad-based price index. Thus, if prices rose by 1.2 percent this month and your last month's wage was $1,000, your wage this month would be $1,012 ($1,000 × 1.012). By making as many contracts as possible payable in dollars of constant purchasing power, those involved could protect themselves against unanticipated changes in inflation.

indexing use of payment contracts that automatically adjust for changes in inflation

Why Is Indexing Not Used More Extensively?

Indexing seems to eliminate most of the wealth transfers associated with unexpected inflation. Why then is it not more commonly used? One main argument against indexing is that it can worsen inflation. As prices go up, wages and certain other contractual obligations (e.g., rents) also automatically increase. This immediate and comprehensive reaction to price increases leads to greater inflationary pressures. One price increase leads to a second, which in turn leads to a third, and so on.

Other Problems Associated with Indexing

We might ask, so what? If prices rise rapidly, but wages, rents, and so forth move up with prices, real wages and rents remain constant. However, if inflation gets bad enough, it could become almost impossible administratively to maintain the indexing scheme. The index, to be effective, might have to be changed every few days, but the information to make such frequent changes is not currently available. To get the necessary information quickly, then, might be quite expensive, involving a small army of price-checking bureaucrats and a massive electronic communications system. Other inefficiencies occur as well. During the German hyperinflation of the early 1920s, prices at one point rose so rapidly that workers demanded to be paid twice a day, at noon and at the end of the workday. During their lunch hour, workers would rush money to their wives, who would then run out and buy real goods before prices increased further.

© Jonathan Larsen/Diadem Images/Alamy

Other big problems include the fact that indexing reduces the ability for relative price changes to allocate resources where they are more valuable. Not everything can be indexed, so indexing would cause wealth redistribution. In addition, costs would necessarily be incurred as a result of renegotiating cost-of-living (COLA) clauses.

Excessive inflation, then, leads to great inefficiency, as well as to a loss of confidence in the issuer of money—namely, the government. Furthermore, inflation influences world trade patterns. Limited indexing, in fact, has already been adopted, as some wage and pension payments are changed with changes in the cost-of-living index. Whether on balance those escalator clauses are "good" or "bad" is a debatable topic—a normative judgment that we will leave to the reader to make.

SECTION CHECK 3 ANSWERS

1. Proponents of active monetary and fiscal policy view the economy as inherently unstable and believe that contractionary and expansionary fiscal and monetary policy can stabilize the economy. Critics believe that lags and uncertainty make stabilization polices more often counterproductive.

2. Targeting could enhance credibility and "anchor" inflationary expectations. Critics argue that the central banks need flexibility, and competent leaders can do the job without rules or targeting.

3. Indexing reduces the impact of inflation on the distribution of income but may also intensify the inflationary effects of expansionary monetary policy by increasing inflationary pressures.

17-4 The Financial Crisis of 2007–2009

SECTION CHECK 4

Keep the following questions in mind as you read through this section.

1. What impact did low short-term interest rates have on the housing market?

2. What role did relaxed standards for mortgage loans have on the housing market?

3. What impact did the higher interest rate of 2005 have on the housing market?

The best word to sum up the financial crisis of 2007–2009 is *debt*. In technical terms, it is called excessive leverage. In short, too many homeowners and financial firms had assumed too much debt and taken on too much risk. Why did this happen? There is plenty of blame to go around—poorly informed borrowers, predatory mortgage lenders, incompetent rating agencies, lax regulators, misguided government policies, and outright fraud.

Many economists believe the crisis started in the housing market with declining housing prices caused by overbuilding, excessive appreciation, and aggressive (i.e., risky) mortgages—a formula that only works when housing prices are rising.

Housing prices were rising at an extraordinary rate from 2000–2006. Housing prices peaked in 2006 and fell sharply in 2007; with the worst of the housing decline concentrated in California, Florida, Arizona, and Nevada.

17-4a LOW INTEREST RATES (2002–2004) LED TO AGGRESSIVE BORROWING

After the 2001 recession, the Fed pursued an expansionary monetary policy that pushed interest rates down to historically low levels. The federal funds rate was maintained at 2 percent or lower for almost three years. Economists disagree on whether this was the correct government policy. Some argue that the Fed pursued the appropriate policy to stimulate economic growth and employment after the 2001 recession and terrorist attacks in order to head off potential deflation. Once deflation sets in, it is very difficult to successfully use expansionary

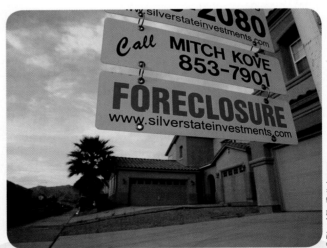

The housing market in Nevada was one of the hardest hit during the financial crisis. In October 2008, nearly 1 in every 74 Nevada homes had received foreclosure filings.

monetary policy. In addition, worldwide interest rates were very low at this time due to the large amount of savings in emerging markets. Because the U.S. financial markets appeared relatively safe, many of these global funds flowed into the United States, lowering the interest rate and eventually helping to fuel the housing bubble.

Critics of the Fed argue that it lowered interest rates too much for too long in a growing economy. Most would agree that monetary policy was "too loose for too long" in the United States and around the world.

But whatever the reason for the low interest rates, there is common agreement that the low interest rates increased aggressive borrowing that encouraged less qualified buyers to purchase houses. The low interest rates set off a housing boom, especially in California, Florida, and the Northeast.

17-4b DEREGULATION IN THE HOUSING MARKET AND SUBPRIME MORTGAGES

In the last several decades, the federal government encouraged the mortgage industry, especially Fannie Mae and Freddie Mac, to lower lending standards for low-income families in an effort to increase home ownership. Fannie Mae and Freddie Mac are the government-sponsored enterprises that fund or guarantee the majority of mortgage loans in the United States.

Specifically, lenders devised innovative adjustable rate mortgages with extremely low "teaser" rates, making it possible for many new higher-risk buyers to purchase houses, often with little or no money as a down payment and, in some cases, no documentation of income. Most of these loans ended up in the hands of high-risk borrowers. These loans were called subprime loans because the borrower had less than a prime credit rating and many would not have qualified for a conventional loan.

In 2006, almost 70 percent of the subprime loans were in the form of a new innovative product called a hybrid. These loans started at a very low fixed rate for the initial period, say three to seven years, and then reset to a much higher rate for the remainder of the loan. Many subprime borrowers just expected to refinance later—thinking their property would continue to appreciate and interest rates would remain low. In retrospect, borrowers and lenders focused too much on the borrower's ability to cover the low initial payment and not enough on risk.

Speculators flipped (quickly bought and sold) properties with inflated appraisals and outright lying on loan applications. In addition, excessive credit provided to subprime borrowers (individuals who may not have qualified for conventional loans) fueled the housing bubble. Mortgage originators were not worried about making risky loans because they could pass on the risk to others (particularly Fannie Mae and Freddie Mac, who were aggressively buying such loans). Because origination fees on loans were due up front, and others would buy the loans, lenders were less concerned if the loan was ever repaid. It is safe to say that if mortgage companies had given loans only to safe investors, the United States would not have had a financial crisis.

Subprime mortgages jumped from 8 percent of the total in 2001 to 13.5 percent in 2005, as shown in Exhibit 17.7 on the next page. These new buyers pushed housing prices higher. The increase in the lending to "subprime" borrowers helped inflate the housing bubble. The rising housing prices then led to overly optimistic expectations with both borrowers and lenders thinking that with housing prices increasing, the risks were minimal. (After all, housing prices jumped almost 10 percent a year nationally from 2000–2006, as shown in Exhibit 17.8 on the next page.)

Lenders were eager to make loans to anyone because they thought the prices for housing would continue to rise and, if borrowers defaulted, lenders would be left with an asset worth more than they were owed.

In short, the relaxed lending standards, backed by the government, put many low-income families into homes they could not afford. Unscrupulous mortgage brokers even falsified loan application forms so clients could qualify for larger loans. Many borrowers also did not completely understand the terms of their loans.

17-4c WHO BOUGHT THESE RISKY SUBPRIME MORTGAGES?

Many of these risky subprime mortgages were sold to investment banks such as Bear Stearns and Merrill Lynch. They pooled them with other securities into packages and sold them all over the world. Part of the impetus for them was the great demand for mortgage-backed securities in the global market. A mortgage-backed security (MBS) is a package of mortgages bundled together and then sold to an investor, like a bond. Foreign investors were hungry to invest in these securities because the U.S. housing market traditionally has been strong and stable. These mortgage-backed securities were also thought to have minimal risk because of the diversity of mortgages in each portfolio and because they had high security ratings. Security rating agencies gave their highest ratings to these securities—AAA (Standard and Poor's) and Aaa (Moody's). High ratings encouraged investors to buy securities backed by subprime mortgages, helping finance the

EXHIBIT 17.7 The Subprime Share of Home Mortgages Grows Rapidly before the Big Decline (1995–Q2 2008)

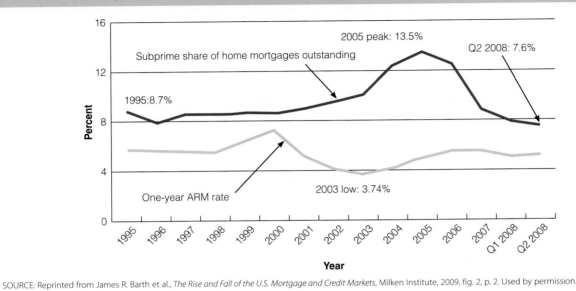

SOURCE: Reprinted from James R. Barth et al., *The Rise and Fall of the U.S. Mortgage and Credit Markets*, Milken Institute, 2009, fig. 2, p. 2. Used by permission.

housing boom. The rating agencies clearly underestimated the risk of these securities. The risk was spread among many different investment institutions, but no one knew exactly where the bad loans had ended up.

Consumers Borrowing against Their Equity

To complicate matters further, consumers borrowed hundreds of billions of dollars against the equity from the appreciation in their homes, fueling consumption

EXHIBIT 17.8 The Recent Run-Up of Nominal Home Prices Was Extraordinary (1890–Q2 2008)

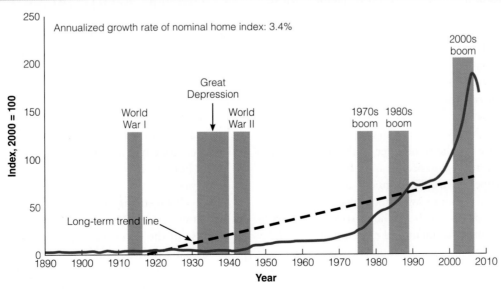

NOTE: The annualized growth rate is the geometric mean.
SOURCE: Reprinted from James R. Barth et al., *The Rise and Fall of the U.S. Mortgage and Credit Markets*, Milken Institute, 2009, fig. 5, p. 9. Used by permission.

spending and an increase in household debt, combined with a fall in personal saving. The low interest rates subsidized massive borrowing, and credit market debt soared as well.

17-4d FED INTEREST RATE INCREASES AND THE HOUSING BUST

The low interest rates of the 2002–2004 period and other factors led to the Fed becoming concerned about rising prices. In 2005–2006, therefore, the Fed reversed course and pushed short-term interest rates up. For those holding new adjustable rate mortgages (ARMs), it meant their monthly payments rose. Higher interest rates and falling housing prices were a recipe for disaster. Consequently, many homes went into default and foreclosure—both subprime borrowers and prime borrowers lost their homes. (The default rate was much lower on those holding fixed mortgage rates.)

When housing prices crashed, not only did too many homeowners find themselves over their heads, but there was also a huge excess inventory of new homes. From 2006–2008, housing construction fell by a whopping $350 billion—a huge hit on the economy. And by December of 2007, the United States was officially in a recession.

As housing prices fell and interest rates rose, foreclosures jumped. Once home prices fell below loan values, borrowers could not qualify to refinance and many were forced into foreclosure. When houses turn "upside down"—people owe more on their loan than the house is worth—many walk away from their houses. If a homeowner had put 20 percent down and had an appreciable amount of equity, she would have a greater incentive to make it work. Zero-down mortgages meant more defaults, especially when given to someone with a poor credit rating and little documentation of income. There was a major mispricing of risk in the mortgage markets.

When housing prices fell and mortgage delinquencies soared, the securities-backed subprime mortgages lost most of their value. When subprime borrowers defaulted, the investors that took the hit started demanding their money back by surrendering these securities to the banks. The result was a large decline in the capital of many banks and financial institutions, tightening credit around the world. One investment bank went bankrupt (Lehman Brothers in September 2008) and two were sold at fire-sale prices to other banks (Bear Stearns in March 2008 and Merrill Lynch in September 2008). The failures of three of the five largest investment banks augmented the instability in the global financial system. The remaining two investment banks, Morgan Stanley and Goldman Sachs, opted to become commercial banks, thereby subjecting themselves to more stringent regulation.

Banks ended up receiving a double hit. Their securities investors started demanding money and their borrowers were failing to pay their loans. And troubled banks were not able to raise more money, because other banks and investors sensed that they were in trouble and refused to lend to them.

It is also easy to see why the government-sponsored financial intermediaries, Freddie Mac and Fannie Mae, collapsed. Many economists believe it had to do with moral hazard, when individuals take additional risks because they are insured. Investors knew that the government supported Freddie and Fannie mortgage-backed securities, so they considered them very low risk. With the government behind them, Freddie and Fannie had an incentive to issue risky securities and buy risky mortgages from banks. Banks knew that Freddie and Fannie would buy almost any mortgage they created. However, when people stopped paying their mortgages, the two giant intermediaries lost billions of dollars. Their stocks became worthless and the government had to take control of both Fannie Mae and Freddie Mac.

Financial markets depend on lenders making funds available to borrowers. When lenders become reluctant to make loans, it becomes difficult to assess credit risk. This happened in 2008, and led the Federal Reserve and other central banks around the world to pour hundreds of billions of dollars (euros, pounds, etc.) into credit markets to ease the pain of the financial crisis. In addition, the government has enacted large fiscal stimulus packages of close to $1 trillion. The borrowing and spending is intended to offset the reduction in private sector demand caused by the crisis. We will return to this topic in the chapter entitled "Fiscal Policy."

In sum, we saw several factors contribute to the financial crisis. First, there was a decline in asset prices. In the case of the financial crisis of 2007 to 2008, the asset was housing, which had its worst downturn in over 70 years. Second, many financial institutions became insolvent as a result of investments in the real estate market. When housing prices fell, some homeowners stopped paying their loans, and financial institutions holding those loans were compromised.

Third, the financial crisis led to a decline in confidence and a credit crunch. Because a number of financial institutions were in trouble, many borrowers had a difficult time securing a loan, even for promising investment projects. This led to a reduction in overall demand for goods and services in the economy. The good news is that financial crises do eventually end.

17-4e THE RECESSION OF 2008–2009: THE *AD/AS* MODEL

The U.S. experienced a strong expansion from 2003–2007. Housing and stock prices were rising. Increases in wealth caused the aggregate demand curve to shift right.

By early 2007 and the first half of 2008, energy prices were soaring. The *SRAS* shifted to the left as gas prices and other energy prices almost doubled from early 2007 to mid-2008. Recall that unanticipated increases in key input prices can cause negative supply shocks and shift the *SRAS* curve to the left, as shown in Exhibit 17.5. However, by mid-2008 oil prices reversed themselves and now the economy faced a much bigger problem—a powerful negative demand shock. Housing prices started falling in 2006 and by 2008 were falling sharply. Stock prices were also rapidly declining; together they led to the destruction of trillions of dollars of wealth. Consequently, there was a substantial reduction in consumption and investment spending, causing a leftward shift in the aggregate demand curve. The price level fell from PL_1 to PL_2 and real output fell from $RGDP_{NR}$ to $RGDP_1$ as the economy moved from point A to point B as shown in Exhibit 17.9.

The Fed changed course to reverse the decline in *AD* beginning in September 2007 by pumping reserves into the banking system and lowering interest rates. But its actions were not enough to increase *AD*. Expansionary fiscal policy was also used, but its effects were both slow to appear and had a limited effect in combatting the fall in *AD*. Even by mid-2009, only about 15 percent of the over $800 billion of American Recovery and Reinvestment Act (ARRA) money had made it into the economy.

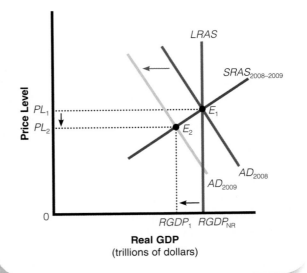

EXHIBIT 17.9 The Recession of 2008–2009

© Cengage Learning 2014

SECTION CHECK 4 ANSWERS

1. Maintaining very low interest rates for a substantial period of time contributed to the housing price run-up. The rapid increase in housing prices during the housing bubble made both borrowers and lenders expect that the risks of subprime lending were not great.

2. The standards for low-income families to qualify for home loans were reduced, increasing the number of high-risk borrowers.

3. After several years of maintaining low real interest rates, the Fed began pushing short-term interest rates up in 2005. The higher interest rates and falling housing prices pushed many homeowners into default and foreclosure.

Chapter 17: Self-Review

Now that you are finished reading the chapter, review the questions below. You can write your answers in the space provided, then go online to see the answers at www.cengagebrain.com.

17-1 PROBLEMS IN IMPLEMENTING FISCAL AND MONETARY POLICY

1. What is the crowding-out effect?

2. True or False: The lag time for adopting policy changes is shorter for fiscal policy than for monetary policy.

3. True or False: The activities of global and nonbank institutions weaken the Fed's influence on the money market.

17-2 RATIONAL EXPECTATIONS

4. Fill-in-the-Blanks: In a world of rational expectations, it is _____ to reduce unemployment below its natural rate but potentially _____ to reduce inflation rates.

5. True or False: According to rational expectations theory, both expected and unexpected changes in inflation can affect real wages and unemployment.

6. Give an example of a positive productivity shock.

7. Fill-in-the-Blanks: Real business cycle theorists as well as rational expectations economists believe that wages and prices are _____ and that markets adjust _____.

17-3 CONTROVERSIES IN MACROECONOMIC POLICY

8. What is a political business cycle?

9. What are the arguments against inflation targeting?

10. True or False: If each possible good were indexed to changes in the general price level, it would be easy for relative price changes to signal changing relative scarcities.

17-4 THE FINANCIAL CRISIS OF 2007–2009

11. Why were those who took out hybrid loans at far greater risk of foreclosure when the Fed began raising interest rates?

12. Why was home building such an important factor in the crisis?

13. Fill-in-the-Blanks: After several years of maintaining _____ real interest rates, the Fed reversed course and pushed short-term interest rates _____.

		BUY	SELL
🇺🇸	USD	1.6110	1.5410
🇬🇧	GBP	0.8110	0.7770
🇦🇺	AUD	1.6760	1.5800
🇨🇦	CAD	1.6400	1.5460
🇨🇭	CHF	1.6560	1.5610
🇸🇪	SEK	9.6750	9.1120

If you lived in Canada

and you were leaving the country, you would need to convert your money into the currency of the country you were going to so that you could make purchases there. Why do the rates matter, though? And what makes them different? Where would you get the most advantageous deal when exchanging currencies? If you were a firm doing business, how would these different exchange rates affect the profitability of your business in other countries?

Test your Economics *street-smart* knowledge and see how you compare against other students! Scan here or visit CourseMate for Survey of ECON2.

JPY	172.329	162.??1

© iStockphoto.com/funart

18

International Economics

conomics is largely about exchange. But up to this point we have focused on trade between individuals within the domestic economy. In this chapter, we extend our coverage to international trade. Why do countries trade? Hong Kong has no oil—how are they going to get it? Bananas could be grown in the most tropical parts of the United States or in expensive greenhouses; however it is easier to import bananas from Honduras.

Stop for a moment and imagine a world without international trade. Chocolate is derived from cocoa beans that are imported from South America and Africa. There are imported cars from Germany and Japan, shoes and sweaters from Italy, shirts from India, and watches and clocks from Switzerland. Consumers love trade because it provides us with more choices. It is good for producers, too; and the speed of transportation and communication has opened up world markets. In addition, lower costs are sometimes the result of economies of scale. Free trade gives firms access to large world markets. It also fosters more competition, which helps to keep prices down.

In the first half of this chapter we will study the reasons for the importance of trade. We will also look at the arguments for and against trade protection. In the second half of this chapter we will discuss international finance.

18-1 The Growth in World Trade

SECTION CHECK 1

Keep the following questions in mind as you read through this section.

1. What does the United States export and import?

2. Who trades with the United States?

The importance of the international sector varies enormously from place to place across the world. Some nations are virtually closed economies (no interaction with other economies), with foreign trade equaling only

383

EXHIBIT 18.1 Major U.S. Trading Partners

Top Trading Partners—Exports of Goods in 2011			Top Trading Partners—Imports of Goods in 2011		
Rank	Country	Percent of Total	Rank	Country	Percent of Total
1	Canada	19	1	China	18.4
2	Mexico	13.3	2	Canada	14.2
3	China	7	3	Mexico	11.7
4	Japan	4.5	4	Japan	5.8
			5	Germany	4.4

SOURCE: Central Intelligence Agency, *North America: United States, The World Factbook.*

a small proportion (perhaps 5 percent) of total output, while in other countries trade is much more important.

18-1a U.S. EXPORTS AND IMPORTS

U.S. exports of goods and services amounted to 14 percent of GDP in 2011. U.S. exports include services (transportation, insurance, banking, education and tourism), capital goods (like aircraft), industrial supplies (like chemicals and plastics), consumer goods (pharmaceuticals and entertainment products), food, and automobiles. U.S. imports of goods and services in 2011 amounted to 18 percent of GDP. U.S. imports include industrial supplies (crude oil and refined petroleum products), consumer goods (pharmaceuticals), capital goods (computers), services, autos, and food.

18-1b TRADING PARTNERS

In the early history of the United States, international trade largely took place with Europe and with Great Britain in particular. Now the United States trades with a number of countries, the most important of which are Canada, Mexico, China, Japan, Germany, and the United Kingdom, as seen in Exhibit 18.1.

SECTION CHECK 1 ANSWERS

1. U.S. exports include capital goods, automobiles, industrial supplies, raw materials, consumer goods, and agricultural products. U.S. imports include crude oil and refined petroleum products, machinery, automobiles, consumer goods, industrial raw materials, food, and beverages.

2. Some of the United States' most important trade partners include Canada, Japan, Mexico, China, Germany, and the United Kingdom.

18-2 Comparative Advantage and Gains from Trade

SECTION CHECK 2

Keep the following questions in mind as you read through this section.

1. Does voluntary trade lead to an improvement in economic welfare?

2. What benefits can a nation derive from specialization?

Using simple logic, we conclude that the very existence of trade suggests that trade is economically beneficial. Our conclusion is true if we assume that people are utility maximizers and are rational, are intelligent, and engage in trade on a voluntary basis. Because almost all trade is voluntary, it would seem that trade occurs because the participants feel that they are better off because of the trade. Both participants in an exchange of goods and services anticipate an improvement in their economic welfare. Sometimes, of course, anticipations are not realized (because the world is uncertain); but the motive behind trade remains an expectation of some enhancement in utility or satisfaction by both parties.

Granted, "trade must be good because people do it" is a rather simplistic explanation. The classical economist David Ricardo is usually given most of the credit for developing the economic theory that more precisely explains how trade can be mutually beneficial to both parties, raising output and income levels in the entire trading area.

18-2a THE PRINCIPLE OF COMPARATIVE ADVANTAGE

Ricardo's theory of international trade centers on the concept of comparative advantage. As we discussed in Chapter 2, persons, regions, or countries can gain by specializing in the production of the good in which they have a comparative advantage. That is, if they can produce a good or service at a lower opportunity cost than others can, we say that they have a *comparative advantage* in the production of that good or service. In other words, a country or a region should specialize in producing and selling those items that it can produce at a lower opportunity cost than other regions or countries.

Comparative advantage analysis does not mean that nations or areas that export goods will necessarily be able to produce those goods or services more cheaply than can other nations in an absolute sense. What is important is *comparative* advantage, not *absolute* advantage. For example, the United States may be able to produce more cotton cloth per worker than India can, but this capability does not mean that the United States should necessarily sell cotton cloth to India. For a highly productive nation to produce goods in which it is only marginally more productive than other nations, the nation must take resources from the production of other goods in which its productive abilities are markedly superior. As a result, the opportunity costs in India of making cotton cloth may be less than in the

COMPARATIVE ADVANTAGE AND ABSOLUTE ADVANTAGE

Q&A

Q: Renee Saunts is a successful artist who can complete one painting in each 40-hour workweek. Each painting sells for $4,000. As a result of her enormous success, however, Renee is swamped in paperwork. To solve the problem, Renee hires Drake to handle all the bookkeeping and typing associated with buying supplies, answering inquiries from prospective buyers and dealers, writing art galleries, and so forth. Renee pays Drake $300 per week for his work. After a couple of weeks in this arrangement, Renee realizes that she can handle Drake's chores more quickly than Drake does. In fact, she estimates that she is twice as fast as Drake, completing in 20 hours what it takes Drake 40 hours to complete. Should Renee fire Drake?

COMPARATIVE ADVANTAGE AND ABSOLUTE ADVANTAGE

Q&A

A: Clearly Renee has an absolute advantage over Drake in both painting and paperwork, because she can do twice as much paperwork in 40 hours as Drake can, and Drake cannot paint well at all. Still, it would be foolish for Renee to do both jobs. If Renee did her own paperwork, it would take her 20 hours per week, leaving her only 20 hours to paint. Because each watercolor takes 40 hours to paint, Renee's output would fall from one painting per week to one painting per two weeks.

When Drake works for her, Renee's net income is $3,700 per week ($4,000 per painting minus $300 in Drake's wages); when Drake does not work for her, it is only $2,000 per week (one painting every two weeks). Even though Renee is both a better painter and better at Drake's chores than Drake, it pays for her to specialize in painting, in which she has a comparative advantage, and allow Drake to do the paperwork. The opportunity cost to Renee of paperwork is high. For Drake, who lacks skills as a painter, the opportunity cost of doing the paperwork is much less.

United States. With that, both can gain from trade, despite potential absolute advantages for every good in the United States.

18-2b COMPARATIVE ADVANTAGE, SPECIALIZATION, AND THE PRODUCTION POSSIBILITIES CURVES

Wendy and Calvin live on opposite ends of a small town. Wendy can produce either food or cloth. On a daily basis, she can produce 10 pounds of food, 5 yards of cloth, or any linear combination of the two goods along her production possibilities curve in Exhibit 18.2 (to simplify the calculations, we have drawn linear production possibilities curves). If Wendy spends the whole day producing food, she can produce 10 pounds. If she spends the whole day producing cloth, she can produce 5 yards. Recall that the production possibilities curve represents the maximum possible combinations of food and cloth she can produce, given her fixed set of resources and technology. The negatively sloped production possibilities curve means that when she produces one good, with her fixed resources, she gives up the opportunity to produce another good.

What is Wendy's opportunity cost of producing cloth? It is what Wendy gives up in food production for each unit of cloth production, which is 2 pounds of food per yard of cloth. Therefore, her opportunity cost of producing a yard of cloth is 2 pounds of food. What is the opportunity cost of Wendy producing food? It is what she gives up in cloth production for each unit increase in food production—1 yard of cloth per 2 pounds of food. That is, for each pound of food Wendy produces, she gives up producing 1/2 yard of cloth.

Calvin, who lives on the other side of town, can also produce food or cloth. On a daily basis, he could produce 3 pounds of food, 4 yards of cloth, or any linear combination of the two along his production

EXHIBIT 18.2 Wendy's Production Possibilities Curve

$$OC_{CLOTH} = \frac{\text{loss in food}}{\text{gain in cloth}} = \frac{10}{5} = \frac{2 \text{ pounds of food}}{1 \text{ yard of cloth}}$$

$$OC_{FOOD} = \frac{\text{loss in cloth}}{\text{gain in food}} = \frac{5}{10} = \frac{1 \text{ yard of cloth}}{2 \text{ pounds of food}}$$

or

1 yard of cloth costs 2 pounds of food.
1 pound of food costs 1/2 yard of cloth.

© Cengage Learning 2014

EXHIBIT 18.3 Calvin's Production Possibilities Curve

$$OC_{CLOTH} = \frac{\text{loss in food}}{\text{gain in cloth}} = \frac{3 \text{ pounds of food}}{4 \text{ yards of cloth}}$$

$$OC_{FOOD} = \frac{\text{loss in cloth}}{\text{gain in food}} = \frac{4 \text{ yards of cloth}}{3 \text{ pounds of food}}$$

or

1 yard of cloth costs 3/4 pounds of food.
1 pound of food costs 4/3 yards of cloth.

© Cengage Learning 2014

possibilities curve in Exhibit 18.3. When he spends the day producing cloth, he can produce 4 yards. When he spends the day producing food, he can produce 3 pounds. To produce cloth, Calvin must decrease his production of food. What is Calvin's opportunity cost of producing cloth? It is what he gives up in producing food for each unit of cloth production, which is 3 pounds of food per 4 pounds of cloth. Therefore, his opportunity cost of producing cloth is 3/4 pound of food. What is Calvin's opportunity cost of producing food? It is what he gives up in cloth production for each unit of food production, which is 4 yards of cloth per 3 pounds of food. Therefore, the opportunity cost of producing a pound of food is 4/3 yards of cloth per day.

Absolute and Comparative Advantage

Now let us compare Wendy's production possibilities curve to Calvin's production possibilities curve to see who has an absolute advantage in producing cloth and who has an absolute advantage in producing food. An absolute advantage occurs when one producer can perform a task using fewer inputs than the other producer. In Exhibit 18.4 on the next page, we see that Wendy is

more productive than Calvin at producing food. Along the vertical axis, we can see that if Wendy uses all of her resources to produce food, she can produce 10 pounds of food per day. If Calvin devotes all of his resources to producing food, he can only produce 3 pounds of food per day. We say that Wendy has an absolute advantage over Calvin in the production of food.

Along the horizontal axis in Exhibit 18.4, we can see that Wendy is also more productive than Calvin at producing cloth. If Wendy devotes all of her resources to producing cloth, she can produce 5 yards of cloth per day. If Calvin devotes all of his resources to producing cloth, he can only produce 4 yards of cloth per day. We say that Wendy also has an absolute advantage over Calvin in the production of cloth. She has an absolute advantage in producing both food and cloth. Therefore, should Wendy produce both food and cloth and Calvin produce nothing? No!

Recall from Chapter 2 that a comparative advantage exists when one person can produce a good at a lower opportunity cost than can another person. So who has the comparative advantage (lowest opportunity cost) in producing food? In this case, Wendy's opportunity cost of producing food is less than Calvin's.

EXHIBIT 18.4 Absolute and Comparative Advantage

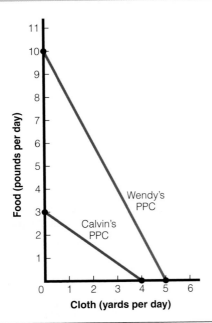

	Cloth (yds/day)	Food (lbs/day)	OC of Cloth	OC of Food
Wendy	5	10	2 lb of food	1/2 yd of cloth
Calvin	4	3	3/4 lbs of food	4/3 yds of cloth

© Cengage Learning 2014

Wendy's opportunity cost of producing a pound of food is 1/2 yard of cloth, whereas Calvin's opportunity cost of producing 1 pound of food is 4/3 yards of cloth. Therefore, Wendy is the more efficient producer of food—she gives up less in cloth when she produces food, compared to Calvin. Remember, comparative advantage is always a relative concept.

Who has the comparative advantage in producing cloth? That is, who can produce cloth at the lowest opportunity cost? That would be Calvin, because he gives up only 3/4 pound of food to produce 1 yard of cloth. If Wendy were to produce a yard of cloth, she would have to give up 2 pounds of food. The lowest opportunity cost producer of cloth is Calvin. In other words, to produce one more yard of cloth, Calvin gives up fewer pounds of food than does Wendy. Therefore, Calvin is the more efficient producer of cloth—he gives up less in food when he produces cloth, compared to Wendy. Calvin has a comparative advantage in producing cloth.

Gains from Specialization and Exchange

Suppose Wendy and Calvin meet and decide to specialize in those activities in which they have a comparative advantage. Wendy would specialize in the production of food and Calvin would specialize in the production of cloth. By specializing, Wendy can produce 10 pounds of food per day (point B' in Exhibit 18.5) and Calvin can produce 4 yards of cloth per day (point B in Exhibit 18.5). *However, to achieve any of the gains from comparative advantage and specialization, there must be trade.*

After specializing in the good in which they have a comparative advantage, suppose Wendy and Calvin agree to trade at the exchange "price" of 1 pound of food for 1 yard of cloth. If Wendy trades 3 yards of cloth for 3 pounds of food, she can obtain a position along the new production possibilities curve which is beyond her original production possibilities curve, point C' in Exhibit 18.5. Wendy can now have 7 pounds of food and 3 yards of cloth—a combination she could not have obtained without specialization and trade.

Calvin also benefits from specialization and trade. In the trade, he receives 3 pounds of food for 3 yards of cloth and now can enjoy 3 pounds of food and 1 yard of cloth a combination, at point C in Exhibit 18.5, he could not have obtained without specialization and trade. In sum, the exchange has allowed both Wendy and Calvin to produce and consume a combination of the two goods beyond what would have been attainable if it were not for specialization and trade.

Individuals and Nations Gain from Specialization and Trade

Just as Calvin and Wendy benefit from specialization and trade, so do the people of different nations. Because of specialization, according to comparative advantage, both nations can be better off, even if one nation has an absolute advantage in both goods over the other. Furthermore, the greater the difference in opportunity cost between the two trading partners, the greater the benefits from specialization and exchange.

Note that when we say nations trade with nations, we really mean that the people of a nation trade with people of other nations. When China trades clothes to the United States for Boeing 787 jetliners, they both benefit from the exchange, because they are able to obtain them at a lower cost than if they produced those goods themselves. Free trade does not guarantee that each individual will be better off or that everyone will receive the same benefits, but it does mean that collectively, the population of each

EXHIBIT 18.5 The Gains from Specialization and Trade

Wendy's PPC

Calvin's PPC

nation will benefit from the trade. Indeed, unskilled workers in high-wage countries may temporarily lose jobs. Recall that when NAFTA was passed, its critics argued that low-skilled workers would lose jobs because of U.S. trade with Mexico. However, that does not appear to have happened to any large extent. Instead, consumers have been enjoying lower-priced goods because of the trade.

SECTION CHECK 2 ANSWERS

1. Voluntary trade occurs because participants feel that they are better off as a result of the trade. Through trade and specialization in products in which it has a comparative advantage, a country can enjoy a greater array of goods and services at a lower cost.

2. A nation can gain from trade if it can produce the good or service relatively more cheaply than can anyone else. That is, a country should specialize in producing and selling those items that it can produce at a lower opportunity cost than can other countries.

18-3 Supply and Demand in International Trade

SECTION CHECK 3

Keep the following questions in mind as you read through this section.

1. Who benefits and who loses when a country becomes an exporter?

2. Who benefits and who loses when a country becomes an importer?

Recall from Chapter 4 that the difference between the most a consumer would be willing to pay for a quantity of a good and what a consumer actually has to pay is called *consumer surplus*. The difference between the lowest price for which a supplier would be willing to supply a quantity of a good or service and the revenues a supplier actually receives for selling it is called *producer surplus*. With the tools of consumer and producer surplus, we can better analyze the impact of trade. Who gains? Who loses? What happens to net welfare?

18-3a FREE TRADE AND EXPORTS— DOMESTIC PRODUCERS GAIN MORE THAN DOMESTIC CONSUMERS LOSE

Using the concepts of consumer and producer surplus, we can graphically show the net benefits of free trade. Imagine an economy with no trade, where the equilibrium price, P_{BT}, and equilibrium quantity, Q_{BT}, of wheat are determined exclusively in the domestic economy, as shown in Exhibit 18.6. Suppose that this imaginary economy decides to engage in free trade. You can see that the world price (established in the world market for wheat), P_{AT}, is higher than the domestic price before trade, P_{BT}. In other words, the domestic economy has a comparative advantage in wheat, because it can produce wheat at a lower relative price than the rest of the world can. So this wheat-producing country sells some wheat to the domestic market and some wheat to the world market, all at the going world price.

The price after trade (P_{AT}) is higher than the price before trade (P_{BT}). Because the world market is huge, the demand from the rest of the world at the world price (P_{AT}) is assumed to be perfectly elastic. That is, domestic wheat farmers can sell all the wheat they want at the world price. If you were a wheat farmer in Nebraska, would you rather sell all your bushels of wheat at the higher world price or the lower domestic price? As a wheat farmer, you would surely prefer the higher world price. But this preference is not good news for domestic cereal and bread eaters, who now have to pay more for products made with wheat because P_{AT} is greater than P_{BT}.

Graphically, we can see how free trade and exports affect both domestic consumers and domestic producers. At the higher world price, P_{AT}, domestic wheat producers are receiving larger amounts of producer surplus. Before trade, they received a surplus equal to area e + f; after trade, they received surplus b + c + d + e + f, for a net gain of area b + c + d. However, part of the domestic producers' gain comes at domestic consumers' expense. Specifically, consumers had a consumer surplus equal to area a + b + c before the trade (at P_{BT}), but they now have only area a (at P_{AT})—a loss of area b + c.

Area b reflects a redistribution of income, because producers are gaining exactly what consumers are losing. Is that good or bad? We cannot say objectively whether consumers or producers are more deserving. However, the net benefits from allowing free trade and exports are clearly visible in area d. Without free trade, no one gets area d. That is, on net, members of the domestic society gain when domestic wheat producers are able to sell

EXHIBIT 18.6 Free Trade and Exports

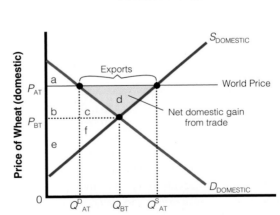

Domestic Gains and Losses from Free Trade (exports)			
Area	Before	After	Change
Consumer Surplus (CS)	a + b + c	a	−b − c
Producer Surplus (PS)	e + f	b + c + d + e + f	+b + c + d
Total Welfare from Trade (CS + PS)	a + b + c + e + f	a + b + c + d + e + f	+d

© Cengage Learning 2014

EXHIBIT 18.7 Free Trade and Imports

World Market

Price of Shirts (world) vs. Quantity of Shirts (world)

S_{WORLD}, D_{WORLD}, P_{WORLD}

Domestic Market

Price of Shirts (domestic) vs. Quantity of Shirts (domestic)

$S_{DOMESTIC}$, $D_{DOMESTIC}$

a, b, c, d

P_{BT}, P_{AT}

Net domestic gain from trade

World

Imports

Q^S_{AT}, Q^D_{AT}

Domestic Gains and Losses from Free Trade (imports)			
Area	**Before Trade**	**After Trade**	**Change**
Consumer Surplus (*CS*)	a	a + b + d	b + d
Producer Surplus (*PS*)	b + c	c	–b
Total Welfare from Trade (*CS* + *PS*)	a + b + c	a + b + c + d	+d

© Cengage Learning 2014

their wheat at the higher world price. Although domestic wheat consumers lose from the free trade, those negative effects are more than offset by the positive gains captured by producers. Area d is the net increase in domestic wealth (the welfare gain) from free trade and exports.

18-3b FREE TRADE AND IMPORTS— DOMESTIC CONSUMERS GAIN MORE THAN DOMESTIC PRODUCERS LOSE

Now suppose that our economy does not produce shirts as well as other countries of the world. In other words, other countries have a comparative advantage in producing shirts, and the domestic price for shirts is above the world price. This scenario is illustrated in Exhibit 18.7 above. At the new, lower world price, the domestic producer will supply quantity Q^S_{AT}. However, at the lower world price, the domestic producers will not produce the entire amount demanded by domestic consumers, Q^D_{AT}. At the world price, reflecting the world supply and demand for shirts, the difference between what is domestically supplied and what is domestically demanded is supplied by imports.

At the world price (established in the world market for shirts), we assume that the world supply to the domestic

market curve is perfectly elastic—that the producers of the world can supply all that domestic consumers are willing to buy at the going price. At the world price, Q^S_{AT} is supplied by domestic producers, and the difference between Q^D_{AT} and Q^S_{AT} is imported from other countries.

Who wins and who loses from free trade and imports? Domestic consumers benefit from paying a lower price for shirts. In Exhibit 18.7, before trade,

tariff a tax on imports

consumers only received area a in consumer surplus. After trade, the price fell and quantity purchased increased, causing the area of consumer surplus to increase from area a to area a + b + d, a gain of b + d. Domestic producers lose because they are now selling their shirts at the lower world price, P_{AT}. The producer surplus before trade was b + c. After trade, the producer surplus falls to area c, reducing producer surplus by area b. Area b, then, represents a redistribution from producers to consumers; but area d is the net increase in domestic wealth (the welfare gain) from free trade and imports.

SECTION CHECK 3 ANSWERS

1. With free trade and exports, domestic producers gain more than domestic consumers lose.

2. With free trade and imports, domestic consumers gain more than domestic producers lose.

18-4 Tariffs, Import Quotas, and Subsidies

SECTION CHECK 4

Keep the following questions in mind as you read through this section.

1. What are the effects of a tariff?

2. What are the effects of an import quota?

3. What is the economic impact of subsidies?

In this section we will discuss three mechanisms of trade protection: tariffs, import quotas, and subsidies.

18-4a TARIFFS

A **tariff** is a tax on imported goods. Tariffs are usually relatively small revenue producers that retard the expansion of trade. They bring about higher prices and revenues for domestic

producers, and lower sales and revenues for foreign producers. Moreover, tariffs lead to higher prices for domestic consumers. In fact, the gains to producers are more than offset by the losses to consumers. With the aid of a graph we will see how the gains and losses from tariffs work.

18-4b THE DOMESTIC ECONOMIC IMPACT OF TARIFFS

The domestic economic impact of tariffs is presented in Exhibit 18.8, which illustrates the supply and demand curves for domestic consumers and producers of shoes. In a typical international supply and demand illustration, the intersection of the world supply and demand curves would determine the domestic market price. However, with import tariffs, the domestic price of shoes is greater than the world price, as in Exhibit 18.8. We consider the world supply curve (S_W) for domestic consumers to be perfectly elastic; that is, we can buy all we want at the world price (P_W). At the world price, domestic producers are only willing to provide quantity Q_S, but domestic consumers are willing to buy quantity Q_D—more than domestic producers are willing to supply. Imports make up the difference.

As you can see in Exhibit 18.8, the imposition of the tariff shifts the perfectly elastic supply curve from foreigners to domestic consumers upward from S_{WORLD} to $S_{WORLD+TARIFF}$, but it does not alter the domestic supply or demand curve. At the resulting higher domestic price (P_{W+T}), domestic suppliers are willing to supply more, Q_{iS}, but domestic consumers are willing to buy less, Q'_D. At the new equilibrium, the domestic price (P_{W+T}) is higher and the quantity of shoes demanded (Q'_D) is lower. But at the new price, the domestic quantity demanded is lower and the quantity supplied domestically is higher, reducing the quantity of imported shoes. Overall, then, tariffs lead to (1) a smaller total quantity sold, (2) a higher price for shoes for domestic consumers, (3) greater sales of shoes at higher prices for domestic producers, and (4) lower sales of foreign shoes.

Although domestic producers do gain more sales and higher earnings, consumers lose much more. The increase in price from the tariff results in a loss in consumer surplus, as shown in Exhibit 18.8. After the tariff, shoe prices rise to P_{W+T}, and, consequently, consumer surplus falls by area c + d + e + f, representing the welfare loss to consumers from the tariff. Area c in Exhibit 18.8 shows the gain to domestic producers as a result of the tariff. That is, at the higher price, domestic producers are willing to supply

Tariffs lead to:

1) Smaller total quantity sold

2) Higher price for domestic consumers

3) More sales at higher prices for domestic producers

4) Lower foreign sales

EXHIBIT 18.8 Free Trade and Tariffs

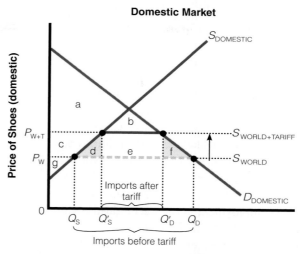

Gains and Losses from Tariffs			
Area	Before Tariffs	After Tariffs	Change
Consumer Surplus (CS)	a + b + c + d + e + f	a + b	−c − d − e − f
Producer Surplus (PS)	g	c + g	+c
Government Revenues (Tariff)	0	e	+e
Total Welfare from Tariff (CS + PS + Tariff Revenues)	a + b + c + d + e + f + g	a + b + c + e + g	−d − f

© Cengage Learning 2014

more shoes, representing a welfare gain to producers resulting from the tariff. As a result of the tariff revenues, government gains area e. This is the import tariff—the revenue government collects from foreign countries on imports. However, we see from Exhibit 18.8 that consumers lose more than producers and government gain from the tariff. That is, on net, the deadweight loss associated with the tariff is represented by area d + f.

18-4c ARGUMENTS FOR TARIFFS

Despite the preceding arguments against trade restrictions, they continue to be levied. Some rationale for their existence is necessary. Three common arguments for the use of trade restrictions deserve our critical examination.

Temporary Trade Restrictions Help Infant Industries Grow

A country might argue that a protective tariff will allow a new industry to more quickly reach a scale of operation at which economies of scale and production efficiencies

can be realized. That is, temporarily shielding the young industry from competition from foreign firms will allow the infant industry a chance to grow. With early protection, these firms will eventually be able to compete effectively in the global market. It is presumed that without this protection, the industry could never get on its feet. At first hearing, the argument sounds valid, but it involves many problems. How do you identify "infant industries" that genuinely have potential economies of scale and will quickly become efficient with protection? We do not know the long-run average total cost curves of industries, a necessary piece of information. Moreover, if firms and governments are truly convinced of the advantages of allowing an industry to reach a large scale, would it not be wise to make massive loans to the industry, allowing it to begin large-scale production all at once rather than slowly and at the expense of consumers? In other words, the goal of allowing the industry to reach its efficient size can be reached without protection. Finally, the history of infant industry tariffs suggests that the tariffs often linger long after the industry is mature and no longer in need of protection.

Tariffs Can Reduce Domestic Unemployment

Exhibit 18.8 shows how tariffs increase output by domestic producers, thus leading to increased employment and reduced unemployment in industries where tariffs have been imposed. Yet the overall employment effects of a tariff imposition are not likely to be positive; the argument is incorrect. Why? First, the imposition of a tariff by the United States on, say, foreign steel is going to be noticed in the countries adversely affected by the tariff. If a new tariff on steel lowers Japanese steel sales to the United States, the Japanese will likely retaliate by imposing tariffs on U.S. exports to Japan, say, on machinery exports. The retaliatory tariff will lower U.S. sales of machinery and thus employment in the U.S. machinery industries. As a result, the gain in employment in the steel industry will be offset by a loss of employment elsewhere.

Even if other countries did not retaliate, U.S. employment would likely suffer outside the industry gaining tariff protection. The way that other countries pay for U.S. goods is by getting dollars from sales to the United States—imports to us. If new tariffs lead to restrictions on imports, fewer dollars will be flowing overseas in payment for imports, which means that foreigners will have fewer dollars available to buy our exports. Other things being equal, this situation will tend to reduce our exports, thus creating unemployment in the export industries.

Tariffs Are Necessary for Reasons of National Security

Sometimes it is argued that tariffs are a means of preventing a nation from becoming too dependent on foreign suppliers of goods vital to national security. That is, by making foreign goods more expensive, we can protect domestic suppliers. For example, if oil is vital to operating planes and tanks, a cutoff of foreign supplies of oil during wartime could cripple a nation's defenses.

The national security argument is usually not valid. If a nation's own resources are depletable, tariff-imposed reliance on domestic supplies will hasten depletion of domestic reserves, making the country even *more* dependent on imports in the future. If we impose a high tariff on foreign oil to protect domestic producers, we will increase domestic output of oil in the short run; but in the process, we will deplete the stockpile of available reserves. Thus, the defense argument is of questionable validity. From a defense standpoint, it makes more sense to use foreign oil in peacetime and perhaps stockpile "insurance" supplies so that larger domestic supplies would be available during wars.

Are Tariffs Necessary to Protect against Dumping?

Dumping occurs when a foreign country sells its products at prices below their costs or below the prices for which they are sold on the domestic market. For example, the Japanese government has been accused for years of subsidizing Japanese steel producers as they attempt to gain a greater share of the world steel market and greater market power. That is, the short-term losses from selling below cost may be offset by the long-term economic profits from employing this strategy. Some have argued that tariffs are needed to protect domestic producers against low-cost dumpers because they will raise the cost to foreign producers and offset their cost advantage.

The United States has antidumping laws; if a foreign country is found guilty of dumping, the United States can impose antidumping tariffs on that country's products, thereby raising the price of the foreign goods that are being dumped. In practice, however, it is often difficult to prove dumping; foreign countries may simply have lower steel production costs. So what may seem like dumping may in fact be comparative advantage.

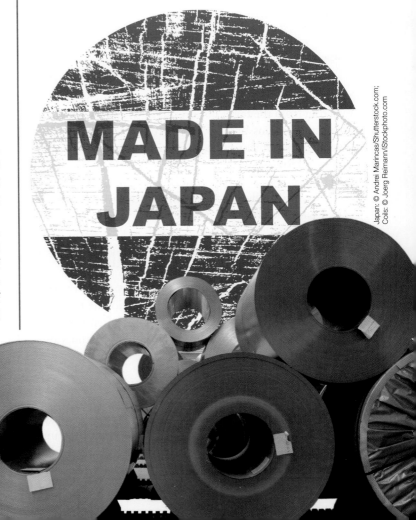

18-4d IMPORT QUOTAS

Like tariffs, **import quotas** directly restrict imports, leading to reductions in trade and thus preventing nations from fully realizing their comparative advantage. The case for quotas is probably even weaker than the case for tariffs. Unlike what occurs with a tariff, the U.S. government does not collect any revenue as a result of the import quota. Despite the higher prices, the loss in consumer surplus, and the loss in government revenue, quotas come about because people often view them as being less protectionist than tariffs—the traditional, most-maligned form of protection.

Besides the rather blunt means of curtailing imports by using tariffs and quotas, nations have devised still other, more subtle means of restricting international trade. For example, nations sometimes impose product standards, ostensibly to protect consumers against inferior merchandise. Effectively, however, those standards may be simply a means of restricting foreign competition. For example, France might keep certain kinds of wine out of the country on the grounds that they are made with allegedly inferior grapes or have an inappropriate alcoholic content. Likewise, the United States might prohibit automobile imports that do not meet certain standards in terms of pollutants, safety, and gasoline mileage. Even if these standards are not intended to restrict foreign competition, the regulations may nonetheless have that impact, restricting consumer choice in the process.

18-4e THE DOMESTIC ECONOMIC IMPACT OF AN IMPORT QUOTA

The domestic economic impact of an import quota on sugar is presented in Exhibit 18.9 on the next page. The introduction of an import quota increases the price from the world price, P_W (established in the world market for sugar) to P_{W+Q}. The quota causes the price to rise above the world price. The domestic quantity demanded falls and the domestic quantity supplied rises.

Consequently, the number of imports is much smaller than

it would be without the import quota. Compared with free trade, domestic producers are better off, but domestic consumers are worse off. Specifically, the import quota results in a gain in producer surplus of area c and a loss in consumer surplus of area c + d + e + f. However, unlike the tariff case, where the government gains area e in revenues, the government does not gain any revenues with a quota. So the difference between a tariff and a quota is that the tariff brings in revenue to the government while the quota benefits the foreign producer who is lucky enough to receive an import license. They are lucky because they can sell their allotted amount of output at the higher domestic price rather than the lower world price. In the United States, import licenses are given to foreign producers of clothes and, to a lesser extent, sugar. However, if the government charges a fee for the import license, then it is very similar to the tariff—especially if the fee is the difference between the domestic and world

> **import quota** a legal limit on the imported quantity of a good that is produced abroad and can be sold in domestic markets

Tariffs on foreign exports can lead to retaliatory tariffs on domestic exports.

EXHIBIT 18.9 Free Trade and Import Quotas

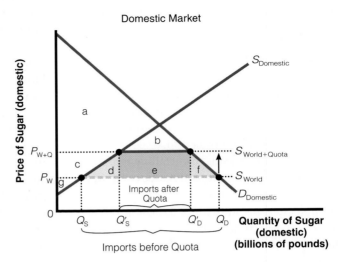

Gains and Losses from Import Quotas			
Area	**Before Quota**	**After Quota**	**Change**
Consumer Surplus (*CS*)	a + b + c + d + e + f	a + b	–c – d – e – f
Producer Surplus (*PS*)	g	c + g	+c
Foreign Producers (import license)	0	e	+e
Total Welfare (*CS* + *PS*) from Quota	a + b + c + d + e + f + g	a + b + c + g	–d – f

With an import quota, the price rises from P_W to P_{W+Q}. Compared with free trade, consumers lose area c + d + e + f, while producers gain area b. Foreign producers who have an import license gain area e. The deadweight loss from the quota is area d + f. Under quotas, consumers lose and producers gain.

From Exploring Economics, 6e, by Robert L. Sexton, ISBN: 9781111970307

rent seeking efforts by producers to gain profits from government protections such as tariffs and import quotas

price. In this case, the import quota and the tariff would be identical. In reality, countries very seldom sell their import licenses, so the gains accrue to the firms that receive the licenses. Consequently, the deadweight loss is even greater with quotas than with tariffs.

If tariffs and import quotas hurt importing countries, why do they exist? The reason they exist is that producers can make large profits or "rents" from tariffs and import quotas. Economists call these efforts to gain profits from government protection **rent seeking**. Because this money, time, and effort spent on lobbying could have been spent producing something else, the deadweight loss from tariffs and quotas will likely understate the true deadweight loss to society.

18-4f THE ECONOMIC IMPACT OF SUBSIDIES

Working in the opposite direction, governments sometimes try to encourage exports by subsidizing producers. With a subsidy, revenue is given to producers for each exported unit of output, which stimulates exports. Although not a barrier to trade like tariffs and quotas, subsidies can distort trade patterns and lead to inefficiencies. How do these distortions happen? With subsidies, producers will export goods not because their costs are lower than those of a foreign competitor but because their costs have been artificially reduced by government action, transferring income from taxpayers to the exporter. The subsidy does not reduce the amounts of actual labor, raw material, and capital costs of production—society has the same opportunity costs as before. The nation's taxpayers end up subsidizing the output of producers who, relative to producers in other countries, are inefficient. The nation, then, is exporting products in which it does not have a comparative advantage. Gains from trade in terms of world output are eliminated or reduced by such subsidies. Thus, while usually defended as a means of increasing exports and improving a nation's international financial position, subsidies are usually of dubious worth to the world economy and even to the economy doing the subsidizing.

According to the World Bank and the International Monetary Fund (IMF), world trade has benefited enormously from greater openness in trade since 1950. Tariffs on goods have fallen from a worldwide average of 26 percent to less than 9 percent today. On average, trade has grown more than twice as fast as world output.

Some countries might use methods other than tariffs and import quotes to restrict trade. For example, France might impose quality standards on certain products such as imported wine.

SECTION CHECK 4 ANSWERS

1. Tariffs bring about higher prices and revenues to domestic producers and lower sales and revenues to foreign producers. Tariffs lead to higher prices and reduce consumer surplus for domestic consumers. Tariffs result in a net loss in welfare because the loss in consumer surplus is greater than the gain to producers and the government.

2. Like tariffs, import quotas restrict imports, lowering consumer surplus and preventing countries from fully realizing their comparative advantage. The net loss in welfare from a quota is proportionately larger than for a tariff because it does not result in government revenues.

3. Sometimes government tries to encourage production of a certain good by subsidizing its production with taxpayer dollars. Because subsidies stimulate exports, they are not a barrier to trade like tariffs and import quotas. However, they do distort trade patterns and cause overall inefficiencies.

18-5 The Balance of Payments

SECTION CHECK 5

Keep the following questions in mind as you read through this section.

1. What is the balance of payments?
2. What are the three main components of the balance of payments?
3. What is the balance of trade?

The record of all of the international financial transactions of a nation over a year is called the balance of payments. The **balance of payments** is a statement that records all the exchanges requiring an outflow of funds to foreign nations or an inflow of funds from other nations. Just as an examination of gross domestic product accounts gives us some idea of the economic health and vitality of a nation, the balance of payments provides information about a nation's world trade position. The balance of payments is divided into three main sections: the current account, the financial account, and an "error term" called the statistical discrepancy. These are highlighted in Exhibit 18.10 on the next page. Let us look at each of these components, beginning with the current account, which is made up of imports and exports of goods and services.

18-5a THE CURRENT ACCOUNT

A **current account** is a record of a country's imports and exports of goods and services, net investment income, and net transfers.

Export Goods and the Current Account

Any time a foreign buyer purchases a good from a U.S. producer, the foreign buyer must pay the U.S. producer for the good. Usually, the foreign buyer must pay for the good

balance of payments the record of international transactions in which a nation has engaged over a year

current account a record of a country's imports and exports of goods and services, net investment income, and net transfers

EXHIBIT 18.10 U.S. Balance of Payments, 2011 (billions of dollars)

Type of Transaction				
Current Account			**Financial Account**	
1. Exports of goods	$ 1,497		10. U.S.-owned assets abroad	$−484
2. Imports of goods	−2,236		11. Foreign-owned assets in the United States	1,001
3. Balance of trade (lines 1 + 2)		−739	12. Capital account balance (lines 10 + 11)	517
4. Service exports	606		13. Statistical discrepancy	−51
5. Service imports	−427		14. Net Balance (lines 9 + 12 + 13)	$0
6. Balance on goods and services (lines 3 + 4 + 5)		−560		
7. Unilateral transfers (net)	−133			
8. Investment income (net)	227			
9. Current account balance (lines 6 + 7 + 8)		−466		

SOURCE: Bureau of Economic Analysis

in U.S. dollars, because the producer wants to pay his workers' wages and other input costs with dollars. Making this payment requires the foreign buyer to exchange units of her currency at a foreign exchange dealer for U.S. dollars. Because the United States gains claims for foreign goods by obtaining foreign currency in exchange for the dollars needed to buy exports, all exports of U.S. goods abroad are considered a credit, or plus (+), item in the U.S. balance of payments. Those foreign currencies are later exchangeable for goods and services made in the country that purchased the U.S. exports.

Import Goods and the Current Account

When a U.S. consumer buys an imported good, however, the reverse is true: The U.S. importer must pay the foreign producer, usually in that nation's currency. Typically, the U.S. buyer will go to a foreign exchange dealer and exchange dollars for units of that foreign currency. Imports are thus a debit (−) item in the balance of payments, because the dollars sold to buy the foreign currency add to foreign claims for foreign goods, which are later exchangeable for U.S. goods and services. U.S. imports, then, provide the means by which foreigners can buy U.S. exports.

Services and the Current Account

Even though imports and exports of goods are the largest components of the balance of payments, they are not the only ones. Nations import and export services as well. A particularly important service is tourism.

When U.S. tourists go abroad, they are buying foreign-produced services in addition to those purchased by citizens there. Those services include the use of hotels, sightseeing tours, restaurants, and so forth. In the current account, these services are included in imports. On the other hand, foreign tourism in the United States provides us with foreign currencies and claims against foreigners, so they are included in exports. Airline and shipping services also affect the balance of payments. When someone from Italy flies American Airlines, that person is making a payment to a U.S. company. Because the flow of international financial claims is the same, this payment is treated just like a U.S. export in the

When foreigners purchase tourism services inside a country, these actually count as exports for that country. Tourism could provide the country with foreign currencies and claims against foreign consumers.

balance of payments. If an American flies on Alitalia, however, Italians acquire claims against the United States; and so it is included as a debit (import) item in the U.S. balance-of-payments accounts.

Net Transfer Payments and Net Investment Income

Other items that affect the current account are private and government grants and gifts to and from other countries. When the U.S. gives foreign aid to another country, a debit occurs in the U.S. balance of payments because the aid gives foreigners added claims against the United States in the form of dollars. Private gifts, such as individuals sending money to relatives or friends in foreign countries, show up in the current account as debit items as well. Because the United States usually sends more humanitarian and military aid to foreigners than it receives, net transfers are usually in deficit. In 2011, net unilateral transfers for the United States were $-133 billion.

Net investment income is also included in the current account (line 8)—U.S. investors hold foreign assets and foreign investors hold U.S. assets. Payments received by U.S. residents are added to the current account and payments made by U.S. residents are subtracted from the current account. In 2011, a net flow of $227 billion came into the United States.

The Current Account Balance

The balance on the current account is the net amount of credits or debits after adding up all transactions of goods (merchandise imports and exports), services, and transfer payments (e.g., foreign aid and gifts). If the sum of credits exceeds the sum of debits, the nation is said to run a balance-of-payments surplus on the current account. If debits exceed credits, however, the nation is running a balance-of-payments deficit on the current account.

The Balance of Trade and the Balance of the Current Account

The balance of payments of the United States for 2011 is presented in Exhibit 18.10. Notice that exports and imports of goods and services are by far the largest credits and

debits. Notice also that U.S. exports of goods were $739 billion less than imports of goods. The import/export goods relationship is often called the **balance of trade.** The United States, therefore, experienced a balance-of-trade deficit that year of $739 billion. However, some of the $739 billion trade deficit is offset by credits from a $179 billion surplus in services. This difference leads to a $-560 billion deficit in the balance of goods and services. When $133 billion of net unilateral transfers (gifts and grants between the United States and foreigners) and $227 billion of investment income (net) from the United States are added (the foreigners gave more to the United States than the United States gave to the foreigners), the total deficit on the current account is $466 billion. Exhibit 18.11 on the next page shows the balance of trade since 1975.

> **balance of trade** the net surplus or deficit resulting from the level of exportation and importation of merchandise

18-5b THE FINANCIAL ACCOUNT

How was this deficit on the current account financed? Remember that U.S. credits give us the financial means to buy foreign goods and that our credits were

The financial account records foreign purchases or assets in the United States (a monetary inflow) and U.S. purchases of assets abroad (a monetary outflow).

derived demand the demand for an input derived from consumers' demand for the good or service produced with that input

If it takes $1 to buy 1 euro, then the exchange rate is $1 per euro. From the German perspective, the exchange rate is 1 euro per U.S. dollar.

18-6b CHANGES IN EXCHANGE RATES AFFECT THE DOMESTIC DEMAND FOR FOREIGN GOODS

Prices of goods in their currencies combine with exchange rates to determine the domestic price of foreign goods. Suppose the cuckoo clock sells for 100 euros in Germany. What is the price to U.S. consumers? Let us assume that tariffs and other transaction costs are zero. If the exchange rate is $1 = 1 euro, then the equivalent U.S. dollar price of the cuckoo clock is 100 euros times $1 per euro, or $100. If the exchange rate were to change to $2 = 1 euro, fewer clocks would be demanded in the United States, because the effective U.S. dollar price of the clocks would rise to $200 (100 euros × $2 per euro). The higher relative value of a euro compared to the dollar (or, equivalently, the lower relative value of a dollar compared to the euro) would lead to a reduction in U.S. demand for German-made clocks.

18-6c THE DEMAND FOR A FOREIGN CURRENCY

The demand for foreign currencies is known as a **derived demand**, because the demand for a foreign currency derives directly from the demand for foreign goods and services or for foreign investment. The more that goods from a foreign country are demanded, the more of that country's currency is needed to pay for those goods. This increased demand for the currency will push up the exchange value of that currency relative to other currencies.

18-6d THE SUPPLY OF A FOREIGN CURRENCY

Similarly, the supply of foreign currency is provided by foreigners who want to buy the exports of a particular nation. For example, the more that foreigners demand U.S. products, the more of their currencies they will supply in exchange for U.S. dollars, which they use to buy our products.

18-6e DETERMINING EXCHANGE RATES

We know that the demand for foreign currencies is derived from the demand for foreign goods, but how does that affect the exchange rate? Just as in the product market, the answer lies with the forces of supply and demand. In this case, it is the supply of and demand for a foreign currency that determine the equilibrium price (exchange rate) of that currency.

18-6f THE DEMAND CURVE FOR A FOREIGN CURRENCY

As Exhibit 18.12 shows, the demand curve for a foreign currency—the euro, for example—is downward sloping, just as it is in product markets. In this case, however, the demand curve has a negative slope because as the price of the euro falls relative to the dollar, European products become relatively more inexpensive to U.S. consumers, who therefore buy more European goods. To do so, the quantity of euros demanded by U.S. consumers will increase as U.S. consumers buy more European goods as the price of the euro falls. For this reason, the demand for foreign currencies is considered to be a derived demand.

18-6g THE SUPPLY CURVE FOR FOREIGN CURRENCY

The supply curve for a foreign currency is upward sloping, just as it is in product markets. In this case, as the price, or value, of the euro increases relative to the dollar, U.S. products will become relatively less

EXHIBIT 18.12 Equilibrium in the Foreign Exchange Market

expensive to European buyers, who will thus increase the quantity of dollars they demand. Europeans will, therefore, increase the quantity of euros supplied to the United States by buying more U.S. products.

18-6h EQUILIBRIUM IN THE FOREIGN EXCHANGE MARKET

Equilibrium is reached where the demand and supply curves for a given currency intersect. In Exhibit 18.12, the equilibrium price of a euro is $1.25. As in the product market, if the dollar price of euros is higher than the equilibrium price, an excess quantity of euros will be supplied at that price; that is, a surplus of euros will exist. Competition among euro sellers will push the price of euros down toward equilibrium. Likewise, if the dollar price of euros is lower than the equilibrium price, an excess quantity of euros will be demanded at that price; that is, a shortage of euros will occur. Competition among euro buyers will push the price of euros up toward equilibrium.

SECTION CHECK 6 ANSWERS

1. The price of a unit of one foreign currency in terms of another is called the exchange rate.

2. The exchange rate for a currency is determined by the supply of and demand for that currency in the foreign exchange market.

3. If the dollar appreciates in value relative to foreign currencies, foreign goods become more inexpensive to U.S. consumers, increasing U.S. demand for foreign goods.

18-7 Equilibrium Changes in the Foreign Exchange Market

SECTION CHECK 7

Keep the following questions in mind as you read through this section.

1. What factors cause the exchange rate to change?

2. What factors cause the supply and demand curves for a currency to shift?

The equilibrium exchange rate of a currency changes many times daily. Sometimes, these changes can be quite significant. Any force that shifts either the demand for or supply of a currency will shift the equilibrium in the foreign exchange market, leading to a new exchange rate. Among such factors are changes in consumer tastes for goods, income levels, relative real interest rates, and relative inflation rates, as well as speculation.

18-7a INCREASED TASTES FOR FOREIGN GOODS

Because the demand for foreign currencies is derived from the demand for foreign goods, any change in the U.S. demand for foreign goods will shift the demand schedule for foreign currency in the same direction. For example, if a cuckoo clock revolution sweeps through the United States, German producers will have reason to celebrate, knowing that many U.S. buyers will turn to Germany for their cuckoo clocks. However, because Germans will only accept payment in the form of euros, U.S. consumers and retailers must convert their dollars into euros before they can purchase their clocks. The increased taste for European goods in the United States will, therefore, lead to an increased demand for euros. As shown in Exhibit 18.13, this increased demand for euros shifts the demand curve to the right, resulting in a new, higher equilibrium dollar price of euros.

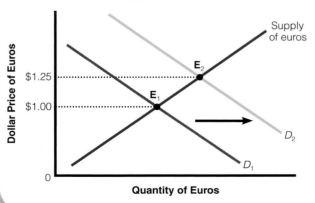

EXHIBIT 18.13 Impact on the Foreign Exchange Market of a U.S. Change in Taste, Income Increase, or Tariff Decrease

© Cengage Learning 2014

18-7b RELATIVE INCOME INCREASES OR REDUCTIONS IN U.S. TARIFFS

Any change in the average income of U.S. consumers will also change the equilibrium exchange rate, *ceteris paribus*. If on the whole incomes were to increase in the United States, Americans would buy more goods, including imported goods, hence more European goods would be bought. This increased demand for European goods would lead to an increased demand for euros, resulting in a higher exchange rate for the euro. A decrease in U.S. tariffs on European goods would tend to have the same effect as an increase in incomes, by making European goods more affordable. Exhibit 18.13 shows that it would again lead to an increased demand for European goods and a higher short-run equilibrium exchange rate for the euro.

18-7c INCREASES IN EUROPEAN INCOMES, REDUCTIONS IN EUROPEAN TARIFFS, OR CHANGES IN EUROPEAN TASTES

If European incomes rose, European tariffs on U.S. goods fell, or European tastes for American goods increased, the supply of euros in the euro foreign exchange market would increase. Any of these changes would cause Europeans to demand more U.S. goods and therefore more U.S. dollars to purchase those goods. To obtain these added dollars, Europeans would have to exchange more of their euros, increasing the supply of euros on the euro foreign exchange market. As Exhibit 18.14 demonstrates, the result would be a rightward shift in the euro supply curve, leading to a new equilibrium at a lower exchange rate for the euro.

18-7d HOW DO CHANGES IN RELATIVE REAL INTEREST RATES AFFECT EXCHANGE RATES?

If interest rates in the United States were to increase relative to, say, European interest rates, *ceteris paribus*, the rate of return on U.S. investments would increase relative to that on European investments. European investors would then increase their demand for U.S. investments and therefore offer euros for sale in order to buy dollars to buy U.S. investments, shifting the supply curve for euros to the right, from S_1 to S_2 in Exhibit 18.15.

In this scenario, U.S. investors would also shift their investments away from Europe by decreasing their demand for euros relative to their demand for dollars, from D_1 to D_2 in Exhibit 18.15. A subsequent, lower equilibrium price ($1.25) would result for the euro as a result of the increase in U.S. interest rates. That is, the euro would depreciate, because euros could now buy fewer units of dollars than before. In short, the higher U.S. interest rates would attract more investment to the United States, leading to a relative appreciation of the dollar and a relative depreciation of the euro.

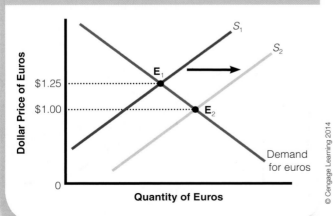

EXHIBIT 18.14 Impact on the Foreign Exchange Market of a European Change in Taste, Income Increase, or Tariff Decrease

© Cengage Learning 2014

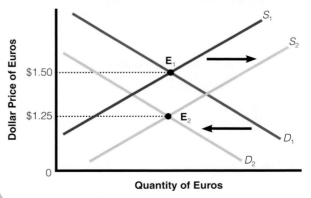

EXHIBIT 18.15 Impact on the Foreign Exchange Market from an Increase in the U.S. Interest Rate

© Cengage Learning 2014

18-7e CHANGES IN THE RELATIVE INFLATION RATE

If Europe experienced an inflation rate greater than that experienced in the United States, *ceteris paribus*, what would happen to the exchange rate? In this case, European products would become more expensive to U.S. consumers. Americans would then decrease the quantity of European goods demanded and thus decrease their demand for euros. The result would be a leftward shift of the demand curve for euros.

On the other side of the Atlantic, U.S. goods would become relatively cheaper to Europeans, leading Europeans to increase the quantity of U.S. goods demanded and thus to demand more U.S. dollars. This increased demand for dollars would translate into an increased supply of euros, shifting the supply curve for euros outward. Exhibit 18.16 shows the shifts of the supply and demand curves and the new lower equilibrium price for the euro resulting from the higher European rate.

18-7f EXPECTATIONS AND SPECULATION

Every trading day, roughly a trillion dollars in currency trades hands in the foreign exchange markets. Suppose currency traders believe that in the future the United States will experience more rapid inflation than will

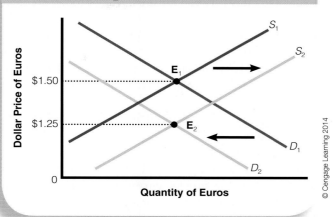

EXHIBIT 18.16 Impact on the Foreign Exchange Market from an Increase in the European Inflation Rate

Japan. If currency speculators believe that the value of the dollar will soon be falling because of the anticipated rise in the U.S. inflation rate, those who are holding dollars will convert them to yen. This move will lead to an increase in the demand for yen—the yen appreciates and the dollar depreciates relative to the yen, *ceteris paribus*. In short, if speculators believe that the price of a country's currency is going to rise, they will buy more of that currency, pushing up the price and causing the country's currency to appreciate.

Determinants of Exchange Rates

Q How will each of the following events affect the foreign exchange market?

  a. American travel to Europe increases.
  b. Japanese investors purchase U.S. stock.
  c. U.S. real interest rates abruptly increase relative to world interest rates.
  d. Other countries become less politically and economically stable relative to the United States.

A a. The demand for euros increases (demand shifts right in the euro market), the dollar will depreciate, and the euro will appreciate, *ceteris paribus*.

  b. The demand for dollars increases (demand shifts right in the dollar market), the dollar will appreciate, and the yen will depreciate, *ceteris paribus*. Alternatively, you could think of it as an increase in supply in the yen market.

  c. International investors will increase their demand for dollars in the dollar market to take advantage of the higher interest rates. The dollar will appreciate relative to other foreign currencies, *ceteris paribus*.

  d. More foreign investors will want to buy U.S. assets, resulting in an increase in demand for dollars.

18-7g IS IT BETTER TO HAVE A STRONG DOLLAR OR A WEAK DOLLAR?

Exchange rates between most currencies today are flexible. That is, their value floats with supply and demand. For example, changes in the supply of and/or demand for the dollar can create a stronger dollar (which exchanges for more foreign currency) or a weaker dollar (which exchanges for less foreign currency). However, governments also sometimes buy or sell currencies in order to affect exchange rates, resulting in what is called a "dirty float" system.

Is a strong dollar (dollar appreciates) good? It depends on who you ask. U.S. consumers like it because they pay less for foreign currencies. That is, foreign goods become relatively less expensive; so the price of Japanese cars and Italian shoes fall. Foreign producers are happy as their sales rise. However, domestic producers are hurt by the higher relative prices of domestic goods as consumers buy more imports and fewer substitute domestic goods. In addition, foreigners buy fewer U.S. exports. In sum, when the dollar gets stronger, U.S. goods and services cost more to foreigners, so they buy fewer U.S. exports; foreign goods and services cost U.S. consumers less, so they buy more foreign imports. A stronger dollar leads to an increase in imports and a decrease in exports.

A weak dollar (dollar depreciates) benefits U.S. producers. Why? Foreigners pay less of their currency for dollars, so U.S. goods become relatively less expensive to foreign buyers. However a weak dollar is not good news for domestic consumers of foreign goods or foreign producers. The prices of imported goods rise, from Italian shoes to Japanese cars, causing U.S. imports to fall. Foreign consumers also increase their purchases of the relatively lower-priced U.S. goods. In sum, when the dollar becomes weaker, U.S. goods and services cost less to foreigners, so they buy more U.S. exports; foreign goods and services cost U.S. consumers more, so they buy fewer foreign imports. A weaker dollar leads to an increase in exports and a decrease in imports.

While one might think that a stronger dollar is good and a weaker dollar is bad, the truth is that exchange rate changes produce both winners and losers. Domestic exporters prefer a weaker dollar and domestic importers prefer a stronger dollar.

Which is preferable can also depend on the condition of the domestic economy. When the economy is below full employment, a weaker dollar can increase net exports, and thus increase *AD*, real output, and employment; when the economy is beyond full employment, a stronger dollar can reduce net exports and *AD*, offsetting an unsustainable economic boom.

SECTION CHECK 7 ANSWERS

1. Any force that shifts either the demand or the supply curves for a foreign currency will shift the equilibrium in the foreign exchange market and lead to a new exchange rate.

2. Any changes in tastes, income levels, relative real interest rates, or relative inflation rates will cause the demand for and supply of a currency to shift.

Chapter 18: Self-Review

Now that you are finished reading the chapter, review the questions below. You can write your answers in the space provided, then go online to see the answers at www.cengagebrain.com.

18-1 THE GROWTH IN WORLD TRADE

1. True or False: U.S. producers and consumers should be more concerned about Canadian trade restrictions than Swedish trade restrictions.

18-2 COMPARATIVE ADVANTAGE AND GAINS FROM TRADE

2. True or False: A country cannot have an absolute advantage in producing one good or service without also having a comparative advantage in its production.

18-3 SUPPLY AND DEMAND IN INTERNATIONAL TRADE

3. Fill-in-the-Blank: If the world price of a good is greater than the domestic price prior to trade, it implies that the domestic economy has a _____ in producing that good.

4. True or False: When a country has a comparative advantage in the production of a good, domestic producers gain more than domestic consumers lose from free international trade.

18-4 TARIFFS, IMPORT QUOTAS, AND SUBSIDIES

5. Fill-in-the-Blanks: Tariffs _____ domestic producer surplus but _____ domestic consumer surplus.

6. True or False: Subsidizing exports by industries without a comparative advantage tends to harm the domestic economy.

18-5 THE BALANCE OF PAYMENTS

7. True or False: British purchasers of U.S. goods and services must first exchange pounds for dollars.

8. True or False: A Nigerian family visiting Chicago enjoys a Chicago Cubs baseball game at Wrigley Field. This expense should be recorded as an export of services on the balance-of-payments account.

18-6 EXCHANGE RATES

9. How are each of the following events likely to affect the value of the dollar relative to the euro?
   a. Interest rates in the European Union increase relative to those in the United States.
   b. The European Union price level rises relative to the U.S. price level.
   c. The European central bank intervenes by selling dollars on currency markets.
   d. The price level in the United States falls relative to the price level in Europe.

18-7 EQUILIBRIUM CHANGES IN THE FOREIGN EXCHANGE MARKET

10. What will happen to the supply of dollars, the demand for dollars, and the equilibrium exchange rate of the dollar in each of the following cases? Fill in the table below.

	Supply of Dollars	Demand for Dollars	Equilibrium Exchange Rate
Americans buy more European goods.			
Europeans invest in the U.S. stock market.			
European tourists flock to the United States.			
Europeans buy U.S. government bonds.			
American tourists flock to Europe.			

INDEX

C

Canada
  abundance of natural resources, 254
  Bank of Canada, 374
  growth in real GDP per capita (2003–2012), 251
  health-care system, 97
  no bank runs during Great Depression, 337
  revenues and government spending as percentage of GDP, 304
Canadian Medical Association Journal (CMAJ), 97
capital, 4
capital gains taxes, 242
capital intensive, 43
capital stock, 331
Card, David, 81
Carlyle, Thomas, 46
Carnegie, Andrew, 248
cartels, 190
cash transfers, 219
Castaway (film), 44
catch-up effect, 587
causation, 16
Cellar-Kefauver Act (1950), 172
central banks, 341–342, 366, 373, 375
ceteris paribus, 14
change in demand, 51, 55
change in quantity demanded, 51, 55
change in quantity supplied, 56–57
change in supply, 56–57
Chicago Board of Trade (CBOT), 138, 140
Chile
  inflation rate in, 374
  private retirement investment in, 299
  revenues and government spending as percentage of GDP, 304
China
  growth in real GDP per capita (2003–2012), 250–251
  revenues and government spending as percentage of GDP, 304
  Rule of 70, 250–252
circular flow model, 11, 252
classical macroeconomic model, 289–291
Clayton Act (1914), 172
clean environment, cost vs. benefit, 106
Cleveland, Jeffrey, 234
Clinton, Bill, 315, 365
collective bargaining, 211–212
college tuition, as price discrimination, 177
collusion, 190
collusion and cartels, 189–194
  antitrust and mergers, 193–194

antitrust and pricing strategies, 194
  collusive oligopolies, 191
  easy entry, 192–193
  joint profit maximization, 190
  market entry deterrence, 193
  price leadership, 191–192
  uncertainty and pricing decisions, 190
Combs, Sean "Diddy," 8
command economy, 42
commercial banks, 329
common resource, 108
comparative advantage, 35
comparative advantage, in international trade, 384–389
competitive market, 48
complements, 52
concentration ratios, in manufacturing, 188
conglomerate merger, 193–194
Congressional Budget Office, 84, 309, 315–316
constant-cost industry, 153
constant returns to scale, 134
consumer preferences, 53–54, 403
consumer price index (CPI), 237–238
consumer sovereignty, 41–42
consumer surplus, 87
consumption
  in measurement of total production, 261–262
  positive externalities in, 104–106
contraction, 244
contractionary fiscal policy, 303–304
contractionary monetary policy, 354–357
cooperative game, 195
copyrights, as monopoly, 168–169
corporate income taxes, 302
corporate scandals (2001), 285, 353, 354
correlation, 16
Costco, 239
cost of living allowance (COLA), 243, 376
cost-push inflation, 285
coupons, as price discrimination, 177
credit cards, 325
credit unions, 329
crowding-out effect, 364
Crowe, Russell, 198
currency, 323
current account, 397–398
cyclical unemployment, 231

D

Day-O'Connor, Sandra, 20
deadweight loss, 91
De Beers, 163
debit cards, 325

debt. *See* national debt
decreasing-cost industry, 155–156
deflation, 237
Dell, 187
demand, law of, 48–55
  available income and, 52–53
  changes in, 50–51, 55
  consumer expectations, 54–55
  consumer preferences and, 53–54
  individual demand curve, 49
  individual demand schedule, 49
  market demand curve, 49–50
  new product information, 54
  number of buyers, 53
  prices of related goods and, 51–52
  shifts in, 51
  wants vs. needs, 48–49
demand deposits, 324
demand-pull inflation, 284
demand shifts, 51
Denmark, capital taxes in, 311
Depp, Johnny, 202, 203
depreciation, 263
depression, 245
derived demand, 204, 402
developing countries
  child labor in, 259
  costs of education, 259
  lack of property rights, 257
  lower tax burdens in, 304
  nonmarket transactions, 267
  underground economies, 269
diamond monopoly, 163
diminishing marginal product, 126–127
discount rate, 345
discouraged workers, 225–226
diseconomies of scale, 134
disinflation, 237
disposable personal income, 263
dollar, 406
dominant strategy, 195
double counting, 260
Dow Jones Industrial, 371
Dubner, Stephen J., 8
dumping, 394

E

Earned Income Tax Credit (EITC), 219
East Asia, economic growth due to education, 259
econometric models, formulation of, 246
economic behavior, 6–8
  incentives, 8
  rational behavior and, 7–8
  self-interest and, 7
economic fluctuation in business cycles, 244–245
economic goods, 5
economic growth, 249–250

Section Summaries

1-1 Economics: A Brief Introduction

Economics is the study of the choices we make among our many wants and desires given our limited resources. Scarcity forces us to ch[...] choices are costly beca[...] give up other opportu[...] we value—this is the e[...] problem. Our scarce re[...] grouped into four cate[...] land, capital, and entre[...] Entrepreneurship is the process of combining labor, land, and capital to produce goods and services. Goods are tangible items that we value or desire, and services are intangible acts for which people are willing to pay. Everyone faces scarcity, and it cannot be eliminated.

> Each Review Card contains summaries for each chapter section. These will provide an overview of the basic concepts from each chapter.

1-2 Economic Behavior

Economists assume that individuals act as if they are motivated by self-interest and respond in predictable ways to changing circumstances. Self-interest to an economist is not a narrow monetary self-interest. A person acting in self-interest might pursue personal gain, but that does not necessarily exclude helping others. Rational behavior [...] ple do the [...] their values [...] current and [...] nstances. [...] ek [...] e them better off, we can predict what will happen when incentives are changed.

> Some cards have images from the chapter which can be used as memory prompts to help you recall the information in the written summary.

1-3 Markets

A market is the process of buyers and sellers exchanging goods and services. In most countries, resources are allocated through a market economy. Efficiency is achieved when the economy gets the most out of its scarce resources. Voluntary exchange and the price system guide people's choices and help determine what goods are produced and how they are produced. Market failure occurs when the economy fails to allocate resources efficiently on its own. We [...]ular flow model to illustrate [...] of goods and services. [...]lds and firms interact with [...]er in product markets (where [...]ds buy and firms sell) and [...] arkets (where households [...] and firms buy).

1-4 Economic Theory

A theory is an established explanation that accounts for known facts or phenomena. Specifically, economic theories are statements or propositions about patterns of human behavior that occur expectedly under certain circumstances. Theories use abstraction to weed out relevant from irrelevant information. A theory begins with a hypothesis, which is tested through empirical analysis. If the data collected supports the hypothesis, it can be tentatively accepted as an economic theory.

Conventionally, we distinguish two main branches of economics: microeconomics, which deals with smaller units in the economy, and macroeconomics, which deals with the aggregate or total economy.

1-5 Pitfalls to Avoid in Scientific Thinking

The two major pitfalls to avoid are confusing correlation with causation and the fallacy of composition. The fact that two events usually occur together (correlation) does not necessarily mean that the one caused the other to occur (causation). The fallacy of composition tells us that if a thing is true for an individual, it is not necessarily true on a group level.

Key Terms

> Key Terms from the chapter's margins appear in this column (and continue on the back of the card) in alphabetical order.

aggregate the total amount—such as the aggregate l[...]

bads iter[...] where less[...] terrorism, s[...]

bar grap[...] comparison[...]

capital the equipment and structures used to produce goods and services (pg. 4)

causation when one event brings about another event (pg. 16)

ceteris paribus holding all other things constant (pg. 14)

correlation when two events occur together (pg. 16)

economic goods scarce goods created from scarce resources—goods that are desirable but limited in supply (pg. 5)

economic problem scarcity forces us to choose, and choices are costly because we must give up other opportunities that we value (pg. 4)

economics the study of choices we make among our many wants and desires given our limited resources (pg. 4)

efficiency when an economy gets the most out of its scarce resources (pg. 9)

empirical analysis the use of data to test a hypothesis (pg. 14)

entrepreneurship the process of combining labor, land, and capital to produce goods and services (pg. 4)

factor (or input) markets markets in which households sell the use of their inputs (capital, land, labor, and entrepreneurship) to firms (pg. 11)

fallacy of composition the incorrect view that what is true for the individual is always true for the group (pg. 17)

goods items we value or desire (pg. 5)

human capital the productive knowledge and skill people receive from education, on-the-job training, health, and other factors that increase productivity (pg. 4)

hypothesis a testable proposition (pg. 13)

intangible goods goods that we cannot reach out and touch, such as friendship and knowledge (pg. 5)

(continues)

Section Summaries - Continued

1-6 Positive and Normative Economics

Positive analysis deals with factual stater... explain the world. Normative analysis de... judgments trying to improve the world. A... distinction is that positive statements ca... normative statements cannot.

1-7 Why Study Economics?

Perhaps the best reason for studying eco... many of the things of concern in the worl...

least partly economic in character. The study of economics ...natic, disciplined way of thinking.

...NDIX: Working with Graphs

...se of visual aids, such as graphs, greatly ...lerstanding of a theory. This textbook will ...ghout to enhance the understanding of ...nic relationships. This appendix provides ...o read and create your own graphs.

How to Use this Card:

1. **Look over the card to preview new concepts you'll be introduced to in the chapter.**

2. **Read the chapter to fully understand the material.**

3. **Go to class (and pay attention).**

4. **Review the card one more time to make sure you've grasped the key concepts.**

5. **Don't forget, this card is only one of many ECON Survey learning tools available to help you succeed in your economics course.**

Key Terms - Continued

labor the physical and human effort used in the production of goods and services (pg. 4)

land the natural resources used in the production of goods and services (pg. 4)

macroeconomics the study of the whole economy, including the topics of inflation, unemployment, and economic growth (pg. 15)

market the process of buyers and sellers exchanging goods and services (pg. 8)

market failure when the economy fails to allocate resources efficiently on its own (pg. 10)

microeconomics the study of household and firm behavior and how they interact in the marketplace (pg. 15)

negative relationship when two variables change in opposite directions (pg. 24)

normative statemen... contestable statement th... describe what should be ...

...ve size of various quantities that add up to 100 percent (pg. 22)

positive relationship when two variables change in the same direction (pg. 24)

positive statement an objective, testable statement that describes what happens and why it happens (pg. 17)

product markets markets in which households are buyers and firms are sellers of goods and services (pg. 11)

rational behavior people do the best they can, based on their values and information, under current and anticipated future circumstances (pg. 7)

resources inputs used to produce goods and services (pg. 4)

scarcity exists when human wants (material and nonmaterial) exceed available ...g. 4)

...intangible items of value provided ...rs, such as education (pg. 5)

simple circular flow model an illustration of the continuous flow of goods, services, inputs, and payments between firms and households (pg. 12)

slope the ratio of rise (change in the Y variable) over run (change in the X variable) (pg. 25)

tangible goods items we value or desire that we can reach out and touch (pg. 5)

theory a statement or proposition used to explain and predict behavior in the real world (pg. 13)

time-series graph visual tool to show changes in a variable's value over time (pg. 22)

variable something that is measured by a number, such as your height (pg. 22)

X-axis the horizontal axis on a graph (pg. 22)

Y-axis the vertical axis on a graph (pg. 22)

The list below offers a wide range of tools to help you review and sharpen your understanding of economic concepts from this chapter.

For More Review Tools Visit www.cengagebrain.com.

Online Study Tools

At www.cengagebrain.com, you can

❑ **Download printable Key Term Flash Cards**

❑ **Study online with interactive Key Term Flash Cards**

❑ **Complete Practice Quizzes with instant feedback**

❑ **Play "Beat the Clock" to master concepts**

❑ **Complete the Crossword Puzzle to review key terms**

❑ **Watch the Ask the Instructor video "Why do economists talk about money and wealth? Do they really believe that people are motivated only by money?"**

❑ **Download and review Exhibit Worksheets**

❑ **Access Economic Application "Economic Analysis"**

❑ **Access Graphing Workshop "Working with Graphs"**

❑ **Check your answers to the Chapter 1 Self-Review on page 21 on the e-book in CourseMate.**

CHAPTER 4

Price Elasticity of Demand

$$\text{Price elasticity of demand } (E_D) = \frac{\text{Percentage change in quantity demand}}{\text{Percentage change in price}}$$

Total Revenue (TR)

$TR = P \times Q$

Price Elasticity of Supply

$$\text{Price elasticity of supply } (E_S) = \frac{\%\,\Delta \text{ in the quantity supplied}}{\%\,\Delta \text{ in price}}$$

CHAPTER 6

Profits

profit = total revenue − total cost

Accounting Profits

accounting profits = total revenue − total explicit costs

Economic Profits

economic profits = total revenue − (explicit costs + implicit costs)

Marginal Product (MP)

marginal product = change in total output of a good that results from a one-unit change in input

$MP = \Delta Q/\Delta V$

Total Cost (TC)

total cost = total fixed cost + total variable cost

$TC = TFC + TVC$

Average Total Cost (ATC)

average total cost = total cost/output

$ATC = TC/Q$

Average Fixed Cost (AFC)

average fixed cost = total fixed cost/output

$AFC = TFC/Q$

Average Variable Cost (AVC)

average variable cost = total variable cost/output

$AVC = TVC/Q$

Marginal Cost (MC)

marginal cost = change in total cost resulting from a one-unit change in output

$MC = \Delta TC/\Delta Q$

CHAPTER 7

Average Revenue (AR)

average revenue = total revenue/number of units sold

$AR = TR/q$

Marginal Revenue (MR)

marginal revenue = increase in total revenue resulting from a one-unit increase in sales

$MR = \Delta TR/\Delta q$

Profit Maximizing Level of Output

$MR = MC$

CHAPTER 10

Marginal Revenue Product (MRP)

marginal revenue product = marginal product × price of the product

$MRP = MP \times P$

CHAPTER 11

Unemployment Rate

$$\text{unemployment rate} = \frac{\text{number of unemployed}}{\text{civilian labor force}}$$

Price Index

$$\text{price index} = \frac{\text{cost of market basket in current year} \times 100}{\text{cost of market basket in base year}}$$

CHAPTER 12

Gross Domestic Product (*GDP*)

gross domestic product = consumption + investment + government purchases + net exports

$GDP = C + I + G + (X - M)$

Real GDP

$Real\ GDP = \dfrac{Nominal\ GDP}{price\text{-}level\ index} \times 100$

CHAPTER 14

Aggregate Demand

aggregate demand = consumption + investment + government purchases + net exports

$AD = C + I + G + (X - M)$

Marginal Propensity to Consume (*MPC*)

marginal propensity to consume = change in consumption spending/change in disposable income

$MPC = \Delta C/\Delta DY$

Marginal Propensity to Save (*MPS*)

marginal propensity to consume = change in savings/change in disposable income

$MPS = \Delta S/\Delta DY$

Multiplier Formula

$Multiplier = 1/(1 - MPC)$

Budget Deficit and Budget Surplus

Budget Deficit: Government Spending > Tax Revenues
Budget Surplus: Tax Revenues > Government Spending

CHAPTER 15

M1

M1 = Currency + Checkable deposits + Traveler's checks

M2

M2 = M1 + Savings deposits + Small-denomination time deposits + Noninstitutional money market mutual fund shares + Money market deposit accounts

Required Reserves

required reserves = deposits × reserve ratio

Excess Reserves

excess reserves = actual reserves − required reserves

Money Multiplier

potential money creation = initial deposit × money multiplier

CHAPTER 16

Equation of Exchange

money supply × velocity of money = price level × real output

$M \times V = P \times Q$

Velocity of Money

velocity of money = nominal GDP/money supply

$V = Nominal\ GDP/M$

Growth Version of the Quantity Equation

Growth rate of the money supply + Growth rate of velocity = Growth rate of the price level (inflation rate) + Growth rate of real output

Inflation Rate

Inflation Rate = Growth rate of the money supply − Growth rate of real GDP

Section Summaries

1-1 Economics: A Brief Introduction

Economics is the study of the choices we make among our many wants and desires given our limited resources. Scarcity forces us to choose, and choices are costly because we must give up other opportunities that we value—this is the economic problem. Our scarce resources can be grouped into four categories: labor, land, capital, and entrepreneurship. Entrepreneurship is the process of combining labor, land, and capital to produce goods and services. Goods are tangible items that we value or desire, and services are intangible acts for which people are willing to pay. Everyone faces scarcity, and it cannot be eliminated.

1-2 Economic Behavior

Economists assume that individuals act as if they are motivated by self-interest and respond in predictable ways to changing circumstances. Self-interest to an economist is not a narrow monetary self-interest. A person acting in self-interest might pursue personal gain, but that does not necessarily exclude helping others. Rational behavior merely means that people do the best they can, based on their values and information, under current and anticipated future circumstances. Because most people seek opportunities that make them better off, we can predict what will happen when incentives are changed.

1-3 Markets

A market is the process of buyers and sellers exchanging goods and services. In most countries, resources are allocated through a market economy. Efficiency is achieved when the economy gets the most out of its scarce resources. Voluntary exchange and the price system guide people's choices and help determine what goods are produced and how they are produced. Market failure occurs when the economy fails to allocate resources efficiently on its own. We use a circular flow model to illustrate the flow of goods and services. Households and firms interact with each other in product markets (where households buy and firms sell) and factor markets (where households sell and firms buy).

1-4 Economic Theory

A theory is an established explanation that accounts for known facts or phenomena. Specifically, economic theories are statements or propositions about patterns of human behavior that occur expectedly under certain circumstances. Theories use abstraction to weed out relevant from irrelevant information. A theory begins with a hypothesis, which is tested through empirical analysis. If the data collected supports the hypothesis, it can be tentatively accepted as an economic theory.

Conventionally, we distinguish two main branches of economics: microeconomics, which deals with smaller units in the economy, and macroeconomics, which deals with the aggregate or total economy.

1-5 Pitfalls to Avoid in Scientific Thinking

The two major pitfalls to avoid are confusing correlation with causation and the fallacy of composition. The fact that two events usually occur together (correlation) does not necessarily mean that the one caused the other to occur (causation). The fallacy of composition tells us that if a thing is true for an individual, it is not necessarily true on a group level.

Key Terms

aggregate the total amount—such as the aggregate level of output (pg. 16)

bads items that we do not desire or want, where less is preferred to more, such as terrorism, smog, or poison oak (pg. 5)

bar graph visual display showing the comparison of quantities (pg. 22)

capital the equipment and structures used to produce goods and services (pg. 4)

causation when one event brings about another event (pg. 16)

ceteris paribus holding all other things constant (pg. 14)

correlation when two events occur together (pg. 16)

economic goods scarce goods created from scarce resources—goods that are desirable but limited in supply (pg. 5)

economic problem scarcity forces us to choose, and choices are costly because we must give up other opportunities that we value (pg. 4)

economics the study of choices we make among our many wants and desires given our limited resources (pg. 4)

efficiency when an economy gets the most out of its scarce resources (pg. 9)

empirical analysis the use of data to test a hypothesis (pg. 14)

entrepreneurship the process of combining labor, land, and capital to produce goods and services (pg. 4)

factor (or input) markets markets in which households sell the use of their inputs (capital, land, labor, and entrepreneurship) to firms (pg. 11)

fallacy of composition the incorrect view that what is true for the individual is always true for the group (pg. 17)

goods items we value or desire (pg. 5)

human capital the productive knowledge and skill people receive from education, on-the-job training, health, and other factors that increase productivity (pg. 4)

hypothesis a testable proposition (pg. 13)

intangible goods goods that we cannot reach out and touch, such as friendship and knowledge (pg. 5)

(continues)

Section Summaries - Continued

1-6 Positive and Normative Economics

Positive analysis deals with factual statements trying to explain the world. Normative analysis deals with value judgments trying to improve the world. An important distinction is that positive statements can be tested but normative statements cannot.

1-7 Why Study Economics?

Perhaps the best reason for studying economics is that so many of the things of concern in the world around us are at least partly economic in character. The study of economics provides a systematic, disciplined way of thinking.

A1-1 APPENDIX: Working with Graphs

Sometimes the use of visual aids, such as graphs, greatly enhances our understanding of a theory. This textbook will use graphs throughout to enhance the understanding of important economic relationships. This appendix provides a guide on how to read and create your own graphs.

Key Terms - Continued

labor the physical and human effort used in the production of goods and services (pg. 4)

land the natural resources used in the production of goods and services (pg. 4)

macroeconomics the study of the whole economy, including the topics of inflation, unemployment, and economic growth (pg. 15)

market the process of buyers and sellers exchanging goods and services (pg. 8)

market failure when the economy fails to allocate resources efficiently on its own (pg. 10)

microeconomics the study of household and firm behavior and how they interact in the marketplace (pg. 15)

negative relationship when two variables change in opposite directions (pg. 24)

normative statement a subjective, contestable statement that attempts to describe what should be done (pg. 17)

pie chart visual display showing the relative size of various quantities that add up to 100 percent (pg. 22)

positive relationship when two variables change in the same direction (pg. 24)

positive statement an objective, testable statement that describes what happens and why it happens (pg. 17)

product markets markets in which households are buyers and firms are sellers of goods and services (pg. 11)

rational behavior people do the best they can, based on their values and information, under current and anticipated future circumstances (pg. 7)

resources inputs used to produce goods and services (pg. 4)

scarcity exists when human wants (material and nonmaterial) exceed available resources (pg. 4)

services intangible items of value provided to consumers, such as education (pg. 5)

simple circular flow model an illustration of the continuous flow of goods, services, inputs, and payments between firms and households (pg. 12)

slope the ratio of rise (change in the Y variable) over run (change in the X variable) (pg. 25)

tangible goods items we value or desire that we can reach out and touch (pg. 5)

theory a statement or proposition used to explain and predict behavior in the real world (pg. 13)

time-series graph visual tool to show changes in a variable's value over time (pg. 22)

variable something that is measured by a number, such as your height (pg. 22)

X-axis the horizontal axis on a graph (pg. 22)

Y-axis the vertical axis on a graph (pg. 22)

For More Review Tools Visit www.cengagebrain.com.

Online Study Tools

At www.cengagebrain.com, you can

❑ Download printable Key Term Flash Cards

❑ Study online with interactive Key Term Flash Cards

❑ Complete Practice Quizzes with instant feedback

❑ Play "Beat the Clock" to master concepts

❑ Complete the Crossword Puzzle to review key terms

❑ Watch the Ask the Instructor video "Why do economists talk about money and wealth? Do they really believe that people are motivated only by money?"

❑ Download and review Exhibit Worksheets

❑ Access Economic Application "Economic Analysis"

❑ Access Graphing Workshop "Working with Graphs"

❑ Check your answers to the Chapter 1 Self-Review on page 21 on the e-book in CourseMate.

Section Summaries

2-1 Choices, Costs, and Trade-Offs

We all face scarcity, and as a consequence, we must make choices. Economics is about understanding the effects that scarcity has on our decision making. In a world of scarcity, we all face trade-offs; when we make choices, we forgo other valued alternatives. Society must make trade-offs as well. The highest or best forgone opportunity resulting from a decision is called the opportunity cost. Opportunity costs can include both monetary and nonmonetary costs, such as time. It is easy to mistake "free" for a zero monetary price. Many allegedly free goods may not cost consumers any money, but they still use society's scarce resources.

2-2 Marginal Thinking

Many choices we face involve *how much* of something to do rather than *whether* to do something or not. Marginal thinking is concerned with additional, or marginal, choices; marginal choices involve the effects of adding or subtracting, from the current situation, the small (or large) incremental changes to a plan of action. The rule of rational choice tells us that individuals will pursue an activity if the expected marginal benefits are greater than the expected marginal costs. The net benefit is the difference between the expected marginal benefits and the expected marginal costs.

© Sergei Bachlakov/Shutterstock.com

2-3 Specialization and Trade

People generally specialize in what they produce because of opportunity costs. By concentrating their energies on only one, or a few, activities, individuals can make the best use of (and thus gain the most benefit from) their limited resources. If an individual can produce a good or service at a lower opportunity cost than others, we say that she has a comparative advantage in the production of that good or service.

The primary advantages of specialization are that employees acquire greater skill from repetition, they avoid wasted time in shifting from one task to another, and they do the types of work for which they are best suited. Specialization also promotes the use of specialized equipment for specialized tasks.

Trade, or voluntary exchange, directly increases wealth by making both parties better off. Standards of living can be increased through trade and exchange. The economy as a whole can create more wealth when each person specializes in the task that he or she does best. Through specialization and trade, a country can gain a greater variety of goods and services at a lower cost.

Key Terms

capital intensive production that uses a large amount of capital (pg. 43)

command economy economy in which the government uses central planning to coordinate most economic activities (pg. 42)

comparative advantage occurs when a person or country can produce a good or service at a lower opportunity cost than others (pg. 35)

consumer sovereignty consumers vote with their dollars in a market economy; this accounts for what is produced (pg. 42)

increasing opportunity cost the opportunity cost of producing additional units of a good rises as society produces more of that good (pg. 38)

labor intensive production that uses a large amount of labor (pg. 43)

marginal thinking focusing on the additional, or marginal, choices; marginal choices involve the effects of adding or subtracting, from the current situation, the small (or large) incremental changes to a plan of action (pg. 33)

market economy an economy that allocates goods and services through the private decisions of consumers, input suppliers, and firms (pg. 42)

mixed economy an economy in which government and the private sector determine the allocation of resources (pg. 42)

net benefit the difference between the expected marginal benefits and the expected marginal costs (pg. 34)

opportunity cost the value of the best forgone alternative that was not chosen (pg. 31)

production possibilities curve the potential total output combinations of any two goods for an economy (pg. 37)

rule of rational choice individuals will pursue an activity if the expected marginal benefits are greater than the expected marginal costs (pg. 33)

specializing concentrating on the production of one or a few goods (pg. 35)

Section Summaries - Continued

2-4 The Production Possibilities of an Economy

The production possibilities curve represents the potential total output combinations of any two goods for an economy, given the inputs and technology available to the economy. It illustrates an economy's potential for allocating its limited resources in producing various combinations of goods in a given time period.

An economy cannot operate outside the production possibilities curve because in the given time period, it does not have sufficient resources to produce that level of output. If, however, the economy operates inside the production possibility curve, it is not producing at full capacity and is operating inefficiently. Efficiency requires society to use its resources to the fullest extent—getting the most from its scarce resources and wasting none.

The law of increasing opportunity cost tells us that the opportunity cost of producing additional units of a good rises as society produces more of that good. This is because some resources and skills cannot be easily adapted from their current uses to alternative uses.

The economy can only grow with qualitative or quantitative changes in the factors of production—for instance, advancement in technology or improvements in labor productivity. Growth, however, does not eliminate scarcity. An economy can also grow by increasing its capital stock.

2-5 Economic Systems

Every economy must answer three fundamental questions: (1) What goods and services will be produced? (2) How will the goods and services be produced? (3) Who will get the goods and services produced? Consumer sovereignty explains how individual consumers in market economies determine what is to be produced. Economies can be organized as command economies, market economies, and mixed economies. When deciding how to produce goods and services, firms may face a trade-off between using more machines (capital) or more workers (labor). This decision will depend on relative factor prices. In a market economy, the goods and services an individual can obtain depend on her income.

© S_L/Shutterstock.com

For More Review Tools Visit www.cengagebrain.com.

Online Study Tools

At www.cengagebra in.com, you can

❏ Download printable Key Term Flash Cards

❏ Study online with interactive Key Term Flash Cards

❏ Complete Practice Quizzes with instant feedback

❏ Play "Beat the Clock" to master concepts

❏ Complete the Crossword Puzzle to review key terms

❏ Download and review Exhibit Worksheets

❏ Access Economic Applications "Scarcity, Choice, and Opportunity Cost" and "Production Possibilities Frontiers"

❏ Access Graphing Workshop "Production Possibilities"

❏ Check your answers to the Chapter 2 Self-Review on page 45 on the e-book in CourseMate.

Section Summaries

3-1 Competitive Markets

Buyers determine the demand side of the market. Buyers include the consumers who purchase the goods and services and the firms that buy inputs. Sellers determine the supply side of the market. Sellers include the firms that produce and sell goods and services and the resource owners who sell their inputs to firms—workers who "sell" their labor and resource owners who sell raw materials and capital.

A competitive market is one in which a number of buyers and sellers are offering similar products, and no single buyer or seller can influence the market price. Because many markets contain a large degree of competitiveness, the lessons of supply and demand can be applied to many different types of problems. The model of supply and demand is very good at predicting changes in prices and quantities in many markets, large and small.

3-2 Demand

The law of demand states that the quantity of a good or service demanded varies inversely (negatively) with its price, *ceteris paribus*. The horizontal summing of the demand curves of all the individuals in an economy is called the market demand curve. A change in a good's own price is said to lead to a change in quantity demanded. The other factors that influence the demand curve are called *determinants of demand,* and a change in these other factors shifts the entire demand curve. Important determinants of demand are the prices of related goods, income, number of buyers, consumers' preferences and information, and expectations.

It is important to understand the difference between the change in the price of a good (a movement *along* a demand curve) and a change in one of the determinants of demand (a shift in the demand curve).

3-3 Supply

According to the law of supply, the quantity supplied will vary directly with the price of the good. The market supply curve may be thought of as the horizontal summation of the supply curves for individual firms. A change in the price of the good in question is shown as a movement along a given supply curve, leading to a change in quantity supplied. A change in any other factor that can affect supplier behavior results in a shift in the entire supply curve, leading to a change in supply. The determinants of supply are input prices, prices of related products, expectations, number of suppliers, technology, regulation, taxes and subsidies, and weather. Essentially, if there is a change in the good's own price, it leads to a change in the quantity supplied. If one of the other factors influences sellers' behavior, we say it results in a change in supply.

3-4 Market Equilibrium Price and Quantity

The market equilibrium is found at the point at which the market supply and market demand curves intersect. The price at the intersection of the market supply curve and the market demand curve is called the equilibrium price, and the quantity is called the equilibrium quantity. At the equilibrium price, the amount that buyers are willing and able to buy is exactly equal to the amount that sellers are willing and able to produce.

Key Terms

change in demand the prices of related goods, income, number of buyers, tastes, and expectations can change the demand for a good; that is, a change in one of these factors shifts the entire demand curve (pg. 51)

change in quantity demanded a change in a good's own price leads to a change in quantity demanded, a move along a given demand curve (pg. 51)

change in quantity supplied a change in a good's own price leads to a change in quantity supplied, a move along a given supply curve (pg. 57)

change in supply input prices, prices of related products, expectations, number of suppliers, technology, regulation, taxes and subsidies, and weather can change the supply for a good; that is, a change in one of these factors shifts the entire supply curve (pg. 57)

competitive market a market in which the many buyers and sellers have little market power—each buyer's or seller's effect on market price is negligible (pg. 48)

complements two goods are complements if an increase (decrease) in the price of one good shifts the demand curve for another good to the left (right) (pg. 52)

equilibrium price the price at the intersection of the market supply and demand curves; at this price, the quantity demanded equals the quantity supplied (pg. 61)

equilibrium quantity the quantity at the intersection of the market supply and demand curves; at the equilibrium quantity, the quantity demanded equals the quantity supplied (pg. 61)

individual demand curve a graphical representation that shows the inverse relationship between price and quantity demanded (pg. 49)

individual demand schedule a schedule that shows the relationship between price and quantity demanded (pg. 49)

individual supply curve a graphical representation that shows the positive relationship between the price and quantity supplied (pg. 56)

individual supply schedule a schedule that shows the relationship between price and quantity supplied (pg. 56)

(continues)

Section Summaries - Continued

If a surplus (or excess quantity supplied) exists, frustrated suppliers will cut their prices and cut back on production; as prices fall, consumers will buy more, eliminating the surplus. If a shortage (or excess quantity demanded) exists, frustrated buyers will be forced to compete for the existing supply, bidding up the price. In turn, the higher price will decrease the quantity demanded and also encourage producers to increase the quantity supplied until the equilibrium is reached.

Often both supply and demand shift in the same time period. When this happens we can predict the change in one variable (price or quantity), but we are unable to predict the direction of the effect on the other variable with any certainty. The change in the second variable, then, is said to be indeterminate.

As the foundations of the market system, supply and demand determine the prices of goods and services and how scarce resources are allocated. Within the market system, market prices are critical for communicating important information to both buyers and sellers. This communication results in a shifting of resources from those uses that are valued less to those that are valued more.

Key Terms - Continued

inferior good   a good for which demand decreases if income decreases and demand increases if income decreases (pg. 52)

law of demand   the quantity of a good or service demanded varies inversely with its price, *ceteris paribus* (pg. 49)

law of supply   the quantity of a good or service supplied varies directly (positively) with its price, *ceteris paribus* (pg. 55)

market demand curve   the horizontal summation of individual demand curves (pg. 50)

market equilibrium   the point at which the market supply and market demand curves intersect (pg. 61)

market supply curve   a graphical representation of the amount of goods and services that suppliers are willing and able to supply at various prices (pg. 56)

normal good   a good for which demand increases if income increases and demand decreases if income decreases (pg. 52)

shortage   a situation in which quantity demanded exceeds quantity supplied (pg. 62)

substitutes   two goods are substitutes if an increase (decrease) in the price of one good causes the demand curve for another good to shift to the right (left) (pg. 52)

surplus   a situation in which quantity supplied exceeds quantity demanded (pg. 62)

For More Review Tools Visit
www.cengagebrain.com.

Online Study Tools

At www.cengagebrain.com, you can

❏ Download printable Key Term Flash Cards

❏ Study online with interactive Key Term Flash Cards

❏ Complete Practice Quizzes with instant feedback

❏ Play "Beat the Clock" to master concepts

❏ Complete the Crossword Puzzle to review key terms

❏ Download and review Exhibit Worksheets

❏ Access Economic Applications "Supply and Demand" and "Equilibrium"

❏ Access Graphing Workshops "Demand," "Supply," and "Market Equilibrium"

❏ Check your answers to the Chapter 3 Self-Review on page 67 on the e-book in CourseMate.

Section Summaries

4-1 Price Elasticity of Demand

The price elasticity of demand measures the responsiveness of quantity demanded to a change in price. Specifically, price elasticity is defined as the percentage change in quantity demanded divided by the percentage change in price. When the quantity demanded moves proportionately more than price, demand is considered elastic. When the quantity demanded moves proportionately less than price, demand is considered to be inelastic. A good is said to be unit elastic if the quantity demanded changes in direct proportion to the price.

For the most part, the price elasticity of demand depends on three factors: (1) the availability of close substitutes, (2) the proportion of income spent on the good, and (3) the amount of time that has elapsed since the price change.

4-2 Total Revenue and the Price Elasticity of Demand

Total revenue (TR) is the amount sellers receive for a good or service. Total revenue is simply the price of the good (P) times the quantity of the good sold (Q): $TR = P \times Q$. Total revenue varies inversely with price if demand is relatively price elastic—if the demand curve is relatively inelastic, total revenue will vary directly with a price change.

We can see how the slopes of demand curves can be used to estimate their relative elasticities of demand: the steeper one demand curve is relative to another, the more inelastic it is *relative* to the other. Although the slope remains constant, the elasticity of a linear demand curve changes along the length of the curve—from relatively elastic at higher price ranges to relatively inelastic at lower price ranges.

4-3 Price Elasticity of Supply

The price elasticity of supply is the measure of the sensitivity of the quantity supplied to changes in price of a good. The price elasticity of supply is calculated in much the same manner as the price elasticity of demand. Goods with a supply elasticity that is greater than 1 ($E_s > 1$) are said to be relatively elastic in supply. Goods with a supply elasticity that is less than 1 ($E_s < 1$) are said to be inelastic in supply. In a condition of *perfectly inelastic supply*, an increase in price will not change the quantity supplied. At the other extreme is a perfectly elastic supply curve, where the elasticity equals infinity. Time is usually critical in supply elasticities, because it is more costly for sellers to bring forth and release products in a shorter period.

4-4 Supply, Demand, and Policies of Government

Price controls involve the use of the power of the state to establish prices different from the equilibrium prices that would otherwise prevail. A price ceiling is a legal maximum price;

Key Terms

consumer surplus the difference between the price a consumer is willing and able to pay for an additional unit of a good and the price the consumer actually pays; for the whole market, it is the sum of all the individual consumer surpluses (pg. 87)

deadweight loss net loss of total surplus that results from an action that alters a market equilibrium (pg. 91)

elastic percentage change in quantity demanded is greater than the percentage change in price ($E_D > 1$) (pg. 71)

health maintenance organization (HMO) an organization that contracts with physicians, medical facilities, employers, and individuals to provide medical care to a group of individuals. Health care services are usually provided at a fixed price per patient. The cost of providing care is contained through the rationing of health care resources (pg. 95)

indemnity coverage compensation toward the cost of medical services in the event of illness or injury (pg. 95)

inelastic percentage change in quantity demanded is less than the percentage change in price ($E_D < 1$) (pg. 71)

marginal cost (MC) the change in total costs resulting from a one-unit change in output (pg. 89)

preferred provider organization (PPO) is a network of doctors who agree to provide services to a health plan's enrollees at discounted fees (pg. 95)

price ceiling a legally established maximum price (pg. 79)

price elasticity of demand the measure of the responsiveness of quantity demanded to a change in price (pg. 70)

price elasticity of supply the measure of the sensitivity of the quantity supplied to changes in price of a good (pg. 76)

price floor a legally established minimum price (pg. 79)

producer surplus the difference between what a producer is paid for a good and the cost of producing that unit of the good; for the market, it is the sum of all the individual sellers' producer surpluses—the area above the market supply curve and below the market price (pg. 88)

(continues)

© Blue Jean Images/Alamy

Section Summaries - Continued

rent control is a common example of a price ceiling. A price floor is a legal minimum price; minimum wage laws are examples of price floors. Though well intentioned, these kinds of price controls can have unintended consequences. Policy makers must be aware of such effects.

The relative elasticity of supply and demand also determines the distribution of the tax burden for a good. If demand is relatively less elastic than supply in the relevant tax region, the largest portion of the tax is paid by the consumer. If demand is relatively more elastic, the largest portion of the tax is paid by the producer.

4-5 Consumer Surplus, Producer Surplus, and the Efficiency of Markets

Consumer surplus is the monetary difference between the amount a consumer is willing and able to pay for an additional unit of a good and what the consumer actually pays (market price). Marginal willingness to pay falls as more is consumed of a given good in a given period. Producer surplus is the difference between what a producer is paid for a good and the cost of producing one unit of that good. Producers would never knowingly sell a good that is worth more to them than the asking price. Marginal cost is the cost of producing one more unit of a good. The total welfare gains to the economy from trade in this good is the sum of the consumer and producer surpluses created. A deadweight loss is the net loss of total surplus that results from the misallocation of resources.

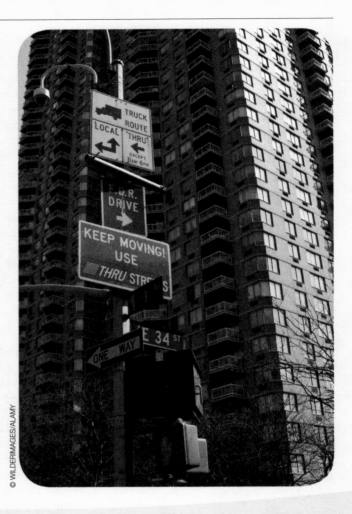

© WILDERIMAGES/ALAMY

Key Terms - Continued

total revenue (*TR*) the amount sellers receive for a good or service, calculated as the product price times the quantity sold (pg. 74)

total welfare gains the sum of consumer and producer surpluses (pg. 91)

unintended consequences the secondary effects of an action that may occur after the initial effects (pg. 82)

unit elastic demand demand with a price elasticity of 1; the percentage change in quantity demanded is equal to the percentage change in price (pg. 71)

For More Review Tools Visit www.cengagebrain.com.

Online Study Tools

At www.cengagebrain.com, you can

- ❏ Download printable Key Term Flash Cards
- ❏ Study online with interactive Key Term Flash Cards
- ❏ Complete Practice Quizzes with instant feedback
- ❏ Play "Beat the Clock" to master concepts
- ❏ Complete the Crossword Puzzle to review key terms

- ❏ Download and review Exhibit Worksheets
- ❏ Access Economic Application "Elasticity"
- ❏ Access Graphing Workshops "Demand, Price Elasticity, and Total Revenue" and "Consumer/Producer Surplus"
- ❏ Check your answers to the Chapter 4 Self-Review on page 93 on the e-book in CourseMate.

Section Summaries

5-1 Externalities

Sometimes the market system fails to produce efficient outcomes because of side effects economists call externalities. In the case of negative externalities (such as pollution), the market supplies too much. With positive externalities (such as education), the private market supplies too little of the good in question.

With negative externalities, the government can use taxes or other forms of regulation to correct the underallocation problem.

With positive externalities, the government can provide subsidies or other forms of regulation to correct the underallocation problem. Individuals sometimes act independently, without government prompting, to reduce negative externalities or create more positive externalities.

5-2 Public Goods

Public goods can be another source of market failure. Most goods in the economy are private goods, which means they are rival and excludable. Public goods are neither rival nor excludable—that is, anyone can enjoy their benefits and it would be too costly to prevent an individual from doing so. It would also be difficult to force individuals to pay for such goods. This can create a free-rider problem, in which people try to take advantage of benefits that they do not pay for. If everyone was a free rider, however, the ride would no longer exist. In these cases, the government must finance or provide the good or service, as no private company could profitably supply efficient levels of the goods. Everything that the government produces, however, has an

opportunity cost, and these must be considered by policy makers.

5-3 Asymmetric Information

When the available information is initially distributed in favor of one party relative to another, asymmetric information is said to exist. This can reduce market efficiency, as lower-quality goods can drive higher-quality goods out of the market. A situation in which an informed party benefits in an exchange by taking advantage of knowing more than the other party is called adverse selection. Adverse selection can be reduced if the buyer can acquire more information. Ideally, the seller would reveal her superior information to the buyer; however, this would not be rational if the product is of inferior quality. The threat of punishment could provide adequate incentives for the seller to be truthful. Sellers can also use reputation and standardization to convince buyers that their products are high quality. Moral hazard is another potential problem, where individuals might take more risks if they know they will not have to shoulder the full consequences of their actions.

Key Terms

adverse selection a situation in which an informed party benefits in an exchange by taking advantage of knowing more than the other party (pg. 109)

asymmetric information occurs when the available information is initially distributed in favor of one party relative to another in an exchange (pg. 109)

common resource a rival good that is nonexcludable (pg. 108)

externality a benefit or cost from consumption or production that spills over onto those who are not consuming or producing the good (pg. 102)

free rider a consumer who derives benefits from something he or she has not paid for (pg. 107)

median voter model a model that predicts candidates will choose a position in the middle of the distribution (pg. 115)

moral hazard taking additional risks because you are insured (pg. 112)

negative externality occurs when costs spill over to an outside party who is not involved in producing or consuming the good (pg. 102)

positive externality occurs when benefits spill over to an outside party who is not involved in producing or consuming the good (pg. 102)

private good a good that is rival in consumption and excludable (pg. 106)

public good a good that is nonrival in consumption and nonexcludable (pg. 106)

rational ignorance lack of incentive to be informed (pg. 116)

special-interest groups groups with an intense interest in particular voting issues that may be different from that of the general public (pg. 117)

winner's curse a situation that arises in certain auctions in which the winner is worse off than the loser because of an overly optimistic value placed on the good (pg. 113)

© iStockphoto.com/Brian Behunin

Section Summaries - Continued

5-4 Public Choice

When the market fails, as in the case of an externality or a public good, it may be necessary for the government to intervene. Government intervention, however, can make matters worse. Public choice theory is the application of economic principles to politics. It assumes that the behavior of individuals in politics will be guided by self-interest, just as it is in the marketplace. Scarcity and competition are present in the public sector as well as in the private sector. On the other hand, the individual consumption-payment link, which is present in the private sector, breaks down, as public choices are often made by majority rule. The median voter model predicts that politics will generally tend toward the middle of the political spectrum. One of the keys to an efficiently working democracy is a concerned and informed electorate, but this can be costly and the issues can be complicated. Public choice economists refer to the lack of incentive to become informed as rational ignorance. Special-interest groups may have intense feelings about and a degree of interest in particular issues that are at variance with those of the general public.

For More Review Tools Visit www.cengagebrain.com.

Online Study Tools

At www.cengagebrain.com, you can

- ❏ Download printable Key Term Flash Cards
- ❏ Study online with interactive Key Term Flash Cards
- ❏ Complete Practice Quizzes with instant feedback
- ❏ Play "Beat the Clock" to master concepts
- ❏ Complete the Crossword Puzzle to review key terms

- ❏ Download and review Exhibit Worksheets
- ❏ Access Economic Applications "Taxes, Spending, and Deficits" and "Economics and the Environment"
- ❏ Access Graphing Workshop "Externalities"
- ❏ Check your answers to the Chapter 5 Self-Review on page 118 on the e-book in CourseMate.

Section Summaries

6-1 Firms and Profits: Total Revenues Minus Total Costs

Explicit costs are the input costs that require a monetary payment. Implicit costs do not require an outlay of money. Accountants do not include implicit costs in the firm's total cost; economists do.

Economists generally assume that the ultimate goal of every firm is to maximize its profits, the difference between what they give up for their inputs and the amount they receive for their goods and services. A zero economic profit means that the firm is covering both explicit and implicit costs—the total opportunity costs of its resources. Sunk costs should be ignored when making economic decisions, because they have already been incurred and cannot be recovered.

6-2 Production in the Short Run

The short run is defined as a period too brief for some production inputs to be varied. The long run is a period in which a firm can adjust all production inputs. The production function illustrates the relationship between the quantity of inputs and the quantity of outputs.

The marginal product (*MP*) of any input is the increase in the quantity of output obtained from one additional unit of input used. The initial rise in the marginal product is the result of more effective use of fixed inputs as the number of workers increases. As additional workers are added, machines are brought into efficient operation

and thus the marginal product of the workers rises. Adding more and more of a variable input to a fixed input, however, will eventually lead to diminishing marginal product. A point will ultimately be reached beyond which marginal product will decline.

6-3 Costs in the Short Run

The short-run total costs of a business fall into two distinct categories: fixed costs and variable costs. Fixed costs are those costs that do not vary with the level of output, such as insurance premiums or property taxes. The sum of the firm's fixed costs is called the total fixed cost (*TFC*). Variable costs, such as expenditures for wages and raw materials, vary with the level of output, increasing as output increases. The sum of the firm's variable costs is called the total variable cost (*TVC*). The sum of the total fixed costs and total variable costs is called the firm's total cost (*TC*).

Sometimes we find it convenient to discuss these costs on a per-unit-of-output or average basis. Average total cost (*ATC*) is the per-unit cost of operation; total cost divided by output. Average fixed cost

Key Terms

accounting profits total revenues minus total explicit costs (pg. 122)

average fixed cost (*AFC*) a per-unit measure of fixed costs; fixed costs divided by output (pg. 128)

average total cost (*ATC*) a per-unit cost of operation; total cost divided by output (pg. 128)

average variable cost (*AVC*) a per-unit measure of variable costs; variable costs divided by output (pg. 128)

constant returns to scale occur in an output range where *LRATC* does not change as output varies (pg. 134)

diminishing marginal product as a variable input increases, with other inputs fixed, a point will be reached at which the additions to output will eventually decline (pg. 126)

diseconomies of scale occur in an output range where *LRATC* rises as output expands (pg. 134)

economic profits total revenues minus explicit and implicit costs (pg. 122)

economies of scale occur in an output range where *LRATC* falls as output increases (pg. 134)

explicit costs the opportunity costs of production that require monetary payment (pg. 122)

fixed costs costs that do not vary with the level of output (pg. 128)

implicit costs the opportunity costs of production that do not require monetary payment (pg. 122)

long run a period over which all production inputs are variable (pg. 125)

marginal cost (*MC*) the change in total costs resulting from a one-unit change in output (pg. 129)

marginal product (*MP*) the change in total output of a good that results from a one-unit change in input (pg. 126)

minimum efficient scale the output level where economies of scale are exhausted and constant returns to scale begin (pg. 134)

production function the relationship between the quantity of inputs and the quantity of outputs (pg. 125)

(continues)

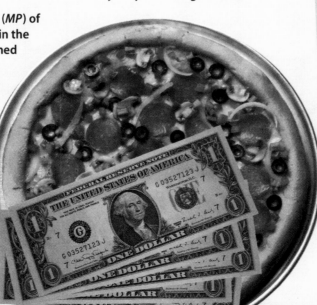

Pizza: © iStockphoto.com/DNY59; Money: © Chapel House Photography

Section Summaries - Continued

(*AFC*) is the per-unit measure of fixed costs; fixed costs divided by output. Average variable cost (*AVC*) is the per-unit measure of variable costs; variable costs divided by output. Marginal cost (*MC*) shows the change in total cost associated with a change in output by one unit.

6-4 The Shape of the Short-Run Cost Curves

If an additional worker's marginal product is lower (higher) than that of previous workers, marginal costs increase (decrease). The relationship between the marginal and the average amount is simply a matter of arithmetic; when a number (the marginal cost) being added into a series is smaller than the previous average of the series, the new average will be lower than the previous one. Likewise, when the marginal number is larger than the average, the average will rise. A declining average fixed cost is the primary reason for the decline in the average total cost curve. The average total cost rises at high levels of output because of diminishing marginal product. When the average variable cost is falling, marginal costs must be

less than the average variable cost; and when the average variable cost is rising, marginal costs are greater than the average variable cost. The same relationship holds for the marginal cost curve and the average total cost curve.

6-5 Cost Curves: Short-Run versus Long-Run

The main difference between short-run and long-run cost curves is that in the long run, firms can substitute lower-cost capital. In the short run, however, firms can only increase output by increasing variable inputs, such as workers and raw materials.

By examining the long-run average total cost curve for a firm, we can see three possible production patterns. Economies of scale occur in an output range where the long-run average total cost falls as output increases. Firms that expand beyond a certain point encounter diseconomies of scale; that is, they incur rising per-unit costs as their output grows. Firms experience constant returns to scale when their per-unit costs remain stable as output grows.

Key Terms - Continued

profits the difference between total revenues and total costs (pg. 122)

short run a period too brief for some production inputs to be varied (pg. 125)

sunk costs costs that have been incurred and cannot be recovered (pg. 124)

total cost (*TC*) the sum of the firm's total fixed costs and total variable costs (pg. 128)

total fixed cost (*TFC*) the sum of the firm's fixed costs (pg. 128)

total output (*Q*) the total amount of output of a good produced by the firm (pg. 125)

total variable cost (*TVC*) the sum of the firm's variable costs (pg. 128)

variable costs costs that change with the level of output (pg. 128)

For More Review Tools Visit www.cengagebrain.com.

Online Study Tools

At www.cengagebrain.com, you can

❏ Download printable Key Term Flash Cards

❏ Study online with interactive Key Term Flash Cards

❏ Complete Practice Quizzes with instant feedback

❏ Play "Beat the Clock" to master concepts

❏ Complete the Crossword Puzzle to review key terms

❏ Download and review Exhibit Worksheets

❏ Access Economic Application "Production and Costs"

❏ Access Graphing Workshop "Production and Cost"

❏ Check your answers to the Chapter 6 Self-Review on page 136 on the e-book in CourseMate.

Section Summaries

7-1 A Perfectly Competitive Market

A perfectly competitive market is characterized by (1) many buyers and sellers, (2) identical (homogeneous) products, and (3) easy market entry and exit. When there are many buyers and sellers, each firm is so small in relation to the industry that its production decisions have no impact on the market. Perfectly competitive firms are called price takers because they must accept the market price. In a perfectly competitive market, firms sell identical (homogeneous) products. Perfectly competitive markets have no significant barriers to entry or exit. Firms can enter or exit the market freely.

7-2 An Individual Price Taker's Demand Curve

As price takers, perfectly competitive firms must sell at the market-determined price, where the market price and output are determined by the intersection of the market supply and demand curves. Likewise, individual sellers can change their outputs, and it will not alter the market price. When the market price for the given product increases, say as a result of an increase in market demand, the price-taking firm will receive a higher price for all its output. However, if the price decreases, the firm will receive a lower price. The perfectly competitive model does not assume any knowledge on the part of individual buyers and sellers about market demand and supply—they only have to know the price of the good they sell.

7-3 Profit Maximization

The objective of the firm is to maximize profits. To maximize profits, the firm wants to produce the amount that maximizes the difference between its total revenues and total costs. Total revenue (TR) from a product equals the price of the good (P) times the quantity (q) of units sold. Average revenue (AR) equals total revenue divided by the number of units sold of the product. Marginal revenue (MR) is the additional revenue derived from the production of one more unit of the good. The firm will maximize its profits at the level of output that maximizes the difference between total revenue and total cost—that is, when marginal revenue equals marginal cost.

7-4 Short-Run Profits and Losses

Determining whether the firm is generating economic profits can be done in three easy steps. First, find the profit-maximizing output level, where marginal revenue equals marginal cost. Second, identify the market price and find total revenue at the profit-maximizing output level. Third, multiply the average total cost by the output level to find the total cost. If total revenue is greater than total cost, the firm is generating economic profits, and if total revenue is less than total cost then the firm is generating economic losses. If total revenue and cost are equal, the firm has zero economic profit—a normal return.

A firm making an economic loss must decide whether to continue producing or shut down. If it cannot cover its average variable cost, the firm will shut down in the short run.

Key Terms

allocative efficiency where $P = MC$ and production will be allocated to reflect consumer preferences (pg. 156)

average revenue (AR) the total revenue divided by the number of units sold (pg. 143)

constant-cost industry an industry in which input prices (and cost curves) do not change as industry output changes (pg. 153)

decreasing-cost industry an industry in which input prices fall (and cost curves fall) as industry output rises (pg. 156)

increasing-cost industry an industry in which input prices rise (and cost curves rise) as industry output rises (pg. 155)

marginal revenue (MR) the increase in total revenue resulting from a one-unit increase in sales (pg. 143)

perfect competition a market structure characterized by many buyers and sellers, identical (homogeneous) products, and easy market entry and exit (pg. 140)

price taker a perfectly competitive firm that takes the price it is given by the intersection of the market demand and market supply curves (pg. 140)

productive efficiency where a good or service is produced at the lowest possible cost (pg. 156)

profit-maximizing level of output a firm should always produce at the output level at which $MR = MC$ (pg. 144)

short-run market supply curve the horizontal summation of the individual firms' supply curves in the market (pg. 148)

short-run supply curve the portion of the MC curve above the AVC curve (pg. 148)

total revenue (TR) the product price times the quantity sold (pg. 142)

Section Summaries - Continued

The short-run market supply curve is the summation of all the individual firms' supply curves (that is, the portion of the firms' *MC* above *AVC*) in the market.

7-5 Long-Run Equilibrium

If the firm is able to make economic profits with the goods it produces, it will increase the resources devoted to producing that good. These profits will draw other firms into the market and create a supply response, shifting the market supply curve to the right. This will cause the equilibrium market price to fall, returning the firm to zero economic profits.

The equilibrium condition in the long run in perfect competition is for each firm to produce at the output that minimizes average total cost—that is, the firm is operating at its minimum efficient scale. At this long-run equilibrium, all firms in the industry earn zero economic profit.

7-6 Long-Run Supply

Long run supply varies based on the type of industry. The three major types are constant-cost, increasing-cost, and decreasing-cost industries. In a constant-cost industry, the prices of inputs do not change as output is expanded. In an increasing-cost industry, the cost curves of individual firms rise as the total output of the industry increases. In decreasing-cost industries, an expansion in the output of an industry can lead to a reduction in input costs and shift the *MC* and *ATC* curves downward, and the market price falls because of external economies of scale. For markets to operate efficiently, they must achieve both productive efficiency, where firms produce goods and services in the least costly way, and allocative efficiency, where firms produce the goods that reflect society's preferences.

Harald Sund/Brand X Pictures/Gettyimages.com

For More Review Tools Visit www.cengagebrain.com.

Online Study Tools

At www.cengagebrain.com, you can

❏ Download printable Key Term Flash Cards

❏ Study online with interactive Key Term Flash Cards

❏ Complete Practice Quizzes with instant feedback

❏ Play "Beat the Clock" to master concepts

❏ Complete the Crossword Puzzle to review key terms

❏ Download and review Exhibit Worksheets

❏ Access Economic Application "Perfect Competition"

❏ Access Graphing Workshop "Short-Run Supply Decision"

❏ Check your answers to the Chapter 7 Self-Review on page 158 on the e-book in CourseMate.

Section Summaries

8-1 Monopoly: The Price Maker

A true or pure monopoly exists when a market consists of only one seller of a product with no close substitute and natural or legal barriers to prevent entry competition. Monopolists are price makers that try to pick the price that will maximize their profits based on the market demand curve. Pure monopolies are rare. Some public utilities are provided by one producer. Governments are the sole suppliers of some goods as well.

A monopolist might create barriers to entry by establishing legal barriers, taking advantage of economies of scale, or controlling important inputs.

8-2 Demand and Marginal Revenue in Monopoly

In monopoly, the demand curve is downward sloping—the firm cannot set both the price and the quantity it sells. Because a monopolist's marginal revenue is always less than the price, the marginal revenue curve will always lie below the demand curve. A monopolist will never knowingly operate on the inelastic portion of its demand curve, because increased output will lead to lower total revenue in this region and total costs will rise.

8-3 The Monopolist's Equilibrium

The monopolist, like the perfect competitor, will maximize profits at the output where $MR = MC$. The same basic three-step method discussed in Chapter 7 can be used to determine whether the firm is generating an economic profit, an economic loss, or zero economic profits at the profit-maximizing level of output. In monopoly, profits can persist in the long run, because barriers to entry will keep new firms out of the market.

If demand is insufficient to cover the monopolist's average total costs, the monopolist will incur a loss.

The government uses patents and copyrights to confer a form of monopoly. These provide producers incentives to incur the upfront costs of producing some goods, such as prescription drugs.

8-4 Monopoly and Welfare Loss

To most economists, the most serious objection to monopoly is that monopolies result in market inefficiencies. Compared to the perfectly competitive market, monopolists charge higher prices and produce less output. This situation may also be viewed as "unfair," in that consumers are burdened more than under the alternative competitive arrangement. Since the monopolist produces at a level where price is greater than marginal cost, this means that the monopolist is not producing enough from society's perspective. This is the welfare or deadweight loss.

Key Terms

average cost pricing setting price equal to average total cost (pg. 174)

monopoly the single supplier of a product that has no close substitute (pg. 162)

natural monopoly a firm that can produce at a lower cost than a number of smaller firms can (pg. 162)

price discrimination the practice of charging different consumers different prices for the same good or service (pg. 176)

Section Summaries - Continued

8-5 Monopoly Policy

Antitrust policies and regulation are the two major approaches for dealing with monopoly situations. Through antitrust policies, the government can make monopolistic practices illegal and impose costs on monopolists that would decrease their profits. The Sherman Antitrust Act, the first important law regulating monopoly, prohibited practices such as price fixing and collusion.

Under government regulation, a company would not be allowed to charge any price it wants. This is common when the government does not want to break up a natural monopoly, such as in the water or power industries.

Monopolistic firms also cannot perform at the optimal output, because they would operate at a loss. Regulators might encourage an average cost pricing strategy. Costs can be difficult to calculate, however, and monopolists may have little incentive to keep costs down.

8-6 Price Discrimination

Price discrimination is the practice of charging different consumers different prices for the same good or service. For price discrimination to be possible, three conditions must be met: the firm must hold monopoly power, the demand curves for various groups within the market must differ, and the buyer must not be able to easily resell the product. Price discrimination results from the profit-maximization motive.

> **For More Review Tools Visit**
> **www.cengagebrain.com.**

Online Study Tools

At www.cengagebrain.com, you can

- ❏ Download printable Key Term Flash Cards
- ❏ Study online with interactive Key Term Flash Cards
- ❏ Complete Practice Quizzes with instant feedback
- ❏ Play "Beat the Clock" to master concepts
- ❏ Complete the Crossword Puzzle to review key terms
- ❏ Download and review Exhibit Worksheets

- ❏ Access Economic Application "Monopoly"
- ❏ Access Graphing Workshops "Monopoly Behavior in the Short Run," "Monopoly verses Perfect Competition," and "Price Discrimination"
- ❏ Check your answers to the Chapter 8 Self-Review on page 179 on the e-book in CourseMate.

Section Summaries

9-1 Monopolistic Competition

Monopolistic competition is a market structure in which many producers of somewhat different products compete with one another. Monopolistic competition is based on three characteristics: (1) product differentiation, (2) many sellers, and (3) free entry.

9-2 Price and Output Determination in Monopolistic Competition

Monopolistically competitive sellers are price makers. We can use the same three-step method from Chapters 7 and 8 to determine if the firm is making an economic profit. Since entry is free in monopolistic competition, profits and losses probably will not last in the long run. Long-run equilibrium will occur when demand is equal to average total costs for each firm at a level of output at which each firm's demand curve is just tangent to its *ATC* curve.

9-3 Monopolistic Competition versus Perfect Competition

Both monopolistic competition and perfect competition have many buyers and sellers and relatively free entry. However, product differentiation enables a monopolistic competitor to have some influence over price. It also results in certain inefficiencies.

Firms in monopolistic competition do not produce at the minimum point of *ATC*, failing to meet productive efficiency, and they do not charge a price equal to marginal cost, failing to meet allocative efficiency. The inefficiency of monopolistic competition is a result of product differentiation. Because consumers value variety, the loss in efficiency must be weighed against the gain in increased variety.

9-4 Oligopoly

Oligopolies exist, by definition, where relatively few firms control all or most of the production and sale of a product. Oligopoly is characterized by mutual interdependence among firms; each firm shapes its policy by constantly observing and anticipating the moves of rival firms. Substantial economies of scale are often present in oligopoly markets, creating a barrier to entry, as small scale production for new firms can be very unprofitable.

9-5 Collusion and Cartels

Because the actions and profits of oligopolists are dominated by mutual interdependence, the temptation is great for firms to collude—to agree to act jointly in pricing and other matters to increase profits. A cartel is a collection of firms making an agreement. Cartels lead to joint profit maximization, in which firms together will set optimum price and output levels according to mutually estimated demand and cost schedules.

Most strong collusive oligopolies are rather short lived for two reasons: First, in the United States and many other nations, collusive oligopolies are illegal. Second, for collusion to work, firms must cooperate in setting the price, but there is a great temptation for firms to cheat by slightly lowering their price.

Tacit collusion can occur when a single large firm in a market acts as a price leader; the price leader will publicly announce its pricing decisions and other firms in the

Key Terms

cartel a collection of firms that agree on sales, pricing, and other decisions (pg. 190)

collusion when firms act together to restrict competition (pg. 190)

cooperative game collusion by two firms in order to improve their profit maximizations (pg. 195)

dominant strategy strategy that will be optimal regardless of opponents' actions (pg. 195)

excess capacity occurs when the firm produces below the level at which average total cost is minimized (pg. 185)

game theory firms attempt to maximize profits by acting in ways that minimize damage from competitors (pg. 195)

joint profit maximization determination of price based on the marginal revenue derived from the market demand schedule and marginal cost schedule of the firms in the industry (pg. 190)

monopolistic competition a market structure with many firms selling differentiated products (pg. 181)

mutual interdependence when a firm shapes its policy with an eye to the policies of competing firms (pg. 188)

noncooperative game each firm sets its own price without consulting other firms (pg. 195)

oligopoly a market structure in which relatively few firms control all or most of the production and sale of a product (pg. 187)

payoff matrix a summary of the possible outcomes of various strategies (pg. 195)

predatory pricing setting a price deliberately low in order to drive out competitors (pg. 194)

price follower a competitor in an oligopoly that goes along with the pricing decision of the price leader (pg. 192)

price leader a large firm in an oligopoly that unilaterally makes changes in its product prices that competitors tend to follow (pg. 191)

price leadership when a dominant firm that produces a large portion of the industry's output sets a price that maximizes its profits, and other firms follow (pg. 192)

(continues)

Section Summaries - Continued

market, called price followers, will match that pricing decision.

   There are three types of mergers: horizontal, vertical, and conglomerate mergers. Most antitrust issues arise with horizontal mergers. Antitrust laws also forbid predatory pricing, price discrimination, and tying.

9-6 Game Theory and Strategic Behavior

Game theory analyzes oligopoly equilibrium price and output as a strategic game, in which firms in such circumstances act in a way that minimizes damage from competitors. Most games are noncooperative games, in which each firm sets its

own price without consulting other firms. A famous game that has a dominant strategy and demonstrates the basic problem confronting noncolluding oligopolists is known as the prisoners' dilemma. At a Nash equilibrium, each firm is said to be doing as well as it can given the actions of its competitor. Most oligopolistic interactions are repeated games, which makes cooperation possible.

© iStockphoto.com/adventtr

Key Terms - Continued

prisoners' dilemma the basic problem facing noncolluding oligopolists in maximizing their own profits (pg. 195)

product differentiation goods or services that are slightly different, or perceived to be different, from one another (pg. 182)

tit-for-tat strategy used in repeated games, the strategy in which one player follows the other player's move in the previous round; leads to greater cooperation (pg. 199)

For More Review Tools Visit www.cengagebrain.com.

Online Study Tools

At www.cengagebrain.com, you can

- ❑ Download printable Key Term Flash Cards
- ❑ Study online with interactive Key Term Flash Cards
- ❑ Complete Practice Quizzes with instant feedback
- ❑ Play "Beat the Clock" to master concepts
- ❑ Complete the Crossword Puzzle to review key terms
- ❑ Download and review Exhibit Worksheets

- ❑ Access Economic Applications "Monopolistic Competition" and "Oligopoly"
- ❑ Access Graphing Workshops "Short-Run Equilibrium in Monopolistic Competition," "Long-Run Equilibrium in Monopolistic Competition," and "Game Theory"
- ❑ Check your answers to the Chapter 9 Self-Review on page 201 on the e-book in CourseMate.

Section Summaries

10-1 Input Markets

Input markets are the markets for the factors of production used to produce output. In input or factor markets, the demand for an input derived from consumers' demand for the good or service produced with that input is called a derived demand.

10-2 Supply and Demand in the Labor Market

In a competitive labor market, the demand for labor is determined by its marginal revenue product (*MRP*), which is the additional revenue that a firm obtains from one more unit of input. The marginal resource cost (*MRC*) is the amount that an extra input adds to the firm's total costs.

The downward-sloping demand curve for labor indicates a negative relationship between wage and the quantity of labor demanded. Marginal revenue product is equal to marginal product (*MP*) multiplied by marginal revenue.

Profits are maximized if the firm hires only to the point at which the wage equals the expected marginal revenue product.

In the market supply curve, a positive relationship exists between the wage rate and the quantity of labor supplied.

10-3 Labor Market Equilibrium

The equilibrium wage and quantity in competitive markets for labor is determined by the intersection of labor demand and labor supply. The demand curve for labor can be shifted by increases in labor productivity and changes in the output price of the good. The labor supply curve can be shifted by immigration and population growth, worker preferences, nonwage income, and amenities.

10-4 Labor Unions

Labor unions were formed to increase their members' wages and to improve working conditions. The union negotiates with firms through a process called collective bargaining. Labor unions influence the quantity of union labor hired and the wages, primarily through their ability to alter the supply of labor services.

10-5 Income Distribution

In many economies, some individuals will have high income and others will have low income. Factors such as age, demographic factors, institutional factors, and governmental

© Helga Esteb/Shutterstock.com

Key Terms

cash transfers direct cash payments such as welfare, Social Security, and unemployment compensation (pg. 219)

collective bargaining negotiations between representatives of employers and unions (pg. 212)

derived demand the demand for an input derived from consumers' demand for the good or service produced with that input (pg. 204)

Earned Income Tax Credit (EITC) a welfare program that allows the working poor to receive income refunds that can be greater than the taxes they paid during the last year (pg. 219)

in-kind transfers transfers in the form of goods and services instead of money, including food stamps, school lunch programs, housing subsidies, and Medicaid, among others (pg. 215)

marginal product (*MP*) the change in total output of a good that results from a one-unit change in input (pg. 205)

marginal resource cost (*MRC*) the amount that an extra input adds to the firm's total cost (pg. 204)

marginal revenue product (*MRP*) marginal product times the price of the output (pg. 204)

means-tested income transfer program program in which eligibility is dependent on low income; food stamps, Medicaid, and housing subsidies are examples of means-tested income transfer programs (pg. 219)

poverty line a set of money income thresholds, established by the federal government, that vary by family size and are used to detect who is poor; if a family's total income is less than the established family threshold, then that family, and every individual in it, is considered poor (pg. 218)

poverty rate the percentage of the population who fall below the poverty line (pg. 218)

progressive tax system tax system that imposes higher marginal tax rates on higher incomes; the federal income tax is designed to be a progressive tax system (pg. 219)

(continues)

Section Summaries - Continued

redistribution activities influence income distribution data. Studies indicate that income mobility is significant in the United States—there will always be high- and low-income earners, but the people in those segments are likely to change. Reasons for income differences include age, skill, human capital, and preferences toward risk and leisure. While income inequality within nations is substantial, it is far less than income inequality among nations.

10-6 Poverty

The federal government measures poverty by using a set of money income thresholds that vary by family size. The poverty rate is the percentage of the population that falls below income threshold set by the government, called the poverty line.

A variety of programs are designed to reduce poverty and redistribute income. These include taxes, transfer payments, welfare programs, and government subsidies.

Key Terms - Continued

Supplemental Security Income (SSI) a welfare program designed for the most needy, elderly, disabled, and blind (pg. 219)

Temporary Assistance for Needy Families (TANF) a welfare program designed to help families that have few financial resources (pg. 219)

For More Review Tools Visit www.cengagebrain.com.

Online Study Tools

At www.cengagebrain.com, you can

❑ Download printable Key Term Flash Cards

❑ Study online with interactive Key Term Flash Cards

❑ Complete Practice Quizzes with instant feedback

❑ Play "Beat the Clock" to master concepts

❑ Complete the Crossword Puzzle to review key terms

❑ Download and review Exhibit Worksheets

❑ Access Economic Applications "Labor Markets" and "Income Distribution and Poverty"

❑ Access Graphing Workshops "Demand for Labor," "Union Effects on Wages," and "The Effects of a Wage Differential"

❑ Check your answers to the Chapter 10 Self-Review on page 221 on the e-book in CourseMate.

Section Summaries

11-1 Macroeconomic Goals

Nearly every society has three major macroeconomic goals: (1) maintaining employment of human resources at relatively high levels, (2) maintaining prices at a relatively stable level, and (3) achieving a high rate of economic growth. We use the term *real gross domestic product* (RGDP) to measure output or production.

11-2 Employment and Unemployment

Relatively high rates of unemployment are viewed almost universally as undesirable. To calculate the unemployment rate, divide the number of unemployed by the number in the civilian labor force. In periods of prolonged recession, some individuals think that the chances of landing a job are so bleak that they quit looking. These people are called discouraged workers.

Education, age, sex, and race can be factors in unemployment. Categories of unemployed workers include job losers, job leavers, reentrants, and new entrants. The duration of unemployment tends to be greater when the amount of unemployment is high and smaller when the amount of unemployment is low. The percentage of the working age (16 years and older) population that is in the labor force is what economists call the labor force participation rate.

11-3 Types of Unemployment

The three types of unemployment are frictional, structural, and cyclical unemployment. Frictional and structural unemployment are unavoidable in a vibrant economy, resulting from imperfections in the labor market. In years of relatively high unemployment, some joblessness may result from short-term cyclical fluctuations in

the economy. Most attempts to solve the cyclical unemployment problem emphasized increasing aggregate demand to counter recession. Many economists consider the natural rate of unemployment to be around 5 percent.

11-4 Reasons for Unemployment

Economists cite three reasons for the failure of wages to balance the labor demand and labor supply equilibrium—minimum wages, unions, and the efficiency wage theory. Because minimum wage earners are a small portion of the labor force, most economists believe the effect of minimum wage on unemployment is small. If union officials are able to increase wages, then unemployment will rise in the union sector. Some economists follow the efficiency wage model, which is based on the belief that higher wages lead to greater productivity.

Although the unemployment insurance is intended to ease the pain of unemployment, it also leads to prolonged periods of unemployment. The widespread belief that technological advances inevitably result in the displacement of workers is not necessarily true.

11-5 Inflation

The continuing rise in the overall price level is called inflation. When the overall price level is falling, it is called deflation. The higher the inflation rate, the greater the rate of decline in purchasing power. A price index attempts to provide a measure of the prices paid for a certain bundle of goods and services over time. The most well-known index is probably the consumer price index (CPI). We can calculate a price index by dividing the cost of the market basket in the current year by the cost in the base

Key Terms

boom period of prolonged economic expansion (pg. 245)

business cycles short-term fluctuations in the economy relative to the long-term trend in output (pg. 244)

consumer price index (CPI) a measure of the cost of a market basket that represents the consumption of a typical household (pg. 237)

contraction when the economy is slowing down—measured from the peak to the trough (pg. 244)

cyclical unemployment unemployment due to short-term cyclical fluctuations in the economy (pg. 231)

deflation a decrease in the overall price level, which increases the purchasing power of money (pg. 237)

depression severe recession or contraction in output (pg. 245)

discouraged worker an individual who has left the labor force because he or she could not find a job (pg. 226)

efficiency wage model a theory stating that higher wages lead to greater productivity (pg. 234)

Employment Act of 1946 a commitment by the federal government to hold itself accountable for short-run economic fluctuations (pg. 224)

expansion when output (real GDP) is rising significantly—the period between the trough of a recession and the next peak (pg. 244)

frictional unemployment the unemployment that results from workers searching for suitable jobs and firms looking for suitable workers (pg. 230)

GDP deflator a price index that helps measure the average price level of all final consumer goods and services produced (pg. 238)

hyperinflation extremely high rates of inflation for sustained periods of time (pg. 241)

inflation a rise in the overall price level, which decreases the purchasing power of money (pg. 237)

job leaver a person who quits his or her job (pg. 227)

job loser an individual who has been temporarily laid off or fired (pg. 227)

labor force the number of people aged 16 and older who are available for employment (pg. 225)

(continues)

Section Summaries - Continued

year and multiplying by 100. Unanticipated and sharp changes in the price level are almost universally considered to be "bad" and to require a policy remedy.

11-6 Economic Fluctuations

We sometimes call the short-term fluctuations in economic activity business cycles. The period of expansion is when output (real GDP) is rising significantly. The contraction, also called a recession, is a period of falling real output and is usually accompanied by rising unemployment and declining business and consumer confidence. Some fluctuation in economic activity reflects seasonal patterns. Businesses, government agencies, and consumers rely on economic forecasts to learn of forthcoming developments in the business cycle.

Key Terms - Continued

labor force participation rate the percentage of the working age population in the labor force (pg. 229)

leading economic indicators factors that economists at the Commerce Department have found typically change before changes in economic activity occur (pg. 246)

menu costs the costs imposed on a firm from changing listed prices (pg. 242)

minimum wage rate an hourly wage floor set above the equilibrium wage (pg. 233)

natural rate of unemployment the median, or "typical," unemployment rate, equal to the sum of frictional and structural unemployment when they are at a maximum (pg. 231)

new entrant an individual who has not held a job before but is now seeking employment (pg. 227)

nominal interest rate the reported interest rate that is not adjusted for inflation (pg. 242)

peak the point in time when expansion comes to an end, that is, when output is at the highest point in the cycle (pg. 244)

potential output the amount of real output the economy would produce if its labor and other resources were fully employed, that is, at the natural rate of unemployment (pg. 232)

price index a measure of the trend in prices paid for a certain bundle of goods and services over a given period (pg. 237)

price level the average level of prices in the economy (pg. 237)

real gross domestic product (RGDP) the total value of all final goods and services produced in a given period, such as a year or a quarter, adjusted for inflation (pg. 224)

real interest rate the nominal interest rate minus the inflation rate; also called the inflation adjusted interest rate (pg. 242)

recession a period of significant decline in output and employment (pg. 244)

reentrant an individual who worked before and is now reentering the labor force (pg. 227)

relative price the price of a specific good compared to the price of other goods (pg. 237)

seasonal unemployment unemployment that occurs because of seasonal factors such as weather or fluctuations in the demand for some goods or services during different times of the year (pg. 230)

shoe-leather cost the cost incurred when individuals reduce their money holdings because of inflation (pg. 242)

structural unemployment the unemployment that results from workers not having the skills to obtain long-term employment (pg. 231)

trough the point in time when output stops declining, that is, when business activity is at its lowest point in the cycle (pg. 244)

underemployment a situation in which a worker's skill level is higher than necessary for a job (pg. 228)

unemployment rate the percentage of the population aged 16 and older who are willing and able to work but are unable to obtain a job (pg. 224)

For More Review Tools Visit
www.cengagebrain.com.

Online Study Tools

At www.cengagebrain.com, you can

❏ Download printable Key Term Flash Cards

❏ Study online with interactive Key Term Flash Cards

❏ Complete Practice Quizzes with instant feedback

❏ Play "Beat the Clock" to master concepts

❏ Complete the Crossword Puzzle to review key terms

❏ Download and review Exhibit Worksheets

❏ Access Economic Applications "Employment, Unemployment, and Inflation;" "Output, Income, and the Price Level;" and "Recession"

❏ Check your answers to the Chapter 11 Self-Review on page 247 on the e-book in CourseMate.

Section Summaries

12-1 Economic Growth

Economic growth is usually measured by the annual percentage change in real output of goods and services per capita (real GDP per capita). The Rule of 70 shows how long it will take a nation to double its output at various growth rates. Growth rates vary widely across different countries. Productivity is the amount of good and services a worker can produce per hour. Sustained economic growth occurs when workers' productivity rises.

12-2 Determinants of Long-Run Economic Growth

Labor productivity is the output per unit of worker. The four major factors that contribute to productivity growth include (1) physical capital, (2) human capital, (3) natural resources, and (4) technology. New Growth Theory argues that economic growth can continue unimpeded, as long as we keep coming up with new ideas.

12-3 Public Policy and Economic Growth

One of the most important determinants of economic growth is the saving rate. To consume more in the future, we must save more now. Infrastructure is also critical to economic coordination and activity. Research and development consists of the activities undertaken to create new products and processes that will lead to technological progress. Economic growth rates tend to be higher in countries where the government enforces property rights. Allowing free trade can also lead to greater output because of the principle of comparative advantage. Education, investment in human capital, may be just as important as improvements in physical capital.

12-4 Measuring Economic Growth and Its Components

Gross domestic product (GDP) is defined as the value of all final goods and services produced within a country during a given period. GDP also measures the value of total income, since every dollar of spending ends up being a dollar of income for a seller. We can use the circular flow model to show the flow of money in the economy.

12-5 Measuring Total Production

With the expenditure approach, GDP is calculated by adding how much market participants spend on final goods and services over a specific period of time. Economists usually group spending into four categories: consumption (C), investment (I), government purchases (G), and net exports ($X - M$).

The Bureau of Economic Analysis (BEA) also computes five additional measures of production and income: gross national product, net national product, national income, personal income, and disposable personal income.

© Robyn Mackenzie/iStockphoto.com

Key Terms

consumption purchases of final goods and services (pg. 261)

depreciation annual allowance set aside to replace worn-out capital. (pg. 263)

disposable personal income the personal income available after personal taxes (pg. 263)

double counting adding the value of a good or service twice by mistakenly counting the intermediate goods and services in GDP (pg. 260)

economic growth an upward trend in the real per capita output of goods and services (pg. 249)

expenditure approach calculation of GDP by adding the expenditures by market participants on final goods and services over a given period (pg. 261)

factor payments wages (salaries), rent, interest payments, and profits paid to the owners of productive resources (pg. 263)

gross domestic product (GDP) the measure of economic performance based on the value of all final goods and services produced within a country during a given period (pg. 260)

gross national product (GNP) the difference between net income of foreigners and GDP (pg. 263)

indirect business taxes taxes, such as sales tax, levied on goods and services sold (pg. 263)

innovation applications of new knowledge that create new products or improve existing products (pg. 254)

investment the creation of capital goods to augment future production (pg. 262)

labor productivity output per unit of worker (pg. 253)

national income (NI) a measure of income earned by owners of the factors of production (pg. 263)

net national product (NNP) GNP minus depreciation (pg. 263)

personal income (PI) the amount of income received by households before personal taxes (pg. 263)

(continues)

Section Summaries - Continued

12-6 Problems in Calculating an Accurate GDP

The primary problem in calculating accurate GDP statistics is changes in the overall price level for goods and services over time. To compare GDP values over time, the calculations must use a common, or standardized, unit of measure, which only money can provide.

Real GDP is equal to the nominal GDP divided by the price-level index times 100. To calculate real GDP per capita, we divide the real GDP by the total population to get the value of real output of final goods and services per person.

12-7 Problems with GDP as a Measure of Economic Welfare

The accuracy of real GDP as a measure of economic welfare fails to account for certain factors, including nonmarket transactions, the underground economy, leisure, externalities, and the quality of the goods purchased.

© ALEXANDER CHAIKIN/SHUTTERSTOCK.COM

Key Terms - Continued

productivity the amount of goods and services a worker can produce per hour (pg. 252)

real gross domestic product per capita real output of goods and services per person (pg. 264)

research and development (R&D) activities undertaken to create new products and processes that will lead to technological progress (pg. 257)

For More Review Tools Visit www.cengagebrain.com.

Online Study Tools

At www.cengagebrain.com, you can

❑ Download printable Key Term Flash Cards

❑ Study online with interactive Key Term Flash Cards

❑ Complete Practice Quizzes with instant feedback

❑ Play "Beat the Clock" to master concepts

❑ Complete the Crossword Puzzle to review key terms

❑ Download and review Exhibit Worksheets

❑ Access Economic Application "Productivity and Growth" and "National Income Accounts"

❑ Access Graphing Workshop "The Circular Flow Model"

❑ Check your answers to the Chapter 12 Self-Review on page 271 on the e-book in CourseMate.

Section Summaries

13-1 The Aggregate Demand Curve

The aggregate demand curve reflects the total amount of real goods and services that all groups together want to purchase in a given period. Three complementary explanations exist for the negative slope of the aggregate demand curve: the real wealth effect, the interest rate effect, and the open economy effect.

13-2 Shifts in the Aggregate Demand Curve

Each of the three factors—real wealth, interest rate, and open economy effects—generates a movement along the aggregate demand curve, in reaction to changes in the general price level. Anything that changes the amount of total spending in the economy (holding price levels constant) will affect the aggregate demand curve. An increase in any component of GDP (C, I, G, or $X - M$) will cause the aggregate demand curve to shift rightward. Conversely, decreases in C, I, G, or $X - M$ will shift aggregate demand leftward.

13-3 The Aggregate Supply Curve

The aggregate supply (AS) curve is the relationship between the total quantity of final goods and services that suppliers are *willing* and *able* to produce and the overall price level. In the short run, the aggregate supply curve is upward sloping. Two possible explanations for this are the profit effect and the misperception effect. The long-run aggregate supply curve is vertical, reflecting the fact that the level of RGDP producers are willing to

supply is not affected by changes in the price level.

13-4 Shifts in the Aggregate Supply Curve

Any change in the quantity of any factor of production available— capital, land, labor, or technology— can cause a shift in both the long-run and short-run aggregate supply curves. Some important factors that only shift the short-run aggregate supply curve are wages and other input prices, productivity, and unexpected supply shocks.

13-5 Macroeconomic Equilibrium

The short-run equilibrium level of real output and the price level are given by the intersection of the aggregate demand curve and the short-run aggregate supply curve. Equilibrium can occur at less than the potential output of the economy (a recessionary gap), beyond the potential output (an inflationary gap), or at potential GDP.

Demand-pull inflation occurs when the price level rises as a result of an increase in aggregate

Key Terms

aggregate demand curve graph that shows the inverse relationship between the price level and RGDP demanded (pg. 273)

aggregate supply (AS) curve the total quantity of final goods and services suppliers are willing and able to supply at a given price level (pg. 277)

cost-push inflation a price-level increase due to a negative supply shock or increases in input prices (pg. 285)

demand-pull inflation a price-level increase due to an increase in aggregate demand (pg. 284)

inflationary gap the output gap that occurs when the actual output is greater than the potential output (pg. 284)

long-run aggregate supply (LRAS) curve the graphical relationship between RGDP and the price level when output prices and input prices can fully adjust to economic changes (pg. 277)

recessionary gap the output gap that occurs when the actual output is less than the potential output (pg. 284)

short-run aggregate supply (SRAS) curve the graphical relationship between RGDP and the price level when output prices can change but input prices are unable to adjust (pg. 277)

stagflation a situation in which lower growth and higher prices occur together (pg. 285)

supply shocks unexpected temporary events that can either increase or decrease aggregate supply (pg. 282)

wage and price inflexibility the tendency for prices and wages to only adjust slowly downward to changes in the economy (pg. 287)

Today's Special
—
higher menu costs

Section Summaries - Continued

demand. If the aggregate demand curve did not increase significantly but the price level did, then the inflation was caused by supply-side forces, which is called cost-push inflation. A decrease in aggregate demand can also cause a recessionary gap. Eventual recoveries from a recessionary gap occur because of increases in aggregate demand. Downward wage and price inflexibility may prolong the duration of a recessionary gap. During an inflationary gap, suppliers will continue to seek higher prices for their inputs until they reach the long-run equilibrium.

13-6 The Classical and the Keynesian Macroeconomic Models

The classical school of thought believed that wages and prices adjust quickly to changes in supply and demand. According to Say's law, "supply creates its own demand." The classical school focused on the economy at full employment; prolonged unemployment is impossible according to the long-run classical model.

According to Keynes, the problem with the classical model is that not all income generated from output need be used to buy goods and services; it can also be saved, hoarded, or taxed away. Supply does not automatically create an adequate demand. Keynes argued that wages and price are inflexible downward. Most macroeconomists now believe that wages and prices do tend to be less flexible when excess capacity is available.

Money: © Chapel House Photography; Falling man: © iStockphoto.com/gradts

For More Review Tools Visit
www.cengagebrain.com.

Online Study Tools

At www.cengagebrain.com, you can

❏ Download printable Key Term Flash Cards

❏ Study online with interactive Key Term Flash Cards

❏ Complete Practice Quizzes with instant feedback

❏ Play "Beat the Clock" to master concepts

❏ Complete the Crossword Puzzle to review key terms

❏ Download and review Exhibit Worksheets

❏ Access Economic Application "Aggregate Demand/ Aggregate Supply"

❏ Access Graphing Workshops "Aggregate Demand," "Changes in Aggregate Demand," "Aggregate Supply," and "Types of Inflation"

❏ Check your answers to the Chapter 13 Self-Review on page 293 on the e-book in CourseMate.

Section Summaries

14-1 Fiscal Policy

Fiscal policy is the use of government purchases, taxes, and transfer payments to alter RGDP and the price level. Sometimes it is necessary for the government to use fiscal policy to stimulate the economy during a contraction (or recession) or to try to curb an expansion in order to bring inflation under control.

Government spending that exceeds tax revenues causes a budget deficit. When tax revenues are greater than government spending, a budget surplus exists. Expansionary fiscal policy is associated with increased government budget deficits. Contractionary fiscal policy will tend to create or expand a budget surplus or reduce an existing budget deficit.

14-2 Government Spending and Taxation

A large majority of government activity is financed by taxation. Fifty percent of tax revenues come in the form of income taxes. Progressive taxes are designed so that those with higher incomes pay a greater proportion of their income in taxes. With a regressive or payroll tax, a person's tax as a proportion of income falls as the person's income rises. An excise tax is a sales tax on individual products such as alcohol, tobacco, and gasoline. A flat tax is designed so that everybody would pay the same percentage of their income.

The ability to pay principle is simply that those with the greatest ability to pay taxes should pay more than those with the least ability to pay taxes. The benefits received principle means that the individuals receiving the benefits are those who pay for them.

14-3 Fiscal Policy and the *AD/AS* Model

Increased government purchases, tax cuts, and/or increases in transfer payments, *ceteris paribus*, can shift the aggregate demand curve to the right. This would increase the price level. If this stimulus is of the right timing and magnitude, it can stimulate the economy and close the recessionary gap.

If the government decides to reduce its purchases, increase taxes, or reduce transfer payments, the aggregate demand curve will shift leftward. This will lower the price level and close the inflationary gap.

14-4 The Multiplier Effect

When an increase in purchases of goods or services occurs, the ultimate increase in total purchases tends to be greater than the initial increase. This is known as the multiplier effect. The marginal propensity to consume (MPC) is the fraction of additional disposable (after-tax) income that a household consumes rather than saves. The marginal propensity to save (MPS) is the proportion of an addition to your income that you would save. The larger the MPC, the larger the multiplier effect.

14-5 Supply-Side Effects of Tax Cuts

Supply-sider economists believe that if the government reduced individual and business taxes, deregulated, and increased spending on research and development, these policies could generate greater long-term economic growth by stimulating personal income, savings, and capital formation.

Key Terms

ability to pay principle belief that those with the greatest ability to pay taxes should pay more than those with less ability to pay (pg. 301)

automatic stabilizers changes in government transfer payments or tax collections that automatically help counter business cycle fluctuations (pg. 313)

benefits received principle the belief that those receiving the benefits from taxes are those who should pay for them (pg. 302)

budget deficit occurs when government spending exceeds tax revenues for a given fiscal year (pg. 296)

budget surplus occurs when tax revenues are greater than government expenditures for a given fiscal year (pg. 296)

excise tax a sales tax on individual products such as alcohol, tobacco, and gasoline (pg. 300)

fiscal policy use of government purchases, taxes, and transfer payments to alter equilibrium output and prices (pg. 295)

flat tax a tax that charges all income earners the same percentage of their income (pg. 300)

marginal propensity to consume (MPC) the additional consumption resulting from an additional dollar of disposable income (pg. 305)

marginal propensity to save (MPS) the change in savings divided by the change in disposable income (pg. 305)

multiplier effect a chain reaction of additional income and purchases that results in total purchases that are greater than the initial increase in purchases (pg. 305)

progressive tax a tax designed so that those with higher incomes pay a greater proportion of their income in taxes (pg. 299)

regressive tax as a person's income rises, the amount his or her tax as a proportion of income falls (pg. 299)

vertical equity different treatment based on level of income and the ability to pay principle (pg. 301)

Section Summaries - Continued

14-6 Automatic Stabilizers

Changes in government transfer payments or tax collections that automatically tend to counter business cycle fluctuations are called automatic stabilizers. The most important automatic stabilizer is the tax system.

Personal income taxes vary directly in amount with respect to income. Incomes, earnings, and profits all fall during a recession so the government collects less in taxes. When you work less, you are paid less and therefore pay less in taxes—an automatic tax cut. Automatic stabilizers are not strong enough to completely offset a serious recession, but they can reduce the severity.

14-7 The National Debt

One method the government can use to finance a budget deficit is to print money; however, this method is highly inflationary. Typically, the budget deficit is financed by issuing debt. Budget deficits can provide the federal government with the flexibility to respond appropriately to changing economic circumstances.

In the short run, running a larger deficit is the same as running expansionary fiscal policy. In the long run, when the government borrows to finance a budget deficit, it causes the real interest rate to rise, which decreases private investment, reduces the growth in the nation's capital stock, and retards the growth rate of potential GDP.

The real issue of importance regarding budget deficits is whether the government's activities have benefits that are greater than their costs.

© Dwight Smith/Shutterstock

> **For More Review Tools Visit**
> **www.cengagebrain.com.**

Online Study Tools

At www.cengagebrain.com, you can

- ❏ Download printable Key Term Flash Cards
- ❏ Study online with interactive Key Term Flash Cards
- ❏ Complete Practice Quizzes with instant feedback
- ❏ Play "Beat the Clock" to master concepts
- ❏ Complete the Crossword Puzzle to review key terms
- ❏ Download and review Exhibit Worksheets

- ❏ Access Economic Applications "Fiscal Policy" and "Taxes, Spending, and Deficits"
- ❏ Access Graphing Workshops "Discretionary Policy and a Contractionary Gap," "Closing a Contractionary Gap," and "Responses to an Expansionary Gap"
- ❏ Check your answers to the Chapter 14 Self-Review on page 319 on the e-book in CourseMate.

Section Summaries

15-1 What Is Money?

Money is anything that is generally accepted in exchange for goods and services. Money has four important functions in the economy: as a medium of exchange, a unit of account, a store of value, and a means of deferred payment.

15-2 Measuring Money

Currency consists of coins and/or paper that some institution or government has created to be used in the trading of goods and services and the payment of debts. In the United States and most other nations of the world, metallic coins and paper currency are the only forms of legal tender. Legal tender is fiat money—a means of exchange that has been established by government fiat, or declaration.

Today, most money we use is not officially legal tender, but balances in checking accounts in banks, more formally called demand deposits. Transaction deposits can be easily converted into currency or used to buy goods and services directly. Other forms of payments and assets include credit cards, nontransaction deposits, money market mutual funds, stocks, and bonds. Liquidity refers to the ease with which one asset can be converted into another asset or goods and services.

M1 is the narrow definition of money, which includes currency, checkable deposits, and traveler's checks. M2, the broader definition of money, includes M1 plus savings deposits, time deposits (except for some large-denomination certificates of deposit), and noninstitutional money market mutual fund shares.

Until 1933, the currency of the United States operated on an internal gold standard. Today no precious metal is used to back or establish the value of our money.

15-3 How Banks Create Money

Financial intermediaries serve many functions, the most important of which are creating loans and serving as depositories for savings and liquid assets that are used by individuals and firms for transaction purposes. When a bank lends to a person, it usually gives the borrower the funds by issuing a check or by adding funds to an existing checking account. Banks create money when they increase demand deposits through the process of creating loans. Because demand deposits are money, the issuers of new loans have created money.

15-4 The Money Multiplier

New loans create new money directly, but they also create excess reserves in other banks, which leads to still further increases in both loans and the money supply. The money multiplier, calculated by dividing 1 by the reserve requirement, measures the potential amount of money that the banking system generates with each dollar of reserves. Potential money creation is equal to initial deposits times the money multiplier. This money creation is only potential because some banks might hold on to some of their excess reserves or some borrowers might not immediately spend all of their newly acquired deposits.

Key Terms

balance sheet a financial record that indicates the balance between a bank's assets and its liabilities plus capital (pg. 331)

barter direct exchange of goods and services without the use of money (pg. 322)

commercial banks financial institutions organized to handle everyday financial transactions of businesses and households through demand deposit accounts and savings accounts and by making short-term commercial and consumer loans (pg. 329)

credit unions financial cooperatives made up of depositors with a common affiliation (pg. 329)

currency coins and/or paper created to facilitate the trade of goods and services and the payment of debts (pg. 323)

demand deposits balances in bank accounts that depositors can access on demand (pg. 324)

excess reserves reserve levels held above that required by the Fed (pg. 331)

fiat money a means of exchange established by government declaration (pg. 324)

fractional reserve system a system that requires banks to hold reserves equal to some fraction of their checkable deposits (pg. 330)

gold standard defining the dollar as equivalent to a set value of a quantity of gold, allowing direct convertibility from currency to gold (pg. 327)

Gresham's Law the principle that "cheap money drives out dear money"; given an alternative, people prefer to spend less valuable money (pg. 327)

legal tender coins and paper officially declared to be acceptable for the settlement of financial debts (pg. 324)

liquidity the ease with which one asset can be converted into another asset or into goods and services (pg. 326)

M1 the narrowest definition of money; includes currency, checkable deposits, and traveler's checks (pg. 326)

M2 a broader definition of money that includes M1 plus savings deposits, time deposits, and noninstitutional money market mutual fund shares (pg. 326)

(continues)

Section Summaries - Continued

15-5 The Collapse of America's Banking System, 1920–1933

In 1920, 30,000 banks were operating in the United States; by 1933, the number declined to about 15,000. By early 1933 the decline in depositor confidence had reached the point that the entire banking system was in jeopardy. President Roosevelt declared a two-week bank holiday, allowing only the healthy banks to reopen. The passing of federal deposit insurance also helped improve depositor confidence.

There were four major reasons for the collapse. First, the U.S. had lots of small banks, which were vulnerable to bank runs. Second, government aid was weak and too late. Third, deposit insurance did not exist. And fourth, the broader economic downturn further eroded depositor confidence.

The combination of the Federal Deposit Insurance Corporation (FDIC) and the government's greater willingness to assist distressed banks has reduced the number of bank failures in recent times.

Key Terms - Continued

means of deferred payment the attribute of money that makes it easier to borrow and to repay loans (pg. 323)

medium of exchange the primary function of money, which is to facilitate transactions and lower transaction costs (pg. 322)

money anything generally accepted in exchange for goods or services (pg. 321)

money market mutual funds interest-earning accounts provided by brokers who pool funds into such investments as Treasury bills (pg. 326)

money multiplier measures the potential amount of money that the banking system generates with each dollar of reserves (pg. 335)

near money nontransaction deposits that are not money but can be quickly converted into money (pg. 325)

nontransaction deposits funds that cannot be used for payment directly but must be converted into currency for general use (pg. 325)

required reserve ratio the percentage of deposits that a bank must hold at the Federal Reserve Bank or in bank vaults (pg. 331)

reserve requirements holdings of assets at the bank or at the Federal Reserve Bank as mandated by the Fed (pg. 330)

savings and loan association financial institution organized as cooperative associations that holds demand deposits and savings of members in the form of dividend-bearing shares and makes loans, especially home mortgages loans (pg. 329)

secondary reserves highly liquid, interest-paying assets held by the bank (pg. 330)

transaction deposits deposits that can be easily converted to currency or used to buy goods and services directly (pg. 324)

traveler's checks transaction instruments easily converted into currency (pg. 324)

> **For More Review Tools Visit www.cengagebrain.com.**

Online Study Tools

At www.cengagebrain.com, you can

- ❏ Download printable Key Term Flash Cards
- ❏ Study online with interactive Key Term Flash Cards
- ❏ Complete Practice Quizzes with instant feedback
- ❏ Play "Beat the Clock" to master concepts
- ❏ Complete the Crossword Puzzle to review key terms

- ❏ Download and review Exhibit Worksheets
- ❏ Access Economic Application "Money and the Financial System"
- ❏ Check your answers to the Chapter 15 Self-Review on page 339 on the e-book in CourseMate.

Section Summaries

16-1 The Federal Reserve System

A central bank performs many functions. First, the central bank is a "banker's bank." Second, the central bank performs a service function for commercial banks. Third, the central bank serves as the primary bank for the central government. Fourth, the central bank buys and sells foreign currencies and assists in financial transactions with other countries. Fifth, the central bank serves as the "lender of last resort." And sixth, the central bank monitors the stability of the banking system and the money supply.

In the United States, the central bank is composed of 12 banks, closely tied together and collectively called the Federal Reserve System. The Federal Reserve Board of Governors, which controls major policy decisions, is appointed by the president of the United States. Historically, the Fed has enjoyed a considerable amount of independence from both the executive and legislative branches of government.

16-2 How Does the Federal Reserve Change the Money Supply?

The Fed uses three major methods to control the supply of money: open market operations, changing reserve requirements, and/or changing the discount rate. Open market operations, the Fed's most important tool, involve the purchase and sale of government bonds. If the Fed wants to reduce the money supply or reduce the rate of growth in the money supply, it will sell bonds, raise reserve requirements, and/or raise the discount rate. If the Fed wants to increase the money supply, it will buy bonds, lower reserve requirements, and/or lower the discount rate.

16-3 Money, Interest Rates, and Aggregate Demand

The money market is the market in which money demand and money supply determine the equilibrium *nominal* interest rate. When the Fed acts to change the money supply by changing one of its policy variables, it alters the money market equilibrium.

Why do people hold money instead of other financial assets? Transaction purposes, precautionary reasons, and asset purposes are three of the major determinants of the demand for money.

The quantity of money demanded varies inversely with the nominal interest rate. The money supply is almost perfectly inelastic with respect to interest rates over their plausible range, as controlled by Federal Reserve policies. When the Fed changes policy to increase the money supply, the interest rate falls in the short run. At lower interest rates, households and businesses invest more and buy more goods and services, shifting the aggregate demand curve to the right. The Fed cannot target both the money supply and interest rates at the same time.

Key Terms

discount rate interest rate that the Fed charges commercial banks for the loans it extends to them (pg. 345)

federal funds market market in which banks provide short-term loans to other banks that need cash to meet reserve requirements (pg. 346)

money market market in which money demand and money supply determine the equilibrium interest rate (pg. 348)

open market operations purchase and sale of government securities by the Federal Reserve System (pg. 344)

quantity theory of money and prices a theory of the connection between the money supply and the price level when the velocity of money is constant (pg. 358)

velocity of money a measure of how frequently money is turned over (pg. 357)

Section Summaries - Continued

16-4 Expansionary and Contractionary Monetary Policy

When the Fed engages in expansionary monetary policy, it increases the money supply, interest rates fall, and the aggregate demand curve shifts to the right.

The Fed may engage in contractionary monetary policy if the economy faces an inflationary gap. When the Fed decreases the money supply, it increases the interest rate, and the aggregate demand curve shifts to the left.

16-5 Money and Inflation

There is a positive relationship between the money supply, the price level, the growth in the money supply, and the inflation rate. The equation of exchange, $M \times V = P \times Q$, explains the relationship between money and the price level, where M is the money supply, P is the price level, Q is RGDP, and V is the velocity of money. The velocity of money refers to its "turnover" rate, or the intensity with which money is used. The faster money circulates, the higher the velocity. The quantity theory of money explains the connection between the money supply and the price level when the velocity of money is constant.

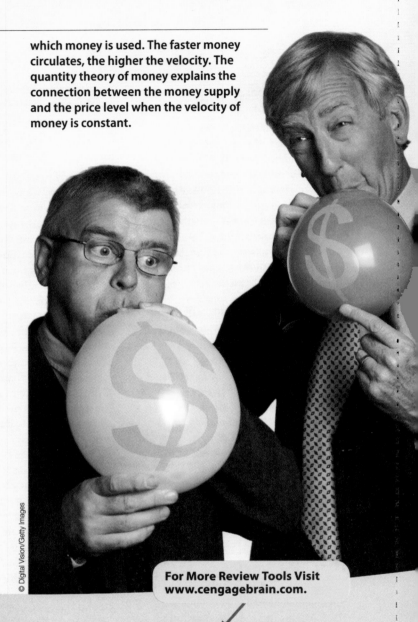

© Digital Vision/Getty Images

For More Review Tools Visit
www.cengagebrain.com.

Online Study Tools

At www.cengagebrain.com, you can

❏ Download printable Key Term Flash Cards

❏ Study online with interactive Key Term Flash Cards

❏ Complete Practice Quizzes with instant feedback

❏ Play "Beat the Clock" to master concepts

❏ Complete the Crossword Puzzle to review key terms

❏ Download and review Exhibit Worksheets

❏ Access Economic Application "Monetary Policy"

❏ Access Graphing Workshops "The Money Market" and "Open Market Operations"

❏ Check your answers to the Chapter 16 Self-Review on page 361 on the e-book in CourseMate.

Section Summaries

17-1 Problems in Implementing Fiscal and Monetary Policy

When implementing fiscal stimulus, the multiplier effect assumes all other things will remain equal; however, this may not always hold true. For example, when an increase in government purchases stimulates aggregate demand, it also drives up the interest rate. This in turn dampens private spending on goods and services, reducing the overall impact of the fiscal stimulus. This is known as the crowding-out effect.

Fiscal stimulus usually takes time before its effects are fully realized. Three types of time lags that occur are recognition lags, implementation lags, and impact lags.

The lag problem inherent in adopting fiscal policy changes is less acute for monetary policy because the decisions are not slowed by the budgetary process. The full effects of monetary policy changes on productivity, unemployment, and inflation, however, can take much longer. One limitation of monetary policy is that it ultimately must be carried out through the commercial banking system. Also, its ability to influence nonmember banks, international banks, and nonbank institutions is limited.

A further macroeconomic problem arises if the federal government's fiscal decision makers differ with the Fed's monetary decision makers on policy objectives or targets. The timing of fiscal policy and monetary policy is crucial.

17-2 Rational Expectations

Rational expectations theory asserts that workers and consumers incorporate the likely consequences of government policy changes into their expectations by quickly adjusting wages and prices. Rational expectations economists believe that wages and prices are flexible and that government economic policies designed to alter aggregate demand to meet macroeconomic goals are of limited effectiveness. The only way that monetary or fiscal policy can change output in the rational expectations model is with a surprise—an unanticipated change. Critics of rational expectations theory suggest that households and firms may not be completely informed about the impact of monetary and fiscal policy.

17-3 Controversies in Macroeconomic Policy

Many economists believe that in the short run, policy makers have the ability to alter aggregate demand. Other economists believe that aggregate demand stimulus cannot keep the rate of unemployment below the natural rate. Other economists, rational expectations theorists, believe that government economic policies designed to alter aggregate demand are not all that effective. The real business cycle theorists believe that economic fluctuations are the result of external shocks to the economy. Most macroeconomists believe both that monetary and fiscal policy can shift the aggregate demand and that the intervention can be counterproductive. Other economists believe that the potency of expansionary fiscal policy will be diminished by the crowding-out effect.

Most economists believe that monetary policy should take the lead

Key Terms

crowding-out effect theory that government borrowing drives up the interest rate, lowering consumption by households and investment spending by firms (pg. 364)

Indexing use of payment contracts that automatically adjust for changes in inflation (pg. 375)

theory of rational expectations belief that workers and consumers incorporate the likely consequences of government policy changes into their expectations by quickly adjusting wages and prices (pg. 369)

Section Summaries - Continued

in stabilization policy and that the central bank should be independent and insulated from political pressure to avoid political business cycles. Some believe that the central bank should attempt to keep the inflation rate within a certain range for a specified period of time. One means of protecting parties against unanticipated price increases is to write contracts that automatically change the prices of goods or services whenever the overall price level changes, effectively rewriting agreements in terms of dollars of constant purchasing power. This method is known as indexing.

17-4 The Financial Crisis of 2007–2009

One of the biggest factors in the financial crisis of 2007–2009 was debt, or excess leverage. After the 2001 recession, the Fed pursued an expansionary monetary policy that pushed interest rates down to historically low levels, which persisted until 2004. This, accompanied by deregulation in the mortgage markets, resulted in low interest rates and aggressive borrowing that encouraged less qualified buyers to purchase houses. The Fed reversed its policy in 2005–2006,

which pushed interest rates up. As homeowners found themselves caught between rising interest rates and falling housing prices, many mortgages began to default and homes went into foreclosure. Many of these mortgages were held by major investment banks, which began to lose a lot of money on these assets. Lehman Brothers eventually went bankrupt, and Bear Stearns and Merrill Lynch were bought out at fire-sale prices. As credit markets began to seize up, the Federal Reserve and other central banks around the world responded by pouring money into the ailing credit markets. The United States also enacted a stimulus package worth nearly $1 trillion.

© Jamie Farrant/iStockphoto.com

For More Review Tools Visit www.cengagebrain.com.

Online Study Tools

At www.cengagebrain.com, you can

❏ Download printable Key Term Flash Cards

❏ Study online with interactive Key Term Flash Cards

❏ Complete Practice Quizzes with instant feedback

❏ Play "Beat the Clock" to master concepts

❏ Complete the Crossword Puzzle to review key terms

❏ Download and review Exhibit Worksheets

❏ Access Economic Application "Global Financial Crisis"

❏ Check your answers to the Chapter 17 Self-Review on page 381 on the e-book in CourseMate.

Section Summaries

18-1 The Growth in World Trade

In a typical year, about 15 percent of the world's output is traded in international markets. In the last three decades, the sum of U.S. imports and exports has increased from 11 percent of GDP to roughly 30 percent.

Major U.S. trading partners include Canada, China, Japan, Mexico, Germany, and the United Kingdom.

18-2 Comparative Advantage and Gains from Trade

Both participants in an exchange of goods and services anticipate an improvement in their economic welfare. Persons, regions, or countries can gain by specializing in the production of the good in which they have a comparative advantage. What is important is comparative advantage, not absolute advantage.

The production possibilities curve illustrates how one partner in trade might have a comparative advantage in production of a good though they do not have an absolute advantage. To achieve any of the gains from comparative advantage and specialization, however, there must be trade. The greater the difference in opportunity cost between the two trading partners, the greater the benefits from specialization and exchange.

18-3 Supply and Demand in International Trade

Using the concepts of consumer and producer surplus, we can graphically show the net benefits of free trade. With exports, domestic producers gain more than domestic consumers lose. With imports, domestic consumers gain more than domestic producers lose.

18-4 Tariffs, Import Quotas, and Subsidies

In this section, we discuss three mechanisms of trade protection: tariffs, import quotas, and subsidies. A tariff is a tax on imported goods. Tariffs lead to (1) a smaller total quantity sold, (2) a higher price for domestic consumers, (3) greater sales at higher prices for domestic producers, and (4) lower sales of foreign products.

Import quotas directly restrict imports, leading to reductions in trade and thus preventing nations from fully realizing their comparative advantage. Domestic producers are better off under quotas, but domestic consumers are worse off.

With a subsidy, revenue is given to producers for each exported unit of output, which stimulates exports. While usually defended as a means of increasing exports and improving a nation's international financial position, subsidies are usually of

Key Terms

balance of payments the record of international transactions in which a nation has engaged over a year (pg. 397)

balance of trade the net surplus or deficit resulting from the level of exportation and importation of merchandise (pg. 399)

current account a record of a country's imports and exports of goods and services, net investment income, and net transfers (pg. 397)

derived demand the demand for an input derived from consumers' demand for the good or service produced with that input (pg. 402)

exchange rate the price of one unit of a country's currency in terms of another country's currency (pg. 401)

financial account records the foreign purchases or assets in the domestic economy (a monetary inflow) and domestic purchases of assets abroad (a monetary outflow) (pg. 400)

import quota a legal limit on the imported quantity of a good that is produced abroad and can be sold in domestic markets (pg. 395)

rent seeking efforts by producers to gain profits from government protections such as tariffs and import quotas (pg. 396)

tariff a tax on imports (pg. 392)

Beach: © Inspirestock/Getty Images; Paper ships: © Hiroshi Watanabe/Getty Images

Section Summaries - Continued

dubious worth to the world economy and even to the economy doing the subsidizing.

18-5 The Balance of Payments

The balance of payments is a statement that records all the exchanges requiring an outflow of funds to foreign nations or an inflow of funds from other nations. A current account is a record of a country's imports and exports of goods and services, net investment income, and net transfers. The import/export goods relationship is often called the balance of trade. The capital account records the foreign purchases or assets in the United States and U.S. purchases of assets abroad (a monetary outflow). Finally, the statistical discrepancy is included to account for any errors or omissions, and to make sure the balance of payments is balanced.

18-6 Exchange Rates

The price of a unit of one foreign currency in terms of another is called the exchange rate. Prices of goods in their currencies combine with exchange rates to determine the domestic price of foreign goods. The demand for foreign currencies is known as a derived demand. The equilibrium price (exchange rate) of a foreign currency is reached where the demand and supply curves of that currency intersect.

18-7 Equilibrium Changes in the Foreign Exchange Market

Any force that shifts either the demand for or supply of a currency will shift the equilibrium in the foreign exchange market, leading to a new exchange rate. Among such factors are changes in consumer tastes for goods, income levels, relative real interest rates, and relative inflation rates, as well as speculation.

For More Review Tools Visit www.cengagebrain.com.

Online Study Tools

At www.cengagebrain.com, you can

- ❏ Download printable Key Term Flash Cards
- ❏ Study online with interactive Key Term Flash Cards
- ❏ Complete Practice Quizzes with instant feedback
- ❏ Play "Beat the Clock" to master concepts
- ❏ Complete the Crossword Puzzle to review key terms
- ❏ Download and review Exhibit Worksheets

- ❏ Access Economic Applications "International Trade" and "International Finance"
- ❏ Access Graphing Workshops "Foreign Exchange Market (euros)" and "Foreign Exchange Market (yen)"
- ❏ Check your answers to the Chapter 18 Self-Review on page 407 on the e-book in CourseMate.